MARGOT ASQUITH'S GREAT
WAR DIARY 1914–1916

'Mrs. Asquith's diaries are both entertainingly and splendidly edited by the late Michael Brock and his wife Eleanor and copious footnotes add hugely to the context, accuracy, and frequent inaccuracy, of the writings. Perhaps even more valuable than Margot's own record is the editors' 147-page introduction and its corrective to the reputation of her husband Herbert, and the events of his war-time premiership and government'

David Filsell, *Stand-To: Magazine of The Western Front Association*

'The diaries may be 100 years old, but political life has changed little, it seems'

Chris Green, *Suffolk & Norfolk Life*

'The diaries never cease to entertain, and they turn out to be remarkably enlightening too'

Ferdinand Mount, *London Review of Books*

'Lovingly edited'

Andy McSmith, *Independent*

'In a mass of new volumes on the First World War, Margot Asquith's diaries stand out'

The Oldie Review of Books

'This is one diary that pulls no punches'

Steve Craggs, *Northern Echo*

'The diaries start with the lead-up to war and end with the fall of the last Liberal government and David Lloyd Georges extraordinary coup against the prime minister. Mrs Asquith is well placed to watch it all. Michael and Eleanor Brock have done a fine job as editors. Their footnotes signpost all the major events of the great war and provide the reader with some delicious quotes'

The Economist

'[A] beautiful work of conjugal editorship by Eleanor Brock and her late husband'   Miranda Seymour, *Daily Mail*

'They may not constitute the most important historical work published in this centenary year, but by a country mile they are the most entertaining'

Max Hastings, *Sunday Times*

'Michael and Eleanor Brock have edited Margot's writing with meticulous academic precision. This diary is an invaluable and fascinating text, and we must be thankful to the Brocks for producing it'   Jane Ridley, *Literary Review*

'Reading these diaries has been a pleasure enhanced by its editors, who have set the stage and introduced the cast with lucidity and scholarship'

Lawrence James, *The Times*

'This book offers a first-hand insight into what was happening, from the perspective of someone who was at the centre of things ... Once it's on the library shelves it will be worth taking down'   *Methodist Recorder*

MARGOT ASQUITH'S GREAT WAR DIARY 1914–1916

THE VIEW FROM DOWNING STREET

Selected and Edited by
Michael and Eleanor Brock

With the assistance of Mark Pottle

OXFORD
UNIVERSITY PRESS

OXFORD

UNIVERSITY PRESS

Great Clarendon Street, Oxford, OX2 6DP,
United Kingdom

Oxford University Press is a department of the University of Oxford.
It furthers the University's objective of excellence in research, scholarship,
and education by publishing worldwide. Oxford is a registered trade mark of
Oxford University Press in the UK and in certain other countries

First published 2014
First published in paperback 2016

Impression: 1

Published in the United States of America by Oxford University Press
198 Madison Avenue, New York, NY 10016, United States of America

British Library Cataloguing in Publication Data
Data available

Library of Congress Cataloging in Publication Data
Data available

ISBN 978–0–19–822977–3 (Hbk.)
ISBN 978–0–19–873772–8 (Pbk.)

Printed and bound by
CPI Group (UK) Ltd, Croydon, CR0 4YY

To Patricia

PREFACE

Presented here are the diaries kept by Margot Asquith—the wife of H. H. Asquith, the British Prime Minister from 1908 to 1916—from the outbreak of the First World War in August 1914 until her husband's departure from office in December 1916. These years were as catastrophic for the Asquiths as for British society at large, and Margot offers a unique perspective of H. H. Asquith as a wartime Premier, seen through his marriage.

Margot was a regular diarist, but wrote more during 1915 than in any other single year. She did not always understand the enormous changes that she was recording, or comprehend the full significance of the events that she witnessed, and although she possessed some narrative skill she was an opinionated egotist, often inaccurate, the victim of flattery, and occasionally prone to fantasy. For this war period, however, even more than during peacetime, these faults are outweighed by her advantage: she was closer to the Prime Minister, and thus to the centre of events, than anyone else.

The years 1914 to 1918 were to alter British society more profoundly than any comparable period since the end of the seventeenth century. They were also to break Asquith politically, and lead to the division and almost terminal decline of the once great party that he led. On the eve of war Asquith's Liberal government had been in office for more than six of the most turbulent years in modern British history, but Asquith had shown consummate skill in riding every crisis, and had retained that mastery of the House of Commons that had so impressed his former chief and predecessor, Sir Henry Campbell-Bannerman. When faced with particular difficulty in the House 'C.B.' would send for Asquith, telling his aides: 'Go and bring the sledge-hammer.'[1] Asquith seldom disappointed, and his great authority as Premier was internationally recognized on the eve of war. Within a relatively short time, however, his premiership had ended. As the fighting on the Western Front ground on his incomparable skill in parliamentary debate counted for less, and he did not establish a compensatory mastery over extra-parliamentary councils. Problems in dealing with the Allies, with the Press, and the trade unions multiplied with every reverse on the battlefield, and doubts grew whether Asquith was still capable of meeting each new threat. Against the background of the Somme, which claimed the life of his eldest son, Raymond, he was forced out of the premiership, and resigned on 5 December 1916. He never held high office again. Margot unwittingly chronicles his fall, and the very fact that she did not anticipate it, although she claimed to be a close student of politics, sheds light on one of its principal causes: his belief, shared fully by her, that he was indispensable.

The Introduction offers a concise biographical sketch of Margot and HHA, describing their pre-war triumphs and troubles, and focusing in some depth on the period covered by the diary, from late July 1914 to early December 1916. It suggests that the experiences of peacetime had ill equipped the Asquiths to face the momentous challenges of a war that repeatedly bore out the veracity of one of HHA's favourite sayings: 'The expected does not happen.'

---

[1] Gardiner, *Prophets*, 54.

ACKNOWLEDGEMENTS

We were invited to undertake this editing by the late Lord Bonham-Carter soon after 1982, when our edition of Asquith's *Letters to Venetia Stanley* had been published. He knew that we had other work on hand to which we would have to give priority. One of us was working then for Nuffield College, Oxford, and later for the College of St George, Windsor Castle, and we are grateful to both institutions for allowing us to pursue the early researches needed for the production of this edition, and to the Wolfson Foundation for a grant which helped us with those researches.

Those writings of Margot and H. H. Asquith that were still unpublished in 1989 will be in copyright until 2039, and our first thanks go to Christopher Osborn and to Lord Bonham-Carter's daughters, the copyright holders for Margot's writings and her husband's respectively. The Hon. Virginia Brand, who manages the copyright questions arising from H. H. Asquith's pen, has shown us much kindness over many years. Our debt to Dr Mark Pottle is beyond measurement. He has contributed over a long period unstinted and extensive technical help in preparing this edition; and, being himself an experienced and meticulous editor of the Asquith and other collections, he has made us free of his unrivalled knowledge about the issues involved. Without his devoted aid in overcoming many obstacles, we could not possibly have published this book. The editors also acknowledge the generous assistance of Dr Mark Curthoys, of the *Oxford Dictionary of National Biography*. We have been greatly helped, over many years, by the staffs of the Bodleian Library, Oxford, especially by Mary Clapinson, Colin Harris, and Helen Langley; of the Imperial War Museum; of the India Office Records and Private Papers, the British

Library; of the National Archives of Scotland, especially Alison Lindsay; of Nuffield College Library, especially Elizabeth Martin and her colleagues; of the Oxford Union Society's Library; and of the staff over many years of Oxford University Press, especially by Anne Gelling, Ruth Parr, and Stephanie Ireland.

We record in grateful memory the help which we received during our researches from six people who had particular knowledge of the scenes portrayed in the Diaries—Lord David Cecil, Lady Diana Cooper, the Right Hon. the Lord Glenconner, the Right Hon. the Lord Jenkins of Hillhead, the Right Hon. the 2nd Earl of Oxford and Asquith, and the Right Hon. the Earl of Stockton. We express our thanks for their help to Lady Berlin, Lady Bonham-Carter, the Hon. Elena Bonham Carter, Oliver Brock, Dr Christopher Collins, Professor R. J. W. Evans, Professor Robert Franklin, Professor Zara Steiner, and Professor Hew Strachan. If we have omitted any others who should have been mentioned we apologize to them.

We owe much good advice to Professor Vernon Bogdanor, and to George and David Brock. To the latter we also owe the map of the Western Front. We have derived much benefit from the expert typing of Judith Godley, Elaine Herman, Margaret Hunt, and Catherine Brocklehurst.

We thank the following persons and institutions for leave to consult and make use of unpublished items which they hold, or of which they control the copyright, and in some cases, for both of these permissions:

The Arthur Asquith Papers: the Hon. John Rous, Clovelly Court; the Papers of the Rt. Hon. the Earl of Oxford and Asquith, OBE, Mells; Correspondence of Lady Elizabeth Balfour: the National Archives of Scotland; Professor N. W. Ellenberger: an unpublished doctoral dissertation on 'The Souls'; The Hankey Papers: the Churchill Archives Centre, Churchill College; The Kipling Papers: the University of Sussex; the Lloyd George Collection: the Rt. Hon. the Earl Lloyd George of Dwyfor; The Papers of Leo Maxse: the West Sussex Record Office and Mr Anthony Maxse; The Papers of E. S. Montagu: the Master and Fellows of Trinity College, Cambridge; The Papers of J. A. Pease: the Rt. Hon. the

Lord Gainford and the Warden and Fellows of Nuffield College, Oxford; The Marquess of Reading's Papers: the India Office Records (Private Papers), The British Library; The Henry Wilson Papers: The Trustees of the Imperial War Museum.

M.G.B.

E.H.B.

CONTENTS

LIST OF ILLUSTRATIONS

EDITORIAL NOTE

Margot Asquith's first diary is dated 1876, when she was 12 years old. The sequence runs until 1923, but is not continuous: there seem to be no extant diaries for 1886–92, for 1900–4, or for 1919–20. Margot wrote in *More Memories* (1933) that she hardly ever looked at her diaries, which she 'ceased to write' after her *Autobiography* had been published (1920, 1922).

The handwriting and arrangement of the diary of 1904–6 (Bodleian Library, MS Eng. d. 3204) show that Margot had resolved in 1904 to compose more carefully. At the same date she decided to divide 'family' content from 'political', and kept two diaries, with some overlap in time and material; this division ended in March 1913. The text of the present edition is drawn from six of the 'joint' diaries, beginning with that of February 1912–September 1914 (d. 3210) and ending with that of July 1916–August 1917 (d. 3215).[1] The year 1915, a critical time in H. H. Asquith's career, was chronicled by Margot in remarkable detail, and occupies two whole volumes, with parts of two others.

The twenty-two volumes of the Diary, along with other papers, were presented to the Bodleian Library in 1998 by the late Mrs Priscilla Bibesco-Hodgson, Margot's granddaughter.

The writing of the Diary

By 1914 Margot had been writing diaries for nearly forty years. She was accustomed to scribble down pencil notes as soon as possible after the

---

[1] For full bibliographical references for the diaries see the list at the end of this Editorial Note.

events to be recorded, with a view to 'writing up' the diary at a later date. Sometimes these acts of reconstruction occurred a considerable time after the event, and as a result errors and inaccuracies inevitably crept into the record. Margot nevertheless persisted in believing that this method ensured the diary's truthfulness, in spite of criticism on this point.[1] Certainly her method had many disadvantages, to which she herself was not blind: notes were lost, or muddled, or accumulated in such quantities that she was overwhelmed at the prospect of working through them: 'I see huge envelopes of notes, but to put them in order depresses me so much.'[2] Above all, her method made for confusion in the dating of entries. Margot would have been cavalier about dates however she had composed her diary, such was her temperament, but often the date that she placed at the head of an entry seems merely to denote the date at which she started the 'writing up' process. In some cases an entry is dated only by the month in question, without further refinement. The editors have not corrected Margot's dating, or disturbed the order in which she wrote her diary entries, but they have added the day of the week, and the year where necessary, and provided footnotes to explain any particularly misleading entry-dating.

Margot does not seem, however, to have misused her notes much when writing her diary: certainly it is a more accurate record than her later published writings. She became far less careful, and took much greater poetic licence, when she wrote retrospectively for publication. In her last book, which appeared in 1943, she wrote that she had been present in the House of Commons when her husband had delivered his much admired obituary tribute to Alfred Lyttelton, 7 July 1913. Yet, as the relevant diary entry makes clear, she did not know in advance that the premier was going to give the tribute, and bitterly regretted her absence from the occasion.[3] And in her *Autobiography*, which appeared in two volumes in 1920 and 1922, Margot used and misused the diary repeatedly.

---

[1] See, for instance, Lady Frances Balfour to Margot, 21 Sept. 1920: c. 6670, fo. 182.
[2] Diary, 2 Sept. 1912.
[3] *Off the Record*, 157. Text of speech, *Off the Record*, 158–9; and *Parl. Deb.*, 7 July 1913, 55.61–2.

In her diary entry of 24 August 1914 she records that General Cowans warned her to be prepared for heavy losses in the BEF in France, observing: 'I'm very much afraid these restless Frenchmen have done some folly.' In the *Autobiography* the pungency of this last remark has been lost. Cowans instead says: 'I'm afraid the French have been too dashing or wrong in their strategy.'[1]

Other changes illustrate the essential difference between a diary and any kind of retrospective. A diary, if it is honestly composed and nothing is excised or altered later, shows the author's attitudes at—or at least very close to—the time of the event, and might include statements or sentiments of which he or she later became ashamed. In the early evening of 29 July 1914, for example, Asquith told his wife, who was resting, that 'the precautionary telegram' about possible British participation in the European war had been sent all round the Empire:

(I never saw Henry so keen outwardly—his face looked quite small and handsome. He sat on the foot of my bed.)

M. (passionately moved, I sat up, and felt 10 feet high.) How thrilling! Oh! Tell me, aren't you excited, darling?

H. (who generally smiles with his eyebrows slightly turned, quite gravely kissed me, and said) It will be very interesting…

In her *Autobiography*, which was of course written in the full light of the horrors of that conflict, Margot subtly alters this account, to make it appear less jarring: 'Deeply moved, and thrilled with excitement, I…said: "Has it come to this?"'[2] Six days later, on Tuesday 4 August, Margot records seeing her husband 'for one moment' in his room after he had announced the British ultimatum to Berlin in the Commons.

He was sitting writing in his room. We looked at each other.

M. 'So it is all up?'

H. 'Yes, it is all up.' He had tears in his eyes.

---

[1] *Autobiography*, ii. 205.
[2] *Autobiography*, ii. 159.

This is practically the end of the diary entry in question, but in the *Auto-biography* Margot embellishes it, suggesting that she went on to write in her journal: 'What was he thinking of?...His sons?...My son was too young to fight.'[1] This does not accord with what we know of Asquith's feelings at the time. In particular two comments in his letters to Venetia Stanley, about their mutual friend Edward Horner, suggest strongly that on 4 August 1914 he had little fear about any of his sons being called on to fight abroad.[2]

Margot chose stout volumes bound in red cloth for most of her diaries, but occasionally also used a white vellum binding. Heavy locks were screwed on to many of the covers. By 1910 she wrote on the right-hand pages only, using the left for brief reminders and marginal comments, and for pasting in letters and newspaper cuttings. In later diaries many letters were left loose. Margot was advised at one point by A. J. Balfour to leave broad margins on her pages, as this would allow room for later comments. She took this advice, which later redounded to the detriment of the giver: in 1921 she added a note against a contemporary passage praising Balfour: 'I think I am wrong here, he is an obstinate man and a bitter, jealous and even an unfair enemy.'

Margot wrote the diary usually in bed in the early morning, and most of her untidy narratives show every sign of haste and impatience (see illustration, p. xxii). She worked too fast to be particular about punctuation, and made frequent use of dashes and of a rudimentary ampersand.

From girlhood Margot had lived a full life in society, and had acquired a large acquaintance, and she did not allow either motherhood—she had two children with Asquith—or the role of stepmother to five others to inhibit her social activities. These loom large in the earlier diaries in particular, but in order to concentrate on the political events of Asquith's

---

[1] Asquith had four sons by his first marriage, and one with Margot—Anthony—to whom she here refers (see Biographical Notes).

[2] *Autobiography*, ii. 195. HHA to BVS, 10 and 11 Aug. 1914: *Asquith–Stanley*, 62, 165; Asquith told Venetia, 11 Aug., that Edward Horner, though 'full of zeal' for soldiering, was 'not likely to get nearer the front than Winchester'. For a glaring instance of rearrangement of material in the *Autobiography* (ii. 209–17) see its treatment of her Diary entry for 12 Dec. 1914, pp. 58–60 below.

premiership—with which she was closely involved—the editors have excluded most of her musings on her family, as well as lists of many of the guests that she entertained, and also passages where there is obvious repetition. All omissions are marked with ellipses.

Margot was apt to be stimulated to reflection by starting or completing a Diary volume; for the reader these breaks come fortuitously, and, apart from them, her narrative is continuous. The editors have divided the material in the 1914–16 diaries into nine parts, and the text into paragraphs, with the dialogues indented, for greater clarity. The narrative has been more fully punctuated than Margot allowed, with brackets, apostrophes, inverted commas, or full stops added where these are deemed necessary. Stops after initials have been made uniform: for example, Margot had four different ways of abbreviating 'Lloyd George', and 'Ll.G.' has been preferred. Obvious mistakes, such as 'flaunt' for 'flout' have been silently corrected; and contractions such as 'sd' and 'wd' have been expanded.

Margot was on the whole a careful speller, although, when in a hurry, she could write 'crisiss' for the plural of 'crisis', or render a term such as 'stellenbosched' as 'stellenboshed' (see Glossary). She used French words and phrases freely. Her most curious habit was to write words beginning with 'ex' without the 'e': this has not been reproduced. On the other hand the editors have retained the many capital letters scattered throughout the narrative, usually for emphasis or in moments of strong feeling. Two examples may suffice: 'The capacity to feel deeply, to <u>Love</u> <u>Really</u>, to give of yourself <u>Freely</u>'; and her transcription of Lloyd George's remark about Lord Selborne as 'a Real Donkey of the best type'.[1]

As the former of these examples suggests, underlining was used by Margot for emphasis, particularly as an outlet for her indignation at times of crisis: one, two or even three lines might be used. These have been retained, although her triple-underlining has perforce been rendered as double-underlining. Foreign words are italicized, as are also names of

---

[1] Diary, 7 May 1915 (below, pp. 103–5) and 11 Nov. 1912 respectively.

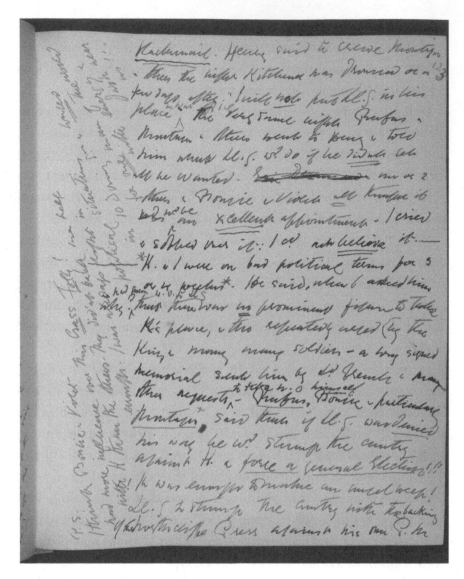

FIGURE 1 Margot's handwriting on the morning of 16 December 1916, the day on which she and Henry left Downing Street, recounting the events of 5–15 December 1916.

newspapers and of ships. The object in all of this has been to preserve the character of the diaries while eliminating stylistic oddities which the reader might find awkward.

Biographical footnotes accompany the diary text, but not the introductory essay, and they are as a rule given at the first mention of the individual in question. Where a prominent character is mentioned in the diary without an accompanying biographical note, it is likely that they will be found in the extended appendix of Biographical Notes: this is indicated with an asterisk against their name in the Index, and at the first mention of their name in the diary text. Also included as appendices are a Bibliography, Chronology, Family Trees, and Map of the Western Front.

The bibliographic references for the six volumes of the diary on which this edition is based are as follows:

Diary Dates	Bodleian Reference
February 1912–September 1914	M.S.Eng. d. 3210
October 1914–May 1915	M.S.Eng. d. 3211
May–July 1915	M.S.Eng. d. 3212
July–November 1915	M.S.Eng. d. 3213
December 1915–July 1916	M.S.Eng. d. 3214
July 1916–August 1917	M.S.Eng. d. 3215

Bodleian Library references for all of Margot's diary volumes are given in the Bibliography.

ABBREVIATIONS USED IN THE TEXT AND NOTES

BEF	British Expeditionary Force
Bt.	Baronet
Ch.	Chapter
CID	Committee of Imperial Defence
CIGS	Chief of Imperial General Staff
cr.	created
d.	died
GHQ	General Headquarters
Kt.	Knight
m.	married
memo.	memorandum
Nat. Lib. Fed.	National Liberal Federation
n.	note
OED	*Oxford English Dictionary*
p., pp.	page, pages
Parl. Deb.	*Parliamentary Debates*, i.e. Hansard
PPS	Parliamentary Private Secretary
QMG	Quartermaster General
RGA	Royal Garrison Artillery
RND	Royal Naval Division
s.	succeeded
WO	War Office

ABBREVIATIONS OF NAMES USED IN THE TEXT AND NOTES

Ann	Ann Dickson-Poynder, Lady Islington
A.J.B./Arthur	Arthur James Balfour
Austen	Austen Chamberlain
Beb	Herbert Asquith
B.L.	Bonar Law
Bongie/Bongy	Maurice Bonham Carter
Bron	Auberon Herbert
Charty	Charlotte Monkton Lister, Lady Ribblesdale, née Tennant
Clemmie/Clemmy	Clementine Churchill (née Hozier)
Cys	Cyril Asquith
Da	David Davies
E/Eliz.	Elizabeth Asquith
Edgar	Edgar D'Abernon, né Vincent
Eric	Eric Drummond
Etty/Ettie	Ethel Grenfell, Lady Desborough
F.E.	Frederick Edwin Smith
H/HHA	Herbert Henry Asquith
Jack	John Poynder Dickson-Poynder, 1st Baron Islington
Joe	Joseph Chamberlain
K/K. of K.	(Horatio Herbert) Lord Kitchener
Laura	(Octavia) Laura Lyttelton, née Tennant
Ll.G.	David Lloyd George
Loulou	Lewis Harcourt

Lucy	Lucy Graham-Smith née Tennant
M	Margot Asquith
Master (the)	Alexander Murray, Master of Elibank
McK	Reginald McKenna
Oc	Arthur Asquith
Pamela	Pamela Tennant née Wyndham
Patrick	Patrick Shaw-Stewart
Puffin/Puff	Anthony Asquith
Rufus	Rufus Isaacs, Lord Reading
St John	St John Brodrick, Viscount Midleton
Venetia	Venetia Stanley/Montagu
V/Violet	Violet Asquith (later Bonham Carter)
Walter	Walter Long
Winston	Winston Churchill

INTRODUCTION

1. Margot Asquith née Tennant

Margaret Emma Alice Tennant, known to everyone as 'Margot', was born on 2 February 1864, the sixth daughter and eleventh child, from his first marriage, of Sir Charles Tennant, a Scottish industrialist and entrepreneur, who amassed a fortune in chemicals and mining.[1] By 1882, when Margot, his youngest daughter, had her first London season, Tennant had become a well-established figure in society, with an estate at Glen in Peeblesshire, where he was Liberal MP for the local constituency of Peebles and Selkirk, and a London house in Grosvenor Square. He collected Reynolds, Constables, and Turners, and was known for his sociability and generosity, one party guest at his London home remembering it 'ablaze with lights and alive with flunkeys; the drawing rooms full of people'.[2] Margot inherited much of his quick mind and bold temperament, and all of his naive egotism and tactlessness; and, though good-hearted and fearless, she was extremely wilful and assertive.[3] These inherited defects were exacerbated by her upbringing. Her mother, who had lost her first four children, made little attempt to control her. She did not undergo the social discipline of schooling; and at Glen she had been, in her own words, 'as wild as a hawk, a kind of queen', living what Gladstone's daughter Mary called 'a spoiling life'.[4] At seventeen she was well known for her pluck on the hunting field, where, according to Winston

[1] For Sir Charles Tennant (made a Baronet in 1885), see *Autobiography*, ed. Bonham Carter, xvi–xix; Bennett, *Margot*, 19–20; and Biographical Notes.

[2] Symonds, *Letters*, ii. 250.

[3] For Margot on her father see diary, 6 June 1906: d. 3204 fos 157–64, *Autobiography*, i .9. For her resemblance to him see O. T. Falk, 13 Feb. 1961: d. 3279 fo 233. For her capacity to offend, Lady F. Balfour's reproof, 5 Mar. 1912: c. 6670 fos 131–8; Cynthia Asquith, *Diaries*, 68, 210, *Remember*, ii. 16; Drew, *Acton*, 140; Brock, *Asquith–Stanley*, 9; Ziegler, *Diana Cooper*, 60–1.

[4] D. 3199, fo. 177; Drew, *Acton*, 136; Mrs Mary Drew, who had known Margot since 1882, was Gladstone's second daughter; Margot wrote 28 Aug. 1916 (marginal note) that when on honeymoon, she had been 'the most spoilt…egotistical creature': d. 3199 fo. 151. For her kindness see Spender and Asquith i. 225; *Tom Jones Diary*, 1931–50, 59; Horner, *Time Remembered*, 162; Hankey diary: Hankey Papers, HNKY 1/1 (10 Dec. 1916). For Margot's lifelong inability to change her ways see *Autobiography*, i. 283–4 (Morley's advice, 1894); d. 3200, fo. 150; d. 3204 fo. 19; d. 3210 fo. 185; Gardiner, *People*, 71; *Belloc Lowndes Diaries*, 271. For the period she spent in a 'hyper-refined seminary for twelve young ladies' see *Autobiography*, i. 72–7: it hardly represented 'schooling'.

Churchill, she 'came sometimes to grief, but always to the fore'.[1] Ten years later Benjamin Jowett, the Master of Balliol College, Oxford, told her that her 'cleverness almost amounted to genius', while chiding her for wasting 'her time and her gifts'.[2] The waste was greater even than Jowett knew. Within a year or two of coming to London for her debut Margot had formed a romantic attachment with an athletic and equestrian ne'er-do-well named Peter Flower, some years older than herself.[3] This attachment delayed for her the serious pursuit of a husband.

By the 1880s girls in Britain were being given increased freedom and a better chance to shine. London society was changing fast under the impact of 'new money', where family wealth was not derived from inherited land.[4] The Tennant girls, daughters of 'one of the earliest provincial industrialists to become a major metropolitan figure', were products and beneficiaries of this trend.[5] The most beautiful, Charlotte ('Charty') Tennant, married an eligible hunting peer, Lord Ribblesdale, in 1877, and the most charming, Laura, used her considerable social grace to smooth the way for her youngest sister in London society. After a slow start both girls achieved a remarkable success, and in 1885 Laura married Alfred Lyttelton, cricketer and politician, and a man revered among his contemporaries as an exemplar of the English character.[6] Margot was devastated by Laura's death after just eleven months of marriage, following childbirth, but the tragedy consolidated her social position. Henceforth she became a central figure in a select group of friends who had known and admired Laura, and who were drawn to one another in her memory. They had no formal organization, but their association became recognizable during

[1] *Daily Mail*, 4 Nov. 1920.
[2] *Autobiography*, i. 104. For Jowett, see Biographical Notes.
[3] Peter Lewis (/Louis) Flower (1856–1902); younger brother of 1st Baron Battersea. See *Autobiography*, i. 229–60.
[4] In Nancy W. Ellenberger's forty 'original' Souls, 1887, Margot and Edith Balfour were the two members who lacked any aristocratic connections: Ellenberger, thesis, 7.
[5] Richard Davenport-Hines, *ODNB*, 'Tennant, Sir Charles'.
[6] For Laura see *Autobiography*, i. 33–7; Bennett, *Margot*, 39; Horner, *Time Remembered*, 31, 161; *Hawarden Letters*, 173; for Alfred Lyttelton, see H. C. G. Matthew, *ODNB*, 'Lyttelton, Alfred'; and see also Biographical Notes.

1887. By this date serious discussion in a gathering which included women had become socially acceptable,[1] and the group soon had a reputation for earnest explorations into the spiritual problems that occupied British intellectual circles during the post-Darwinian era. Because of this they were given the nickname 'the Souls',[2] and their existence pointed to a social and religious change: during the era of Gladstone and Salisbury discussion of the deepest matters was thought apt to undermine religious faith, but during the next era it was held by many of the elite to be the foundation on which Protestant faith could best be built.[3]

Although the nickname of 'The Souls' had been conferred derisively, membership of the group represented admission to Britain's young and aspiring elite, and Margot's mental agility, effrontery, and hunger for attention brought her special prominence. She was portrayed in one of the century's most widely read novels, Mrs Humphry Ward's *Robert Elsmere* (1888), where the beautiful, stylish, and spirited Rose Leyburn is supposedly modelled on her. But occupying the limelit place was not the same as attracting an eligible fiancé: and the Souls, though far more interesting in membership than the aristocratic set led by the Prince of Wales, did not include many potential suitors for Margot. Moreover, some of the stories about her conduct at Glen were far from reassuring. There were only three unmarried girls among the twenty women Souls of 1887: Margot was, of course, one, but the other two were not allowed to visit her at Glen.[4]

The Souls flourished during the aftermath of a great political change, and amid the bitter controversies which it had engendered. Under the

---

[1] Cannadine, *Aristocracy*, 351. For one symptom of the increasing 'independence' allowed to young, upper-class women, see figures for university attendance by 1880, *Nineteenth-Century Oxford*, ii (Howarth), 239–40. Henry James's early novels portray this development: *Portrait of a Lady* was published in 1881.

[2] Balfour, *Autobiography*, 231–3; Liddell, *Notes*, 212; Ellenberger, 'The Souls and London "Society"', 133–4; *More Memories*, 147 n. 1.

[3] *Autobiography*, i. 120–1; Sutherland, *Ward*, 94–5. For the clash in 1879–80 between the two religious attitudes mentioned see *Nineteenth-Century Oxford*, ii. 245–7 (founding of Lady Margaret Hall and Somerville Hall).

[4] They were Edith ('DD') Balfour and Betty Ponsonby. Mrs A. L. Smith thought Margot 'fast'. See Raymond Asquith to H. T. Baker, 25 Aug. 1901: Jolliffe, *Raymond Asquith*, 82.

franchise reforms of 1884–5, which were in operation until 1918, the electorate of the United Kingdom was expanded and reorganized so that it would include some three-fifths of adult males, arranged in constituencies largely of the single-member type. The system created was the outcome of a compromise between the two main parties, the Liberals and Conservatives.[1] Seen in conjunction with the birth of a popular press, which would soon cater to the needs of a mass readership that owed its literacy to the passage of the 1870 Education Act,[2] the new system was expected to strengthen the radical elements in both parties. This was thought likely to entail, first, a gradual drift away from the Liberals of their most aristocratic anti-radical section, the Whigs; and secondly, the advancement of Lord Randolph Churchill, who was seen as the Conservatives' answer to the radicalism of Joseph [Joe] Chamberlain. These expectations were proved wrong when, in December 1885, Gladstone's conversion to Irish Home Rule was incautiously revealed by his son Herbert.

The prospect of a Liberal government committed to granting Irish self-government, entailing the dismemberment of the Union, changed the political landscape, and the Whigs' gradual defection to Conservatism became a stampede. Joe Chamberlain moved with them most reluctantly, for a variety of reasons, his dislike of Whiggism ultimately being overborne by a belief that English radicals could not be converted en masse to reversing the Union with Ireland. A return of the Chamberlainites to their old Liberal allegiance was expected once the Liberals had repented of trying to give the Irish their own Parliament. There could, however, be no such reunion while Gladstone retained the Liberal leadership; and he did so until March 1894, more than eight years after he had first raised the Home Rule flag. Meanwhile the Liberals had lost much of Joe Chamberlain's following, in the Commons and in the constituencies,

---

[1] *Ensor, 1870–1914*, 88. For the extent to which the 1884–5 system fell short of manhood suffrage and of 'one man one value', see N. Blewett, 'The Franchise in the UK, 1885–1918', *Past and Present*, 32 (1965), 27–56.

[2] George Newnes's weekly *Tit-Bits*, started in 1880, was the harbinger of a new style in journalism: *Ensor, 1870–1914*, 145.

and most of their strength in the Lords. In June 1886 their first Home Rule Bill was defeated there on its second reading by the narrow margin of 343 votes to 313: in September 1893 their second such bill was rejected by the crushing majority of 419 votes to 41, the Conservative opponents of Home Rule augmented by the flood of 'Liberal Unionist' peers.

Laura Tennant's widower, Alfred Lyttelton, was a key figure in the process whereby the Conservative Party, with the Souls' help, absorbed quondam Liberals following the Home Rule split. In spite of being Mrs Gladstone's nephew, Lyttelton was moving towards Conservatism; and his combination of sporting prowess with a good brain made him a popular Soul. One of his fellow benchers in the Inner Temple was an ambitious and promising young MP, Herbert Henry Asquith, whom he introduced in 1890 to the Souls, and to Margot.[1] Asquith, a star from Jowett's Balliol in its greatest decade, and a firm Liberal,[2] was soon accepted as an agreeable late arrival by the Souls, and particularly by Margot; and he was welcomed at first by Margot's mother as a distraction from the hazards of Peter Flower. By July 1891, despite having a young and charming wife, Helen, and five children, Asquith was writing to Margot in intimate terms: 'You have made me a different man and brought back into my life the feeling of spring time.'[3] Though Margot was responsive to him, he was not the sole focus of her attentions, and in the same month that he wrote to her, she wrote in encouraging terms to his friend Alfred Milner, an extremely eligible bachelor, and another of Jowett's Balliol stars: 'I want you to like me always. I feel as if I could give my friends a good deal.'[4]

[1] Spender and Asquith, i. 97: date given wrongly as 1891 in *Autobiography*, i. 261. Asquith had been known in youth as Herbert: his second Christian name was used only by Margot, and later by a few close friends.

[2] Asquith's Liberalism was more firmly grounded than Alfred Lyttelton's: his uncle Willans had married Edward Baines's daughter. Baines, whose family owned the *Leeds Mercury*, was a Congregationalist, a teetotaller, and a radical Member for Leeds. Asquith was taken to the House of Commons in 1865, when he was 12, to hear Baines moving a Bill for extending the Borough franchise: Spender and Asquith, i. 27–8; Koss, *Asquith*, 3–5. Lyttelton, despite his Gladstonian connection and comparative poverty in youth, was a peer's son and the most prominent Etonian sportsman of his day.

[3] *Autobiography*, i. 247; Asquith to Margot, 22 July 1891.

[4] Bennett, *Margot*, 95. Evan Charteris (1864–1940) was another who had received indiscreet encouragement from Margot: Diary, d. 3217, fo. 74; Davenport-Hines, *Ettie*, 75.

At the time that those two letters were written Lady Tennant was planning to bring Margot into Alfred Milner's company whenever possible. Margot needed, as her mother thought, not another admirer, however eminent he might be, but a capable husband. The situation changed dramatically when, on 11 September 1891, Helen Asquith died of typhoid while the Asquiths were holidaying on the Island of Arran. The grieving widower turned to Margot: 'There is no one else,' he wrote to her a month later, 'to whom I can talk freely, or from whom I get in return light and help and hope.'[1] This was the start of an ardent courtship which ended, after some hesitation on Margot's part, when they were married on 10 May 1894, the marriage register being signed by four Prime Ministers, past, present, and future.[2]

2. Margot and Henry

It is not difficult to see why Asquith eventually succeeded in persuading Margot to shoulder the obligations which his love for her entailed. By the end of 1893 she knew that she must marry.[3] E. F. Benson's novel *Dodo*, portraying a scatterbrained society girl of that nickname, was achieving a large sale; and it was widely taken to portray the most criticized woman in the Souls.[4] That group came into a bad light after revelations had appeared in the press about the sexual indiscretions of a founder member,

---

[1] Spender and Asquith, i. 102, where Ch. 9 consists largely of selected passages from Asquith's letters to Margot, Oct. 1891 to May 1894. For the date of the letter quoted see Margot's Papers MSS.Eng.c. 6685, fo. 104. Asquith also corresponded during those years, and after his second marriage, with 'Ettie' Grenfell (from Dec. 1905, Lady Desborough): Davenport-Hines, *Ettie*, 58–60.

[2] Gladstone, Rosebery, Balfour, and Asquith himself.

[3] Margot's time in the Souls was less 'triumphant' than she recalled: for the term see d. 3204 fo 175 (Diary, 29 Oct. 1906), *Autobiography*, i. 214; Diary, 11 November 1918: 'I had 10 years of the most remarkable girlhood any female ever had': d. 3216 fo 250r. See *Fortnightly Review*, 312, 1 Dec. 1892, for a critical assessment of the Souls by W. H. Mallock (1849–1923). For later favourable views of the group see D'Abernon, *Portraits*, 94; R. Cecil, *All the Way*, 44–5; Davenport-Hines, *Ettie*, 365 (quoting Violet Bonham Carter, Oct. 1947).

[4] Between 1893 and 1914 sixteen editions of *Dodo* were published. For a skit derived from it see *Punch*, 14 Oct. 1893. A. F. Lascelles, writing in 1945, thought it 'as bad a best seller as ever was'. For an even earlier fictional reference to Margot see A. C. Benson's *Memoirs of Arthur Hamilton, B.A., by Christopher Carr* (1886).

Harry Cust.[1] Margot had once said that she meant to marry a future Prime Minister,[2] and having become Home Secretary at the age of 41 Asquith seemed to be exactly that. His quality as a parliamentary speaker was already beyond doubt, and ministerial office proved him to be equally capable in administration. Once, when Margot was on the verge of breaking off her engagement to him, she was told by her sister Charty: 'Don't be a fool, darling. You are more than lucky to have made… Mr Asquith fond of you. It is high time that you married. If you are not very careful no decent man will marry you.'[3]

Asquith's love for Margot was connected with three prominent features of his personality: he was notably self-confident, conservative in habit, and pleasure-loving. The Balliol of the 1870s had left a deep mark on him. He combined great optimism and confidence about the power which his intellectual grasp and debating ability gave him, with a certain conservatism, not in his political views but in personal habits.[4] Finally, straitened years in boyhood and at the start of his bar career had given him a hunger for luxury and high life. On the rebound from what he saw as his first wife, Helen's, restrictive influence and relative lack of ambition for him, he was attracted to Margot's great social confidence and éclat. He could not see that his idea of the kind of wife he needed was no longer suitable to an aspiring *Liberal* leader. He had fallen deeply in love with a woman who was certainly equipped to shine in London society, and who, despite her extravagance, might well obtain, by gift and inheritance, the resources that his political career would need; but these attributes came at a cost, and marrying Margot represented a gamble redolent of a man who was slow to recognize change, and whose amazing self-confidence had made him a little arrogant.

---

[1] For Cust's marriage with Nina Welby-Gregory see Ellenberger, thesis, 213–14; Davenport-Hines, *Ettie*, 84–6. Cust lost his parliamentary seat when Lord Brownlow's backing was withdrawn. Balfour's unsuccessful efforts to find him another in Manchester encountered opposition from Millicent Fawcett and others, and led to press publicity. See *New York Herald Tribune*, 25 Feb. 1894.

[2] For Margot's remark to the Duchess of Devonshire about marrying a Prime Minister see *Autobiography*, i. 145.

[3] *Off the Record*, 96.

[4] Churchill, *Great Contemporaries*, 137.

A junior barrister of this era would be thought particularly unwise to stand for Parliament, because he was expected to be available in court at any time—MPs were not then paid a salary—and it had thus been risky for Asquith to enter the Commons in 1886 before he had taken silk. That bold step was nevertheless rewarded when a brilliant cross-examination during the proceedings of the Parnell Commission in 1889[1] enabled him to become a QC the following year, with appropriately higher earning potential. And while still a junior barrister he had taken the astonishing decision not to become either a law officer or a judge, thus eschewing the route that traditionally allowed an impecunious lawyer to combine political advancement with a degree of financial security. Instead, as he told his pupil John Roskill, he aimed to become Home Secretary. The audacity of this plan lay in the fact that while a high law officer, for example an ex-Attorney General, might return to his legal practice, there seemed to be no precedent for an ex-Home Secretary to do this. Asquith assured Roskill that he was not deterred by this; but, should he be successful politically and climb to the highest office, this would not solve the danger of financial insecurity, but simply defer it, since an ex-Prime Minister would not be able to return to his legal practice. A successful law officer, by contrast, had a good chance of becoming Lord Chancellor; and an ex-Lord Chancellor, unlike an ex-premier, was entitled to a pension.

When the political furore and party schism of the later 1880s subsided some of the Liberal leaders realized that social prominence was no longer as important for them as it had once been. Walter Bagehot had written in 1875 that a Prime Minister needed to be active in London society in order to keep abreast of movements of opinion within the elite of his party, and must 'combine the vivacity of an idle man with the assiduity of a very laborious one'.[2] But in 1891 Edward Hamilton recorded John Morley's view

---

[1] For Asquith's cross-examination of D. J. Macdonald, the manager of The Times, see Spender and Asquith, i. 62.

[2] Economist, 2 Jan. 1875. Writing after the enactment of the 1867 franchise extension, Bagehot assumed the two main political parties to be practically identical in social composition. For this see also Ensor, 1870–1914, 1; Ellenberger, thesis, 252 (Ishbel Aberdeen and Edith Balfour echoing Bagehot).

that, where members of the opposite party were concerned, 'every out-ward form of courtesy should be observed but there should be no social intimacy'.[1] Unlike Morley, Asquith did not grasp how quickly Bagehot's world had vanished, or the extent to which his advice represented a snare to any Liberal aspirant for the premiership. Nine-tenths of London so-ciety were likely to be his political opponents; and mingling in it might incline his middle-class followers to suspect the strength of his allegiance to his party's principles. Asquith did not need a wife who had been taught by the Souls to take a prominent social role, to absorb ideas and seek friendships among the leading members of both parties, and to give advice to all and sundry on her husband's behalf. A. J. Balfour told Mar-got, in October 1905, that the task of a politician's wife was 'to make and keep the peace'; he was criticizing Mary Curzon for failing, despite her love for her husband, to do this.[2] There is no sign in the diary that Margot took the remark as possibly applying to herself.[3] A wife who was econom-ical, and modest in her social pretensions, would help Asquith to save enough from his official emoluments to sustain his family when, on the swing of the political pendulum, those had been lost. An extravagant wife who might or might not inherit a share of her father's fortune (in the event Margot *did not*), and who overrated a set of political notions gained from a group of intimate friends who were predominately Conservatives and Liberal Unionists, would not fit easily into that long-term pattern.

All of this pointed to a second marriage, not with Margot, but with someone who, while possessing an ample private income, was in other ways not unlike his first wife, Helen.[4] Above all, her death had left the widower in need of a wife who was capable of fulfilling the difficult role

---

[1] Edward Hamilton's diary, 6 Oct. 1891: Ellenberger, thesis, 256.

[2] George Curzon (1859–1925), Viceroy of India 1899–1905, and prominent Soul, mar-ried, 1895, Mary Victoria Leiter (1870–1906), the daughter of a Chicago millionaire and philanthropist.

[3] Diary, d. 3204 fo. 63ᵛ.

[4] For Helen's income see Spender and Asquith, i. 42, 45. For her character see Spender and Asquith, i. 73, 98; Haldane, *Autobiography*, 103; Bonham Carter, *Diaries, 1904–1914*, 335; Koss, *Asquith*, 15; *Autobiography*, i. 262–3, 284; diary, d. 3217, fos 213–14. Margot's remarks about Helen should be read in the light of Clifford, *Asquiths*, 6–23, 32–5. Helen's letters to Asquith are in Bonham Carter Papers, Bodleian Library, 623–35.

FIGURE 2 The Asquith family and friends at Glen, Easter 1904. Left to right: Elizabeth Asquith, H. H. Asquith, Olive MacLeod (standing at back), Margot Asquith (seated, foreground), Katharine Horner (seated in profile), Violet Asquith (seated at back), H. T. Baker (standing at back), Arthur Asquith (seated at back), Cyril Asquith (seated in front), Edward Horner, Raymond Asquith.

of a stepmother. Margot proved reasonably successful with Asquith's four boys, the eldest and most formidable of whom, Raymond, wrote to her from Oxford in 1898: 'I would certainly consult you if I got into any difficulty for I think you know more of the world and take a saner view of it than almost anyone else.'[1] Her main trouble soon proved to be Asquith's only daughter, Violet. A girl of great ability, who had lost her mother at the age of 4, and who from then on had been specially attached to her father,[2] Violet would have tested the skills of a stepmother far more tactful than Margot. In the event she proved almost more than Margot could manage, and the difficulty in their relations continually taxed the man to whom they were both, in different ways, devoted.

---

[1] Jolliffe, *Raymond Asquith*, 35.
[2] Bonham Carter, *Diaries, 1914–1945*, 85–8, shows how close this relationship was.

Most political leaders reach the top several decades after they have formed their guiding ideas, and much depends on the extent to which reflection and imaginative insight enable them to adjust in middle age to the changing scene. Asquith's second marriage did not encourage him in this direction. He and Margot were outwardly so dissimilar in personality that neither they nor most of their contemporaries realized how similar were their trajectories. Both of them symbolized the start of the immense industrial and social transformation which would soon widen and enlarge the British elite from being a small group based largely on hereditary privilege into today's professionalized ruling class. Both had experienced, when young, an early and highly intoxicating phase of that transformation. This had made both of them over-optimistic about the future, and their role in it, and yet fundamentally backward-looking. They were strangely blind to some of the social and political realities of the Edwardian age—to the increasing power and influence of the popular press, for example, and of the need to show some signs of conforming, outwardly at least, to the mores of a mass electorate.

In career terms at least, Margot's much-discussed marriage started well. Sir Charles Tennant settled capital worth £5,000 a year on her, and obtained a West End mansion for the pair, which, though expensive to run, was at least very fashionable.[1] When the Rosebery government collapsed in June 1895 Asquith's return to his bar practice was accepted without adverse comment, despite the prediction of a leading parliamentary journalist that this would prove to be 'an act of political suicide unparalleled in recent history'.[2] A period in opposition could be faced without great alarm. When the leadership of the opposition became vacant at the end of 1898 Sir Charles declined a plea from the Unionist leader and Soul, A. J. Balfour, that he should provide funds that would allow Asquith to accept the position, and it went instead to Sir Charles's fellow

[1] 20 Cavendish Square: Bennett, *Margot*, 128–9. Used as a family home, in which many guests were entertained, this house needed a staff of about fourteen. By the 1890s such establishments were commoner among the Conservative leaders than among the Liberal.
[2] Lucy, Diary, i. 106. The theory was that an aspiring politician ought to be available whether his party was in or out of office. Lucy was giving the accepted view.

Glaswegian Sir Henry Campbell-Bannerman.[1] This was no more than a minor setback for the Asquiths. C.B.'s health was indifferent, and the Liberals had no immediate prospect of regaining office. Nor was there any sign that Sir Charles's refusal to help had resulted from a withdrawal of his favour, or from the prospect of his fresh parental responsibilities: Lady Tennant had died in 1895, and Sir Charles remarried three years later, but Margot received further largesse from him around the turn of the century.[2]

More serious was the impact of the political troubles that followed the fall of the Liberal government, and in particular the elevation of imperial affairs in national politics. The Salisbury administration formed in 1895 was a coalition of Conservatives and Liberal Unionists, in which Joe Chamberlain had become Colonial Secretary. With the prospects of a return to Liberal ranks now all but gone, Chamberlain adroitly used his new office to cement his personal standing among the party that he had joined; in so doing he caused a realignment in Liberal ranks also. The younger generation of British intellectuals, viewing the strength of the recently formed German Empire, were convinced that, if the British were to keep their place in this new Europe, they must cherish and develop their overseas heritage. This was made more practicable by the technological advances of the era: the development of the trans-continental railway, and of the ocean liner, steel-built and powered by triple-expansion engines. These changes were widely recognized, and most of the Souls, including Margot, thought that a more imperial outlook would replace the old 'parochial' politics.[3] But few foresaw the skill with which Joe Chamberlain would transfer his demagogy from radical causes to an aggressive imperialism that would be welcomed by many Tories. The outbreak of the Boer War, in 1899, provided him with an ideal opportunity to capitalize

---

[1] *Ensor, 1870–1914*, 239 n. 1; Young, *Balfour*, 169–70; Koss, *Haldane*, 44.

[2] 31 Jan. 1900, Williamson Hill and co. to Sir C. Tennant; 20 October 1901, Asquith to same; Glenconner Papers. Margot, however, told Mary Curzon at a lunch party, May 1901, that her finances were distressing: Bradley, *Lady Curzon*, 97.

[3] *Autobiography*, i. 139 ('the old parochialisms'); Ellenberger, thesis, 276–8. See Wells, *New Machiavelli*, 365, for Balfour's view expressed by 'Evesham', a fictional character based on A.J.B., who accepted the likeness: Asquith, C., *Remember*, ii. 5–6.

on the imperial issue, while presenting his old party with a dilemma. In its response the Liberal Party fractured into 'pro-Boer' and 'Liberal imperialist' elements. The actual divergence between Campbell-Bannerman, a leader of the former camp, and Asquith, a representative of the latter, was not great when the war began, but as it progressed it widened. C.B., and most of his followers, were not outright opponents of the war; but they deplored the British policies which had preceded it, and, unlike Asquith, they did not respect the judgement of Alfred Milner, then High Commissioner for South Africa, who was thought by critics to have precipitated it. The reasonable view about the war which Asquith shared with Rosebery, leader of the Liberal Imperialists, seemed in some Liberal circles too similar to the 'swaggering aggressiveness' encouraged by Chamberlain, which all Liberals abhorred.[1] In fact both 'C.B.-ites' and Rosebery's group deplored the concentration camps which Kitchener used in conducting the campaign, but the Conservatives were able to exploit these divisions to electoral advantage, and these years dented even Asquith's optimism. His hostess at a dinner party in November 1902, Beatrice Webb, observed that he had become 'disheartened with politics...He has resigned himself to missing [the Liberal] leadership.'[2]

A mere five months later Chamberlain came unintentionally to Asquith's rescue. The Boer War had brought the price of militant Empire building home to the British electorate. A new variety of Unionist populism was needed, and Chamberlain switched to an economic version of imperialism. In May 1903 he declared for Tariff Reform, whereby tax revenue would be raised on foreign imports, with preferential rates for goods from within the empire. In September 1903 he threw the Unionists (as the now-permanent coalition between Conservatives and Liberal Unionists was to be known) into disarray by resigning from Balfour's cabinet in order to campaign for it. The system of import duties which he advocated was intended to favour the colonies' agricultural products, thus strength-

---

[1] For the phrase see Ensor, 1870–1914, 250. The Unionist sneer about Campbell-Bannerman being a pro-Boer was wholly unjustified.
[2] Webb Diary, ii. 263 (28 November 1902). See also Webb Diary, 235–6.

ening imperial ties; to create 'work for all', by protecting British industries from 'unfair' foreign competition; and to provide the revenue needed for financing health and unemployment insurance. But Chamberlain's grand scheme was somehow to exclude foreign goods while providing a revenue by admitting them: the finer details had not been thought out with enough care; nor had the attachment of many British voters to free trade and 'cheap bread' been properly anticipated.[1] This was the ideal issue for Asquith to contest. His debating mastery in the House could not be questioned, but he now showed that he could be equally effective on the platform. He travelled up and down the country answering Chamberlain speech by speech, and quickly became the foremost advocate for free trade.[2]

Balfour managed to stay in office for more than two years after Chamberlain had precipitated a Unionist split by declaring for Tariff Reform. He was determined to hang on as Prime Minister because he was initiating important defence developments which, as he feared, an incoming Liberal administration might well have delayed or cancelled. By doing so he put the Committee of Imperial Defence (CID) on a businesslike basis; ensured that Britain obtained a modern, quick-firing field gun, the 18 pounder; and took the lead in naval building, with 'all big-gun' battleships of unprecedented speed and power—the famed 'Dreadnoughts'. But in securing these benefits for his country he greatly enhanced his opponents' electoral prospects, allowing them a lengthy period in which they could campaign on the platform of Free Trade, popularly interpreted as promising a 'bigger loaf'. When Balfour at last resigned, in December 1905, Asquith became Chancellor of the Exchequer in the government led by Campbell-Bannerman, Sir Charles Tennant providing some more financial help.[3] By the end of January 1906, when the Liberals had won a

---

[1] Amery, Julian, *Chamberlain*, iv. 531–2.

[2] Asquith saw at once how the Liberals could gain; *Autobiography*, ii. 53. For his mastery of the free trade case see Amery, Julian, *Chamberlain*, iv. 450. For Campbell-Bannerman's praise for these speeches see Wilson, *CB*, 415.

[3] Sir Charles paid the Asquiths the equivalent of the annual rent for 20 Cavendish Square and so relieved them from the need to move into 11 Downing Street.

startling landslide victory in the general election, Asquith was the recognized heir to an elderly premier who was far from robust, and who headed a party riding the crest of a strong electoral wave.

3.10 Downing Street: 'the wish of my life and the ambition of his'

When the Asquiths at last came, in this way, within reach of 10 Downing Street, both of them showed some of the scars of life. By the summer of 1900 Margot had undergone the misery of losing two of her three children within a few hours of their birth—the surviving child was her daughter Elizabeth, born in 1897—and a year later Mary Curzon, by then the Indian Viceroy's wife, thought her 'perhaps a little left behind in the race of life'; soon afterwards she wrote to her husband that 'Margot's nervous state had developed a tendency of always hurting and wounding'.[1] The birth of a son, Anthony, in 1902 raised Margot's morale for a time, but the happiness of the Souls' years did not return.

Lady Curzon did not limit her criticisms of the Asquiths to reflections on Margot's nervous complaints. She also reported on Asquith's 'amorous interest in various people [and] his reckless consumption of champagne'.[2] Unlike most of his Liberal critics she did not attribute this recent deterioration to Margot's influence. R. B. Haldane, whose close friendship with Asquith dated from the early 1880s, later recounted how Asquith had referred, when young, to John Bright as 'the only man in public life who had risen to eminence without being corrupted by London society'. That society, Haldane later wrote, 'came particularly after his second marriage to have a great attraction for [Asquith], and he grew by degrees diverted from the sterner outlook on life which he and I for long shared'. The words 'particularly after his second marriage' were expunged

---

[1] Bradley, *Lady Curzon*, 88, 122. For the three tragedies see Bennett, *Margot*, 137 (May 1895), 165 (early 1900), 174 (Dec. 1906, date from Margot's Diary). For the two who survived, Elizabeth (b. 1897) and Anthony (b. 1902), see 'family diaries', d. 3205, 3207, 3209, and Biographical Notes.

[2] Bradley, *Lady Curzon*, 122; *Crawford Journals*, 121.

FIGURE 3 Margot with her two surviving children, Elizabeth and Anthony ('Puffin').

before the statement was published.[1] Many political leaders have differed markedly from the bulk of their followers in style and attitudes: few have shown less concern about it than Asquith did. Margot's supposed negative influence on his habits was one of the few points on which Rosebery's views coincided with those of Campbell-Bannerman. In private conversation with his family Rosebery 'deplored the bad influence which Margot had upon her husband', while C.B. told A. G. Gardiner of the *Daily News*: 'Asquith *qua* Asquith is a fine fellow, an honest man and a sincere liberal. But Asquith *cum* Margot is a lost soul.'[2] By 1906 W. T. Stead, the veteran

[1] Haldane, *Autobiography*, 103; Koss, *Asquith*, 16. For Haldane's reflections on the Souls and the Tennant sisters see his *Autobiography*, 120–4; they are characterized by the egotism of nearly all such reflections.

[2] Rhodes James, *Rosebery*, 438 n. 2; Wilson, *CB*, 466. Rosebery, like Queen Victoria, had been among those who deplored the marriage when it was first announced: Bennett, *Margot*, 117, 122.

newspaper editor, was appealing to Margot in the *Review of Reviews* to release her husband from 'the treadmill of society'.[1]

These views were not shared by every Liberal leader or publicist; and
they remain extremely questionable. It seems likely that Margot's influence on her husband's political bearing was neither very great, nor very
welcome to him. While she helped to make him more demonstrative in
public, and sometimes saw the dangers ahead more clearly than he did,
her refusal to recognize her own political ignorance often led him to dis-
regard the specks of gold in the dross of her advice.[2] She was proud of her
perceptiveness in politics, and told her stepson Arthur in July 1915 that
she was 'a sort of political clairvoyant'.[3] In reality her perceptiveness concerned individuals only, and could be overborne by resentments even
with them. Certainly Asquith plunged into the high life at his own wish,
and not at Margot's dictation. Unlike her he did not think consorting with
the grander Unionists to be part of his mission; and there was no danger
of his being seduced from the social reform views entertained in Liberal
circles by 1900. He liked the grandees' champagne, as Hugh Cecil shrewdly
realized, better than their company. Beneath Asquith's Balliol veneer lay
the boy of 12 who had been brought to the Commons' gallery to hear
Edward Baines propound the case for electoral reform; and Jowett's
Balliol had been no nest of toryism. Asquith's Liberal and reforming
views were firm; but he shared his wife's obtuseness in refusing to recognize some contours in the new political landscape. This refusal originated in his conservatism of habit; and his arrogance, concealed by a
pleasant manner, reinforced it.[4] As has already been noted, the periods

---

[1] *Esher Journals*, ii. 304. See also Beatrice Webb on the influence of Asquith's 'brilliant and
silly wife': *Webb Diary*, ii. 64, 77, 236. While some perceptive observers realized that Margot
was not a snob—see, for instance, Drew, *Acton*, 133—when she happened to list her '3 greatest
friends' in her diary in March 1911 they were all prominent Unionist peers: Selborne, Midleton, and Curzon: d. 3208, fo. 132r.

[2] See, for instance, Margot's diary entry of 13 June 1915, p. 156 below.

[3] 18 July 1915, Margot to Arthur Asquith, Arthur Asquith Papers, AMA/05/08.

[4] For Asquith's conservative habits see Spender and Asquith, i. 212 (Cyril Asquith); Bentley,
Those Days, 194–5; Keynes, *Collected Writings*, x. 38–9; Roskill, *Hankey*, i. 234. For his boyhood
visit to the Commons, mentioned earlier, see Koss, *Asquith*, 3–5, 101–2. For his 'natural intellectual scorn' see Margot's preface, xi, to *Memories*, i.

of privation earlier in his life had given him a hunger for luxury, which Margot had some of the means to satisfy. She enlarged his access to society, and encouraged him to dress more fashionably and to drop Yorkshire traces from his speech.[1]

But the two most conspicuous changes in his personal habits during the later 1890s, and the ones which were thought to betray the influence of London society, could hardly have originated in Margot's prompting. Her horror of drunkenness was well known; and, while she was tolerant of her husband's liking for the company of pretty girls, to attribute this feature in his habits entirely to her would be patently absurd.[2] By failing to provide a restful home environment, however, she may have made it more likely that he would seek relief from the pressures of office in wine and in the company of young women. Asquith took to mitigating the strain of living with Margot in middle age by encouraging the 'companions in brightness', in Violet's phrase, who could solace his leisure hours. For some years Margot did not object to what she called her husband's 'little harem'; but in January 1912 he formed a serious romantic attachment to the group's most capable member, Venetia Stanley; and this continued until she revealed her engagement to Edwin Montagu in May 1915. As his correspondence to her makes evident, the intensity of Asquith's feelings for Venetia varied with the strain to which his work was subjecting him. He had been much worried by the labour unrest of early 1912, 1913 being quieter, but in January 1914 the flow of letters and the incidence of meetings rose again.[3] No one suggested in these years that Asquith's drinking interfered materially with his public speaking or transaction of business; but it undoubtedly reduced his moral authority in a party

[1] Diary, d. 3216 fo. 189ʳ. For continuing sneers in the elite at Asquith's personal traits see *Asquith–Stanley*, 118 (W. S. Blunt on 'the square-toed A', Earl Grey on A's 'little bourgeois legs'); Bradley, *Lady Curzon*, 128 (Curzon: 'You cannot transplant the middle classes'). For a similar sneer about Margot's 'want of breeding' from Lady Pembroke see diary, d. 3207, fo. 11. Significantly, Lloyd George thought Asquith 'a stranger…in any other home' than the Nonconformist world of his boyhood: *War Memoirs*, i. 611.

[2] Asquith, C., *Diaries*, 100; Bennett, *Margot*, 166, 253–5.

[3] For the historical importance of the letters from Jan. 1914 onwards see *Asquith–Stanley*, 615–20.

greatly concerned with the harm that drink was doing among the poor, and in the long term it damaged his own health. Balfour told David Lindsay, later 27th Earl of Crawford, in July 1910 that during the Constitutional Conference Asquith was showing 'all his old quickness and ability'; but the two of them agreed, in the light of the premier's 'physical coarsening', that 'he cannot last ten years longer'.[1]

Some months after Asquith became Chancellor of the Exchequer he and Margot received an unexpected and devastating financial blow. When Sir Charles Tennant died in June 1906, leaving more than three million pounds, the daughters of his first marriage received none of it, his will stating that provision had been made for them through their respective marriage settlements during his lifetime.[2] He naturally provided for his widow and the three young children of his second marriage; but neither that marriage, nor his desertion of the Liberals in favour of Tariff Reform, had suggested that the bequests to his first family would all go to his three sons.[3] The effect of this very public reverse for a self-made statesman who had developed expensive tastes, and seemed unwilling or unable to curb his wife's extravagance, was extremely hurtful. Asquith made little attempt to conceal his anger. According to Charles Hobhouse he was 'so sulky at Sir C. Tennant's will that he would take no part in anything'.[4] And from this time onwards he was vulnerable to the accusation that he clung to office, in defiance of principle and conscience, because he could not afford to leave it.[5]

That suspicion, though largely ill founded, dogged him for the rest of his career. It was particularly damaging to a leading statesman who, while

[1] Taylor, 1914–1945, 15 n.1; *Crawford Journals*, 161. For signs that Asquith's sobriety improved during the period of his intense association with Venetia Stanley see *Asquith–Stanley*, 10–11.
[2] See *The Times*, 24 July 1906, 9f, when probate had been granted. Gross estate £3,151,974; net of estate, legacy, and succession duties £2,864,874; at the price levels of 2009 the equivalent to £243,332,393 and £221,168,273. See also short report, *The Times*, 19 June 1906, 11e.
[3] For Sir Charles's membership of Joseph Chamberlain's 'Tariff Commission' see Amery, Julian, *Chamberlain*, v. 305, vi. 473, 531, 532 n. 3.
[4] *Hobhouse Diaries*, 55. See Margot, diary, 20 Jan. 1909 (d.3207, fo. 9) on her father's 'foolish will'.
[5] See, for instance, *National Review*, 62. 894 (Feb. 1914). For Crawford's private reflections on the question see *Crawford Journals*, 280.

much valued for his dominance of debate, was not greatly respected for his conduct and bearing. Having disagreed with many of his party's activists over the Boer War, Asquith seemed, by the date when he became premier, to have cooled on his party's central Gladstonian commitment to Home Rule. Even more dangerous than the Unionist gossip about his dependence on a government salary was the fear among committed Liberals that their Prime Minister might care less for his party's principles than for expensive pleasures of which they disapproved. What would make Asquith so vulnerable in the future was his unflagging insistence on retaining the premiership, and the high salary that went with it, as long as the Liberals held office. More than once he could have protected both his reputation as a statesman of principle, and his income, if he had been prepared to relinquish his place at the 'tip top of the greasy pole' in a reconstruction of the government. If that had ended his tenure of 10 Downing Street he would almost certainly have been offered the Lord Chancellorship, which was named several times before his eventual resignation in December 1916 as an office for which he was extremely well qualified; and, as was mentioned earlier, it carried not merely a good salary but a pension. Champagne and brandy, consumed rather too liberally, were not good for Asquith; but they damaged him less than a substance which Trollope, when depicting a fictional premier (Plantagenet Palliser), had called 'the poison of power'.

The Asquiths' financial setback was followed in December 1906 by Margot's loss of a third baby after a few hours of life: she was ill for much of 1907, and was told by her doctors that she must not have any more children.[1] It was against this sad domestic background that Asquith made his claim on the premiership unassailable. He deployed his power in debate in loyal and highly effective service to C.B., and in his budget for 1907 skilfully made provision for the launch of old age pensions in the following year, thereby establishing that this landmark legislation, a cornerstone in

---

[1] Bennett, *Margot*, 174–5. Lord Carrington, after a weekend as a fellow guest at Nuneham with the King and the Asquiths, noted, 11 July 1909: 'Margot is really an excellent sort, very kind but all nerves and excitement': Carrington MSS Film 1106.

the social reforms of New Liberalism, did not involve a reckless disruption of national finance. Later that year, in June, he concluded several nights of debate on the Prime Minister's motion for reform of the House of Lords with one of his most powerful speeches.[1] In the two years following the Liberals' great electoral victory Asquith had made himself indispensable to his party, and well before Campbell-Bannerman became mortally ill, in February 1908, he had effectively taken the reins. For some weeks that spring even Margot's hunger for drama was satisfied, after Asquith was told to ready himself for the King's summons to 'kiss hands'.

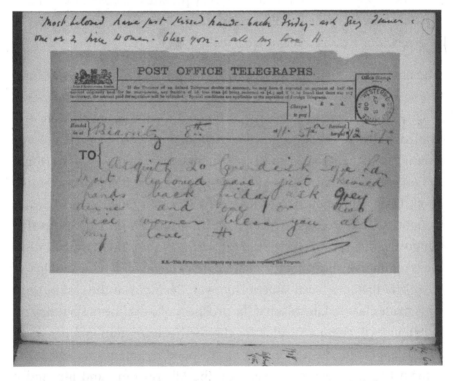

FIGURE 4 Telegram 8 April 1908. H. H. Asquith to Margot Asquith from Biarritz where he had 'kissed hands' in King Edward VII's hotel room on taking office as prime minister.

[1] The effect of this speech on the House was enhanced by Asquith's confession that he was a fairly recent convert to C.B.'s solution for the pressing problem of the Lords' veto power: *Parl. Deb.*, 26 June 1907, 176.1507.

He did so, controversially, in a hotel room at Biarritz, where the King was holidaying, on 8 April 1908.[1] When he had arrived at Charing Cross from Biarritz on 10 April Asquith's first stop was at Downing Street to 'ask after' Campbell-Bannerman, and while waiting outside No. 10 Margot 'wondered for how long we should live there and what we should make of it all'.[2] Reflecting in her diary on the heady days in which her husband became Prime Minister, Margot betrayed the sense of financial insecurity that had clouded her happiness:

> the wish of my life and the ambition of his was accomplished, gloriously happy I felt; but I shed a few very private tears to think...if it could have happened while Papa was alive, how he wd. at once have given £3 or £4,000 a year to do it well.[3]

The absence of financial support, however, would not deter her from 'doing it well', and this ultimately added to her husband's list of worries.

During the interval when Asquith acted for his dying chief he was confronted with three problems which were to dominate his pre-war premiership: spending on naval armaments; the veto power of the House of Lords; and the Irish Nationalists' demand for Home Rule. On 10 March 1908, faced with evidence of increased German facilities for 'Dreadnought' battleship construction, Asquith promised the Commons that the government would provide in the spring of 1909 'not only for a sufficient number of ships, but for such a date of laying down those ships' as to ensure Britain's naval superiority over Germany at the end of 1911.[4] This made clear to Liberals that the prospect of a decline in spending on armaments, leaving a surplus for the forthcoming national pensions, had disappeared: the notion that naval spending might threaten social reform had not been anticipated by the Liberal rank and file, and it marked an abrupt and unwelcome change in the party's direction.

---

[1] Spender and Asquith, i. 194–9. C.B. appeared in the Commons for the last time, 12 Feb. 1908. Asquith's first 'cabinet letter' went to the King, 17 Feb. 1908.

[2] Diary, d. 3205, 10 Apr. 1908.

[3] Diary, d. 3205, 13 Apr. 1908.

[4] Parl. Deb., 10 Mar. 1908, 185, 1338. See also 1180–2 (Balfour), 1190 (A. Chamberlain).

Asquith's task was to reassure them, but constitutional difficulties then arose that threatened the Liberals' ability to govern.[1] In February 1908, while still Chancellor, he introduced the government's Licensing Bill in the Commons: the measure was controversially rejected by Unionist peers, by 272 votes to 96, on 27 November 1908. The killing of this bill was an ominous demonstration of the Unionists' ability to disrupt at will their opponents' legislative programme, using the veto power of the Upper Chamber, where they could always assemble an overwhelming majority, and clearing this constitutional logjam presented Asquith with one of his greatest challenges. Finally, on 30 March 1908, Asquith was called on to give the government's response to an Irish Nationalist Home Rule motion. While stressing that Home Rule remained the Liberals' objective, he also stated that until 'the British people' were convinced of the need for the measure the government could not 'travel an inch' towards it. The Irish Nationalist Tim Healy replied at once that he and his friends were not minded to wait until the Liberals had nerved themselves to confer the boon. Like all insurgents, the Irish for whom Healy spoke wanted to make their liberation their own achievement, rather than a gift presented by their 'oppressors'. In lightly coded language he indicated that Nationalists meant to extort Home Rule as soon as a Liberal cabinet depended on their votes in the Commons, and by the spring of 1908 that dependency did not seem distant.[2] The government that Asquith inherited from C.B. thus faced a formidable list of difficulties. It had to obtain a substantial revenue increase, while remaining thoroughly popular; it had to enact its legislative agenda, even though its bills were at the mercy of the Unionist majority in the Lords; and it

---

[1] For a reminder of the Liberals' 'pledges' to reduce defence spending see *The Nation*, ii. 557, 18 Jan. 1908. 'Dreadnought' is used here, and by Margot in the Diaries, for all of the new, 'all-big-gun' capital ships, whether battleships or battle cruisers, but in a strict classification the battleships alone would be called Dreadnoughts. For Asquith's perception that he had to prove financing 'social reform' to be possible 'on free trade lines', to avoid 'a return to Protection', see Koss, *Asquith*, 103.

[2] *Parl. Deb.*187. 228 (Asquith), 233–4 (Healy). The government lost seven seats in the twenty by-elections of 1908. The Unionists' vote went up, while the Liberals' vote declined, in all twenty.

needed to win the next election by a majority large enough to allow it at least a degree of independence from the Irish Nationalists, while also persuading the King to promise the creation of peers that would alone guarantee Lords' reform. It also had to address the insistent demands of women suffragists and suffragettes for the vote, and of organized labour for improved working conditions. Despite his failings, Asquith was well equipped to deal with this formidable raft of problems, but he faced an additional trouble of a different kind.

On the opening page of her 1904 diary Margot promised to record 'with absolute fidelity and indiscretion the private and political events of the coming years', but the impulse to tell the truth, *as she saw it*, was irresistible to her, and never likely to be confined to paper. In April 1908, when Viscount Esher asked W. T. Stead 'what he thought the rock ahead of the government, the reply was "Mrs Asquith"'.[1] It was perhaps not a surprising answer: three years earlier Margot had received a stiff royal rebuke, which included the threat of a withdrawal of future invitations to Windsor, after she had proved unable to resist dining out on an incident at Court, and not long before the First World War Raymond Asquith commented that his stepmother 'says and does things that you never forget, and remembers things that you never say or do'.[2] At the start of the second 1910 general election campaign she had taken it upon herself to caution Lloyd George about his political language: '…don't, when you speak on platforms, arouse what is low and sordid and violent in your audience. It hurts the members of your party that are fighting these elections.' Irked by this, Ll.G. wrote Margot a heavily sardonic reply, which she interpreted, with a degree of shame, as proof that she had hurt him. It stimulated her to write a passionate letter of apology, and to collect the whole correspondence in her diary, where she observed:

Hurting people's feelings seems to be my prevailing vice (I! who cannot bear to see a tear in any one's eye, and am more full of pity

[1] *Esher Journals*, ii. 304.
[2] Jolliffe, *Raymond Asquith*, 261 n. 1.

and compassion than I dare even show—I! who find callous, temperamentless corpses peopling the places I most frequent and among my best friends!)

In fact she, rather than Ll.G., had been scorched by this exchange, and in March 1914 she lamented: 'How I pray I may be improved by the d—d amount of pain moral and physical I have gone through…but…I am haunted by what mama always said: "Dear Margot! She never improves"'.[1]

4. Naval and military planning: 'little navy-idiots' and 'little Englanders'

In 1908 the influential Liberal newspaper editor and journalist A. G. Gardiner published a prescient sketch of the new premier:[2]

> Asquith's…is incomparably the most powerful intellect in the…Commons today—not the finest, nor the subtlest, nor the most attractive, but the most effective.…[3] The sentences of his orderly speech march into action like disciplined units, marshalled and drilled.…He creates the impression of visible overthrow.…Violence and recrimination find in him no response.…This detachment from the pettiness and meanness of controversy is largely the source of the growing authority he has established over the House.…His power of work is unequalled, for the strength of his mind is backed by a physique equal to any burden.…His succession to the premiership was a matter of course.

Gardiner noted Asquith's 'reticence and dislike of display' as a characteristic which would probably prevent him from gaining more than 'a small hold upon the affections of the public'; and, in two mildly critical asides,

---

[1] Diary, March 1914, d.3120 fo. 471; see also *Esher Journals*, ii. 323.

[2] Gardiner, *Prophets*, 54–5, 58–60.

[3] Herbert Samuel, writing thirty years later about Asquith's speaking, quoted Ben Jonson on Lord Chancellor Bacon: 'He commanded where he spoke': Samuel, *Memoirs*, 87.

he connected this, first, with the new premier's 'easy-going' temperament, which was, 'in strange contrast to his intellect, a little flaccid'; and,
secondly, with his university career in Jowett's Balliol. Gardiner, who was
born in 1865, missed the full significance of Asquith's arrival at Balliol in
October 1870, at the start of Jowett's mastership. The Act of Parliament
abolishing Oxford's remaining religious test in 1871 symbolized the victory of Balliol's philosophy tutors over the university's Tractarians and
the High Churchmen.[1] It was the overthrow of religiosity by rationalism,
and represented an intoxicating liberation that marked Asquith for life. It
led him to presume, first, that a reasoned argument, presented with force,
could be expected to prevail, and, secondly, to suspect, and even to disre-
gard, views which had emerged since the 1870s.[2] Asquith could see that
the Liberals' triumph in the 1906 election had not eliminated the rifts in
the party which had opened during the Boer War. But he could not see
that the twenty years since he had become an MP had eroded the social
basis of Gladstonian Liberalism. He was not primarily an intellectual in
the Balfourian style of constant reflection about received ideas; nor did
he possess all of Lloyd George's aptitude as a 'man of action'; and he
lacked John Simon's immense persuasiveness as an advocate. He was, as
Gardiner wrote, above all else, an incomparably ready and powerful
debater.

Asquith's performance during his first four years as premier was masterly. By the end of 1911 his government had shown that building battleships could be combined with paying a national old age pension—the
achievement of Lloyd George's famous 1909 'People's Budget'. That same
measure had begun a hard-fought constitutional battle to reform the
House of Lords, which ended with the 1911 Parliament Act, which greatly
restricted the Unionists peers' ability to disrupt future Liberal Bills.

[1] *Nineteenth-Century Oxford*, ii. 30.
[2] John Buchan suggested to Asquith, after Lytton Strachey's iconoclastic *Eminent Victorians*
had been published in 1918, that it was time to subject John Stuart Mill and the other Victorian saints of rationalism to the treatment which the household of faith had received from
Strachey; Asquith, according to Buchan, 'was really shocked' by this suggestion: Buchan,
Memory, 155.

These signal triumphs had led to the retirement of A. J. Balfour from the leadership of the opposition, while Asquith's ascendancy over his own party, and in parliamentary debate, had been put beyond doubt. In 1909 he had won a particularly important debate among Liberals about the number of Dreadnought battleships to be built. The Liberal opponents of this policy, termed 'the little-navy idiots' by Margot, were encouraged from inside the cabinet by Lloyd George and Churchill.[1] The premier told his wife that Winston had 'proved himself to be a thoroughly untrustworthy fellow', and signs of Margot's resentment at the 'bluff swagger and leakiness' of this 'little treacherous gutter genius' were not confined to the pages of her diary.[2] This, however, was a passing trouble. Churchill soon realized that, pacific as most Liberals were, they insisted, like their compatriots, on the continuing predominance of the British Navy.[3]

Dealing with 'the little-navy idiots', however, did nothing to reduce the problem of the German battle fleet and the Kaiser's naval ambitions. Germany's victory over France in the war of 1870–1, and her remarkable industrial growth since 1880, had engendered ambitions of worldwide power, which Bismarck's successors were unable to control.[4] Britain's industrial working class had grown slowly enough for adjustments to be made between employers and employees, and political developments had broadly kept pace with those in society. The same was not true during the German Empire's earliest years. The Kaiser and his ministers inherited a complex governmental system compounded of federalism, semi-feudal aristocratic militarism, Prussian ascendancy, hereditary rule, and universal male suffrage,[5] and they tried desperately, by demagogic displays of

---

[1] Marder, *Royal Navy*, i. 159–60.
[2] Margot, diary, 10 Apr. 1909: d. 3206, p. 171.
[3] Churchill, *World Crisis*, i. 40.
[4] M. R. Gordon, 'Domestic Conflict and the Origins of the First World War: The British and German Cases', *J. Mod. H.* 46 (June 1974), 191–226; Röhl, *Delusion*, 34–5. Between 1890 and 1900 German steel production grew from 2.3 to 6.7 million tons per year. Taylor, *Struggle*, xxx.
[5] Craig, *Germany*, 43, 45, 158. In Prussia manhood suffrage was balanced by a three-class voting system which favoured propertied people.

grandeur and naval strength, to keep their hold on a working class exposed to Marxist and anti-regime doctrines.[1]

This would have been a dangerous line of policy however skilful those operating it, but those who ran Wilhelm II's *Reich* were not their predecessors' equals: to adapt Macaulay's aphorism, the men who created a united Germany had been succeeded by the lesser men whom that Germany had created. The Kaiser himself was thought in Europe's governmental circles to be on the edge of insanity; and he never succeeded in establishing coherent governmental arrangements.[2] His naval supremo, Admiral Tirpitz, had embarked on an ambitious naval building programme, but in so doing he challenged the British on ground that they could never concede. The unwisdom of this German strategy was identified by A. T. Mahon in 1902: 'Great Britain', he wrote, 'cannot help commanding the approaches to Germany by the mere possession of the very means essential to her own existence as a state of the first order.'[3] But Britain's control of the shipping lanes to the North Sea posed no intrinsic threat to Germany: it was inconceivable that the Royal Navy would be used in peacetime to block Germany's trade routes, while the Boer War had warned the British not to aim at further imperial expansion; nor were they capable of doing so now that they were the only great power in Europe which lacked a large army.

Asquith remained calm and sensible in the face of aggressive German statements and gestures, and in the first of his annual Guildhall speeches as premier, 9 November 1908, he struck a conciliatory note edged with realism:

[1] For the policy dilemma behind the demagogy see Taylor, *Struggle*, 395–6.
[2] Macaulay, *Essays*, i. 200 (Sir William Temple). The Kaiser's mental instability was well known to Asquith, and others in public life, though hardly recognized by Margot: diary, d. 3204 fo. 123; 24 May 1911, Asquith to Knollys (Cecil, *Wilhelm II*, 379 n. 83). Grey thought the Kaiser 'not quite sane, and very superficial'; Esher agreed: *Esher Journals*, ii. 344. On the chaos at the top in Germany, see Haldane, *Before the War*, 70–1 ('not one foreign policy but three'). See also Goschen, after 3 months as ambassador, reporting to Hardinge that, in dealing 'with so many Ministers of Foreign Affairs', he found 'more muddle—more confusion—than I have found in any country in my 35 years' experience': 26 Feb. 1909, Goschen Diary, 28.
[3] Marder, Royal Navy, i. 431.

Nothing will induce us...to falter or fall short in any one of the special engagements which we have undertaken...; but...we have neither animosities to gratify nor selfish interests to advance, and...we shall not be reluctant to grasp any hand that is extended to us in goodwill and good faith.[1]

In July 1910 he reported in the House of Commons that an approach had been made to the German government, with a view to limiting Dreadnought construction, but that the German government had responded that any modification to its programme would not have the support of public opinion in Germany:[2]

These are the governing and unalterable facts of the situation for the moment. We must deal with them as facts and make our provision for them. We feel that there is no body of men in this country who would, with more unfeigned satisfaction, put a stop to the construction of these necessary, expensive and wasteful instruments of warfare and thereby divert the money which is so employed to purposes for the welfare and progress of our people.

A year later, in July 1911, the German government sent the gunboat *Panther* to the port of Agadir, on Morocco's Atlantic coast, in a maladroit attempt to disrupt the *Entente Cordiale* between Britain and France: that diplomatic arrangement, dating from 1904, became the basis of a close working relationship between the erstwhile colonial rivals, who recognized Morocco and Egypt as, respectively, French and British spheres of influence. The Kaiser had first tested the Entente in March 1905, with a provocative speech in Tangier aimed at challenging French influence in Morocco, but this had the effect of riveting rather than splitting the new alliance.[3] And two years later, in 1907, the British reached an understanding with France's

---

[1] Spender and Asquith, i. 246.

[2] Parl. Deb., 14 July 1910, 19. 638, 644–5. For the concern which this statement gave to the German government, since it seemed to suggest that negotiations over battleship strengths might have been held, see *Goschen Diary*, 211.

[3] Evans and von Strandmann, *First World War*, 1.

ally Russia, raising the prospect of a 'Triple Entente' to rival the 'Triple Alliance' of Germany, Austria-Hungary, and Italy. The Agadir crisis of 1911, like its predecessor in 1905, was resolved by negotiation, but in a manner humiliating to German imperial ambitions, and on 23 August 1911, in response to the heightened tensions in Europe, the respective war plans of the War Office and Admiralty were put before the CID by Henry Wilson, the Director of Military Operations, and Sir A. K. Wilson, the First Sea Lord.

It was on this occasion that Henry Wilson disclosed that since early 1906 secret military 'conversations' had been conducted with the French about the possible use of a British Expeditionary Force (BEF) on the Continent, in response to a German attack on France. Wilson explained that a German war plan was likely to be based on a south-western advance to Paris by the most direct route, south of the Meuse–Sambre river line: this would entail at most an incursion into Belgian territory in the Ardennes, and not a wholesale invasion of that neutral country.[1] Pressed by Churchill and others about the possibility that the German staff might be planning a wider sweep than this into central Belgium, Wilson replied that Germany lacked the troops needed to capture the fortress town of Liège, which barred the way. A detour to the north of Liège would have involved invading the Netherlands, through the Maastricht appendix that projected south between Germany and Belgium, and it was known by 1911, to Haldane and others, that the German General Staff had no intention of doing this,[2] since they had identified Rotterdam as the neutral port through which German war supplies would be imported.[3]

Apart from its logistical drawbacks, the full-scale assault on Liège would make the Belgians fight seriously, and in all probability appeal for help to the British under the terms of the 1839 Treaty by which the European Powers jointly guaranteed the independence and neutrality of

---

[1] The part of Belgium south of that line constituted about a third of its area, but contained no more than a small proportion of its population.

[2] Haldane, *Autobiography*, 275.

[3] Brock, *Britain Enters*, 150.

Belgium.[1] It therefore seemed overwhelmingly likely that in order to avoid this the German army would move through the Ardennes south of the Meuse–Sambre river line.[2] In September 1911 the Belgian Foreign Minister was asked by a British Legation official what the Belgian army would do if an invasion of this nature took place. He replied:

> I do not say that if the invasion took place in that corner of the Kingdom...we should make our last stand there or that we should die there to the last man. We should probably fall back under the pressure of overwhelming forces on the line of our fortifications.

A few weeks later the Military Attaché reported on the possibility that the Brussels government would meet an invasion 'south of the Meuse' with a 'sufficient show of force' to comply with the terms of the 1839 Treaty, and would avoid calling upon the guaranteeing powers for assistance. This view, as he added, did not 'hold good for...a direct attack, such as an on-slaught on Liège, which would certainly rouse the country'.[3] These statements put into diplomatic language what was generally known. The Belgian high command made no secret about predicting that their troops would be lined 'up...along the road' taken by the German army, provided that it stayed south of the Meuse–Sambre line: 'a few shots might be fired outside Liège or Namur', but that would be all.[4] Those 'few shots' would be enough to fulfil the Belgian government's duty under the 1839 Treaty to protect its neutrality; moreover, any army entering Belgium to resist the Germans would probably be treated in Brussels as an enemy. This represented a reasonable Belgian decision: remaining anything other than neutral, at least until it became clearer which side was likely to win

[1] For L. C. F. Turner's view that 'trying to maintain more than 600,000 men through the narrow aperture of Liège' was 'a fatuous blunder' see Kennedy, *War Plans*, 213.

[2] It was foreseen that the German forces might be able to cross the Meuse at Huy without triggering a Belgian appeal to the guarantor powers. That would have been a minor incursion into central Belgium by comparison with an assault on Liège.

[3] 29 Sept. 1911, Macleay to Nicolson, *BDW*, viii. 386; 19 Oct. 1911, Bridges to Villiers, *BDW*, viii. 390. These predictions were made before the enlargements of the German army in 1912 and 1913. For a more balanced forecast see *Round Table*, 3 (June 1913), 418–24.

[4] The first of the quoted phrases was used by Kühlmann, the second by Churchill; Tuchman, *Guns*, 41, 507; Churchill, *World Crisis*, i. 202.

the war, would be folly. To the Belgian government the British were no longer potential saviours; rather, they were the potential ally of France and Russia, in a struggle against Germany and Austria-Hungary, to be fought, if necessary, across the small country which had so often been the cockpit of Europe.

Appalled by the revelations about the secret military 'conversations' between Britain and France, the isolationist cabinet ministers who had not been invited to the CID meeting on 23 August 1911 insisted, on 15 November, on an agreement that any new communications between Britain's military and naval staffs and those of the other two Entente powers 'should not be entered into without the previous approval of the cabinet'.[1] Twelve days later the Foreign Secretary, Sir Edward Grey, answered his critics by telling the Commons, in a much applauded speech, that Britain's Ententes with France and Russia, while not alliances, had become more than arrangements to deal with old colonial trouble spots: if Britain failed to stand by its Entente partners in a crisis it would soon be building warships 'not against a two-Power standard, but probably against the united navies of Europe'.[2] That scale of naval building would entail a ruinous level of taxation for Britain; and if, despite such an effort, the country lost its naval supremacy, it would cease to be a sovereign power. Greatly as Margot admired Grey, and his speech, it is doubtful whether she understood this passage in it. Like many others she continued to talk as if the British Navy could continue to rule the waves whatever combination of fleets might be brought against it.[3] So engrained was this mentality that some 'little Englanders' behaved as if talk about the risk of a war involving Europe's great powers did not concern the British, since there should be no suggestion

[1] Robbins, *Grey*, 246–7. This policy was limited in operation to new agreements; the Franco-Russian Entente had been formed in 1907.

[2] *Parl. Deb.*, 32.60. Bonar Law had been told what Grey would say. Faced with this argument in July 1911 C. P. Scott seems simply to have told Grey that 'England...so long as she retained her sea-power could not be coerced': *Scott, Diaries*, 51. The 'two power standard' was defined in 1889 by the then First Lord of the Admiralty, Lord George Hamilton, as ensuring 'that our establishment should be on such a scale that it should be at least equal to the naval strength of any two other countries': *The Times*, 24 January 1907, 8a.

[3] Diary, 16 Feb. 1912.

FIGURE 5 H. H. Asquith and Margot Asquith at Penrhos, July 1912; Maurice Bonham Carter ('Bongie') in the background.

that Britain, a naval power, might become involved in a war fought on the Continents. These Liberals did not realize that in order to deal a devastating blow against the French, the Central Powers, under the guidance of Moltke, Chief of the German General Staff, would be willing to provoke Britain into becoming Germany's adversary, whether by sea *or* land.

The poor performance of the First Sea Lord, A. K. Wilson, at the CID meeting on 23 August 1911 had convinced Asquith that the Admiralty had done no war planning worth the name, and he therefore arranged for Churchill and Reginald McKenna to exchange offices, Winston becoming First Lord of the Admiralty and McKenna Home Secretary. The new First Lord lost no time in initiating an Admiralty War Staff; and he introduced a new class of 'super-Dreadnoughts', armed with fifteen-inch guns, an innovation which led to the substitution of oil fuel for coal throughout the fighting units of the fleet.[1] But strengthening the British battle fleet could not obscure the fact that, through its alliance with France, Britain was now moving, uncertainly, towards a continental commitment that it did not have the military means to uphold, a paradox that would not be resolved until after the fighting had begun.

5. The advent of war: 'we cannot be more Belgian than the Belgians'

By the end of 1912 Admiral Tirpitz had lost his influence, reflecting a change in German policy, which henceforth emphasized expansion of the army rather than the navy. Ironically the German Chancellor, Bethmann Hollweg, supported the enormous enlargement of the German military in 1913 because he saw in it a possibility of avoiding Britain's enmity: he realized that the British were much more easily alarmed, where Germany's military power was concerned, by threats to the Royal Navy's supremacy than by any increase in German land forces,[2] and the sense in Britain that this supremacy was once again secure encouraged a misguided sense of optimism towards Anglo-German relations. In August 1913 Margot, noting the praise of 'every ambassador' for Grey's conduct of foreign policy, observed: 'For the moment, it would seem as if we were on better terms than we've ever been with all our neighbours.'[3] According to *The Nation*, in December 1913, 'nothing more than a memory [was] left of the old Anglo-German antagonism', and it was the increased Naval Estimates of that year which aroused some protests.[4] 'Our relations with Germany', Haldane said some weeks later, 'are twice as good as they were two years ago.'[5] This pacific tone was echoed in the Northcliffe press, the

[1] Marder, *Royal Navy*, i. 440.

[2] Marder, *Royal Navy*, i. 430–1. Between 1911 and 1914 the peacetime strength of the German army was increased from 612,000 (some 54 per cent of the manpower available) to 864,000. Fear of a vast Russian army was a factor in overcoming fears that recruits from Germany's growing cities might prove politically unreliable: Howard, *First War*, 24–5.

[3] Diary, 16 Aug. 1913.

[4] Diary, 16 Aug. 1913; *The Nation*, 13 Dec. 1913, xiv. 483.

[5] 1 Dec. 1913, to the Royal Scottish Corporation. In retrospect the absence of 'incidents' does not seem a reliable indicator that the Germans had no hostile intentions against Britain.

Evening News referring to the Kaiser in October 1913 as a 'peace preserver and a very gallant gentleman'.[1] In May 1914 the Committee of Imperial Defence authorized its Overseas Defence Committee 'to act on the assumption that the present international situation [was] likely to continue for the next three to four years',[2] and in June a British naval squadron was permitted to attend the celebrations that marked the completion of the widening of the Kiel Canal. That this project would make easier the deployment in the high seas of German Dreadnought class battleships illustrates how relaxed the British elite had become once they considered their naval ascendancy to be assured, and on leaving Kiel the squadron commander, Sir George Warrender, signalled to his hosts: 'Friends in [the] past and friends forever.'[3]

The opposition, far from warning against the illusions of these years, actually increased the mood of détente. Bonar Law, the Unionist leader, had none of his predecessor Balfour's interest in defence issues, and was too intensely absorbed with the cause of Protestant Ulster.[4] Austen Chamberlain, by contrast, realized that any repetition of the Agadir fiasco 'would leave the [German] government [with] no choice but war, for the only alternative to war would be a revolution in which the government itself would be overthrown'.[5] He had grasped the truth which had escaped Margot. Her expectation, after a visit to Paris, was that Agadir and the Kaiser's electoral losses in the January 1912 election would have persuaded him 'to get on some sort of terms with us. He has not the power he had, and no sane German wants war, not even the Kaiser.'[6] Margot did not

[1] *Evening News*, 17 Oct. 1913.

[2] Roskill, *Hankey*, 135: CID, 126th Meeting, 14 May 1914.

[3] Massie, *Dreadnought*, 853. Nicolson had told the British Ambassador, St Petersburg, 7 Apr. 1914, that the possibility of a BEF being sent to the Continent on the outbreak of a war was 'extremely remote': Steiner, *Foreign Policy*, 130. Hankey's claim, in 1928, that Britain's defence policy at the outbreak of the war had been 'quite clear', exaggerated the extent of agreement achieved on it: Roskill, *Hankey*, 134–5.

[4] For Bonar Law's reluctance, pre-war, to attend to defence issues see *Lee Diaries*, 129.

[5] Chamberlain, *Down the Years*, 65. Austen Chamberlain saw Grey and suggested that the Entente with France should be changed into a 'formal alliance'. He soon realized that the Liberals could not have secured enough parliamentary support to make that change; and by 1935 he had abandoned the view that such an alliance might have deterred the German government from aggression.

[6] Diary, 16 Feb. 1912.

understand that, while a British government's further loss of prestige might entail its unpopularity, a similar setback could bring the Kaiser's regime crashing down in anarchy and chaos while he fled into exile. Moltke made no concealment of his fury about Germany's humiliation over Agadir.[1] He was not obliged to reveal his detailed planning to the Kaiser, still less to the Chancellor. He now made a war plan which would produce for Germany either a great triumph or an unexampled disaster. In an island country equipped with a stable system of responsible government, and one which had not known conscription, it was hard to believe that the Germans might take such risks of war against the Franco-Russian alliance, particularly since their firms already owned much of Russian, and even of French, industrial capacity.[2]

The enlargements of the German army in 1912 and 1913 had induced the French to revert to a three-year military service system, and the Russians to plan a large extension of their strategic railways.[3] On 12 May 1914 Moltke told his Austro-Hungarian counterpart, Conrad, that the moment for action had come:[4] the French change to the three-year conscription system would mean that for a year from November 1913 they would have only one annual class of trained men in their standing army. The German Ambassador in London, Lichnowsky, meanwhile was reporting that the Ulster troubles would prevent Britain from aiding her Entente partners in war. Neither Moltke nor Conrad was confident of victory in the war on which they were proposing to embark; but both believed that, if they waited for two years, they would face a vast and irresistible Russian army, a situation which they saw as the ultimate disaster.[5] In June 1914 Moltke

[1] Craig, *Germany*, 329.
[2] Taylor, *Struggle*, 519.
[3] Taylor, *Struggle*, 500–1.
[4] Cf., meeting, Feb. 1913, when Moltke had told Conrad that, although a struggle between Germanism and Slavism was inevitable, it should be postponed until the Balkan league broke up: Taylor, *Struggle*, 495, 514–15.
[5] For Lichnowsky see *National Review*, 72 (1918), 335. The view that the chances in war, though not very good in 1914, would deteriorate in two more years of peace is reflected in Tirpitz, *Memories*, i. 272; Ritter, *Sword and Sceptre*, ii. 235–6; Strachan, *First World War*, 55, 78, 102; Offer, *Agrarian Interpretation*, 352.

asked Jagow, the career diplomat who had succeeded Kiderlen as German Foreign Minister, to devise the scenario for a so-called preventive war. This met with a refusal; but Edward House, who was in Europe as President Wilson's representative, thought Jagow 'not forceful', and feared that such requests would end with a compliance.[1] At this time Nicolson, Grey's Under-Secretary of State, greeted with scepticism alarming reports from the British embassies, letting it be known that in his view the Kaiser, being 'most pacifically inclined…would be very unwilling to find himself compelled to initiate…a European war'.[2] Grey, for his part, was reported on 27 June to consider the German government 'in a peaceful mood and…very anxious to be on good terms with England'.[3] He did not perhaps see that German cooperation over negotiations about the Portuguese colonies and the Baghdad railway might reflect, not so much a 'peaceful mood' in Germany, as a determination to put an end to quarrels on other continents in preparation for gaining ascendancy in Europe. On 28 June the need for Jagow to concoct Germany's case for starting a preventive war disappeared, when a Bosnian Serb assassinated Archduke Franz Ferdinand, heir to the empire and kingdom of Austria-Hungary, and his wife, while they were visiting Sarajevo.[4]

Until the last days of July Margot was preoccupied by the dangers of civil war in Ulster. Churchill later recalled how, at its meeting on Friday

---

[1] Evans and Von Strandmann, *First World War*, 113; *Page Letters*, i. 296. Jagow had been German Ambassador in Rome. In strict parlance he was Prussia's Foreign Minister.

[2] *BDW*, x. 2. 727, 745. See also *Goschen Diary*, 273. Nicolson was thought in Berlin to be notably anti-German: Wilson, *Empire and Continent*, 66. In the sense that he was implacably opposed to any policy which might weaken the Triple Entente this view was not entirely mistaken: Wemyss, *Wester Wemyss*, 127–8.

[3] Robbins, *Grey*, 287. Nicolson and Grey neglected the fact that Moltke was not under any obligation to reveal his plans to Bethmann Hollweg and Jagow; and they did not share Moltke's belief that Britain's Dreadnought superiority had lost its effect in the age of the U-Boats and their long-range torpedoes. He was equally optimistic in his belief that the British would not dare to interfere with American supplies to Germany via Rotterdam. By the end of 1913 the more alert of the British knew that the enlargement of the German army had provided Moltke with the troops needed for a wide swing through central Belgium. They did not know that a high-angle howitzer of 420mm calibre, constructed in secrecy and capable of destroying Liège's forts in a few days, was awaiting its final tests: Tuchman, *Guns of August*, 192–3.

[4] For Nicolson's hope, 30 June, that the assassinations would not be followed by 'complications' see Nicolson, *Carnock*, 410.

24 July, the cabinet was about to depart, having 'toiled around the muddy by-ways of Fermanagh and Tyrone' in their search for a solution to that crisis, when Sir Edward Grey read aloud the Austrian note to Serbia: 'This note was clearly an ultimatum...such as had never been penned in modern times. As the reading proceeded it seemed absolutely impossible that any State in the world could accept it, or that any acceptance, however abject, would satisfy the aggressor.'[1] The same day Asquith wrote to Venetia Stanley that there was no need for the British to be anything more than 'spectators' of the unfolding crisis, but on 28 July Austria-Hungary declared war on Serbia, and at midday the next day the cabinet agreed to initiate the so-called 'precautionary period', putting British armed forces all over the world on high alert.[2] As the armies of Austria-Hungary, Germany, Russia, and France all began to mobilize the rationale for Britain's isolation grew weaker. On 31 July Asquith lunched with Kitchener: '[He] is very strong that if we don't back up France when she is in real danger, we shall never be regarded or exercise real power again.'[3] To the premier naval support seemed the appropriate method by which Britain could 'back up' France, and as German armies moved westwards on 2 August the cabinet discussed whether the British were to wage a *naval* war in alliance with their two Entente partners. Grey was authorized to tell the French ambassador, Paul Cambon, that the German fleet would not be allowed to enter the Channel in order to bombard the French coast. Opinions were divided on the chances of the German government accepting this restriction, and Churchill tried to brace Lloyd George about facing a possible refusal, passing to him a scribbled note across the cabinet table: 'The naval war will be cheap—not more than 25 millions a year.'[4]

---

[1] Churchill, *World Crisis* (one vol. 1964 edition), 113–14.

[2] See Asquith's letter to the King, 30 July 1914, reporting on the cabinet's discussion, 29 July, about Britain's obligation under the 1839 Treaty on Belgium, and the despatch of the 'precautionary telegram': Spender and Asquith, ii. 81. For his remark to Venetia, letter of 24 July, see *Asquith–Stanley*, 123: 'Happily there seems to be no reason why we should be anything more than spectators.'

[3] *Asquith–Stanley*, 138; their luncheon host was Churchill.

[4] Robbins, *Grey*, 295–6; *Churchill*, ii. 718.

During that morning a message arrived from Bonar Law and Lansdowne announcing the Unionist opposition's 'unhesitating support' for France and Russia, and for 'any measures' which the government might consider necessary in providing that support. Significantly, the letter did not mention the 1839 Treaty on Belgian neutrality.[1] In replying to Bonar Law's letter the Prime Minister rehearsed six basic principles that he had outlined in a letter to Venetia Stanley earlier:[2]

(1) We have no obligation of any kind either to France or Russia to give them military or naval help.
(2) The despatch of the Expeditionary force to help France at this moment is out of the question & wd. serve no object.
(3) We mustn't forget the ties created by our long-standing and intimate friendship with France.
(4) It is against British interests that France shd. be wiped out as a Great Power.
(5) We cannot allow Germany to use the Channel as a hostile base.
(6) We have obligations to Belgium to prevent her being utilised and absorbed by Germany.

In his letter to Bonar Law he added, first, that Cambon had been told about the Channel pledge; and secondly, that before deciding what action, if any, to take over the 1839 Treaty, the cabinet would 'need to know the circumstances and conditions of any German interference with Belgian territory'.[3]

Late that morning the Belgian situation was clarified by a diplomatic 'keep out' notice from the Brussels Legation. It read:

Minister of Foreign Affairs states that the Belgian Government have no reason whatever to suspect Germany of an intention to violate

---

[1] Blake, *Bonar Law*, 222. Maxse later stressed the effect of the opposition leader's letter: *National Review*, 71 (Aug. 1918), 744–52. Asquith denied that it had influenced the cabinet: letter to St Loe Strachey, 11 Aug. 1918.

[2] Asquith to Venetia, Sunday 2 Aug., *Asquith–Stanley*, 146. That day the Unionists do not seem to have been unanimous about sending the BEF abroad at once: see *Sandars Diaries*, 80.

[3] Blake, *Bonar Law*, 223–4.

neutrality. He says that Belgian Government have not considered idea of appeal to other guarantee powers, nor of intervention should a violation occur; they would rely upon their own armed force as sufficient to resist aggression, from whatever quarter it might come.[1]

The inner meaning of this apparently preposterous statement was clear. The Belgian government would not offer serious resistance to a German incursion which remained south of the Meuse–Sambre river line; and they were confident that the German advance on Paris would be restricted to the Ardennes area south of that line. When the cabinet reassembled at 6.30 p.m. on that Sunday, 2 August, they needed to brief Grey for his speech in the Commons on the next day, Monday 3 August. The watchword of the non-interventionists, led by Lewis Harcourt, was: 'We cannot be more Belgian than the Belgians.'[2] The Prime Minister, the Foreign Secretary, and at least four of their colleagues stood in opposition to this view.[3] They wanted war declared if there should be *any* German incursion into Belgium. This group made no pretence of being primarily concerned with the Belgians' interests: they saw the provisions of the 1839 Treaty primarily as a way of backing France, without arousing all the horror felt by the more isolationist Liberals at the prospect of a continental entanglement. At the end of this session it was agreed, in the words of Crewe's letter to the King, 'without any attempts to state a formula that...a substantial violation of [Belgian] neutrality would...compel us to take action'.[4] To Harcourt and his allies a 'substantial violation' would be one going north of the Meuse, while to the Prime Minister's group it meant any incursion larger than

---

[1] BDW, xi. 271. Received London, 1.25 p.m. 2 Aug. This message (BDW ii. 271) is not mentioned in Grey, *Twenty-Five Years*, or Strachan, *First World War*, although both give prominence to the Belgian government's assurance, 1 Aug., of its intention to defend its neutrality (BDW, ii. 218; Grey, *Twenty-Five Years*, ii. 9; Strachan, *First World War*, 97). This may give a slightly unbalanced impression of the Belgian cabinet's attitude in the hours before they learned of the German ultimatum.

[2] Brock, *Britain Enters*, 154.

[3] Asquith, Churchill, Grey, Haldane, Hobhouse, McKenna.

[4] Spender and Asquith, ii. 82.

that of a German detachment or two straying over the Belgian border. The one certainty, as those Sunday cabinet sessions ended, was that an isolationist government was no longer in prospect. Asquith, foreseeing an unpreventable cabinet spilt, said to Pease at lunch on that Sunday: 'Jack, we have turned many awkward corners; but I don't see how we are to get round this.'[1]

After the end of the second of the Sunday cabinets Herbert Samuel wrote to his wife:

> I still have hopes that Germany will neither send her fleet down the Channel nor invade Belgium, and that we shall be able to keep England at peace while rendering France the greatest of all services— the protection of her northern coasts from the sea and the protection of her 150 miles of frontier with Belgium. If we can achieve this, without firing a shot we shall have accomplished a brilliant stroke of policy.

Grey and Haldane were less optimistic. While dining together they were brought a telegram indicating that a German army corps had occupied a position close to the Belgian frontier. They went to Downing Street and suggested that the army should be mobilized at once. Asquith agreed and wrote out the order which was to be taken to the War Office the next morning.[2] The night of 2–3 August provided a startling illustration of Asquith's 'favourite axiom...that the Expected does not Happen'.[3] Early on Monday, 3 August, a news agency reported that the Belgian government had been presented with a German ultimatum that gave them twelve hours in which to agree to allow German troops unimpeded passage through any part of Belgium. Asquith, reporting to Venetia on the

---

[1] Pease, *Journals*, 1914, 47.

[2] Haldane, *Autobiography*, 274–6. This was not an order for movement to embarkation ports. The dispatch leading to mobilization was probably *BDW*, xi. 281 (no. 5070). The telegram was from the Ambassador, Paris, and was based on information from the French War Office: a German army corps was stated to be 'about thirty miles north-west of Trèves [Trier]', i.e. opposite the Belgian border immediately north of the Grand Duchy.

[3] *Asquith–Stanley*, 61.

German ultimatum, called it a piece of 'almost Austrian crassness';[1] and Spender's 'leader' in that afternoon's *Westminster Gazette* was equally contemptuous. Years later two notable figures—one German, the other Austrian—declared that the ultimatum to Brussels had given Grey and Asquith the chance to inflict a serious moral defeat on the Central Powers: Germany's Crown Prince looked back to Sunday 2 August 1914 as the day 'when we Germans lost the first great battle in the eyes of the world', while Count Czernin recalled it as the day of 'our greatest disaster'.[2]

Asquith informed Bonar Law and Lansdowne of the ultimatum when, discontented with his reply to their Sunday letter, they called on him early on that Monday morning before the cabinet assembled. He told them that, while the news report had affected his views, the government could not say more until the information had been confirmed. The opposition leaders saw that the wind had changed, and in sharp contrast to their earlier letter they now 'laid great stress upon Belgian neutrality'.[3] When Morley reached the cabinet room after a Privy Council meeting, Lloyd George mentioned the ultimatum to him and said that 'it had changed [Walter] Runciman's line and his own'.[4] The resignations of Simon and Beauchamp had been determined and were announced early in the proceedings. Faced with four gaps in his cabinet Asquith said again that 'nothing would induce him to separate himself from Grey'; and he indicated that he meant to carry on: no experienced politician could doubt that four replacements could be found from within the Liberals' ranks; there would be no coalition with the Unionists unless the number of defectors rose above that figure; and the morning's news made such a rise most unlikely.[5] Lloyd George begged

---

[1] *Asquith–Stanley*, 146–8; Morley, *Memo.*, 24–5. Churchill saw the arrival of a Belgian appeal for British protection as being crucial.

[2] Text in Asquith, *War*, 13–19. For the Crown Prince and Czernin see Tuchman, *Guns*, 147.

[3] Chamberlain, *Down the Years*, 103; *Asquith–Stanley*, 148.

[4] Pease, *Journals, July–August 1914*, 48. Lloyd George had originally been 'very strongly anti-German' but had 'veered round' in deference to the 'anti-war' stand of the Liberal press: *Hobhouse Diaries*, 179. See an exchange of notes during the Monday morning cabinet meeting: *Churchill*, ii. 717, where heading gives date wrongly.

[5] Asquith had told Samuel this on the afternoon of 2 Aug.: Wasserstein, *Samuel*, 163. He told Venetia Stanley in his letter, 4 Aug., how Burns and Morley were being replaced: *Asquith–Stanley*, 150.

those resigning 'to say nothing today [3 Aug.] and to sit in their accustomed places in the House' during Grey's speech. No one with a mind as quick as his could have failed to see that the case for British intervention was close to becoming overwhelming. The previous day's discussion about being 'more Belgian than the Belgians' would be unreal as soon as the Belgians asked for Britain's 'protection'.

When Grey arrived back in the Foreign Office at two o'clock Lichnowsky was waiting for him. The Ambassador, realizing that the news of the ultimatum might drive Britain into intervening in the war, said that 'he could not suppose' the German General Staff to be planning 'a serious violation' of Belgian neutrality; but it might be 'part of the plan for German troops to go through one small corner perhaps of Belgium'.[1] After a quick lunch Grey was at the House by three o'clock. He received two pieces of information shortly before he reached it. One was that the German government would be prepared, if the British would pledge themselves to neutrality, not to 'attack the northern coast of France'. The other reported a 'supreme appeal' from King Albert to George V for Britain's 'diplomatic intervention...to safeguard the integrity of Belgium'.[2] It is not certain that Moltke had expected even this degree of resistance from the Belgians to the ultimatum. He was neglectful enough of political obstacles to express the hope that the Belgian government would come to an understanding with him when they 'realized the seriousness of the situation'. The American Ambassador in Berlin was asked as late as 9 August 1914 to approach the Belgian government in this sense. The American ministers at Brussels and The Hague both refused to convey the message; but, through the Dutch government's offices, it reached King Albert on 12 August. He refused to modify his country's attitude.[3]

During the first part of his speech on 3 August, when he reviewed British foreign policy in the years before the present crisis, Grey was well sup-

---

[1] Grey, *Twenty-Five Years*, ii. 13.

[2] *Parl. Deb.*, 3 Aug. 1914, 65. 1818, 1821.

[3] Brock, *Britain Enters*, 173; Tuchman, *Guns*, 206–7. For the doubts of the Belgian Foreign Minister until 4 August whether Belgium was in 'real danger from Germany' see Fay, *World War*, 541–2.

ported by cheers from the opposition benches, while the Liberal Members remained silent.[1] The second part, on Belgium, drew applause from all parts of the House. Grey's argument was essentially the same as the one which he had presented in November 1911.[2] He refused to pledge Britain to neutrality on the basis of a 'narrow' German agreement not to attack France's northern coast. He referred to the possibility of France being 'beaten in [this] struggle of life and death, beaten to her knees', so that she would lose her position as a Great Power, and become 'subordinate to the will and power of one greater than herself'. That catastrophe might be accompanied by Belgium falling 'under the same dominating influence, and then Holland, and then Denmark'. He rejected the idea that Britain could keep out of the war and then, 'at the end of it, intervene with effect to put things right'. If, he said, 'in a crisis like this, we run away from those obligations of honour and interest as regards the Belgian Treaty, I doubt whether, whatever material force we might have at the end, it would be of very much value in face of the respect that we should have lost'.[3] Grey stopped short of actually saying what his whole argument implied, namely, that a German victory over France and Russia would expose the Royal Navy to a struggle against impossible odds, since it would have given Germany control over all the navies of continental Europe and practically over the whole coastline of the North Sea.

Grey's speech was regarded almost everywhere as an unanswerable triumph. The Labour leader Ramsay MacDonald had contended during the ensuing debate that the Labour Members would have supported Grey if they had been persuaded that the country was in danger, but they were not: in fact

[1] Grenfell, *Memoirs*, 204; Hazlehurst, *Politicians at War*, 44 (Charles Trevelyan); Nicolson, *Carnock*, 422.

[2] See above, lxii; it was put by Grey in blunter terms to the CID in July 1912: the British ought to envisage as possible 'a situation something like that in the old Napoleonic days...Our concern that there did not arise a supremacy in Europe which...would deprive us of the command of the sea...might [compel us] to take part in [a] European war....The naval position underlies our European policy': Marder, *Royal Navy*, i. 429. J. L. Garvin's 'leader' in Sunday's *Observer*, 2 Aug., had given the same argument before the ultimatum had been delivered in Brussels: Gollin, *Garvin*, 430.

[3] *Parl. Deb.*, 3 Aug., 65.1822. See also D. C. Watt, 'The British Reactions to the Assassinations at Sarajevo', *European Studies Review*, 1.3, 233–49.

his MPs refused to support his stand, and he resigned at once from the chairmanship of the parliamentary party.[1] Christopher Addison's comments on the effect of Grey's speech are particularly striking, because he was a member of the isolationist Liberal Foreign Affairs Committee. His diary entry reads:

> [Grey] satisfied, I think, all the House, with perhaps three or four exceptions, that we were compelled to participate; that the Kaiser meant to ride roughshod over Belgium and get to the Channel coast; and that unless we were prepared to see both France and Belgium wiped out, with no guarantee that we ourselves would not be the next victims, we must join with France and Belgium—apart altogether from the fact that we were pledged, as much as a nation could be, to defend Belgium.[2]

German troops entered Belgium in strength early in the morning of 4 August. By the time the cabinet met on that Tuesday Simon and Beauchamp had withdrawn their resignations; and at noon King Albert appealed for 'concerted and common' *military action* by guarantor countries to repel this invasion. Asked to account for Belgium's heroic stand Albert disdained poses and replied: 'We were cornered into it.'[3] Asquith wrote to Venetia later that day: 'We got the news that the Germans had entered Belgium, and had announced to "les braves Belges" that, if necessary, they would push their way through by force of arms. This simplifies matters. So we sent the Germans an ultimatum to expire at midnight.'[4]

'All happened', Margot wrote in the Diary for 4 August 1914, 'in such a short time', and the pace of events was indeed bewildering. It originated in the nature of Germany's military strategy, and in the strains which

---

[1] *Parl. Deb.*, 65.1830. For MacDonald's view of the war's causes see *Labour Leader*, 5, 29 Aug. 1914. When Keir Hardie spoke against British intervention in the war on 6 Aug. in his Merthyr Tydfil constituency, he was howled down after uttering a few sentences: Wilson, *Myriad Faces*, 155.

[2] Diary passage dictated at the end of August 1914: Addison, *Years*, i. 32.

[3] Brock, *Britain Enters*, 162.

[4] *Asquith–Stanley*, 150; the ultimatum, requiring the Germans 'to give a like assurance with the French that they wd. respect Belgian neutrality', was to take effect as Big Ben struck 11 p.m.

were developing between the civil and military leaders in Berlin and those in Vienna. Moltke planned to defeat France decisively within six weeks. If he achieved this he would be able to turn his divisions eastwards before the Austro-Hungarian army had been overwhelmed by the Russians, who could not complete their mobilization quickly. On 30 July 1914, when he realized that the German force in Poland might be overwhelmed before France had been subdued, he pressed Vienna to bring general war nearer by declaring general mobilization at once, but these insistent signals coincided with equally peremptory ones from Bethmann Hollweg urging Berchtold, the Austrian Foreign Minister, to exercise restraint and to open negotiations with Russia; and on 31 July Berchtold asked sarcastically: 'Who rules in Berlin, Moltke or Bethmann?'[1] Certainly it was not Bethmann. Like the Kaiser he had not realized until that day how the German offensive in the West was to start with a full-scale assault on Liège.[2] Yet Moltke could hardly be said to 'rule' in the sense of 'having the last word' in shaping German policy. His strength was that, in the chaos at the top among the Kaiser's ministers, he made the crucial decisions. When Margot and the Russian Ambassador Benckendorff, had their 'altercation' a day or so later about the Germans who were to blame for warmaking, she was wholly wrong in thinking that the Kaiser still controlled events, whereas 'Bencky', in naming the German 'war party', came somewhere near to the truth.[3]

These factors may be held to explain the haste with which the Germans plunged themselves and their continental opponents into war. They do not explain the speed with which the British turned towards war directly they received a Belgian appeal for their help. The first explanation for this remarkable response from the most detached and the least militarized of the European powers relates primarily, but by no means exclusively, to the rank and file Liberals. The impact on them was described twenty

[1] Turner, *Origins,* 109.
[2] Ritter, *Sword and Sceptre,* ii. 266–7. Moltke had drafted the ultimatum to Belgium on 26 July 1914, and it had been sent to Brussels on 29 July in a sealed envelope: Fay, *World War* (ii), 502.
[3] Diary, 1 Aug. 1914, p. 9 below.

years later by R. C. K. Ensor. 'For years past', he wrote, 'the Liberals...had been making it an article of party faith that militarist Germany was not so black as it was painted. Now in a flash it seemed to them self-revealed as much blacker.'[1] On 29 July or thereabouts 'a very active Liberal Member.' told Grey in the Lobby of the House 'in a dictatorial tone...that under no circumstances whatever ought [Britain] to take part in the war if it came'. Grey asked, as he recorded:

'Suppose Germany violates the neutrality of Belgium?'...He said with emphasis, 'She won't do it'. 'I don't say she will, but supposing she does?' 'She won't do it', he repeated confidently...[2]

One difficulty about evaluating post-war statements such as Grey's, even when they come from people as reliable as he was, lies in the fact that the German ultimatum to Brussels altered the way in which British observers referred to the violation of Belgian neutrality. Because of the attitude of the Belgians themselves, the inner circles of British politics and journalism had ceased to regard a German traverse through the south of that country as a serious infringement of the 1839 Treaty. But during the war, and for a few years after it, British politicians and publicists paid minimal attention to the time when Belgium's stance had been less than heroic. The Belgian warning of 2 August to the guarantor powers to 'keep out' was omitted tactfully from the British White Book on the start of the war.[3] This marked the beginning of a trend which lasted for some time. 'It is a mistake', wrote the Liberal journalist Harold Begbie in 1920, 'to say that Mr Asquith carried England into the war. England carried Mr Asquith into the war.... A House of Commons that had hesitated an hour after the invasion of Belgium would have been swept out of existence by the wrath and indignation of the people.' This was a simplification of the historical

---

[1] *Ensor, 1870–1914*, 575. Ensor had been the secretary, under Lord Courtney's presidency, of the Foreign Policy Committee set up after Agadir to demand 'a friendly approach to the German government': Taylor, *Trouble Makers*, 118–19.

[2] Grey, *Twenty-Five Years*, i. 337–8.

[3] This omission from CD7476 meant that many comparatively well-informed British people did not know about the message from Brussels, 2 Aug. 1914, until the publication of *BDW* 11.271 some years later.

fact. The people's wrath would have become irresistible, not so much by failure to react to *any* invasion of Belgium, as by failure to respond to King Albert's appeal for support, that is, by a refusal to resist an invasion which the Belgians themselves were resisting strongly, and against which they were calling for their guarantors' help.[1] During August 1914 it was practically forgotten in Britain that a German march on Paris, confined to the Ardennes and hardly resisted by the Belgian army, would also have been an 'invasion of Belgium'.

In the same way the German ultimatum probably had more effect on Liberal stalwarts in the provinces than it did on those nimble Liberal politicians who had recognized for some time that there was no place for British isolationism in a Europe dominated by two hostile alliances, and had merely been waiting for an interventionist surge which did not smack of Tory jingoism.[2] But by producing a threat about a German occupation of the Belgian coast, the ultimatum to Brussels did far more than give Liberals a 'pretext' for intervention:[3] by menacing the Royal Navy's supremacy it touched a sensitive nerve. It altered, not what Asquith and Grey were inclined to do, but what they had the popular backing to do. On 3 August R. C. K. Ensor had made out a case for non-intervention in his leader for the *Daily Chronicle*, the largest circulation Liberal daily newspaper:

> [There is] no particular reason to think that we or our interests are to be attacked....The neutrality of Belgium is...different [from that of Luxemburg]; but...its violation is not yet reported, and...though

[1] [Begbie], *Mirrors*, 43–4. Grey wrote privately, 9 Aug. 1914: 'But for Belgium we should have kept out of it.' At the time the ambiguity of the phrase passed unnoticed: see also Eyck, *Gooch*, 327; *Manchester Guardian*, 25 Oct. 1928.

[2] Frances Stevenson's prayer that an invasion of Belgium would give Lloyd George 'a heaven-sent excuse for supporting a declaration of war' may be noted: Stevenson, *Years Past*, 73–4.

[3] As Professor Zara Steiner concedes when using the term: Steiner, *First World War*, 237. Isolationist Liberals finally admitted that 'maintaining the balance of power', when the rulers of Germany showed signs of 'Napoleonic' ambitions, stood for preserving Britain's position as an independent country. It freed them from the party dogma under which the balance of power was for them, as for John Bright, a 'foul idol' (Bright's Birmingham speech, 18 Jan. 1865: in *Bright's Speeches*, ed. J. E. Thorold Rogers (1869), 332).

we have a generally recognized interest in it, it is not one that, standing by itself, would compensate us for the risks and losses of war....

But in his leader the next day, 4 August, Ensor cast the Belgian issue in a completely different light:

> Germany has...committed herself to an entirely unprovoked war on Belgium, made with full knowledge that Great Britain is pledged by treaty to defend Belgium, and also that she regards Belgian neutrality as a British interest.... [That] neutrality is strategically important in two ways—by sea to us and Germany, by land to Germany and France. If we abandoned it in its land aspect, we should find nobody, not even the Belgians, willing to defend it when it was threatened in its sea aspect.[1]

Another who changed course was Harcourt, who had been one of the cabinet's strongest isolationists while intervention looked to him like trying to be 'more Belgian than the Belgians'. In response to the wholesale German invasion of that country he too came around to war, and on 5 August 1914 recorded the reasons why:

> I have acted not from any obligation of Treaty or of honour for neither existed...; but there were three overwhelming British interests which I could not abandon:
> (1) That the German fleet should not occupy, under our neutrality, the North Sea and the English Channel.
> (2) That they should not seize and occupy the north-western part of France opposite our shores.
> (3) That they should not violate the ultimate independence of Belgium and hereafter occupy Antwerp as a standing menace to us.[2]

---

[1] *Daily Chronicle*, 3 Aug. 1914, 4c; 4 Aug., 4b. Ensor allowed it to be known later that he had written both leaders. He was well informed on Belgium: his mother and sister had lived in Brussels for some years. See also Spender, *Fifty Years*, 419–20. A similar comparison between *Daily News* articles, 3 and 4 Aug., is included in Lloyd George, *War Memoirs*, i. 41–2.

[2] Hazlehurst, *Politicians at War*, 114. See also 2 Aug. and 9 Aug. entries, *Holt Diary*, 33–4.

Both Ensor's pronouncements and Harcourt's show the extreme sensitivity of Britain's public men for the maintenance of their country's naval supremacy. No German observer who had taken an unprejudiced look at the naval acceleration crisis of 1909 could have had a doubt about that truth; and Metternich's stress on it to the Kaiser had cost him his London Embassy.[1] The threat was not immediate in August 1914; but, if the British waited until it was actually mounted, they would be worsted. The British Navy would not be strong enough to defeat the Germans if the latter could acquire, by defeating France and Russia, a very substantial increase in naval strength and in harbour facilities. The irony, and the tragedy, of August 1914 is that in order to defend its naval supremacy Britain relied, in the first instance, on a tiny army that had almost no deterrent value.

It is not surprising that the peace demonstrations in Britain of Sunday 2 August received relatively little support. The struggle was generally expected to be short, and the young men who shouted for war seemed unlikely to be called to defend their country, unlike their French contemporaries. Some London youngsters indulged in a noisy jingoism on 4 August, to the disgust of their more responsible elders, and Asquith was not the only leading man in London to recall Walpole's remark that those ringing the bells would soon be wringing their hands.[2] As the British later looked back on the long misery of the war, the ministers who had led their country into it came to seem callous and irresponsible. There was no basis for this view. For most of the cabinet the war crisis was a nightmare.[3] On 4 August Asquith told Venetia, 'We are on the eve of horrible things,' while the architect of British involvement, Sir Edward Grey, hated the war policy to which he had now to give a voice.[4] Of recent years both men have been criticized for neglecting the chance to give the

---

[1] See Mechtilde Lichnowsky's remark: diary, 2 Aug. 1914, p. 11 below.

[2] For Asquith see *Asquith–Stanley*, 148: for Crawford see *Crawford Journals*, 341.

[3] For the accusation see Spender and Asquith, ii. 94. For the atmosphere in the cabinet room, 3 Aug. see Pease, *Journals, July–August 1914*, 48. C. F. G. Masterman published a description of the experience in the *Daily Chronicle* a year later: quoted in *Masterman*, 266.

[4] Congratulated on his speech, Grey groaned, 'I hate war': Nicolson, *Carnock*, 422; Steiner, *First World War*, 240; Sitwell, *Great Morning*, 298; Maurice Bonham Carter to Violet Bonham Carter, 9 Oct. 1917: Bonham Carter Papers, 259.

German government early warning that, if France and Russia were challenged, the British would stand solidly with their Entente partners.[1] This
charge too is open to question. Asquith did not know until the German
ultimatum had reached Brussels whether the electorate would support
him in such a stand; and he and Grey were determined not to promise
support which they might prove unable to give.[2] Nor was Moltke likely to
have been deterred by any British warning—he assumed that he would
be opposed by all three members of the Entente—while on the French
side Poincaré and Joffre were fully prepared to fight without the BEF's
help, though doubtless they welcomed it.[3] The Kaiser refused to notice
the warning signs from Britain until the moment for acting on them had
passed; and, in any case, he was not in control of events.

In his *War Memoirs*, Lloyd George blamed Grey for failing to give the
German government an early warning that if they sent their troops
through Belgium 'they would encounter the active hostility of the British
Empire'.[4] Couched in such terms the issue of Belgian neutrality appears
deceptively straightforward: and by not invoking it as a possible *casus belli*
Grey culpably let slip an opportunity for avoiding war, with disastrous
consequences. But can Lloyd George really have forgotten the distinction
that he himself drew, between a lesser and a greater violation of Belgian
neutrality? According to C. P. Scott, at an early point in the crisis Ll.G. had
urged his colleagues to allow the German army to occupy 'the extreme
southerly point of Belgium...by Luxemburg', and had said that he would
resign rather than permit that limited occupation to be 'a *casus belli*' for
Britain.[5] On 4 August, however, after the wholesale invasion of Belgium,

---

[1] See Lord Adonis, 'A Liberal Tragedy', *Prospect*, Apr. 1908, 15.
[2] Grey, *Twenty-Five Years*, i. 313, 330–1, 341.
[3] Taylor, *Struggle*, 501, incl. n. 2.
[4] See Lloyd George, *War Memoirs*, i. 93–6 (6 vol. edn), and Chapter III passim.
[5] For the warning to Germany conveyed by Haldane, Dec. 1912, through Lichnowsky see Craig,
Germany, 331. For the Kaiser's delayed regrets see Tuchman, *Guns*, 95 ('We have run our heads into
the noose'), 143. For Lloyd George's attitude during the crisis see his *War Memoirs*, i. 58, and, more
reliably, *Scott, Diaries*, 96–7; W. George, *My Brother*, 238–9. For Churchill's attitude to a German
traverse limited to the Ardennes see *Masterman*, 265. Lloyd George probably exaggerated to C. P.
Scott how suddenly the German ultimatum to Belgium had converted him: see *Riddell War Diary*,
6. He became particularly adept at concealing that a German traverse of the Ardennes would have

he supported the cabinet's ultimatum to Berlin. Belgian neutrality, enshrined in what Lichnowsky lamentingly described to Margot as 'that old, old treaty' of 1839, proved an insufficient instrument to avert Armageddon. So long as the Belgians were not prepared to resist a German invasion of their country, no one else could do so on their behalf; but once they were committed to resist, their appeal for support would prove impossible to ignore. As George V exclaimed to the American Ambassador: 'My God, Mr Page, what else could we do?'[1]

6. The only possible Prime Minister: 'Henry knocks all the others into a cocked hat'

Asquith's performance during the first weeks of the war was masterly enough to deserve Margot's superlatives. He started with the prestige of a leader who had brought his country united into the war, and he possessed the right temperament and the ideal technique for dealing with all of the early war shocks. Maurice Hankey later wrote: 'I was very much impressed by his [Asquith's] clear, orderly mind, his coolness, courage and decision, and his amazing power of seizing on essentials. He inspired me.'[2] The pace of events was bewildering: on 2 August Asquith told the opposition's leaders that the cabinet did not 'contemplate...the immediate despatch of an expeditionary force' to France, but on 6 August the cabinet sanctioned, and 'with much less demur' than the Prime Minister had expected, the embarkation of all but two divisions of the BEF.[3] On 8 August Kitchener, the new Secretary of State for War, called for a hundred thousand men to volunteer for overseas service, the beginning of

been an invasion of Belgium: see his interview with H. B. Needham, *Pearson's Magazine*, Mar. 1915; speech, Savoy Hotel, 12 Apr. 1917. For this confusion see also Brock, *Britain Enters*, 175.

[1] *Page Letters*, i. 309.

[2] Hankey, *Supreme Command*, i. 160.

[3] *Asquith–Stanley*, 158; Cassar, *Kitchener*, 201, 204; Magnus, *Kitchener*, 299. The extent to which cabinet ministers' views changed between the start of Grey's speech on the afternoon of 3 Aug and the expiry of the British ultimatum to Berlin, 11 p.m. 4 Aug., is indicated by Churchill's statement (*World Crisis*, i. 220) that the terms of the ultimatum were never decided 'at any cabinet'. This remark (which is easily disproved by, for instance, *Asquith–Stanley*, 150) shows that Churchill thought the great issue to have been decided once Grey had made that speech.

the new armies who would ultimately deliver victory more than four years later; and on 8 September he told Asquith that he expected to have a million newly trained troops, ready to go anywhere within six months. By then the daily total of volunteers had reached 30,000. Five days in August 1914 had transformed Britain's war plans, and to an extent which many people could not comprehend at once. Far from waging war at sea, but not on land, the British had taken the first steps towards becoming a military power on a continental scale.

Asquith was seldom rattled, and his powers of exposition, whether in the Commons or on the platform, were unequalled.[1] He deployed them between August 1914 and March 1915 to the admiration of every audience. Indeed the brilliance of his performance during these eight months helped to delay the stage at which his, and to some degree his wife's, wartime defects would attract widespread notice, and this war 'honeymoon' intensified their over-confidence. Margot became convinced that Henry had the right equipment for coping with all war problems. She did not know how quickly war conditions, and the demands made on a war premier, would change. 'Henry', she wrote in November 1914, 'knocks all the others into a cocked hat … I feel proud of being near so great a man.'[2] The Unionists' leaders and newspapers contributed as freely as their Liberal counterparts to the acclamations of praise. The Liberal Harold Begbie observed:

> It was said in the early months of the war by the most able of his political opponents that it passed the wit of man to suggest any other statesman at that juncture for the office of Prime Minister.[3]

Critics on the Unionist fringe, the 'radical right', who were outraged at the Liberals' theft of their patriotic clothes, hardly managed to interrupt the chorus.[4]

---

[1] For Asquith's composure see *Riddell War Diary*, 63–4; Diary, 31 July 1914, p. 7 below.
[2] Diary, November 1914.
[3] [Begbie], *Mirrors*, 45.
[4] For Henry Wilson's anger at 'Squiff's sham patriotism' see his letter, 25 Sept. 1914, to Leo Maxse: Maxse Papers, vol. 469, fo. 549.

The Prime Minister's first wartime speech, on 6 August 1914, which Balfour thought 'the finest thing he had ever heard',[1] was given, as the premier mentioned to Margot, after 'about five minutes' of preparation, between the meeting at which the cabinet decided to send four divisions of the BEF to France, and the second 'War Council' session, when the details of that movement were arranged. Asquith contrived to allude to the threat to British independence without suggesting that the French army might be in danger of defeat, and according to *The Times* the premier 'once more exposed the common fallacy that parliamentary oratory is dead', praise that was echoed in the *Daily Mail*, where it was suggested that he had risen 'to heights which oratory is seldom competent to gain'.[2] Margot drove back from the House one afternoon with Harry Chaplin, who had been a Conservative MP since 1874, and who told her: 'I am proud to be seen with you.'[3] Radical voices had been raised even earlier than this in repentance and praise for the government that had declared war. The Quaker-controlled *Daily News* and the *Manchester Guardian*, which had both stood out against British intervention, came round at once after news of the German ultimatum to Belgium. Having only recently described a British decision to remain neutral as 'the greatest service to humanity in history', the *Daily News* now conceded 'that to have maintained peace under German conditions would have been a crime'. And C. P. Scott recorded a meeting with a contrite John Simon, who acknowledged that:[4]

he had been entirely deceived about Germany and that I ought to know that...the party which had got control of the direction of

---

[1] See below, p. 15; Spender and Asquith, ii. 111–16 for text. Balfour was equally admiring of Grey's 3 Aug. speech: *Riddell War Diary*, 31; and in Sept. 1918 Lloyd George and Bonar Law took a similar view: *Riddell War Diary*, 357.

[2] *The Times*, 7 August 1914, 7e; *Daily Mail*, 7 August 1914.

[3] Chaplin, Diary, 10 Aug. 1914.

[4] *Scott, Diaries*, 96. Simon did not realize that, much as most German leaders would have liked to abandon Vienna, they had recoiled, at the last moment, from risking the loss of their only ally by 'checking' Berchtold. The Austrian army formed an essential part of Moltke's plans; and even the most pacific German had trembled at the thought of his country's soldiers facing the Russian hordes without any help from Austria.

FIGURE 6 Margot at the ministerial gathering at Brodick Castle, Isle of Arran, 28 September 1913. 'After lunch a few amateur Kodaks were taken of all of us... The Ministers sat in a semi-circle under the trees – Seely [outside edge of frame], Winston [Churchill], then Henry [Asquith] and Ll.G., and Runciman. I insisted on their being photographed. I went behind H. for one, but am sure it will turn out <u>grotesque</u>!'.

affairs throughout the crisis had deliberately played for and pro-voked the war.... Beyond question Germany could have held Aus-tria in check... but the party in power did not wish to do so.

Robertson Nicoll, editor of the *British Weekly*, had told Lloyd George on 1 August 1914 'that he and the Free Churches would strongly oppose any war', but on 5 August he wrote an article declaring his support for British intervention. The *Daily Chronicle* confessed in a leader on 7 August, 'We feel that past Liberal criticisms of Sir Edward Grey have often done him much less than justice,' while H. W. Massingham of *The Nation* wrote to Margot on 11 August about his own change of mind: 'Sir Edward Grey's case seems to me unbreakable at every point.' As this spate of confessions shows, most of the radical critics of Grey's foreign policy had been, not 'pacifists' in the modern sense of that term, but people whose hatred of militant imperialism had blinded them to the more dangerous features of the European scene. The example of German aggression now before them however changed the picture, and after Asquith had expressed the 'sympathy and admiration' of the Commons for Belgium, on 27 August, *The Times* suggested that his words should be posted up 'in every town and village in these islands'. At the end of September 1914 A. G. Gardiner wrote that Britain now stood for 'the spirit of light against the spirit of darkness'.[1]

These parliamentary triumphs and paeans of praise were succeeded by a series of platform speeches designed to stimulate recruiting. The first of them, in the Guildhall on 4 September, led the *Daily Telegraph* to report that the premier had 'delivered the greatest speech of his career', while the *Observer*, another paper of Unionist inclinations, called it a 'surpassing oration'. To earn such praise without saying anything to offend French or Russian susceptibilities was a remarkable feat, since these early speeches were delivered against a background of alarming war news. Esher had written on 5 August 1914 that 'Unless the Kaiser turns out to be Napoleon, he will be done a month hence when Russia advances',[2] but within that space of time the Russians, advancing before their mobilization had been completed in order to help the French, had suffered a heavy defeat in the Battle of Tannenberg; and by mid-September 1914 they had been defeated again around the Masurian Lakes. In these battles they had lost more than 300,000 men and some

---

[1] *Riddell War Diary*, 11, on Robertson Nicoll's volte-face. Massingham to Margot, 11 Aug. 1914: c. 6679 fo. 190; A. G. Gardiner's attitude early in Aug. 1914 had not been that of the *Daily Chronicle* and Massingham. On 6 Aug. he pronounced: 'It would have been just and prudent and statesmanlike for England to have remained neutral ... [but] a mistaken course of policy, pursued over ten years, has led us to the terrible conflict in which we are now engaged ... [and] being in ... we must win': Howard, *War and Liberal Conscience*, 74.

[2] *Esher Journals*, iii. 175. See heading in *The Times*, 18 Aug. 1914: 'The Russian Avalanche'.

650 guns. The French had also failed, and incurred substantial losses, in their early attacks.[1]

On 3 September Margot was told by her husband: 'Nothing can be more serious than our position—indeed than the whole situation at the front.'[2] By the next day, when Asquith was speaking in London's Guildhall, the British Expeditionary Force was some 25 miles south-east of Paris, having retreated more than 200 miles from their first position at Mons. At that moment it was more than ever essential not to offend Britain's hard-pressed allies by stressing that in this conflict the British were fighting to ward off a deadly threat to their own independence. That degree of candour would not have been possible, and Asquith had to stress instead the duty imposed by the 1839 Treaty. His invariable preoccupation with the Liberals' isolationists may have led him to refer less than Grey had done to Britain's interests. In saying that, in the government's conviction, it was the 'duty as well as the interest of this country to go to war' he may be judged to have said as much as was prudent at that moment.[3]

The reverses suffered by the Entente powers during these early days of the war probably increased the reputation of the premier and of his most famous minister, Kitchener. The government's pre-war strategy had rested on the belief that the French would be able to hold their own in the West until the Russians could bring their enormous armies into use against Germany in the East. But Kitchener had no faith either in the Russian 'steamroller' or in the competence and sound planning of the French army, and had shown his conviction that the war would be anything but short by a recruiting drive designed to give Britain an army capable of

[1] Cruttwell, *Great War*, 18, 48 n. 1. For an analysis of the effect of the French losses see Strachan, *First World War*, 230–1. Two German corps had been transferred from the Western to the Eastern Front to meet this unexpectedly early Russian advance. The Russians' losses in the north should be seen in relation to their success in Galicia, where, by 11 Sept. 1914, the Austrian army had lost in the Battle of Lemberg some 350,000 men: Strachan, *First World War*, 349–56.

[2] Diary, 3 Sept. 1914, below, p. 30. Namur had fallen after two days of bombardment by 420mm. howitzers, just after *The Times* (24 Aug., 7a) had predicted that it would hold out for months. Asquith was not exceptional in failing to appreciate what had happened to the Liège forts.

[3] Spender and Asquith, ii. 114.

taking a decisive part in a long war. Asquith gave full backing to his new War Secretary, and against the background of bad news from the front they appeared as shock-proof realists. They emerged, with Churchill, as the 'dominant triumvirate in the cabinet'.[1] And it seemed that there were no possible challengers for the premiership. The threat to Grey's sight precluded him, while Crewe remained virtually unknown to the public, and Lloyd George still laboured under the cloud of the Marconi scandal. When invited by the newspaper proprietor George Riddell 'to make a speech explaining why we were at war', on 19 August 1914, Lloyd George said that 'he did not feel like speaking'. The leading pro-Boer of 1901 could not change his public image overnight. 'It is a great wrench', he said at the City Temple in November 1914, 'for most of us, who have during the whole of our lives been fighting against militarism, to be driven by irresistible force of conscience to support a War.'[2] The reason behind Lloyd George's delay in speaking points to a paradox about the praises bestowed on Asquith in these first weeks of the war: they came more easily from his political opponents than from his own party. The Unionists who gave them were setting partisanship aside for a moment in acknowledgement that the war had induced the premier to express their long-held convictions. The more radical of the Liberals, by contrast, were confessing that some of their own most deeply held convictions had been misdirected. Robertson Nicoll, for instance, while he never went back on his stand for intervention, struck Riddell as 'very broken by the war' at the start of December. His prompt endorsement of Grey's ultimatum to Berlin had not been approved by *all* of his following.[3]

[1] Keith Neilson, *ODNB*, 'Kitchener, Horatio Herbert'.
[2] Grey, *Twenty-Five Years*, ii. 57–61 (Grey's eye trouble). *Riddell War Diary*, 14. Once Lloyd George joined in the recruiting drive he surpassed all others. His Queen's Hall speech to the London Welsh, 19 Sept. 1914, was reprinted as a pamphlet, 2.5 million copies being distributed. By November Ll.G. was ready to show Nonconformity that fighting for the right consorted with their deepest belief, and carried no taint of militarism. Flanked by the veteran Baptist leader Dr Clifford, and Robertson Nicoll, he gave this message with great success in the City Temple, which belonged to the Congregationalists, on 10 November 1914: Grigg, *Lloyd George, 1912–1916*, 161–7, 183–7; *Stevenson Diary*, 2, 11.
[3] *Riddell War Diary*, 44.

The shocks suffered by all the belligerents during the early weeks of the war showed Asquith to possess the imperturbable quality needed in a war leader. His personal bearing reinforced the message of his speeches. Massingham wrote in November 1914:

> If you want a tonic... have a look at the Prime Minister. Unquestionably, Mr Asquith is carrying his burden with great courage; with a steady, massive, self-reliant, and unswerving confidence which is in itself a moral asset of no slight value.[1]

But by the end of December 1914 it was becoming clear that this quality of imperturbability coexisted with an inability not merely to adapt to rapid changes, but even, where they were not wholly obvious, to recognize that they were occurring. The 'deadlock' on the Western Front by the end of the first Battle of Ypres, 17 October–13 November 1914, presented the British government with a host of problems, most of which were hardly, if at all, of the premier's making. Moltke's successor Falkenhayn claimed in his memoirs that he had aimed, with the first Battle of Ypres, to secure the Belgian harbours, and thus endanger Britain's command of the seas, but in fact his primary objective had been to achieve victory for Germany in the west before the year ended. He failed in both objectives, largely because of the heroic resistance of the BEF, which had arrived in the battle zone just in time to arrest the German advance. The battle has been described as the 'chief glory' of the original Expeditionary Force, which 'practically ceased to exist' as a result of its losses there.[2] The 7th Division, for example, had arrived in Belgium in early October with nearly 18,000 men, but was taken out of the line at Ypres on 5 November with less than a half of this number. The Allies were learning painfully that to deprive the Central Powers of victory was very different from subjecting them to defeat.

The trench system along the Western Front represented an unprecedented challenge to both sets of combatants, and after experiencing high

---

[1] *The Nation*, 21 November 1914. See also *British Weekly*, 3 Sept. 1914.
[2] Cruttwell, *Great War*, 106.

command in the Second World War, Field Marshal Earl Wavell wrote privately that the British commanders of 1914–17 operated as if they were engaged in 'Open Warfare at the Halt', whereas the reality confronting them 'was Siege Warfare and should have been treated as such'.[1] The stalemate, and the terrible logic of attrition that ensued, subjected both sides to a degree of nerve-strain previously unknown, and justified Kitchener's observation to Rosebery, that the cabinet deserved the Victoria Cross 'for their courage in declaring war without any adequate supplies of arms, ammunition, and general military equipment'.[2] A very percipient Prime Minister might have been overcome by finding that he had leapt into a horrific new world, but Asquith's much admired composure, though greatly preferable to agitated alarm, carried its own dangers. He was neither open-minded nor imaginative enough to grasp the baffling implications—for diplomacy, military strategy, industrial organization—of the stalemate on the Western Front, and the defects of his virtues now became obtrusive: he was unshaken by the unexpected, but had no aptitude for innovation.

His failure to manage the issue of conscription is the most glaring example of this, and the one that ultimately proved most damaging to his premiership. The need for government to take a tighter control of the economy and of society became increasingly apparent after August 1914, and this naturally posed more problems for the Liberals than for their party opponents. Some Liberal tenets were bound to be put into 'cold storage' while the war lasted, if only on pragmatic grounds, but Asquith was slow to accept this logic. Margot's remark in the diary on 26 November 1914 that the weekly recruiting figure stood at 30,000 was close enough to the fact; but she did not add that two months earlier it had been 116,000. The tailing off of volunteering, coupled with the likely duration of the war, pointed in the obvious direction of military conscription, but this was alien to the majority of Liberals, and Margot's belief that the

[1] The Germans occupied nearly a tenth of France, including the industrial area of Lille, Roubaix, and Tourcoing which included some four-fifths of her coal and nine-tenths of her iron resources: Cruttwell, *Great War*, 107–13. David French, *The RUSI Journal*, 131 (1986), 1, 61.

[2] Rhodes James, *Rosebery*, 476.

Unionists' growing support for 'compulsion', as it came to be called, would mean 'an enormous lift' for her own party enshrined a lethal illusion, from which her husband was not altogether free.[1]

The prolonged deadlock on the Western Front that left the French deprived of their most important industrial area obviously posed problems for the Entente powers; but Britain was soon able to bring her naval supremacy to bear in a way that produced some degree of corrective to this. The Declaration of London, 1909, had defined categories of contraband cargoes, under three headings. Absolute contraband included practically all warlike weapons. Conditional contraband, which included food, was confiscable only if en route to a military or naval destination. Non-contraband goods could not be seized by a combatant if carried in a neutral ship. On 20 August 1914 the government proclaimed, in response to an American enquiry, that they would act in accordance with the Declaration 'as far as may be practicable', subject to certain modifications.[2] By the end of 1914 it was clear that, although this adherence prevented trouble with the United States, it entailed neglecting a weapon of great potential power.[3] In February 1915 the Germans gave Asquith the chance to remedy this. They announced that their U-Boats would be liable to sink, without warning, any British or neutral ship approaching the European Continent by a route other than the one north of Scotland.[4]

The resulting protest in Margot's diary—'a form of naval warfare—piracy, and indeed murder—unheard in the world's History'—though excitedly phrased, is substantially correct: under the accepted usages a belligerent sinking a ship and its cargo was obliged to save its passengers and crew. This task could hardly be performed by a submarine; and complaints about the cruelty of starving an opponent's women and children were unconvincing when they came from the country which had starved

[1] Adams and Poirier, *Conscription*, 62.
[2] Grey, *Twenty-Five Years*, ii. 101 n. 1.
[3] *Page Letters*, i. 364–97.
[4] Cruttwell, *Great War*, 196–7. Fisher had predicted this German move, which Churchill and Battenberg believed would never be made 'by a civilized power': Churchill, *World Crisis*, ii. 280; Marder, *Royal Navy*, i. 363–4.

Paris into submission in 1871.[1] Moreover the Germans' peremptory move was unwise. They did not yet possess a submarine force capable of starving Britain of food and supplies;[2] and Asquith had been given a cast-iron case for imposing a British naval 'blockade', since a belligerent had an undisputed right of reprisal.[3] In calling Asquith's reply to the German threat 'probably the greatest speech Henry has ever delivered', Margot did not exaggerate, and he had secured much more than an ephemeral parliamentary triumph. The visit paid by the American Ambassador and his daughter to the Asquiths shortly afterwards, when they were staying at Walmer Castle, could not have been more timely. W. H. Page was Britain's firm friend, and the understanding which Grey forged with him proved crucial to the success of British blockade policy. Moltke had paid a high price for leaving the port of Rotterdam in neutral hands: he had believed that the British would not risk the enmity which preventing American cargoes from reaching it might arouse.[4] That was not the least of Germany's pre-war illusions. Most American firms did not mind which belligerent paid them for a consignment of war material, so long as they were paid promptly and at top rates. The British had the financial resources to fulfil these conditions.[5]

---

[1] Asquith–Stanley, 406; The Times, 7 Apr. 1916, 9a, b (Leader, German Chancellor's speech).

[2] In Jan. 1915 only 21 German U-Boats were available. All had a short range and limited endurance; and needed long periods in port. Eight of them were of an obsolete type: Offer, Agrarian Interpretation, 355.

[3] 'Reprisal' freed the British government not only from the orbit of the 1909 Declaration of London, but from uncertainty about the status of a distant blockade in international law. Once the Admiralty had abandoned close blockade (from fear of submarine attacks) in 1912, it had been questionable whether the navy's closure of the passage from the North Sea to the Atlantic north of Scotland had given Britain the legal authority needed by a belligerent claiming to impose a 'blockade'. During 1915 the Royal Navy's patrols intercepted, under Britain's right of reprisal, 3,098 ships on the northern route: only nineteen evaded the patrols. No ship is known to have passed the Straits of Dover unnoticed.

[4] See Page Letters, ii. 118. In Moltke's memo. on Western Front strategy (1911 or earlier) Rotterdam is called 'the windpipe through which we breathe': Ritter, Schlieffen Plan, 166–7. Moltke had feared (and expected) prolongation of the war, since he could neither be sure that the British would avoid intervening to help France, nor that occupying Paris quickly would lead to an early surrender by both France and Russia.

[5] President Wilson's proposal for 'freedom of the seas' would have become formidable had American exporters believed that the British could neither protect their cargoes, nor pay for those which were stopped by the Royal Navy when en route to Germany. In 1915 the exporters saw no evidence that the navy would fail to protect, or that the British government would be unable to pay: Page Letters, i. 435–6.

7. The Asquiths in wartime

Faithful to what she had been told at the end of July 1914 about Kitchener's views, Margot was prepared to bet with Montagu that the war 'would not be over till…November or December 1915', but although she was reconciled to a long war her ignorance of the political and social changes that this might entail remains striking. She underestimated the need for collective action, and still saw the cabinet's control of the war effort in essentially personal terms, as a series of 'little stunts' by individual ministers. More damaging still, she discounted how differently the electorate might think and act during wartime, and continued to regard conscription and protection as political liabilities, opposition to which would 'always give the Liberal Party a long lease of life'.[1] Her diary conveys no impression that the first months of the conflict induced her to reconsider pre-war notions and behaviour that quickly looked outdated, not least her obvious admiration for Germany and its army. When she and the premier met Charles Grant at dinner late in November she was given a staff officer's view of First Ypres, but whereas in writing to Venetia Stanley of this encounter Asquith focused on Grant's impressions of the 'extraordinary bravery' and resource of the BEF, Margot characteristically concentrated on his praise for 'the amazing courage of the Germans'.[2] Ever since she had stayed in Dresden as a girl she had made no secret of her liking for German people, but she could not see that her habit of speaking her mind on all occasions, which had been troublesome enough in peacetime, was far more dangerous in war. The attacks on her during the war as a pro-German, though unfair, seem to have been provoked by her own re-

---

[1] Below, pp. 47, 46, 53. For Lloyd George's regret, 26 Oct. 1912, that neither party could command enough support to introduce compulsory military training see McEwen, *Riddell Diaries*, 49–50 (26 Oct. 1912). Although nearly all acknowledged supporters of conscription were Unionists, it had never been part of that party's programme: Morris, *Scaremongers*, ch. 16.

[2] General Sir Charles Grant (1877–1950) had commanded a company of the 1st Coldstream Guards in France during the retreat to the Marne, and during the fighting on the Aisne. For Asquith's strikingly different selection from Grant's remarks see *Asquith–Stanley*, 318. For the last two German attacks which Grant was describing, 10–11 Nov. 1914, see Farrar-Hockley, *Death of an Army*, 172–9; Strachan, *First World War*, 277–8.

marks,[1] and sometimes she insisted on proclaiming her convictions even if she knew that doing so might damage her husband. In May 1915, when told by Lady Frances Balfour that her protests at anti-German riots 'did H. harm, as I was suspected of being pro-German', she replied that she 'didn't care a damn'.[2] Charlie Grant, as a sophisticated staff officer, was ready enough to agree with her that the Germans would have been greatly preferable to the French as allies, since they were 'much more like us'; but those who read the ½d. papers, and more still the journalists who wrote for them, held such views to be wicked and indecent. For them the Germans were the monsters who massacred Belgian civilians, used gas against British boys in the trenches, torpedoed passenger liners, and executed the British nurse Edith Cavell.

Asquith was no more ready than Margot to bow to popular notions of what was acceptable conduct in wartime, and he showed a loyalty to friends that would have been admirable in a less prominent man, but which was dangerous for the leader of a country in great peril. He scorned the idea of avoiding Sir Edgar Speyer, whose brother James was one of America's principal pro-Germans, but by 1916, amid mounting British casualties, and the agony and hysteria which they caused, such an attitude aroused much detraction.[3] The Asquiths continued to visit Ottoline Morrell at Garsington Manor, although her husband Philip was in trouble with his Liberal constituents for his pacifism. The Garsington pacifist coterie included Robbie Ross, whose long association with Oscar Wilde had not been forgotten. Maurice Hankey and his wife, arriving at Sutton Courtenay from Walton Heath on a Sunday in November 1916, noticed with amusement the contrast between the suburbanism of the Ll.G. household and the ultra-smart fashionableness of the Asquiths' home. It

---

[1] Early in October 1915 the Herefordshire gentry apparently thought Margot to be in German pay despite her successful prosecution of the *London Mail* four months earlier: Holroyd, *Strachey*, 602.

[2] See below, p. 112; also *Rasp*, 127.

[3] For Edgar Speyer's illegal doings during the war see *Parl. Pp.* 1922, vii. 141–56, CMD 1569 (revocation of naturalization cert.).

is noticeable that the Asquiths' habits were subjected to harsh and unreasonable censure, while those of Lloyd George, who practised a carefully calculated scorn for the world's opinion, remained almost uncriticized. As he told Frances Stevenson in October 1915: 'If you pay homage to [the world] in certain things, you can defy it in others as much as you like'. During the war Asquith went his own way in his personal life because he was too arrogant to conform to the public's expectations. Lloyd George was much bolder in his habits, but also immensely more circumspect.[1]

As was often remarked, when others were being required to risk all in their country's service, it was fair to ask the nation's leaders to make a wartime sacrifice of their views and their lifestyle, but the Asquiths had already shown over the women's suffrage problem an astonishing inability to respond to changed circumstances. They harboured none of the introspection and reflective self-doubt which later elites were to derive from the psychologist and the sociologist; and the thought of adjusting their habits or their views in order to gain popularity, when the world was turning upside down, was alien to them. Asquith had the inner arrogance of a prize-man from Jowett's Balliol. He shrank from anything which he saw as irrational; but, for a statesman, refusing to take popular irrationalities into account is far from rational, and a detached manner is not suitable in a leader when he alone has the authority to ensure timely action on issues of life and death, and, equally as important, must be seen to be exerting himself to exercise that authority. Asquith had achieved his ascendancy by exposing the irrationalities inherent in his opponents' tariff reform policy. He was politically too unimaginative to realize that the war had deprived some Liberal views of their obvious basis in right reason.[2]

The Asquiths' failure to adapt to a way of life suitable for wartime is often attributed to Margot, although her husband does not seem to have

[1] Gwynne, *Rasp*, 40, 43, 293; *Asquith–Stanley*, 292–3, 295; Darroch, *Ottoline*, 172–3; Hyde, *Other Love*, 189–90 (Ross), Jenkins, *Asquith*, 379–80. For Lloyd George's wartime private life see *Stevenson Diary*, 69, and Campbell, *Frances*, chs 6–12.

[2] Gardiner, *Prophets*, 57; Churchill, *Great Contemporaries*, 137. Asquith warned Venetia Stanley in June 1914 that 'introspection [was] a dangerous and debilitating habit': *Asquith–Stanley*, 80.

helped her to make the adaptations needed. Only during the comparatively short period of his great popularity early in the war was Asquith more or less immune from the criticisms directed at his wife's conduct. Many of these criticisms focused on Margot's failure to conform to the prevailing mood of self-sacrifice, and she still behaved like the much-indulged mascot of the Souls. She showed no recognition of the wartime trend to economize, and neglected a heaven-sent chance to clear the debts which had worried her so badly in recent times.[1] Fashionable clothes in particular came to be viewed as an extravagance, and possibly even an indication that the wearer had gained from war profiteering, and one contemporary observed: 'As the months passed women of the upper classes dressed more and more plainly, even shabbily....Smart clothes were looked upon with disfavour.'[2] Margot ostentatiously ignored the trend, describing Mrs Lloyd George in her diary, in May 1915, as 'a little woman inferiorly dressed and with no distinction of appearance'. A month later Maurice Bonham Carter reported to Violet: 'Margot has not changed. Instead of having big dinner parties of 20, she has frequent ones of 12, her clothes seem still very new & her bridge not less expensive, but I may be unjust as I really have seen very little of her.'[3] It was also hard to believe that the Asquiths needed to maintain a domestic staff of fifteen or sixteen in wartime, or that Margot could find so little time for the humble and more visible kinds of war work. Even in war the Prime Minister was obliged to undertake a good deal of entertaining, and no one expected his wife to

[1] Margot provided generous allowances for Raymond and Violet, and covered numerous costs incurred by her large family; she wrote in her diary, 19 Nov. 1913: 'My bankers informed me I was heavily in debt...I was not surprised. I shall be much more in debt when I have paid all the operations, nurses, homes, journeys to Riviera and Khartoum, hotel bills, and doctors all over the world! I wrote to my brothers for money: they refused to help me': d. 3210. The hotel-and-doctors' bills at Khartoum had been incurred by Violet and Cys. The Riviera bills referred to Margot's own stay at Antibes. The inheritance of Edward Tennant ('Eddy') had been twice as large as those for each of his brothers. In giving Margot £850, 8 Apr. 1910, he had warned her to reduce her 'unnecessary' entertaining: c. 6697, fo. 160. H. J. Tennant was equally concerned about his sister's extravagance: see, for instance, his warning to her, 13 Jan. 1917: c. 6697, fo. 188. For wartime reductions in ministerial salaries, see *Stevenson Diary*, 80; *Riddell War Diary*, 213–14; Grigg, *Lloyd George, 1912–1916*, 410.

[2] Peel, *How We Lived*, 52.

[3] Diary, 18 May 1915, p. 120 below; Bonham Carter, *Diaries, 1914–45*, 69.

tackle substantial administrative tasks such as those being shouldered by Clementine Churchill, for example; but Margaret Lloyd George was showing what a wife could achieve from Downing Street, and, had Margot done a two-hour shift in a nearby hospital pantry, she would quickly have attracted press photos entitled 'Helping the lads'. Her war work mentioned in the diary—'the Queen's needle work committee' and lifts for war blinded officers from St Dunstan's—smacked more of the grand world and the officers' mess than of the private soldiers' welfare.[1]

Margot was too set in her ways to assume a sufficiently humble role, and curb her self-indulgence and grand style, even in the face of wartime austerity;[2] these traits were reflected in the arrangements for her stepdaughter Violet's wedding to her husband's private secretary, Maurice Bonham Carter, in November 1915. The ceremony and reception drew much adverse comment because of its expense. Andrew Clark, the Rector of Great Leighs, Essex, noted in his diary on 7 January 1916:

> The village gossips are much exercised over the Government's exhortations to practise economy, addressed to a village like this where no-one has ever done anything else and where there is no increase of money received, since no-one has war work....If extravagance is sinful (as the Government says), why did Mr Asquith not check it in the case of his daughter's marriage?[3]

The 'village gossips' doubtless did not know that on this occasion Margot's inherent inability to economize had been reinforced by her wish to get on better terms with her stepdaughter, with whom she had long

---

[1] Soames, *Clementine*, 148; Kennet, *Self-Portrait*, 129, 131, 135; Venetia Montagu to A. M. Henley, 22 June 1916; Grigg, *Lloyd George, 1912–1916*, 402; Asquith, C, *Diaries*, 281; Diary, 10 Aug. 1914; [May 1916].

[2] For Grey on Margot's self-indulgence see below, p. 57. In war, as always, Margot could show great kindness; but she tended to do so in fairly private situations: see below, p. 83; also; Clifford, *Asquiths*, 343, 408.

[3] Clark, *Echoes*, 106. Clark (1856–1922) was Rector of Great Leighs from 1894 to his death. For Asquith's attempts to reduce what the *Daily Chronicle* termed the 'normal panoply' of his daughter's wedding see Bonham Carter, *Diaries, 1914–1915*, 84–5; Asquith, C., *Diaries*, 106–7. For Margot's insistence on the need for a trousseau even in wartime see Bonham Carter, *Churchill*, 413.

quarrelled. But a month later William Sutherland, who had been in France, told Frances Stevenson that 'The French cannot understand the attitude of a Prime Minister who allows such a display in his family at a time when everyone is preaching economy and sacrifice, and the necessity of abandoning everything to get on with the war.'[1] When Lloyd George's daughter Olwen was married in June 1917, the wedding and reception were simple, the wedding cake being a cardboard imitation.[2] Just a few weeks after Violet's wedding, her sister-in-law, Cynthia Asquith, recorded her amazement at the entertainment provided one evening at Downing Street, where she spent the night:

> [W]hat a dinner it was in wartime! incomprehensible enough as it would have been in peace. Over twenty people—with few exceptions their only status was as bridge players. If you must have bridge, why not one or even two tables? Why shock London by feeding twenty bores in order that you may have your bridge? It does seem a great pity.[3]

Asquith's predilection for after-dinner bridge was well known, but his devotion to the game, in the context of a war that was going badly, was potentially damaging, and it drew critical comment from so balanced an observer as Hankey.[4]

Neither Asquith nor Margot managed to grasp, until it was too late, that in war they needed to satisfy not merely the Liberal voters, but the whole adult population. It would of course be mistaken to suppose that all of those who lacked the vote in 1914—some two-fifths of the United Kingdom's men and all of its women—were incapable of understanding public affairs; but the proportion of the electorate who had gained any

---

[1] Grigg, *Lloyd George, 1916–1918*, 146–7.

[2] *Stevenson Diary*, 97.

[3] Asquith, C., *Diaries*, 146; Cynthia had observed of Violet's wedding: 'There is something terribly grim about a pompous wedding now. It seems so unnecessary and irrelevant…': Asquith, C., *Diaries*, 106.

[4] F. Bouillon visiting London was jarred by 'the whole tone' of this recreation while 'people were…being killed every hour': *Scott, Diaries*, 162–3; for Asquith's long-standing devotion to bridge see Pease, *Journals*, 67 (3 Oct. 1908). For an example of the Asquiths' ample wartime domestic staff see below, p. 144, 2 June 1915: 'third footman…and butler'.

real secondary education was pathetically small, and among non-electors it was almost certainly smaller.[1] The vast majority of the British were technically literate, but an ability to read Northcliffe's *Daily Mail* was no guarantee of an equal ability to follow the arguments for and against particular war policies as they were presented in Parliament, or on the platform. It was hard enough to convince even those who were used to political argument of the basic, but unpalatable, fact that Britain was a member of a war alliance, and could not act independently. People who had never cast a vote represented a still greater problem. A great many people could judge only by appearances, and the men who were enduring terrible bombardments at the front, and the families back at home who dreaded the loss of a loved one, needed to see some sacrifice by the Prime Minister and his wife, which would show them both to be utterly intent on curtailing war's horrors in a decisive victory. C. E. Montague reported that George V's pledge at the end of March 1915 to give up 'all alcoholic liquor' while the war lasted had a profound effect on public opinion, and on those at the front. Later in the war Montague reported:

> The one good word that the average private had for his unseen 'betters'…was for the King. 'He did give up his beer' was said a thousand times by men whom that symbolic act of willing comradeship with the dry throat on the march and war-pricked household at home had touched and astonished.[2]

Neither of the Asquiths had had the slightest intention of following the royal example, and in a retrospective diary entry written in May 1915 Violet Asquith recorded:

> Father gave a pathetic account of his visit to Windsor shortly after the temperance régime set in—almost complete silence prevailed at

---

[1] In 1902 9 per cent of British children had been in full-time education at 14: *British Political Facts*, 312.

[2] Montague, *Disenchantment*, 192. For circumstances of the King's pledge see below, pp. 90–3. C. E. Montague (1867–1928) dyed his grey hair in 1914 to enlist and saw service at the front.

meals—broken only by Margot's hunting stories—'She'd had her jorum of brandy before coming down' Father wld. explain.[1]

8. Coalition: 'If things go wrong, we shall be flayed'

In March 1915, in a humorous skit written for Venetia about the 'qualities of temperament' that helped him most in his career, Asquith put first 'energy under the guise of lethargy', and a predisposition to good luck 'in external things...above all (at a most critical and fateful moment...) in the sudden outburst of the Great War'.[2] The advent of war had indeed saved Asquith from the crisis over Home Rule that threatened to envelop his government, but even in a moderately jocular passage these were notably impercipient remarks, and none could have illustrated more clearly his complacency and lack of imagination after more than seven months of war. Weeks earlier Lady Tree had asked him: 'do you take an interest in the war?' There is no sign that he saw the question as more than merely quaint.[3]

Ironically things began to go badly wrong on the very day on which Asquith told Venetia what luck the war's outbreak had brought him. On 10 March 1915 Sir John French launched his first planned offensive, at Neuve Chapelle: a cleverly executed initial breakthrough there was not exploited, and after three days of heavy fighting, which cost Haig's First Army almost 13,000 casualties, all forward movement was ordered to cease, a decision necessitated 'by the fatigue of the troops, and, above all, by the want of ammunition'.[4] The naval attack at the Dardanelles that followed on 18 March could also be viewed as a costly failure, entailing as it did the loss of three battleships—two British and one French—without appreciable gain. Neuve Chapelle made Crawford feel 'suicidal', while the losses at Gallipoli were judged 'a very considerable disaster' by

[1] Bonham Carter, *Diaries, 1914–45*, 36.
[2] *Asquith–Stanley*, 470.
[3] Jenkins, *Asquith*, 348.
[4] French's communication to Kitchener: in Edmonds, *1915*, i. 149.

The Times.[1] In fact neither event represented a calamitous reverse, but they did suggest to those near the centre of affairs that Britain's war effort was not being controlled to good effect. 'If things go wrong', Runciman had written weeks earlier, 'we shall be flayed', and, stimulated by these signs that the government were not tackling their problems, *The Times* and *Morning Post* went after the Prime Minister in full cry, to the indignation of many Liberals.[2] On 29 March the *Daily Chronicle*'s editor, who was in touch with McKenna, published a counterblast to the press criticism, in which he denounced the 'innuendoes and suggestions' that Asquith was 'not fit for his task'. It was a perception encouraged in some quarters by Lloyd George, who McKenna suspected of intriguing for the premiership. On 7 March Ll.G. had told Riddell:

Balfour is a very useful member of the committee of Defence. He possesses a searching, probing and penetrating mind... very different from Asquith whose mind is entirely judicial... Asquith... lacks initiative and takes no steps to control or hold together the public departments... During a great war the Prime Minister should direct and overlook the whole machine. No one else has the authority.

The constant praise for the Chancellor of the Exchequer, and criticisms of the Prime Minister, in the Northcliffe press, were quite enough to feed McKenna's ineradicable distrust of Lloyd George.[3]

---

[1] *Crawford Journals*, 350; *The Times*, 29 Apr. 1915, 9a. On the day after the naval failure in the Dardanelles Hankey recorded the warnings he had given about the strategy for forcing the Straits when the measure had first been proposed: 'I warned the PM, Lord K's Chief of Staff, Lloyd George and Balfour that Fleet could not effect passage without troops, and that all naval officers thought so': Roskill, *Hankey*, 168. See also 21 Jan. 1915, Fisher to Jellicoe: '200,000 men [needed] in conjunction with the Fleet': Rhodes James, *Churchill*, 69 n. 2. The Dardanelles operation would have presented serious difficulties even if correctly planned.

[2] Runciman wrote this in February 1915; Hazlehurst, *Politicians at War*, 142 (to Chalmers, 7 Feb. 1915). Cf. *Asquith–Stanley*, 471.

[3] *Riddell War Diary*, 65. See also Fisher's remarks to Riddell, 3 Feb. 15, *Riddell War Diary*, 58. McKenna had distrusted Lloyd George since clashing with him over the 1909 Naval Estimates. For *The Times* on Ll.G.'s 'courage and imagination' see 1 Mar. 1915, 9a; 19 Mar. 9a. Balfour told his niece and biographer that, as a war premier, Asquith had been 'an arbitrator... I never heard him originate or suggest': Dugdale, *Balfour*, ii. 157.

While Ll.G. may already have begun to test the political water, he did not at this time command the backing needed for an assault on the premiership, and it is doubtful whether even by 1916 he aimed specifically at being Prime Minister.[1] The *Daily Chronicle* article represented a sign, not that Asquith was in danger of being deposed, but simply that his capacity for war leadership was being questioned. In peacetime Asquith's ascendancy had been maintained through his grip in Parliament and on the platform. During the war both of these institutions were devalued, while the influence of the press, which he had neglected and despised, was correspondingly enhanced. Everyone wanted the latest war news and newspaper circulations rose accordingly. It is not easy nowadays to envisage an embattled Britain in which, in the absence of radio broadcasting and television, most people derived all their information about the war from a single newspaper. Those who bought any of them wanted to read of the Allies' victories, or at least to be assured that the government was straining every nerve, and would stick at nothing, to secure some.[2] But Unionist writers of the wilder kind began to insinuate that the premier and his wife did not really wish their country to win the war.[3] Margot had made no secret of her liking for Germans, and the *Morning Post* did not hesitate to class her with those leading Liberals who did not want to see the enemy defeated. Early in November 1915 its editor sent Bonar Law a draft statement dividing the British population into:

(1) The Free-Trade, pro-German, and Voluntary Service party.
(2) The British, Protection, and National Service party, [who] will naturally seek to concentrate on the prejudice against Conscription.

---

[1] Lloyd George said, 30 July 1916, that he 'should be glad and proud to serve under' Carson: *Riddell War Diary*, 206.

[2] For a detailed account of press doings during the first half of the war see Koss, *Political Press*, ii, chs. 7 and 8. Northcliffe had opposed the despatch of the BEF to France on 5 Aug. 1914: Thompson, *Northcliffe*, 223–4.

[3] See Gwynne, *Rasp*, 127. The publicists of the 'Radical Right' were not subject to the restraints acknowledged by the Unionists' parliamentary leaders. They held no brief for the Unionists' pre-war doings. Leo Maxse had taken a leading part in ousting Balfour from the party leadership in 1911. Arnold White was not even a Unionist party member.

Among the least educated and most credulous of the population such slanders were bound to do the Liberal Party some damage, and the Asquiths a good deal.[1]

The Liberals were not strong in press coverage. Northcliffe, whose holdings included both *The Times* and the *Daily Mail*, bestrode the newspaper field. His reduction of *The Times's* price to a penny just before the war, while the *Daily Mail's* circulation was reaching a million, had consolidated his position.[2] Though certainly no Liberal, he was not a Unionist of the usual kind. He had gained his peerage in Balfour's Resignation Honours List, but by Edward VII's initiative, not by Balfour's.[3] Margot thought that he must be pro-German, since his papers often included war stories that seemed calculated to encourage Britain's enemies.[4] She was wrong. Northcliffe was an irresponsible and rather unbalanced patriot, whose criticisms of government conduct of the war inevitably entailed the publication of statements that might occasionally give the enemy comfort.[5] He thought it his particular duty to expose the follies and evasions of Liberal ministers, and it was characteristic of him to start his campaign for military conscription as soon as his papers had helped to discredit the one Liberal minister, Haldane, who had declared, as early as January 1915, that its application in wartime did not in the least contravene Liberal principles.[6] Asquith clearly could not possibly have adopted Margot's formula for suppressing all press criticism of the government,

[1] Gwynne, *Rasp*, 148–9. In temperament the *Morning Post's* editor, H. A. Gwynne, 'was never far from paranoia': Gwynne, *Rasp*, 321.

[2] Searle, *1886–1918*, 575. For Margot's comment on the penny *Times* see Diary, p. 32 below. The dip in circulation when Northcliffe attacked Kitchener over the shell shortage, 21 May 1915, in *The Times* and *Daily Mail*, and both papers were burned ceremonially in the streets, was short-lived. Both had recovered by July, and Northcliffe regarded himself as the author of the Liberal government's fall: Thompson, *Northcliffe*, 240–5.

[3] Thompson, *Northcliffe*, 126.

[4] For Northcliffe's fluctuating attitude to the Kaiser before the War see Morris, *Scaremongers*, 8.

[5] Northcliffe told a member of his staff that the comments on 'the Amiens' despatches' (for which see below, p. 33 n. 1) had hurt him 'more than anything else in his life': Thompson, *Northcliffe*, 228. See diary, 9 June 1915, for Margot's belief that Northcliffe had emphasized the 'shells scandal' in order to sell his papers. For the evidence that he had recognized the damage which attacking Kitchener on shells would do to his papers see Thompson, *Northcliffe*, 240–2.

[6] See *Parl. Deb.*, Lords, 18.378, 1002–4.

on the ground that it was bound to encourage the enemy; but he could certainly have spoken more often to meetings of the newspaper owners and editors, most of whom had no great love for Northcliffe. He was however reluctant to convene such gatherings, even though, when he did so, he enjoyed considerable success. J. L. Garvin was one of the leading editors who attended the press briefing given at 10 Downing Street in January 1916, during which Asquith explained the difficulties of conducting the naval blockade of Germany: 'though some of my colleagues proposed very simple, rash and impossible policies', Garvin recalled, 'I came away very much impressed as one so often is by the troubles of Government.'[1]

Many of the initiatives that turned out badly in the war fell somewhere between being regarded as 'mistakes' and 'misfortunes', but there can be no doubt that Asquith's speech at Armstrongs' Tyneside armament works, on 20 April 1915, falls into the former category.[2] Asquith sought reassurance against the suggestion that the country's armament workers might have failed the troops, because alcoholic self-indulgence had reduced output, and he was supplied with a confirmatory written statement by Kitchener, who had consulted French. Kitchener wrote that French 'would have as much artillery ammunition... as his troops [will] be able to use during the next forward movement'.[3] Margot, like many others then and since, doubted whether French should have given even this limited assurance to his chief, and thus to the premier. But quite apart from this, Asquith produced a grossly exaggerated version of French's words in his Tyneside speech. He said:

> I do not believe that any army... has ever either entered upon a campaign, or been maintained during a campaign, with better or more

---

[1] J. G. Garvin to his son Ged, 26 Jan. 1916; Asquith's performance struck Riddell as highly effective: *Riddell War Diary*, 151.

[2] See Diary, 21 Apr. 1915 (p. 101 below), where Margot misdates the speech to 21 Apr. 1915; *Asquith–Stanley*, 560.

[3] *Asquith–Stanley*, 558–9. For Asquith's explanation of the episode, 2 June 1919, see Spender and Asquith, ii. 144–51. French's assurance to Kitchener must have been based on a highly optimistic estimate about the ammunition needed for the Aubers Ridge attack.

adequate equipment [than the BEF's]. I saw a statement the other day that the operations... of our army... were being crippled, or at any rate hampered, by our failure to provide the necessary ammunition. There is not a word of truth in that statement.[1]

Those remarks haunted Asquith for the rest of the war and beyond it. They ran contrary to the experience of Neuve Chapelle, and indeed to statements by other members of the government, as the press quickly pointed out.[2] Even more dangerously they were known by almost everyone on the Western Front to be untrue. They could not have been made by anyone who had visited that front with eyes and ears open. The premier had converted a limited assurance about a particular attack then being planned into a general statement about the BEF's armament and ammunition. It was true that the original BEF had crossed the Channel fairly well equipped for the campaign in which it was expected to be involved, although even then there were notable deficiencies; but it was anything but well supplied for the kind of 'siege warfare' in which it had been engaged since November 1914.[3]

Asquith's words at Tyneside revealed disastrously that he did not know enough about conditions at the front, and the 'guise of lethargy', which was of questionable value in the pre-war years, now told heavily against him. Sir Edward Cook noted in his diary early in April 1915 J. A. Spender's private admission that the 'real foundation' for the 'recent press outcry' against the Prime Minister had been 'A's laziness and lack of ideas'. 'It was not unknown', Austen Chamberlain recorded after the

---

[1] For a reference to this statement in May 1940 see *Dalton War Diaries*, 9. The assertion about the completeness of the BEF's initial equipment is in (the official) *History of the Great War*, i. 10. Robertson was sceptical of that, and stressed that the navy's priority in pre-war expenditure questions had entailed denying the army some of the equipment known to be necessary: Robertson, *Private to Field-Marshal*, 192–3. For the defects in the British Navy's equipment when the war began see Marder, *Royal Navy*, i. 435. Maurice explained why shrapnel had been preferred for the BEF before the war: Maurice, *Haldane*, i. 371.

[2] Koss, *Asquith*, 181.

[3] The German army was better equipped for this change largely because rapid destruction of the forts at Liège and Namur had been a crucial feature of its pre-war planning. For the British Army's difficulties in producing weapons needed urgently in trench warfare see Lloyd George, *War Memoirs*, i. 369–70 (the Stokes mortar).

war, 'for the Prime Minister to be writing letters while the discussion proceeded'; and in war much more was expected of the occupant of that office than the prompt and careful dispatch of current business.[1] Asquith had not set up a machinery that would ensure that he would know everything afoot. He happened to learn in December 1914, for example, that self-inflicted wounds had become quite common at the front, and saw from this 'what a shattering thing [life in] the trenches must be'; but it was five months before he crossed the Channel to learn more about such problems at first hand, even though he had been 'pressed strongly' by French in December 1914 to visit the BEF for '2 or 3 days'.[2] Margot had seconded French's pleas, and she realized that Asquith's delay until 30 May 1915 in making his visit was most damaging. He always made a good impression with the officers and men of the BEF when he did visit, and, unlike Ll.G., was untroubled by the risk which approaching the battle zone entailed.[3] Northcliffe had paid the first of many visits to the front early in October 1914; and a few days later Lloyd George and Simon had met most of the leading French generals during a visit. Hobhouse found Ll.G.'s account to the cabinet on return 'vivid and useful'.[4] Inevitably comparisons were drawn between Lloyd George and his chief. Morley told Sir William Robertson Nicoll in 1915: 'Asquith is a fine fellow; but he will never carry the business through. He is much too casual…'; and in passing this view on to another well-known Nonconformist minister

[1] Spender and Asquith, ii. 230; Koss, *Political Press*, 272; Chamberlain, *Down the Years*, 111; Bonham Carter, *Diaries, 1914–45*, 83.

[2] *Asquith–Stanley*, 334; for the stream of distinguished visitors to the British front in Apr. 1915 see Charteris, *At GHQ*, 87.

[3] See the account of Asquith during an air raid on London, 7–8 Sept. 1915: Bonham Carter Papers, 257; 'under shellfire', Fricourt, 6 Sept. 1916: Hankey, *Supreme Command*, 513. Cf. Grigg, *Lloyd George, 1912–1916*, 383–6: Ll.G. seldom visited the front-line troops when War Secretary. John Grigg gave a convincing statement of the reasons for his failure to spend time in and near the trenches. 'His fear of explosives', Grigg wrote, 'was no doubt one reason; but the main [one] was his squeamishness. All his life he had recoiled from illness, injury and death, so it was inevitable that the physical consequences of war should be so abhorrent to him that he could not trust himself to contemplate them at close quarters.'

[4] Thompson, *Northcliffe*, 229; Grigg, *Lloyd George, 1912–1916*, 179–81; Lloyd George, *War Memoirs*, i. 90–6; *Hobhouse Diaries*, 199.

Nicoll added: 'Lloyd George has been…infinitely the most useful member of the government since the War began.'[1]

By August 1914 Asquith was well used to the trials of the premiership, having presided over one of the most turbulent periods in modern British politics, but the onset of war engendered a degree of strain such as even he had not previously encountered. One manifestation of this was a marked increase in the number of his letters to Venetia Stanley. To a remarkable extent these deal with political and public events, rather than personal matters. Venetia's replies have not survived, but it is clear from contemporary accounts that she was a highly intelligent and well-read young woman, described by one male friend as having 'a masculine intellect' and 'fine brain'.[2] She evidently enjoyed political discussion, and, though notably discreet, must have prized the confidences that Asquith regularly bestowed upon her. By January 1915 she was receiving two or three letters a day, and in April Margot, fearing that her position as her husband's chief confidante was being usurped by a much younger rival, wrote to him seeking reassurance. He answered, soothingly, by return of post:[3]

> But you would have just reason for complaint, & more, if it were true that I was transferring my confidence from you to anyone else. My fondness for Venetia has never interfered & never could with our relationship.

Margot's inability to be a restful companion, whether alone or in company, represented however an insoluble problem: Bongie told Violet in January 1915 that a large contingent of weekend guests had merely made her 'the more edgy',[4] and she was incapable of giving her husband what he now needed most, and which Venetia *could* supply—the restful companionship of someone who could keep a secret, and knew how to reassure a

---

[1] Attenborough, *Living Memory*, 77. Nicoll had been a Minister in the Scottish Free Church. He was writing, Oct. 1915, to Dr J. D. Jones.

[2] L. E. Jones, *An Edwardian Youth* (1956), 214.

[3] *Asquith–Stanley*, 546–8.

[4] *Asquith–Stanley*, 459, 511; see also 381.

FIGURE 7 Venetia Stanley

heavily burdened leader with responsive sympathy and tactful advice. Ever since Roy Jenkins first revealed publicly the story of the premier's prolific and amorous correspondence to Venetia, in his 1964 biography, there has been speculation about the nature of that relationship, and modern readers have perhaps too readily assumed a physical dimension. The tone of the letters is that of courtly rather than carnal love, and speaks of an *amitié amoureuse*—a form of communication, and perhaps even of feeling, that may be difficult to comprehend in the digital age.

Writing letters to Venetia clearly had a therapeutic value for Asquith, and they perhaps enabled him to organize more clearly his thoughts about events, but the fact that some of them were written, in whole or part, during official proceedings has damaged his reputation. The number written in those circumstances seems to have been small, and as a proportion of those written to Venetia it is minuscule: 6 from the Treasury bench in the House, 4 during cabinet discussions, 3 during committees, 1 during a CID meeting, and 1 during a War Council meeting. But Asquith's letter-writing on the latter occasion, 13 January 1915, represents a serious dereliction of duty, as a crucial decision about the Dardanelles was taken during that meeting.[1] How far that lapse may have affected the outcome cannot, of course, be known,[2] but the subsequent costly failure of the Gallipoli adventure focuses attention now, as then, on Asquith's management of the cabinet at a crucial stage in the war. The first use of gas by the Germans, at Ypres on 22 April; the failure of the Gallipoli landings on 25 April, with heavy casualties; and the sinking of the *Lusitania* by a U-Boat off the south coast of Ireland on 7 May, with the loss of 1,198 lives, including 124 Americans, all heralded a new and much grimmer phase of the war, and the premier now needed to exemplify not merely confidence, but ceaseless activity and indomitable will.

During the first two weeks of May 1915 the war situation worsened markedly, with important political ramifications. The failure of the Dardanelles expedition made it less likely that Italy would enter the war on the Allied side, an event viewed in London as being of great strategic significance. On 13 May the Salandra government, which favoured the Allies, resigned.[3] The next day *The Times* included a dispatch from its military correspondent, Charles à Court Repington, about the failure of the British attack, five days earlier, at Aubers Ridge in northern France; as at Neuve Chapelle, a lack of ammunition was cited as a key reason for the failure. Repington, who had been quite deliberately briefed by French himself, reported:

> The attacks were well planned and valiantly conducted...but...the want of an unlimited supply of high explosive was a fatal bar to our success.[4]

[1] *Asquith–Stanley*, 375–7.

[2] See Hankey, *Supreme Command*, i. 265–7.

[3] Cassar, *Asquith, War*, 98; Taylor, *Struggle*, 544–7. The Italians had promised to join the Allies in the war under the Treaty of London, 26 Apr. 1915. The opponents of intervention in the Chamber, who had forced Salandra to resign, found how limited their influence was when the crowd broke the Chamber's windows. On 23 May Italy declared war on Austria-Hungary.

[4] Cassar, *Kitchener*, 354. French wrote to Mrs Bennett, 8 May 1915: 'I am just on the eve of commencing what I believe will grow into one of the greatest battles in the history of the world.'

Several government meetings were held on 14 May in the shadow of this report, and the atmosphere in the War Council, which convened after an eight-week interval, was gloomy. The following morning, 15 May, the government's problems were compounded when 'Jackie' Fisher, the First Sea Lord, sent his ninth resignation to his chief, Churchill, and to the Prime Minister. This time he meant it. He vacated his office and vanished. Fisher gave as his reason for resigning 'incompatibility of views with Churchill', but the root cause was his chief's mismanagement, as Fisher saw it, of the navy's resources at Gallipoli.[1]

The authors of the May crisis, French and Fisher, had aimed not at Asquith, but at their 'departmental' chiefs Kitchener and Churchill. Neither of those two had any great talent for cooperating with cabinet colleagues, or understanding a subordinate's grievances. Neither realized how important maintaining the balance between civilian control and professional expertise would be in wartime; but a Prime Minister who meant to establish his control over his colleagues would, at least, have set up a War Council in the first month of the war, and not in the fourth, and would have shown its importance by giving it, not merely a small secretariat, but explicit authority to question officials, and a limited power of decision. Kitchener thought of himself more as the army's Supreme Commander than as a cabinet minister.[2] His immense prestige, and Churchill's outstanding ability, enabled each to act independently of the other, when they should have been working in harness. Unfettered by proper

Montagu had told Sylvia Henley that the 9 Apr. attack was to be the BEF's 'big push': 11 May, Sylvia to her husband: Bodleian, MSS Eng. Lett. c. 641, fo. 78. Margot referred to this attack in writing to Arthur Asquith, 13 May, as 'a very big offensive carefully planned by Haig'. See French, 1914, 357: 'I immediately gave instructions that evidence should be furnished to Colonel Repington, military correspondent of The Times, who happened to be then at Headquarters, that the vital need of high-explosive shells had been a fatal bar to our Army success on that day.'

[1] *Fisher Correspondence*, iii. 228; Marder, *Royal Navy*, ii. 278–9.

[2] For Asquith's description of the War Council's operations see his *Memories*, ii. 87–8. Asquith did not always show any great respect for the War Council. He did not circulate Fisher's statement of objections to the Dardanelles plan to it, but saw Churchill and Fisher immediately before its meeting, 28 Jan. 1915: Hankey, *Supreme Command*, 269–71; Churchill, *World Crisis*, ii. 154–7; Roskill, *Hankey*, 168. Ll.G. concluded that Kitchener's main idea in cabinet meetings 'was to tell the politicians as little as possible…and get back to his desk at the War Office as quickly as he could decently escape': Lloyd George, *War Memoirs*, i. 51.

cabinet control they were also able to have their own way when it clashed with predominant professional views, including those held by their principal subordinates, French and Fisher. Yet both were deficient in professional knowledge about the kind of conflict in which they were now involved: Kitchener had won his reputation in a totally different kind of warfare, while Churchill was simply a brilliant amateur, whose innovative flair was sometimes marred by a dominant care for his own reputation.[1]

In response to what became known as the shells shortage scandal, and Fisher's theatrical flight from the Admiralty, Asquith quickly reached agreement with Bonar Law, on 17 May, on the need for a coalition government. As he told Margot: 'The fact is, there are too many difficulties just now: we can't have a debate on munitions with Germany watching us. We can't have a Gen. Election: we can only carry on with the full support of the opposition.'[2] There has been speculation that in agreeing to the Coalition Asquith was adversely affected by Venetia Stanley's confession to him, in a letter of 11 May, that she was engaged to marry his protégé Edwin Montagu. Asquith had not suspected their affair, and was devastated by the news.[3] That the blow adversely affected his judgement at this crucial hour may, however, be doubted, and in the longer term the break with Venetia was probably beneficial.[4] The friendship was no longer helping him quite as it had done during the first weeks of the war: his state had turned from dependence into obsession. Edwin [Montagu] was not an impartial judge; but he may have been right when he told Venetia in April

[1] As Balfour reminded the premier, 23 Sept. 1915: Spender and Asquith, ii, 187, Asquith Papers, 28 fo. 185 for date; See Cassar, *Kitchener*, ch. 12; Marder, *Royal Navy*, ii. 270 for Churchill's interpretation of the First Lord's role in war; and H. W. Richmond, *Churchill Companion*, ii. 430, for Fisher in 1914–15.

[2] Diary, 17 May 1915, p. 120 below; Asquith apparently told Margot that he 'could have weathered the Winston storm'; but the conjunction of that with the shells shortage allegations had made the formation of a Coalition inevitable: Margot to Arthur Asquith, 19 May 1915: Arthur Asquith Papers.

[3] Edwin Montagu had written to Venetia, 19 Apr. 1915: 'I am not the only member of the cabinet writing to you during its deliberations': *Asquith Stanley*, 554.

[4] For an assessment of its impact on his handling of the May crisis see *Asquith–Stanley*, 598–9.

1915 that the Prime Minister's relationship with her spelled 'trouble for him…and possibly loss of grip eventually'.

In spite of this severe emotional blow, Asquith continued to function, and managed the coalition-building process now at hand with considerable dexterity. But Venetia's letter had shattered his romantic idyll, and deprived him of what had become his principal means of solace in the preceding nine and a half months of war; and soon after its receipt he lost his other principal source of restful companionship, when Violet Asquith left for Egypt to visit her brother Arthur, who had been wounded at Gallipoli. Shortly after departing, on 19 May, Violet recorded in her diary a telling conversation with her father:[1]

> He came up into my bedroom later on & talked to me till nearly 3 about every sort of thing—politics—Venetia—Margot. Poor darling he said: 'I have sometimes walked up & down that room till I felt as tho' I were going mad. When one needed rest to have a thing like the *Morning Post* leader flung at one [by Margot]—all the obvious reasons for & against things more controversially put even than by one's colleagues'.

'Venetia', Violet observed, 'rested him from all this.'

9. Conscription: '…would be Insanity'

Asquith's first task as a Coalition premier was to reassure his Liberal followers over his sudden decision to broaden his government. In performing this he was helped by a skilful appeal to the Liberal MPs, as Margot records, and perhaps by the fact that Bonar Law lacked the experience necessary to press him harder, having never been a cabinet minister.[2] By adroit Coalition building Asquith was able to associate the Unionists with the government, while denying them much

---

[1] Bonham Carter, *Diaries, 1914–45*, 55.

[2] Asquith failed to realize that, while it might make sense to take advantage of Bonar's comparative inexperience, to give the Liberals as much advantage as possible, it was essential for him to treat his opposite number with the greatest respect. Asquith seemed reluctant to remember how dependent the Coalition was on the continuing goodwill of the largest party contingent in the Commons and of its leader.

control over it, a strategy that served him well at the time, but which carried a high cost in the longer term. A preoccupation with the balance between the parties ran counter to the essential task of reforming the governmental apparatus, with the result that a machinery already recognized as ill suited to waging war became still more inefficient. Yet the creation of the Coalition had made effective reform more essential than ever. The Liberal cabinet had seldom questioned the War Council's proposals, but a Coalition cabinet, reflecting a wider range of views and talents, was certain to be more assertive: unless the Council could be given some defined power of decision, delays would result. Asquith, however, partly from a sense of constitutional propriety, was reluctant to delegate cabinet authority. He had been confronted by an increased need to reform the machine, while being furnished with an excuse for dodging the issue.[1]

The most notable Liberal casualty of the Coalition was Haldane. Margot believed that in sacrificing him her husband had yielded with the utmost reluctance to Unionist pressure, and Spender wrote that the decision almost reduced the premier 'to despair'.[2] According to Austen Chamberlain, however, Asquith had suggested Haldane's removal from the Woolsack on the very first day of the discussions with Bonar Law, on 17 May.[3] Chamberlain was a comparatively reliable reporter, and his statement is not implausible. Haldane, apart from being the target for scurrilous attacks 'as a thinly veiled friend of Germany', had not maintained the prudent silence on military conscription which the Prime Minister had expected from his Liberal colleagues.[4] Bonar Law and his allies would have insisted that Haldane must go whatever the premier had said on

[1] For views, May 1915, on creating a small body to run the war, and keeping the cabinet in the background, from the Marquess of Salisbury (1861–1947) and Birrell, see Koss, *Asquith*, 188–9. For Carson's similar suggestions, 2 Nov. 1915 see Hyde, *Carson*, 396. For Asquith's view about war business, 12 Mar. 1915, which was 'much better done' in a committee of five 'than in a huge, unwieldy cabinet', see *Asquith–Stanley*, 475.

[2] See below, p. 70; Bonham Carter, *Churchill*, 394–5; Spender and Asquith, ii. 167.

[3] Koss, *Haldane*, 191.

[4] For the attacks, see *Asquith–Stanley*, 322–4; Haldane, *Autobiography*, 282–7. The particulars of his 1912 conversations in Germany were not published either then or during the war: a silence much to his disadvantage.

17 May, but Asquith may not have been quite so unhappy to comply with their insistence as Margot and Spender made out.[1] Constructing a well-balanced coalition was extremely difficult. It left no room for the claims of old friendship, or for recognizing Haldane's outstanding achievement as Secretary of State for War. Asquith must have hated appearing to comply with the deplorable demands of the Unionists' mud-slingers; but when the appearance of complying was needed, he did not hesitate. A less complacent premier would have recognized the attack on Haldane to be the prelude to one on his own position. Both of them were in the sights of the radical right: the polemical journalist Arnold White had told Leo Maxse, owner-editor of the *National Review*, that a failure to destroy Haldane could leave 'the Radical boches' in office 'for thirty years'.[2]

While the Coalition was being formed Massingham proclaimed conscription to be the Liberals' 'all-dominating anxiety', and the question of whether or not to compel young men to serve in the army was sure to be a dangerous one for the Prime Minister. His party's traditions were libertarian. He was always afraid of any charge of departing from them; and on this issue his optimism and inclination to delay action were very powerful. It took more than a year of war for most British people to realize that the inventions which had transformed weaponry and explosives since 1890 favoured the defence, and made a long war a virtual certainty; but by the summer of 1915 the more perceptive of the elite realized that Kitchener's plan of hoarding his army until it could be used to dominate the Entente's victory advance was impracticable. No French government would approve of those British inclinations while a tenth of

[1] Bonar Law was not invulnerable on pro-German accusations: see his expression of admiration for German literature: *Parl. Deb.*, 27 Nov. 1911, 32.68. He no doubt thought that Haldane had 'stepped over the line' by saying, 20 June 1914 (speech, Hartley University College, Southampton): 'I am not in the least afraid of the invasion of German armies, but … very much afraid of the invasion of people who have been trained in German universities and schools'. Haldane's exclusion showed how much the outbreak of war had strengthened the publicists of the 'Radical Right' such as Maxse and Arnold White; see Koss, *Haldane*, 136.

[2] Koss, *Haldane*, 134. The fact that Asquith did not write to Haldane about this decision may have been connected with the ambiguity of his position. Perhaps he baulked at expressing regret for an exclusion which he had virtually initiated.

France, and a high percentage of its industrial resources, remained in enemy hands. The volunteering effort had been wonderful; but by the time the Coalition had been formed the steady fall in the recruiting figures constituted a powerful case for compulsion. The adoption of military conscription was probably the only measure which would have convinced French people as a whole that the British meant to put everything into the war, and take their proper share of the suffering involved without any thought about having the largest army when it came to peacemaking.[1]

This was not the only reason for supposing that adhering indefinitely to a voluntary system of army recruitment might be unwise. Kitchener's highly successful appeal for his volunteer armies had deprived all the main war industries of some of their keenest and most expert workers. By January 1915 the need for a national register, to show how a further outflow might be prevented, without crippling the new armies, was obvious and urgent;[2] but, from fear that compiling one would be seen as a first step to conscription, Asquith hesitated to put it in hand. In so doing he missed the best chance of showing that there was no Liberal objection of principle to military conscription *during war*. When some of the leading Unionist peers called for this register in the Lords on 8 January 1915 Haldane told the Upper House, in the words of *The Times*' report, 'that compulsory service was not foreign to the Constitution, and declared, with grave emphasis, that the government barred nothing out in principle'.[3] If Asquith had supported his Lord Chancellor in a Commons statement he could have killed the wicked suggestions that Haldane was Germany's

[1] Curzon, speaking to the Primrose League, 30 Apr. 1915, compared Britain's 700,000 mustered for the front from a population of 45 million, with France's 2.5 million in the field out of 40 million. At Manchester, he said, there were '30,000 [men] looking on at 22 other men knocking a leather ball about': *The Times*, 1 May 1915. Curzon had been prominent in the National Service League since 1909. Like other peacetime supporters of conscription he spoke as if all of these 30,000 spectators at a football match were fit and available for army service in France, and should have undergone military training before the war.

[2] See Midleton and others: *Parl. Deb.*, Lords, 8 Jan. 1915, 18.347–58 (Midleton), 387–94 (Curzon) and, for figures about effects on war industry, Adams and Poirier, *Conscription*, 90–1.

[3] *The Times*, 9 Jan. 1915, 9b; see also *Parl. Deb.*, Lords, 8 Jan. 1915, 18.378. Haldane had indicated as early as 1909 that Britain might well need to adopt conscription during war.

friend,[1] reassured the French, and pointed his countrymen towards a sensible distribution of manpower. Indeed Crawford, who was an exceptionally experienced judge, thought early in February 1915 that 'the radicals might well accept Conscription if passed by their own government'.[2] Once the agitation in the press began, and the Coalition took office, however, Asquith's conscription problems were vastly increased. The change to compulsion began to look, as Margot wrote, like part of an attempt to 'smash the Prime Minister' and upset the Coalition.[3] The Asquiths' sneers about those who initiated the 8 January debate symbolized what was wrong with Britain's wartime leadership.[4]

Massingham saw only four 'ardent' conscriptionists in the new cabinet; and he predicted that the outcome would depend on the 'Facing-both-ways' cohort, or, in more dispassionate phrasing, on politicians whose stance changed with events and with shifts in popular attitudes.[5] It took a mere twelve days from the government's formation for a leading Liberal to start moving towards the 'ardent' conscriptionists. Lloyd George had received the premier's effusive thanks for his self-forgetfulness in helping to construct the Coalition,[6] but he had hardly been the Coalition's Minister of Munitions for a week when he began to fall from Margot's good graces. In opening his munitions campaigning at Manchester on 3 June 1915 he remarked that, although a compulsory system was not yet needed for the army, some move towards it might be used for adding to Britain's industrial strength.[7] He was quickly reminded of

---

[1] Professor Oncken of Heidelberg stated in an article late in 1914 that Haldane had called Germany his 'spiritual home'. Long afterwards it became known that Haldane had used the phrase of Lötze's classroom at Göttingen, where he had attended the philosophy seminar in 1874. Sommer, *Haldane*, 318–19.

[2] Crawford Journals, 347 (2 Feb. 1915).

[3] Diary, 18 Aug. 1915, p. 168 below.

[4] Diary, 10 Jan. 1915, pp. 69–70 below; *Asquith–Stanley*, 365.

[5] Massingham was presumably referring to publicly declared conscriptionists. This could have excluded Churchill. For Bunyan's Mr Facing-both-ways see *Pilgrim's Progress*, part 1.

[6] Lloyd George, *War Memoirs*, 140–1 (facsimile); Hazlehurst, *Politicians at War*, 249.

[7] Grigg, *Lloyd George, 1912–1916*, 263–4.

what Robert Smillie, the miners' leader, had told the Prime Minister late in April 1915. As summarized by Riddell, Smillie's message was: 'while the men are willing to sacrifice themselves in the national interest, they are not prepared to do so in the interests of the masters.'[1]

This second effort by Ll.G. to establish himself as an effective warrior, without alienating his Nonconformist following, proved no more successful than his earlier appeal for wartime teetotalism had been. His remarks at Manchester on 3 June aroused what Christopher Addison called 'something of a storm' in the Commons. The most diehard Unionists had expected Bonar to require military, not industrial, conscription as the price of adhesion. The two most prominent conscriptionist commoners in the new government, Austen Chamberlain and Walter Long, made clear to their cabinet colleagues that they did not favour industrial conscription. Austen's friend, F. S. Oliver, although friendly to conscription of both kinds, advised caution on this. 'If you attempt', he told Austen on 10 June, 'to have compulsory *industrial* service—which nobody understands—without first setting up compulsory *military* service—which everybody understands—you will, I think, come somewhere near revolution.' Balfour and the new Labour leader Arthur Henderson also advanced an anti-compulsion argument, which applied to industrial conscription with particular force, namely, that it would bear hardest on the working class.[2] Lloyd George quickly concluded that military conscription represented the only route to a nation disciplined for war.

The Coalition lost no time in promoting the national registration measure from which the Liberal government had shrunk. Sunday 15 August was made Registration Day. In preparation for the figures which it would reveal Asquith appointed on 11 August what was soon called the War Policy Committee, under Crewe's chairmanship. This body in-

---

[1] *Riddell War Diary*, 80. See also Wolfe, *Labour Supply*, 42.

[2] Bonar Law did not demand military conscription as a condition for joining the government, though he had been expected to do so: Adams and Poirier, *Conscription*, 87, 91–2, 95–6, 114–15. The die-hard peer Willoughby de Broke was particularly angry at the failure to extract a conscription pledge: Koss, *Asquith*, 197. His conscriptionist views had led him, in March 1914, to sponsor a bill under which those entering the 'higher professions' should undergo mandatory training: Adams and Poirier, *Conscription*, 261 n. 43.

cluded, with the chairman, four committed conscriptionists, and Arthur Henderson, the cabinet's only Labour member. It was given the task of establishing 'the main facts' needed by the cabinet so that they could determine the size of the army which Britain would try 'to keep in the field during...1916'.[1] As all of 'the facts' were imponderables the chances of an agreed report were small. The probable rate of casualties, and the extent to which war production processes, hitherto performed by fit and trained young men, could become the work of half-trained women and older men, were, for instance, entirely unknown.

Once Lloyd George had plunged incautiously into the control of strong drink, and into a still more disastrous suggestion about industrial conscription, Margot concluded that his efforts to turn himself into a war leader had merely made him 'a sort of low comedian'[2]. She was wrong. In giving evidence to the Crewe Committee on 18 August 1915 Lloyd George said that 'every man and woman was bound to render the services which the State required of them, and which in the opinion of the State they could best render'. He added that he was 'certain you will have to come to [this]', but that for the present 'a general compulsion [was not] essential:...If you had compulsory military service you could work the rest all right.'[3] This was a more realistic, and therefore to conscription's opponents a more dangerous, position than the one which Ll.G. had taken early in June 1915. The Minister of Munitions was not aiming at being able to dictate the armament concern for which a man worked, nor at creating a very large army. He aimed to ensure that, if a fit man, aged between 18 and 41 and engaged in essential war work, left his job without permission, he would risk finding himself in the trenches.[4] He wanted, as he told the Crewe Committee, to ensure that these younger men would be serving wherever they could contribute most effectively to the war effort.

[1] Adams and Poirier, *Conscription*, 104.
[2] Diary, 13 July 1915; see below, p. 166.
[3] Grigg, *Lloyd George, 1912–1916*, 327–8.
[4] Under the first Military Service Act a man of military age who lost his exempted status, by leaving his job in war industry, was given a two-month grace period to find another one before being 'called up': Adams and Poirier, *Conscription*, 141.

Achieving this would not necessarily increase the numbers at the front. Ll.G. had grasped, somewhat tardily, that the opposition to conscription from the organized section of the working class, while far more formidable than the libertarian scruples of elderly Liberals, would fade away once it was clear that the absence of compulsion would delay victory and even invite defeat.

Each day's evidence to the Crewe Committee was circulated to the cabinet, but Asquith may not have read the passage giving Lloyd George's argument, and it seems doubtful whether he ever really understood its importance. In her diary on 19 August 1915 Margot wrote of a revealing exchange on conscription with Maurice Bonham Carter ('Bongie'):

[Bongie] 'I'm afraid the Prime Minister is going to be obstinate about Conscription. I'm inclined to think we shall have to come to this.'

M. 'Good Heavens, Bongie, are you also wobbly!? Well, I don't know exactly what line H. will take, but I would rather be out of public life altogether if he goes in for Conscription: it would be <u>Insanity</u>.'

Four days earlier, when speaking to Edwin Montagu, Margot had claimed much greater certainty about her husband's views:

Montagu told me after dinner he rather hoped H. would come down on the side of Conscription, which need never come into force, as we were recruiting very well: it would be a sop to the agitators, and if the war went on another year we might need it; that Curzon was out for mischief, and the whole gang intended forcing a Gen. Election, and smirching the late Gov, and Henry. I told him I had never discussed Conscription in my life with Henry, but that I was <u>passionately</u> against it, and <u>knew he was</u>.

Margot habitually assumed not only that she knew her husband's private views, but that she had a duty to proclaim them. In peacetime the harm done by her political indiscretions was mitigated by her Liberal partisanship: her husband's followers might not like her friendships with prominent Unionists, or her taste for London society; but, if they were at all fair-minded, they recognized her to be a staunch and devoted Liberal. The dynamics of wartime politics, however, deprived her of that protective shield. Faced with issues of a highly controversial nature, Margot felt that she could not stay silent, but the effect on her husband's premiership was the opposite to the one that she intended. She could not see that by her remarks on conscription, for example, she curtailed the freedom of manoeuvre that, as a Coalition Prime Minister, it was essential for him to maintain; her unscripted interventions on the subject were devastatingly effective in making his later attempts to modify his position, notably in the Commons on 2 November 1915, sound insincere. Her recantation on conscription in a marginal note of the diary—'I was wrong. It had to come.'—came much too late for both of them.[1]

Asquith was acutely aware that many of the active Liberals in the constituencies suspected him of veering towards the Tories; but this awareness hardly accounts for the rigid opposition to wartime conscription which Margot imputed to him. Both of his oldest political associates had declared for it,[2] and he had appointed a War Policy Committee with a membership of two-to-one in its support. He does not seem to have examined the case for it with great care. He probably thought Ll.G.'s flirtation with industrial conscription merely a sign that the best judge of the popular breeze despaired of Liberal support for the military version.[3] Above all, there was an excuse for delay: it might be possible to win the war while maintaining Britain's unique tradition of a volunteer army. And late in August 1915 Asquith told Sylvia Henley of two objections to military compulsion which he thought 'vital matters'. The first of these fears proved to be mistaken; the second, though true, needed to be carefully qualified. The premier believed that a mixed BEF, containing both

---

[1] D. 3213 fo. 157ʳ (19 Aug. 1915).

[2] Haldane made known his views in the Lords in January 1915, and had repeated them in May 1915. It accorded with his pre-war position. For Grey's memo. (not sent), 14 May 1915, to the premier on the need for military compulsion see Adams and Poirier, *Conscription*, 85–6.

[3] For Asquith's pre-war reliance on Ll.G.'s judgement of the public's views (as a 'foolometer') see *Esher Journals*, iii. 61.

volunteers and conscripts, would be very difficult to manage. Kitchener seems to have shared this fear; but the officers at the front were far too anxious to fill the ranks effectively to worry about a possible problem such as that. More plausibly, Asquith suspected that with the large claims on manpower made by the armaments industry, food production, shipping and shipbuilding, conscription would yield no more than 'a small residuum of the dregs of the nation' for the army.[1] He was right to suppose that compulsion would not supply the generals with as many men for the BEF as they expected; but Lloyd George, newly appointed as Minister of Munitions, wisely saw military conscription as a crucial component in an overall manpower policy that was essential to winning the war.

The Crewe Committee's finding were circulated to the cabinet on 8 September, and of the several reports given, that of Arthur Henderson was particularly important. If conscription were to gain general consent, Henderson argued, the support of young men of the working class was crucial, and he gave this warning:

> Party and class are coming to coincide as they did before the war.... On the alternative of Conscription or defeat [the classes] will be united again. But they cannot be brought to that alternative suddenly.... They must have time. And if time is spent in a final endeavour, made after the most solemn appeal and on a full and reasoned statement of our obligations to our Allies, to meet those obligations voluntarily, I believe that... either Conscription will be accepted without serious injury to the nation, or it will be proved to be unnecessary.[2]

In the second half of 1915 Britain's heavy obligations to its principal ally meant agreeing to French battle plans in the West that were driven more by political considerations than by military: when Churchill protested

---

[1] Asquith, *Memories*, ii. 109; Cassar, *Kitchener*, 444–50.

[2] Asquith, *Memories*, ii. 114–15; and Gwynne, *Rasp*, 128 (confidential report to Gwynne on the Trades Union Congress).

against Britain's agreement to join in 'useless slaughter on a gigantic scale' in the West, Kitchener grimly admitted: 'There was a great deal of truth in what Mr Churchill said; but unfortunately we had to make war as we must, and not as we should like to.' Kitchener told Britain's senior commanders that it was Britain's duty to help the French in this crisis 'even though, by doing so we suffered very heavy losses indeed',[1] and British casualties at the Battle of Loos, 25 September to 14 October 1915, came close to 50,000, or rather more than double the number suffered by the enemy. The failure of an offensive at Gallipoli in August had placed renewed emphasis on the campaign in the West, and the experience of Loos encouraged a sober realization that the war would extend into 1916, and in all likelihood beyond. The British Army would soon need more recruits than the voluntary system could supply, convincing Kitchener, and consequently the premier, that a move towards conscription could not be avoided.

The operative word here is *towards*: on 19 October the government announced a new registration initiative that, however, fell short of conscription. The eponymous Derby Scheme was the invention of the Earl of Derby, whose appointment as Asquith's Director of Recruiting had been announced on 5 October 1915.[2] On 16 October Bonar Law wrote to Asquith, with his Chief Whip's agreement, to indicate the Unionists' assent to the plan, with the proviso that, if it failed, conscription must follow. Under the scheme all of the men aged 19 to 41 on the National Register who were not yet in uniform were invited to 'attest' their willingness to serve in the army when called. It was made clear that skilled men in key trades would not be called, and married men were promised that the call-up would not apply to them until all of the bachelors and childless widowers had been taken.[3] There was some joking about the choice between being compelled to volunteer or volunteering to be compelled,

---

[1] Cruttwell, *Great War*, 169.

[2] Cruttwell, *Great War*, 169 n. 1. Derby declined both a salary and a military commission.

[3] The prospect of a great many war widows' pensions was regarded as formidable. For an indication of this see *Asquith–Stanley*, 276–7, 297, 313. For Margot's views on taking the bachelors first see diary, 3 Aug. [1915], p. 170 below.

but the scheme embodied Henderson's principle of consent: working-class people would come to accept conscription once they realized that the only alternative would be defeat; but that conclusion should be presented to them carefully, and they ought to be given enough time to consider it. Compulsion would be recognized as unnecessary in the event of the Derby Scheme's success, and as unavoidable for single men in that of failure.

On 2 November 1915 Asquith outlined the government's conscription policy in an important statement in the Commons. He explained:

> That for the purpose of the war compulsion was a pure question of practical expediency.... The sole limitation... was that, if compulsion were to be applied, it must be with something of the nature of general consent.[1]

Asquith could well have added that adopting military conscription for the war did not carry any implication that industrial conscription was also necessary; nor did it indicate an intention to continue any form of compulsion after the war. Both additions would have been welcomed in Liberal and trade union circles, and if a basic declaration of this sort had been made when the Coalition was first formed it would have been very useful. By the time that it was made, on 2 November 1915, its force had been lost. Margot's anti-conscription statements during the preceding months had made believing the premier's personal commitment to it too difficult. As she judged every political position in terms of the leading people supporting and opposing it, she seldom knew whether popular support for it was likely to increase, as in the case of military conscription, or to decline. The later stages of the conscription controversy brought into focus the larger question of Asquith's war leadership. The existing governmental structure, which had survived the Coalition of May 1915, was proving too cumbersome to be effective, and much of the blame for this could be laid at the door of the man popularly perceived as

---

[1] *Parl. Deb.* 72.521.

the 'wait and see' premier.[1] War policy was too often reactive, a step behind events, rather than a step ahead. During the debate on 2 November 1915, Sir Edward Carson had defined what was needed as: 'A small body of competent men—the smaller the better—sitting not once a week, but from day to day, with the best expert advisers you can get, working out the problems that arise.' He had entered the cabinet in the May 1915 Coalition as Attorney-General, but resigned that October in protest at the running of the war. His stock among Unionists rose correspondingly, and he emerged as the leader of the Unionist War Committee, a 'ginger group' formed at the close of the 1915–16 parliamentary session, and which, like its much smaller Liberal counterpart, pressed for a more active war policy. Carson considered the establishment of a small decision-making body as essential to this, and had told Craig two months before his November 1915 speech that he wanted 'a cabinet of about 7 with power by Order in Council to pass such ordinances as are necessary'.[2] When, later that month, Asquith finally moved in this direction, proposing a reduction in the size of the War Committee that oversaw management of the war, he identified as its members himself, Balfour, Lloyd George, McKenna, and Kitchener, characteristically leaving out Bonar Law: in reluctantly reversing this omission he was obliged to recognize the latter's growing influence.

The Derby Scheme significantly increased enlistments, but the final figures, which were discussed by the cabinet on 22 December 1915, made its ultimate failure undeniable.[3] They showed that well over half a million unmarried men had not attested at all. Before the cabinet started to discuss Derby's report several developments had strengthened the case in favour of a bill providing for a call-up of the lagging bachelors. On 25 November 1915 the victory of a conscriptionist, C. B. Stanton, was announced after a by-election at Merthyr Tydfil following Keir Hardie's

---

[1] The famous music hall artiste and comedian George Robey (1869–1954) added a verse on Asquith to his famous song 'In other words': 'Just stem this tide of ignorant conjecture, | Remain inert and dormant just like me, | And cultivate spontaneous quiescence, | In other words, Wait and See!!!'; R. B. McCallum, *Asquith* (1936), 121.

[2] Hyde, *Carson*, 391, 396.

[3] *Parl. Deb.*, 2 Nov. 1915, 75, 523–4; Cassar, *Asquith*, 159; Wilson, *Myriad Faces*, 207.

death. The accredited Labour Party candidate had been beaten by 4,000 votes despite union support, as well as that of Arthur Henderson and several other party heavyweights. The effect of this result in a solidly working-class constituency, with miners predominating, was very great. Stanton interpreted his triumph as 'a message of good cheer to the boys in the trenches and certainly a setback to the pro-German section'.[1] A second important development was Kitchener's surrender, on 10 December 1915, of control of strategic movements to the new CIGS, William Robertson.[2] 'Wully', as he was usually called, surpassed 'K of K' in determination, but also in ability to deal with politicians. His demands for men were not limited to the 1916 campaign; he was sure that winning the war would take longer than that.[3] He saw no purpose in trying to state the army's needs in terms of the number of British divisions needed in the field. The number of casualties to be expected, now that the war had become one of attrition, would falsify any such calculation. He realized that he would be competing with the claims of war industry, shipbuilding, and shipping. He meant his claims to come first.[4]

Margot wrote fully about the week of hectic negotiation that preceded Asquith's introduction of the first Military Service Bill—'the Bachelor's Bill'—on 4 January 1916. John Simon, who objected on principle to compulsion for military service, was the only cabinet minister to resign. 'Does anyone really suppose', he asked during the debate, 'that, once the principle of compulsion has been conceded...you are going to stop there?'[5] In old age he thought that this decision had been mistaken. To give Britain's

---

[1] *The Times*, 27 Nov. 1915, 8d. See *Stevenson Diary*, 81–2. J. H. Thomas, an anti-conscriptionist Labour MP, had spoken against Stanton. Relations between the miners and the railway unions, for which Thomas spoke, were not very cordial.

[2] Cassar, *Kitchener*, 434–7.

[3] Cassar, *Kitchener*, 197, 453; *Esher Journals*, iv. 16–17. Kitchener feared that if Robertson and Haig were allowed too many men, they might use them in attacks which, by consuming Britain's reserves, might frustrate his plan to have the most powerful army when peacemaking began.

[4] See, for instance, Robertson to Clive Wigram, 12 Jan. 1916: Adams and Poirier, *Conscription*, 146.

[5] i.e. stop with single men only; *Parl. Deb.*, 5 Jan. 1916, 77.962–78. For Asquith's speech see *Parl. Deb.*, 5 Jan. 1916, 77.949–62.

Allies, and its own anxious families, the only proof which they would recognize that the government meant to stick at nothing to win the war should, as he had come to think, have overborne his Liberal principles.[1] On 4 February 1916 the three-man committee appointed on 31 December 1915 to apportion manpower between the army and the war industries (the Military Finance Committee) recommended that the cabinet should aim at an army of sixty-two divisions in the field with full reserves.[2] It seemed by then almost certain that the brunt of the summer offensive would be borne by the British, and pressure from both sides was increasing: volunteering had fallen off sharply, while newly built state armaments works were opening all the time. On 2 March 1916 Derby declared in the Lords for conscription of married men; and on 28 March Carson emerged from some weeks of illness to take the chair of the Unionist War Committee in the Commons, where some 130 Unionist members resolved to require their ministers to resign from the government unless the conscription of married men was enacted within a reasonable time.[3]

There could have been very few left at the end of March 1916 who supposed that compulsion could 'stop' at the bachelors, but among them was the Prime Minister. At the end of March he wrote to Sylvia Henley: 'Aren't you amused to see how they are trying to engineer a new Conscription agitation? B. Law (as usual) is in a state of pigeon-livered perturbation'; and on his return from a visit to France and Italy, 26 March to 6 April, he observed to the same correspondent: 'People here seem to have been suffering from a series of acute attacks of the nerves.'[4] Although Margot was 'assuring' her husband that he faced 'the worst crisis in all his political life', he 'absolutely' disbelieved her; and on 9 April he apparently expected to have 'rather fun with all these silly [conscriptionists] this week'. This last comment seems to have represented more than an attempt to head

[1] Simon, *Retrospect*, 106–7.
[2] Adams and Poirier, *Conscription*, 146.
[3] *Parl. Deb.*, Lords, 21.268–78, esp. 272 (2 Mar. 1916); Adams and Poirier, *Conscription*, 153.
[4] *Belloc Lowndes Diaries*, 70; Asquith to Sylvia Henley, 23 Mar., 6 Apr. 1916, 606, 609.

off Margot's tiresome questions by bolstering her confidence. Margot was so erratic in her views that Asquith may have had some excuses for disregarding her apprehensions; but it is remarkable that he should have laughed at Bonar Law's. The basic reason for his insouciance was a reluctance, if not to recognize a rapid change in public feeling, then certainly to respond to it. The Merthyr Tydfil by-election result had revealed a profound shift in working-class opinion. By 1916, while Labour was as hostile as ever to industrial conscription, the pre-war condemnation of military conscription as an instrument for enslaving the workers was fading.

10. Resignation: 'Some radical change must be made'

The crisis which began with the Unionist War Committee threat of 28 March 1916 was not resolved until the second Military Service Act became law on 25 May. Hankey heard Asquith introduce that measure before the Commons on 2 May:

> He did not much like the job and was not at his best. The House was astonishingly cold. The fact was that the people who wanted compulsory service did not want Asquith, and those who wanted Asquith did not want compulsory service.[1]

Asquith faced the situation, Hankey noted, 'with his usual courage', but the later phase of the conscription controversy revealed the extent of his unpopularity. 'If I were Margot', Cynthia Asquith had written in August 1915, 'I would whitewash the Prime Minister's face. He is so much attacked for callousness because he looks rosy and well.'[2] By then 'the guise of lethargy' had become horribly effective, and even Violet became worried that her father's manner might indicate, on war problems, a certain insouciance. When in October 1915 he contemplated taking on Kitchener's role

[1] Hankey, *Supreme Command*, 476; for Asquith in debate, 2 May 1916, *Parl. Deb.*, 81.2611–16.
[2] Asquith, C., *Diaries*, 72 (23 Aug. 1915), 119. See Holroyd, *Strachey*, 652–3, 663–4, 734; *The Times*, 15 Jan. 1972.

as War Secretary, during the latter's absence on a fact-finding mission to the Mediterranean theatre, she wrote to Bongie:

> [I] am <u>delighted</u> to hear of Father's contemplated move. . . . I welcome it because quite apart from W.O. administration it will bring him to closer grips with the <u>war</u> itself & give him a more <u>personal</u> sense of responsibility about it. I have felt sometimes lately as if his clutch hadn't got in—as if the full force of his mind was not in it & driving it forwards. . . .[1]

The Prime Minister evidently did not exude the air of one who was straining every nerve to end the slaughter by winning the war, and in February 1916, after nine months' experience of Coalition government, Bonar Law wrote to him: 'In war it is necessary not only to be active but to seem active.'[2] This excellent advice was not heeded, and Asquith took no extra steps to keep himself in the public eye. When 'off duty' he maintained a lifelong practice of refusing to refer to work problems, but this disinclination to talk war 'shop' gave the impression that he cared much less than in fact was the case. A few weeks after he had received Bonar's cautionary letter he sat next to Cynthia Asquith at a lunch at Walmer Castle, and she noted: 'P.M. sniffs and looks bored at any mention of shrapnel or anything to do with the war.'[3] Cynthia knew her father-in-law well enough to see through his guise of indifference, but it rendered him vulnerable to criticism from those who were instinctively averse to his politics. In March 1916 J. L. Garvin's wife Christina wrote to their son in France: 'I'm dead sick of Asquith—pig and Nero, whichever you like to call him—only he can't fiddle, just swill.'[4] The same month Bonar Law remarked to Lloyd George: 'Asquith has no idea how unpopular his government is'; yet Bonar still believed at this date that Asquith was the best available premier, and Lloyd George was emphasizing that 'he would not

---

[1] 10 Oct. 1915, Bonham Carter, *Diaries, 1914–45*, 83.
[2] Spender and Asquith, ii. 230. See also Spender and Asquith, ii. 177.
[3] Asquith, C., *Diaries*, 147.
[4] Christina Garvin to her son Ged, 13 March 1916: Garvin, *Tomorrow*, 157.

be prepared to replace Asquith by Bonar Law'.[1] Nor would Bonar have been prepared to replace Asquith by Ll.G.: when asked by the latter in April 1916 for 'a heart-to-heart talk Bonar replied: "I do not confide in you because I do not agree with you."'[2] Yet Lloyd George came much closer to Bonar's ideal, and that of other Unionists', as to what a war premier should be, and after Kitchener was drowned when the cruiser carrying him to Russia struck a mine and sank off the Orkneys, in June, Bonar supported Ll.G.'s claim to be the new War Secretary.

Margot's violent reaction to the decision to appoint Lloyd George as War Secretary proved disastrously mistaken, and the stridency of her opposition alienated her for a time from her husband.[3] He did not like to confess to her that his political position was no longer strong enough to enable him to refuse the War Office to Ll.G. In December 1916 Bonar Law talked to Riddell about his own part in promoting Lloyd George's appointment. He had apparently told Asquith:

> You must appoint Ll.G. He wants the job and you will have to give it to him.... If you had wanted to break with him, perhaps at one point you might have done so, but now he is too strong for you. If you stand in his way he will probably crush you.[4]

Also in December 1916, when no longer the premier's wife, Margot wrote:

> Directly Ll.G. was put in the War Office...I knew it was our doom. It has been....In a war like this...delays are unavoidable; but they have been made twice as bad by two avoidable things—the first by Ll.G. telling Northcliffe every cabinet secret...and second, that when the thing was fixed, and decisions arrived at, they were never made known or enforced quickly. We had three schoolboys—

---

[1] Gwynn, *Redmond*, 466; *Riddell War Diary*, 164, 165; *Lee Diaries*, 148; Spender and Asquith, ii. 246–7.
[2] *Riddell War Diary*, 178.
[3] Diary, 26 June 1916, pp. 268–9 below.
[4] *Riddell War Diary*, 183 (21 May 1916), 189, 235.

Bongie, Davies and Ed. Marsh to push them forward, and a whip...without the <u>faintest</u> authority, and <u>unable to stage-manage anything</u>.[1]

Margot's basic contention, that Lloyd George was in close touch with people who were planning to remove Asquith from the premiership, was correct; but on everything else she was astray. Lloyd George had revealed comparatively few cabinet secrets to Northcliffe while War Secretary. Most of the 'delays' had resulted, not from defects in Asquith's private secretaries, but from the insistence of cabinet ministers on re-discussing the War Committee's recommendations.[2] John Gulland was probably a less competent Chief Whip than his predecessors had been; but unlike them he was required to cope with Coalition conditions, and he seems to have received little guidance on that from the premier.[3]

Margot was also unaware that the War Secretaryship had ceased to be the most important post, after the premier's, during the war. While in office Lloyd George failed to claw back any of the powers that Robertson, the CIGS, had obtained from the War Secretary in Kitchener's time. And far from strengthening the link between Northcliffe and Lloyd George, as Margot feared, the appointment helped to drive them apart; Northcliffe actually tried to prevent Ll.G. from accepting the post, on the ground that it would 'give the government a new lease of life and...it will be impossible to turn them out'.[4] Nor, despite Margot's obsessional belief, was Northcliffe the linchpin of the opposition to her husband. His powerful help was welcomed by the premier's opponents and critics; but he did not stand close to the more fastidious of them; and they were wary of him. Most of the self-styled 'Monday Night Cabal' were as determined to oust Asquith as Margot supposed; and they were ready to accept the aid of Northcliffe, or of almost anyone else, to achieve that; but they were not in

---

[1] Those named were Asquith's private secretaries during the war. For John Gulland, the Chief Whip, see Asquith, C., *Diaries*, 242 (5 Dec. 1916).

[2] Hankey, *Supreme Command*, 556, 557; Roskill, *Hankey*, 317–18.

[3] Crawford noted, 25 Jan. 1915, on Gulland's appointment: 'On the whole Asquith has made the right choice': *Crawford Journals*, 347. See below, p. 299.

[4] McEwen, *Riddell Diaries*, 160.

spirit Northcliffe's men.[1] F. S. Oliver, who was one of the Cabal, revealed, when dining at Austen Chamberlain's in May 1916, his wish to see Northcliffe interned 'along with Asquith'.[2]

During the summer of 1916 Margot could see nothing except her husband's treacherous rival gaining a position of enormous prestige, and taking all the credit if Haig's 'great offensive' succeeded, while shifting the blame should it fail.[3] According to Riddell, Montagu advised Asquith that at the War Office 'Ll.G. would probably be engulfed by the machine, and...would have the credit for the many casualties which were certain to result from the new offensive'.[4] In the event the Somme Battle was neither a complete success nor a complete failure,[5] but Lloyd George did not enhance his reputation at the War Office, and he was anything but the press tycoon's favourite while there. In September 1916 he questioned Foch about the abilities and tactics of the British generals. This gaffe did not remain a secret; and on 28 September the *Morning Post* carried a hint of it.[6] By 11 October Northcliffe had heard of Ll.G.'s plan to send British troops to the aid of Romania: he stormed into the Secretary of State's office, and told the official there that 'if this sort of thing went on [he] would...expose it, both in the House of Lords and in his own newspapers'.[7] At the same time the *Morning Post's* editor followed up his paragraph of 28 September with a friendly warning to Ll.G. to 'let the army alone'. On 13 October Asquith told Sylvia Henley with misplaced complacency:

---

[1] Thompson, *Northcliffe*, 254. 15 Aug. 1915, Milner to Gwynne: Gwynne, *Rasp*, 113–15; Adams and Poirier, *Conscription*, 153. The 'Monday Night Cabal', also called the 'Ginger Group', was instituted by Leo Amery in January 1916 'to co-ordinate Unionist opposition to the Asquith government and build links with potential Liberal rebels'; it brought together Milner and Lloyd George: Alex May, *ODNB*, 'Kerr, Philip Henry'.

[2] Kennet, *Self-Portrait*, 142.

[3] For the phrase 'great offensive', see Hankey's diary, Roskill, *Hankey*, 266; diary, 26 June 1916, p. 268 below.

[4] Wilson, *Myriad Faces*, 417. Thompson, *Northcliffe*, 258; McEwen, *Riddell Diaries*, 167; *Stevenson Diary*, 109–10; Guinn, *British Strategy*, 142.

[5] Roskill, *Hankey*, 286.

[6] Gwynne, *Rasp*, 189, n.1.

[7] Thompson, *Northcliffe*, 258; *Stevenson Diary*, 115. In Beaverbrook's version the remarks are more violent, and probably less accurately reported.

Northcliffe is apparently starting a new press campaign. He has apparently given me up as a bad or unprofitable job; and his new objectives are Winston and Lloyd George! The latter came to see me in some perturbation this morning, and I gave him the good old advice to lie low and say nothing: which is not congenial to his temperament.[1]

The events leading to Asquith's resignation, however, were precipitated not by Ll.G. or Bonar in the first instance, but rather by Sir Edward Carson. Early in November 1916 this formidable parliamentary speaker decided to challenge the Coalition over the arrangements for enemy properties confiscated in Nigeria. The government proposed that bidding would be restricted to Allied firms, or to firms known to be at least 'genuinely neutral'. Carson sponsored an amendment restricting sales to 'natural born British subjects of companies wholly British'. This represented an ingenious appeal to the Unionists' opposition to free trade, and, more generally, to the nationalism engendered by war.[2] Bonar Law called the motion for this amendment one of 'want of confidence in the government'; and he made clear in debate that, should a majority of his party vote for it, he would resign, and so bring the Coalition to an end. That result was narrowly avoided, and without the votes of the Unionist office-holders Bonar Law would have been in a minority within his party.[3] In a memorandum of 30 December 1916 he recorded the effect that the Nigerian debate and division had had on him, and his consequent actions:

After the debate I had very strongly the feeling that the Unionist party in the House was not only hostile to the government but was fast reaching a point where their hostility would make it impossible for me, and probably for other Unionist ministers, to remain in the

---

[1] Gwynne, *Rasp*, 194; see Asquith to Sylvia Henley, 767. Robertson backed Lloyd George in the December crisis: *Tom Jones Diary, 1916–1925*, 7.

[2] Blake, *Bonar Law*, 298; *Parl. Deb.*, 87.364 (8 Nov. 1916).

[3] Of the 286 Unionists in the Commons on 8 Nov. 1916 148 either voted with Carson or failed to vote. Bonar gained the support of 73 Unionists against Carson's 65 (and secured an overall majority by 231 votes to 117).

cabinet....I said to Mr Asquith that in my judgement we could not go on as we were, and that some radical change must be made in the government...at once.

Asquith rejected Bonar Law's plea. In his view, as he said, Bonar was 'simply exaggerating a passing discontent due to a want of military success in the War'. The discussion ended with Bonar, his opinion unshaken, undertaking to return to the premier when he had 'something definite to propose'.

The critical tone of Bonar Law's statement to Asquith in November 1916 stands in contrast to the confidence that he expressed to Redmond in March 1916, when he said that the premier was the best available, and Balfour's view of the premier had also changed significantly in intervening months. In April 1916 he had told a member of his family that the Prime Minister's worst troubles did not arise from personal errors or defects: they would assail any possible successor. By November 1916 his assessment of the political scene was different. To the suggestion that Lloyd George 'wanted to be a dictator' A.J.B. replied: 'Let him be....If he thinks he can win the war, I'm all for his having a try.'[1] Both of those Unionist leaders were people of judgement. What had happened during these eight months to induce them to change their views? Both had been involved in decisions associated with the setbacks of 1916. Both knew that none of those setbacks were in themselves really dangerous. The surrender at Kut on 29 April 1916 had been a humiliation; but it involved relatively small numbers. A tactical victory had eluded Jellicoe in the Battle of Jutland, 30–1 May, and Margot's criticism of the depressing first report of the engagement, authorized by Balfour, was well justified: someone reading it might not have foreseen Hankey's later verdict, that *strategically* Jutland had been 'as sweeping a success as Trafalgar'.[2] But the battle did not lift the national mood, and neither did Haig's grand offensive on the Western

---

[1] Dugdale, *Balfour*, ii. 157. Lady Frances Balfour told Margot of this remark in a letter, 19 Jan. 1917: c. 6670, fo. 118. See also 30 Dec. 1916, Betty to Frances Balfour: Balfour Papers, Whitt., 358.103.

[2] Young, *Balfour*, 363–4; Hankey, *Supreme Command*, 493. For Lord Wemyss's reaction to the first report see Asquith, C., *Diaries*, 169–70: 'While I was dressing Papa, with very blue face, told me our Fleet had been smashed in the North Sea ...'

Front: the British casualties during the first day of the Somme were appalling, but if the 142 days of that battle are seen as a whole, a pronouncement by Asquith in November 1917 has to be accepted. Taken with the successful defence of Verdun, Haig's 'aggressive on the Somme', Asquith said, 'saved the whole situation, and did at least as much [or] more than anything [else] in ... the War to damage the prestige of the German command and the *morale* of the German army'.[1] Those remarks have been confirmed by the inquest of history. In November 1916, however, the long weeks of the Somme had created a mood, not of defeatism, but certainly of bitter disappointment.

The governmental system had come close to collapse. The War Committee met fifteen times during November 1916. These were, as Hankey recorded, 'really dreadful War Committees'. The eleven members were mostly departmental ministers. Each was hard pressed to cope with his department's affairs, let alone attend both the War Committee and the cabinet, while knowing that the endless discussion of gloomy reports in both bodies would probably be inconclusive. The cautious pessimism of the reports by McKenna and Runciman did not suggest a willingness to defy precedent and make experiments in order to win the war. Addison called Runciman's shipping losses report of 9 November 'the most invertebrate and hopeless memorandum ever presented to the government during the war by a responsible head of a department on a great issue'.[2] Calls for a reform of the cabinet system had been made, and resisted, ever since the Coalition had been formed. Asquith still seemed largely unaware of its defects.[3] If he had at last become aware of them, did he, in the shadow of his son Raymond's death on the Somme, have the energy and the authority to put the changes needed in hand? On 27 November 1916 Milner told H. A. Gwynne:

---

[1] *Parl. Deb.*, 99.891 (19 Nov. 1917).

[2] Hankey, *Supreme Command*, 557–8; Addison, *Politics*, ii. 10.

[3] See Asquith to Sylvia Henley, 19 Aug. 1916, 723; Hankey, *Supreme Command*, 439–41; Blake, *Bonar Law*, 292. Austen Chamberlain wrote: 'When the War Committee was first appointed I ... suggested that it should be made the cabinet': Chamberlain, *Down the Years*, 112.

Any slight chance…of retrieving the situation depends on getting the government into stronger hands. But every attempt to do this is regarded as an 'intrigue'.…The only chance seems to be a break up of the Government from within.…Perhaps it is not yet too late for Lloyd George to come out, and take at least one or two others with him. That would, I think, shortly produce a collapse and the possibility of a reconstruction. But it is desperately late.[1]

This letter pointed to a problem which Margot could not face. Did Lloyd George believe adopting his policies in general, and conscription in particular, to be essential for bringing the Allies nearer to victory in the war? Bonham Carter had heard in September 1915 from Eric Drummond of the latter's conviction that Ll.G. had 'a wholly sincere belief' to that effect.[2] If this was the case, was Ll.G. to blame for intriguing?

Asquith's refusal to countenance Bonar's November plea for a 'radical change' can be explained by the combination of three Asquithian attitudes, all of which are illustrated repeatedly in Margot's diary, namely, his ingrained conservatism; his persistent failure to realize what a formidable politician Bonar Law could be; and his lack of awareness about how unpopular his government had become. He was accustomed to disregarding Bonar's warnings. Perhaps he had forgotten that when, in March 1916, he had referred to Bonar Law's mood as being one of 'pigeon-livered perturbation' over conscription, the apprehensions at which he had sneered had proved to be remarkably well justified. His disparagement was echoed later by Margot and Violet in their attempts to explain the government's fall. 'On the night of the Nigerian debate', Margot wrote, 'Bonar was subjugated'; and on 26 December 1916 Violet, writing to Mary Herbert, referred to 'poor Bonar's terror of Carson' as a cause of the government's 'shipwreck'.[3] But nearly three-quarters of the Unionists in the Commons had either voted with Carson or failed to vote on 8 November

[1] Gwynne, Rasp, 202–3.
[2] Bonham Carter, Diaries, 1914–45, 77 (13 Sept. 1915—Maurice Bonham Carter to Violet Asquith).
[3] Diary, 14 Dec. 1916, p. 310 below; Bonham Carter, Diaries, 1914–45, 98.

1916; and it was well known in parliamentary circles that Carson's Unionist War Committee meetings had been attracting an attendance of up to 150 MPs. The vote on 8 November 1916 had proclaimed to everyone what political 'insiders' already knew, and to accuse Bonar of being needlessly terrified of Carson on the evidence of the Nigerian episode capped a long series of Asquithian slights.[1]

Shortly after the Nigerian vote Asquith visited Lady Scott, and he related to her how Bonar Law had arrived before him 'with his teeth chattering'. Asquith proceeded to review his years in office, and Lady Scott noted:

> He...is heartily sick of it....I reminded him that five or six years ago he had said to me, 'I'm like a rat in a trap'. He said, 'Yes, and that was before the war'. I asked him point-blank whether he would really like to go. He said that...if he kept his faculties and his activity, it might be an irritation to want to do things and to be powerless to do them. I said he would probably get suddenly old and gaga; he said he thought that one might perhaps just die.

The Prime Minister who spoke like this was bereaved and weary, and as impercipient as ever.[2] He also gave the impression of being dangerously dependent on the stimulus of alcohol.[3] But he still held one winning card on which he clearly placed great reliance: his critics and would-be supplanters were disunited among themselves. According to Bonar Law's close friend 'Max' Aitken, the Unionist leader had 'formed the opinion that in matters of office and power Lloyd George was a self-seeker...who considered no interests except his own';[4] and in November 1916 Bonar

---

[1] Hyde, *Carson*, 400. For Asquith's determination, May 1915, to prevent Bonar Law becoming Chancellor of the Exchequer, see Blake, *Bonar Law*, 251 (including sentence omitted from Spender and Asquith, ii. 171).

[2] Asquith's eldest son Raymond had died of wounds near Trônes Wood during the Somme Battle, 15 Sept. 1916; he was a lieutenant in the Grenadier Guards.

[3] Kennet, *Self-Portrait*, 148. See *Crawford Journals*, 2 Aug. 1916, 358 (Crawford had joined the cabinet from France in July 1916); Diana Manners to Katharine Asquith: 'The old boy...I fear lately too conspicuously buffed': Ziegler, *Diana Cooper*, 60.

[4] Beaverbrook, *Politicians*, 329–30. For Aitken Beaverbrook, see Biographical Notes.

was not alone in suspecting that Ll.G. cared about no administrative reforms except those which would give the War Secretary complete authority over the CIGS.[1] Margot's many references to Lloyd George in her
diary help to explain why he did not 'inspire trust'; and the picture which
they give is confirmed by Mrs Wilfrid Spender's jotting (10 Sept. 1916)
about a private meeting at which all present were agreed in denouncing
Asquith:

> Bonar Law said: 'There is one man I distrust more' (i.e. Lloyd George).
> But Sir Edward [Carson] said: 'No, that one is a plain man of the
> people and shows his hand, and, though you mayn't trust him, his
> crookednesses are all plain to see. But the other is clever and pol-
> ished and knows how to conceal his crookedness'. And Bonar Law
> said: 'Well, perhaps you're right'.[2]

Late in March 1916 Bonar had explained to Sir Henry Wilson why he was
determined to keep Asquith's Coalition going if he possibly could. To
break it up, by leading the Unionist members out of it, would, as he
wrote, entail a wartime election. To conduct one in full view of the
enemy would be lamentable. Each seat would be fought, in Bonar's
phrase, 'with almost the usual amount of party bitterness': 'The first
effect…would be to discourage our Allies and make our enemies feel
certain that we could not stay the course.'[3] By November 1916 Bonar's
Law's control over his parliamentary following had shrunk. He was no
longer in a position to decide whether to prolong the Coalition's life. By
the end of that month about half of the Unionists in the Commons were
attending the party's War Committee meetings. Its members were close
enough to the centre of the elite to be experiencing not merely disappointment but alarm. Monthly shipping losses by U-Boat attack had increased significantly during the year, and by October 1916 stood at
120,000 tons a month; and there seemed to be no effective Admiralty

[1] Beaverbrook, *Politicians*, 335.
[2] Hyde, *Carson*, 407 n. For Captain Wilfrid Bliss Spender and his wife see Stewart, *Ulster Crisis*, 83 and foll.
[3] Blake, *Bonar Law*, 280–1.

plan for coping with this menacing sign of improvement in the U-Boats' design and performance.

After Bonar's November 1916 visit to Asquith, Max Aitken quickly arranged a meeting between Bonar, Carson, and Ll.G. Bonar told the Prime Minister that its object would be to create a small body 'to conduct the War'. Asquith, while still unfavourable to such a project, raised no objection to the meeting. By 25 November this Triumvirate—crucial members of the 'little gang of brigands', as Margot called them—had drawn up their proposals in the form of a statement to be issued by the Prime Minister. This would call for 'a Civilian General Staff' of four, with the premier as 'President'. The three others would 'have no portfolio[s] and [would] devote their whole time…day by day' to war problems. Lloyd George would preside as the chairman at any meeting which 'pressure of other duties' prevented the premier from attending. The statement would end:

> I propose that the body should have executive authority subject to this—that it shall rest with me to refer any questions to the decision of the cabinet, which I think should be brought before them.

The new feature in the situation now confronting Asquith lay, not in the proposals themselves, but in the fact that they were made by a trio who had just combined, and who in combination held the power to bring the Coalition to an end. Bonar Law recorded that, in presenting them to Asquith, he said:

> In my opinion, if this change were made by him entirely on his own initiative…it could be made without the smallest loss of dignity; but, if it came about as a result of pressure either in the cabinet, or, still worse, in the press, it would be almost impossible to carry it out.[1]

For Asquith the time for parleying had already passed: he could not keep all of his power as well as his dignity and official emoluments; but his self-confidence had not yet been dented. He found little attraction in a re-

---

[1] Blake, *Bonar Law*, 248.

stricted premiership, and no difficulty, when replying to Bonar on 26 November, in lighting on a clear defect in the arrangement outlined.[1] The two other members of the proposed 'War Council', though not named in the rebellious trio's document, were obviously to be Carson and Bonar Law. Hankey noted in his diary on 3 December: 'The new War Ctee. is really ridiculous. Bonar Law is by common consent the poorest figure on the present War Ctee. Carson, on the old Dardanelles Ctee. was positively pitiful and worse than Bonar Law.'[2] Apart from such personal questions, this kind of small directing body clearly had to include both people of great political standing and others of equally great executive talent. During the next two years Lloyd George was to show that, though difficult to achieve, this requirement could be met.

The week which elapsed between the reply to the trio's memo. of 25 November and that diary note by Hankey revealed how uneasy an agreement between Asquith and the trio was bound to be. On 29 November Hankey, prodded apparently by Margot about dangers ahead, put pressure on the premier to end shilly-shallying in the War Committee; and on 30 November the committee decided to recommend 'industrial Conscription' for British men to the age of 60. The immediate result of this belated boldness on the manpower problem was a stiff protest from Runciman. He asked Hankey to record that the recommendation had been made in his absence and without adequate consultation.[3] On the following day,

---

[1] Bonar was not surprised by this negative reply. Late in 1922 he told C. P. Scott: 'All Prime Ministers suffer by suppression. Their friends...tell them what they want to hear': Blake, *Bonar Law*, 439. See also *Tom Jones Diary, 1916–1925*, 221–2 (12 Nov. 1922). Asquith had been very difficult to warn in 1916.

[2] Roskill, *Hankey*, 325. In modern works on the war it has become usual to use the term 'War Committee' for an entirely subordinate body, and 'War Council' for one which had some power of decision: see Blake, *Bonar Law*, 302 n. 1. This practice does not correspond to all First World War usage, e.g. the subordinate body formed in November 1914 was called the War Council. Carson became First Lord of the Admiralty in Lloyd George's December 1916 government, but 'proved a surprisingly ineffective minister.... Carson's real power lay, as it did in his legal career, in his strength of critical attack' (D. George Boyce, *ODNB*, 'Carson, Edward Henry').

[3] Roskill, *Hankey*, 322. The issues went beyond the structure of the government. As the *Westminster Gazette's* editor wrote (issue of 4 Dec. 1916), the cabinet's critics were calling for revised ideas on what was 'financially and industrially necessary in order to put the largest number of fighting soldiers into the field'.

1 December, Asquith sent his counter-proposal to Lloyd George. This scheme, which had originated with Lord Robert Cecil, entailed the creation of 'a Committee of National Organization to deal with the purely domestic side of war problems'. Should this counter-proposal be brought into effect, re-discussion and delay, far from being reduced, would increase, since the cabinet could be called on to decide which committee ought to be dealing with the problem. Clearly the premier did not agree with the most basic feature of the trio's scheme, namely, that the new small War Council, composed of ministers freed from departmental duties and meeting daily, should have authority to *decide* on *all* war problems except for any which the Prime Minister might insist on bringing before the cabinet. Asquith had resisted that particular scheme when Carson had brought it before the Commons on 2 November 1915, and his dislike of it had not lessened.[1]

Apart from this, the week had brought the development which would be fatal, as Bonar had warned, to the peaceful adoption of any radical change in the governmental system: the press had been alerted to a political crisis. News of this appeared in the morning papers on Saturday, 2 December. The *Daily Chronicle* and *Daily Express* were better informed than their Northcliffe-controlled competitors, in that, briefed by Aitken, they named the trio's members. The front page of the *Daily Chronicle*, a widely read Liberal daily, expressed dissatisfaction with the conduct of the war and gave the names of the proposed War Council.[2] Despite this the Asquiths went to Walmer for the weekend, as usual, on 2 December, and, according to Margot, her husband spoke optimistically to her that evening. She sent this account of the evening's conversation to Montagu:[3]

[1] Beaverbrook, *Politicians*, 388–9. For the origin of Asquith's counter-proposal see Cecil's memo. for cabinet, 27 Nov. 1916; *Memories and Reflections*, ii, 147–9. The Liberal *Daily Chronicle* called, 29 November, for a War Council, reduced to four members, which would command 'the widest powers of prompt action'.

[2] Beaverbrook, *Politicians*, 398.

[3] Margot to Edwin Montagu, from Walmer, late 2 or early 3 Dec. 1916: Margot Asquith Papers, d. 3273, fos. 76, 77.

H. I shall dish the lot.... They all think me a fool and [that] I am too kind and soft, but there they are <u>wrong</u>. I shall call a party meeting and ask what they want—me or Ll.G., Northcliffe and Co. and I'll bet you they won't have 10 men.

Me. My darling, if only you and your friends had realized it was <u>bound</u> to come to this, it need never have come. If Ll.G. died Carson's power would not terrify Bonar. Now I fear they all long [to] go.

H. I don't think so: it would be grossly unpatriotic in serious times—I at any rate shall not go.

Much now depended on the view of Bonar's Unionist colleagues in the cabinet. They had protested on 30 November when first told of the plan to hand over control of an all-powerful War Council to Lloyd George. They met Bonar Law on the morning of Sunday 3 December in a mood of some outrage. On that Sunday *Reynolds News* had included an article which went well beyond the press revelations of the preceding day. It said that Lloyd George, as the moving spirit of the trio, was ready to resign and to appeal to the public against the government, if his demands for change were not met. It predicted that Bonar Law would resign at the same time, and would join Ll.G. and Carson in this opposition campaign.[1]

The views of the Unionist ministers, as they were expressed at this Sunday meeting, were summarized in Austen Chamberlain's letter, 8 December 1916, to Chelmsford, the Viceroy of India. Each of the four ministers concerned—Walter Long, Robert Cecil, Chamberlain, and Curzon (Long and 'the three Cs')—had his own view; but Austen was an honest reporter, and (especially when writing as Secretary of State for India to the Viceroy) he is unlikely to have been seriously misleading. He wrote:

It had been for some time apparent to all of us that the late government could not continue without some vital reconstruction of that

---

[1] *Reynolds News* was controlled by Sir Henry Dalziel, a disruptive Liberal MP of Lloyd Georgian views, who is mentioned in Margot's diaries in both peace and war: diary, 21 Feb. 1910, 15 June 1915 (p. 158 below), and 9 July 1915 (p. 165).

part of the machinery which was especially concerned with the management of the war. Asquith has many virtues [but he] lacks the power to drive....Any committee...is apt to dissolve in talk unless the chairman...makes it his business to secure from them a decision on each question as it is raised. Asquith never so understood his duties....He no doubt often averted conflict, but he never contributed a suggestion. He only once in my experience directly helped us to a rapid decision....On...Dec 3rd...the Sunday papers known to be in close relation with Lloyd George announced that he had presented his terms to the Prime Minister....The situation was quite intolerable. Lloyd George was in revolt and the controversy on his side was being carried on in the press, by partial and inaccurate revelations....We thought that...the man who had made the government impossible should be faced with his responsibilities. If he could form a government well and good. If not, he must take his place again as a member of an Asquith administration, having learned the limits of his power and deprived thenceforward of the opportunity for intrigue. In any case, power and responsibility must go together and the man who was Prime Minister in name must be also Prime Minister in fact. It seemed to us...that the only hope of a stable government still lay in combining somehow...in one administration the separate forces represented by both Asquith and Lloyd George....It was not for us to say which of the rival Liberals could secure the greatest...support in the Liberal party and in the parties which habitually worked with it....In our view, the publicity given to Lloyd George's intentions had rendered internal reconstruction no longer possible, and we advised the Prime Minister that he should tender his own resignation carrying with it that of all his colleagues, and, if he was unable to accept this advice, we requested Bonar Law to hand to him our collective resignation.[1]

[1] Chamberlain, *Down the Years*, 116–18.

The manoeuvres which followed this meeting of the Unionist ministers on 3 December 1916 have been much described and analysed, and only the most summary account of them is needed here. Asquith had been brought back from Walmer by Bonham Carter on that morning, as Margot recounts; and in the afternoon he saw Bonar Law and learned that his Unionist colleagues were not prepared to give him outright support against Lloyd George. In the light of this information he agreed provisionally to adopt the trio's reform programme, provided the problem of personnel could be solved satisfactorily. Margot spent much of the evening, and of the early hours of the night, in warning her husband against conceding too much to the 'brigands'. Asquith receded from this agreement on Monday, 4 December, when it was represented in *The Times* as a humiliating surrender. On 5 December Asquith met 'the three Cs', and asked, in Chamberlain's account:

> whether we should 'be prepared to go on with him whilst Lloyd George and Bonar Law resigned'.... We answered with a perfectly definite negative. This was evidently a great blow to [Asquith].... He then asked us what our attitude would be towards Lloyd George if he attempted to form an administration. We replied... that our only object was to get a stable government capable of conducting the war successfully.... We should be prepared to support, to join or to serve under any government which offered a prospect of fulfilling our conditions.... Bob Cecil had the courage to suggest to him [Asquith] that the finest and biggest thing that he could do would be to offer to serve under Lloyd George; but he would not allow Cecil to develop this idea, which he rejected with indignation and even with scorn.[1]

Asquith was confronted at last with the fact that Bonar Law, Carson, and Lloyd George had formed a close alliance which was unopposed among the Unionists, and that this trio were capable of forming a government.

---

[1] Chamberlain, *Down the Years*, 124. For Cecil's letter to Asquith, embodying this suggestion, see Grigg, *Lloyd George, 1912–1916*, 465–6.

He submitted his resignation to the King at 7 p.m. on that evening, 5 December 1916.

Later that evening Bonar Law accepted the King's invitation to form a government. He did so by agreement with Lloyd George in the expectation that Asquith, while almost certainly unwilling to serve under Ll.G., might be readier to take office under the Unionists' leader or under a 'neutral' Prime Minister; but Asquith declined to serve under either Bonar or Balfour.[1] On the morning of 6 December the trio met at Bonar's house and decided to consult Balfour, who suggested that the King should be invited to call a conference.[2] This took place at 3 p.m. that afternoon in Buckingham Palace. It was attended by Bonar Law, Lloyd George, Balfour, Asquith, and Arthur Henderson. The proceedings were dominated by the widely shared conviction, already encountered in Chamberlain's remarks about the Unionist ministers' meeting on 3 December, that the best chance of forming a stable government lay in an agreement between Asquith and Lloyd George. Much had happened since Bonar Law had handed the trio's proposals to Asquith on 25 November. Not only had the newspapers been given time to make difficulties, as Bonar had warned that they would, but, whereas there had been a chance on 3 December of the administration being reformed and rebalanced under the existing premier, three days later a reform on that scale would depend on Asquith's acceptance of a subordinate office. Balfour, Bonar Law and Henderson pleaded with him to accept one; but, although the pleas probably represented the King's wishes as well as those of these three, he reserved his position. 'The result of the meeting', Stamfordham wrote, 'was an agreement that Mr Asquith should consider the proposals made to him' to take subordinate office. If he declined again, 'Mr Bonar Law would not form a government, but Mr Lloyd George would try to do so.'[3]

---

[1] Asquith, *Memories*, ii. 134 (Crewe); Blake, *Bonar Law*, 337.
[2] Balfour, though not the only person to suggest this conference, was the most influential.
[3] Nicolson, *George V*, 290–1. For the King's hope that Asquith would accept subordinate office see diary, 14 Dec. 1916 (p. 304 below) and Asquith, *Memories*, ii, 135 (Crewe).

Lloyd George could rely on substantial support from the Liberal back-benches. Christopher Addison and F. G. Kellaway, having renewed an earlier survey, were soon able to report to him that he had 'forty-nine out-right supporters' there, while '126 others...would support heartily if he could form a government';[1] and at midday on 7 December he had a not-able success with the members of Labour's National Executive, who, im-pressed with the dangers faced by the Entente powers, were inclined to cooperate with him. Bonar Law had already secured an equally signifi-cant triumph on Ll.G.'s behalf when Balfour agreed to become Foreign Secretary;[2] and in the afternoon Curzon, Chamberlain, Robert Cecil, and Long climbed aboard. Leo Maxse had urged that the 'useless rubbish' from the last government should be dropped whether Unionist or Lib-eral; but Lloyd George was in no position to slight the leading Unionists when he had the support of little more than half of the Liberal MPs. He promised 'the three Cs' and Long that neither Churchill nor Northcliffe would be invited to take office, and that he had no plans to change the army command.[3] At 7.30 p.m. on 7 December 1916, as George V wrote in his diary, 'Mr Lloyd George came...and informed me that he is able to form an administration and told me the...names of his colleagues. He will have a strong government. I then appointed him Prime Minister and First Lord of the Treasury.' While the new premier was far from free of all restraint, his appointment marked an important change of style. Britain now had a leader who advertised his readiness to circumvent any obs-tacle which stood in the way of a victory for the Allies. He was always looking for a 'way round' the obstruction.[4] This transition was not an edifying spectacle; but it showed the strength of the only great nation en-gaged in the war which benefited from a parliamentary system and re-sponsible cabinet government.

[1] Addison, *Years*, i. 274. These figures, derived from the survey, 4–6 Dec. 1916, were specula-tive: Lloyd George reckoned on 136 Liberal MPs as supporters: Taylor, *War Politics*, 33.

[2] 'I was all for Ll.G. being given a free hand': A.J.B. as quoted by Lady Betty Balfour to Lady Frances, 30 Dec. 1916, Balfour Papers, Whitt., GD433/2/358.

[3] Grigg, *Lloyd George, 1912–1916*, 480–1.

[4] Taylor, *War Politics*, 145.

FIGURE 8 Margot at the window of The Wharf, Sutton Courtenay.

Margot probably exaggerated Crewe's respect for her 'political advice' during the war; but he may have thought, as the diary states, that Asquith would not have been ousted had he sometimes taken it in the later part of 1916.[1] She had seen the approaching danger, but lacked the temperament and knowledge needed for mitigating it.[2] That Asquith's aversion to what Bonar Law called 'seeming active' damaged his reputation, and eventually lessened his effectiveness as a wartime premier, remains beyond doubt: 'The agonized nation', Churchill wrote, 'demanded a frenzied energy at the summit; an effort to compel events rather than to adjudicate wisely and deliberately upon them.'[3] Moreover, the heroes of the hour were no longer to be found campaigning on the parliamentary battlefield, where Asquith's greatest strengths lay. In January 1916, after attending a

[1] Diary, 14 Dec. 1916, p. 305 below.
[2] Diary, 10 Apr. 1916, p. 250 below.
[3] Churchill, *Great Contemporaries*, 149.

debate on conscription, J. L. Garvin described the Commons as 'that mixed, haphazard mob of civilians left over from irrelevant elections of years ago....They were like men at a fire objecting to the use of fire-engines.'[1] Asquith, the commanding debater, might have lost a little of his mastery, but the chamber where he performed had lost a great deal, and he had neither the skills nor the inclination that were necessary to adapt to the new political landscape. Nor did he have the support of a wife capable of keeping her controversial views to herself. Neither properly saw the challenges that faced them after August 1914, and their incomprehension was enduring. After reading the second volume of Margot's *Autobiography* Crawford wrote in his journal:

> To those who remember...[Asquith's] tedious indolence in 1916—his dilatory slacknesses and indecisions, the book is utterly misleading...Asquith...never seems to have shaken off his desire for ease and self-indulgence....By Xmas 1916 it was high time that a change of government was made. Ll.G. may have been wrong in a hundred things then and thereafter; but he at least galvanized us into effort.[2]

Asquith had been a commanding presence in British politics for more than eight years, and his peacetime record of legislative achievement should not be overshadowed by his wartime inadequacy. On the basis of his achievements 1908 to 1914 he must rank among the greatest British statesmen of any era. The war, though, cruelly exposed his limitations, and those of his brilliant but erratic wife. They were blessed with tremendous talents, but hampered by an inability to adapt those to changing circumstances. In Margot's equestrian phrase: 'The Almighty is a wonderful handicapper. He will not give us everything.'[3]

M. G. B.

---

[1] J. L. to R. G. Garvin, 6 Jan. 1916: Garvin, *Tomorrow*, 133. 'J.L.G.' was reporting on the introduction, 5 Jan., of the first Conscription Bill (single men).

[2] Birrell, *Redress*, 251; *Crawford Journals*, 471 (28 Nov. 1922).

[3] *Off the Record*, 44. Asquith too was fond of this saying: *Asquith–Harrisson*, i. 145.

PART I

24 JULY–7 AUGUST 1914

In June 1914 Margot proudly recorded in her diary the high standing in which her husband was held throughout continental Europe: 'Count Constantine Benckendorff[1] told me that there was not a doubt Henry (so the Russians thought) was the biggest figure in European politics; and James Rothschild[2] said "In Paris and throughout France, the very name of Asquith amazes and stuns them."' 'Henry's success this year has been alarming', she added, 'and his speeches unsurpassed. I can't say I feel quite the same about his colleagues.' The cabinet was then embroiled in the bitter controversy over Irish Home Rule, and laboured in its search for a constitutional solution to a problem that raised a realistic prospect of civil war. This crisis, though, faded into the background with the advent of a European war, proving the wisdom of Asquith's favourite axiom 'that the Expected does not Happen'. He seems not to have been greatly surprised when, on 23 July, Austria 'sent a bullying and humiliating Ultimatum to Servia who cannot possibly comply with it'. With his usual confidence he attributed this move, not to the Austrians' policy, but simply to their being 'quite the stupidest people in Europe'. Such views were known to very few, and did little harm, since detailed negotiations with Europe's chancelleries were conducted not by the premier, but by his Foreign Secretary, Sir Edward Grey*.[3] It was Asquith's handling of the various views among the members of his cabinet that gained him much praise during the war crisis. Margot's reactions to events, as recorded in her diary, are revealing. The dispatch of the 'precautionary telegram' on 29 July 1914 'thrilled' her; and this delight was enhanced when the premier announced the next day that the Irish Home Rule proceedings were to be postponed. Her joy that the insolent Tory ladies were to be deprived of what she saw as 'their civil war' in defence of Protestant Ulster reveals, with startling vividness, how bitter inter-party strife had become in Britain. Margot's assurance to Edwin Montagu,* on the evening of 31 July, that her husband would not be deflected, where the decision whether to support France and Russia was concerned, looks to have been soundly based. By that Friday evening Asquith may not yet have made up his mind whether Britain ought to intervene. He probably expected, on the basis of much experience, that, provided he could keep his colleagues together, something would soon occur to decide the question. That event occurred on the night of the 2–3 August when, as he later told Venetia Stanley*: 'The Germans, with almost Austrian crassness ... delivered an ultimatum to Belgium.' The next day, 4 August, German troops entered Belgium. 'This simplifies matters', Asquith wrote, 'so we sent the Germans an ultimatum to expire at midnight ... We are on the eve of horrible things.'[4]

[1] Constantine Benckendorff (1880–1959), son of the Russian Ambassador, Count Alexandre de Benckendorff (see below, p. 9 n. 2).

[2] James Armand Edmond (Jimmy) de Rothschild (1878–1957), born in Paris; he took British citizenship after the First World War, in which he served with the British Army in France and Palestine; Liberal MP for the Isle of Ely 1929–45.

[3] An asterisk against a name indicates inclusion in the Biographical Notes.

[4] Asquith–Stanley, 61, 122–3, 126, 148, 150–1.

Friday 24 July 1914

(The Austrian note to Servia was published 22nd July, the answer 25th).[1] H[enry]. told the House that the Amending Bill would be put off on 30th July.[2] I went into his bedroom in morning, and he told me Bonar Law's* motor was at the door; he said: 'I don't know why I have to be bothered like this.' When he came back, he told me that B. Law's motor had whisked him down to the latter's rooms in Kensington, where he found Carson*, and they had both asked H. to put off Amending Bill, as things were so gloomy abroad.

The gallery was <u>packed</u>, Ly Londonderry[3] and the Diehards sitting near Mrs Lowther[4]—myself and Liberal ladies the other side of the gallery. The beautiful, incredibly silly Muriel Beckett[5] and M. Lowther rushed round me, and others, pressing up, said 'Good Heavens, Margot, what does this mean? How frightfully dangerous! Why, the Irish will be fighting tonight— what does it all mean?' M. 'It means your civil war is <u>postponed</u>, and you will, I think, never get it.' I looked at these women who had been insolent to me all the session, when I added 'If you read the papers, you'll find we are on the verge of a European war.'

Redmond* told H. that afternoon that if the Government liked to re-move every soldier from Ireland, he would bet there would never be one

[1] Friday 24 July, the date given to this diary entry, indicates no more than the start of the final crisis. The Austrian note was addressed to Belgrade on 23 July and notified to various powers on the morning of the 24th.

[2] Margot means that on 30 July Asquith informed the Commons of the postponement of the Amending Bill that would determine how the Irish Home Rule Bill would affect the six mostly Protestant counties of Ulster; a few hours before he was due to introduce the Amending Bill Asquith had been asked by Bonar Law and Carson to postpone it, in the interests of national unity, for the duration of the war crisis, to which request he assented: see *Asquith–Stanley*, 69, 84–5.

[3] Lady Theresa Vane-Tempest-Stewart née Chetwynd-Talbot (1856–1919), Marchioness of Londonderry, perhaps the leading Unionist political hostess of the pre-war era; her affair with Harry Cust imposed a great strain on her marriage to the 6th Marquis (see below), but their later married years were marked by warmth and mutual support.

[4] Mary Frances née Beresford-Hope, m. 1886 James William Lowther (see Biographical Notes). Diehards: those who refuse to make compromises or retreat; the term originated in the stand of the 57th of Foot at Albuera in the Peninsular War; in the years before the First World War it was frequently applied to the hotter sort of Unionist Peer, who typically rejected the Liberals 1909 'People's Budget', 1911 Parliament Act, and 1912 Home Rule Bill.

[5] Muriel Helen Paget (d. 1941), m. 1896 Rupert Evelyn Beckett.

hitch; and that both his volunteers and Carson's would police Ireland with ease.

War! War!—everyone at dinner discussing how long the war would last. The average opinion was 3 weeks to 3 months. Violet* said 4 weeks. H. said nothing, which amazed us! I said it would last a year. I went to tea with Con, and Betty Manners told me she had heard Kitchener* at lunch say to Arthur Balfour* he was sure it would last over a year.[1]

Wednesday 29 July 1914

Bad news from abroad. I was lying in bed, resting, 7.30 p.m. The strain from hour to hour waiting for telegrams, late at night; standing stunned and unable to read or write; two cabinets a day; crowds through which to pass, cheering Henry wildly—all this contributed to making me tired. H. came into my room. I saw by his face that something momentous had happened. I sat up and looked at him. For once he stood still, and didn't walk up and down the room (He never sits down when he is talking of important things.)

H. Well! We've sent what is called 'the precautionary telegram' to every office in the Empire—War, Navy, Post Office, etc., to be ready for war. This is what the Committee of Defence have been discussing and settling for the last two years. It has never been done before, and I am very curious to see what effect it will have. All these wires were sent between 2 and 2.30 marvellously quick.[2] (I never saw Henry so keen

---

[1] Betty Constance Manners (1889–1962), daughter of Lord John and Lady Constance ('Con') Manners, who were old friends of Margot's. Betty married Arthur ('Oc') Asquith in 1918. That the war would be over in a few weeks was one of 1914's popular fallacies, and the 'diners' failed to see that, while Germany and Austria-Hungary might possibly win a quick victory, an initial German repulse was unlikely to end the war. The members of the CID did not expect the war to end in an Allied victory until the Germans had felt that pressure on their trade and imports which the British Navy would exercise through blockade. This pressure was unlikely to become fatal to Germany for at least eighteen months. For Hankey's account of the stress on 'economic pressure' in British planning until the outbreak of war see Roskill, *Hankey*, 134 (H. to G. Blake, 3 September 1928).

[2] For Hankey's account of this process see his *Supreme Command*, i. 154–6; by 'Committee of Defence' HHA means the CID.

outwardly—his face looked quite small and handsome. He sat on the foot of my bed.)

M. (passionately moved, I sat up, and felt 10 feet high.) How <u>thrilling</u>! Oh! Tell me, aren't you excited, darling?[1]

H. (who generally smiles with his eyebrows slightly turned, quite gravely kissed me, and said) It will be very interesting. We've had a Press Committee, which we also decided to have at Committee of Defence, to which papers can send a delegate; and we tell them what they may not publish. (The Press has behaved very well. Only *The Times* has indicated how near we are to war.)[2] I shall be curious to know if there will be anything in the papers tomorrow (tomorrow being July 30th 1914).

I went to the House in the afternoon, and saw Redmond and Dillon[3] going to H.'s room. I asked him afterwards if they were reasonable.

H. Poor devils! They're anxious not to be dropped down too much. I should think there must be a settlement. The others[4] are also in a funk over the situation.

M. Is the situation <u>really</u> so serious, Henry?

H. I'm afraid so. In any case, we must not be caught napping.

Friday 31 July 1914

At 11 a.m. H. came into my bedroom, and said that though he himself had no hope, there was an idea that things were better.[5] He went down to the cabinet. After the cabinet, he lunched at Admiralty. He then spent an hour with the King [George V]*. I was waiting for him to make his statement at House of Commons....He told me that the Bank of England men had

---

[1] In the *Autobiography*, ii. 159, Margot toned down her reaction to this announcement.

[2] The purpose of the 'Press Committee' was to prevent the publication of statements that might help a potential, or actual, enemy.

[3] John Dillon (1851–1927), Irish National politician, and MP 1885–1918; a supporter of John Redmond as Chairman of United Party, 1900.

[4] i.e. Bonar Law and Carson.

[5] The mediation proposals, on the basis of the Austrian forces halting in Belgrade (late 29 and 30 July 1914), are summarized in Fay, *World War*, ii. 434–8.

given him infinite trouble—Cunliffe,[1] the boss, whom I know, looks like a jolly, red-faced farmer; Currie, a little man like a caraway seed; Schuster,[2] a man who is frightened when he hears his own name mentioned; and five others—'the greatest ninnies and funks I've ever had to tackle' ('like so many old women having tea in a cathedral town', Montagu told me afterwards that he had said.)[3]

Edward Grey came in after dinner, and played bridge with me, Cys* and Micky.[4] He was very grave and silent, but in quite good form. In crises, he seems to get right away from himself, and my love for him returns.... [He] is as unupsettable as Henry is. Two more different men never sat in one cabinet. Very devoted to each other, they share an unexpressed intimacy, which suits them both....[5]

Montagu jumped up from the card table (when masses of FO boxes drove Grey away, and Crewe* and Haldane* came in), seized my arm, and in a violent whisper said

[Montagu] We ought to mobilize tomorrow, and declare it! How I wish Simon* could be crushed right out! His influence is most pernicious. He and Ll.G.*, my chief, are against this.[6]

---

[1] Walter Cunliffe (1855–1920), cr. Baron 1914; Governor of Bank of England, 1913–18.

[2] Sir Felix Otto Schuster (1854–1936), Bt. 1906, Governor Union Bank of England and Smith's Bank Ltd., 1895–1918. Currie has not been identified.

[3] On 31 July the City of London was still preventing the Unionists from being as interventionist as the Unionist press made out: Oliver, *Anvil*, 79–80. For Lloyd George's view that in these days 'money was...frightened and trembling' see Lloyd George, *War Memoirs*, i. 45.

[4] Roderick Sinclair Meiklejohn (1876–1962), KBE, 1931; CB 1911; Private Secretary to Asquith as Chancellor of the Exchequer and Prime Minister, 1905–11; Deputy Controller of Supply Services in HM Treasury; First Civil Service Commissioner, 1928–39.

[5] Grey's anger at the German Chancellor Bethmann Hollweg's bid for British neutrality (received 30 July) was aroused by the realization that this was not an attempt to lessen the crisis, but a bid for victory in war by ensuring that the British would not join their Entente partners against Germany. The incident provided a striking illustration of the psychological difference, stressed by Margot, between the Prime Minister and his Foreign Secretary. Asquith's indignation at the 'bid', to which he gave eloquent expression in his speech on 6 August (Spender and Asquith, ii. 111–16), had been exceeded on 30 July by his contempt at its ineptitude. He told Venetia Stanley on that day: 'There is something very crude and almost childlike about German diplomacy': *Asquith–Stanley*, 186.

[6] It is not clear whether Montagu referred to mobilization of army or navy: probably army, recommended 31 July by Nicolson (Nicolson, *Carnock*, 418). On the evening of 1 August Churchill was authorized to mobilize the navy: Churchill, *Great Contemporaries*, 148. Haldane took the order for army mobilization to the War Office, a.m. 3 August.

M. (knowing as I did how passionately McK[enna].* resented the idea of us sending an Expeditionary Force to France in the German crisis over Morocco).¹ What about McK.?

Montagu He is the best of the lot.²

M. Haven't I <u>always</u> told you, that after Grey, Crewe and Haldane, McKenna is Henry's most loyal and devoted colleague. Haven't you all laughed at me?—except Henry; and I'll say more: he has got the best of heads.

Montagu (in a frenzy) George is mad not to see we <u>must</u> mobilize at once.

M. Don't fret. Neither Ll.G. or Simon will have the faintest effect on Henry.³

Saturday 1 August 1914

I wrote to Redmond and told him he had the opportunity of his life if he made a great speech, offering his Volunteers, or if he were to write to the King.... On the 3rd August, he made [a] wonderful speech. I told <u>no</u> one, as I was so anxious Redmond should be fully appreciated.⁴ F. Lawson and

¹ i.e. during the Agadir crisis of 1911.

² Early on 2 August Geoffrey Robinson* (from 1917 Dawson), editor of *The Times*, met McKenna and was pleased to discover that he was 'at least on the fence'; and Asquith, in his letter that day to Venetia Stanley, called Crewe, McKenna, and Samuel* 'a moderating intermediate body' in the cabinet. McKenna apparently told Robinson at this meeting that the government was powerless 'unless the people are behind them, and the people are against war': Morris, *Scaremongers*, 361, *Asquith–Stanley*, 146.

³ On 1 August Asquith wrote to Venetia Stanley that Morley and perhaps Simon wanted an immediate declaration that '*in no circumstances* will we take a stand [but that] Lloyd George—all for peace—[was] ... for keeping the position still open'. The premier added that he and Grey would never agree to an 'uncompromising position of non-intervention at all costs': *Asquith–Stanley*, 140. Margot was right in predicting that the outright non-interventionists would not influence the premier.

⁴ Redmond was the second member to speak, after Bonar Law, in reply to Sir Edward Grey's statement on 3 August. In keeping with the patriotic spirit of the moment he pledged the Irish Volunteers to the defence of Britain; the Volunteers were a Nationalist military organization formed in 1913, ostensibly in response to formation of the Ulster Volunteers the previous year. As civil war loomed over Home Rule the two volunteer forces stood in opposition to one another, but in his speech on 3 August Redmond proclaimed: 'I say that the coast of Ireland will be defended from foreign invasion by her armed sons, and for this purpose armed Nationalist Catholics in the South will be only too glad to join arms with the armed Protestant Ulstermen in the North' (*Parl. Deb.*, 3 Aug. 1914, 65. 1828–9). In the event a significant minority of the Irish Volunteers rejected his leadership, and supported in the Easter Rising of 1916.

masses of old, crusted Tories, raved about the speech. I heard it, and was thrilled by the words and the delivery. Coming after Edward Grey's <u>won-derful</u> pronouncement[1] (in its way the most remarkable utterance in a unique crisis that has been made in my lifetime), made its reception more noticeable. I daresay he would have made the speech even if I had not written, but (in his letter to me) he does not give the impression of being mad keen.

Benckendorffs dined.[2] He and I had an altercation. He says it is not the Kaiser*, but his war party, that is to blame for declaring war. I will <u>never</u> believe the Kaiser is not boss of his soldiers. I also said Alliances were a bore—not at all tactful, but Bencky didn't mind. We luckily have no alliance with any country.[3]

Saturday 15 August 1914

I am writing from notes taken on the spot, while everything is fresh in my memory. Further on I will make a simple diary of what happened from old *Timeses*, which I have not got here.[4]

<u>Germany declared war on Russia on Sat. August 1st</u>. The Stock Exchange was closed.[5] Henry made his statement in the House . . . on 31st. All

---

[1] *Parl. Deb.*, 3 Aug. 1914, 65. 1809–27. Balfour thought Grey's 'the most important speech delivered in the House of Commons during the past hundred years', and Lloyd George and Bonar Law agreed with him: *Riddell War Diary*, 31, 357. Lord Hugh Cecil called this speech 'the greatest example of the art of persuasion that I have ever listened to': Trevelyan, *Grey*, 265.

[2] Alexandre, Count de Benckendorff (Bencky) (1849–1917), Russian Ambassador in London from 1903, and Sophie, Countess de Benckendorff, née Comtesse de Schouvaloff; they married in 1879; according to Lady Diana Cooper they had 'the happiest embassy in London' (Asquith, C., *Diaries*, 488).

[3] Technically true, although Britain had Ententes with France (1904) and Russia (1907). Margot put a marginal note against the end of the entry: 'I would not particularly like one [an alliance] with Russia. As some wag said "Britons *never, never*, never will be Slavs"': Diary, d. 3210, fo. 623ʳ. She was unaware that Britain had long been allied to Japan; and was doubtless surprised when Britain shortly concluded a wartime alliance with France and Russia. Nor did Margot see that by August 1914 the Kaiser's control over the German army was largely mythical; the Kaiser disagreed entirely (i) with the view of Moltke, Chief of the German General Staff, about Britain's inevitable alignment with Russia and France, and her comparative impotence, (ii) with the Austrian Foreign Minister Berchtold's conviction about the need to defeat Serbia in war.

[4] Margot was at Hopeman Lodge, Moray: *Asquith–Stanley*, 167.

[5] It had been closed at 10 a.m., 31 July. The bank rate had been raised to 8 per cent, the highest rate since 1873.

the papers on 1st Aug. made it pretty sure we were going to join with France to crush Germany.[1]

Aug. 3rd 1914 the papers published the declaration[s] of war....

Sunday 2 August 1914

We were all in 10 Downing St. Various people dined with us, among others Mr Montagu (now Financial Secretary to the Treasury). After dinner:

Mr M.   Till last night I thought we might be kept out of this war. My views have quite changed. My chief (Lloyd George) is intriguing with that scoundrel Simon (our Attorney-General, a very old young man, honourable, kind, mulish, dusty, and shocked at the mention of a new-laid egg), Beauchamp,[2] Morley* and the Peace party. I said to Simon yesterday: 'Have you heard what Ll.G. is going to say about specie tomorrow?' He said he had <u>glanced</u> at it. I then said 'do you, or do you not, know what he is going to say?' He replied 'Don't worry; there may be no Chancellor of the Exchequer tomorrow'[3]— and this, Margot, at a time when both my chief and Simon should be working night and day.

    M.   Will they all resign at tomorrow's cabinet?

Mr M.   I don't think so.

Sunday 2 August 1914

Elizabeth* and I, and our married governess and her husband, Frau and Herr Meyer, went to St. Paul's Cathedral, and all took the Holy Communion.

---

[1] The bewildering speed of events in the week before war was declared bemused Margot as much as her countrymen, and she was not discerning enough to understand all of the press reports that appeared during this hectic period. The Liberal press did not take an interventionist line until 3–4 August, i.e. until the effect of the German ultimatum to Brussels had become apparent in Britain. Germany declared war on France between 6 and 7 p.m., Monday, 3 Aug. 1914: Tuchman, *Guns*, 145–6. News of this did not appear in the daily papers until 4 Aug.

[2] William Lygon (1872–1938), 7th Earl of Beauchamp, Lord President of the Council, 1910, 1914–15.

[3] A Royal Proclamation, 2 August, granted a month's moratorium for bills of exchange and prolonged the Bank Holiday, 3 August, by three further days: Hurwitz, *Intervention*, 66.

I felt intensely sorry for her, as I knew he would have to be called back to Germany to fight.

After St. Paul's, I went to see the German Ambassador [Lichnowsky]* and his dear wife Mechtilde Lichnowsky*, friends of ours. ... He looks like a Goya picture. He told me that he had said to the Kaiser when he (K.) sent him over here 'I am not your man, if you are going to have any row about England.' M. 'Did you think then that there was much ill feeling in Germany?' (This talk was when the Lichnowskys first came). Prince L. 'Certainly not (in his high hoarse voice). I have never seen better feeling than there is now, but as you know (with an innocent smile), our Kaiser is very impulsive.'

[The Princess] was lying on a green sofa, with her little dachshund, who yapped drearily at me from habit, feeling no hostility, only pity for his lady. Her eyes were starved from crying. The Prince was walking up and down in silence. He caught me by the hands, and said 'Oh! say there is surely not going to be 'warr' (pronouncing it like 'far'). Dear, dear Mrs Asquith, can we not stop it?' (wringing his hands). I put my arms round Mechtilde on the sofa, while we both cried. She got up and pointed to the trees and sky, and said:

[Pss. L.] To think that we should bring such sorrows to an innocent, happy people! I have always hated and loathed our Kaiser—have I not said so a thousand times, dear little Margot. He and his friends are all brutes! I will never cross his threshold again.

Pr. L. I do not understand what has happened. What is it all about?

M. I can only think his genius—

Pr. L. The Kaiser is no genius! He is ill-informed, impulsive, mad!— never listening or believing one word that I say, never answering telegrams!!

M. He treated Metternich[1] just the same. He can't bear the truth. He is a fiend and megalomaniac.

[1] Count Paul Wolff-Metternich (1853–1934), German Ambassador in London until May 1912, when his prescient warnings about the dangers inherent in Anglo-German naval rivalry led to his recall: Marder, *Royal Navy*, i. 285.

Pr. L.   Some say it is not so much his—
Pss. L.   They say what they like, it is him and his idiot son, and that horrible, hard, brutal war party that surrounds him.

I stayed on, doing all I could, but quite powerless to console them. The Prince had large tears rolling down his thin cheeks when I said goodbye....

On 4th [August]...he saw me a moment [at the Embassy]...and said 'So it is all over. You will declare war tonight; and you knew we <u>must</u> go through Belgium—there is no other way. We never counted that old, old treaty.[1] Oh dear! Oh dear! Don't, don't go to war—just wait.' (Holding my hands). I felt too sad to speak. We sat and cried on the green sofa. Pce. 'You will be much for peace, and far more useful—do keep out. All your men will be killed. Why should they be killed?' I said goodbye....

Tuesday 4 August 1914

We declared war. It was an agonizing day and night. I asked H. at night if he had had a bad day. He said 'Six of my men have resigned: John Morley, Burns*, Simon, Beauchamp and Trevelyan.[2] As you know, John Morley resigned, and Burns, two days ago. I tried to persuade Morley to stay.'...H. gave [a letter from Morley] to me and said 'One of the most distinguished men living, and certainly the best talker. I shall miss him very much.' He persuaded Simon and Beauchamp to stay on, but Trevelyan and the other two left.

[1] A reference to the 1839 Treaty of London, by which the European Great Powers recognized and guaranteed the independence and neutrality of Belgium. Assuming Margot's account to be true, Lichnowsky, like many other Germans, could not understand that, to the British, a German invasion of all Belgium was quite different from a German traverse through the Belgian Ardennes. Lichnowsky, visited by Harold Nicolson in 1927, referred to Margot as having been 'courageous and generous' in making this second visit on Tuesday 4th Aug. after her first on Sunday 2nd: Lees-Milne, *Nicolson*, i. 325.

[2] The identity of the sixth is not clear. In fact only three of the five who are named actually resigned. The third was Charles Philips Trevelyan (1870–1958), s. as 3rd Bt. 1928; Liberal MP 1899–1918; Labour MP 1922–31; under-secretary, Board of Education, 1908–14.

WAR

We went to the House of Commons. I sat breathless while Henry announced that an ultimatum had been sent to Germany, on the question of the neutrality of Belgium.[1] He spoke with extraordinary gravity, and in his most deliberate tones. The House was packed. 'We have asked that the reply to that request, and a satisfactory answer to the telegram of this morning, should be given before midnight.' These words called forth a roll of cheers from every part of the House. Henry then got up, and walked down to the bar of the House, in a roar of cheers, was then called on [by] the Speaker [Lowther*], and announced 'A message from His Majesty, signed by his own hand.'[2] This announcement was received with cheers, which went on as H. walked up the floor of the House, and handed his document to the Speaker.

I can truthfully say that this has been the greatest moment of my Life, and the greatest moment in British politics since Waterloo. I was glad the Speaker's gallery was dark, and that no one could hear my heart beat, or see the thousand hammers in my brain. No one really at that time would have turned a hair if we had all screamed or fainted. Even the least imaginative was rivetted.... We can't hear a word the Speaker says from our gallery, so reading the King's message conveyed nothing to me. I went downstairs and saw H. for one moment (Before I could say more than one word in his ear, he was invaded by men who had appointments.) He was sitting writing in his room. We looked at each other. M. 'So it is all up?' H. 'Yes, it is all up.' He had tears in his eyes.

All happened in such a short time.[3] On 30th July everyone was talking of Ireland. The cry of 'Civil war! Civil war!' to which *The Times* and the

---

[1] A stilted, but strictly correct, phrase. Did Margot understand Lichnowsky's remark, in his conversation with her that day, about 'that old, old treaty'?

[2] *Parl. Deb.*, 4 Aug. 1914, 65.1927. The King's message is pasted in Diary, d. 3210 fo. 644; it announces the imminent calling out of the army reserve, with directions for 'embodying the Territorial Force' and for making arrangements 'for units or individuals whose services may be required in other than a military capacity'.

[3] Once the ultimatum from Vienna had gone to Belgrade, Moltke needed to move quickly: the German forces could be mobilized and readied for action much more rapidly than the Russian, but his divisions had to win in the west and turn eastwards before the Austrians had become too embroiled against Serbia in the south; and, moreover, the German units attacking Liège needed to occupy the ground between the forts before the Belgian defenders did.

Tories treated us every day has been stilled in five days, and now we read in tears a silenced Press, with the sound of <u>real</u> war waving like wireless telegraphy round our heads.

Thursday 6 August 1914

The White Book, an official record of all the diplomatic correspondence, was placed in the hands of everyone. Henry's parliamentary under-secretary, Mr Lyell, gave me a copy of it.[1] It is a thick book, but amazing reading!! Germany's arrogance and insolence justify the whole of Europe joining to rid the world of such a menace to civilization.

I forgot to say that on 3rd August 1914, the day Henry stopped K[itchener]. going to Egypt, he sounded him about taking the W. Office.[2] Henry came into his dressing-room, as he always does when Elizabeth and I are in our baths. He leaves his door open, and we talk. This is one of the most amusing parts of my day. Henry is always at his best, and most indiscreet!...

H. I've just been sounding K., as I can't go on with this heavy work.

M. I suppose he jumped at it?

H. Not he! He didn't want it <u>at all</u>. He doesn't fancy taking the post, now that every detail of our plans has been made (by Haldane, Henry and Com. of Defence).[3]

[1] Charles Henry Lyell (1875–1918), Liberal MP for East Dorset, 1904–10; South Edinburgh, 1910–17; PPS to Sir Edward Grey, 1906, and to Asquith, 1910; gazetted captain in Fife RGA, September 1914; on active service 1915–17; Margot was unimpressed with him in the capacity of PPS to the premier, writing in 1912: 'Lyell ... useless and probably not in the House' (i.e. not regular in attendance: diary, 11 November 1912).

[2] This appointment received widespread press support on 5 Aug. 1914. It had been mentioned as a possibility in 1903–4 by Rosebery, in 1909 by Esher, and in Apr. 1914 (in *John Bull*) by Horatio Bottomley. For Kitchener's doings between about 12.50 p.m., 3 Aug. 1914, when he left the cross-channel steamer to motor back to London, and 1 p.m., 5 Aug., when Asquith told the King of his decision to surrender the seals of the War Office to the great soldier (he had held them since the resignation of John Seely in March 1914, over the Curragh 'mutiny'), see Cassar, *Kitchener*, 173–7. Kitchener's attitude was perhaps best summarized by his remark: 'May God preserve me from the politicians.'

[3] Cf. Kitchener's critical remark to Rosebery, that the cabinet 'deserved the Victoria Cross' for declaring war in a state of such unpreparedness.

I wondered in my heart of hearts whether K. was waiting to be pressed. The next day I took Etty* to [the] House. She is a great friend of K.'s, and said to me 'Isn't it <u>splendid</u> of K. to have offered his services <u>at once</u> to the Government! He says there is nothing he will not do for the Gov. in W. Office.' I had to point out to her that, though K. might have said this to <u>her</u>, it was not what he said to Henry. (It was a side-light on K.'s methods.) I <u>knew</u> after that that he would accept, which he did. I saw Sir W. Tyrrell,[1] who said 'I am <u>very</u> sorry the PM is to be succeeded by K. I am sure he will prove a difficulty.' I thought so too, but as all was settled, and he had to get the Home defence ready, he was the very man to do this.[2]

Thursday 6 August 1914

August 6th Henry made his great speech to a packed House.[3] Arthur Balfour told Cambon[4] that it was the finest thing he had ever heard, and most people were amazed by it. He [Henry] told me afterwards that he had not prepared a word, only jotted down headings (that are in *The Times*). I never saw him so worked up as he was…. Arthur B. was clever enough to spot that H. was unprepared….[5]

---

[1] Sir William George Tyrrell (1866–1947), KCMG 1913, cr. Baron 1929; principal private secretary to Sir Edward Grey, 1907–15. By May 1915 Asquith was not far from Tyrrell in opinion: see below, p. 119. Asquith expected it to 'be amusing to see how [Kitchener would] get on in the cabinet', while Raymond and Violet were soon retailing stories about K's loquacity at the cabinet table on Welsh Disestablishment. For the premier and his colleagues at least the joke soon palled: *Asquith–Stanley*, 158; Jolliffe, *Raymond Asquith*, 192; Fitzherbert, *Greenmantle*, 130.

[2] Margot was soon to learn that Kitchener's plans went far beyond ensuring the readiness of 'the Home Defence'. On 6 August Asquith told Venetia of the cabinet's decision to send most of the BEF to France: *Asquith–Stanley*, 158. Northcliffe had wanted the *Daily Mail* to pronounce on 5 August against any British solder leaving Britain: he had been dissuaded by his editor from publishing a leader to that effect: Thompson, *Northcliffe*, 224.

[3] Asquith spoke bullishly in support of an extraordinary vote of credit of £100,000,000 to the government for the pursuance of the war: he also announced that Kitchener 'with that great public spirit and patriotism that everyone would expect from him', had agreed to serve as War Secretary: see Spender and Asquith, ii. 111–116; *Parl. Deb.*, 65. 2073–83.

[4] Paul Pierre Cambon (1843–1924), French Ambassador in London, 1898–1920.

[5] Asquith had come from a cabinet meeting and went on to the 'War Council' meeting at which it was virtually decided that the BEF should be sent to the Continent to operate 'on the left of the French army'. This complied with the only plan which had been 'worked out by the two staffs in great detail'. The decision represented the crucial step to Britain's 'continental commitment': *Asquith–Stanley*, 158; Hankey, *Supreme Command*, 170–1, 193–4.

Friday 7 August 1914

Henry was dragged away early from bridge in 10 Downing St.

M. (when saying good-night to H.) Why did you have to go to [the] cabinet room?

H. I had Bonar Law and Ll.G. with me. I don't know which is the most foolish and unreasonable—B. Law or the Irish. Illingworth* told me that Ll.G. and Redmond had a long talk, which ended with them both being so <u>furious</u> that Redmond went out and banged the door, and Ll.G. went out by the window. They are all so jealous and suspicious of each-other, and think that proroguing the session may mean the loss of the Home Rule Bill, or vice versa.[1] I've just had a long letter from the Archbishop, talking about the Welsh Bill.[2] What little minds they've all got! I should call the Archbishop's letter hypocritical.

M. Why bully you about these things just now!

Austria declared war on Russia.... The first fruits of the war have been that our *Amphion*, light cruiser hunting the mine-layer *Königin Luise*, first sank her, and then were sunk themselves [*sic*] on a mine. Over 100 of our men were killed by the explosion. All not killed were taken to Shottley, both Germans and English.

---

[1] For the problem presented by the Home Rule Bill once Britain had gone to war, see *Asquith–Stanley*, 173–5. The Nationalists did not want the parliamentary session ended by prorogation until the Speaker had certified that the bill had been passed by the Commons in three sessions under the Parliament Act, and could therefore receive the Royal Assent. The Unionists naturally wanted to see the session ended before Home Rule (even with a suspension provision for the duration of the war) had reached the Statute Book.

[2] i.e. Randall Thomas Davidson, Archbishop of Canterbury (see Biographical Notes). The Bill for disestablishing the Welsh Church had been accepted by the Commons in three sessions, like the Home Rule Bill, and was ready for the Royal Assent which was given in September 1914. It came into force in March 1920.

PART II

10 AUGUST–
21 DECEMBER 1914

During the nineteen weeks with which this part deals, the premier and Margot encountered various vagaries of fortune. On 3 September Asquith, telling his wife of the French government's flight to Bordeaux, added: 'Nothing can be more serious than ... the whole situation at the front.' By contrast, Henry Wilson,[1] replying to a question from a French counterpart eleven days later, expected, unless some serious blunder was made, to 'cross into Germany ... in four weeks'. On 13 December 1914, when Margot was at Rawlinson's[2] headquarters, a French officier de liaison 'spoke ... as if the Germans were done'. Margot was amazed; and, in the event, the front lines in the west did not move by more than 10 miles either way until March 1917. By that date Margot had bemoaned repeated British losses incurred in foredoomed efforts to recover France's main industrial area, which the Germans had seized during their initial advance. This first phase of the fighting in the west evoked some of Margot's most striking Diary passages—for instance, Charlie Grant's[3] remarks on the Battle of Ypres (19 November 1914), her description of Earl Roberts's* funeral in St Paul's; and her sketch of Winston Churchill* at 40. Margot recorded on 26 October 1914 that she had 'never felt the same since the War began'. Her views, however, unlike her feelings, survived unchanged. She still saw the government's contribution to the war effort in terms of 'little stunts' by individual ministers. She continued to view public affairs with the partisan eye of peacetime, and to believe that if the Tories were to 'go in for Conscription ... we should romp in at next Gen. Election'.

Monday 10 August 1914

The French, Germans and Belgians opened the war at Liège.[4] As the Press is now rigorously censored, I know none of the details, but we know how wonderfully the Belgians fought, and how, thanks to them, Germany's

[1] Henry Hughes Wilson (1864–1922), Bt. 1919. Principal advocate of military cooperation with France in event of attack by Germany. Director of Military Operations 1910–14; chief liaison officer with French HQ 1915; commanded IV Army Corps 1915–16; CIGS 1918. Described by Asquith, to whom he was grossly disloyal, as 'that poisonous mischief-maker' (Nov. 1914, *Asquith–Stanley*, 311). For the damage done to his reputation when extracts from his diaries were posthumously published, 1927, see Jeffery, *Henry Wilson*, 291–3.

[2] Henry Seymour Rawlinson (1864–1925), cr. 1st Baron Rawlinson 1919; Officer Commanding the Antwerp force (7th Division and 3rd Cavalry Division), October 1914; later GOC, IV. Corps, and Fourth Army; played an important role in the Somme offensive, and the successful counter-offensive that led to the breaking of the Hindenburg Line in September 1918; later Commander-in-Chief, India, 1920–5.

[3] Charles John Cecil Grant (1877–1950), KCB 1937; DSO 1915; entered Coldstream Guards, 1897; Brigade Major, France, 1914; GSO2, 1914–15; GSO1, 1915–17; Brig.-Gen. and commanded 1st Infantry Brigade, 1917–18; he married, 1903, Lady Sybil Myra Caroline Primrose, daughter of the 5th Earl of Rosebery.

[4] The French were not involved at Liège. The Belgian resistance was delaying the German advance briefly. The last of Liège's twelve forts fell on 16 August the German army's advance

plans have been knocked. Ld K. has asked the country to give him a new army of 100,000 men (out of the despised Territorials, etc.!)...I drove away from the House with dear old H. Chaplin.[1] He dropped me in his taxi at Downing St. '<u>I am proud to be seen with you</u>. If anyone had told me that <u>any</u> prime minister could have come to this House, and asked for a vote of credit of a hundred million, and got a unanimous vote, I should have said the thing is impossible. I'm not saying it because I'm an old pal, but, my dear Mrs. Asquith, I think—and I am not the only one—that <u>your</u> <u>husband is the most remarkable man living. He and Grey have started</u> <u>this war in a memorable way</u>.'

I forgot to say on 9th Aug. 1914 I was sent for to Buckingham Palace, by Ly Ampthill,[2] a delightful woman (married to a most unprepossessing, conceited lout), to ask if I would be on the Queen's (Mary)[*] committee for needle work. I said yes. Ly Bertha Dawkins[3] gave me tea. They seemed very cheerful—I felt very low myself.

I went to our first meeting, 4.30 pm—an infernal hour. I wanted to be in H. of Commons, where every day something of interest happens. Questions go on till 4....I sat next to Pss Mary,[4] then the Queen, both on my left; next to me, on my right, was Ly Lansdowne.[5] I observed Ly Northcliffe,[6] May Harcourt,[7] Mrs Spender. The suggestions were all right. I said I would make shirts and night-shirts for men, etc....After

through Belgium, scheduled to start on 15 August, started two days later. A few days earlier the *Daily Mail* had quoted a consensus that the forts 'would never be taken', a view supported by H. G. Wells: Tuchman, *Guns*, 215, 220; Bertrand Russell, *The Listener*, 418, 10 Sept. 1953.

[1] Henry Chaplin (1840–1923), cr. 1st Viscount 1916; Conservative (and Unionist) MP 1868–1916; President of Local Government Board 1895–1900; listed his recreations in *Who's Who* as 'Sport of all kinds—hunting, racing, deerstalking, shooting'.

[2] Lady Margaret Lygon (1874–1957), m. 1894, 2nd Baron Ampthill; she was a Lady of the Bedchamber to Queen Mary from 1911.

[3] Lady Bertha Mabel (1866–1943), widow of Major Arthur Dawkins.

[4] Princess Mary (1897–1965), daughter of George V; Margot added a marginal note here: 'The Queen has mobilised her smile, and, considering we were only looking at agenda and flannel patterns, she was inappropriately gay.'

[5] Lady Maud Evelyn Hamilton (1850–1931), m. 1869, 5th Marquess of Lansdowne; a Lady of the Bedchamber to Queen Alexandra, 1905–9; for Lansdowne, see Biographical Notes.

[6] Mary Elizabeth Milner (1867–1963), m. 1888, Alfred Harmsworth, later Lord Northcliffe (see Biographical Notes).

[7] Mary Ethel Burns, m. 1899, Lewis Harcourt (see Biographical Notes).

dinner H., Montagu and I were talking together. Montagu was saying what a wonderful financial brain McKenna had; that he was in fact quite beyond words quick, clever and resourceful; that he and the Ld Chief Justice (Rufus Isaacs*, who has given all his time to helping Ll.G.) really did the whole thing. Henry: 'I suppose if we left them to themselves, they could do everything, and you and I, Montagu, would be like their clerks!'

Tuesday 11 August 1914

I said goodbye to Sir John French*, the man who will command the Expeditionary Force. I love General French, and felt infinitely sad to say goodbye to him. He put his arm round me, and blessed me. I gave him a little sort of medallion of a saint, which he said he would wear through the war. We could not speak. Henry came in and took him away out of my room—he took my two hands and whispered 'I shall never, never forget you.' I heard him say 'Well, sir—' as he shut the door which divides Henry's room from mine....

Sir Edward Goschen[1] lunched (our ambassador in Berlin). He is a brother of my dear old friend,[2] who was for so many years in the Tory Government: a good-looking, attractive man, who told us quite amazing things of the barbaric brutality of the Germans in Berlin. They had assaulted and hurt several members of the Russian embassy as they left, and beaten the First Sec. and his American wife over their heads, and spat in their faces.

The German soldiers held up the special train with the French ambassador and suite in it, and demanded £200 in gold; then made each sit in the centre of a different carriage, daring them to move or look out of the windows, or they would shoot them—a German soldier at the door of

[1] Sir (William) Edward Goschen (1847–1924), KCMG 1901, Bt., 1916; ambassador to Vienna 1905–8, to Berlin 1908–14.
[2] George Joachim Goschen (1831–1907), cr. Viscount 1900; Liberal, later Liberal Unionist, MP 1863–1900; First Lord of the Admiralty 1871–4 and 1895–1900; Chancellor of the Exchequer 1886–92.

each corridor carriage, with loaded revolvers in their hands. 'I was more fortunate, as the Berlin mob only broke all the windows of the Embassy, so that the Kaiser had to apologize.'...[1]

Wednesday 19 August 1914

Alice Keppel*, Edward VII's mistress—the last declared lady of any King, I should say...was a Scotch girl, and I knew her when I was a girl—Alice Edmonstone. She is a typical *femme maitresse*....She is coarse, kind, truthful and gay. She is a woman who has done what she liked all her life....Alice is clever, and essentially kind and good-hearted. I allowed Elizabeth to pay her first visit alone (since she came out) to Holland, to stay with Alice—a strange choice, you might say, for me to have made—but my experience is that women like Alice Keppel are more careful with their girls than most women....Elizabeth returned August 1st, when war looked near....None of the party believed in the war, but laughed at her....

Sunday 23 August 1914

Have stuck up Gen. French's ADC General's badges by the side of my bed. The star is beautiful, and all three emblems very precious....

H. arrived in motor from Lympne at 2 am. He looked anxious and worried.... To be here just now, with a European war raging at the end of a wire is terribly interesting; and I must watch to see that Henry's health is good, and that little things go smoothly for him. Sometimes his windows are shut, and I go in every night to see that they are wedged and wide open. Alas! there is so little I can do for him just now. I never felt so helpless, but I am observant, and he doesn't resent my carefulness.

---

[1] See Gerard, *Four Years*, 91–5; *BDW* xi. 350–4; *Goschen Diary*, 48–50. These three sources cited bear out much of what Margot wrote. Goschen's official report was released to the press, 27 Aug., which gave it prominence, 28 Aug. 1914.

Monday 24 August 1914

At 8 am the housemaid brought me tea....Henry came into the room, looking very grave. H. 'Bad news—the Germans have taken Namur.' We've been driven back with the French; terrible fighting since Saturday; only one name—dangerously wounded, young Ld Leven.² We shall have an awful list of casualties. I <u>cannot</u> understand how Namur <u>can</u> have fallen, if it's as strongly fortified as we are told. The position now is very serious. I must go and see K., then we have a cabinet.'³

I saw at once that H. was terribly upset. It came like a thunderclap to me. The very first time our fresh, keen, wonderful force were in battle, to have to <u>retreat</u>!⁴ H. told me K. had cursed and sworn, and that he (H.) much feared the French had been out-generalled by the Germans; and only wondered if our lot had been in any way cut off.

<u>A Black Day</u>
Gen Cowans⁵ lunched.

Gen. C. I expect we've lost about 6000 men, all told.⁶ If so, it's very good.

   M. (appalled) Would this be considered <u>good</u>?

Gen. C. Certainly. The losses, my dear Mrs Asquith, will be <u>tremendous</u> in this war. I'm very much afraid these restless Frenchmen have done some folly. (At lunch [he] told us he had had an order from the front to send out 1,200 <u>miles</u> of tenting. They had already sent out 600 miles. He was interesting about K.)

---

¹ It had been abandoned by the Belgian 4th Division at midday, 23 Aug.
² Archibald Alexander Melville (1890–1947), who had succeeded as 15th Earl of Leven and Melville in 1913.
³ *The Times* had expected Namur to withstand a siege for six months: Tuchman, *Guns*, 295. Kitchener seems already to have told Churchill the news: *World Crisis*, i. 268–9.
⁴ Margot's ignorance about military affairs prevented her from realizing how small the BEF was by comparison with the continental armies.
⁵ General Sir John Steven Cowans (1862–1921), KCB 1913; Quarter-Master General, and a member of the army council, 1912–19.
⁶ The BEF suffered just over 1,600 casualties at Mons, 23 August, and was forced to retreat to south of the Marne, marching around 200 miles in thirteen days (the 'retreat from Mons').

Gen. C. You have to <u>know</u> K. to work with him, or you're done. He gives impossible orders, always to the wrong men. I never think of obeying, but just pass the order on to the right man. I assure you, he caused chaos and despair at first. You cannot get a new army: you <u>must</u> use the machinery that is there. Ld Haldane's Territorial machinery he thought he could put away. He made a fool of himself. Luckily, some strong hints from the PM and Haldane made him change at once.

M. That is the jolly part of K.

Gen. C. Yes, but he put everyone out, and created a lot of unnecessary worry and chaos in the War Office.[1]

H. Up to now, K. has been perfectly right in his forecast of the German plan of campaign.[2]

Apropos of this, Haldane said in his dreamy way to me 'K. is a very clever man. The difficulty at first was that he is a man of <u>great</u> authority, and considerable ignorance, but this will improve'. I know K. well, and am amazed often at his ignorance, but as H. and Haldane say, he is teachable, not obstinate, and very clever. He gets on well with H., who likes him, and finds him quick, which with <u>Henry</u> is everything. K. <u>never</u> bores.

After lunch, we had an agonizing day. The general impression was that the French had run away! Gen. French's wire, which H. read to me in the morning, said our men had reluctantly retreated, and they seem to have been retreating ever since. The retreat was quite wonderfully executed, we hear, but we know nothing. All that afternoon, we waited, wondering if our poor fellows had been cut off....I feel quite sure Joffre* is a d---d fool, and that, as usual, the French have no generals.[3] How I hate a nation

---

[1] Cassar, *Kitchener*, 198–202.

[2] *Asquith–Stanley*, 177–8. Cf. the judgement given on Henry Wilson's performance, 23–4 Aug. 1914, in Terraine, *Mons*, 24, 86–8. In Kitchener's view the German high command would not have committed themselves to invading central and north Belgium unless they had seen a heavy concentration on that route as the means of securing a quick victory over France. He realized that, in a German view, it would be worth attacking Liège and alienating the British in order to deal rapidly and decisively with the main French army.

[3] Margot's comment provides a characteristic mixture of insight and error. Joffre had been slow to react to the danger from the German right wing; but from 25 August he conducted

of this type. The Germans in this war up to now have shown themselves to be great, coarse, savage brutes, valuing their own lives, and other people's, as little as Chinamen: but take the best German, and the best Frenchman, and I know which of the two I would like to go tiger-hunting with!! I know nothing of what has happened and may be quite wrong. There is perfect silence in Downing St., but I see by H.'s face that some terrible blunder has been made.

We waited till nearly 2 a.m. for news, sitting like people in a Maeterlinck play:[1] Oc*, myself, a friend of Cys's, Williams, in khaki, waiting for marching orders: the Harcourts*; Blackwell from Home Office; Sir C Mathews,[2] public prosecutor; our two secretaries, Bongie*, [Eric] Drummond*. I made H. play bridge. Anxious minister after minister called to ask for news.

(We had finished bridge, and were sitting chatting or silent.)

Drummond (to H.) A dispatch has come in, Sir, and is being decyphered at War Office.'[3] (Fearful excitement. H. went down to cabinet room. Crowds of men waiting; nothing more arriving. Eric rushes across to War Office—no K. there—no decyphered message, it had gone to K. Where was K.? Why did he have a bed and bath put into WO, if he doesn't sleep there?)

Someone: I hear he was dining with A. Balfour.

Another: He won't make Arthur sit up after 11 o'clock.

An authority: Ly Wantage has lent him her house: telephone there.[4]

a re-grouping which was the basis of the allied victory on the Marne. French generalship during the opening battles suffered from the degree to which, from 1900 to 1904, proven republicanism had been a precondition for promotion. Some of Joffre's 1914 commanders were too old to stand the strain of war. By 6 September he had dismissed three army-, seven corps-, and thirty-four divisional-commanders: Strachan, *First World War*, 226–7; for Joffre's pre-war planning, 189–98.

  [1] Maurice Maeterlinck (1862–1949), Belgian playwright, poet, and essayist, and leading figure in the Symbolist movement; awarded the Nobel Prize in Literature in 1911.

  [2] Sir Charles Willie Mathews (1850–1920), Kt. 1907, Bt. 1917: Director of Public Prosecutions, 1908–20.

  [3] This telegram from French was not, in strict terms, a 'dispatch'.

  [4] Lady Harriet Sarah (d. 1920), widow of 1st Baron Wantage, placed her house, 2 Carlton Gardens, at Kitchener's disposal until March 1915.

This was done at once—confused return to telephone—irritable talk. Eric 'Hullo? I'm the PM's secretary. Who? Who? Yes, the butler—all right, tell Ld Kitchener the P. Minister wants to see the message from Gen. French at once. Hullo?' (to all of us listening, 'Oh, damn!—he's not the butler; he has gone.') After much irritation, and various men being sent off, I went to H. in cabinet room. H. (very angry) 'Tell Bongie or Drummond to go to K., and say I must have the dispatch <u>at once</u>. D—d cheek. Don't let this happen again.'

Loss of over 2000.[1] Fighting since Sat. 22nd, but all in line again after hideous losses on both sides. A sigh of relief. At any rate the flower of the British army has not been cut off. The lines of communication are open still.[2]

Thursday 27 August 1914

We all went to the House, and heard Henry move the resolution expressing the admiration of H. of Commons for the heroic resistance offered by Belgium to the invader, and pledging the support of this country to its gallant ally. *The Times* said Henry's speech would become historic.[3] All the papers raved about it, and I must say I trembled with admiration.

---

[1] The losses at Mons were very largely in the 2nd Corps which had performed brilliantly. For the charge of the 9th (Queen's Royal) Lancers 'to save the guns' see Buchan, *Grenfells*, 193–201. The 2nd Corps and 4th Division together lost over 8,000, 26 Aug., in a successful defensive battle at Le Cateau—more than Wellington at Waterloo: Searle, *1886–1918*, 666.

[2] Margot was right to stress this. Von Kluck, who commanded the German First Army, was intent on working round the BEF's left wing; by 24 August he was convinced that it would now retreat westwards to the Channel ports. His failure to ascertain what Sir John French and his corps commanders were actually doing was one reason for the survival of the BEF and their ability to take part in the Allied victory on the Marne: Strachan, *First World War*, 233. Von Kluck's insubordinate attitude, when he had been made temporarily von Bülow's subordinate, also helped the BEF: Strachan, *First World War*, 235.

[3] Asquith paid tribute in the Commons, 27 Aug., to the Belgian resistance to the German invasion, acknowledging the large debt that Britain owed to that small country: 'Future generations of Englishmen will assuredly read with pride Mr Asquith's orations on the war.' (*Times*, 28 Aug. 1914, 9e).

Friday 28 August 1914

Henry looked dog-tired. At lunch, he told us that one of our officers had come home this morning from the war, with a very slight wound. He had asked to see K. The latter asked if he had come from General French. When K. heard he had not, he said 'Then arrest him.' H. and I motored *à deux* two and a half hours, past Hatfield. I referred to K.'s action, and said I thought it was horrid, as the poor young man might have known no better, and had real news to tell us, which would be refreshing, since we were so completely in the dark.

H. It's a side-light on K.'s methods.

(I saw on a poster 300,000 Germans against our men.)

M. Is it possible?

H. Yes, they are three to one now, if not more, fighting against our poor devils.

(I could not speak—it appalled me. On the next poster I saw 'Indians come to help'.)

M. Is that true?

H. Yes, we decided it at yesterday's cabinet. They will land at Marseilles—our native troops. They were going to Egypt, but now we think we must have every man we can in France.

(We flew like swallows through rather empty streets.)

M. Will the Indians be in time?

H. It depends what time means: there are more French than Germans, if they will only fight![1]

---

[1] At the War Council on 5 August it was decided to transport two Indian divisions to Egypt; the severity of the fighting in France and Belgium ensured their onward passage, however, and eventually four Indian divisions (Indian Expeditionary Force A) were deployed in the Ypres salient in October 1914, having arrived at Marseilles from the end of September. The French difficulty was that originally too few divisions had been placed opposite the German right wing, where the BEF was heavily outnumbered, and forced into the famous retreat from Mons to the Marne; but Joffre's transfer of troops to this sector had begun several days before Margot wrote this diary entry, and so the balance had begun to shift. The three German right-wing armies (24.5 divisions) confronted 17.5 Allied divisions, 23 Aug., but 41 divisions, 6 Sept.: Strachan, *First World War*, 242–3.

I sat quite still to make H. sleep, which he did between these short intervals of speech. I could see he was tired and low. He constantly said 'I can't <u>think</u> why we get no news. It's all the fault of the French. We've been fighting since 22nd: it is now 28th, and we've got none of the names of dead and wounded. It is terrible.' I found the secretaries, when I got home, angry with K. for not having attempted to get news from the arrested officer. I can see K. is far from popular. He advertises himself in rather a boring way. I saw a Mrs Munro, who brought our governess Frau a letter from her husband. (Frau left on 26th August, Lucy [Graham-Smith]*, V., E. and I seeing her off 9.30 Victoria.) This lady told us that the little children in Coblenz were marching up and down with little sticks singing out 'We're going to dide in London!! 1914!! 1914!!'—meaning 'dine' in London. She says there is a bitterness and savagery of feeling against us in every German breast, from the tiniest to the oldest, which is past belief.[1]

Sunday 30–Monday 31 August 1914

We spent Sunday 30th August 1914 at Lympne, with my cousin, Frances Charteris, and Guy and Dinah.[2] I was, and indeed we all were, becalmed from the strain of an agonizing week—the first week of the greatest and most savage European war that has ever been known. What times to live in! At first I thought I was lucky to be alive, but I was beginning to feel that, before it is over, I shall see all I love best in deep incurable sorrow, and wonder if I <u>am</u> so lucky![3] We motored to the Folkestone Hospital, and

[1] The Kaiser's optimism during Aug. 1914 (telling departing troops: 'You will be home before the leaves have fallen') was for public consumption. Once he was sure that Britain would enter the war he feared defeat: Tuchman, *Guns*, 95, 143–4, 206. The bitterness reflected general resentment against the British for turning against the country which was ethnically closest to them, and for supposedly concealing until the last moment that this 'treachery' was being planned: see Tuchman, *Guns*, 154.

[2] Frances and Dinah were Margot's nieces. Frances Lucy Tennant (1887–1925) m. 1912, Guy Lawrence Charteris (1886–1967), brother of Cynthia Asquith. Geraldine Bryde Tennant ('Dinah') (1889–1974) m. 1915, Sir Ian Colquhoun of Luss, Bt. (1887–1948).

[3] Margot was not unusual in either her initial excitement at the prospect of war (diary, 29 July 1914, p. 6 above) or her later reaction. The embittered poets of the war's later years had been writing about it earlier as romantically as Rupert Brooke or Julian Grenfell: see (Wilfred) Owen, *Poems*, i. 116, ii. 504; Silkin, *Out of Battle*, 27 (Rosenberg), 133 (Sassoon);

I saw, for the first time, our wounded: men that had fought from the first day.

I concentrated on a Tommy in Gough's[1] cavalry (the whole cavalry is under [Allenby]).[2] He was a bright, sharp fellow. He had put his arm and shoulder out, and broken some fingers, so was not very ill. He told me he and 'three others took ten of the Kaiser's Death Heads.[3] Our lances are bamboo, the Germans' much heavier. They hate steel, and won't face bayonets or lances. Before we came up full tilt, they dismounted and put down their lances. They aren't good soldiers. None of us mind them at all, and they've no idea of shooting, but they have heaps of machine guns and big guns, and clouds of aeroplanes give the range. Why, I tell you, they fairly came on into the lot of us, wave after wave of closely packed men, and our line very thin.' He had never seen a Frenchman, nor had any of the men I saw. This, of course, accounted for the order to retreat—those awful days of perpetual retreat from 22nd till 26th, when our men stopped fighting.

31st no news. Henry came into my room, looking almost ill from worry. He told me that K. had gone off to Paris at 3 a.m., after the Monday 31st cabinet.[4] He said K. and he were so upset at getting no messages or proper news, that Tuesday 1st at 3 a.m. he thought K. had better go: so no one at War Office even knows, and he will be back tomorrow night.

Winter, *War and People*, 289 (Sorley). Some of the privileged young did not greet the war's outbreak simply as a glorious adventure: see Mrs Brooke on Rupert's hatred of 'the idea of war', and Arthur Asquith on the '*beastly* duty' of fighting: Bonham Carter, *Diaries, 1914–45*, 44, 205.

[1] General Hubert (de la Poer) Gough (1870–1963), KCB 1916; commanded 3rd Cavalry Brigade, 1914; 2nd Cavalry Division and 7th Division, 1915; I Army Corps 1916; V Army, 1916–18.

[2] Maj.-Gen. Edmund Henry Allenby (1861–1936), KCB 1915, cr. Viscount 1919; commanded 1st Cavalry Division on arrival in France, and the Cavalry Corps on its formation in October 1914; succeeded Plumer as commander, V. Corps, 6 May 1915; commander, Third Army, 1915–17; C.-in-C., Egyptian Expeditionary Force, 1917–19; conducted victorious campaign in Palestine.

[3] Death Heads: those wearing the *totenkopf*, the skull and crossbones emblem in use over hundreds of years by German regiments.

[4] The decision to send Kitchener was taken not at the cabinet, as Margot implies, but at a midnight 'conference', and he left at about 1.30 a.m. by special train: see *Asquith–Stanley*, 212–13.

Thursday 3 September 1914

K. saw Millerand,[1] who said he was neither hopeful of winning, nor des-pairing; a great mistake had been made by Joffre, and a sort of mutual misunderstanding, but that the effect of this had been to make the present position all right. I confess I felt amazed and stunned, that the French weren't more miserable, but perhaps they are.[2]

Edgar Vincent,[3] Violet and I were waiting for lunch when H. said, sud-denly coming through the folded doors, 'Nothing can be more serious than our position—indeed, the whole situation at the front. The French Government has left Paris, and gone to Bordeaux. (I saw in the papers that that they were jeered at—'There you go, you runaways! Off you go!')....

Friday 4 September 1914—Hackwood[4]

Henry and I went down to George Curzon's* to meet the Queen of the Belgians.[5] It was the first time I had met George to speak to since he had written his ridiculous letter (May 17th), saying that my meeting his guests might have provoked a scene at his ball—poor old boy; but I never turn a hair if I'm really fond of anyone, so I was quite at my ease, walking into the garden to join him and Ly Lansdowne[6] at tea (at Hackwood, Basingstoke).

They were full of excitement over the first joint party meeting, held that morning in the Guildhall. George, I could see, longed to have been

[1] Alexandre Millerand (1859–1943), French Minister of War, 1912–13, and 26 Aug. 1914–Oct. 1915.
[2] Joffre was already planning his attack on the Marne. His orders for it were issued 10 p.m. 4 Sept.: it began a.m., 6 Sept.: Strachan, *First World War*, 251–2.
[3] Sir Edgar Vincent (1857–1941), cr. Baron d'Abernon 1914; Viscount, 1926; served in dip-lomatic service and was ambassador to Berlin 1920–6; former Unionist MP, he became a Liberal over tariff reform; a close friend of the Asquith family, and godfather to HHA's granddaughter Cressida Bonham Carter.
[4] Hackwood Park, Hampshire: a late 17th-century house, remodelled early in the 19th by Lewis Wyatt; leased from 1907 by Lord Curzon.
[5] Elisabeth (1876–1975), m. 1900 Albert I, King of the Belgians.
[6] Lady Lansdowne: after meeting her Asquith wrote to Venetia Stanley: 'She is nice but *au fond* quite a cat': *Asquith–Stanley*, 221. A term used then for a lady liable to use her claws.

there. It was very striking seeing Henry, Arthur and Bonar Law all on the same platform, moved to the core by this horrible war, and the false pretensions which led up to it. I described the vast mass of men standing in silence, the wonderful depth of their enthusiasm, and the effect of Henry's fine speech. George listened like a boy.[1]

As I was smoking my cigarette, I took note of the party we were asked to meet. George meandered off, and brought the Queen up to us—a woman of no significance, dull, sensible, short, with no sort of charm, and a poor understanding; she spoke broken English, and nothing would make her speak French; Ly Lansdowne, always charming, limited, with a courteous *acceuil*[2] and faint atmosphere of old-fashioned humour; Bonar Law, mediocre and flat; then a surprising semi-professional couple!—Mr and Mrs Rubens, second-rate Jewish, and full of small, cheap change and social alacrity....

George arranged his dinner-table very well. He took in the Queen, but put her between Lansdowne* (who took me in) and Henry. He put himself next to Henry, and I had Bonar Law the other side of me. Thanks to H. and George, and my talking across the table, we had one of the sort of general talks which I love, and was brought up on, and which no young people can carry on now, unless the table is very small....

Bonar Law asked me if it was true Kühlmann* (First Sec. to Lichnowsky) had given wrong information to the Kaiser. I had to say that I thought Kühlmann believed in civil war in Ireland as certainly the Kaiser did, and that the army would not fight for the Liberal Party. 'How perfectly childish,' was all he said.[3] Anyone more out of his *assiette*[4] than Bonar Law in society, is difficult to imagine. I have come to the conclusion that [he] is of that Scotch blood so difficult to describe. He is cun-

[1] For text see Asquith, *War*, 13–19. When this speech was delivered the BEF was some 25 miles south-east of Paris.
[2] Fr. 'welcoming manner'.
[3] In Aug. 1917 Theodore Roosevelt told G. W. Russell: 'Carson, Smith and Company, and the English Tories who backed them, are more responsible for this War than any other...men in the world except the German General Staff': *Theodore Roosevelt Letters*, viii. 1220–1. Such statements should be treated with reserve. It became known in Britain in 1918 that Lichnowsky had also assured the Kaiser about Britain's inability to intervene effectively in a European war.
[4] Fr. 'to be ill at ease'.

ning, cautious and shallow; very quick, hopelessly uneducated and naïf. A feeling of half-mourning clings to his personality. He invests everything with dullness.[1]

After dinner, we all went out together. The Queen, who was dying to talk alone to H., sat on the edge of a hard, but very red, velvet sofa, and began talking—H. said, very sensibly—about the war, and her King, etc. George and I had a little tête-à-tête. I asked him if, before he had quarrelled with Kitchener in India, when he delighted in him, he had found him business-like, at which he was hugely pleased. Dear old boy! he is easily drawn, and his laugh is delicious. After describing the chaos that K. always brought about, he said he was all the same a <u>very</u> clever man, full of energy and drive, and, he thought, would help recruiting. I can see K. is not a great favourite with the opposition. Bonar Law said to me he was (K.) like Ld Northcliffe* of *The Times*—he didn't mind much <u>how</u> he did things, as long as he got them done.

I could not resist saying to B. Law that I thought the Editor of *The Times* a treacherous brute, and that publishing the stuff he did had brought our fine *Times* newspaper down very, very, low, quite as much as making it a 1d paper (instead of 3d, which it was till this year).[2] Bonar Law looked a little suspicious, and said

[B. Law] You need not warn me, Mrs Asquith, against Northcliffe. I know
him exceedingly well. You can't expect me to take such a severe
view of F. E. Smith* as you do.

M. Why not? Politics has got nothing to do with the blunders he
has made in his censorship. The article about our failures, which
he [allowed to be] published in Sunday's *Times* ([30] August
1914) was translated into every language, and widely circulated.

---

[1] The text from 'I have come to the conclusion...' to the end of the paragraph takes the form of a marginal note.

[2] The price (already lowered to twopence) had been reduced to one penny, 16 Mar. 1914. The Liberals had no daily of *The Times'* standing. The *Daily Chronicle* cost ½d. Margot told Bonar Law that, in allowing these articles which would give the enemy comfort, Northcliffe and F. E. Smith had combined in committing a treacherous act.

> At times when Italy and Turkey are up for auction, this kind of thing does a lot of harm.
>
> B. Law   Poor F.E., he has suffered a great deal over his mistake, and has not been fairly treated by *The Times*.[1]
>
> M.   Oh! I'm sorry if he has suffered.

George thought the evening was fading, so asked Mrs Rubens to sing. I admired Bonar Law. He got up and went as far as he could from the piano. George settled himself comfortably down in a huge red velvet and gold Venetian chair, and listened with a pained but interested expression to a variety of songs, sung with frightening gusto and perfect ease by Mrs Rubens,[2] standing well away from the piano. In every interval, H. and the Queen dashed into conversation, like canaries—the more music, the more conversation....

Just as H.'s motor was announced (he went back to London at 11 after dinner) Mrs Rubens had the bad inspiration to sing 'something light' at my request. She placed one knee on a chair, and with pretty hands on slim hips, sang a nigger song 'Kissing at the gate'—luckily short, and wonderfully vulgar. I amused myself watching the faces of the audience—Bonar Law looking like a Scotch grieve who had heard that the effect of the war 'had held back the bidding for black-faced rams at the sale in Lanark' (as I read in the *Scotsman*); the Queen, with immobile *profile-perdu*,[3] appeared like a shocked Swiss nursery governess; Ld Lansdowne erect, but with an attentive, if rather chilly smile; Ly Lansdowne yawning; and H. in such a position that no one could see his face.

---

[1] Two articles on the BEF's retreat had appeared in Northcliffe papers on Sunday, 30 August. Both were rather alarmist in tone. Arthur Moore's 'Amiens dispatch' had been published in a special Sunday edition of *The Times*. Neither that paper nor the *Weekly Dispatch* had expected F. E. Smith, the censor, to allow publication, and Northcliffe, when attacked about both, let it be known that Moore's dispatch had in fact been 'carefully edited for publication' by Smith's office (*The Times*, 1 Sept. 1914, 9a). Smith had been appointed press censor on the outbreak of war, a 'spectacularly inappropriate' job for him: 'He was not a success, and lasted only a few weeks' (John Campbell, *ODNB*, 'Smith, Frederick Edwin').

[2] The songs included what Asquith called 'the most wall-and-ceiling penetrating version of "Annie Laurie"'; *Asquith–Stanley*, 221. For Esher's admiration of Mrs Rubens's singing see *Esher Journals*, iii. 45–6.

[3] Fr. 'portrait showing more of the back of the head than face'.

Saturday 5 September 1914

At breakfast next day, B. Law and I had a tête-à-tête talk, apropos of Arthur Balfour. He said he was probably one of the greatest men living today. I said that if Arthur had gone in for anything but politics, he would certainly have been a greater man. He agreed with me.

BL I suppose he is a considerable philosopher.

M. I wonder: to me his philosophy is interesting, like all the speculations of a deeply religious man who writes well would be.

BL Surely, Mrs Asquith, you would not call Mr Balfour a religious man—not an orthodox man.

M. I should say yes: orthodox is a very awkward word, and conveys different things to different people; but I should say, taken in its widest form, Arthur Balfour's religion is orthodox. (His Gifford lectures this year were of the deepest interest.)...[1]

Monday 7 September 1914

Arthur Balfour dined: he, Henry, Baker,[2] and Winston, Violet, Elizabeth, Venetia and I made eight. Winston was in great form. He is the one happy man, Henry says, in his cabinet. (Grey has nearly broken down.) He said he was all for dash on land, but caution at sea. I can't remember all he said, but will ask Violet to write one or 2 sentences for me. I walked Arthur back to Duke of York's monument. He told me to read Cramb,[3] a little book on Germany's feeling towards us. I never saw him more charming. He walked me back again to the garden at No. 10.

---

[1] Given at Glasgow University, and published, 1915, as *Theism and Humanism*.

[2] Harold Trevor Baker (1877–1960), a Winchester contemporary and lifelong friend of Raymond Asquith, whose Oxford success he rivalled (New College, 1896–1900); Liberal MP for Accrington, Lancashire, 1910–18; parliamentary private secretary at War Office, 1910–11, and financial secretary, 1912–15.

[3] *England and Germany* by Professor J. A. Cramb (1862–1913); an edition of lectures given in 1913; described by Asquith as 'a rhetorical prejudiced book', *Asquith–Stanley*, 230.

September 1914

[Francis Grenfell] wrote and asked me to go and see him in…hospital on 3rd Sep 1914; he was the first officer I've seen returned (wounded in 3 places).[1] I met one or two of my sillier friends who told me he was certain to get the Victoria Cross—he had shown quite amazing courage and resource.…I observed that if Ld K. overheard this sort of talk Francis would have no chance of getting decorated.

I felt thrilled when the nurse showed me into a bleak bed-room with my beautiful friend lying in bed, his arm and half his body bandaged. There is Spanish blood in the Grenfells and Francis has a very handsome face.…He was very restless but perfectly well except for his wounds. He had two bullets through the leg, another he told me blew the heel off his boot, and a fourth pierced his coat sleeve without hurting him and three of his fingers are put out of action.

He told me how he and Rivvy (twin brother) and a handful of men kept the line…how no French troops came to help them.…'I don't remember very clearly what happened but the first voice I heard, when I had been taken God knows where, was Rivvy's—"Bless the old boy," I said, "so you're alive."…just as we were getting comfortable he came galloping in and said "Hurry out! The Germans are coming"—out we crawled—I don't suppose we shall ever see any of those who couldn't crawl again; that's the worst of a retreat, leaving our grand fellows in the hands of brutes like the Germans. I hid in the grass at the side of a road and by the

---

[1] The twin brothers Francis (1880–1915) and Riversdale ('Rivvy' or 'Rivy') (1880–1914) Grenfell belonged to a distinguished military family, and both saw action with the 9th (Queen's Royal) Lancers, at Mons, 23–4 Aug. 1914, where they held the rank of captain. Francis was sufficiently badly wounded on the 24th to need a tourniquet, the application of which was delayed, as it took his friends some time to find the relevant instructions in the Field Service Regulations. For his actions that day he was awarded the VC: he was one of nine gazetted 16 Nov. 1914. By this date his brother, Riversdale, was already dead, killed in action on 14 Sept. while directing fire on German positions; the brothers are the subject of John Buchan's *Francis and Riversdale Grenfell, a Memoir* (1920). Rivy, after meeting Margot at Hatfield in December 1905, reported: 'I made great pals with [her]…she is an absolute clinker': *Francis and Riversdale Grenfell*, 79.

luck of the devil heard a motor. I shouted out and there was Westminster:[1] he shoved me into his car and drove me right away to the sea. Poor little Garstin, I'm afraid he is killed.'[2]

Just as Francis was telling me this the nurse came with Sir W. Garstin's card.[3] 'Oh! what can I say to him—he is devoted to this only boy'. M: 'Don't see him—after all you don't know if his boy is killed or not'...When I went downstairs I met Sir W. Garstin...he looked anxiously at me to see if I had heard of his son. I said nothing except that Francis would get all right. I could not trust myself to speak—something in his wooden pathetic face made me jump into the motor as fast as I could.

Friday 18 September 1914—Edinburgh

Henry, Violet, Raymond*, Cys and Katharine arrived just before dinner from London. He looked well, I thought, though tired.

The Lord Provost[4] took me in to dinner at Sir William and Ly Haldane's.[5] He told me he had asked Rosebery* to help him over the huge [Edinburgh] meeting. 'He said he would do nothing, so I just said "I press no one." It got into the papers that his lordship had been asked to speak, and refused, but I know him well—he'll speak all right, but we never asked him!'

This, the 2nd meeting for recruiting, (Guildhall was the first joint party meeting) was even more wonderful in size than the London meeting; but, though Henry had a <u>marvellous</u> reception, I don't think the audience was

[1] Hugh Richard Grosvenor (1879–1953), 2nd Duke of Westminster; he had served briefly in the Royal Horse Guards at the time of the Boer War, and at the outbreak of hostilities in 1914 'went to the front in an indeterminate position on Sir John French's staff, taking with him a Rolls-Royce car with a Hotchkiss machine-gun in the after compartment. With this he succeeded in waging minor war with the enemy' (*The Times*, 21 July 1953, 8d); he later served in France and Egypt with the RNVR, and at the Ministry of Munitions.

[2] Charles William North Garstin (*c*.1884–1914), killed in action, 24 Aug., when a lieutenant serving with the 9th (Queen's Royal) Lancers; he was originally 'reported as unofficially killed'.

[3] Sir William Edmund Garstin (1849–1925), civil engineer, and a British government director of the Suez Canal Company.

[4] Robert Kirk Inches (1840–1918), Kt. 1915, Lord Provost of Edinburgh 1912–16.

[5] Sir William Stowell Haldane (1864–1951), WS, Kt. 1912, and Lady Haldane, were the brother and sister-in-law of R. B. Haldane (see Biographical Notes).

as striking.[1] They were too respectable. He made a grand speech, and was listened to with great intensity. Ld Balfour of Burleigh,[2] and Clyde,[3] a Tory member for one of the Edinburgh divisions, were on the platform. I sat between Puffin* and Elizabeth, and watched Puffin's dear little keen face. It was his first big meeting, and I could see he was enjoying himself hugely.

H. was carried off to the overflow meeting, and the family went with him. I stayed, as I thought it was more civil to Mr. Clyde, the other speaker: the latter made a boring speech. It is easy to make a bad speech on the war, but <u>very</u>, <u>very</u> difficult to make a good one. Henry's abilities are peculiarly fitted for great occasions. He is a man whose imagination, even more than his experience, has made him acquainted with grief. There is something authentic and restrained in his unrivalled gift of expression, which commands attention. It is difficult to listen to anyone after him.

When Clyde had sat down, there were great cries for 'Rozbery', who was seen leaving his seat in the dress circle. His lordship, who, as the Lord Provost rightly prophesied, had a careful speech up a careless sleeve, came forward and advised us all to go to bed, with characteristic Napoleonic abruptness; but his audience, more curious than expectant, would not have this, and after a little shouting, he sprang forward, and spoke for fifteen minutes—loud and soft, booming and oracular. He shouted 'Lies! <u>Lies</u>! Lies!' three times, but I remember nothing else.[4] It wasn't good, but had that little touch of humour and pomposity which the people in Edinburgh like, and are familiar with. Raymond put his glass in his eye, and looked on at this little drama with good humour....

[1] Asquith told Venetia Stanley that the overflow meeting was more successful: see *Asquith–Stanley*, 246–7.

[2] Alexander Hugh Bruce (1849–1921), 6th Baron Balfour of Burleigh, Secretary for Scotland 1895–1903.

[3] James Avon Clyde (1863–1944), cr. Baron 1920; Unionist MP 1909–20.

[4] See Rhodes James, *Rosebery*, 475.

Sunday 20 September 1914

Ly Frances Balfour lunched.[1] She said Henry putting the H. Rule Bill on statute book (on 15th September 1914) had brought back all the venom into the opposition.[2] I said he had done the only thing possible, and that the Amending Bill would come into operation at the same time as the Home Rule Bill; and that by the time the war was over, things would look very different. Frances agreed, and said people would soon forget this in such times as we were living in.

I said no one would forget Bonar Law's vile speech. Violet and Henry told me that <u>no</u> one liked Bonar Law's speech. I am not bitter, but no cad that was ever bred could have made a viler speech. Knowing, as Bonar Law knew from Henry's own lips, exactly what was going to be done, and having made no sort of objection in private,[3] shows me conclusively what a cunning, unreal creature the leader of the great Tory party is.

Monday 26 October 1914

This is the 84th day of the war.

It began on the 4th of August, and speaking for myself I have never felt the same person since. I don't mean to say I have <u>improved</u>! On the contrary, I think I am more impatient and alas <u>much</u> more irritable (others

[1] Lady Frances Balfour née Campbell (1858–1931), suffragist leader and churchwoman, the fifth daughter of the 8th Duke of Argyll, a Whig-Liberal government minister of long standing and some renown; she married, 1879, Eustace James Anthony Balfour (1854–1911), youngest brother of A. J. Balfour.

[2] On 15 Sept. 1914 the government placed its Home Rule Bill on the statute-book, while undertaking not to put it into operation until after the war, when the controversy over the accompanying Amending Bill would be resolved. It was an uneasy compromise in response to a complex political and constitutional problem, but Unionists objected to the hated measure even progressing this far during the war, and they walked out of the Commons en masse in protest. Asquith describes the scene, and Bonar Law's speech (the 'vile speech' referred to here), in a letter to Venetia Stanley: *Asquith–Stanley*, 239. By 15 Sept., however, few except for committed Ulsterians thought the fate of Fermanagh and Tyrone more important than that of Britain, France, and Russia.

[3] Margot was wrong: Bonar Law wrote to Asquith, 11 Sept. 1914, that the policy on which the government had decided was 'a distinct breach of the definite pledge given by you in the…Commons and repeated to me by yourself in conversation': Blake, *Bonar Law*, 229.

are that too! I think it is the awful—awe full—<u>strain</u> of the war, the impossibility of sleeping restfully even if you sleep at all.)...

I have no son in the war, thank God. Anthony is only 11 (he will be 12 on 9th Nov.) but I have Oc*, our beloved boy, who has already been in the Antwerp fiasco¹ and who will probably go out again....I have also 3 nephews in the war:² John Tennant, aged 15, on the cruiser *Bacchante*; Christopher Tennant on the *Lord Nelson* (commanded by a very dear friend, Sir Cecil Burney);³ Edward Tennant in the R. Army Flying Corps. Charlotte [Ribblesdale]'s* 3 girls⁴ married soldiers: Diana's boy-husband, Percy Wyndham, was shot on the 14th Sep. 1914; and Lovat and Harry Wilson are training the Lovat Scouts and Middlesex Yeomanry, expecting to be called to the front every day.

Ld K. seems to think it a good plan to tell all the Territorials in turn that they must be prepared to go out in 10 days or 2 weeks, but in his heart of hearts he has made up his mind not to send them out for ages! Telling the truth is not his strong point, and disappointing people puts him in good spirits (some day I must ask how K. made his reputation: I think it must have been in diplomacy)....He is a man of good judgement and bad manners; a man brutal by nature and by pose, a man of <u>no imagination</u> though

---

¹ The Allies were tardy in the extreme in lending support to the Belgians to defend Antwerp from the inevitable German assault, and the dispatch of the 7th Division and 3rd Cavalry Division under Rawlinson in the first week of October came too late. On 3 Oct., when it seemed that the Belgians were about to abandon the city, Churchill himself had arrived to stiffen its defence, his mission emanating from a consultation with Kitchener and Grey late the previous night. Churchill did much to organize the city's defences, but the three battalions of the Royal Naval Division that he summoned, and in which 'Oc' Asquith and Rupert Brooke, among others, served, were poorly equipped, and badly caught out, and Churchill was severely criticized in the press when the city fell. The most recent authoritative account of the episode (Strachan, *First World War*, 270–3), while not supporting 'fiasco', is hardly favourable to Churchill, whose failure to prolong the defence of Antwerp resulted largely from King Albert's determination to keep an area of his country west of it in Belgian hands.

² John, son of Harold Tennant; Christopher Grey Tennant, Edward Tennant's (Lord Glenconner's) second son (later 2nd Baron Glenconner); and Edward Wyndham ('Bimbo') Tennant, Edward's eldest son, who was killed in 1916.

³ Vice-Admiral Sir Cecil Burney (1858–1929), KCB 1913, Bt. 1921; second-in-command under Jellicoe, 1914; at Jutland, 1916.

⁴ The three daughters of Margot's deceased elder sister Charlotte, Lady Ribblesdale (see Biographical Notes), were: Barbara (1882–1943), m. 1905, Sir Mathew Wilson 4th Bt.; Laura (1892–1965), m. 1910, 14th Baron Lovat; Diana (1893–1983), m. 1913, Percy Wyndham.

not without ideas. Slow and cumbersome in mind (totally ignorant of most things), he is clever and even teachable in practice; a bad organizer, good administrator, he has been the despair of the War Office since he succeeded Henry.

Poor old Sir Charles Douglas[1] who lunched with us only the other day—chief of the staff here—died yesterday, to my horror. I've no doubt after what he said to me at lunch K. had helped to wear him out! Henry thinks much more of K. than I do: I wonder how long he will think so well of him!—and if I am all wrong. At present the thing I like best about him is that for an advertiser and a newspaper-man he hasn't scrupled to *flout The Times*, and what I like least about him is that he hasn't got a good character: he is very unscrupulous. Bonar Law said to me at Hackwood that K. was like Northcliffe but there he is wrong—K. is a much better fellow than Northcliffe (the latter is a wicked man for whom I have real contempt).

To return however to K., the British public and Tory party think him a god! and as I said to M. St. Clair Deville (the inventor of the great French gun)[2] 'Here in England it may or may not be difficult for a man to make a reputation, but it is impossible to lose it.' (This apropos of the French removing their generals after their first mistake in going up to Alsace and obliging us to retreat. 'Ah! *Madame, chez nous, nous avons la loyauté de circonstance.*'[3] was his reply. He congratulated England on being able to have a voluntary Army.)

I was saying that I have never felt the same since the war began—I will go further and say I don't think I shall ever feel the same. I hear a lot of

---

[1] General Sir Charles Whittingham Douglas (1850–1914), KCB 1907; Inspector-General, Home Forces, 1912–14; CIGS, Mar.–Oct. 1914; he became CIGS after resignation of Sir John French, and the demands of office took a heavy toll of his health.

[2] The 75 millimetre gun was much more effective in mobile warfare than in siege conditions or against entrenched troops. General Deville (1862–1928) had come to London, at the request of the War Office, on 22 Oct. 1914 to discuss artillery ammunition problems. For Kitchener's investigation of the fuses for the French 'seventy fives', and their modification for British use, see Cassar, *Kitchener*, 336–7.

[3] Fr. 'Ah! Madame, with us loyalty depends on the circumstances.'

people saying this!—but though it sounds horrid, I think they not only are the same but that they will <u>remain</u> the same. Those that have spoken to me have not suffered personally. There are a great many <u>very</u> rotten people in the London or England of today. This war has caught us at our worst.

The Church never had less influence than it has today. Art is down—meaningless, grotesque pictures (cubists, Futurists, etc.); invertebrate, washy, pretentious music (Debussy, etc.). Law is set at defiance—Suffragettes, Carson's army (lives threatened, churches and gardens burned, pictures in galleries torn; the gentry of Ireland, the Court and the West End encouraging, advertising, promoting and expecting 'civil war'); the army cajoled, and here and there bribed, Field Marshals signing covenants against the King's Government, Generals asking for guarantees (Gough in the Curragh row).[1] Politicians losing all sight of truth and courtesy, hurling the foulest charges against their enemy and using the ugliest language; cutting, forgetting and trying to oust all their oldest friends; and Society so flippant, callous, idle and blasphemous as to ultimately arouse in the Denis dénouement a storm of indignation and letters of protest from complete outsiders.[2] All these things I have watched from far back, growing, growing: and now that shrapnel is killing an entire generation, we are left staring at God. . . .

---

[1] As brigadier-general commanding the 3rd Cavalry Brigade, Gough was closely implicated in the Curragh 'incident' of Mar. 1914, in which troops under his command sought assurances that they would not be 'called upon to enforce the present Home Rule Bill on Ulster': see *Asquith–Stanley*, 56–8.

[2] During the evening of 2 July 1914 a group of friends that included Raymond and Katharine Asquith, Constantine Benckendorff, Diana Manners (later Lady Diana Cooper, Viscountess Norwich), and Sir Denis Anson (1888–1914, s. as 2nd Bt. 4 June 1914), held a party on a river steamer on the Thames tideway. In circumstances that are unclear Anson dived into the river, soon ran into difficulties, and drowned, along with a musician on the steamer who had come to his aid. Those at the party were the nucleus of a group known as 'the coterie', or less flatteringly the 'corrupt coterie', and which included several children of 'Souls'; the coterie affected to be 'unafraid of words, unshocked by drink and unashamed of "decadence" and gambling' (Cooper, *Rainbow*, 109–12), and were critical of their elders, and notably Margot, who disapproved of their cynical attitude, which she believed, however unjustly, was strongly in evidence in the Anson affair: see Ziegler, *Diana Cooper*, 43–5.

Sunday 25 October 1914

We spent Sunday with the Jekylls[1] at Godalming and motored over to see the German prisoners,[2] soldiers and civilians at Aldershot. It was a villainous day—sousing rain.... The wire entanglements round the interned camp are terrifying things!—no sort of cutting would ever disentangle these hideous impediments. It is a clever invention, looking so transparent and yet being so formidable. At first I felt it was painful seeing all the Germans wandering about behind the wire, but in some ways I think it was a little change for them seeing us. We were conducted round by our head soldier and an Irish Dr and one or two English soldiers.

The first camp, where the German civilians were, was <u>horrible</u>—highly uncomfortable, but very waterproof, tents—some, though few, on mud, and the others with wooden floors. One of our colonels said his tent had no wooden pavement. I asked Why? and added it was foolish to get rheumatism unnecessarily, and they said the WO could not get them wood enough, wh. I thought absurd. These poor devils complained of the discomfort and bad drainage and sanitary arrangements. Henry said they were better off than our soldiers, but I could see he was rather shocked....

(McKenna, motoring back, said he was quite horrified at the hideous discomfort and would see that it was altered.

McK. 'It is all K.'s fault! 6 weeks ago I asked him to let <u>me</u> at the Home Office take over the civilians and leave him the soldiers, but he refused, and <u>this</u> is what we see! He is a <u>most</u> trying man.')

We drank the camp tea and ate the bread—as near the sour, horrible German bread as they could make it. It was quite good. The <u>soldiers</u> were <u>quite</u> happy, singing and laughing, only too glad to be out of the war

[1] Sir Herbert Jekyll (1846–1932), late of the Royal Engineers, was a brother of the artist and garden designer Gertrude Jekyll, and Assistant Secretary at the Board of Trade 1901–11; he married, 1881, (Dame) Agnes ('Aggie') née Graham (1861–1937), DBE 1918, philanthropist and political hostess; both of their daughters married Liberal MPs, and the younger, Pamela, was the wife of Reginald McKenna; they lived at Munstead House near Godalming, Surrey.
[2] The camp was at Deepcut, near Frimley in Surrey; prisoners and internees were transferred from it in the following month.

of which they are getting heartily tired. They wore different forms of uniform—green-grey for wood fighting, blue-grey and grey. The German boss who looks after their money and wants was a nice fellow. He said to me rather grimly in English 'Your khaki is not very invisible:[1] it is too yellow. It does well enough on hard veldt ground, but in green countries it's not as good as ours....'

[Monday 26 October 1914]

Violet returned with Beb* from the front,[2] where she went in a motor with Cynthia and a new friend of mine Mr J. Dunn,[3] a very nice, clever little Canadian—I was very anxious she should have some real experience. At first she and Henry were discouraging, and said amateurs weren't wanted at the front, and other conventionalities; but she went, had a very interesting and wonderful time. The hideous waste among the wounded, the sordid quarrels, the confusion, incompetence and red tape of the War Office and Red Cross, all moved her deeply....

Tuesday 27 October 1914

I went down to see John Morley at his villa Flowermead, Wimbledon Common. He has undercurrents of bitterness over the War; this comes from faint jealousy, not so much of individuals as of the situation—he wonders if he was right in leaving the cabinet; he feels out of it, and both praises and blames Ed. Grey in the same sentence....

John spoke highly of Seely's[4] courage and stupidity (the latter seems to have asked Sir John French to give the Victoria Cross to his chauffeur,

---

[1] Like so much in the British Army, khaki uniforms had been devised for hot countries such as India: 'khaki' is an Urdu word meaning 'dusty'.

[2] For an account of this expedition see Bonham Carter, *Diaries, 1914–45*, 9–14.

[3] James Dunn (1874–1956), financier. Asquith writes in June 1914 that Dunn was not to be in that month's honours list, but he was made a baronet in 1921; see *Asquith–Stanley*, 90 n. 6.

[4] (Major-General) John Edward Bernard Seely (1868–1947), cr. Baron Mottistone 1933; Unionist MP 1900–4, Liberal MP 1906–24; Sec. of State for War 1912–14; obliged to resign over Curragh affair; on French's staff 1914; commanded Canadian Cavalry Brigade in France 1915–18. CB 1916, CMG 1918, five times mentioned in dispatches; considered by Hankey one of the bravest men he had ever known.

and when asked Why? he said 'He has driven me everywhere and never left me once.')

On the war, Morley was not really interesting. He pretended it might have been avoided, but when I squared up to him and asked 'How?' and 'When?', he was ragged and very unconvincing. All the men who are against the war on our side—or who were against it, and who don't go in heart and soul—are devoured by self-consciousness, I find....[1]

I feel the war so acutely that I am quite frightened of seeing certain people who don't feel it. When the details of the great retreat (with wh. the war opened) of our men began to come in, I felt physically ill; and one morning in Mrs Leo Rothschild's[2] house, just before one of the Queen's Committee Meeting[s], I broke down and sobbed in Peggy Crewe's[3] presence. Luckily for me she pulled me sharply together and really scolded me for 'showing so little self-control, when others much more directly concerned were showing such Pluck!' It did me a world of good. Netty Henderson[4] also, with great tenderness, implored me to keep very very calm, as terrible things would happen before the end of this war....

Wednesday 28 October 1914

Henry told me that Lloyd George and K. had had a regular row at the cabinet—'most unpleasant'. It was over giving the Colours [to] and indeed setting up the Irish and Welsh Battalions in the new army.[5] It is hardly possible to conceive K.'s stupidity and want of imagination over

[1] Margot had the stronger case. The evidence is overwhelming that no British government could have delayed the decision about intervention once it was certain that the Belgians would resist the ultimatum.

[2] Marie Perugia (d. 1937), m. 1881, Leopold de Rothschild, brother of 1st Baron Rothschild.

[3] Lady Margaret Etienne Primrose ('Peggy') (1881–1967), daughter of 5th Earl of Rosebery; m. (as his second wife), 1899, 1st Earl of Crewe (cr. Marquess 1911).

[4] Henrietta Dundas (d. 1959), m. 1895, Lt Gen. David Henderson (1862–1921), KCB 1914, General Officer Commanding RFC, 1914–17. She was created DBE in 1919.

[5] Asquith, writing to Venetia (Asquith–Stanley, 343), refers to 'badges' for the new 'Irish, Welsh and Ulster Divisions'. Margot probably did not realize that colours were a regimental matter. Kitchener was not good at keeping in his mind that any privilege accorded to regiments drawn from Ulster had to be accorded also to those from the rest of Ireland.

these things!! For example, I told him that the recruiting on Horse Guards Parade, just outside my bedroom window, went on from early morning, wet or fine, without of course shelter of any kind except a small tent in which names were registered.

I suggested that bands should play, so that the new men—many of whom were making enormous sacrifices of money, etc.—should feel elated, and that their womenfolk, often in passionate tears, should feel they were heroes.... K. was, however, obdurate: so I wrote to the King (after waiting for 3 weeks and getting any amount of letters complaining of the grim silence in which the new army started, and the cold comfort and muddle in which it continued).[1]

To return to the row—K. refused to do this, that, and the other over the Welsh and Irish battalions. Ll.G. lost his temper completely! (I was enchanted to hear it.) Ll.G. (shaking his fist at K.) 'You think you are a Dictator! You are only 1 of 18!!' K. 'All right, if you think you can do things so much better than I can, come over and do my job' (pointing towards War Office out of the window). Henry told me this, and continued:

[H.]   They both lost their tempers. Ll.G. was ill-mannered and insolent, and they both resigned.[2] After lunch Ll.G. was quite normal.

Montagu   I'm not at all sorry that K. caught it! I'm told Ll.G. said when K. said 'No one wants colours in khaki,' 'I never heard a more sterile remark! you show a complete want of imagination.'

H.   It was Edward Grey said that—not Ll.G. Grey thought K. quite wrong.

M.   I'm too glad K. was sat on! He richly deserves it after snubbing Jack Pease* in his admirable plan of amusing the new army in the evening, and in his treatment of German civilians.

[1] Margot's plea soon had the support of such influential people as the Lord Mayor of London and Rudyard Kipling: Kipling, *Letters*, 284 n. 2; *Daily Telegraph*, 29 Jan. 1915, reporting Manson House meeting, 27 Jan.

[2] Margot seems to have exaggerated a little here. Asquith merely told Venetia (*Asquith–Stanley*, 291): 'They came to very high words, and it looked as if either or both of them wd. resign.' Hobhouse thought that the 'rebuff' to Kitchener 'did him good': *Hobhouse Diaries*, 204.

Montagu (to Henry) Don't you think Rufus Isaacs,[1] with his Stock Exchange, Ll.G. with his Big Guns, McKenna with his sugar,[2] and in a smaller way Winston with his Antwerp[3]—each with a little stunt of their own—have performed extraordinary feats, Prime Minister?

   H. Yes. I think McKenna is the most remarkable of the lot in what he has done.

Montagu (who works with Rufus and Ll.G. for hours in the Treasury over the Stock Exchange and city things) Rufus has come out of all this marvellously! You know, PM, when you asked him when he was going back to his work, he thought you were snubbing him!

   H. What rot!! I'll write to him, if you like.

Montagu (laughing) Oh! no, I told him that you never thought of such a thing.

  Margot I would never have guessed that Rufus, with his rather commonplace mind, would have shown such resource.

Montagu I know! The most obvious talker I ever met: but you can't think how good he is—<u>so</u> unselfish, giving up hours of time. He said a very good thing to Ll.G. apropos of his row with K.: 'You know, any Minister may resign in time of Peace, but you must learn that in times of War <u>this is impossible!</u>'

This conversation between H. and myself and Montagu took place after a dinner party we had here, at about midnight.

---

[1] For the help given by Isaacs (Lord Reading) with the financial arrangements in the war's first weeks see *Riddell War Diary*, 42; *Asquith–Stanley*, 288.

[2] Some two-thirds of Britain's sugar had come from Germany and Austria-Hungary. A Royal Commission was formed, 20 Aug. 1914, empowered to buy, sell, and regulate the supply of sugar: Hurwitz, *Intervention*, 72.

[3] Churchill was in Antwerp from a.m. 3 to p.m. 6 Oct. 1914. He claimed to have gained time to enable the Allies to secure the Channel ports by preventing Antwerp's surrender until 10 October, a claim disputed in Strachan, *First World War*, 272–3. The episode, like the earlier one of the 'Dunkirk circus', had Kitchener's sanction; but both exposed Churchill to much unfair criticism: Birkenhead, *Churchill*, 310, 313.

Montagu before he went away betted me the war would be over by the 8th of June—no more shots fired after 8th June 1915 (This bet was made and taken on 28th October 1914). Henry said Montagu ought to give me a shade of odds. I stuck to it that the war would not be over till summer was gone, Nov. or December in 1915: but I went to bed happier.

Sunday 1 November 1914

Henry and I dined at Wimbledon with John Morley. There was a distinguished company....

I heard Henry chaff Rosebery very much about speaking from the dress circle at the Edinburgh meeting on Sep. 18th 1914. Ld R. kept his tail up, as he has a fine temper, but I could see he felt just a little foolish. 'You've got no idea how funny you all look on a Platform' was all he could think of to say!...

Saturday 7 November 1914

I motored over from the Wharf[1] to Summer Fields at 2.15 and took Puffin for his exeat back with me, promising to take him back to school by 8 o'clock on Sunday. His 12th birthday was Monday 9th, but we kept it Sunday 8th. I was very grateful to Dr. Williams[2] for giving his father and me this little treat. We both want cheering up. It is a great strain living in times of War....

I do hope and pray Anthony won't lose his [vitality] like Cys has. Raymond and Beb have no sort of vitality. Henry has more than any of his children. Violet has a certain amount, but I think she appears to have more than she has. The Tennants are so tremendously vital that after them no one seems to me to have much Life. When I look at my beautiful, delicious

---

[1] The Wharf, Sutton Courtenay, Oxford: riverside house acquired by the Asquiths (partly from Lady Tree) in 1911; the 18th-century structure was converted and enlarged by Walter Cave. In the grounds was The Barn, a separate building that Margot appropriated for her own use.

[2] The Revd Charles Eccles Williams (1851–1941), headmaster of Summer Fields preparatory school, 1896–1918.

daughters-in-law, I almost wonder by what impulse they move at all! (Cynthia* is less of a Spectator than Katharine*.) I expect my restless energies have a damping effect, though they worship me and I adore them.

The German spy in our midst is causing a great deal of talk. The Press, balked in every way by censorship at home and no correspondents abroad, has been making our flesh creep, and attacking the Home Office in violent language. I suppose it is always difficult to know what to do in times of war with the enemy living in the country. Thousands of Germans live in England. Unpopular as it is to say so, I confess the German is the only foreigner I have ever met who reminds me of ourselves. (However much you may like or dislike Americans, they are never like us au fond. They are always strangers on the make. I have never met one that I didn't bump up against morally and spiritually and they have not the education or intellect or simplicity of the best German.) The French are fun-people—delicious, brilliant, pleasure people to laugh with, and at, but never to count on too heavily one way or another....

There is no bitterness of feeling against the Germans in this country! We like each other: at least we like them. The Germans, however, hate us! It is curious why they should and a mystery to most of us, but it is true.... [Germany] has brought up its youth to believe that England is the enemy and would attack. (The younger generation, I am told, seriously believe we made war on Germany!!!!) ... I suppose if you lie often enough, you may end by believing what you say. (This reminds me of the widely spread lie that H. never mentioned H. Rule at the last Elections!!! I believe some Tories really believe this Lie! Or the lie about the great 'plot that failed', to coerce Ulster, which Winston, Crewe, Ll.G. etc. hatched without H.'s knowledge)....

Spy funk is not a bad test of people's character, or perhaps I should say nervous system to be fairer: Grey has suffered much from nerves in this war and he quite lost all sense of proportion about spies.[1] In consequence

---

[1] Asquith noticed signs of 'strain' in Grey as early as 9 Aug., and Grey had recently requested a week's leave; see *Asquith–Stanley*, 161, 288. Hankey soon concluded that society gossip was the main source of 'leakage': see, for instance, Roskill, *Hankey*, 185.

of a violent Press attack our First Sea Lord, Prince Louis Battenberg,[1] resigned. I was sorry for the reasons, but for the conclusion, <u>no</u>!! He is the best fellow in the world but <u>not clever</u>, and the patrolling of our coasts has not been well done. The concerted action of the Fleet has been splendid but individual actions foolish and blameworthy....

November 1914

Henry made a memorable speech at the Guildhall to a crowded assembly on 9th Nov. 1914. The speech was conspicuous by its frankness over Turkey.[2] In consequence of the *Goeben* and *Breslau*[3] joining the Turkish navy we are at war with Turkey.... Kitchener sat the other side of Henry at Guildhall—we talked across. He is certainly jolly and alive. He got a great reception, so did Winston.

Henry knocks all the others into a cocked hat. His calm, sweetness of temper, perfect judgment, sympathy, imagination and un-irritability <u>have amazed me</u>. I feel proud of being near so great a man, and told him frankly that his goodness and power have never been more felt and by

[1] Admiral Prince Louis Alexander of Battenberg (1854–1921), Austrian-born son of Prince Alexander of Hesse; he became a naturalized British subject and entered the Royal Navy in 1868; First Sea Lord, 1912–14; on 26 July 1914, in Churchill's absence (he was at Cromer, with his family), Battenberg gave the crucially important order to the First Fleet, then at Portland, not to disperse after its manoeuvres, 25–7 July, thus ensuring that at the declaration of war it was fully mobilized (see Churchill, *World Crisis*, i. 198); notwithstanding this, Battenberg was compelled to resign his post, 29 Oct., because of his 'German origins'; in 1917, at the request of George V, he changed his name to Louis Alexander Mountbatten, 1st Marquis of Milford Haven; his son, Earl Mountbatten of Burma, served with distinction during the Second World War, and was the last Viceroy of India.

[2] Reported in *The Times*, 10 Nov., 9f. Britain had declared war on Turkey, 5 Nov. 1914: Strachan, *First World War*, 680, 735–42; Howard, *First War*, 53–4; Jeffery, *Henry Wilson*, 104–5. The low estimate of the Turkish Army's capacity formed by both German and British generals after the Balkan Wars was held also by Asquith: *Asquith–Stanley*, 414–15 (Turkish failure against Suez Canal, 2–4 Feb. 1915). Gallipoli forced a revision of this estimate.

[3] The failure of the Royal Navy to intercept the *Goeben* and *Breslau*, a battle cruiser and light cruiser, respectively, before they reached Constantinople, early in Aug. 1914, contributed to the Ottoman Empire later joining the war on the side of the Central Powers. Asquith told Venetia Stanley in Aug. 1914 that the ships were to be sold to Turkey, and manned by a Turkish crew. On 29–30 Oct., however, with the *Breslau* and a Turkish squadron, the *Goeben* made an extremely destructive raid on Russian shipping and installations in the Black Sea; see Hough, *War at Sea*, 69ff.; *Asquith–Stanley*, 168.

more people than since this war began. He chaffs Elizabeth, listens to Puffin, never snubs or snaps and seems to have no self at all.

H. told me driving out to dinner one evening that the King had begged K. to let the Prince of Wales[1] go to the front—K. <u>absolutely</u> refused. The King said 'I suppose you think he will be killed?' K. 'Oh! no not that particularly, but he may be taken prisoner, which would be a score for the Enemy.'…(On 16th Nov. 1914 the Prince of Wales was allowed to go to the front.)…

Lord Roberts* died at 8 o'clock in the night of 14th Nov. 1914 at the front in France.…He was a cheerful, charming little man of sweet temper, good manners, and no mind of any kind. Although vain, he was open-minded till he fell under political influences. He was jealous of Gen. Sir John French, and in the Curragh incident and the whole Home Rule controversy came out badly. He had a lot of smallness and envy in him. He had, however, one great gift: he could make himself loved more than any soldier of our day. He <u>was</u> Tommy Atkins.…Instead of working with Haldane in his fine idea of the Territorials he did his very best to crunch and snub the whole movement.…[2]

Ld Roberts was a violent Tory and in conjunction with Milner* started the English Covenant.…[3] Gen. French [and two of his colleagues] all told me that they blushed for the money and trouble the upper Ulster Irish were using to influence the soldiers against our Government. (It was in consequence of this awfully rotten corruption, luckily localized, that Henry took the War Office).…

[1] Edward, Prince of Wales (1894–1972), Edward VIII; at the start of war he left Oxford and was commissioned in the Grenadier Guards; he hoped to see action, but this was out of the question, Kitchener insisting that there must be no risk of his being captured, and he was given instead a largely ambassadorial role in France, and was much at GHQ: Edward VIII, *King's Story*, 111–12; his frequent appearances in the battle area, however, whether in his royal Daimler or on a bicycle, did much to associate the royal family with the war effort, and involved some danger: his driver was killed by shrapnel at Loos while the Prince was visiting the front line.

[2] Among Haldane's many achievements as War Secretary, 1905–12, was the creation of the Territorial Force (later Territorial Army), an important augmentation of Britain's army reserve strength.

[3] The version of the Ulster Covenant, a mass protest against the government's Home Rule Bill, that was used on the British mainland. On 26 Aug. 1914 Lord Roberts visited Asquith in Parliament and, 'rather *émotionné*', asked him '"to forget the past" (I suppose the Curragh business &c) and assured me that he was now entirely on my side!': *Asquith–Stanley*, 198.

Thursday 19 November 1914

We dined at the Leo Rothschilds at Gunnersbury 19th [Nov.] 1914. I sat next to Charlie Grant, Ld Rosebery's son-in-law—one of the nicest fellows and best soldiers I have ever known. He had just got 3 nights leave from the trenches—60 days and nights he had been fighting, and you could see it in his eyes.[1] He is on one of the Haig* division staffs and in comparative comfort. He could hardly speak of the hardships of our poor fellows, or the amazing courage of the Germans. He said the French were very incalculable, often telling him of the impossible positions they were going to take, and never making a move towards carrying this out: <u>always</u> late and invariably restless, but very brave and on the whole calm for them. When I said I would personally rather have had Germany for an ally, as the German was much more like us, he <u>quite</u> agreed. He also agreed that Germany, not France, was the nation of the future.

He spoke very highly of Robertson and said our men had <u>everything</u> except sleep—heaps of first-rate food and clothes—but that the rain and cold was awful, and the perpetual, unresting fighting.[2] He said he was a little afraid the Indians were holding up their left hands so as to be faintly wounded and get out of the fighting line. The Roberts funeral in St Paul's cathedral was a very beautiful sight.... The old man was buried under the dome just in front of the choir steps. The last post was bugled out from the whispering galleries. It was a pea soup wet day and this gave the lighting of St Paul's great beauty. Newly placed candles of great height stood as sentinels round the coffin; the atmosphere of the cathedral was foggy so that the candle flames looked isolated as stars from their surroundings. Beautiful old soldier-faces and khaki all around—stars and decorations gleaming here and there.

Ld. Kitchener looked better than any one: he has a really grand figure, and if you can get over a very persistent ugliness his appearance

---

[1] Grant recounted his experiences of the First Battle of Ypres, Oct.–Nov. 1914.

[2] Gen. Sir William Robert ('Wully') Robertson (1860–1933), KCVO 1913, cr. 1st Bt. 1919; Director of Military Training 1913–14; QMG GHQ France Aug. 1914–Jan. 1915; CIGS Dec. 1915–Feb. 1918; rose from private to field marshal, but did not change his style with the ascent.

certainly has great authority. I expect it has contributed much to his reputation.[1]

Thursday 26 November 1914

About a week after Roberts['s] funeral K. dined. I asked him if Roberts was a really great man.

[K.] Certainly not. He was much too unforgiving, slightly vindictive, but he was a great soldier.

M. How would you compare him with Wolseley?[2]

K. Oh! not at all! They could not be put together. Ld Wolseley was a very great man.

M. How stupid of Roberts to abuse French.

K. He always disliked French long ago in S. Africa....

I never saw K. so nice as that night. He was quite playful.... [His] whole soul and mind is in this war. <u>Everything</u> is subordinate to it. His loathing of War as a factor in Human life, his perfect appreciation of the horrors of it, his ungrudging gift of all his time and his powers to finishing this war, all raise him in one's estimation. He is quite a study, but very likeable...

Considering we have not got a big army, and never meant to have one, our army is the <u>wonder of the world</u>. The answer to Simon's [Lovat's] Conscription[3] is that we <u>have</u> got a million men, and that they recruit 30,000 a week. Any form of compulsion would stop the whole fine spirit and set all wise men by the ears.

---

[1] Alfred Leete's poster of Kitchener with outstretched finger, captioned 'Your Country Needs You', had appeared in Sept. 1914.

[2] Field Marshal Sir Garnet Joseph Wolseley (1833–1913), cr. Visc. 1885; Commander-in-Chief of the Army 1895–1900.

[3] After the death of Lord Roberts, Margot had written critically about him to Simon Joseph Fraser (1871–1933), 14th Lord Lovat, an army officer and landowner who was married to her niece Laura. He replied on 23 Nov. 1914, deploring her remarks on Roberts's 'brain power', and strongly defending his conscriptionist views. Margot had not grasped either that the case for conscription was much stronger in war than it had been in peacetime, especially when Britain's two largest Allied powers had long relied on conscript armies, or that political thinking in party terms was inappropriate when the country was fighting for its life.

From a political point of view, if the Tories go in for Conscription, it would be an enormous lift for us. I think we should romp [in] at next Gen. Election! Conscription and Protection will always give the Liberal Party a long lease of life. It is a wonderful mind! the <u>kind</u> of mind that does not see the fatal effects Conscription and Protection have had on Foreign nations!...

I never thought Germany would take on such a big job. I certainly would <u>never</u> have believed that she would have blown up and bombarded Libraries, cathedrals and glorious old Buildings! A civilized nation that destroys Rheims Cathedral and kills Belgian women and children— of which we have seen several eyewitnesses—deserves universal condemnation...[1]

November 1914

London is <u>crowded</u>. It is odd to see one's husband's name in vast letters in Trafalgar Square: 'No price can be too high where Honour and Freedom are at stake. Mr Asquith'. This, out of one of his recruiting speeches, is printed in huge letters on a board which is placed between 2 of the lions in Trafalgar Square. I look at it every day of my life (here).

The terrible losses among our men in the last fighting reported fully by French Saturday made us all <u>very</u> unhappy. Many of my friends are dead. My nephew in Gordon Highlanders, Lachlan Gordon-Duff;[2] an old sporting lover, Eustace Crawley,[3] one of the best fellows I ever knew, 12th. Lancers (He commanded his regiment for 6 weeks, bird happy!) was killed; Lovat's brother, Hugh Fraser, killed....[4]

[1] Rheims Cathedral was hit by an incendiary shell on 19 Oct. 1914, and the fierce fire which broke out caused much destruction. The cathedral was subjected to repeated bombardment until 1918. It was very close to the front line, and the Germans thought that the French were using it as a look-out post. For reports and accusations about German atrocities in Belgium and France, see Strachan, *First World War*, 1117–23; although 'much exaggerated', such accounts 'were almost certainly not without some foundation' (Strachan, *First World War*, 1118 n. 18).

[2] Lachlan Gordon-Duff (1880–1914), the only son of Margot's deceased sister Pauline.

[3] Eustace Crawley (1868–1914), m. 1904 Lady Violet Finch, d. of 8th Earl of Aylesford.

[4] Hugh Joseph Fraser (1874–1914), brother of 14th Baron Lovat.

Tuesday 1 December 1914

Winston Churchill was 40 today. I wrote and congratulated him upon his youth. He has done a great deal for a man of 40. When I look round and see as I do a few young men of 35 with amazing brains, and see how much less they have done; knowing that superiority of character pure and simple is not exactly what Winston has got, 'I put myself this question' (as the dreary peer in H. of Lords started most of his speeches), and I suppose I lay myself open to the same retort as the peer 'And a d—d dull answer you will get!'

What is it that gives Winston his pre-eminence? It certainly is not his mind. I said long ago, with truth, Winston has a noisy mind. Certainly not his judgement: he is constantly very wrong indeed (he was strikingly wrong when he opposed McKenna's modest naval programme in [1909] and roughly speaking he is always wrong in his judgements about people).

It is of course his courage and colour, his amazing mixture of industry and enterprise. He can, and does always—all ways put himself in the pool. He never shirks, hedges, or <u>protects</u> himself—though he thinks of himself perpetually. <u>He takes huge risks</u>. He is at his very best just now: when others are shrivelled with Grief, apprehensive, silent, irascible and self-conscious morally, Winston is intrepid, valorous, passionately keen, sympathetic, longing to be in the trenches, dreaming of war, big, buoyant—happy, even. It is very extraordinary: he is a born soldier…

Monday 7 December 1914

Henry went to see the King on his return from visiting his troops. He told H. the vile weather rather spoilt it for him, but that he never saw so many cheerful sanguine people—particularly Poincaré (I never saw a Frenchman who wasn't either jumpy or sanguine.)…[1]

---

[1] During George V's first visit to the front, in Dec. 1914, he held long conversations with Poincaré; see Nicolson, *George V*, 259. Raymond Nicolas Poincaré (1860–1934) was Prime Minister of France 1912, President 1913–20.

Henry looked tired which always makes me sad—just as I am getting so very well, he looks to me <u>very</u> tired. I'm glad to say he had a little snooze in the afternoon after a little golf. He never thinks of himself. I don't suppose any of us have ever known so big a man so simple, easy, affectionate, light in hand and sweet in sympathy....

Thursday 3 December 1914

I went to see Queen Alexandra* on 3rd Dec. at Marlborough House. It was her 70th birthday. No one could say she looked more than 40 or 45. I never saw her look more beautiful than she did that day. In black, but not ostentatiously so, pearls round her neck, a little white lace falling half over them, and a miniature of the King round her neck the size of an oval half-crown; her skin clear, her eyes not half as bloodshot as they used to be, her beautiful, calm, finely-shaped forehead and lovely eyebrows; her wonderful gesticulations, divine, gay laugh, with her amazing grace and quickness of movement all combine to make her the most attractive, fascinating and beautiful woman in Europe. She is different to other Royal people. She is gloriously at her ease and impulsive. I quite forget anything but the sort of prestige that goes with a woman of her distinguished appearance and fine manners....

The Q. 'Why don't you send "Henry" to see me? I suppose he is very tired and busy—can he come tomorrow?' M. 'No, but he will go to you next day. He longs to see you, ma'am, for he loves you as much as I do.' (When Henry did go, she made him rock with laughter, describing Queen Victoria's death-bed and how [the Kaiser] would sit on his mother-in-law's bed till Alexandra and the nurse combined to give him 'a good push'.) ...

Tuesday 8 December 1914

Eric Drummond, H.'s 2nd secretary (a most intelligent, observant, delightful man: unique in temper, humour, kindness and courage, as well as <u>remarkably</u> clever) said to me tonight that he thought the Admiralty made a mistake in not announcing that one of our best battleships had been blown up by a German mine off the coast of Ireland: guns and ship at the bottom of the sea (over 3 weeks ago), but luckily 800—in fact the whole crew—saved. I said from what I had heard keeping it quiet was not a bad thing to do, as our men were very exhausted at that time in the long Ypres–Calais coastline, and that the news, had it reached the Germans, would have cheered them up dangerously; but that now the Germans knew through the American papers, I thought it was silly not to announce it.[1]

Eric said that sort of concealment was always dangerous, as it led the British public to think other naval disasters had happened and been kept dark. I asked Henry about this, and he said that at the Cabinet he and Ll.G. were strongly of the opinion that nothing should be kept dark (except of course news that could help the enemy in the field); but that the whole cabinet were against them, especially our 1st Admiral, Jellicoe*, in command of the whole Fleet. 'In face of Jellicoe* I could not stand out....'

H. made up his mind (after much halting and many semi-promises to the cabinet) to rid himself finally of the Aberdeens, at which she wrote both Violet and H. most wrong and undignified letters, and ever since they have been fussing and trying to stay on.[2] As Viceroys they are both abject failures, and both Redmond and Birrell* feel it (latter acutely)....I have come to the reluctant conclusion that the Aberdeens are fussy, self-important, vain people—saints in some ways, small in others; their want of self knowledge and thickness of skin is past all belief!! She is open to every form of flattery, and he is, poor darling, a perfect donkey! I am sure they will pull every string to stay on and struggle to be made Duke

[1] The sinking of the *Audacious*, one of the newest Dreadnoughts, by a German mine, had been reported by Churchill on 27 Oct. (see *Asquith–Stanley*, 287). The crew were saved because the ship sank very slowly. The *Olympic's* passengers had seen this sinking, and a photo of it had been produced, 14 Nov., in the *Philadelphia Public Ledger*.

[2] John Campbell Gordon (1847–1934), 7th Earl of Aberdeen, cr. Marquess 1915, Lord Lieutenant (i.e. Viceroy) of Ireland 1906–15; m. 1877 Ishbel Maria (1857–1939), daughter of 1st Baron Tweedmouth. For Violet's friendship with their deceased son, Archie, see next note.

and Duchess at the New Year! Had it not been for dear Archie Gordon they would have gone long ago.[1]

Thursday 10 December 1914

Sir Ed. Grey lunched in Downing St. I told him I was going to Belgium to stay with the King and Queen of the Belgians with Major Gordon (sec. to the D. of Wellington, a gentle, good, stupid man who would have put the fear of God into the Iron Duke!).[2]

Sir E. G.   I'm sorry you are going abroad; it is a great mistake. In doing these things you should always say to yourself 'What good do I do?'

M.   (I could not help thinking what a complacent ass I should be if I went about thinking I was doing good!) Perhaps it would be better to say what harm?

Sir E. G.   (looking cross) It is pure self-indulgence.

M.   Most things are self-indulgence—to some it is self-indulgent to be cheerful, to some indulgent to grouse; to some it is self-indulgent to stay at home and knit, to others it is self-indulgent to go abroad and sit with the Tommies in the Hospitals. Just now none of us can do right. Everyone is crabbed. You are laughed at for turning your house into a Hospital, and abused if you don't. I've long made up my mind that I don't mind criticism. I shall do no harm to any one going abroad, and in any case my sins will be over in 5 days.

I turned to Edgar Vincent (now Ld D'Abernon), who was delighted that I had the prospect of such an interesting visit. A little later on at lunch Grey,

---

[1] Violet Asquith had become unofficially engaged to Archie Gordon, the Aberdeens' youngest son, shortly before he died on 16 Dec. 1909 as the result of a motoring accident, and for a time she remained close to his parents. Aberdeen wanted his marquisate, which came upon his retirement from the lord lieutenancy of Ireland, to be associated with Tara, Ireland's mythical capital, but the Heralds' College were invited to discover that this most unsuitable title was not vacant; and Temair was chosen as the second title for the Aberdeens: *Asquith–Stanley*, 392.

[2] Arthur Charles Wellesley (1849–1934), s. as 4th Duke of Wellington 1900; he died at the age of 85 on the anniversary of his ancestor's victory at Waterloo.

with a little more sweetness, warned me to be very careful what I said to the King about Ld K. He said he had heard I had abused K. before people at tea. I could not deny that when I heard the English cursed for not recruiting, or Haldane cursed for believing in and having started the Territorials (as against Conscription), I have abused K., but I said I would not mention his name except to praise it.

What gossips people are, and I suppose ever will be! For if war doesn't take away pettiness, nothing will, and constantly repeating is petty. Grey would be the finest soldier in the world, and a little active service would do him a world of good. He needs outlet and outlook and being taken quite out of himself and his little habits. He is far too set and old (though very young when he makes jokes), but a great love in spite of all I'm writing! I am devoted to him. I long for a little red blood in his veins and this sometimes gets the better of me. I like crimson blood.

Eric Drummond, our 2nd secretary and one in 1000, roared with laughter when I told him about Grey. 'What a governess! Some one must have put him out. I totally disagree with him. I'm delighted you're going out, you'll cheer them all up.' I felt grateful for this: I rather miss encouragement in my home circle! I think everyone thinks I'm too old and confident, but au fond I'm very humble and grateful for all I can get (I oughtn't to complain when I can amuse Elizabeth and Puffin, which I can always do if I'm in fair spirits). Bongy, who was also very stuffy about my going (as he knew my one desire was to see Sir John French, naturally), took me to the station, where I met Major Gordon....

Saturday 12 December 1914—Belgium[1]

The King [of the Belgians] was extremely bitter about the French. (I may say all the Belgians of any authority or intelligence are the same—I should

[1] Margot arrived in Belgium on 11 December 1914. Next day she visited the King of the Belgians at his headquarters and later the same day drove to Ypres. She crossed into France, after dining with General Sir Henry Rawlinson on 13 December, intending to leave from Le Havre; but, discouraged by the weather, she eventually sailed from Boulogne on 15 December. She did not succeed in her plan to visit Sir John French. In the account which Margot gives of the visit

say they hate the French <u>quite</u> as much as the Germans). 'They were <u>always</u> late with their soldiers and could never be relied on to fulfil any promise...<u>We</u> were never meant to fight, our neutrality was guaranteed. We did our best. We never ran away. When the French came <u>they</u> ran away!'...[1]

We heard guns on Nieuport fired—the first I had heard—they gave me a thrill and we saw a good many aeroplanes hovering like beautiful birds in a clear pale blue sky...The Belgian trenches look very amateur to my unaccustomed eye. They are like rabbit hutches....The whole country for miles around inundated with sea water and the roads where they are not *pavé* are swamps of clinging nasty mud on each side. The only dry fields are full of the holes of German shells like a solitaire board...the houses are all smashed—avalanches of brick and window frames standing up in the walls like dolls' houses—no inhabitants, but soldiers smoking or cooking in the open doorways of less ruined houses. Every church—and some beautiful—littered with bits of bombs and debris of broken stained glass and twisted lead ribbons—tops of tombs, heads of stone saints, all pell mell in the grass of the cemeteries...

We motored straight to Ypres and saw what must have been a <u>beautiful</u> little town. The Cathedral and town Hall with its saints and prophets all in fragments on the streets...We drove out to the cemetery and got out to put a cross on Ld. Charles Mercer-Nairne's grave.[2] (It was only the other day I met him at the Granards' dinner, In Waiting on the King.)...

The Ypres cemetery will haunt me till I die. No hospital full of wounded ever gave me such an insight into war as that damp crowded quiet churchyard. Most of the names scrawled in pencil on bits of wood were English;

to the Front in her *Autobiography* there are many changes of wording from the diary version, and many omissions and rearrangements.

[1] These 'Belgians of...authority' could hardly have been expected to admit to Margot that, until 3 August 1914, their government had interpreted Belgium's duty as a neutral so strictly that plans by the French (or British) to help had been made almost impossible.

[2] Lord Charles Mercer-Nairne (1874–1914), second son of 5th Marquess of Lansdowne; Equerry to George V, 1910–14; sometime ADC to Field Marshal Earl Roberts; he was killed on 31 Oct. while serving as a major in the 1st (Royal) Dragoons, attached to the staff of the 6th Cavalry Brigade, and is buried in Ypres town cemetery.

where the names had been washed off their little forage caps hung on a stick...A Tommy was digging a grave. Two English officers with their caps in their hands were looking at a grave, just covered....Suddenly there burst on our ears a perfect fusillade of firing. I never heard such a noise...Gordon signed to me to stand on a bit of raised ground and look at the German line. I felt so excited that I was stunned. If there had not been a faint haze on the sky I could easily have seen the bombs; as it was I heard Criack!! criack, <u>Boom</u> !!! in 4s and saw white poplar lines of thin smoke and the flash <u>quite</u> clear. Several French Tommies and an officer came up to me and said I had better go under the shelter of...a wall....They smiled and...asked if I was not afraid: I said not more than they were...[I] shut the motor window and wrote my diary listening to the guns shaking the glass of the Hospital windows (with a noise like rattling wine glasses on finger bowls)....

Sunday 13 December 1914—Merville

I can see Rawly blames Haig for not coming up in time when the 7th Div, caught it <u>so</u> terribly.[1] French blames Rawly. Some day I shall hear how things happened, but as far as I can judge no one but a great military genius would have emerged out of that terrible encounter with the Germans and this certainly General Sir Henry Rawlinson is <u>not</u>.

He said he supposed Ld. K. would be going out to command his own new army in February[2]—it was a new idea to me! I said I should not have thought so and did he suppose French would be Minister of War (Rawly never saw I was pulling his leg)...

[1] The 7th Division formed part of a force under General Rawlinson ('Rawly'), that came under the overall command of Sir John French in early Oct. 1914, and which suffered heavily during the opening engagements of the First Battle of Ypres, from 19 Oct. Although Rawlinson extricated his force from a perilous situation as the Germans attacked, he was considered by French to have shown insufficient aggression, the beginnings of a strained relationship that ended when French was replaced by Haig at the end of 1915. Haig's I Corps was delayed in getting to the Ypres area in Oct. 1914, and this may be the cause of the complaint that Margot records here.

[2] From the end of Aug. 1914 Kitchener talked to his friends, to French's alarm, about possibly adding the post of Supreme Military Commander to that of Secretary of State: Cassar, *Kitchener*, 240; Magnus, *Kitchener*, 288, 301; *Esher Journals*, iii. 253.

At dinner I observed the French swell *officier de liaison*...spoke as if the war was finished, or at any rate as if the Germans were done. <u>This amazed me</u>![1] I said it certainly was not the opinion of either our soldiers or our Government...I myself thought it would last till November or December 1915. I could see...the French swell thought I was cracked. What a wonderful race of up and down people they are! Their sanguineness is <u>terrifying</u>....

Monday 21 December 1914

Winston wrote [a] foolish letter to the Mayor of Scarborough. The reason I call it foolish is not because of...the highfalutin' rubbish but because the one thing in war times that no one can stomach is rhetoric—a <u>lot</u> of words, high words, big words etc. are quite out of place now....[2]

---

[1] In December 1914 some French staff officers may still have believed that, as the German Army had failed to achieve decisive victories in the Battles of the Marne and 'First Ypres', the Allies must be close to victory.

[2] A bombardment of Scarborough, Hartlepool, and Whitby by German battle cruisers on 16 December had killed 133 civilians and wounded 360: see *Asquith–Stanley*, 334–5. The last sentence of Churchill's letter (of 20 Dec. 1914) read: 'Whatever feats of arms the German navy may hereafter perform, the stigma of the baby-killers of Scarborough will brand its officers and men while sailors sail the seas.'

PART III

JANUARY–13 APRIL 1915

In her diary entries written early in 1915 Margot unconsciously reveals both her husband's ability in dealing with immediate problems, and his unreadiness in making long-term plans. Asquith was quick to exploit Bethmann Hollweg's* sanctioning, in February, of Germany's adoption of unrestricted submarine warfare, which he used to extend the scope of Britain's naval blockade: the German command paid a heavy price for outraging international opinion long before they possessed a U-Boat fleet capable of putting their new policy into full effect. But Asquith showed to far less advantage in his response to the call of the Tory peers, Curzon and Midleton,[1] on 8 January, for a national register that would help to coordinate manpower and thus supply and sustain the large army that, it was increasingly recognized, would be essential to winning the war. As the remarkable wave of voluntary enlistment tailed off it was only prudent to prepare for a possible transition to conscription, and Haldane, speaking as Lord Chancellor, sensibly made clear his acceptance of the principle at stake. The premier did not follow suit, and, bolstered by Margot, and sharing the repugnance felt by most Liberals for any form of 'compulsion', he delayed over the national register, because it might open the door to conscription. This did not suggest either careful thought about a central problem of war planning, or an overriding drive for victory, an impression confirmed by evidence that his relationship with Venetia Stanley was sometimes leading him to neglect his duties. The premier's habit of occasionally writing to her while chairing government meetings was damaging enough, but that he should be observed doing so during an important meeting of the War Council on 13 January was particularly unfortunate.[2] That meeting accepted his proposal that 'the Admiralty should ... prepare for a naval expedition in February to bombard and take the Gallipoli Peninsula with Constantinople as its objective'. In his letter to Venetia, Asquith stated that the Council had accepted the proposal 'harmoniously', and while this was not untrue, Churchill's bold Gallipoli venture was far from being uncontroversial. On 19 March, the day after the naval failure in the Dardanelles, Hankey recorded that when the idea had first been proposed he had 'warned the PM, Lord K's Chief of Staff, Lloyd George and Balfour that [the] Fleet could not effect passage without troops, and that all naval officers thought so'.[3] Such misgivings were not invited to be aired at the meeting of 13 January, and this was not an occasion when the chairman should have been writing to his young friend.

---

[1] (William) St John Brodrick succeeded as 9th Viscount Midleton 1907 and, although a Unionist, one of Margot's oldest friends: called by her variously 'St John', 'St John Brodrick', and 'St John Midleton' (see Biographical Notes).

[2] *Asquith–Stanley*, 374–7.

[3] Roskill, *Hankey*, 168.

New Year, January 1915

Ld and Ly Beauchamp[1] have lent us Walmer[2] and I looked forward to going there enormously, but I must say the cold, discomfort, endless unpunctual railway journeys, noisy corridors and small rooms, have made me disappointed in the place. I should <u>hate</u> to live there. It is very distinguished and has distinct charm, but it is noisy and horribly exposed. I hate shingle and never feel well touching the sea. There is not a rock or a pool and no sands, so it is not nice for children. There is a beautiful garden, but in winter of course no garden is nice. We were all ill directly we got there—Raymond, Oc, Beb, Cys, Elizabeth and I—but we were ill before, with a sort of influenza and sore throats....

Two of my greatest friends were at Walmer on New Year's Day—Edgar Vincent...and Edwin Montagu (Financial Sec. to the Treasury). Edgar and Evan Charteris[3] are the 2 oldest friends I see much of. Arthur Balfour and George Curzon are of the same period, but I don't see them so much in London, and beloved George is in some ways <u>so</u> foolish (he has gone back to the old practice of letting politics interfere with friendship).[4] St. John Midleton I still see, and Willy Selborne,[5] both great dears and

[1] William Lygon (1872–1938), 7th Earl of Beauchamp, First Commissioner of Works, 1910–14; Lord President of the Council, 1910 and 1914; Lord Warden of the Cinque Ports 1913–33; he married, 1902, Lady Lettice Mary Elizabeth Grosvenor (1876–1936), younger daughter of Earl Grosvenor, and sister of the 2nd Duke of Westminster; Beauchamp joined the Liberal Party over protection, whereafter 'his great Belgravia house became a London power-house for that party' (Richard Davenport-Hines, *ODNB*, 'Lygon, William, seventh Earl Beauchamp').

[2] Walmer Castle, in Kent, was the official residence of the Lord Warden of the Cinque Ports, to which post Beauchamp was appointed in 1913. During the war Beauchamp lent the property to the Asquiths; they arrived there on 28 Dec. 1914, and HHA wrote to Venetia: 'I am glad to say that Margot thoroughly likes the place.' Although this did not represent Margot's first opinion of Walmer, she became devoted to it: see *Asquith–Stanley*, 330–1, 348.

[3] Evan Charteris (1864–1940), brother of 9th Earl of Wemyss, an old friend and admirer of Margot's, whom she found clever, charming, and hyper-refined; she remained forever grateful, though, that she did not marry him.

[4] Margot was hurt by Curzon's failure to invite her to the ball that he gave in London in May 1914 (see below, p. 141). There was no reason, however, to suppose that such a snub would recur during war.

[5] William Waldegrave Palmer (1859–1942), MP, Liberal, 1885–6, Liberal Unionist, 1886–1895, when he succeeded as 2nd Earl of Selborne; First Lord of the Admiralty, 1900–5; High Commissioner for South Africa and Governor of the Transvaal and Orange River Colonies,

faithful friends, but also blind politicians of not much insight (St. John much cleverer, of course, and I think probably fonder of me than any Tory living).

Thursday 7 January 1915

Sir Ed. Grey communicated to Mr Page, the American ambassador here, a Note on British trade and neutrals, etc.[1] I told Henry what an excellent note I thought this was and he said 'Yes, it was the outcome of very serious deliberation. We've got an unanswerable case.'

Since Henry has been Prime Minister, 2 people have asked him to make them Dukes—one Lord Portsmouth,[2] the other Lord Aberdeen. I always thought these stories were the inventions of journalistic biographers, and that vanity and vulgarity of this kind was quite out of nature, but I was wrong—the Aberdeens wanted to be made Dukes!! They have been made Marquis and Marchioness: they want to take the title of 'Tara', over which the whole of Ireland seems to be not a little furious. (I know what we should think if an Irish, Welsh or Englishman tried to call himself 'Bannockburn'!) I don't feel as if I ever wanted to see them again. Wimborne* is common, but I like him. Alice, his wife, is beautiful and charming, very human and courteous, not clever.[3]

The *Westminster Gazette* quoting from an American paper wrote 'Asquith is the strongest sovereign of Europe at the present time.' ...

On January 19th 1915 the first German Zeppelins came (over Yarmouth, Cromer, King's Lynn) arriving in the dark (at a great height, no human being could see them). They threw down many bombs quite aimlessly

1905–10; Balcarres described him, in a private memo., 31 July 1911, as 'persistent, obstinate and full of common sense': *Crawford Journals*, 206.

[1] Walter Hines Page (1855–1918), American Ambassador to London 1913–18; 'To Page—and to Grey's close friendship with him—we owe it, more than to anyone else, that we were able to carry on our policy of economic warfare without a break with the United States during the first part of the war': Hankey, *Supreme Command*, 357.

[2] Newton Wallop (1856–1917), 6th Earl of Portsmouth; Under-Secretary for War, 1905–8.

[3] The Wimbornes were successors to the Aberdeens in the lord lieutenancy (viceroyalty) of Ireland.

and killed 4 civilians—a shoemaker, an old lady over 70 years old, a widow of 26 and a boy of fourteen.[1]

The English people are the most dogged, the most adventurous, and one of the least timid or intimidable in existence, and these Zeppelin raids only leave them cooler and more determined, while they horrify and disgust every neutral country. I have betted from the first that Zeppelins would come over London.

Sunday 10 January 1915

Winston came to stay with us at Walmer (he, Clemmie* and the 2 McKennas). He sat next to me at dinner. Apropos of H. having to appoint a new Viceroy in India,[2] Winston said to me:

[WSC] I've given up all desire for that now. (He used to say he would like this above all things.) Do you think this is a sign of more modesty or more ambition?

M. More ambition, certainly. No one sinks into greater insignificance than [a] retired Viceroy (aged in arteries, pickled by the climate, poor and bewildered by another kind of political public life, he retires to small and drab quarters in Eaton Place).

Winston My God! this—This is living History. Everything we are doing and saying is thrilling. It will be read by 1000 generations—think of that!! Why, I would not be out of this glorious, delicious war for anything the world could give me (Eyes glowing, but with slight anxiety lest the word 'delicious' should jar on me). I say, don't repeat that I said the word 'delicious'—you know what I mean.

Poor Percy Illingworth, our Chief Whip, died of typhoid.[3] He resigned when we were turned out by a snap Division (engineered by Banbury[4]

---

[1] Fisher proposed to shoot German prisoners in reprisal: *Asquith–Stanley*, 359.
[2] i.e. in succession to Lord Hardinge (see below, p. 84) Viceroy 1910–16.
[3] Illingworth died 3 Jan. 1915; see Biographical Notes.
[4] Sir Frederick Banbury (1850–1936), cr. Bt. 1903, Baron 1924; Unionist MP 1892–1924. Banbury proposed an amendment to the government's Home Rule Bill, and in a 'snap'

and F. E. Smith). When I greeted Henry on the stair on his return from the House, I said to him 'Do you feel it much, darling?' Henry 'Only for poor Illingworth, he has done so well and will be <u>terribly</u> upset.' Of course, Henry didn't accept his resignation.

There was much talk as to who should succeed him. I can hardly believe <u>anyone</u> <u>seriously</u> thought of Montagu—I will find out.... It is inconceivable to me! that Ll.G. should have thought of him—a man invaluable where he is, marked out for Cabinet rank as soon as there is a vacancy; a man full of prejudices about people and genuinely interested in himself, a man of fine brains and bad manners. Gulland', our second Whip, will succeed Illingworth.

Lansdowne being ill, George Curzon had the bright idea of urging on the Lords the importance of sitting and enquiring into the actions of this wicked Gov. In consequence, he led the Lords, and he and Midleton made foolish speeches trying to press us for recruiting figures (just what the Germans <u>most</u> want to know), or what they call 'a standard of recruiting'. They meant no harm but it annoyed people.[1]

K... said to me:

[K.] I could have shot Curzon with my own hand for his abominable speech—great lack of generosity, <u>never</u> praising the splendid fellows going into the new Army—men giving up <u>everything</u>! And how <u>monstrous</u>, telling the Germans what divisions and Brigades mean, etc., then trying to flatter <u>me</u>!![2] (with a good-humoured laugh) He's

division on 11 Nov. 1912 the government was defeated, a highly embarrassing and awkward outcome for Asquith's cabinet. In fact both sides had had fair notice of the division, and Illingworth, who became Chief Whip that year, had warned his side to attend; according to *The Times* 'the real fault lay with slackness in his flock'; Illingworth staved off further incidents, even though they were assiduously plotted by the opposition (*The Times*, 12 Nov. 1912, 8a; 4 Jan. 1915, 5a).

[1] Margot refers to the Lords' debate on 'Army Reinforcements, see *Parl. Deb.*, Lords, 8 Jan. 1915, 18.347–58 (Midleton), 387–94 (Curzon). The need to put a national register in hand at once was undeniable, but it was being delayed solely because of Liberal fears that it could be used as the prelude to conscription. By 'people' Margot means her friends. For Asquith's dismissal of the Unionist criticisms of the government see *Asquith–Stanley*, 365.

[2] Curzon and Midleton wanted the government to reveal what its recruiting policy was, in view of the steady decline in the monthly intake figures, albeit that extracting information

an impossible fellow! I walked out with Derby, who <u>entirely</u> agreed with me.[1]

M. Don't you think these attacks on Haldane quite monstrous?[2]

K. Yes, disgraceful! People get very strange and stupid in war times.

M. I think you should say something to show you, at any rate, don't share the views of the Tory party.

K. (thoughtfully) Does Haldane mind these attacks?

M. Yes, and I expect we all should: after all, England owes him <u>such</u> a lot, it seems hard that because he was educated in the only country where you could get well educated—Germany—that every cur should yap at his heels.

K. Well, I'll see and speak to Haldane; he would like this best, I think.

M. Yes, <u>mind you do</u>.

I have been made <u>very</u> unhappy by low, violent attacks on Haldane. I hear St. John and Selborne are violent about him, and of course the Ulster gang (who are a little disappointed that the Carson Army has not recruited better).[3] I find the political truce <u>very</u> shallow,[4] and have been amazed that a fearful, frightful war like this should have changed people so little. It

about troop numbers from a reluctant government, without helping the enemy, was a difficult process. Robertson Nicoll, who was no Tory, had reckoned, in mid-Nov. 1914, that the monthly figure was 'not doing much more than filling the blanks of the field army': Adams and Poirier, *Conscription*, 62. For Bonar Law's reply to his colleagues' complaints see Blake, *Bonar Law*, 238–9.

[1] Edward George Villiers Stanley (1865–1948), KCVO 1905; s. as 17th Earl of Derby 1908; Unionist MP 1892–1906; Postmaster-General, 1903–5; Director-General of Recruiting, 1915–16; Secretary of State for War, 1916–18, 1922–4; Ambassador to France, 1918–20.

[2] Haldane was the victim of a xenophobic campaign in the Unionist press that 'was utterly misplaced': 'No minister bore greater responsibility for Britain's capacity to engage Germany in 1914…but [his] reputation as an intriguer, his writing of philosophical books, his often opaque statements, the fact that he spoke fluent German (uniquely among the class of executive politicians) made him, in the foetid domestic political atmosphere of the time, an unsurprising target for a frustrated press and party' (H. C. G. Matthew, *ODNB*, 'Haldane, Richard Burdon').

[3] By 'Ulstergang' Margot means Unionist opponents to Home Rule. The 'Carson army' is a reference not to the Ulster Volunteer Force but the 36th Ulster Division, which won immortality on the Somme in 1916: see the division's *History* (1922) by Cyril Falls.

[4] Runciman wrote in Feb. 1915, 'If things go wrong we shall be flayed' (to Chalmers, 7 Feb. 1915; Hazlehurst, *Politicians at War*, 142). Asquith was more complacent about the continuing effectiveness of the political truce.

justifies what I said in the first pages of this diary[1] (I feel a little like the *Spectator*, who always strokes itself down, when I write this). I rather doubt if St. John has done much anti-Haldane work. St. John Brodrick has got the nicest character in the world. He is most generous. No one ever behaved better to his enemy than St. John did to George Curzon (I told George from the first that I was a St. Johnite!)

As a matter of fact, all our best soldiers say Haldane was the greatest war Minister we have had for years. Gen. Sir John Cowans wrote to me 'We have <u>never</u> had a good Tory War Minister. Haldane can well afford to despise and overlook his attackers.' When I heard through Sir Ed. Grey how much Haldane minded, and when Henry told me the latter had actually resigned in case he was hampering the Gov., I was dreadfully upset and asked Ld Derby to come and see me. (Of course, H. would not <u>hear</u> of Haldane leaving him.)[2]

Friday 22 January 1915

Derby came in the morning. He is a nice fellow—stupid, straight, manly and not afraid. He has done wonderful works in the Territorial Force, and behaved like a gentleman through [the] Curragh incident (wh. few of them did).... [He] was wonderfully simple and nice, and praised Haldane's work and the Territorials. He deplored St. John and Curzon pressing for figures in recruiting, and said had they been back-benchers he would have attacked them, but he never liked attacking one of his front-bench men. He had gone to St. John personally, and begged him not to ask questions about recruiting. I told him that Sir John French[3] (whom I forgot to say to my joy had come over to see H. and the cabinet for 3 nights) when he saw

[1] This refers to the volume of the diary (d.3211) that opened with the entry of 26 Oct. 1914: on 27 Oct. Margot wrote, 'I feel the war *so* acutely that I am quite frightened of seeing certain people who don't feel it', see p. 44 above.

[2] Asquith's complacency made him less indignant than Margot about the attacks on Haldane. There is no sign that he saw in them the harbinger of an agitation against himself: see *Asquith–Stanley*, 322–4. For his sacrificing of Haldane in May 1915 see Spender and Asquith, ii. 167; Bonham Carter, *Churchill*, 394–5; Koss, *Haldane*, 191.

[3] Asquith wrote to Venetia Stanley on 13 Jan. 1915, during an important meeting of the War Council: 'Sir J. French is here and sits next me': *Asquith–Stanley*, 375.

me was much annoyed with the Tory peers and furious with the attacks on Haldane....

Saturday 23 January 1915

We all went to Walmer Castle.... It was a triumph getting Lloyd George and the Master. I'm <u>excellent</u> at getting all sorts of people together—no doubt!![1] I've always fought against cliques, though I suppose what Arthur Balfour and I are supposed to have started—'The Souls'—was a clique: but it was just because it was <u>not</u> that my particular lot called 'Souls' was so famous and powerful.

It was like the largest, most beautifully-furnished room, with open doors leading to gardens, moors, woods, rivers or bosks; and inhabited by welcoming hosts (Arthur Balfour, Curzon, Cust,[2] Wyndham,[3] Elchos,[4] Godfrey Webb,[5] St. John, Alf. Lyttelton*, Evan [Charteris], Ribblesdales,[6] etc. etc., Pembrokes,[7] Cowpers,[8] Grenfells, Tennants[9]) all fond of each other, <u>without jealousy</u>, back-biting or disloyalty of any kind. These

[1] Bonham Carter reported to Violet, 25 Jan. 1915: 'Ll.G. seems to have enjoyed Walmer very much': Bonham Carter Papers, 256.

[2] Henry John Cockayne-Cust (Harry Cust) (1861–1917), Unionist MP, newspaper editor, and Soul; transformed the radical *Pall Mall Gazette* into a 'a powerful organ of Unionist opinion'; had a reputation as a womanizer, and was believed to be the father of Diana Cooper née Manners, and not least by her; at his premature death was heir to the barony of Brownlow (*The Times*, 30 Sept. 1955, 11b).

[3] The Wyndham family had close connections with Margot. George Wyndham (1863–1913), Unionist MP, 1889–1913, was an old friend and had been a member of the 'Souls'. One of his sisters, Pamela, was married to Margot's eldest brother, and another, Mary, Countess of Wemyss (below), also a former 'Soul', was the mother of Cynthia Asquith née Charteris, and thus mother-in-law of Asquith's son Herbert ('Beb').

[4] Lord and Lady Elcho, i.e. Hugo Richard Charteris (1857–1937) and Mary Constance née Wyndham (1862–1937), before they became 9th Earl and Countess of Wemyss in 1914.

[5] Godfrey Webb (1832–1901): Margot describes him in the *Autobiography* as 'the doyen of the Souls'.

[6] Thomas Lister, 4th Baron Ribblesdale (1854–1925), politician and huntsman, who married, 1877, Margot's elder sister Charlotte (or 'Charty', see Biographical Notes); after her death in 1911 he married, 1919, Ava née Willing, the American widow of John Jacob Astor (see below, p. 112 n. 2).

[7] George Robert Herbert (1850–95), 13th Earl of Pembroke; m. 1874 Gertrude Frances Talbot (d. 1906).

[8] Francis Thomas de Grey (1834–1905), 7th Earl Cowper; m. Lady Katrine Cecilia Compton (1845–1913).

[9] Margot, Charty, and Lucy Tennant were all 'Souls'.

people encouraged and collected every kind of man and woman to come to their big room. There they found not only the most brilliant general conversation and excellent company but real <u>protection</u> and sympathy. This <u>no</u> group that I have ever seen or heard of since has ever been able to give or get.

The talent for tête-à-tête will always be very great! But for the moment the talent for general conversation is almost extinct among women. Men like Henry, Arthur, Birrell, Morley and all my old friends have got it, but except perhaps DD,[1] Frances Horner,[2] Betty and Frances Balfour, I don't know <u>one</u> woman who, if at this moment she was at the centre of a circle of people, could sustain a first-rate general discussion; it would break off in derision and tête-à-tête. (Self-centredness, desire for an audience, want of real interest in Life and its problems account for this. Lightening instead of weightening conversation turns everything into waste. 'She lived in words; she was exciting and monopolizing; she claimed all and gave nothing. Is it surprising that her circle narrowed?' This exactly describes the young female of today and the reason of her failure.)[3]

Ll.G. said to us before dinner that the opposition was longing for a Coalition. I had heard this before, but I said I didn't think they longed for it as much as to get rid of 2 of our men, Haldane and McKenna.

Ll.G.   We've got their best man—Arthur Balfour: who else is there?[4]

M.   Yes, you're right. I often wonder Arthur didn't discover and bring forward more clever young men when he was PM.

---

[1] Edith Sophy 'D.D.' (1865–1948), second wife of Margot's brother-in-law Alfred Lyttelton. She was made DBE in 1917. Her nickname, 'Didi', was given as 'DD' by those who knew her best.

[2] Frances Horner née Graham (1858–1940), who married, 1883, (Sir) John Francis Horner (1842–1927), KCVO 1907; their daughter Katharine married, 1907, Raymond Asquith; through her father, the Liberal MP William Graham, she had come to know the Pre-Raphaelites, and had been a close friend of Sir Edward Burne-Jones.

[3] This parenthetical comment appears in the diary as a marginal note.

[4] After the outbreak of war Asquith made Balfour a full member of the CID, and in November he joined the War Council, the only member of the shadow cabinet thus recognized; he proved an influential and important counsellor to the Liberal government.

Ll.G.   Oh! He didn't like the tall poppies beside him! He got rid of all his best men. He let Winston, Hicks-Beach, B. of B. and Ld George Hamilton go.[1]

At dinner Ll.G. sat next to me and we had a <u>first rate talk</u>. I was rather surprised to hear him praise McKenna so very highly. I myself am devoted to McKenna, and so is Henry; the family can't appreciate him. His up-to-dateness and other externals put them off. Young women are very superficial in their views of men. Ll.G. said to me:

[Ll.G.]   I don't suppose Violet would ever appreciate McKenna.

M.   No, he is not at all her sort.

Ll.G.   But remember, she is a tremendous Winstonite.[2] I don't think she thinks he can do wrong, though she would criticise him.

M.   Oh! I think she knows Winston's weak spots very well <u>now</u>....

Ll.G.   Really, if it wasn't for Winston's affectionate quality and good temper, I sometimes think I can hardly do with him!

M.   Well, I like Winston much better than I did. What I mind is his incapacity to grow up. I feel it about so many people—<u>they put nothing on themselves</u>: born clever or born geniuses, like Harcourt, Rosebery or many others, but the same in the nursery, the school-room, the cabinet. (It's difficult to say what this comes from, but I think it is the consequence of brains being stronger than character.)

Ll.G.   Winston, like all really self-centred people, ends up by boring people. He's, as you say, such a child! Would you believe it, he,

[1] Michael Edward Hicks-Beach (1837–1916), 9th Bt.; cr. 1st Earl of St Aldwyn 1915; Chancellor of the Exchequer 1885–6 and 1895–1902. Lord (6th Baron) Balfour of Burleigh (1849–1921), Sec. for Scotland 1895–1903. Lord George Francis Hamilton (1845–1927), First Lord of the Admiralty 1885–6 and 1886–1892; Secretary of State for India, 1895–1903. Lloyd George was making no allowance for Balfour's difficulty in holding his government together when Joseph Chamberlain had announced his conversion to tariff reform in 1903. Churchill defected to the Liberals over this issue.

[2] Violet was a lifelong friend and supporter of Winston, who she first encountered at a weekend house party in April 1907: 'He's got the uncertain sense of humour of the last generation—which (for me) invests conversation with a new excitement....' (Bonham Carter, *Diaries, 1904–14*, 127); after his death in 1965 she published the acclaimed *Winston Churchill As I Knew Him*.

Neil Primrose[1] and I dined at the Café Royal and had a very nice evening. I suddenly saw Winston get sulky—what for, I had <u>no</u> notion! Neil said to him 'Shall I motor you home?' Winston answered crossly '<u>No</u>', and got into my taxi. I said to him 'Now what <u>is</u> the matter with you?' He said in a sulky, angry voice 'Didn't you hear the young___[2] say to me "<u>I don't agree with you</u>"?' Of course, I roared with laughter, it's so childishly absurd.

M. Luckily Winston has got no rancour and has a really good heart: these make him lovable.

Later on at dinner Ll.G. asked me what I thought of Fisher*.

M. I don't think he is much use now, though he is awfully clever and vital.

Ll.G. He is not at all gaga.

M. No, not at all, only he sees things so much more coloured than they are, and is so inventive and extravagant and coarse, and has bad judgement....

Ll.G. asked me why I thought some women—specially girls—had such cruel tongues. I said it was want of maternal feeling. It's a lack of perfect womanhood, giving everyone away and not being able to love any man enough.

He asked me what [H. T.] Baker was like, as Montagu was going into the Cabinet.[3] (Masterman* has been without a seat in the H. of Commons since [February 1914], and as <u>no</u> constituency will have him, H. made up his mind to drop him).[4] Baker was very likely to succeed him at the Treasury, and as I had been so right about Montagu, whom he had

---

[1] Neil (James Archibald) Primrose (1882–1917), second son of 5th Earl of Rosebery; Parliamentary Under-Secretary to Foreign Office, Feb.–May 1915; Parl. Sec. to Treasury, Dec. 1916–May 1917; died of wounds sustained during Palestine campaign, Nov. 1917.

[2] Margot has left a blank space here but Neil Primrose is clearly the target.

[3] Montagu entered the cabinet as Chancellor of the Duchy of Lancaster in succession to Charles Masterman, February 1915: see *Asquith–Stanley*, 393.

[4] Masterman, then Chancellor of the Duchy of Lancaster, had lost by-elections at Bethnal Green and Ipswich in February and May 1914, respectively.

disliked the idea of having, he would like to hear my views on Baker. 'Rather a prig, isn't he?' M. 'Not at all. He is deaf, but is the best fellow in the world: never shocked, always kind, not at <u>all</u> touchy and not afraid; full of humour and brains and with reserve.' (I did not say a trifle indiscreet, because <u>no</u> one was more indiscreet than Montagu, but he soon got better: Baker's indiscretions are more social than political.) ...

Thursday 2 February 1915

The House of Commons opened on Tuesday 2nd Feb. 1915. My Birthday.

Elizabeth went to London from Walmer by train with me. She wanted to motor up with Violet and her father, but gave it up at once seeing that I was going alone.

I confess I felt out of spirits—it is sad getting old![1]—I should not feel it so much, or indeed at all, if I was <u>quite</u> sure I would keep my place in the hearts of those I love best: but I am not vain enough to feel <u>sure</u> of this! The hearts of those I love—or of some of them—are not quite the same shape as my own.

I went to Henry's dressing room and hugged him. I said 'You have got <u>everything</u>—Fame, Power, Success, Love, friends, Health, children—<u>everything</u> but a young wife!' He said, with that wonderful emotion which I miss so much in his children, 'I have got the youngest wife in the world!' ...

Monday 8 February 1915

We dined at the French Embassy.[2] Cambon took me in and Delcassé sat on the other side of me. Cambon looked very guilty when I congratulated him on having said, apropos of Italy coming in and fighting for us '*Ils voleront au secours des vainqueurs.*'[3] (The harlot of Europe, as Winston calls Italy.) He pretended he had not said it but I could see that he had.

---

[1] Margot was then 51 years old.

[2] This dinner is described by Asquith as having 'reached the very nadir of dullness': *Asquith–Stanley*, 419. Paul Cambon (1843–1924) had been French Ambassador in London since 1898. Theophile Delcassé (1852–1923) was at this date France's Foreign Minister.

[3] Fr. 'they will rush to the aid of the victors'.

Delcassé was very serious over the war. He said that things would have been very different in the early stages if Joffre had got his present Generals, but that 23 of the French Generals were stellenbosched, among whom 5 were Joffre's most intimate friends.[1] He said...Foch*, Joffre and another whose name I forget all came from the 'Midi'....

Thursday 18 February 1915

Today is 'der Tag', the day the German Government, through Tirpitz their First Sea Lord, has threatened to sink all our ships—merchant ships and others—without warning, by submarines: a form of naval warfare—piracy, and indeed murder—unheard in the world's History. Germany has gone so far as to warn neutrals that they also may suffer, unless they go by a special route round Scotland (or the North Pole!). This has caused the Hell of a Row in America, but has been taken pretty calmly here....

There is a great deal of Talk just now of Germany being hard up for copper and food, etc., but I don't believe a word of it. Our dear governess writes from Munich (and we hear the same from Berlin) that, except for the wounded coming in by train, no one would know there was a war going on. Things go on just the same, and no sort of rise in prices. All the same, the German Government has taken over all food and is dealing out Bread tickets, an awkward thing to start.[2]

The German Gov. pretend that there has been a 'secret order' sent out from our Admiralty advising our merchant ships to abuse neutral flags. I telephoned Masterton Smith[3] and he categorically denies this....

Henry made a wonderful speech on the high prices of food on Thursday 11th Feb. 1915.[4] He declined to fix maximum prices.

[1] In the Boer War unsuccessful British commanders were sent to the camp at Stellenbosch, and Limoges performed the same function for the French army in 1914–15: the unfortunate generals had been 'Limogés'.

[2] For the food and raw materials problems of the Central Powers see Strachan, *First World War*, 1014–49. For use of substitutes for copper see Strachan, *First World War*, 1027–8.

[3] James Edward Masterton Smith (1878–1938), KCB 1919, private secretary to the First Lord of the Admiralty, 1910–17.

[4] *Parl. Deb.*, 11 Feb. 1915, 69.758–76. On 'Necessities of Life (Prices)'. Clynes, who followed for Labour, was unimpressed. He believed that the premier's proposals would 'go but a very

It was characteristic of him to go to Lucy's clergyman's son's wedding (Jack Beresford)[1] at 12 up near Grosvenor Square, and only give himself an hour in which to prepare this <u>remarkable</u> speech. Of course, the figures and statistics were given him, but the building up of a speech of this kind wants a peculiar kind of intellectual vision—a seeing of things Whole—which is one of Henry's most striking gifts. No one else living can do this with the same ease and charm. Every 'statement' made by other men is either terribly boring or superficial or inaccurate. I listened with delight.

He made 3 statements of great importance—1. He would not fix maximum prices for food. 2. That Sir John French will in future send twice a week a communication on the doings of the British Force. 3. That the Government are considering the adoption of more stringent measures against German trade....

Ld Londonderry died on 8th Feb. 1915, in his sixty-third year.[2] He was a stupid, courteous man of no education, pushed into the highest places by a vulgar, courageous, arrogant wife of—at one time—great beauty and audacity. He will be remembered by his tub-thumping speeches against Irish Home Rule.

Wednesday 17 February 1915

Henry said to me in the motor going out to dine with the Walter Burnses:[3]

short way to relieve the masses of the poor of the extreme difficulties under which they now live and labour'.

[1] Jack Beresford was the son of the Reverend John Beresford, vicar of the church at Easton Grey. His sister Dorothy was one of Asquith's 'little harem' in earlier days; see *Asquith–Stanley*, 1.

[2] Charles Stewart Vane-Tempest-Stewart (1852–1915), 6th Marquess of Londonderry, Unionist government minister, and an ultra-opponent of the Liberals' 3rd Home Rule Bill, becoming Protestant Ulster's most vocal defender in the Lords; described by his colleague David Lindsay, 27th Earl of Crawford and 10th Earl of Balcarres, in July 1912 as one of 'the two stupidest men in Britain' (*Crawford Journals*, 277).

[3] Walter Burns (1872–1929), brother of Mrs Lewis Harcourt; m. Ruth Evelyn Cavendish-Bentinck (1883–1978).

[H.] Winston just now is absolutely maddening. How I wish Oc had not joined his beastly naval Brigade!¹ He is having a great Review of them today. He inspects the Brigade in a uniform of his own, which will cause universal derision among our soldiers! (Clemmy said some time ago that inventing uniforms was one of Winston's chief pleasures and temptations.) He has just emerged from a fearful row with K. by the skin of his teeth, and has now got himself into another.

M. Do tell me.

H. K. has just been to see me about it. Sir John writes from St. Omer and tells K. that Winston has offered him 9000 of his Naval Brigade, ready to go into action at once in the trenches, and a squadron of armoured motor cars; and French asks if he may be allowed to remove the guns and use the motors, which shows what he thinks of the use of these expensive follies!! K. is of course furious, and says to me he wonders what Winston would say if he, K., was always writing to Jellicoe, offering to do this and that. Of course, Winston is intolerable. It is all Vanity. He is devoured by vanity.

M. It was curious to me to see how depressed he was when I congratulated him on his remarkably good (naval) speech in the House Monday night (8th Feb. 1915).²

H. It was merely because he thought the newspapers would have praised it more—he is quite childish. I have written him a very stiff letter. It's so trying, just as K. and he had got a 'modus vivendi'.

Saturday 20 February 1915

I asked the American Ambassador Mr Page and his daughter to Walmer Castle for Sunday....I was particularly keen to see him. Now that the German gov. has been foolish enough to say their submarines will take

---

¹ Asquith refers to Churchill's creation, the Royal Naval Division, which was thrown, under-prepared, into the unsuccessful defence of Antwerp, and later used in the disastrous and costly Gallipoli campaign.

² *Parl. Deb.*, 15 Feb. 1915 (not 8 Feb.) 69.919–39, debate on 'Supply (Navy Estimates)'.

no account of neutral ships, the American Headquarters point of view is of great interest and value.

Mr Page is a capital American—ugly, poor, honest, humorous and sound as a bell. He has no distinction either of phrase or personality, but he is a very genuine article and knows his country and their men (Taft, Roosevelt, Wilson, Root etc.). He is not too long and has a certain amount of simplicity and candour—the 2 most engaging qualities in the world, I think!...[1]

Monday 1 March 1915

Henry made [a] speech [on the U-Boat campaign] in the House. This is probably the greatest speech Henry has ever delivered. It is certainly the greatest occasion and moment.... Among his greatest speeches I put his first Free Trade campaign speech, his Colenso, Guildhall and this.[2]

When he came to Great Britain's reply, and the finishing words—'Her [Germany's] opponents are therefore driven to frame retaliatory measures in order, in their turn, to prevent commodities of any kind from reaching or leaving the German Empire. That, Sir, is our Reply.'—there was a perfect roar of cheers. Shivers went down my back. The Press gallery was crowded, also the Speaker's gallery. It was a great speech delivered on a Great occasion.[3]

I rushed down to Henry's room and left him on a glowing note of deep congratulations and Pride. I met Sir Robert Finlay[4] 'You must be proud

[1] See Grey to Page, 2 Sept. 1918: *Page Letters*, ii. 399–401. Balfour, like Grey, had the highest opinion of Page (*Page Letters*, ii. 403). William Howard Taft (1857–1930); Theodore Roosevelt (1858–1919); Thomas Woodrow Wilson (1856–1924); Elihu Root (1845–1937).

[2] For Asquith's first free trade speech, see Spender and Asquith, i. 156, Cinderford speech against Tariff Reform (8 Oct. 1903). His 'Colenso' is probably the speech of 16 Dec. 1899 at Willington Quay; see Spender and Asquith, i. 136 (about the 'Black Week' disasters of 9–15 Dec. 1899, at start of Boer War). Asquith spoke at the Guildhall every 9 Nov. while Prime Minister, so that the particular speech to which Margot refers is uncertain.

[3] Margot omits the important sentence: 'These measures will, however, be enforced by the British and French Governments without risk to neutral ships or to neutral or non-combatant life, and in strict observance of the dictates of humanity': see *Parl. Deb.*, 70.589–603; for the Order in Council, 11 Mar. 1915, see Fayle, *Seaborne Trade*, ii. 15–17.

[4] Robert Bannatyne Finlay (1842–1929), Kt. 1895; Baron 1916; cr. Viscount 1919; Lord Chancellor 1916–18.

of your husband' he said. Henry is so <u>wonderfully free</u> from vanity! I don't believe when his life comes to be written (which I shall not live to see) that one saying or act of his can be recorded which will show any <u>sort</u> of personal vanity. There will be a cloud of witnesses to prove the contrary.[1] I don't know a <u>single</u> man or woman of whom I can say this. Vanity is terribly hereditary, but alas! the glorious unconquerable <u>reverse</u> is not. In varying degrees every one of Henry's colleagues have got vanity—but, I might also add, [so has] every single person I know.

<u>Winston's vanity is septic.</u> He would die of blood poisoning if it were not for a great deal of red blood which circulates freely through his heart and stomach. Runciman*, Samuel*, Grey, Loulou [Harcourt]*, even Bron [Herbert]* and Pease have got a good deal of it (also our new Cabinet minister Montagu, whom I love). I think Kitchener and McKenna and Crewe have the least vanity, and in consequence are the best to talk to about the war. McKenna and Kitchener on the whole have done best (after of course Henry, who now holds a <u>very</u> powerful position in England.) ...

Wednesday 24 February 1915

I woke at 5 a.m. on Feb. 24th...I had the bright idea of going down to Blandford that day....I don't think I ought to have minded so much being deceived over Oc's movements....[2] I wept bitter tears over all this pettiness and was angry with myself for minding *so* much when such <u>very</u> big things are going on (nothing makes me so lonely as being deceived in even <u>tiny</u> things). How I wish I had been born with less candour. I should have much more sympathy and much less sternness. It's a beastly quality candour and I loathe it (at times!) if it goes with <u>great</u> irritability and intolerance like it does with me....

---

[1] The danger for Asquith was not vanity, but arrogance.

[2] Violet had heard 'accidentally through Lady Essex at lunch' on 22 Feb. of the Naval Division's impending embarkation for Gallipoli; the Division had been training at Blandford in Dorset: Bonham Carter, *Diaries, 1914–45*, 25. She had no difficulty in gaining confirmation from Churchill. Margot presumably meant by 'being deceived' that Violet had not passed the information to her; but she, Margot, had apparently learned the news independently from Oc, who was in London, on 22 Feb.: d. 3211, 475r.

Ly Wimborne's[1] motor took me over to see Oc and Rupert Brooke,[2] his great friend (a delightful boy and a poet).... Oc and Rupert dashed down the rutty road and jumped into my car....

Dinner <u>wonderfully</u> dull, long and cold. Like all very rich people, Ly Wimborne has no idea of comfort. The fires were not even lit, and we all ran and put on fur coats. The bath water was cold, which disappointed the boys. I wd. have given <u>anything</u> for them to have had boiling baths....

Thursday 25 February 1915

We all got up very early and motored to Blandford to see the whole Naval Brigade reviewed by the King. Clemmy and Violet rode: they neither of them looked quite horsemen to my professional eye....

I wore a white cloth coat and skirt and very thick underclothes.[3] Though quite beautiful in the sun, it was <u>arctic</u>! and the ground hard and white with frost. The whole 9000 men were drawn up on the glorious downs, and Winston walked round and inspected them before the King arrived. I felt quite a thrill when I saw Oc and Rupert with walking-sticks standing in front of their men, looking quite wonderful!

Rupert is a beautiful young man and we get on well: he has so much intellectual temperament and nature about him. He told Oc he was quite <u>certain</u> he would never come back, but be killed. It didn't depress him at all, but he was just <u>convinced</u>. I shall be curious to see if this turns out to be a true instinct....

[1] Lady Cornelia Henrietta (1847–1927), widow of 1st Baron Wimborne, daughter of 7th Duke of Marlborough. Her residence, Canford Manor, Wimborne, was 'lent', and Margot stayed at 'Lake House' with Henry Guest.

[2] Rupert Chawner Brooke (1887–1915), poet, and fellow of King's College, Cambridge, 1912; made famous by his five 'war sonnets' which appeared in the last issue of *New Numbers*, 1914–15, and which included *The Soldier*; he joined the RND as a sub-lieutenant, Sept. 1914; served Antwerp, Oct.; sailed for Gallipoli, 28 Feb. 1915; died of septicaemia, on board the French hospital ship *Duguay-Trouin* off Skyros, 23 Apr. 1915.

[3] Bonham Carter, *Diaries, 1914–45*, 27, refers to Margot 'nipping feverishly in a very short Russian ballet skirt and snowboots'.

The King was pleased and told me they all marched wonderfully. I told him he ought to have ridden: he said he hadn't thought of it, but that it was so cold he didn't mind. I sat for 10 min in Ld Alington's phaeton next to their beautiful young son (in the Coldstream), who was wounded by shrapnel in the spine and is now paralysed.[1] I felt my heart go out to him. He asked me to sit beside him, and told Alice Keppel I was a kind woman.

We lunched in Oc's mess room. I felt horribly depressed and tired. I sat between 2 of Oc's brigade. They gave us champagne and every sort of luxury. Pat Shaw-Stewart looked like death; even Oc and Rupert were very white: they had been up since 6 am....[2]

I motored over in early morning and said Goodbye to Oc (nearly an hour from Lake House.) I stopped at Poole bank and got £50 in gold sovereigns, 10 of which I gave Rupert and 40 to Oc: they were most grateful and sweet. Rupert kissed me. I wondered if I would ever see him again. I talked to Oc sitting on a wooden case outside his hut for half an hour. He said he hoped V. would marry Bongy: that he felt very strongly her life was not at all satisfactory, and that marriage would be the making of her. I said she would make an excellent wife, if she would only give up dialectics; and that really, if she could only see ahead, being an old maid would be a real fiasco for her, more than for most women. Oc was very much of my opinion, and told me to be patient, and that he understood my domestic difficulties and had always seen them from the first. He took my hand and patted it, and put his arm round me like a lover.... I cried bitter tears....[3]

---

[1] Humphrey Napier Sturt (1859–1919), 2nd Baron Alington; his elder son, Gerald, referred to here, died 1918.

[2] Patrick Houston Shaw-Stewart (1888–1917), a Balliol contemporary of Cys Asquith and Charles Lister, and fellow of All Souls, 1910; sub-lieutenant, RND, Sept. 1914; lieutenant-commander, Gallipoli, 1915; killed in action in Flanders, Dec. 1917.

[3] As the Hood Battalion sailed away, 28 Feb. 1915, Violet thought of the Athenians' disastrous Syracusan expedition, 413 BC: Bonham Carter, *Diaries, 1914–45*, 30. Margot's letters to 'Oc' Asquith for this period show how sympathetic she found him: Arthur Asquith Papers, MA to AMA, for the years 1911 to 1932.

Sunday 7 March 1915—Walmer Castle

Henry rather tired. It is terribly hard work being PM in a great war. He has got the best of war temperaments, but he is very human....[1]

He came into my bed-room about 10.15 in the morning Sunday 7th and told me he had had a very characteristic, clever letter from Montagu 'All about himself, etc., but as usual clever.'

H. Winston is far the most disliked man in my cabinet by his colleagues. Montagu is excellent on him, he hates him (the word hate H. only uses for short when talking to me—hate could not describe more than a mood of Montagu's, I think: he is moody and has quick changes in his likes and dislikes though very faithful in the main, but he doesn't <u>hate</u> exactly.)

M. Why does Monty hate Winston? He is rather lovable, I think, and though he often bored me before the war, I've liked him very much since. I <u>love</u> his spirit of adventure: it suits me, and I love his suggestiveness.

H. (irritably) Oh! he is intolerable!—<u>noisy</u>, long-winded and full of perorations. We don't want suggestion, we want wisdom. Crewe, K. and McKenna are far the best just now. Grey is tired out and hysterical, Runciman in his own way admirable, Simon getting better and of more use as the war goes on (Rufus told me Simon was far the best now at the Bar—better than Buckmaster,[2] Carson, F. E. Smith, Finlay[3]—indeed, <u>any</u>.) Montagu oddly enough puts Crewe first and K. second on his list.

M. <u>How</u> amusing! He used to put Crewe down as a bloodless man, merely registering Hardinge's will:[4] a chief impossible to get into close touch with, or to impress or influence in any way, pigeon-holing his (Mon-

---

[1] In the manuscript diary the next words have been excised.
[2] Stanley Owen Buckmaster (1861–1934), Kt. 1913, Baron 1915; a successful barrister, he took silk in 1902; Lord Chancellor, 1915–16, in succession to Haldane.
[3] Lord Finlay succeeded Buckmaster as Lord Chancellor, and was in turn succeeded, 1919, by Birkenhead (F. E. Smith).
[4] Sir Charles Hardinge (1858–1944), KCMG 1904, cr. Baron 1910; Permanent Under-Secretary of State at the Foreign Office 1906–10; Margot thought him 'a man of strong if

tagu's) schemes for India. In fact he told me once he felt suffocated and inclined to commit suicide, as working with Crewe was <u>so</u> Dreary.[1]

H. Yes, but he has learnt after 2 weeks in the Cabinet his <u>exact</u> value, which is very great. We want wisdom above all things now. As for Hardinge, he is, I think, off his head! He refuses to send us troops for Mesopotamia.[2] I should think the next thing we hear of him is his resignation. He hasn't been a success; poor fellow, he has had a lot of sorrow....His son died of blood poisoning from the bungling of a highly fashionable Australian surgeon....[3]

I told Henry that Montagu had got quite furious with me when I had said Ed. Grey had a really <u>bad</u> war temperament, which of course is true: but that now he (Montagu) <u>over-agreed</u> with me!

I <u>love</u> and shall always love Ed. Grey. He is a unique creature, and if he had had a delicious wife and children he would have had just what he misses; but at the same time he is quite by himself....Ld K. said to me 'Grey is such an odd fellow: he feels all sorts of things that don't concern him at all. Now he feels these Labour disputes and strikes acutely. I really believe if we had some awful catastrophe in this war he would go off his head.' M. 'No, I don't think so at all—you'll see, when we are in a terrible plight he will be all right. He is <u>so</u> tired, and he is a very nervous man about his health. Though he thinks he would not mind dying, he is more afraid of his health than anyone I know. He is a lonely man who responds

slightly prejudiced character, very straight, courageous and wise' (diary, July 1908); Hardinge was Viceroy of India 1910–16, and Crewe Secretary of State for India 1910–15.

[1] See *Asquith–Stanley*, 340: 'The Assyrian [Montagu] declares he has a constituent whose wife went mad after hearing Crewe speak for an hour and a half on the land question in the Corn Exchange at Royston'.

[2] In fact Hardinge had pressed for Indian troops to fight on the Western Front alongside their European counterparts, presciently recognizing the impact this would have on Indian commitment to the war effort; he was initially sceptical about the Middle Eastern theatre, but after the early successes of the Mesopotamian expeditionary force 1914–15 became a strong advocate of a campaign designed to take Baghdad, which ended disastrously at the Battle of Ctesiphon, 22–4 Nov. 1915, which was followed by the surrender of General Charles Townshend's remaining forces to the Turks, at Kut, in Apr. 1916.

[3] Edward Hardinge died in Dec. 1914, aged 22, after contracting tetanus from wounds sustained in early fighting in France.

to coozling[1] and loving. He has been unlucky in Life, not meeting quite the right women. We all fall in love with him, and he loves sterling worth, but he is <u>very</u> naïve and easily taken in and is not a fine judge of character. He is a very <u>lovable</u> being, because so remote from the world and so genuinely humble, though quite impenitent and not without a simple sort of vanity. He ought to have met a Clara (in the *Egoist* [by] Meredith)[2]—a sunny, warm, very generous, spontaneous, sensitive-for-others sort of woman of perfect courage and real insight; a woman of fine humour and no sort of artificiality. He has no female friend of that kind.'...

<u>Grey's health wants careful watching</u>. He thinks he is going blind. A clever oculist,[3] taken in I suppose by Grey's impregnable calm and beauty, told him he might very likely go blind (I wish I had heard him say it, as I can't but think Grey exaggerates!) and this has eaten into his very soul. Bridge is his one diversion, and none of us would miss gambling with him for the world. We combine to try and remove this health spectre from his brain.

I forgot to say on 4th March 1915 there was an awful row in the cabinet over the strikes in Clyde—shipping and shell-making, etc. There are always rows on the Clyde: no doubt Scotch employers and foremen are rude and tactless. In this row the employers were dead out.

The men had been promised a raise in wages before the war, and now, stale with overwork, they see their masters making large fortunes and only raising wages in a niggardly spirit, while everything has gone up in price—coal, etc. Their revolt is <u>natural</u>. (Of course, apart from war we shall all sooner or later have to face in the Future the one great question— <u>the Labour question</u>: this is our future revolution, unless we are <u>very</u> careful and clever.)

---

[1] Cosseting.

[2] George Meredith published *The Egoist* in 1879: its heroine, Clara, is famously described as 'a dainty rogue in porcelain'.

[3] Presumably the same as is referred to in *Asquith–Stanley*, 444, as 'a foolish oculist'. The first hint of Grey's eye trouble came as early as May 1914. His eyesight continued to deteriorate, although he never became totally blind. See Grey, *Twenty-Five Years*, ii. 57–61, Trevelyan, *Grey*, 271–3.

When H. told me Ll.G., K. and Winston suggested imprisoning men who would not work in wartime, I felt paralysed by the amazing crass stupidity of such a method!! H. (to me) 'We had a tiring and painful cabinet. K. understood when the situation was explained at once.' M. 'The idea that you will get more work out of more men by imprisoning the tired ones is the high-water mark of folly!! (like trying to put down suicide by the police.)'

Winston is a Tory and knows nothing of the British workman. He looks on him as a mere machine to whom high wages make the whole difference, whereas he is a very good fellow, nearly <u>always</u> mismanaged and overworked. People say to me 'You're a Socialist and of course always sympathize with the employed more than with employer.' I say I myself think when these strikes are gone into, people will find that working overtime and pure physical fatigue (<u>which could have been avoided</u> with a little more foresight on the part of the War Office or K. or Winston) has as much to do with the present Labour difficulties as anything else.

My brother Glenconner* has been 2 years running Lord High Commissioner in Edinburgh.[1] He refuses to be it again, which is a great pity. He did it <u>quite</u> beautifully. H. very properly thought Ld Rosebery, who has nothing <u>earthly</u> to do just now, ought to sacrifice himself and take it. He would have the time of his life as far as popularity went, and in a week it is all over. His letter of refusal…is a masterpiece of egoism and self-consciousness. With all his attractions he is an imperial rotter:— scientifically selfish.

Winston, Ll.G. and Arthur Balfour have been daily confabulating on labour problems. The result of this was pretty easy to prophesy: Winston, who is naturally very indiscreet, and a greenhorn about character, began to tell A.J.B. <u>everything</u> (indeed has, I've no doubt, told him every cabinet secret.) Arthur's non-party, dispassionate manner, his apparent controversial fairness in private life, his ease and almost lofty indifference to self would take in a more observant man than Winston. As a matter of fact Arthur is an

---

[1] The High Commissioner is the sovereign's representative at the General Assembly of the Church of Scotland. See the correspondence in NLS, Rosebery MSS, 10001, fos. 143–5.

impenitent political failure, divorced from ideas, wedded to party in the pettiest, strictest sense of the word; seldom fair in argument—unconvinced and unconvincing; a good critic, a bad judge.

Arthur has no conviction but a good deal of convention. He is fond of Problems of Defence, and thinks H. Rule for Ireland all rot; beyond this, I know nothing that he cares about. Drink, housing, Insurance, wages, education, Tariff [Reform], he doesn't care a hang about. He likes churches and church schools. He has got a fine mind, but not a powerful one in the sense that Henry's is powerful. It is not a sound mind, somehow (at least, Bimetallism and Protection generally mean unsoundness in my experience.) No one else makes much impression on it. The two great failures of Prime Ministers in my lifetime have been Arthur Balfour and Rosebery: two very different men, with different qualities and defects, but both lacking real nature and temperament.[1]

Tuesday 23 March 1915

H. and I motored to dine with Frances Horner. Henry told me that Ll.G. had said to him: 'If Grey needs a holiday and goes away, Winston thinks you should put Arthur Balfour in the Foreign Office.'

[H.] Young puppy! Let him come and suggest this to me and I'll tell him what I think of him!! He really is the greatest donkey! He goes gassing about, abusing K. to Arthur and I've no doubt abusing me, giving him much too much information. He thinks he knows Arthur Balfour: he has not the foggiest idea of what Arthur really is.

[1] For Balfour's brush with bimetallism in the 1890s see Young, *Balfour*, 172–3. By 'protection' Margot means 'imperial protection'—the favouring of empire goods over those from other countries. Her statement that A.J.B. did not 'care a hang about' education overlooks the importance of the Education Act, 1902; Salisbury was more concerned than his nephew about protecting 'Church schools'. Balfour was concerned, during the Tariff Reform controversy, with preventing an open split in Unionism, and this limited his initiative in social reform issues; see Chamberlain, *Down the Years*, 214–15: 'Things which appeared important to him [Balfour] often appeared of little consequence to his followers and to his opponents.' It seems not to have occurred to Margot that the Allies' prospects in the war would have been looking far less hopeful had Balfour not been 'fond of Problems of Defence'.

I thought I would pump Ll.G. about Arthur. I asked him how it was that a man of that futile, feminine brain, starting life as he did with every advantage—Social position, personal fascination, etc., with everything as you might say at his feet—how he succeeded in leading his party to the greatest disaster that has ever befallen any party in this country (1906), and, when they are in the depths, takes his hat off, says he is ill, and leaves his unfortunate friends to be led by a man of 5th rate quality like Bonar Law. This is the man whose counsel and judgement you are taking on delicate, complicated industrial problems.

Ll.G.[1]   The reason Arthur lost everything is that he continually gave way to the Parson, the Publican and the Protectionist.

(Ll.G. is a much more perceiving person than Winston. He knows perfectly well that Arthur is untrustworthy politically.)

[M.]   But, Henry, surely Joe [Chamberlain'] contributed to Arthur's downfall?

H.   Joe! He was an honest fanatic who sacrificed his career to his cause. He had real faiths: Arthur was merely spinning plates—I've no patience with him! No one who was not favoured by fortune like he was could have survived his conduct getting rid of his inconvenient colleagues in [1903] and trying to retain the Duke of Devonshire.[2] Oh! no, Arthur is a very charming fellow but the greatest fraud of our time.

I told Henry I thought at lunch (10 Downing St.), where I had sat between Ll.G. and Arthur, that they were a little tired of each other—they have been seeing too much of each other.

---

[1] Margot's use of the dialogue form seems sometimes to have been idiosyncratic. She is presumably giving here her husband's account of what Ll.G. had said to him.

[2] Spencer Compton Cavendish (1833–1908), 8th Duke of Devonshire; leader of the Liberal Unionists, 1886–1903, and of the Unionists in the House of Lords, 1902–3; Lord President of the Council, 1895–1903; an advocate of free trade, he was prepared to resign from Balfour's government in Sept. 1903, after Chamberlain declared for tariff reform, but remained in response to an appeal from Balfour for government unity in October, though he later resigned when Balfour appeared to lead the Unionists in the direction of fiscal reform.

Apropos of Leo Maxse and the *National Review*, A. said he wasn't a bad fellow in private.[1] I said I thought it was dishonourable to make an income out of the awful lies he published monthly. Ll.G. said he was either mad or bad. I said he was also very, very silly. M. 'He talked of Henry as a "<u>lazy man</u>" which was rather comic.' Arthur (with that touch of feminine claw which I detect now and then in political men of small moral size) '<u>I</u> think he <u>is</u>!'!![2]

Ll.G. burst into fits of laughter, so did Arthur, but though he laughed at this unique idea he looked just a <u>little</u> uncomfortable! I only said '<u>Bravo</u>, Arthur!': but pondered in my heart, and felt for the very first time that Arthur was jealous politically of Henry. Of course, I may be wrong, but though it is very natural he should be jealous, I have not noticed it before; though I've noticed him give H. one in a very good-humoured way fairly often. Arthur is really <u>fond</u> of Henry, but it is perhaps more natural he should <u>feel</u> his enormous success in Life....

Thursday 1 April 1915

Who is to advise the King if he is or is not to drink?[3] Is it true that 'There has been serious delay in the conveyance of necessary reinforcements and supplies to aid our gallant troops at the front'? I can't say I believe

[1] Leopold James ('Leo') Maxse (1864–1932), editor of the *National Review*, which was purchased on his behalf in 1893 by his father, and which he made in his own image: strongly imperialist, protectionist, and Francophile, and highly critical of the Liberal government.

[2] Margot's amused reaction to the perception of Maxse, and Balfour, that her husband was indolent betrayed a complacency that was dangerous at any time, but which in wartime would prove fatal: see above, cxxvii–cxxviii.

[3] Against the background of a national debate about the effect of alcohol consumption on critical war industries, such as armaments, Lloyd George urged the King on 29 Mar. to help war production by abstaining from strong drink during the war, and by imposing the same abstinence on the royal household. The next day Lloyd George reported to the King's private secretary, Stamfordham, the cabinet's feeling 'that, if the King took the lead in [this], the nation would follow him'. On the basis of this assurance a letter disclosing the King's intention was published in the press on 1 Apr. 1915. The starting date for teetotalism at Court was to be 6 Apr. The day before that, disquieted by seeing no sign of governmental activity to stimulate similar decisions, Stamfordham told Lloyd George that the King proposed to delay the Court's starting date. Lloyd George replied that it could not be delayed: the Prime Minister's consent to publication of the letter had given the impression 'that His Majesty had actually issued the order' for the Court's teetotalism: Grigg, *Lloyd George, 1912–1916*, 230–2.

this—it's the first I've heard of it. If it's not correct, what a monstrous thing to say before our enemies! I should think this letter will be posted up in every German village, and cheering up the whole of their armies.[1] I feel pretty sure that this is not Henry's doing, but Ll.G.'s—very sincerely well meant, but intensely Foolish.[2] P.S. (Written on 5th May, M.A.)

Ld Lincolnshire told me today at lunch that Queen Alexandra's old Court Chamberlain,[3] a dodderer physically and mentally, had said to him 'Is the PM and his household following the King's lead?'—to which Lincolnshire answered 'It is not the PM's place to follow the King's lead, but for the King to take a lead from the PM.'...

I dined with Winston. It was Clemmy's birthday. I was shocked by the rot Winston talked about the workmen! (As H. said to me after when I was talking to him before going to bed 'Winston is a regular Tory—I see it constantly in his point of view'.) He said they ought to be shot; if he had his way, he would put a sentry in front of every workman's door, etc. etc. I begged him to believe me that it was not true. Our men could not work as much as they wanted to, because they were far too tired. It was not Drink or Idleness, it was genuine over-work that would account for everything. I could not bear to hear our workmen slandered and misunderstood. Winston said 'I daresay working on Sundays has been a mistake, but you can take it all from me, all my men tell the same tale of drink, and Sunday work has been stopped, hasn't it, Masterton?' Masterton-Smith (secretary) 'No, sir, I've had no orders.' Winston 'Why, I thought I had stopped Sunday work! See that it's done at once.'[4]

---

[1] Stamfordham's letter on behalf of the King (from the *Morning Post*, 1 Apr. 1915) is pasted in MS Eng. d. 3211, fo. 583: 'it is without doubt largely due to drink that we are unable to secure the output of war material indispensable to meet the requirement of our Army in the field' (*The Times*, 1 Apr. 1915, 8a). For the context see Grigg, *Lloyd George, 1912–1916*, 229–37.

[2] Margot may have exaggerated, not the folly of Ll.G.'s move, but the sincerity of his motives in making it. He needed a cause which would both show his zeal as a war-maker and appeal to his Nonconformist followers; and he can hardly have been averse to one which emphasized his temperance by comparison with the Prime Minister's habits. For his uncandid account of the episode see Lloyd George, *War Memoirs*, i. 194–6.

[3] Margot probably refers to Sir Dighton Probyn (1833–1924), who was Queen Alexandra's Comptroller.

[4] For the Admiralty's action on this see *Daily Chronicle*, 16 Apr. 1915, 5b. For the succession of measures by which the consumption of alcohol was reduced during the war see Searle,

The King's silly letter was followed by every sort of letter, which of course ran him in, for the public took it for granted he would not write a letter of the kind without giving up Drink. Kitchener, McKenna, Ll.G. are all pledged to drink nothing till the end of the war. The Archbishop of York went so far as to tell the King he hoped he would let all England know that this state of teetotalism was to last 6 months after peace was signed! (The clergy will always be silly. They stick to their rôle like stage gags, character parts: gamps,[1] mother-in-law, etc; no sex, no sense, little or no spirituality.)

H. said on 6th April 1915 at lunch 'I never saw K. so depressed.' Elizabeth 'Neither the retreat at beginning of War or Neuve Chapelle affected his spirits as badly as 3 days on lemonade.' (We loved Oc's wire from Port Said, 2nd April).[2]

April 1915—Windsor

I went by train to Windsor 12th April 1915. H. followed in his motor. We <u>were</u> a dull lot!—Mary Minto[3] my only friend, and Soveral the only guest.[4] Windsor is a little too big for the present King and Queen. King Edward and beautiful Queen Alexandra were much better suited to castles and palaces.

We all waited before dinner, the men one side and women the other, and when the King was announced by Sir Fritz Ponsonby[5] the Queen

---

1886–1918, 805–6, 815–16. Sales of spirits fell from 35 million gallons in 1915 to 15 millions in 1918.

[1] Umbrellas.

[2] Oc's wire is pasted in the diary, d. 3211, fo. 586ᵛ. It reads: 'Reported spread of temperance alarms and amazes us. Stand Fast. Arthur Asquith.' See also Gwynne, *Rasp*, 81. Oc's Royal Naval Division rested in Port Said before re-embarkin for Gallipoli, via Skyros.

[3] Mary Caroline Grey (1858–1940), m. 1883 4th Earl of Minto.

[4] Marquis de Soveral (1862–1922), lately Portuguese Ambassador in London.

[5] Sir Frederick Ponsonby [Fritz] (1867–1935), KCVO 1910, cr. Baron Sysonby 1935. Assistant Private Secretary successively to Queen Victoria and Edward VII 1894–1910. Equerry in Ordinary and Assistant Private Secretary to George V, 1910, Keeper of Privy Purse 1914; Treasurer to George V 1920. His *Recollections of Three Reigns* were 'prepared for press' by C. Welch, and published in 1951.

walked up the line of men and shook hands, and the King up our line. The remarks they make remind me of the questions we have to put in the game 'acting adverbs' (Do you like travelling? Are you seasick? Did you enjoy yourself today? What do you like doing? etc. What is your favourite flower? etc. etc.) 'You like Walmer? Your little boy is fond of aeroplanes? Do you not feel afraid of Zeppelins so near the sea? etc.'...

The King said to me at dinner that he had been sold![1] as he never intended to give up drink unless the Gov. passed drastic legislation on the subject; that, had this been done, he wanted to say he was ready to share the sacrifices of the poorest of his subjects. He is a dear little fellow and fundamentally humble in spite of his manner (noisy and crude). I sat between him and Soveral at dinner. He said 'My servants, when the cellar man locked up the cellars, arranged a large wreath of empty bottles outside the door and put a crêpe bow on them with a placard and the word 'Dead' written on it.' We both laughed, and he said no German workman had stopped work from strikes or drink, and looked at me as if I didn't believe him. I loathe drink more than anyone. I've suffered from it in grooms and butlers, and seen its fatal effects on the temperaments and intellects of many young men...but I feel the British workman should have his stimulant just the same as all our soldiers have theirs....

[The King] told me his cousin the Tsar was 'the best, straightest, most clear and decided man I know.'[2] He gave H. the sworn and signed written evidence of Vandeleur[3] and his friends, prisoners in Germany, of their

[1] 'Carted' (roughly discarded) was apparently the word used by the Queen to Asquith: Rose, *George V*, 179. See also Bonham Carter, *Diaries, 1914–45*, 36, where Violet quotes her father's description of the dinner: '...Almost complete silence prevailed at meals—broken only by Margot's hunting stories—"She'd had her jorum of brandy before coming down" Father would explain'. Margot drank brandy on doctor's orders. For the improvement in the King's standing with the working class produced by his 'pledge' see Montague, *Disenchantment*, 192. Ironically he owed this added popularity to the fact that very few had 'followed his lead'.

[2] Nicholas II (1868–1918), m. 1894 Princess Alix of Hesse (1872–1918): both were cousins of George V. While Nicholas would have been estimable as a private man he was hardly satisfactory as a ruler.

[3] The treatment of prisoners of war in Germany is described by James Gerard in *Four Years*, ch. 10; Gerard (1867–1951) was the American Ambassador in Berlin, 1913–1917, and made great efforts to obtain improvements in POW camps. Capt. Vandeleur had been imprisoned, and

frightful treatment (shocking reading). He was furious with me when I said I had heard Vandeleur was an exaggerator. He said when the war was over he intended to take this document with his own hands to the Kaiser 'and ask him what he meant by it.'...

Tuesday 13 April 1915—Windsor

I felt terribly depressed and worried over a trifling domestic discouragement which has baffled and bothered me for a long, long time.[1] I wrote a letter to H. about it. I don't know what I said. I told him how <u>much</u> I loved him and how well I knew I was getting older: that I was irritable, and that there <u>were</u> other females in the world, etc.; that I had no common jealousy that would deprive him of unshared leisure or pleasure (that sort of self-loving jealousy which means vanity is unknown to me). On the contrary my Love was constantly re-equipping him for Happiness, but that in moments of discouragement I also wanted re-equipment and a little stimulus...

The enclosed Beautiful letter he wrote immediately on arriving in London for his cabinet.[2] He sent it by special messenger (with an unexpected letter from my little son and Lover) to Windsor. I got it while sitting with the Household at lunch. I read it then and there—all the company and the room fading from my sight.

Rupert Brooke, the beautiful young poet, died of blood poisoning on the night of 23d. April 1915 and was buried at Lemnos[3].... Hearing at

had escaped. The government's intention to disclose his report was announced on 20 Apr. 1915: *Parl. Deb.*, 71.153. Grey had earlier made a statement: *The Times*, 7 Apr. 1915, 9b.

[1] Margot's concern about her husband's friendship with Venetia Stanley became acute around this time. This entry (13 Apr.) seems to have been written over several days; the paragraphs about Rupert Brooke cannot have been written before 23 Apr.

[2] The text of this letter (HHA to Margot, 13 Apr. 1915) is given in *Asquith–Stanley*, 548: 'My own darling—Your letter made me sad, and I hasten to tell you that you have *no* cause for the doubts & fears wh. it expresses, or suggests'. Margot enclosed it with her letter, 16 Apr., to Edwin Montagu (*Asquith–Stanley*, 546–7): 'Dearest Mr Montagu, I value this letter very deeply so return it *at once*.'

[3] In fact on Skyros, 'in a small grove of wild olive trees, up an unfrequented glen, about three-quarters of a mile from the sea' (Arthur Asquith to Violet Asquith, 25 April 1915; Bonham Carter, *Diaries, 1914–45*, 42).

lunch from Bongy that he was ill I sent him a wire by Eddie Marsh in the afternoon 'My Love: thinking of you', but he would never have got it. If one can dare say it, Rupert's death seems an awful, terrible waste! He had all the qualities I love—Goodness and Real Temperament, Freshness, Candour and brains. He had charm and sympathy, immortal youth and no touch of that devastating cleverness that exorcises Holiness, dissects Love and despises God.[1]

I took a copy of *New Numbers* with me for him to write my name in it the last time I saw him. He put his hands on my shoulders and looked at me with his beautiful eyes and kissed me in Oc's little wooden tent at Blandford on 26th Feb. 1915.

---

[1] Edward Howard Marsh (1872–1953), KCVO 1937; personal secretary to Churchill, Admiralty, 1911–15; patron of art and literature; literary executor of Rupert Brooke, whose collected poems he published in 1918. Brooke's less attractive side was not generally revealed until the publication of Nigel Jones's biography in 2000.

PART IV
17 APRIL–19 MAY 1915

By the spring of 1915 Margot had not yet become habituated to disasters, and her use of that adjective to describe the Battle of Neuve Chapelle in March 1915 is questionable. Nevertheless, the reverse experienced there, and at the Dardanelles a few days later, where the navy's attempt to force the Straits ended in failure, contributed to a growing anxiety that the war was not being well managed at the top. Misfortunes in battle were far less damaging to Asquith than his own apparent ignorance of the realities that might lie behind them, and a passage in his speech at Newcastle on 20 Apr. 1915, in particular, was to dog him for the rest of his life. In what Margot judged a 'fine, healing, brave speech', Asquith aimed to refute the suggestion that the country's armament workers might have failed the troops because alcoholic self-indulgence had reduced their output. He had been furnished, as he thought, with proof of this, in a written statement that Kitchener had provided, to the effect that Sir John French 'would have as much artillery ammunition as his troops [will] be able to use during the next forward movement'. This was an unwise statement in itself, but Asquith went well beyond it in suggesting that no army had ever 'entered upon a campaign, or been maintained during a campaign, with better or more adequate equipment'. Such a sanguine estimate ran counter to statements by other members of the government, as the press quickly pointed out, and, even more dangerously, it was known by almost everyone on the Western Front to be untrue. Two days after the Newcastle speech the Germans made the first gas attack of the war, at Ypres; and on 7 May the Lusitania was torpedoed by a U-Boat off the Irish coast, with the loss of 1,198 lives. In the fiercer and more demanding public mood which these setbacks and outrages had created the heads of the army and navy rebelled. On 14 May 1915 The Times published a dispatch in which the respected military correspondent Colonel Repington attributed the failure of the Aubers Ridge attack five days earlier to 'the want of an unlimited supply of high explosive'.[1] His information on the so-called 'shells shortage' scandal came directly from Sir John French. And on the following day, 15 Mar., the First Sea Lord, 'Jacky' Fisher, resigned over the Dardanelles venture, leaving the Admiralty for an undisclosed destination. French and Fisher aimed not at Asquith but at their respective chiefs, Kitchener and Churchill, but their resignations were enough to compel him to enter into a coalition with the Unionists and with Labour, bringing about the end of the Liberal government elected in 1906, and which he had led since 1908.

[1] Charles À Court Repington (1858–1925), military correspondent of The Times, 1904–18. The article gave a highly simplified account of the causes of failure at Aubers Ridge. There was a general shortage of ammunition; but more important in this battle was the shortage of howitzers and heavy artillery.

Saturday 17 April 1915

We spent our last Sunday at Walmer. I had got devoted to it and felt quite sad to leave it. I wish the nation would give it to Henry with a pension for the rest of his life after this war. He deserves everything the King can give him: of this there are not two opinions....

Henry told me his cabinet of 15th April was the saddest and most disagreeable he had ever had in all his term of office.[1] Ll.G. lost his head and temper; Winston was foolish; McK., who ought to have helped, sat silent, unhelpful and gloating over the situation which the 2 men in the cabinet he dislikes—Ll.G. and Winston—had created. K. behaved very well—gave it hot to Ll.G., and practically resigned. M. 'I can't believe K. will ever resign while this war lasts.'

(Crewe told me at Walmer the same about the cabinet. He wasn't so upset by the row as Henry was, because Crewe has a much more bloodless nature. He is very shrewd and said to me there would never be any fear of K. resigning.) No doubt, McK. has a provincial mind and likes small quarrels and seeing his (boring!) suspicions come true....

I forgot to say we've had some baddish times both in France, Flanders and in the Dardanelles (start off).[2] I think Rawlinson is much blamed for the Neuve Chapelle disaster.[3] The Prince of Wales said this to me and added 'We can all make mistakes, Mrs Asquith, but no one will forgive Rawlinson for allowing the blame to rest on Bailey...Capper and others.'...[4]

---

[1] Asquith wrote to Venetia on 16 Apr.: 'The two who came out really worst were Ll.G., who almost got down to the level of a petty police court advocate, & McKenna, who played the part of a wrecker, pure and simple'; see *Asquith–Stanley*, 546.

[2] Margot refers here to the sinking of warships during the naval bombardment of the Dardanelles on 18 March. The army assault began on 25 Apr.

[3] The Battle of Neuve Chapelle, 10–13 Mar., was perhaps not the disaster that Margot suggests: German casualties nearly equalled Haig's, a ratio not matched in a British attack for a considerable time, and 1,600 German prisoners were taken; the enemy had also been taught that 'they could not afford to neglect the British front....In short, Neuve Chapelle marked Britain's debut as a major land power': Terraine, *First World War*, 65, and see also Charteris, *At GHQ*, 81.

[4] The initial success of the British at Neuve Chapelle owed much to Rawlinson's planning, but he subsequently blamed one of his divisional commanders for the failure to exploit this,

Wednesday 21 April 1915

On [20] April 1915 Elizabeth, Violet, Bongy, H. and myself went to New-castle for a speech which H. delivered on munitions. The Tory Press have been attacking him violently for shortage of munitions. This has been a good deal Ll.G.'s fault and of course Winston's. (The top note was struck over both munitions and drink, and of course this is always folly, as we shall all have to climb down; and the Drink legislation, if it is not of the mildest, won't pass in the House.)

Our Newcastle visit was extraordinarily interesting.[1] I like sitting on the platform near H. when he speaks, and at all times loathe a box (He spoke in the theatre) for tho' one is well seen (!!)—as well seen as on the platform—one does not take in the effect of a speech on the audience; and you are of course not in the same boat as it were with one's husband (The strength and joy of my life is to be near Henry or the children when they are being tested—I feel like a second in a duel.)

Henry made a fine, healing, brave speech. He refuses to be rattled in this War, either by his colleagues' screams, or a flow of abuse by the Tory Press. No doubt he has the best war temperament the world has ever seen.

Just now I am watching the strangest evolution of the political truce. [The] *Times* editor, a real blackguard of the lowest kind, has openly boasted he will do for Henry. He wants a coalition Gov.—Ll.G. Prime Minister, Austen [Chamberlain]* Home Office, B. Law Foreign Office (or vice versa) H. Ld. Chancellor, etc. The *Morning Post* who hates Winston first and Henry next has consistently abused us: it is a strong Tory paper: but *The Times* is extremely vindictive and underhand, often praising and struggling to look

when in fact the responsibility lay with himself; only Haig's protection prevented his demo-tion when the sleight was discovered: see Maurice, *Rawlinson*, 126–9. [?]Brigadier-General Vivian Telford Bailey (1868–1938); Major-General Sir Thompson Capper (1863–1915), KCMG 1915; he commanded the 7th Division under Rawlinson at Neuve Chapelle; killed by a sniper at Loos that Sept.

[1] Violet, who was also in the expedition, describes Margot as 'restless and rather dys-peptic' that day: Bonham Carter Papers, Violet Asquith diary, Feb.–June 1915, entry covering 20 Apr.

impartial. Throughout this war no English paper has shown so <u>little</u> patriotism as *The Times*: it was execrated at the front when I was out, and is execrated over here and in Paris. I don't mind it trying to do for Henry, except for the joy it gives the Germans. Garvin of the *Observer* (a Tory) rounded on it last Sunday, which pleased me.[1] Our papers have been outspoken and loyal over this intrigue. The *Daily Telegraph* has behaved best. (Bonar Law seems to me to have behaved well.)[2]

Ll.G. and Winston talked too much with Arthur, F. E. Smith, etc; violent articles began to appear in the <u>whole</u> Harmsworth Press.[3] McKenna met Donald the editor of *Daily Chronicle* and told him to answer these charges.[4] Monday 29th March…the *Morning Post* reached its height of abuse, and our *Daily Chronicle* headed its leader by 'Intrigue against the Prime Minister'. This latter caused a rare rumpus. I've got the articles bound and typewritten, and wish I had written down every word at the time, but I lost my notes, all but one, and as I never write from pure recollection I can only outline what happened.

Ll.G. ran round here (10 Downing St.) and had a most moving scene with H. He cursed McKenna (One of his henchmen told him that McK. and Donald had been seen together) and assured Henry with <u>tears</u> that he (Ll.G.) owed all he possessed to Henry (Marconi trouble);[5] that he would rather retire forever and dig potatoes than intrigue against H. He was in a state of despair—<u>absolutely genuine</u> despair. H. calmed him down, but could not move him about McK., and, fearing a

[1] James Louis Garvin (1868–1947), influential journalist; edited *Pall Mall Gazette*, 1912–15, and the *Observer*, 1908–42; although a supporter of Unionist policies he was not the conventional Tory by any means.

[2] See the *Observer*'s call, 2 May 1915, for an end to the 'harassing fire of criticism' aimed at ministers. On 29 Jan. Bonar Law had explained to Curzon that the Unionists had either 'to go on…without responsibility and with only a very limited amount of criticism…or to face a coalition. The latter proposal I should certainly be against': Blake, *Bonar Law*, 238.

[3] Margot has in mind the newspapers published by Alfred Charles William Harmsworth, Viscount Northcliffe, and notably the *Daily Mail* and *The Times*.

[4] Robert Donald (1860–1933), GBE 1924; editor of the Liberal *Daily Chronicle*, 1902–18.

[5] In June 1913 Asquith had defended Lloyd George and Rufus Isaacs (Lord Reading) in the Commons against charges of impropriety, arising from their unwise dealing in shares in the Marconi company; Margot credited the premier, Balfour, and Grey, all of whom spoke in the relevant debate, with saving their political careers.

serious break in the cabinet, said he would see them both together that afternoon.

(H. hates scenes of all kinds, but when he has to have them he has things radically and fundamentally out. He saw J. Burns and Ll.G. together in a famous row, and many others.)

I wrote to McKenna very privately begging him not to quarrel with Ll.G. I heard afterwards from Donald that McK had said nothing to him against Ll.G., and that he (Donald) had been able to make Ll.G. believe this afterwards; but of course the expression 'intrigue' means from within, so Donald or Ll.G. were to blame for this unlucky expression.

Henry's account of this wonderful interview was very interesting. He said Ll.G. was quite bold and opened at once with a strong attack on McK., saying it was quite evident that the finger was pointed at him (Ll.G.) as the prime intriguer, etc. McK. hotly denied this, and the article was produced. It certainly praised McK. I think there was a slight implication against Ll.G. On the whole the interview was a great success and cleared the air.

H. I blame Winston also: as long as he will see F. E. Smith and discuss every cabinet secret with him, and gas about A.J.B. going to Foreign Office, and coalition Gov., so long we shall have these rows. I can assure you I shan't easily forget my tête-à-tête with Ll.G.

M. Has Winston said anything to you?

H. Oh! No, I'm not going to speak to him about it at all. For a moment I thought of having him in also, but it is no good discussing things with Winston.

Friday 7 May 1915–7.30 a.m.[1]

At the time of writing 2 things are most anxiously awaited: Italy's open action, and the triumph of our Dardanelles expedition. . . .

[1] For the idiosyncrasies of Margot's dating; and, in particular, her habit of apparently mixing up the chronological sequence of her entries, see Editorial Note, p. xviii.

I had just finished [a] wonderful account of the Gallipoli landing which filled me with serious excitement, when as I stood brushing my hair Henry came into the bedroom in his dressing-gown, his eyes streaming with tears, holding a telegram in his hand.[1] (I have been sleeping abominably ever since I knew that Oc was fighting—5, often 3, hours was as much as I seemed able to remain unconscious). I saw Henry in front of me, and felt sure Oc had been killed. I put my hand out to defend myself from the blow and could just say 'Oc is dead?'

Poor Henry! who adores Oc, put his arm round me and read the telegram with me. The relief was so intense that we both cried with a mixture of joy and apprehension. (Henry's wonderful humanness strikes everyone who knows him beyond the surface. I dare say if by some miracle I could survive some fine biography the author would say he was not or at least had not always been very human. Oxford people assure me he was less human before we were married, but this is all nonsense: he would not be where he is if he had been what these people think. I for one would never have married him if he had not been intensely human. The reason Oc is the most loved of my step-children is that he is far the most human of them)....

I ran to tell Violet, who was in her bath, poor darling! She was surprised more than moved—surprised that I could feel emotion over a mere escape, and almost 'put about' that I had frightened her, though she too adores Oc. 'Goodness, I thought by your face and manner he was dead! You gave me an awful fright'!...[2]

Violet would be a wonderful woman if she could be mesmerized into feeling just what others are feeling; if real, disinterested emotion could be added to her many natural gifts. The capacity to feel deeply, to Love Really, to give of yourself Freely would gradually come and transform her into a

[1] The first Gallipoli landings took place on 25 Apr. Oc was luckily not involved in these, but was wounded soon afterwards: 'clean bullet wound left knee' read one telegram, and the Commander-in-Chief there, Sir Ian Hamilton, reported that there was 'no loss of life or limb'.

[2] For Violet's account of this see Bonham Carter, *Diaries, 1914–45*, 47: 'Margot rushed in...making loud sobbing noises and saying "He's not dead! he's not dead! he's not dead,"'.

noble woman....It is grandeur of nature, capacity for Feeling and Emotion,...warmth of Heart and courage of expression, that distinguishes Henry from his fellows.

Monday 3 May 1915

H. said to me 'K. has <u>never</u> been so hopeful as today: he thinks the Germans are retreating; but you must not <u>breathe</u> this.' I saw nothing in the news to make him think this. We have had nothing but bad news and <u>terrible</u> casualties.[1] Winston is always gassing about a coalition Gov.—so disloyal to his PM. I should <u>loathe</u> a coalition, so would H. Winston has no sort of political heart or 'sentiment'.

Saturday 8 May 1915

I had arranged to go by an early train (11.30) to Oxford, to spend 3 hours with Anthony in the sun. Just as I was starting, Frances Horner and my (stepdaughter-in-law) Katharine came in, in great agitation, to say Edward Horner was dangerously wounded in abdomen and they wanted passports to get out to him at once.[2] Henry sat down in the Cabinet room and wrote a note to Cambon. I was much distressed. I love Edward Horner. I was rather struck by K[atharine]'s helplessness. I asked who they were taking out with them—what nurse? what surgeon? etc.—I need hardly say they had never thought of this, though they had known the night before that he had been wounded (7th May 1915). I should have thought that, though both my daughters-in-law have very little Life, Frances Horner would have had complete command of the situation. (How few men or

[1] The German attack at Ypres which had begun, 22 Apr. 1915, with gas and bombardment from 420mm howitzers had been held in check; but Margot was right about the Allied casualties. During the Second Battle of Ypres the British lost 60,000, the French 10,000, the Germans fewer: Cruttwell, *Great War*, 157n.

[2] Edward Horner (1888–1917), eldest son of Sir John and Lady (Frances) Horner, and brother of Raymond Asquith's wife Katharine. He made a recovery from his serious wound and was later sent to Egypt, but pulled strings to get back to the Western Front and was killed at the Battle of Cambrai in 1917.

women there are of action—2 engine drivers to 200 passengers. I believe in the faith that removes mountains more almost than in anything—Faith and Love more than what most people call God and the Church.) I at once motored to the great surgeon Sir Arbuthnot Lane[1] and got his servant to telephone to King Edward's Hospital (where he was performing 5 operations); and he promised to go out by 2 train to Folkstone, Boulogne etc. with K. and Frances. I also got a nurse for them.[2]

Henry… told me in the motor that the Germans had sunk the biggest ship in the world, the *Lusitania,* off the coast of Ireland—masses of Americans and English on board, but luckily no lives lost.[3] I could not help being a little glad as America has played such a poor part in this war; also, I thought it would shock and wake up all the neutrals to the Horrible Threat of a conquering Germany.

When I heard of the loss of life I felt a shudder of Horror at what a highly finished modern nation can resort to, and more than ever felt the uselessness and even temptation of Brains and Education! (compared to Character). What is the use of Culture? Where does Progress of the head lead you to, if you have stagnation in the other parts?

This week has been the most terrible since the 4th Aug. 1914. The Germans have acknowledged they have poisoned wells in S. Africa; they have killed, tortured and suffocated our soldiers by using poisonous gases, and they have sunk the *Lusitania.* One thousand 142 people, women, children and men, have been drowned, 764 saved. The Germans are morally Insane.

What will America do now? I see one of the German papers say[s] America will do nothing: money will satisfy America. What a terrible indictment! Up to now money has satisfied America. Money has been her God, her one great Industry, her Art. She has a chance now of retrieving

---

[1] Sir Arbuthnot Lane (1856–1943), Bt. 1913; consultant at Great Ormond Street, 1883–1916; consulting surgeon, Aldershot Command, 1914–18.

[2] Diana Cooper ascribed these achievements to George Moore: Cooper, *Rainbow,* 144–5.

[3] The *Lusitania* was torpedoed by a U-Boat off the Old Head of Kinsale. First reports of casualties were inaccurate: 1,198 people, including 124 Americans, were drowned.

her Reputation. Will she take it? I have said it before, and felt it <u>always</u>: Progress has gone far ahead of Civilisation in America.[1]

After doing what I could for poor Frances and K. I went by train to Wharf alone as I always do. Henry and Bongy motored. Ll.G., Rufus Isaacs (Ld Reading) and Sylvia Henley* spent Sunday there. The 2nd week of the cuckoo in England is the most beautiful time in the whole year for me, if it is hot and sunny. My little cottage looked a dream—the tulips and all the blossom out; tiny leaves of piercing green shivering in an undeveloped sun and the wind in the East.

Ll.G., having been heavily defeated over his Drink in the House, one might have supposed would have been a little depressed: not at all—I never saw him in better form. He told Montagu he had never enjoyed anything more. He spoke in really genuinely admiring enthusiastic terms of the beauty and particularly of the cleverness of my little property. 'I've never seen a room like this—it is fine, clever, beautiful' he said, standing in the doorway of the Barn (which is my sitting-room). He talked a whole morning.

[Ll.G.] Winston is a difficult fellow: he has not merely <u>bad</u> judgement, but he has <u>none</u>. His Dardanelles expedition gave the Turk a fearful long start. He quarrelled with Enver* and got us at war with the Turk, which he need never have done.[2] The Turk is a formidable fellow, and I don't believe we shall get through this thing with less than 200,000 men. We should have made Fisher and Wilson[3] say what they thought in the War Council. Now Fisher gasses about all over the place saying he was against this expedition—and he <u>was</u>,

[1] Presumably Margot, like many other British people, was unaware that Woodrow Wilson did not yet fear the war ending in a German victory. This fear came much later with the interception, in January 1917, of the Zimmerman telegram. Two days before that, Wilson accused a colleague, who feared a German attack on America, of 'appealing to the Code Duello': Baker, *Wilson*, vi. 471–2.

[2] This probably concerns the requisitioning of two Turkish battleships being built in Britain when war began: Churchill, *World Crisis*, i. 209.

[3] Admiral of the Fleet, Sir Arthur Wilson (1842–1921), s. as 3rd Bt. 1919, First Sea Lord, 1910–11; assistant to Fisher, 1914.

but he should have said so. Neither he nor [Wilson] uttered. Winston said he would do this thing with ships, and that the men would be all right whenever K. could send them.

M.   Winston has a good war temperament, if good spirits and unruffledness is what is wanted. He also has a lot of suggestions and young ideas,—elastic, vital, youthful military ideas: but he is very dangerous, because he has no real imagination, in the sense of seeing deeply into events and probabilities. I've seen it all through his life: when he was a little navyite[1] and intrigued against McKenna—how wicked and above all how <u>Foolish</u> and short-sighted! When he thought out loud over the Curragh affair pre-Curragh, and talked <u>so</u> loud about what he—Winston—would do in the event of such and such, that it almost amounted to a plot. He muddled his Antwerp, and he will again muddle this, I fear. What a strange being! He really likes war. He would be quite damped if he were told now 'The war is over.' He has no imagination of the heart.

Ll.G.   <u>He has none.</u> I shall never forget that night—that 4th August 1914, when war was declared. I dined alone. I was sent for to see the PM about 10.30. I found McKenna and Grey in the cabinet room with the PM. We were all very serious, very anxious. The PM said 'Midnight abroad is 11 here.' We all looked at the clock, and Grey said 'It's not all over yet.' He then told us that a wire from Jagow[2] had been intercepted by our Post office saying Goschen in Berlin had sent for his passports. I said 'It's all over, then'.... Big Ben struck 11: very slowly came the Boom, Boom, Boom. We sat in complete silence I should say for 10 minutes after the last Boom. Winston dashed into the room radiant—his face bright, his manner keen; and he told us, one word pouring out on the other, how he was going to send telegrams to the Mediterranean! the North Sea and God knows where. You could see he was a really happy man. I wondered if this was the state of mind to be in at the opening of

[1] i.e. a pre-war critic of high government spending on the Royal Navy's battleship fleet.
[2] Gottlieb von Jagow (1863–1935), German diplomat; Foreign Secretary, Berlin, 1913–16.

such a fearful war as this. You're right, he has no real Imagination of the kind that counts....

If only this Dardanelles expedition would come off and Italy play up it ought to shorten the war; but I'm sure it will go on another year.

M.   Yes, certainly. They all laughed at me except H. when I betted that it would last till this Xmas....

Ll.G.   My only criticism of the whole cabinet is, I don't believe they realize even <u>now</u> what a big business this is and <u>how</u> difficult the German is to beat.

M.   Oh, I think they do.

Ll.G.   Why, bless your soul, the Germans are the best chemists in the world—they can make munitions out of this grass (kicking the turf under his chair, where we were sitting in the sun under my Barn).[1] I blame K. for not having, in spite of saying the war would last 3 years, got all the factories etc. together from the very first.

M.   (later on) You are rather against the Dardanelles expedition.

Ll.G.   Yes, I am, because I think we shall want many more men, and we can't get them—where are they to come from? 7000 of K.'s new army have gone off to Sir J. French this week, but there aren't many more really equipped and trained.

M.   I'm told there are nearly a million ready.

Ll.G.   Well, I rather think you're right: they will all go out at once, and are going daily.

Wednesday 12 May 1915

H. came into my bedroom much perturbed at his great friend's engagement.[2]

---

[1] See *The Speaker*, 26 Jan. 1907, 490: 'Nitrates from Air'; Strachan, *First World War*, i. 1025–7.

[2] Asquith was informed by Venetia of her plan to marry Edwin Montagu in a letter dated 11 May, which he must have read after midnight: the next day he wrote to her: 'Most Loved—As you know well, *this* breaks my heart. I couldn't bear to come and see you. I can only pray God to bless you—and help me. Yours.' (*Asquith–Stanley*, 592–3).

H. A very sad thing has happened.

M. Is Beb killed?

H. Oh! not as bad as that: but Venetia has engaged herself to Montagu, and I feel, good and devoted fellow as he is, that this will spell disaster and sorrow to both of them.

M. Oh! I don't think so. She is quite old enough to know her own mind, and she knows better than she knows anyone but you, and is fond of him. You are always anti-marriage, but I would rather my children married for a year, even unhappily, than they should never marry at all. An unmarried girl, unless she has exceptional unselfishness and sense of responsibility, is unhappy herself and makes others unhappy. Venetia has never been really in love: she hasn't got the capacity. It is given to few (I must say every day I live, I see how very few have the power to love, even if they have the temperament to fall in love!).

I could not bear to see him unhappy; harassed as he is by everything just now: our West line going badly, the Dardanelles abominably, Italy hanging back, Germany forging forward. My heart went out to him. I jumped out of bed and put my arms round him and said 'My beloved, Venetia is a very sensible girl: if she feels she can't marry him, she won't.'

Thursday 13 May 1915

I met Fisher in Bongy's room.

M. How are things going?

Ld F. As badly as they can: 30,000 casualties in the Dardanelles, 16,000 English 14,000 French; 60 per cent of the French engaged.[1] I was always, as you know, against this mad expedition. The North Sea is the place where we can beat the German. We ought to have taken

---

[1] Fisher's figures seem to have been close to the facts. Between the landing (25 Apr.) and 10 May (the end of the Second Battle of Krithia) the French lost about 12,000. The British 29th Division had lost 10,000: Carlyon, *Gallipoli*, 257.

the island of Borkum,[1] landed these Dardanelles fellows there, and got into Berlin.

M. You know, you have talked too much. All London knows you're against the Dardanelles expedition. Why didn't you resign at the time?

Ld F. It's a lie: I've seen no one, been nowhere. I'm far too busy.

M. But you've talked to a few—enough for all to know.

Ld F. Why, I say I can't even dine or lunch with Mrs Asquith and that sets them up a bit! It's Winston that talks to A.J.B. and F. E. Smith. You can ask A.J.B. if I wasn't against this expedition—taking all our men out there, and our ships will have to go too. It will bleed us white.

M. Well, we're for it and <u>must</u> see it through.

Ld F. Oh! yes, it may turn out all right, but I doubt it.

M. It's helped to bring Italy in. Has she good ships?[2]

Ld F. Mere organ grinders! no use whatever: but it's no good looking backwards!! They say I'm an optimist. Yes, I am....What I want now is a tax levied on every employer who keeps a man doing the work that a woman might do: treat them like motors or dogs—<u>they</u> are taxed and <u>Dogs</u>, that's just what they are, these fellows that won't fight.

M. You would perhaps find it difficult to carry out.

Ld F. Not at all. These things can be done by individuals (I felt like saying 'Then why levy a tax?') Everyone should contribute. Come along and have a Valse.

He seized me by the waist in Bongy's little room, and we valsed round. The old boy is a fine dancer. His last words were 'I'm very glad you told me what they say.'

---

[1] Establishing a base at Borkum, the largest and westernmost of the East Frisian Islands, off the north-western German coast, had been projected some months before; see *Asquith–Stanley*, 365 n. 2. Fisher's ideas for landings on the German coast found little favour.

[2] The Italians had promised to join the Allies in the war under the Treaty of London, 26 Apr. 1915. The opponents of intervention in the Chamber, who had forced Salandra to resign, found how limited their influence was when the crowd broke the Chamber's windows. On 23 May Italy declared war on Austria-Hungary.

Ld Moulton lunched.[1] He is chairman of the Munitions Committee. He told me we had got a wonderful mask against poisonous gases. We had stolen a German one and had much improved on it. I asked him if he was in favour of retaliation. (Certainly not, he said.) M. 'Moral forces, after all, count in war just as much as they count in peace. I should be terribly unhappy if, at this moment when the Germans are doing vile things, we should lose our heads and do the same acts, calling them self-defence. Till your new mask is tried and found wanting, we can't use poisonous gases, after all the cruelty we know this horrible foul invention has caused, and the very proper outcry we've made.' Moulton agreed entirely: he says there is nothing more futile than Revenge.

We dined at Ava Astor's.[2] Evan Charteris quite angry with me because I was against the East End and other riots, which infuriated fools, hooligans, and thieves are getting up against innocent Germans who have lived and worked peacefully for many years amongst us. It's so curious to hear people say England has not woken up, when she has given and is giving all she has got of her very Best. These foolish West Enders!! Will they only be satisfied with an expression of faith from the drunkards and loafers? I loathe these riots and deplore all forms of savagery, and I was angry with Evan and the rest. If our men at the front can face Death daily, can't we face Rumour? Spy panic—all panic—is contemptible. It is called 'indignation', but let these indignant men recruit.

Ly Frances Balfour, who lunched, told me I did H. harm, as I was suspected of being pro German, I said I didn't care a d—n. I would shout against Retaliation till I died.[3] We've got thousands of English soldiers in

[1] John Fletcher Moulton (1844–1921), Kt. 1906; Lord of Appeal in Ordinary and life peer 1912; Liberal MP 1885–6, 1894–5, 1898–1906.

[2] Ava Lowle née Willing (1868–1958); married, 1891, in Philadelphia (where she was born), John Jacob Astor IV (who died with the sinking of the *Titanic* in April 1912); in 1909 she sued successfully for divorce in the state of New York, and in 1911 moved to England with her daughter, where she married, 1919, Thomas Lister, 4th Baron Ribblesdale.

[3] For a warning which Margot received early in the war from two of her 'most intimate friends' about the danger of receiving 'any friend of German name' in Downing Street see *More Memories*, 243–4. Asquith was as careless as his wife in the case of Sir Edgar Speyer (1862–1932); see *Asquith–Stanley*, 292–3, 295. For Speyer's illegal doings during the war see *Parl. Pp.* 1922, vii. 141–56, CND 1569. When this report appeared Speyer's name was struck off the

Germany: even if only for <u>them</u> we should be silent, as certainly they will be very ill-treated thanks to our shouting. We went to H. of Commons, and I heard H. announce the new legislation for rounding up all the Aliens....

What a satire if the coming coalition Gov.¹ of which Winston has gassed so much should not contain him! I know H. too well to suppose this, but there is no doubt if Henry wanted to make himself supremely popular with every party, <u>ours and the others</u>, he would exclude Winston. I would not wish this; there is something lovable in Winston, and he is a real pal, but I should not be surprised if he wrecked the new Gov. If, on the other hand, he behaves really well and gets rid of the awful curse of Himself—reconstructs Himself so to speak, <u>he will come again</u>—will he??

I end this diary with this text.² It describes perfectly what is going on now in this <u>Frightful</u> war, with its aeroplanes, submarines, poisonous gas, grave-digging bombs and general murder and mutilation: 'Woe to the Inhabiters of the Earth and of the sea! for the Devil is come down unto you, having great Wrath, because he knoweth that he hath but a short time.' Revelation XII.12.

I wonder if it <u>will</u> be a short time. The Devil is a very handy name for that horrible spirit which we see displayed by the Germans. No people have ever so departed from the spirit of Christ, both before and since Aug. 4th 1914. I may add we had been moving in something of the same direction before the war, but with the exception of spy panic (Fear always makes people cruel), which I'm glad to say is confined to a few rubbishy people, and panicky papers, we have gone towards the finer spirit since. Certainly our soldiers and our fine ladies have.

list of Privy Councillors, and his British naturalization was revoked, with that of his wife and three daughters.

¹ The latter part of this entry was written later than 13 May 1915.
² The diary volume in question (d.3211) contains some 755 folios, and Margot was coming to the end of them.

Before the war <u>we</u> too had our 'Frightfulness'[1]—Futurists, cubists, etc. etc; we had our 'Hate'—suffragettes burning, destroying churches, blowing up gardens and houses, and threatening in low letters quite innocent people's lives (their children's lives also); and not only <u>threatening</u> but attacking with sticks and stones, dog-whips and axes.

We had many signs of 'Hate'—old friends quarrelling over politics, families cutting and insulting each other (The political ostracism looks peculiarly foolish now!), humiliating and hurting in every way under the guise of 'conviction'. We had soldiers like Ld Roberts electioneering to put the Army against the Government; lawyers like the present Attorney-General Sir Ed. Carson defying the Law; pleasure people watching a man they loved drowned,[2] quite unable either to feel or to wear any form of mourning. We must be careful not to forget our own 'Frightfulness' and 'Hate'.

There is nothing as baffling as war in my spiritual contemplation. I suppose if Life inspired us with the same Heroism as Death—self-surrender, devotion, fortitude, patience, courage, and faith and Hope—there wd. be no more Wars. That God is good I feel more than I have ever felt, but from that we must not infer that he is good-natured.

Saturday 15 May 1915—The Wharf

Henry, Violet and I were as usual in my cottage, the Wharf, entertaining a small party....I ran across after bridge to say good-night to Henry (from my Barn to his bedroom). He told me to my amazement that Fisher had resigned (A week before this I had met Fisher in Bongy's room, and scolded him for not having resigned or held his tongue about Dardanelles expedition.)—and that he (H.) had sent for him. He could not be found anywhere at Admiralty or at his house.

---

[1] Margot may not have realized, even by this stage of the war, how completely *schrecklichkeit* had come to denote a policy of terrorizing a civilian population, as seen in the German massacres of civilians during its invasion of Belgium.

[2] A reference to the 'corrupt coterie' and the death of Sir Denis Anson: see above, p. 41.

H. I sat down and wrote 'By order of the King I command you to return to your post.' I said 'Find Fisher and give him this, even if you've got to get detectives'. (When H. told me this I felt quite numb—a sense of disaster came into my heart.)[1] 'Fisher came to see me. I told him he would cover himself with infamy and ridicule if he resigned <u>now</u>, at the moment we were in difficulties both on our West line and in the Dardanelles: infamy for deserting the ship, and ridicule for not having resigned on the spot the day it was discussed in the War Council. I reminded him that neither he nor Wilson had said <u>one</u> word of protest.

He asked me if before finally deciding he could see McKenna. I shall hear tomorrow, what has happened, as McK will either come or send a messenger. I only hope McK has used and will use all his influence for peace. The worst of McK is that he is <u>so</u> against the Dardanelles expedition, and hates Winston and everything he does.'

Sunday 16 May 1915—The Wharf, Sutton Courtney

It was a beautiful day; all my tulips out—a sort of dream-army of tulips of the Hans Christian Andersen type. McKenna and Pamela motored down, arriving here about 5.30. McK. went up to H.'s room and remained there. Pamela and I had a talk. She takes her husband's point of view politically <u>always</u>, not socially—she is a much better judge of social things than he is....

Neither Pamela or her husband will ever forgive Winston. I am not very surprised. Winston intrigued against and thwarted McK. every time in the cabinets of [early 1909], when Winston belonged to the little navy

---

[1] Lord Reading, when told, 15 May 1915, of Fisher's resignation, thought at once that this 'made a Coalition government inevitable if Fisher meant it': Reading Diary, 15 May, Reading Papers, MSS Eur. F118/153. Asquith's inability to look ahead, and the strength of partisan feeling, are vividly illustrated by his failure to prepare his party for coalition, although he had known for nearly six months that he faced a long war. The Liberals could hardly expect to have sole control of Britain's war effort during such a war despite being slightly outnumbered in the House of Commons by Unionists.

party.[1] They think Winston knocked them out of the Admiralty, but there they are <u>quite</u> wrong. <u>No</u> one was as surprised as Winston when H. told him he was going to make him First Lord! H. had made up his mind to have a change, and this has always been enough—<u>he has his change</u>.

(The common idea that, because H.'s cabinet has stuck together so tight in spite of going their own way so much, he is <u>not</u> a leader who puts his foot down, shows great want of insight, and is quite untrue. No Prime Minister has ever had more grip on his men. It is not necessary to pinch when you squeeze. The world is so crude that unless it sees rows it never believes in remonstrance. Our cabinet would have broken up ages ago, if H. had governessed men of the type of Ll.G. and Winston.)…

I could see by McK.'s face when he joined us that it was all no good. Fisher had stuck to his guns, and said nothing nothing would change him: he would not stay another hour with Winston.

McK. to me: The sad part is that this means the end of Winston: I think Winston and all the Board will resign.

  M. Why do you think the Dardanelles such folly?

 McK. <u>It's impossible</u>. We shall perhaps get 6 ships through, but we shall lose 20.

  M. That's what Fisher says, but he always has a motive behind his opinions, so I never value them so very much.

 McK. Oh! but he's right. We shall have to send more ships till we are bled white (H. tells me this was Bismarck's expression) and so far from shortening, it will lengthen the war. It was thanks to Winston's impulsive action that the Turk went against us at all. I know you think it is mere prejudice on my part, but Winston is a <u>real danger</u>. (Later) The public won't stand Fisher going and Winston remaining, of that I am quite sure.

---

[1] During 1909 McKenna fought with his cabinet colleagues, in particular Lloyd George and Churchill, over the need for increased naval spending in response to a perceived acceleration in German Dreadnought construction; Churchill, then Home Secretary, was an advocate of the social reform policies championed in Lloyd George's 1909 'People's budget', which

The McKs went back to London. I was called up on the telephone by Admiralty and the servants told me Mr and Mrs Churchill were motoring down to dine with us, and would be with us in an hour and [a] half. It seemed hard on Henry, that on such a glorious day he should be kept jawing to colleagues whom he is obliged to see every day of the week.

I went to rest and heard Winston's curious insistent voice under my windows. After he had talked to H., he, Violet and Clemmie walked up and down my solitary paved path, very excited—the 2 females hanging on to his words like maidservants hang on the arms of soldiers in the Park. I wondered, if Winston had had 2 more remarkable female friends, who had, instead of flattering him, really stood up to him, it would have made any difference to him; and I came to the conclusion it would not. No individuals will change Winston. Nothing but experience can teach him. He is devoted to Clemmy, but fonder of himself.

I always think he and Violet would have been good for each other, had they married. Her cleverness would have delighted him, and their mutual egotism would have been an interesting combat. With all his charm and genius, wonderful spirits and good humour, real power of friendship (viz. his keenness for his friends and relations to get office, his fidelity to his mother and cousin[1]), he is light metal and absolutely unprincipled; and I should not be at all surprised if he broke the new Cabinet. Like a parrot I repeat, it will be Winston or Ll.G.; but I must add another name—it may fall to the lot of Kitchener!

[Winston] told me Wilson had promised to succeed Fisher, and the Board would not resign.

---

seemed threatened by the increased naval estimates; but in Oct. 1911 Asquith ordered Churchill and McKenna to swap cabinet seats, a move that the latter resented, and for which he blamed both his successor, and Lloyd George.

[1] Jeanette [Jennie] Jerome (1854–1921), m. 1874 Lord Randolph Churchill (who died in 1895); from 1900 to 1913 she was married to George Cornwallis-West (1874–1951); and 1918–21 to Montagu Porch (1877–1964). Charles Richard John Spencer-Churchill (1871–1934), 9th Duke of Marlborough; served with Yeomanry Cavalry, South Africa, 1900; Paymaster-General, 1899–1902; Under-Secretary of State for Colonies, 1903–5; Parliamentary Secretary, Board of Agriculture, 1917–18.

W. I only wish I could have put it all in the papers tonight just to dish Fisher.

M. (seeing <u>how</u> little Winston realized the inwardness of the situation) How can you be so childish? There will be a tremendous outcry if Fisher goes. It is <u>all-important</u> to patch this up. For God's sake, hurry <u>nothing</u>, as it will only break the Government. You think you'll get on with Arthur Wilson? I'll give you 10 days, or at outside 12.

W. Why! I see him every day, and we get on very well.

M. He is more or less your guest now, but I'm pretty sure you would both hate each other very soon.

We had a rather amusing dinner—W. in great form, with a roving eye, as neither Dolly Gladstone[1] nor I fulfilled his idea of a proper audience. By dint of talking loud, he managed to silence the table, and with the glee of a schoolboy he harangued in his habitual, highly-coloured, amusing way…

Monday 17 May 1915

Henry…came in on Monday night. I was sitting swamped up to my ears in the biggest bath in London.

M. Well, darling, is Fisher resolved to go?

H. Yes. I made him write his reasons. His answer is simple: 'I cannot get on with Winston Churchill.'

M. Oh! <u>How</u> sad, Henry! I <u>am</u> sorry for you.

H. I've had to take very drastic measures. I wrote to all my colleagues to resign.[2] I shall form a Coalition Government. I've just seen Bonar Law. He was pleased and happy; of course, they long to be in it.

This announcement flabbergasted me. I flung the towel round me and said with horrified eyes.

---

[1] Dorothy Mary Paget (d. 1953), m. 1901 Herbert John Gladstone (1854–1930), cr. Viscount 1910.

[2] For the texts of Asquith's letters to his colleagues, 17 May 1915, see Asquith, *Memories*, ii. 95–6.

M. Oh! Darling—so it's come to that!! <u>How</u> terrible! Our wonderful Government and wonderful cabinet—(I could not trust myself to say another word for tears.)

H. Curiously enough, B. Law says none of his men will stand K. They think he has mismanaged, and there is this hideous row over munitions. He and French can't get on. French says K. keeps things back from us, and K. says French keeps things from him. I expect K.'ll have to go, though this will cause the greatest uproar of all. K. is very unhappy himself. I've just seen him. He says he is quite anxious to go (I doubted this, as K. <u>never</u> wants to give up anything.)

M. Who wd. you put in K.'s place?

H. Ll.G., if he'll take it. If not, B. Law, but it's all pretty difficult and quite uncertain. If Ll.G. takes War Office, I shall let B. Law be Chan. of Excheq.[1]

M. Will they have McK.?

H. Oh! yes, they don't mind him, apparently. Isn't it odd, after all their abuse? B.L. seemed quite keen to have him.

M. You are still Boss, darling, I hope?

H. (very simply) Yes: B.L. seems quite agreeable. They won't have a soldier or a sailor at War Office or Admiralty, which is of course right. I've maintained this from the first—professional experts are Hopeless.

While Henry was talking I was wondering and struggling with 1000 thoughts.

M. It seems too sad! Now Winston will get the coalition he has so often gassed about!

H. The satire is he will very likely be excluded. I said to B.L. 'It's obvious to me Fisher wants to make himself First Lord—a position

---

[1] For these possibilities see Blake, *Bonar Law*, 248–52. Neither appointment took place because Northcliffe's criticism of K. aroused such indignation that he was left where he was: Cassar, *Kitchener*, 356–7. On 21 May the *Daily Mail* printed the headline 'The Tragedy of the Shells; Lord Kitchener's grave error'.

corresponding to K.'s in War Office'. B.L. said 'I quite believe it: they had better both go.' (Pause.)

The fact is, there are too many difficulties just now:[1] we can't have a debate on munitions with Germany watching us. We can't have a Gen. Election: we can only carry on with the full support of the opposition.

M. It's patriotic, I suppose, but I mind it <u>fearfully</u>. (I could see H. did too.) Did you think B.L. sensible?

H. Yes, very.

M. Was K. really low?

H. Oh! he's very unhappy indeed about things.

M. What does Ll.G. think?

H. He's keen about the coalition; he always rather wanted it, though he didn't talk like Winston did to outsiders....

Tuesday 18 May 1915

I ran across to 11 Downing St. to see Ll.G. He was out, but I saw his wife. Mrs Ll.G. is a little woman, inferiorly dressed and with no distinction of appearance, or profession of being more than what she is.[2]

She is a most observant, humorous, clever, kind little woman; very true and highly discreet. She knows everything that is going on, and I am very fond of her. She neither entertains or is entertained. She is not ambitious. She has not the beauty or distinction that Henry's wife Helen* had, but much the same want of prominence, and goodness. I found her in one of these dark, tiresome rooms downstairs in No 11. I put my views before her

[1] Asquith apparently told Margot that he 'could have weathered the Winston storm'; but the conjunction of that with the shells shortage allegations had made the formation of a coalition inevitable: Margot to Arthur Asquith, 19 May 1915: Arthur Asquith Papers.

[2] Margaret (Maggie) Lloyd George née Owen (1866–1941), daughter of a prosperous Welsh Methodist farmer, who was initially disapproving of the radical Baptist attorney that she planned to marry; they were wed in 1888, Ll.G. having first made clear: 'My supreme idea is to get on. To this idea, I shall sacrifice everything—except, I trust, honesty. I am prepared to thrust even love itself under the wheels of my Juggernaut if it obstructs the way' (David Lloyd George to Margaret Owen, c.1885, NL Wales, D. Lloyd George MS 20,404C, quoted in Kenneth O. Morgan, ODNB, 'Lloyd George, David').

and could see in a moment that she thought I was right. At the time I spoke I had never heard of a Ministry of Munitions from anyone; it was an entirely original idea as far as I was concerned (I heard afterwards that it is as old as the hills! and that the French have got one, though I don't know who presides over it!)[1]

She said quite frankly she would hate to leave 11 Downing St.

Mrs Ll.G.   When the Marconi was on and we thought there would be a Gen. election, I said to Megan 'If we are beaten, we shall have to leave this house.' She cried! I said 'Well, Anthony will have to leave his house too,' which consoled her very much![2]

This amused Mrs Ll.G., and we both laughed a good deal. I asked her if her husband had minded a letter I had written to him on the sorrows of Coalition (I unfortunately forget what I said, but I gave a rough sketch of the aliens we were interning—B. Law, Austen, Long*, Curzon etc.—in our Cabinet!)

M.   I've forgotten what I said, but I think I said that when H. first became PM I always thought Winston or your husband would break his cabinet. I hope he doesn't mind?

Mrs Ll.G.   Certainly not—he was highly amused. He knows as well as I do that it would have been him if things hadn't gone as he liked and if he didn't love your husband.

M.   Do you really think so?

Mrs Ll.G.   Certainly....

We went on to discuss Mr Ll. G.'s new functions.

M.   Don't let your husband take the War Office. I know what soldiers are: he will get nothing but Kicks. Let the other side get

---

[1] On 18 Mar. 1915 Asquith had revealed to Venetia (*Asquith–Stanley*, 488) that he thought of creating a Directorate of War Contracts under Lloyd George, who would cease to be Chancellor of the Exchequer. See also Adams, *Arms*, ch. 2.

[2] Megan Lloyd George (1902–66) was then 13, the same age as Anthony Asquith; she served as a Liberal MP, 1929–51, and as a Labour MP, 1957–66.

the Kicks. You make your man get the best Committee of real workers to do all the dirty work for him, and let him go about speaking, and speeding up (the workmen would love this.) Let him have a separate office for <u>Munitions only</u>. Let's send for him.

Mrs Ll.G. Certainly.

I followed her to the telephone, and she said to a secretary 'Send the Chancellor to me at once—it is important.' Poor Mr Ll.G. came in from the Treasury quite white. We reassured him and I told him in one telegram the idea (which I could see pleased him.) He said 'This is Right.—I agree but I must be off to quiet Winston down.' He flew out after pressing my hand. Mrs Ll.G. 'Poor man! I should have said it was political business, as I can see he thought it was about Megan (the little girl). How white he went, didn't he?'

Jack Tennant* told me in the course of the day that Kitchener thinks Sir John French's staff is composed entirely of fools. His private secretary is a Stockbroker, Brinsley Fitzgerald.[1] Jack: 'K. said "I hear Sir John's secretary is coming to see me. I don't want him, I'm not going to make any investments".'

Wednesday 19 May 1915

The Liberal Party, after 9½ years of power, met Parliament for the last time (Henry has been Prime Minister since April 1908). I felt like putting on mourning. I slept exactly 3 hours, and began making notes (the ones I am copying out now) for my diary at 5 am. I talked to Henry till 2 am. He was very, <u>very</u> unhappy.

Violet, Cys, Bongy, Henry and I went to Guildhall,[2] after lunching alone early (Sylvia Henley our only guest, a very dear creature and friend of Henry's and now of mine, Venetia Stanley's sister)....

[1] Lt. Col. John Hamilton Brinsley FitzGerald (1859–1931). See *Churchill*, iii. 430 n. 1.
[2] The occasion was 'An Imperial Patriotic Meeting', which Margot described as 'a meeting to praise the services rendered to us by the Indians and Colonials in the war'.

Henry sat on one side of the chairman on the platform and Bonar Law on the other (it was a non-party meeting); Violet and I just behind Henry. They both made good speeches. All the time H. spoke I kept thinking of the announcement he was going to make in the House and the effect it would have on his devoted men (that very afternoon). I felt <u>so</u> restless that, after B.L.'s speech, I got up and sat at the back of the platform, with Albert Grey.[1] We all had to go ages before the meeting was over, and, as many dribbled out after H.'s speech, my moving was not at all conspicuous.

I could not help watching Bonar Law, and feeling how tragic it was for Henry to see this third-rate man, who had called him 'liar', 'cheat', 'fraud'—every name under Heaven—sitting quietly there, wondering which of his followers he could impose upon Henry; and then looking at Henry, who was making up his mind which of our men he would have to sacrifice in his new cabinet.

We motored away from the meeting to the H. of C. H. announced quite casually what we all knew, that he was going to make his statement that evening. Violet tried to get out of him twice at what time he would speak but he didn't know and would not say. We went to Bongy's room. Ll.G. came in and asked me to go and have tea with him. I followed him into his room. Ll.G. 'Well! It is the 2 Tories in our Cabinet that [have] brought this about—K. and Winston.' Just as we were settling down for tea and talk, he was fetched away, and a short time afterwards his secretary told me Henry was going to speak. I flew up to the Speaker's gallery (where, thank God, I have still got my place.)

Just before this, Violet and Bongy had both said they thought the coalition would give strength to the Gov. I totally disagreed. There is no one on the other side that I think will add strength to our wonderful cabinet. It is quite true that both sides joining, and calling themselves a National Government, sounds strong. It is a life-size Imitation of Strength: but

[1] Albert Henry Grey (1851–1917), 4th Earl Grey; Governor-General of Canada, 1904–11.

what is a National Government? It is a phrase, not a fact. I loathe it. I found V. and Bongy taking it without emotion. They didn't even know or suspect that Henry felt it <u>in his blood</u>. He had been so cheerful the night of 18th, and so plucky all day, and at Guildhall. I told them that he and I had cried over it in his bedroom last night, and talked till 2 a.m.

When Henry got up in a thin House and said 'Steps are in Contemplation which involve the reconstruction of the Government on a broader personal and political basis' I shook with Emotion. Not a female in the gallery was moved except myself. <u>Women have no Imagination.</u>

I saw men pouring in through the glass doors, but all too late to hear him. 37 lines of print in next day's *Times*[1] gave our poor fellows who were not in their places no chance.

I went down to [Henry's] room; he was still in the House. I went to Ll.G.'s room and wrote on a card 'It's all up', and dated it, and was going to write more to leave in Henry's room, but I had no time, as I had to get back. I met Donald Maclean,[2] one of our men, on [the] stairs: he could hardly speak to me for rage and surprise. I just said to him in a shaking voice 'Do you not know my husband has done this with his blood?'... Every face I met on our side looked blue and bitter.

I picked up poor crippled Snowden,[3] the Labour member, and took him to Charing Cross Station; he was much upset by the coalition. 'Are we to be governed by Northcliffe and Bottomley?' was printed on huge posters. (I believe a scurrilous, vile rag called *J. Bull* is edited by a horrible man called Bottomley.)[4] The public is getting very tired of the Harmsworth Press (*Daily Mail* and *Times*).

[1] *The Times*, 20 May 1915, 8: part of a brief statement on the '290th day of the war'.
[2] Donald Maclean (1864–1932), KBE 1917, Liberal MP 1906–22, and Deputy Chairman of Ways and Means, House of Commons, 1911–18. Of him C. P. Scott wrote, Jan. 1923, 'He has Liberalism in his bones and never thinks of himself.' Prominent Asquithian in the Liberals' post-war internecine troubles.
[3] Philip Snowden (1864–1937), cr. Viscount 1931; Labour MP for Blackburn 1906–18. In the anti-war Labour group with Ramsay MacDonald during the war. Chancellor of the Exchequer, 1924, 1929–31; he had suffered a crippling spinal illness in 1891.
[4] Horatio William Bottomley (1860–1933), Liberal (nominally) MP 1906–12; Independent MP, 1918–22; founder editor of the sensationalist and colourful weekly *John Bull*, 1906; demagogic, and venomously anti-German, he acted as an unofficial national recruiting sergeant

Just before dinner, H. came as usual to my bedroom and told me what had happened. (From <u>other</u> sources I heard of it, so will write exactly the impression made upon several of the chief actors in this curious drama.) After I left the House, our men held a meeting in one of the committee rooms to protest against their PM's action, and to denounce the coalition and insist on knowing why they had been betrayed, etc. etc. Violent language was used by Henry's oldest and most faithful friends. When H. heard this, he walked quietly into the crowded committee room. Every eye turned on him, a look of guilty surprise and displeasure on every face. He walked up to the chairman, Sir Thomas Whittaker,[1] and made the most wonderful speech he ever made in his life.... He said he could not tell them the truth,[2] he could not give them his reasons for inviting the other side to join him and his party, he could only appeal to their love, their fidelity, their faith and their service. Had he (H.) ever been influenced one way or the other by any paper or person? Did he care one d—n for the Press then, or had he <u>ever</u> cared? <u>No</u>, they knew he never had.

As there were no reporters there, I can't write his exact words, but I will try and ask someone who was there to write it. I only know that when he had finished his speech, which was listened to in dead silence, there was not a dry eye, he had not only melted but moved all his men to the core. With hoarse voices and hot eyes, they cheered him to the echo. (It was a great personal triumph. No P. Minister in my day has been loved like this, not in this intimate, sacrificing way. Gladstone collected great crowds and enthusiasm, and all kinds of newspaper ravings, but he never had the kind of Love that Henry has got now, because he had no Emotion and very little heart. It was purely intellectual, such emotion as he had.)...

during the war; always but a step ahead of the law, he was convicted in 1922 on twenty-three of twenty-four counts of fraudulent conversion, and irredeemably ruined.

[1] Sir Thomas Palmer Whittaker (1850–1919), Kt. 1906; Liberal MP 1892–1919.

[2] At least three important factors were then confidential: the impending declaration of war by Italy; the impossibility of further cooperation between Churchill and Fisher over the Dardanelles; and French's assurance to Kitchener of sufficient ammunition for the Aubers Ridge attack.

We prepared for our big dinner party, both feeling shattered. Ld K. took me in, and Ld Morley sat my other side.[1] My vis-à-vis, on each side of Henry, were Ly Essex[2] and Ly Curzon.[3] (The latter a very good type of decorative West End furniture—beautiful, silly, idle, and wonderfully, amazingly dull; always saying she is a fool and never minding it; never getting accustomed to her beauty, therefore never really interested in anything and with little or no power of admiration.)

In times of war I can't tolerate 'Beauties'—they crush me. Ruby Peto[4] [and] Marjorie Anglesey[5] are crushers. Helen d'Abernon,[6] Milly Sutherland,[7] Gladys Ripon[8] have all come out splendidly, and these are women of real beauty. Venetia Stanley has also been very noble in the way of Hospital work. Most of the young ladies have done something real, but many have done committees only, which alas! useful as it is, is not at all humanizing. It strengthens the head but doesn't soften the heart. The pity, pathos and glory of war, its squalors and Horrors are unknown to the committee girls; for this I am very sorry: it is a great and wonderful opportunity missed and would or might have been the making of many of them.)

As I took K.'s arm he looked at me with a good deal of curiosity. I said 'What a terrible state of affairs!' K. 'Yes, I'm very sorry for the Prime Minister.' He spoke with great earnestness. At dinner I said to him:

[1] John Morley had been made a Viscount in 1908.

[2] Adela Grant (d. 1922), m. 1893 7th Earl of Essex (1857–1916).

[3] Mary Curzon (1887–1962), who married, 1907, her cousin, the politician and motorist Francis Richard Henry Penn Curzon (1884–1964), son of the 4th Earl Howe.

[4] Frances Ruby Linsday (1884–1951), m. 1900 Ralph Harding Peto.

[5] Victoria Marjorie Manners (1883–1946), daughter of 8th Duke of Rutland; m. 1912 6th Marquess of Anglesey.

[6] Lady Helen Vincent née Duncombe (d. 1954), daughter of 1st Earl of Feversham; a famous society beauty, she married, 1890, Edgar Vincent, from 1914 Lord D'Abernon.

[7] Millicent Fanny Sutherland-Leveson-Gower née St Clair-Erskine (1867–1955), dowager Duchess of Sutherland; a society hostess and social reformer, she organized a Red Cross ambulance unit at the outbreak of war, and was at Namur during the German advance; undertook hospital work with Red Cross throughout the war, and was awarded the Croix de Guerre.

[8] Constance Gladys Herbert (1859–1917), widow of 4th Earl of Lonsdale, m. 1885 2nd Marquess of Ripon.

M. K., I want you to tell me as one great soldier might to another—forget that I'm a woman—what do you think of Sir John French?

K. He is the greatest soldier living in the field.

M. How? Why?

K. Well, he has great intuition and courage. If you say 'Mass your men up there', or 'Take this or that position', he will carry out your orders better than any one; but he is the worst organizer, and a stupid man. He can't make a plan of any kind; he is bad at staff work, and has a bad staff.

M. I suppose you don't often find a soldier who combines both field work and the power of making a plan of campaign. If you moved French tomorrow, who would you put there?[1]

K. (shrugging, and looking like a Tom-cat quite straight in my face) I don't know!—perhaps Haig.

M. I don't fancy he would do any better.

K. Well, I can only say the muddle at the front is something <u>awful</u>.

I longed to say, how about munitions? but I forgot to say H. gave me one word of warning before dinner 'Don't mention munitions, darling, as naturally K. is very sore over the Repington article' (in *Times* of 14th May 1915).

K. French is not my French of South Africa. All of you have spoilt him, he won't take orders now. He does things on his own. He has just stellenbosched Smith-Dorrien.[2]

M. You can't object to that, as you've kept that rotten Sir H. Rawlinson, who has made every mistake that can be made (K. never answered).

[1] Margot probably had in mind the rumours that Kitchener wanted to become Commander-in-Chief for the final advance, and thus 'win the war'. For this see above, p. 60.

[2] General Sir Horace Lockwood Smith-Dorrien (1858–1930), KCB 1907; Commander, II. Corps, then Second Army, BEF, 1914–15; his famous stand at Le Cateau, 26 Aug. 1914, which virtually saved the BEF during its retreat from Mons, was against the wishes of French, who had not wanted him as a corps commander; French eventually dismissed him during Second Ypres, and defamed him in his post-war memoir 1914; denied an opportunity publicly to clear his name, Smith-Dorrien, with the assistance of George V, circulated a privately printed defence of his conduct, which was endorsed by the *Official History*.

I turned to Morley, who is so delicious on books and so childish on war.... Later on K. said:

K. If French didn't inspire the Repington article, who did?

M. I think French is a stupid man in many ways, but he is a man of honour, and I will burn my hand off before I would believe he could send that article to the Press.[1]

K. I happen to know it only passed the censor (censor out at front) by special request of Sir J.F. It was all very carefully planned both there and here.

M. I'm quite <u>sure</u> Northcliffe is at the bottom of all this.

K. Perhaps. Sir John saw Northcliffe and Repington. He has, I assure you, believe me, <u>done</u> this—who else wd. have done it?

M. Repington is a hound! You and I knew that in Cairo. There is nothing a blackguard like that wouldn't do.[2] He probably got money from North-cliffe to go over and do this. Sir J. is hypersensitive and listens [to] and believes the awful gossip, mostly gossip at the front; and all soldiers are quarrelsome—I have <u>the</u> greatest contempt for these soldiers and their quarrels in times like these. The Tommies don't quarrel: why do you?

K. I'm not quarrelsome. I can dislike and refuse to see people but this isn't quarrelling. I don't like Curzon, but even <u>you</u> know by now that he is an impossible person....

We played bridge after dinner.... I saw H. (when he was dummy) go into the other room, and sit in perfect silence and in one position in his

---

[1] Margot was mistaken. On 9 May French witnessed the effect of inadequate artillery support on British losses at Festubert: 'I therefore determined on taking the most drastic measures to destroy the apathy of a Government which had brought the Empire to the brink of disaster.' On returning to his headquarters, and learning, as he recalled, that the War Office had sent reserve ammunition to the Dardanelles: 'I immediately gave instructions that evidence should be furnished to Colonel Repington, military correspondent of *The Times*, who happened to be then at Headquarters, that the vital need of high-explosive shells had been a fatal bar to our Army success on that day': French, *1914*, 357.

[2] Margot presumably refers to Repington's passionate and poorly concealed affair in Egypt with Mary Isabella née North (1868–1953), the wife of Sir William Edmund Garstin (see above, p. 36 n. 3), which ended his military career; denied a divorce by his wife, he and Mary Garstin later lived together as a married couple, although his social position was always precarious.

armchair (all the time his hand was played), <u>never</u> moving. I then knew what an effort he was making, and my admiration was profound. What <u>wonderful</u> sweetness, courage, freedom from self, and imperturbability. He looked <u>done</u> to a turn.

We talked till 2 a.m. He told me that practically Violet had made up her mind to marry Bongy, which is what he and I most desire. He longs for her to marry. Girls who don't marry before they are 30 make a cardinal error in life.—I didn't marry before I was 30, but it was not because I could not love enough, but because I loved too much, and was in love for 9 years with one man (with several side affairs). I suffered from just the opposite defect! The present girls have no temperament—I had too much. This is a bad girl era. The conspicuous girls have lots of brains, no concentration or brain output, and complete lack of Loyalty and Heart.

This is the most Fateful Day of my Life (excepting May 10 1894, my Wedding Day).

The Fateful days of my Life:

10 <u>May</u> 1894 (my wedding).
My sister Laura's* engagement to Alfred Lyttelton, Jan. 3d 1885. (On same day 1913 I lost my power of speech and was very very ill the whole year.)
24th April 1886—Laura died, in London.
Jan 21 1895—My mother died, at Glen.[1]
1912 February 19—London, the night before Puffin went to school.
July 14 1914—Wonderful talk with Henry about my difficulties and the children, the first of the kind I ever had.
<u>Feb. 26</u> 1897—At 20 Cavendish Square Elizabeth was born.[2]
<u>Nov. 9 Anthony was born</u> 20 <u>Cav. Square</u> 1902.

[1] A house at Innerleithen in the Borders, built in the 1850s in Scottish Baronial style for Margot's father, Sir Charles Tennant, by David Bryce. Margot had a particular love for Glen and its surrounding countryside, where she had spent much of her childhood and youth.
[2] 18th-century London house bought by Sir Charles Tennant for the Asquiths on their marriage in 1894; after their sojourn in 10 Downing Street (1908–16) they returned to Cavendish Square and lived there until 1919.

PART V
20 MAY–3 AUGUST 1915

The formation of the Coalition in May 1915 enabled Margot to record the full range of her political views. Some of these showed an insider's instinct for preventing trouble; others were, by the diarist's later confession, simply prejudices, never well-based, and by May 1915 dangerously outdated. Her support for putting Lloyd George in charge of Munitions comes under the first category; and her disparagement of Bonar Law and of his Unionist colleagues comes under the second; but her indignant attitude to the revelations of the Northcliffe press is harder to assess. Northcliffe was a patriot of a boyish and irresponsible kind, who thought it his mission to prod a supine government into greater warlike activity. He was not easily bracketed, and while most of the 'radical right' distrusted him, and may have agreed with Margot about the harm that some of his Daily Mail passages might do when republished in the German press, they did not accept her view that he must be a pro-German, who expected 'Germany to win'. Margot 'loathed' the May 1915 Coalition. She saw British politics in terms of the leading figures of the elite. In her view Asquith's 'wonderful cabinet' already had the services of the Unionists' best man, Arthur Balfour, on its War Council; making some other Unionists available for government service merely represented the acquisition of what she called, with typical wit, a group of 'interned aliens'. When repeated, this flagrant indiscretion did harm, but even the most tactful premier's wife could not have given an air of harmony to the new arrangements: the Coalition never looked like more than a short-term solution to a dangerous crisis. Asquith's feat in keeping the Unionists out of the key posts, and preventing either conscriptionists or their opponents from gaining the mastery, was no small one; but by leaving the Coalition cabinet unreformed he was ensuring governmental delays of a lethal kind during war, which would ultimately have an immensely damaging effect on his premiership.

Thursday 20 May 1915

… When Henry was up he showed me [an] <u>amazing</u> letter from Clemmie Churchill.[1] It shows the soul of a servant. That touch of blackmail and insolence, and the revelation of black ingratitude and want of affection, jus-

---

[1] For text see Soames, *Clementine*, 123. Maurice Bonham Carter wrote to Violet, 21 May: 'Clemmie wrote your father a most amazing letter before W's fate was decided. She said "Why do you part with W?…If you throw Winston overboard you will be committing an act of weakness & your Coalition govt will not be as formidable a war machine as the present Govt. etc etc". The question at once arose as to whether this was Winston or Clemmie. I say that W. un-understanding as he is of personalities, could not have perpetrated such a bêtise, & I now learn that he did not inspire it, though he allowed it to go (perhaps without learning its contents). Of course he himself is without an inkling of what the party feels towards him…': Bonham Carter, 1914–45, 57.

tifies everything I have thought of this shallow couple. I expressed myself with vigour to Henry. H. 'After all, it's the letter of a wife.' M. 'A fish-wife, you mean!! But of course, this is Winston, not Clemmie. You don't mean to say you think W. didn't see this letter?' H. 'Yes, I rather agree with you.'...

Ll.G. came in and told H. there was nothing much to do at [the] Treasury: he thought he could keep [the] Chancellorship and new Munition Ministry (Ll.G. has the wits to remember himself sleeplessly, but never to think of himself. He thinks very little.)...Ll.G. turned to me and said 'Your idea of a Ministry of Munitions is going to be adopted, Mrs Asquith. You know, Prime Minister, she ran across to my wife suggesting this, we both thought it excellent.' H. 'Did you, Margot?' M. (anxiously) 'Well, I didn't worry you, as wives with ideas are often boring.' H. (sweetly) 'I don't think so. It's all-important just now.' I confess I clapped my hands like a child, and jumped up and kissed him!

Ll.G. then described my visit to his wife with great graphicness, [and] ended by saying 'I must show you your wife's letter describing the new lot that are coming in—it's the best you ever saw, and amused us both immensely. (I wish I could remember my letter, but not one word do I ever remember of my letters, as I rarely if ever re-read them; sometimes I copy them, but seldom.)

Friday 21 May 1915

St. Loe Strachey[1] came to talk to me about a forecast of our new coalition cabinet which had come out in *Pall Mall*. I told him it mattered little. H. came into the room and said he was sorry Redmond would not come in—(this is a good commentary on Sir George Murray,[2] Queen Alexandra and others, who had said to me H. had broken his word to B. Law and Co. by promising to have no controversial legislation, and then putting

---

[1] John St Loe Strachey (1860–1927), proprietor of the (free-trade Unionist) *Spectator*, 1898–1925.

[2] Sir George Herbert Murray (1849–1936), KCB 1899; Permanent Secretary to Treasury, 1903–11; according to Asquith, 'a very good critic but not a good judge' (diary, 5 May 1908).

Home Rule on the statute books.[1] No Irishman thought this was the end of H. Rule: they knew H. Rule could not be carried till the Amending Bill, or Redmond would have come in)—or Lansdowne, 'a man whose great experience and courtesy and straightness would be a help'.

I determined to see Ly Lansdowne and tell her this. Henry added 'The cargo of actual brains that the opposition bring is not very large. Carson has a good mind and character.' St. Loe 'Almost too much character!' H. 'Yes, perhaps, but I like him: I've always liked him.' St. L. 'Well, he has always liked you very much: he has said so to everyone.'

I motored to Lansdowne House. I met the Dss of Devonshire[2] on my way, and got out [and] walked back with her to Devonshire House (hearing Lansdowne was in Scotland). I asked her how her father was. Dss of D. 'He is very well, and I agree with you he ought to come in.' M. (anxious to put life into her) 'He must come in. Just now we must show a united front, and I don't think Curzon should be the boss of the new lot.' (This had a capital effect as Victor Devonshire[3] doesn't like Curzon.) She said she would persuade her father, and I wrote to Devonshire to wire Lansdowne. I believe Lansdowne was coming in, but I don't know.[4]

Evie Devonshire, in talking of Winston, said she imagined he was 'a kind of mad genius', which amused me. Masterton Smith sat next to me at lunch.... Masterton (pleading for Winston) 'I think it's a danger, changing Winston while the Dardanelles expedition is unfinished.' M. 'My dear friend, Winston is going. Clemmie and he have not come out well in this crisis.... If they only knew how one and all long for H. to get rid of

---

[1] For the government's decision to place the 3rd Home Rule Bill on the statute book, see p. 38 above; it may be observed that a promise about conduct during a relatively confined 'war crisis', i.e. late July/Aug. 1914, could be confused easily with one about doings during the war itself, especially if that war proved long lived.

[2] Evelyn Emily Mary Fitzmaurice (1870–1960), Duchess of Devonshire, daughter of 5th Marquess of Lansdowne; m. 1892 Victor Cavendish, nephew of 8th Duke of Devonshire, who succeeded as 9th Duke, 1908.

[3] Victor Christian William Cavendish (1868–1938), s. as 9th Duke of Devonshire, 1908; Liberal Unionist MP for Derbyshire W., 1891–1908; Financial Secretary to the Treasury, 1903–5; a Civil Lord of the Admiralty, 1915–16; Governor-General, Canada, 1916–21.

[4] Lansdowne joined the cabinet as Minister without Portfolio, and joint Leader (with Crewe) in the Lords, 25 May 1915.

Winston, who, with all his talents, is a danger in <u>any</u> government, they would be stunned. H. would be universally applauded if he left Winston out. Mark my words, he will try and wreck this Gov.—he has no principles whatever.'...

Col. Hankey and I were mad keen to have a proper Press Censorship so was M. Smith....I told some of them after lunch apropos of the Horrible Northcliffe Press (*Times* and *Daily Mail*) that Northcliffe has openly boasted he would get rid of K. and Asquith, and quoted Mr George Moore,[1] Sir J. French's great friend, as having said 'Mrs Asquith, nothing but God can get rid of a man like your husband.'

I sat next to Crewe at dinner and begged him to join Grey in telling H. that they would neither of them serve under Henry if Haldane was ousted by B. Law. He said he would do his best. I appealed for dear Haldane, to whom we owe our whole Army. M. 'H. was more shattered by his talk to Haldane this afternoon than by any thing else in this crisis. All Haldane had said, when H. told him that B. Law would not have him, was "I owe you everything. I would not have gone to the War Office but for you; I would not have gone to the Woolsack but for you; I have nothing to complain of".' (What a grand character.)

Crewe was quite of my opinion. M. 'If you allow the new fellows to blackmail you as to the various offices, you'll regret it. If you want to <u>please</u> H., make a stand for Haldane's inclusion.' (After the foul press campaign—*Times*, *Morning Post*, etc., calling Haldane a spy because he was educated in Germany—letting him go looks <u>terribly</u> like giving way to the Press and Rumour and Lies.)...[2]

---

[1] George Gordon Moore, a wealthy American lawyer and engineer, vividly portrayed in Lady Diana Cooper's *The Rainbow Comes and Goes* (1958); asked in June 1915 when he thought that the war would end, he replied: 'as soon as the production of munitions by the Allies gives them a superiority over the Germans, and that may be in a year....The Allied Armies have the men, they have the *moral*, the money, and 10 months' education. When they have the munitions the end will be in sight' (*The Times*, 28 June 1915, 8e).

[2] Buckmaster, who was Director of the Press Bureau 1914–15 (before succeeding Haldane as Lord Chancellor), explained how such offences could have gone unpunished: 'When strong measures should have been taken', he explained, 'with papers like *The Times* and the *Daily Mail*, my efforts to exercise against them the powers conferred by the Defence of the Realm Act were defeated by one cabinet minister or another'; see Koss, *Political Press*, 244–5.

Whit Sunday 23 May 1915—The Wharf

4th May 1915 Italy denounced the Triple Alliance;[1] on 18th May she practically declared war. I don't think much of Italy. I hope she won't prove as rotten as I think! but I shouldn't be surprised. Sunday 23rd May 1915 Italy declared war on Germany.

I ran across to say Good-night to Henry last night. I asked him how his first real conference with B. Law and Arthur had got on, and this is what he said:

H. We were Crewe, Ll.G., myself, and by an accident McKenna, Law and Arthur Balfour. I began quite informally saying this was the most painful position any public man could be put into—the knocking out of your oldest, most faithful servants to put in new men. They agreed.

I began with Haldane. I said he was my oldest friend, that he had been subjected to a Press campaign, led by *Morning Post*, etc. of the foulest, lowest, most mendacious character fostered by the anti-German mania; and to exclude him just now would not only be personally painful to me but would look as if we had given way to the Press, as well as to pressure. I said Grey felt it so strongly that he had told me he would rather not join and altogether I made a very serious appeal to both of them. B. Law was a little moved, and Arthur very much, but B.L. said the feeling on their side was <u>so</u> strong that it would be quite impossible for them to enter into a coalition at <u>all</u> if he was kept....

We then went on to McK. I said, pointing to him—'I propose to keep my friend here where he is, he is indispensable to me. Have you anything to say?' B. Law made a slight protest, and said he had been much criticized over the aliens. I said I didn't care at all about that, and turning to him said 'Is there any other office you would prefer,' at which McK. said 'I know I've been attacked, so would my successor be, but I prefer my own office. I know the ropes now.'—so this was agreed.

[1] The secret treaty pledging Italy to fight beside the Allies within a month had been signed on 26 Apr. 1915.

I went on to Crewe. I said he had nobly given up the India Office and Loulou the colonies—'2 high posts which should go to you (B.L.), or Austen. What do you say, Crewe?' Crewe said to Bonar 'I think you should succeed me.' I demurred to this, wishing to flatter B. Law, and prevent him interfering in finance with his Tariffs or munitions at the War Office.[1] I said 'The Colonies would welcome him, but if you prefer India, Austen must go to the Colonial Office. What do you say to Austen having the Colonial Office?' Then a most amusing thing happened, which Ll.G. and I watched with acute pleasure. B.L. said 'No, I don't think I could allow that. (M. How lucky Austen wasn't there!) I have been leader of the opposition since [1911]. I could not easily sit in a cabinet with Chamberlain in a higher position than myself.' (I didn't know India was looked on as 2nd. to Colonies, but it showed how much B.L. had jumped at H.'s bait.)

I said 'I quite agree with you. You are indicated for the Colonial Office: you would bring sympathy and knowledge, and everyone would be happy at having a Colonial-born as their representative'. 'What about Simon?' I said next. They both agreed he was indispensable. B. Law said 'He is your handiest man.' It's extraordinary how highly they think of Simon. I had asked Simon to succeed Haldane, you know, and he refused. I don't believe in the whole history of the Bar anyone of Simon's age has ever refused to be Lord Chancellor.

M. I'm sure I wish he hadn't! I rather resent Simon: he played such a poor part in [the] beginning of the war. If it hadn't been for you, he would be out now, by his stupid, self-conscious resignation. I don't think it's

---

[1] Margot may have misinterpreted Asquith here, or he may have given a misleading account of this episode and of its significance; probably both causes of distortion operated. The argument against allowing a tariff reformer in the Treasury was plausible; but Bonar Law was eminently suitable, as a business man from the iron trade, for Munitions. When he saw Asquith and made his claim for the new post, he was referred to Lloyd George, who appealed to him to withdraw it. Bonar did so despite a promise to Chamberlain and others to stand firm: Blake, *Bonar Law*, 249–51, incl. correction to Spender and Asquith, ii. 171.

so very wonderful, refusing the Woolsack. If a man wants a peach, it's easy to reject what to him is a vegetable marrow.[1]

H. I can't say that Simon has been self-seeking. He is incomparably the best advocate at the Bar. He goes to the Local Gov. Board instead of Samuel.

'Now', I said, 'what about our high and mighty friend Ld Curzon?' They hate Curzon—B. Law can't endure him. Arthur pleaded for him. I said I proposed to give him Privy Seal, an office in which he would take precedence over everyone at dinner parties! I suggested leaving Long out: he is ill, and there are more horses than oats; but B.L. said he would be more dangerous out, as he was the most popular man in their party. 'Very well, I will give him Agriculture. I understand you want Selborne and F. E. Smith: the former is safer to exclude than the latter.' I've left this to them.

'Now,' I said, 'we've not yet discussed an important personage in the shape of Mr Winston Churchill. I propose to make him Chan. of the Duchy of Lancaster, which my friend Mr Montagu has vacated of his own free will. I think this is about all. Ll.G. has a separate Ministry of Munitions, as you know.'

M. (thrilled) What an amazing conference. I should think in no country but in England it could have taken place.

H. They retired to consider these proposals. Now, darling, you must go to bed.

Monday 24 May 1915

H. told me he was going to have his first conference with Austen as well as Arthur and B. Law....

As I was having tea with Ann Islington*...Henry sent me a note from the cabinet to ask me to motor with him: so I got on my things, sent away dear old Rothschild, who had just called, and we dashed off to

[1] '...To the man whose mouth is watering for a peach, it is of no use to offer the largest vegetable marrow': from George Eliot, 'Mr Gilfil's Love Story', in *Scenes of Clerical Life* (1858).

Hampstead—a Bank Holiday, the whole heath crowded, and any amount of young men, which saddened us (recruiting wonderful—5000 men a day—but I didn't like so many idle young men).

H. told me he proposed to take Treasury himself, as Ll.G. will have too much to do; and that when he proposed this at the conference, B.L. had the cheek to demur, and say it would make the country think he wasn't giving all his time to the war. This infuriated me. I've always observed that where H. himself is concerned, he is never insistent. I warned him against being blackmailed in these early days. He said it was a painful kind of haggling, which had lasted for 2 hours, and he intended to fix it all up next day (25th May 1915), as he had had enough. B.L. was a little man, and even Arthur had been a trifle shocked at his demands.[1]

Tuesday 25 May 1915

I woke at 5 and wrote this diary. I wrote to Ll.G. to stand firm over H. having exactly what he wanted. H. sent Ll.G. after breakfast to B.L., to say he would have no more nonsense.[2] Before dinner, he amazed E. and me by telling us Simon had H. Office, and McK. was Chan. of Excheq: we were all amazed!! McKenna—what a tribute after all the Abuse!

We all 3, H., E., and self, dined with the McKennas, and after dinner H. drank to the health of the 2 Chancellors, Buckmaster (now Ld Buckmaster) and McK. The company were tiresome—E. and Baker could not be quiet, Pamela laughed in the wrong place, and none of them realized what I did, that H. was keen to make a little speech: he was much moved *au fond*, though none of them perceived it. He spoke of a Baptismal occasion, but I don't remember all he said—it was short and interrupted, which annoyed

---

[1] Margot seems to have been wholly unaware of the crucial importance of Bonar Law's goodwill if the government was to survive; and her tone suggests that her husband was also insufficiently aware of this. Bonar had no illusions about his limitations as a war leader; as he said publicly more than once he would have no value to the premier if he lost the confidence of his Unionist followers: Blake, *Bonar Law*, 304. Bonar's advice on the point in question was wise and, if this apparently 'little' man resigned, the government would fall. The accounts of Asquith's bearing towards him from May 1915 to December 1916 suggest a continuing inability to show a recognition of this basic fact.

[2] Blake, *Bonar Law*, 251.

me. Buckmaster answered cleverly, saying babies at Baptisms didn't answer except by odd sounds, and hoped we would excuse him. McK. began and ended a halting but touching little speech, praising H. and alluding very sweetly to the colleagues who would suffer in this new Coalition. It wasn't well done, but I liked it. 'Ld Buckmaster' is a very nice, <u>excellent</u> fellow—modest, straight and [a] fine lawyer, I am told. He adores Henry. It is an enormous jump for him, going to the Woolsack....

G. Curzon came to lunch, I think 25th. I could not resist saying—as it was the first time I had seen him in this house since he made such an ass of himself over me and his ball, to which he would not ask me—'Well, my dear old man, odd things have happened! <u>Now</u> I suppose <u>I can receive you again</u>!!'[1] He looked very uncomfortable, but is not easily dashed. We had quite an amusing lunch—he one side of me, Ll.G. the other. George C. asked Ll.G. to take Milner in on his Munitions committee (I can see he is afraid St. J. [Midleton] may be used) but I said he had no judgement, and was hopeless, with all his wonderful brains and charm; but I was sure he might be used by some of us. I know he would hate Ll.G., he is so prejudiced, and if they fought over munitions it would be a bore. Ll.G. took G. Curzon, which will do quite well.

Austen lunched one day when Lucy was with us. He is always nice, though <u>very</u> commonplace. He spoke of his father and J. Morley very nicely. H. asked him who was going to write his father's life: Spender* said Buchan would be the best man, to which we all agreed.[2]

---

[1] Curzon held a ball in early May 1914 to which he invited neither Margot, Violet, nor Elizabeth Asquith. Margot wrote in her diary: 'I confess it <u>hurt</u> me deeply. I was his wife's first friend—poor Mary Leiter, that beautiful, natureless being!—and I look upon George almost like I would one of the family. I care less about being asked here or there than most people, as I have <u>such</u> an amusing, thrilling life, and such heaps of friends; but I'm horribly affectionate, and faithful, and to find George such a poop tried me....Oddly enough, George's want of courtesy, and the failure of his ball (he forbade his governess to come down!), flew all over London, and everyone was nicer than the last to me in consequence' (diary, June 1914). Curzon feared that, if Margot, Violet, and Elizabeth came, various Unionists would leave in protest; and he also assumed, quite wrongly, that Margot would share his fears. She would have been quite ready to face a scene.

[2] *The Life of Joseph Chamberlain* (London, 1932–69, 6 vols) was in fact begun by J. L. Garvin, and completed by Julian Amery; the writer John Buchan (1875–1940), author of *The Thirty-Nine Steps* (1915), took no hand in the work.

The row between K. and Sir J. French gets worse daily, and H. arranged to go to the front with Hankey. I begged him to take Bongy, which he did. Sunday 30th he left the Wharf at 4.15 for London, and crossed over that night....

I forgot to say I saw Billy Lambton[1] on 27th or 28th May (Sir J. French's aide-de-camp and closest friend) in Downing St. He was genuinely unhappy over the quarrel between French and K. I said French should never have received men like Northcliffe and Repington (*Times* newspaper)—men who had made up their minds to do both for my husband and Kitchener; that he (Billy) and the staff should have saved their General from that, and that French's shares had gone down frightfully over all these quarrels and brangles.[2] I regret to say my delightful General seems to be making every mistake possible. If he was really so short of shells that he allowed Repington and *Times* to publish their disgusting scandals, why didn't he come directly to Henry? He is my friend: he could have done it through me, or direct to H. if he feared K. would not tell the cabinet.

I blame K. very much. He said in early August that we were in for a 3 years' war: if he really believed this, why has he run so very short of munitions? Has there been terrible shortage of munitions (High explosives)?—if 'Yes', why make so many offensives and kill so many of our splendid men?[3] K. says French has had all he has ever asked for—French says he has had no answers to his appeals for shells; and I suppose this will be his excuse for having allowed the Repington article to appear.[4] It is horrible that war

[1] Major-General William Lambton (1863–1936), military secretary to the Commander-in-Chief of the BEF, 1914–15.

[2] 'A brawl, wrangle, squabble' (*OED*).

[3] Kitchener had warned French, 31 Mar. 1915, 'that continued priority for the Western Front', and by implication his tenure as C.-in-C., depended on whether he could 'make a substantial advance within the next four to six weeks': Cassar, *Kitchener*, 352; Holmes, *French*, 285. Margot did not realize that in Aug. 1914 no one had known how much ammunition would have to be fired to give an attack a good chance of success; and Kitchener may not have seen that putting French 'on notice' came close to persuading him to attack prematurely.

[4] Margot was repeating the mistake which Asquith had made in the Tyneside speech on 20 April), i.e. converting French's very low estimate of the ammunition supply needed for the Aubers Ridge attack, 9 May, into a *general* assurance that his ammunition was adequate. In 1914 (2nd edn.) French denied that he had even assured Kitchener about the 9 May attack. In view of French's statements to (a) Mrs Bennett, 23 Mar. 1915, and (b) to Kitchener, 2 May 1915, this denial must be rejected. For (b) see Arthur, *Kitchener*, iii. 236.

should disclose such quarrels and jealousies and pettiness. French can't be a strong man.

I could see Billy Lambton is genuinely distressed. He is stupid though nice, and a great gentleman. I told him George Moore, French's American friend, was much suspected, but I knew this was all rot; and Billy said Moore's influence was all to the good, but that all visitors from England were a mistake, which is absolutely true. No one should be allowed to go, except on pure business, to the battle line, or Headquarters. I rather think Brinsley FitzGerald has played a foolish part in this quarrel. When the Minister of War and Commander-in-Chief come to loggerheads in the greatest war the world has ever seen, things are getting pretty serious!

Will H. find out when he gets back Thursday (3d [June] 1915) how things can be adjusted between these two men?? If anyone can, he will. Lambton ended his talk (in a secretary's room down stairs) by saying 'You are a sportswoman: if you were riding Sir J. French, do you know what you would do?' M. 'No.' L. 'Well, you would give him one or two over the head, that's what you'd do.'

The casualties and sorrows these last weeks have been heart-rending. Julian Grenfell*, Ettie's beautiful eldest son, was shot in the head, and died in Boulogne Hospital.[1] My splendid friend Francis Grenfell, 9th. Lancers, the first VC, was shot.[2] My 2 cousins—Charlie Tennant, an angel boy,[3] and Willy Tennant,—were killed. We wait daily to hear if our Beb (serving with aeroplane guns[4] in Flanders) is dead or alive. Frances Horner has returned with Edward, who is still very ill. Poor, poor Etty—her first grief, and what a terrible one. No one, I should say, ever got over the loss of a Child.

[1] Julian Grenfell was wounded on 13 May when a splinter from a bursting shell penetrated his skull. He underwent an operation on 16 May and another on 23 May, but died on 26 May: see Mosley, *Grenfell*, 260–5.

[2] Francis Grenfell VC (a cousin of Julian Grenfell) was killed on 24 May 1915 during the final stages of Second Ypres; he had returned to the front in April after being seriously wounded in Oct. 1914; he was *among the first* VCs of the war: see above, p. 35 n. 1.

[3] Four of Margot's cousins were killed in 1915: Charles Alan Tennant, Charles Grant Tennant, John Amherst Tennant, and William Galbraith Tennant. For details see Crathorne, *Tennant's Stalk*, ix, x.

[4] i.e., anti-aircraft guns.

May 1915

I wrote Winston a delightful and kind letter,[1] as I long to cheer him up. I hear he is <u>quite</u> miserable and she weeps. If only they would see me, I'm sure I could help.... Winston has a great opportunity, if he only knew it, just now: but he won't take it, I'm sure. He ought to go out on Ian Hamilton's* staff in the Dardanelles—he would be a great popular hero if he did.

Wednesday 2 June 1915

I am writing this in bed 6.30 a.m. I always thought the day Zeppelins came to London there would be wild excitement, but not a cat took the faintest notice in London yesterday; many didn't even read about this raid in the papers. All I saw was that for once our Censors woke up and reported nothing. (Up till now every newspaper has provided Germany with everything short of a map—sometimes even <u>maps</u> to help her to find her way!); but even I felt not the faintest excitement. What really upset me was my maid telling me that a new and pretty dress of mine (violet silk gabardine with beautiful embroidered belt) and my new gold fencing-jacket were put in a cardboard box on the top of the motor coming back from the Wharf (Eliz. in motor); and had, I need hardly say, been lost on the road. Our second chauffeur, McNicoll, third footman Charles, and butler Yeo are, I suppose, as stupid a trio as were ever made. I can't describe what I've suffered from servants in these last years....

I sent for Sir Ed. Henry head of the Police[2] to ask about Zeppelin damage: he said 8 people had been killed—2 babies, 3 men, the rest old women. 10 were injured. <u>No</u> one had seen anything, and only one man had heard anything. Sir E.H. 'Up till now, Mrs Asquith, not one person in England has seen a Zeppelin, and very few have heard one. The chances are extremely small of them doing much harm. There was no sort of

---

[1] *Churchill Companion*, iii. 957–8.
[2] Sir Edward Richard Henry (1850–1931), KCVO 1906, Bt. 1918; Commissioner of the Metropolitan Police, 1903–18; established central fingerprint bureau.

panic in Whitechapel—the fires put out in a moment. Our organisation is perfect, but I'm sorry to say we have pretty poor anti-aircraft guns. This is the fault of the Admiralty: I've <u>begged for them</u>.' This I thought disquieting, as if the Germans get to know this they will fly quite close, and kill and set fire right and left with surer aim....

Ll.G. has no organising powers, but he can get others to work for him, and if he has a competent board—if—I think he ought to do well. Why H. W. Massingham[1] should want Winston out so much, and then say the new Gov. is not fully supplied with the genius of improvisation, I don't know. Winston is, I should say, the greatest improviser in the world.

I rather doubt if Arthur will do well at Admiralty. When H. and B. Law had their famous first conference, H. told me Arthur didn't think he was at all the man for the place—he said he was too old, etc.; but H. said what is <u>essential</u> just now is that you should have a man of prestige to stop all the intrigue and gossip in the navy, and <u>insisted</u> on Arthur being there. Arthur has plus distinction, a great knowledge of Defence: it is the subject he likes best. I said this to Moulton one day at lunch, and he said he quite believed it: it was a light on his Religion. It was a religion of defence. I said <u>no</u>—only in its expounding. Arthur Balfour is a man of profound faith....

H. wrote [Grey] a slight admonition, telling him he might go on with his holiday, but could not give up his post. We heard no more after that. He has become terribly egotistical, and in consequence unsuggestive.... [He] has not got much heart, and he has at all times very bad nerves. I often thought if anything were to happen to Henry that Grey would succeed him as Prime Minister of the Lib. Party. I am quite sure now he would <u>not</u>—or that if he undertook it, he would break down. He has been useless to Henry throughout this crisis—selfish and quite wanting in sympathy. His eyes have been very bad and alarming, which no doubt has in some ways been the cause, but he was <u>just</u> the same in the

---

[1] Henry William Massingham (1860–1924), editor of *The Nation*, 1907–23; a leading radical 'isolationist' among the Liberals.

coal strike, when his eyes were <u>not</u> threatened. He is a curious study! He has beautiful masculine <u>physique</u>, and manly morals (sense of right and wrong and challenging Truthfulness); he has a schoolboy <u>mind</u>—edgy, touchy, and personal in his taste for books and people and poetry (and a mass of prejudice) though <u>very</u> appreciative and full of genuine admiration for what people call 'favourites'; but he has in his nature a little more of the female than I personally like in any man....

At the Wharf Sunday 30th May Henry got a very hard letter from Grey, insisting on keeping Neil Primrose. H. 'So like Grey! He never thinks of any one but <u>himself</u> in all of this. I've made <u>every</u> personal sacrifice for the sake of the whole; he thinks himself an injured man if he has to make <u>one</u>.' He tore up a dry little letter which he read to me, and threw it in the waste paper basket. Crewe and Haldane wrote Henry delightful letters.

Montagu told me H. had written Ll.G. a wonderful letter, thanking him for his help and sympathy in these sad weeks. Ll.G. showed this letter to Montagu, and said (Ll.G.) 'What would one <u>not</u> do for a man like <u>that</u>!!'—'And then', added Montagu, 'when the PM asks him to give up one of his d-----d Welshmen, Lewis, he refuses!' Believe me, I like George, but he's never lifted a finger to fight for any of us being retained in the new Gov: he has only thought of himself.'...

Thursday 3 June 1915

I went to Charing Cross at 11.30 p.m. to meet Henry, who was due to arrive about then from Dover....² I watched the wounded officers in a very long ambulance train being carried out and put into Red Cross motors at this

---

¹ Asquith's letter to Lloyd George, dated 25 May 1915, spoke of 'your devotion, your unselfishness, your powers of resource, what is...the best of all things your self-forgetfulness'. See Grigg, *Lloyd George, 1912–1916*, 255, for full text. John Herbert Lewis (1858–1933) was Parliamentary Secretary at the Board of Education, 1915.

² Asquith had been visiting the front, and had seen Venetia at Boulogne that day, at her suggestion; she convinced him of her intention both to marry Edwin Montagu, and to convert to Judaism in order to do so; and that night wrote urging him not to allow these facts to affect their friendship; he wrote a long and anguished reply, which ended by asking for time to reconcile himself to events, and signed off: 'Your heart-broken and ever devoted': see *Asquith-Stanley*, 600–2.

strange hour of night or morning. No one allowed in the station but my-self, a huge crowd outside. I never saw anything more beautifully and perfectly arranged than all this. The silence, the ease and quickness with which many of these dying men were conveyed from the train to the motor ambulance was most striking.

I think station light is at all times rather Dickensy and melodramatic. I felt the pathos of these poor fellows, all thrown out of gear even if not dying or in pain. They looked almost green-white, all so clean and beauti-fully dressed in what looked almost new Khaki, lying perfectly flat like so many corpses on the Charing Cross platform....

[Henry,] Bongy, Hankey and G. Howard[1] got out, all dead tired and half-asleep. H. Bongy and I motored (5 min.) to Downing St. H. (in the motor) 'I saw a wonderful operation today done by Sargent[2] (a St. Thomas's man that I had got out to the front through Cheyne's[3] urgings) on the brain of an officer. He bored a hole through his forehead, and with the most powerful magnet ever seen, drew out the bullet (or bit of shell, I'm not sure which). You would have been interested to see this—he is a clever man. Sargent told me poor Julian Grenfell arrived too late for him to save him: he died of septic brain wound.'

(I can't help thinking if Sargent had been on the firing line and had oper-ated at once, Julian might be alive now, but I don't know if this is a wise re-flection.) I kissed Henry and left him in his bedroom terribly tired: he could hardly speak—this distressed me very much. I never saw him so low.

Friday 4 June 1915

Henry came into my bedroom with Elizabeth at 11 a.m., looking just as ill and tired and said he had found no sort of hysteria but perfect confidence

---

[1] Geoffrey William Howard (1877–1935), son of 9th Earl of Carlisle; Liberal MP, 1906–18, 1923–4; Junior Lord of Treasury, 1915.

[2] Sir Percy William George Sargent (1873–1933) Kt. 1928; consulting surgeon to BEF.

[3] Sir (William) Watson Cheyne (1852–1932), cr. 1st Bt. 1908; KCMG 1916; bacteriologist and surgeon; President of the Royal College of Surgeons of England, 1914–17; Consulting Surgeon, RN 1914–15; Temp. Surgeon-General, RN from 1915.

at the front; that all the soldiers <u>bitterly</u> resented the talk over here: what did it amount to? The gravest accusation anyone can make on generals, that they had made a big offensive knowing they had not got munitions, and in consequence exposed hundreds of fellows to unnecessary death: could you have a more <u>awful</u> accusation? It was <u>quite</u> untrue of course. M. 'Then <u>why</u> are *The Times* and *Daily Mail* allowed to write daily "Truth will out", "Crying need for Shells", etc.' <u>It's too wicked</u>, and as long as day in day out Northcliffe is allowed to have his own way, whether in trying to damage Kitchener or Henry, whether spreading Poison and Slander at Home or abroad, <u>so long</u> must we expect not only unrest but actual Panic, should any great reverse happen, either on our West line or in the Dardanelles. (I can <u>never</u> understand why our Gov. is so amazingly weak about the Press. It gets on H.'s nerves my asking him questions, but till I die I shall think this will be one of the stupidest blunders we've ever made in the whole war. I must get some one to explain why we allow Northcliffe to write any and every lie that he thinks 'copy'.) H. 'That is another point: every army is in need of shells.'

Henry is low and edgy about munition talk because there is truth, though not <u>all</u> the truth, in the cry; and because I think he feels as if the new lot, Bonar Law and Co. (men of not very high motives), have slightly blackmailed him—which they certainly <u>have</u>. (I feel pretty sure, had we been in their shoes, we should have done the same: I can see Winston and Ll.G. being even more unpatriotic than Bonar Law and Co., but they would have done it with much more wit and sparkle, and with more <u>brains</u>.)

Both K. and Sir J. French have bungled between them over the question of high explosives.[1] I'm told the villain of the piece is a very slow stubborn fool called Von Donop,[2] but I don't really know—it is probably a little eve-

---

[1] A fair assessment. Kitchener would not accept what enormous amounts of ammunition (especially high explosive in high calibres) were needed on the Western Front. French had launched an attack on the basis of a very over-optimistic assessment about the amount (and type) of ammunition needed.

[2] Major-General Sir Stanley Brenton von Donop (1860–1941), KCB 1914, Master-General of Ordnance 1913–16. See Adams, *Arms*, 160, 168, 178. For an analysis of von Donop's problems and performance see Bidwell and Graham, *Fire-power*, 94–9.

ryone's fault for not foreseeing the magnitude of the war or taking sufficient precautions. It has been in no way Henry's fault.

I attacked K. on his weakness over the Press. M. 'You look like a strong
man, but you aren't! Why didn't you have that cur Northcliffe arrested!
All the generals at the front said to Henry "Germany had got no better
friend in this country than Northcliffe". All he said was 'I got my Garter
through all this, how can I mind??'!'[1]

The new Government met on Thursday 3rd [June] 1915. As the 2 most
interesting figures in the House were away, I did not go to see the National
Government's first meeting. Henry was with Sir John French, and Ll.G.
opening his new Munition campaign in Manchester. I enclose his speech.[2]
Not I think one of his best—it's so very long—but it is praised by most
people.

There is a disgraceful, vulgar, violent campaign going on now by
Northcliffe, the Morning Post and other smaller fry in favour of
Conscription....[3]

Thursday 10 June 1915

I had a painful agonizing day yesterday—but I will begin with Monday.
On Monday 7th Eliz., H. and I motored from the Wharf to London, with
Cys on the box. I never saw H. so silent and taciturn: he never uttered
hardly. It was a mixture of over-fatigue and real depression. He is never
really free from the responsibility and strain of this terrible war....

New National Government sitting in the House of Commons: the first
time I had ever seen it, the first time it sat with its Prime Minister. A painful peculiar impression was made on me; perhaps I shall get accustomed

[1] The birthday honours list included the award of a Garter Knighthood to Kitchener. In
telling him of it Asquith wrote: 'It is a great pleasure to me to couple with this announcement the assurance of my profound gratitude and unabated confidence'; see Magnus, Edward
VII, 341.
[2] See passages in Grigg, Lloyd George, 1912–1916, 263–4.
[3] See Daily Mail, 26 Mar. 1915, 4b; The Times, 6 May, 9a; Gwynne, Rasp, 93–4, 101, 104; Koss,
Nonconformity, 131, for Robertson Nicoll's (radical) British Weekly.

to it. It may work well, but I confess I feel it is a terrible gamble, and it has robbed the H. of Commons of all its interest. It has only one chance of success. If the Press is kept in order, and colleagues and their families and secretaries will be Silent and above all Loyal: but will they be? I fear not. I look on the new National Government with the deepest apprehension.

Sir J. Simon (the new Home Secretary, an able, dusty-minded, ambitious, very old, youngish man of amazing luck) was conducting the emergency Ministry of Munitions Bill (my own rather late invention,[1] which St. John Brodrick told me he had tried to persuade K. to have in September, the second month of the war!)

Henry had Bonar Law sitting on his left, then Winston, then Walter Long. It didn't look so very strange to see Winston between 2 Tories. (He is a Tory, and ought never to have left that party! He would have been their Prime Minister and Leader now, had he stayed; as it is, I think Ll.G. will cut him out on our side, or Sir John Simon.) Harry Chaplin, Valentia,[2] Jack Pease, Hobhouse*, Lambert,[3] Tommy Lough[4] and all sorts of leavings from our side sat on front opposition Bench, and dear Baker. Simon (possibly the happiest man on our front Bench) went drily on.

H. left the House. I felt sad and restless. I went to his room and kissed him. M. 'How sad it all is! The House will have little or no interest now except for set speeches.' (I wondered who I wanted to hear except Henry—perhaps Ll.G. and Winston, but not a cat from the other side, the 'interned aliens' as I call them). Henry was serene and sweet, and said he had asked K. how he liked the new lot, at which he had grunted, and said he preferred the old!

Montagu, Meiklejohn, Eliz., Lucy, Henry...dined....Montagu told E. and me that the whole Treasury were enchanted at having McKenna back again.

---

[1] See Diary, 20 May 1915, pp. 121–2 above.
[2] Arthur Annesley (1843–1927), 11th Viscount Valentia; Unionist MP 1895–1917.
[3] George Lambert (1866–1958), Viscount 1945; Liberal MP 1891–1924, 1929–45; Civil Lord of the Admiralty 1905–15.
[4] Tommy Lough (1850–1922), Liberal MP 1892–1918.

Meiklejohn   It's amazing how <u>hated</u> Ll.G. is and always has been with <u>everyone</u> who works with him.

M[argot]   I don't think he has any real gratitude.

Montagu   I think he is more hated than Winston by his entourage.

Meiklejohn   Oh! 1000 times more. The fact is he never was up to the job of Chan. of Excheq., and all his men know this.

Montagu   Bradbury[1] was so amusing! He said to me apropos of McK's advent 'If it were my habit, I would permit myself to be enthusiastic.'

Tuesday 8 June 1915

We dined with Ld Charles Montagu.[2] I sat between my host and Admiral Sir Hedworth Lambton.[3]

Hedworth   My dear Margot, I've known Jacky Fisher all my life. I grant he's a genius, but he carts away[4] everyone he works with: he's a low, untrustworthy devil, who has played dirty tricks all his life.

M.   I really think he got on <u>personally</u> with Winston.

Hedworth   He liked him very much, but he wanted to knock Winston out, and be a K. in Admiralty[5]—we sailors have known that a <u>very</u> long time.

Ld Charles Montagu   Your husband is the biggest man in Europe: but tell me why he isn't firmer with his colleagues?

---

[1] Sir John Bradbury (1872–1950), KCB 1913, Baron, 1925; Joint Permanent Secretary at Treasury, 1913–19; provided new issue of currency notes, 1914.

[2] Lord Charles William Montagu (1860–1939), son of 7th Duke of Manchester; a member of a prominent Unionist family in Huntingdonshire.

[3] Admiral Sir Hedworth Meux Lambton (1856–1929), KCVO, 1906; brother of 3rd Earl of Durham, he assumed the surname Meux in 1911; Unionist MP for Portsmouth, 1916–18.

[4] i.e. lets down, or disappoints.

[5] Fisher wrote to Asquith on 19 May 1915 with certain conditions, which, if agreed, would enable him to guarantee 'the successful termination of the War and the total abolition of the submarine menace'. The conditions included 'absolutely untrammelled sole command of all the sea forces whatsoever'; and that 'the First Lord of the Admiralty should be absolutely restricted to policy and parliamentary procedure'; see *Fisher Correspondence*, iii. 241.

M.   That is a very superficial observation. If you ride certain horses with big bits they run away. What is it that keeps horses of that type from running amok? <u>Light hands</u>—that is what Henry has got, the lightest hands in the world. In consequence he is adored. You put a 'firmer' man to keep men like Winston, Ll.G. and the rest in their places, and he would not remain PM 2 weeks, or get the best out of any of them.

Ld Charles   I expect that's true. There is no doubt if it were not for him, God knows what would become of this country! There's not a <u>man</u> on my side!!

Charlie and [I] played bridge against Edith Wolverton[1] and the Grand Duke Michael[2]—the latter is a terrible lout with no wits, a snob and a fool, but nice in his family life. I won £7.

Wednesday 9 June 1915

Yesterday I had a <u>great</u> triumph. A Foul paper called *London Mail* wrote enclosed on 29th May.[3] I need hardly say a cutting of this was sent to me, and I insisted on an apology and £100 for Red Cross. I cd. never have got this had it not been for a delightful solicitor (son of the great Ld Russell) Charles Russell.[4] I need hardly say all the old women—Nash,[5] Bongy, Sir J. Simon, my sister Lucy and many others said it would be most undig-

---

[1] Lady Edith Amelia Ward (1872–1956), m. 1895 4th Baron Wolverton.

[2] Grand Duke Michael (1861–1929), a distant cousin of Tsar Nicholas II.

[3] Margot pasted two cuttings in the diary of May–June 1915, d. 3212, fo. 93ᵛ. The first, dated 29 May, alleged that Margot had played tennis with German officer prisoners-of-war at Donnington Hall: several of them were believed to be 'former acquaintances of Mrs Asquith'. The second cutting gave the paper's 'most sincere apologies, regretting any pain and annoyance' and agreeing to the payment to the Red Cross.

[4] Charles Russell (1863–1928), Bt. 1916; solicitor; son of Charles Arthur Russell (1832–1900), Lord Chief Justice, 1894.

[5] Vaughan Nash (1861–1932), Private Secretary to Asquith, 1908–12; Margot wrote of his successor, Maurice Bonham Carter, 'an excellent fellow, but in no ways equal to Nash (the best PM's first secretary that could be made)' (diary, 11 Nov. 1912).

nified of me to take any notice of such a low paper. I hate dignity, and told the Public Prosecutor I would never sit tight, and limp under such an insult.

I would not have minded had this paper not been read by our Tommies: but at the front, when our poor devils are being poisoned by gas and killed like rats in the lowest most treacherous abominable way, for me to be believed to be playing tennis with brother officers of the very men who are shooting and torturing our poor devils, is more than I can stand. I notice in war times like these nothing is too silly or too concocted for people to believe. The credulity of the world just now is past my comprehension....

Ll.G. left early [after dinner], and I took him downstairs as I wanted much to hear of his Winston talk....

Ll.G. We had a most unpleasant but absolutely frank, open talk, but Winston believes I blackmailed the PM over Coalition, threatening to resign, etc.—all pure rubbish.

M. What exactly did happen? (16th May 1915)

Ll.G. On Sunday night McKenna and I were sitting in 11 Downing St. smoking when my servant said 'Will you see Mr. Bonar Law?' I asked McK what he supposed B.L. had come about: we neither of us thought it was munitions, but the Fisher row; but he came in and discussed the whole situation. It was my plain duty to tell the PM first, and on Monday 17th (17th May 1915), when he got back from Wharf, I told him everything, and we made up our minds— not particularly at my instigation—that coalition was inevitable. We could not face a row on munitions, and the K. and French quarrel, in front of the Germans, with Italy not in, etc.

M. Are you sure you and H. were not a little blackmailed?

Ll.G. Well, perhaps we were a little, but sooner or later it was bound to come. (We were sitting in 2 chairs by the big clock outside the cabinet room door.)

M. Did you tell Winston you thought Northcliffe a hero?

Ll.G. No, but I said I thought he had done the right thing over the shells.

M. Then you said a very wrong and foolish thing. Winston will go all over London saying this, and mark my words, I've said this before and I'll say it again as a warning: Ld Northcliffe will run you against Henry. He has already tried and he will go on, and I shall back <u>Henry</u> to score if this happens.

Ll.G. (smiling, and for the first time a little brighter) My dear friend, wicked I may be, but I'm not a d----d fool: as I said to Winston 'Do you <u>really</u> think I don't know what Northcliffe is? Why, he'll turn on me and stab me in the back at any moment.'

M. <u>Then why do you praise him?</u> He is responsible for many, many deaths in this Ypres line by deliberately fostering and encouraging the Generals to quarrel. If it's true we have not obeyed Sir J. French, it's a low thing just to sell your papers to write sensational reports— 'Great Shell Scandal, Shortage' etc., etc., for all the German papers to copy. Why is the *Daily Mail* burnt in the Stock Exchange and on the race courses? Oh! no, I shall <u>never</u> agree with you. The English public is good in this kind of thing, they won't stand foul play; and Northcliffe has run his paper for himself, he doesn't know there is a war going on. He has got no heart. He's a regular Yankee, and has missed a <u>great</u> opportunity.'[1]

Ll.G. Winston is <u>very</u> strong on the point that <u>I</u> should have gone first to him—to Winston—on that fateful Monday, 17th May. I said No, not at all. It is my duty to tell the PM first.

M. I hear you also fancied Coalition. (It is so characteristic to my mind of the kind of men Ll.G. and Winston are, they were the only 2 in Henry's cabinet that wanted Coalition. I should think it was even

---

[1] Northcliffe's leader, 21 May 1915, accusing Kitchener of mishandling ammunition supply, was not written to enhance the *Daily Mail*'s circulation. When he realized that Kitchener would remain at the War Office when the Coalition was formed, Northcliffe told H. W. Wilson, one of his leader writers: 'The thing has to be done! Better to lose circulation than to lose the war': Thompson, *Northcliffe*, 240–4. The leader represented a massive miscalculation; but the motive was not sordid. The *Daily Mail*'s circulation recovered within two months. By 'Yankee' Margot means cunning or coldly calculating.

betting that Winston joined the Tory party some day, and Ll.G. is a natural adventurer who may make or mar himself any day.)

Ll.G.   No one can say I talked about Coalition like Winston has. My discussion of it was purely theory, and to colleagues, <u>never</u> outside.

M.   You'll see, there's no catch in Coalitions,[1] unless they bring brains or great experience: and, with the exception of Curzon, what brains do they bring? <u>None</u>.

Saturday 12 June 1915

We went to Easton Grey[2] 12th June, but in meantime events developed. I had told Bongy and several people that I could see our lot were genuinely unhappy, restless and bewildered by the coalition.... It was obvious to me that <u>something</u> should be done to make [Henry's] leadership felt— more especially as Ll.G. was stumping the country.... Ll.G. has never to my mind shown more greenness, vanity and folly than he is showing now, and making very gassy munition speeches to boot!

I need hardly say Bongy and the others to whom I spoke thought it was nonsense, and that H. had done enough: but thank God the Master of Elibank[*] turned up at tea (11th June 1915), and spoke with amazing insight and cleverness about the situation. He knows <u>everything</u> that is going on and is a really clever man. I miss him every hour in Downing St., as he really has the true instinct of high political life in its personal presentment to the public, and knows better than anyone living when a little drama and colour is needed. Bongy has not one trace of this, H., though he may <u>see</u> it, cares <u>so</u> little for himself that if urged by me alone he would never think of listening.

The Master said it was essential that H. should have a meeting the day before Parliament on 15th. He had a capital excuse not to have done it before: his gov. was only just finished with the Irish law-officerships to

---

[1] By 'no catch in Coalitions' Margot means there is no advantage.

[2] 18th-century Wiltshire manor house on the Avon, and the home of Margot's widowed sister Lucy Graham-Smith. Margot wrote in 1914: 'Easton Grey has been a second home to very very many'.

be published next day. He said Gulland would never see this sort of thing, but that he (Master), Eric Drummond, and Hopwood[1] had been together, and all agreed that Ll.G. was running a show of his own, which upset our men: and that H. had never said a word, or explained his coalition to the public; that our fellows didn't realise it was modesty, but thought it was indifference and callousness.

I need hardly say I jumped with joy that I had found a backer, and engaged the Master to see H. next morning, 12th, at 10.30; and told him I would have Hopwood, Eric and himself to lunch, and that I prayed he would settle it satisfactorily. The Master told me he had made a strong point of this, even if only for Ll.G.'s sake, as he was not consciously disloyal and trying to oust the PM, but just flattered, and allowing himself to be run by Northcliffe. I told the Master with pardonable vanity(!) that I had foreseen this, though no one else had, and I had personally warned Ll.G.

H. wasn't a bit vexed with me for letting him in for a talk with Elibank. He is very fond of him, and they had an excellent talk. The Master came into my drawing room after, and said he thought he had made an impression, and had left H. with 'an open mind'. He would return to lunch, when he would try and clinch things. I felt very anxious. I consider it a most critical moment in the fortunes of the Lib. party.

Sunday 13 June 1915

H. got a clever, very long letter from Mr. Montagu, saying exactly the same things to him, in much better language of course, than I have, about the necessity of his coming out in the open at once. (I dare say I'm vain— I wonder—not au fond, but just a little about 2 things: 1. My political instinct, which in this particular case was so right that I really saw the imperative need for Henry to show himself while his whips and secretaries and colleagues with exception of Montagu were stone blind. 2. My insight into human nature and people....)

[1] Sir Francis Hopwood (1860–1947), KCB 1901, cr. Baron Southborough 1917; Civil Lord of Admiralty 1912–17.

Monday 14 June 1915

I was much relieved to hear Henry <u>had</u> made up his mind to speak in H. of Commons on Tuesday 15th (I wondered if I had been younger and more tactful whether he would have spoken earlier.) ... On night of 14th June H. said to me: 'I had a very long letter from French saying nice things of K. today. I told K. this. All he said was "I shall never forget, to the end of this war, the low trick French has played on me, never!"'

Me.   Does K. still believe French gave special permission, and passed the uncensored Repington article of May 14th?

[H.]   Not <u>himself</u>, but French certainly knew what Repington was doing. K. is the most interesting man in my cabinet in some ways. He has no rancour. They will say he has, but I know he has <u>none</u>. (I quite agree with Henry.) K. comes out of all this shell scandal business with <u>great</u> dignity—never lifted a finger to defend himself, and he has a good case. Oh! no, the <u>really</u> sad thing is that French comes out of it all badly. He is full of pettiness and personal feelings, etc.

M.   And the saddest thing of all, he is not a great general. As Stamfordham* said to me, with broken eyes, 'Neither you nor I, Mrs Asquith, would mind our only sons dying in a Waterloo, but in <u>this</u> muddled, mismanaged war everyone feels the uselessness of their losses'.[1]

Tuesday June 15 1915

Henry made his great Coalition Speech in the House.[2] Frances Balfour and I trembled with excitement. <u>It was quite perfect</u>: touched with just that personal emotion which is rare and distinguished. I ran down and wrote him a little letter. That night I went into his bedroom (next mine) as usual and found him reading my letter with deep emotion. I put my arms around him, and he cried. I realized how frightfully he is taken out of when he has to confess himself, so to speak.

---

[1] Stamfordham's only son, John Neville Bigge, was killed in France on 15 May 1915.
[2] *Parl. Deb.*, 15 June 1915, 72.557–61.

He is also fearfully tired; hates the coalition (though the others are not giving any trouble, and our men are) and is low about Venetia's marriage and Violet's indecision.[1] He was quite wonderful, and said my letter was noble, and infinitely precious to him. We sat a long time together. . . . There never has been anyone like Henry: he makes everyone near him and opposite him like so much waste paper!

Ll.G., I need hardly say, had seen no reason for H. making a speech at all! Rufus Isaacs took me in to dinner that same night, 15th June 1915, at Ly Lewis's; and told me how <u>carefully</u> he had warned Ll.G. of the harm he was doing by letting Northcliffe and his vile press run him.[2] I had been to see Ll.G. that morning: he was out, so wrote and asked him to dine, and also to see me before H.'s speech.

Poor, foolish Ll.G.! He is evidently playing to break with his old party: not consciously to smash H., but he sees that after the war things will completely change, and the man who will be adored in England is the man who helps our poor devils in the trenches. It comes to this: can George and Northcliffe crush Henry and K? The former have for allies the Rt. Hon. Sir H. Dalziel, MP, a hound;[3] Sir A. Markham, a maniac;[4] Sir

---

[1] Violet and Maurice Bonham Carter had been secretly engaged since May 1915, but she had expressed some doubt about her decision to marry. See Bonham Carter, *Churchill*, 413, for this engagement.

[2] Margot had also given Ll.G. this warning (see above, p. 154), and wrote in a letter to 'Oc' Asquith, 18 July 1915: 'Politics have been <u>very</u> sad here. Ll.G. has allowed Northcliffe & his swine to run him in every way against y^r father w^h Rufus & Master of Elibank even have condemned sternly—our rank & file & others w^d have shot Ll.G. any day the last 5 weeks—I with my usual distressing candour told Ll G. that Northcliffe was <u>going</u> to do it—I saw it like fish in a glass bowl (I'm really a sort of political clairvoyante [*sic*]) I warned him <u>not</u> to see Northcliffe or be run by him. He has an odd kind of passion for prominence & incapacity to run straight. I find as I get older you can count on <u>one</u> hand men & women of really fine, candid, unvain unpetty characters—Brains I see terribly often but character never hardly.' Riddell's diary, entries 5 and 6 June 1915, suggest that Ll.G. was wary about Northcliffe's support: McEwen, *Riddell Diaries*, 121.

[3] James Henry Dalziel (1868–1935), Kt. 1908, cr. 1st Bt 1918; Baron 1921; Liberal MP 1892–1921; long associated with, and from 1914 sole owner of, the radical Sunday *Reynolds Newspaper*, which he used in loyal service to Ll.G., especially during the events leading to Asquith's resignation, Dec. 1916; considered by Margot 'a political adventurer' (diary, 21 Feb. 1910).

[4] Sir Arthur Basil Markham (1866–1916), KCB 1903, Bt. 1911; Liberal MP 1900–16. The Asquiths thought his keen interest in the welfare of those in the trenches who were aged less than 19 somewhat fanatical.

G. Riddell, an impostor;[1] Winston, a caprice: and who have Henry and K. got? The Liberal Party in the country and cabinet; devoted friends like McKenna, Crewe, Grey and Montagu, Haldane, and Simon, who has a very warm corner for himself.

Friday 18 June 1915

Eliz.,…H., Puff and I dined early and went to *On Trial*, in the Dress circle. When Henry was recognised, the whole dress circle cheered him. I had the greatest difficulty in making him smile and bow. How foolish parents are not to teach their children gracious manners. It's true manners are a little born, but they are also quite makeable. I've taken great trouble to make E. and A. sweet and grateful to everyone.…

Monday 21 June 1915

Lord Cromer[2] came to see me at 6. He was down on the Coalition. 'Your government were doing magnificently, and full of really clever men: with the exception of Curzon who have you got? I see no brains!! You had Balfour before.' He was furious with Winston and Fisher for hurrying Dardanelles, and genuinely anxious about this up to now ill-starred expedition!…

Thursday 24 June 1915

Yesterday I sent for K. to ask him to tell Ld Hugh Cecil[3] to withdraw his pernicious question to Henry[4] (I didn't know that at H.'s request he was

---

[1] George (Allardice) Riddell (1865–1934), cr. Kt 1909; cr. 1st Bt. 1918; 1st Baron 1920; newspaper proprietor, his titles included the *News of the World*, of which he was managing director 1903; a close ally of Lloyd George.

[2] Evelyn Baring (1841–1917), cr. 1st Earl Cromer 1901; statesman, administrator in India and Egypt.

[3] Hugh Richard Heathcote Gascoyne-Cecil (1869–1956), cr. 1st Baron Quickswood 1941; fifth son of the 3rd Marquess of Salisbury; Unionist MP 1895–1906, 1910–37; Lieut, Royal Flying Corps, 1915.

[4] Hugh Cecil had given notice of his intention to ask a question in the Commons, 23 June, about the source for Asquith's statement on armaments at Newcastle, on 20 Apr., and whether

doing so at the very moment I was talking to K.—this is not the first time that Henry and I have been in telepathic communication. I am very telepathic! Though I don't at all believe in spiritualism. The idea that the existence of God either outside or within one can be proved by a few stray boxes on the ear after dark, is to me repugnant.)

I said to K:

M. You know the Salisburys better than anyone: it is for you to see that Ld Hugh's question to the PM is withdrawn.

K. I would never ask a favour of Hugh Cecil: he is not a good sort.

M. But tell Alice or Jim Salisbury.[1] If the question is not withdrawn, it will bring your quarrel with French up, after all it was to avoid this very thing that we had to have a coalition. Who is Henry's highest authority? You are—it was you who told H. in your letter to him before his Newcastle speech (after The Times article) that you were authorised by Sir J.F. to say he had all the munitions he wanted, and had not been hampered for the want of them: that Newcastle speech, made on your authority, filled our soldiers with despair.[2]

K. I think I enclosed my authority—French's letter.

M. No, you didn't (when I told Henry, he told me what I did not know at the time: that Sir J. French had actually seen K. the day that K. wrote to H., and it was in consequence of their talk together that K. wrote his letter to H. I long to know if French really said that to K., but if French was not satisfied with K. why didn't he see H? and in any case why come over here and not see either of us?)

'the highest possible authority accessible to him…was Lord Kitchener or any other official in the War Office'; when it became clear that Cecil had withdrawn the question, Sir Arthur Markham gave notice of his intention to ask it at a later session, adducing Cecil's silence to government pressure: Parl. Deb., 28 June 1915, 72.1452. Margot regarded a question which reopened the issue whether French had deceived Kitchener (and thus the premier) as 'pernicious'.

[1] James Edward Gascoyne-Cecil (1861–1947), s. as 4th Marquess of Salisbury, 1903; Conservative and Unionist MP, 1885–92, 1893–1903; Under-Secretary for Foreign Affairs, 1900–3; Lord Privy Seal, 1903–5; married, 1887, Lady Cicely Alice née Gore (1867–1955).

[2] Margot misremembers the sequence of events: Kitchener's letter to Asquith was written on 14 Apr. 1915; H.H.A.'s Newcastle speech was 20 Apr.; Repington's article on shell shortage appeared in The Times on 14 May 1915. By 25 June London gossip was giving 'French's letter' as the authority for the Asquith's statement. Asquith, C., Diaries, 47–8.

H. and I were in the dining-room....

H. Bonar Law came to me yesterday, <u>very</u> unhappy over that maniac Ginnell[1] who is going to ask me in the House today what Bonar's relations are or have been to the firm of Jacks, that have just been convicted and punished for selling munitions to Germany. Bonar's brother[2] is in the firm, and it's altogether a very nasty affair. Poor devil, he was ready to give up leading the opposition, in fact chuck <u>everything</u>. I told him not to be a fool. I can't imagine a more idiotic thing to do! I would be sorrier for him, but I can't help thinking, after the way he behaved—believing every low rumour about all our men, attributing the lowest motives to his opponents—that this is retribution....

Friday 2 July 1915[3]

Sir George Murray, Sir Robert Chalmers,[4] <u>one and all</u> have warned me that [Lloyd George] had no ounce of loyalty in him, that he was a traitor and a cad: and yet I've struggled (not to <u>like</u> him—I can't but like him, he has such wonderful charm) to get rid of my disbeliefs in him, to make allowances for his curious nature. It has taken me a long time, but his <u>devotion</u> to Henry, his ease and frankness with me, and his <u>real</u> fondness (so both he and his wife have told me singly) for me too, have succeeded in

[1] Laurence Ginnell (1854–1923), MP for Westmeath North, 1906–23; a notably wild Irish Nationalist.

[2] Until the end of 1901 Bonar Law had been an active partner in William Jacks and Co, an important firm in the Glasgow iron market. His brother John was still a partner when the war began. A ship chartered by William Jacks began unloading her cargo of iron ore for German firms including Krupps on 11 Aug. 1914. The two partners who had made the final arrangements were convicted of trading with the enemy and given short prison sentences in June 1915. Bonar Law's sole connection with the firm then was that it acted as his banker: see Blake, *Bonar Law*, 257–60.

[3] From this point until 24 July 1915 Margot's entries do not follow in a regular chronological sequence: see 13 Apr. 1915 for an equally disorganized passage. She confessed, 12 July, that sometimes she copied her 'pencil notes carelessly', and lacked the time to sort them properly (d. 3213 fo. 17ᵛ; fo. 25ʳ).

[4] Sir Robert Chalmers (1858–1938), KCB 1908, cr. Baron 1919; Permanent Secretary to Treasury 1911–13; Governor General of Ceylon 1913–16.

dispelling my original severity: but I am reverting with horrible certainty and a feeling of inevitability to my original view of his character....[1]

On 30th June or 1st July Violet told me she was going to marry Bongie; that she had told her father, and asked if he thought July or Autumn: he said the sooner the better. I was and am <u>delighted</u>. No girl will ever marry a better fellow. I prefer him to all V.'s admirers, and think she will find he has a much stronger character than she knows (once they are married). I <u>love him</u> and so do many many more. How I pray things may go well for him. I should be miserable if he isn't happy, but he <u>knows</u> Violet better than anyone.[2]

This [2 July 1915] was an important day. Sir John French and Sir William Robertson came over to discuss war in Henry's Cabinet.

At 11.30 (cabinet at 12) Sir John French came to see me. It was the first time I had seen him this year, I think—or at any rate since *The Times* article and shell scandal, and consequent coalition and all its sorrows. I felt <u>indignant</u> at the folly and smallness of my dear friend, though I was sure he had a fair case, as we all have, against K. and V. Donop. His smallness consisted of allowing himself to be <u>exploitéed</u> by Northcliffe; his folly by having <u>such</u> rotten friends as Moore, Fitzgerald and F. Guest.[3] He looked very well—his pretty, keen grey eyes and jolly square head just the same. I took both his hands, and looked at him and said:

M.   If you had hated me and my man, you could not have done us a
     worse turn than you did by seeing swine like Northcliffe and

---

[1] Margot means her pre-1910 view of Lloyd George.

[2] Margot wrote to 'Oc' Asquith, 18 July 1915: 'I was really nervous about V. & thought she had thrown her life away & w[d] never have the <u>resolution</u> to marry but I must say Bongie has shown a great deal of character. He has a much stronger sounder character than she has got, & a much finer & bigger one—I do hope dear fellow he will be happy & that she wont bully him—he deserves the best wife in the world & if Violet can surrender her own will & completely forget herself & her own "ego" she will make the best of wives of this I feel sure. She & Venetia led rotten lives of gossip & shopping & now they are both going to settle down.'

[3] Frederick Edward Guest (1875–1937), DSO 1917, 3rd son of 1st Baron Wimborne, younger brother of Ivor, 2nd Baron and 1st Viscount Wimborne (see Biographical Notes), and cousin and close contemporary of Winston Churchill, whose private secretary he was 1907–10; served in France (ADC to Sir John French), 1914–16, and East Africa, 1916–17; later a Liberal, then Conservative, MP.

Repington. If you had wanted different kind of shells [*sic*],[1] why, if K. didn't answer satisfactorily, didn't you write <u>direct</u> to H. or myself? Would <u>we ever give you away?</u>

Sir J.F.   I've been asking for more munitions since October.

M.   Yes, every General has done this, but if you hadn't enough proper shells, <u>why</u> take offensives? To an amateur it all sounds <u>madness</u>, I think it will strike professionals as the same. (He was pretty silent, and looked quite miserable.) <u>Why</u> do you all quarrel and gossip? Why keep men like Fitzgerald and G. Moore to do you harm?

Sir J.F.   Why, surely you believe nothing against Moore, do you?

M.   No, <u>I</u> don't. I think he is devoted to you, and only wants to do good for you, but I have great contempt for your stockbroker B. Fitzgerald: he is sly and stupid—a bad combination.

Sir J.F.   He wasn't to blame for Repington's article.[2]

M.   Then it was Guest or Moore: but I won't ask you. I can only say, you are <u>badly</u> surrounded. All who get into *The Times's* toils are <u>done</u>: you are a bad judge of character....

Sir J.F.   I'm sorry you are so angry with me. I've been sorry,—very, <u>very</u> sorry for the Prime Minister, I can assure you! Now I must go to the cabinet, but if you'll let me I'll finish this talk after 6, after seeing the King.

He took my 2 hands and looked earnestly at me, full of contrition. I said 'I suppose I shall have to forgive you, but <u>how</u> I wish you would never again see <u>any</u> Press man, and above all, get some good aide-de-camp'. He humbly and rather touchingly kissed me and then kissed my hands, and flew out of the room.

---

[1] i.e. a higher proportion of high explosive and less shrapnel. For the problem of interrupting supply by turning from shrapnel to HE see Cassar, *Kitchener*, 336–8. French stated later (1914, 356) that on 9 May 1915 only 8 per cent of his army's shells were HE. Shrapnel, while effective against troops in the open, was of little use against a well-entrenched opponent.

[2] The culprit was of course French himself, which Margot seems still not to have realized; see above, pp. 127–8, entry for 19 May 1915.

Sir William Robertson lunched with us, and I had a <u>capital talk</u> to him. He is a resolute, sensible man, who ought, I should say, when war is over go to the W. Office and clean out and clean up that organisation, and see who it is that gives such stupid orders to so many people. He said he hated experts!—that a man like Cowans, who <u>got things done</u>, was the kind of man you want.... He was moderate, and wonderfully easy and intelligent. I heard Edgar D'Abernon ask him who was responsible for *The Times* shell scandal, but he was guarded and very ungetatable.

When I was alone with him I told him he would have to keep journalists away from the front, and asked him if <u>I</u> could do anything to help Sir J.F. Sir W. Robertson: 'If you ask me, I think it's only a woman who <u>can</u> do anything.[1] Take his friends away, let them leave him alone, and you'll see it will be much better. I always <u>hope</u> our General will improve.' (with a sweet smile)....

Monday 5 July 1915

Henry, Balfour, K. and Crewe went to Calais to consult with the French PM (Viviani),[2] Delcassé and Millerand [on] the military situation. He returned after midnight on Thurs. 8th July, in nick of time to stop poor Ll.G. and his amazing wickedness and Folly....

Friday 9 July 1915

I was so angry over all this[3] that I wrote a letter and sent it to Haldane, to put in any paper he liked. I've quite forgotten my words but it was defending Haldane's loyalty, and not particularly good!! It gave it hot to papers like the *Morning Post* and *Times*. However, the *Westminster Gazette* had an excellent article saying what I wanted to say, only 1000 times better written than I could ever have done...

---

[1] During 1915 French wrote almost daily to Mrs Winifred Bennett: Holmes, *French*, 278–9.
[2] René Viviani (1863–1925), French premier, June 1914–October 1915.
[3] Margot refers to articles in the press hostile to Haldane; she kept cuttings of these in her diary of July–November 1915.

On Thurs. July 1st a sudden debate arose in the House by a <u>violent</u> attack on V. Donop (and of course K. incidentally) by a microbe called Dalziel,[1] carefully arranged by Northcliffe and fully reported in *Times* of 2nd July (<u>I am going back, as this row looks to me like developing, and in any case has made a profound impression on our men.</u>) Ll.G. never defended this man (though as Minister of Munitions he ought to have defended his head of Ordinance Department) till such men as <u>were</u> on our front bench (H. and others were away) persuaded him to make a lame sort of speech.

Fri. 2nd July: Ll.G. saw Henry the next morning, and this is the account H. gave me of his talk:

H. I saw Ll.G. today and said to him 'I suppose this violent Dalziel attack came as a bolt from the blue to you.' I thought he looked a little un-comfortable, and I believe he wasn't quite speaking the truth, as he hesitated a little and then said, with a good deal of emphasis, that he knew <u>nothing</u> about it....

Tuesday 13 July 1915

Gulland our first whip came in to see me, as he often does on his way to Henry.

G. The PM dealt very well yesterday with the situation! <u>All</u> our men were pleased, and so was the whole House![2]

---

[1] *Parl. Deb.*, 1 July 1915, 72.2090–2112: Henry Dalziel called for the Ordnance Department, of which Von Donop was the head, to be subsumed within Lloyd George's new Ministry of Munitions: 'We demand that the new Ministry of Munitions shall assume all the powers of this Ordnance Department in regard to the supply of munitions, and that it should be robbed of every vestige of its authority in that regard' (2093). Haldane defended Von Donop, 5 July 1915, at the National Liberal Club: 'We have not so many first-class men that we can afford to throw them away' (*The Times*, 6 July, 12d–e). His talk there on 'The Duty of the Nation in this Crisis' gave Liberals, including the premier, a chance publicly to demonstrate their respect for him. On 8 July *The Times* displayed an authorized statement from Ll.G. rebutting Haldane's version of events (*The Times*, 8 July 1915, 8c). Various German papers seized on the evidence of dis-agreement between the two men to announce 'deep divisions' in Britain's government circles (*The Times*, 13 July 1915, 5).
[2] *Parl. Deb.*, 12 July 1915, 73.643–5. In an Oral Answer Asquith deprecated discussion about the causes of munitions shortages. It would, he said, 'be detrimental to the best interests of the nation'.

M. (I was there, and saw how furious the House was at Dalziel, and how tired of this microbe gang!) Ll.G. has been <u>most</u> wrong.

G. But surely you knew what he has always been!

M. Of course, I know he is born disloyal but I had <u>no</u> idea he would ever be light-headed about Henry, to whom he owes his whole soul, or whatever he has got of it, leave alone his political existence (No one ever thought he would recover [from] the Marconi incident.) I confess untrustworthiness to this degree will prevent my ever feeling the same for him. I don't say I hate him, but I don't take him seriously—he becomes a sort of low comedian....

All the soldiers I've seen who come back from the front <u>hate</u> Northcliffe and his shell scandal business. In Lady Ripon's King George Hospital I saw our men who have sent back exchanged from Germany. These poor maimed devils, without arms, legs or hands or feet, have been 10 months in Germany, some well, some badly treated, all a little starved: but what amazed me was they said they would <u>not</u> read *The Times* or *Daily Mail*, as these papers had encouraged Germans throughout this war. They were quoted daily in the German papers.

Every day *The Times* and *Daily Mail* say England is not doing its duty by its allies. One can only imagine Northcliffe is pro-German and expects Germany to win. I think the Coalition idiotic to let him squeal and scream. As for Geof. Robinson*, editor of *The Times*, I will never shake hands with him again....Mr Gulland and I agreed that Ll.G. was to be pitied for being such a purblind fool as to be flatterable and flattered by Northcliffe....[1]

Thursday 8 July 1915[2]

I had a dinner party, and Mr. Bonar Law dined for first time in 10 Downing Street. It was curious entertaining this 5th rate man, who had called

---

[1] For the difficult relationship between Lloyd George and Northcliffe see *Stevenson Diary*, 56.

[2] Margot's anger at Ll.G.'s appointment may have strengthened here her occasional tendency to derange the order of her diary entries.

Henry every name in Heaven, suspected <u>all</u> our men (perhaps with exception of Crewe and Grey) of every crime, and the lowest motives for all they said and did, allowed my husband (his Prime Minister now) to be howled down in the H. of Commons, etc., etc.

His is not an unknown type to me: Glasgow, slim and simple, a good speaker, a man not without courage: he keeps his point of view in an argument and is slightly contentious....

We got on to McKenna. I said to B. Law 'I always told everyone what a clever man McK was but your side never appreciated him.'

B. Law He's not very popular on yours, either.

    M. No, but he is loved by those who know him: he has an excellent heart, and the courage of the devil....

I went to bed at 12.30, and Henry arrived from Flanders at 1 [a.m.] and went to my bedroom. He had had a satisfactory journey with K., Arthur Balfour and Crewe, and an excellent conference.[1] All the French and they 4 sat round a table in Calais Hotel and talked from 10 till 1. Arthur and Crewe returned to England that day (5th July 1915). K. and he had gone on to see King Albert and Ypres, etc. Henry told me he had thought less well of Joffre this time. I must ask him why. I think it is because Joffre is a little jealous, and won't let us hold more of the line—I may be wrong....

Saturday 10 July 1915

Haldane called and told me he was sorry he had put the fat in the fire over Ll.G. in his speech, but that Ll.G. was a very treacherous little man; and he (Haldane) would defend any private friend or public servant with the last breath in his body from such a maniac.

---

[1] If Margot had known the undertaking to produce a British Army of 70 divisions, which Kitchener had given to Joffre at a private session preceding the conference (6 July, not 5 July; the British delegation had arrived at Calais 5 July), she might have been less enthusiastic. There was little sign that a force of this size could be produced by voluntary enlistment: Adams and Poirier, *Conscription*, 103.

Ld H. Ll.G. is out to smash the late Government, and to smash the Prime Minister: but Grey and I intend to stand on each side of him and protect him from such baseness....

Later. Henry told us an excellent story. When he was standing with K. and other officers looking at what is left of Ypres Cathedral, an English officer said, pointing to K.'s face and Tomcat eye glued on such of the early stone saints still left in their niches, 'Those saints are in greater danger now than they have ever been from German shells'.[1]

Wednesday 14 July 1915

I got [a letter] from Sir John French. I am glad he felt that I had given him a good 'd---ing'. Freddie Guest, looking very shame faced, gave me [the] letter.... [He] knows I think Sir John vilely surrounded.

Northcliffe got up a great Press agitation (in his own Press, and no other that I could see) in favour of the House not adjourning for 6 weeks. All the Ministers are dog-tired, and the war news far from satisfactory; every moment wasted in foolish questions in the House is an added irritation. I need hardly say Henry never wavered in his intention, and moved the adjournment till 14th Sep. (6 weeks) on Thurs. 29th July 1915, in an admirable speech....[2]

Henry, in spite of the coalition and his untiring self-effacement, has kept his own men well together this session, and I think the country know him and love him better than ever. I have never admired him more: in all these trying and terrible days he has been human and sweet and quite unrattled. He merely shook himself like a dog getting out of dirty water over the Ll.G. episode. I've never seen the latter yet: he is afraid of meeting me, I think....

---

[1] More probably the Cloth Hall, Ypres, where most of the statues represented counts and countesses of Flanders. Kitchener's appetite as an art collector was notorious: see *Crawford Journals*, 23 July 1910, 163.

[2] Cassar, *Asquith, War*, 150–1. See *Parl. Deb.*, 28 July 1915, 73.2301–12 for Asquith's speech.

Saturday 24 July 1915

24 July we had a little Wharf party which we all enjoyed. Ld Buckmaster (Haldane's successor)...Rufus (Ld Reading), a young soldier, Guy Westmacott,[1] who is fond of Elizabeth, and Sylvia Henley, a nice sister of Venetia's.[2] I liked hearing H. and his two legal friends roaring with laughter over old Bar stories....

Monday 2 August 1915

2nd August I took a group of friends to Blenheim, where we found the little Duke fussy and insignificant.[3] He showed us over the tapestry rooms, halls, etc. It is a wonderful place.

England has always been more grateful or <u>shown</u> more gratitude to her soldiers than to her Prime Ministers. It seems so ridiculous that Henry, who hasn't got a shilling, and whose 4 sons have all left professions to fight, should only get £5,000 a year, and when he goes out of office older and more tired will not get anything. The King ought to give him Walmer Castle for life [and] a pension of at least £5,000 a year. I suggested this to Archbishop of Canterbury, who thought it an excellent idea; also the Master of Elibank, whose eyes shone at the notion (he would no doubt further it if he were still our Chief Whip, but alas he is a partner of Ld Cowdray,[4] the great contractor, and is not 'in touch' with Court and Cabinet.) Henry would not like me to talk like this, I'm sure, but of course it's only fun.

[1] Guy Westmacott (b. 1891), m. 1916 Edith Winn, daughter of 2nd Baron St Oswald.
[2] And also an epistolary substitute: Sylvia became Asquith's confidante, as he struggled to come to terms with the loss of his Venetia idyll: see *Asquith–Stanley*, 595–6.
[3] i.e. Charles Richard Spencer-Churchill, 9th Duke of Marlborough (see above p. 117 n. 1): the family seat, Blenheim Palace, Woodstock, had been given to the 1st Duke by a grateful nation for his victory at the Battle of Blenheim, 1704, during the War of the Spanish Succession.
[4] Weetman Dickinson Pearson (1856–1927), cr. Baron Cowdray 1910; Viscount 1917; contractor and public benefactor.

Tuesday 3 August 1915

K., Winston, Bonar Law and others dined with us. Henry was still at Penrhos. I sat between Winston and K. K. and I had a good talk: he was in great form. I was terribly unhappy at hearing that we had another failure in battle and a lot of casualties—among the killed a dear friend of mine, Billy Grenfell.[1]

I was stunned when Ann Islington told me. In less than 6 months Etty and Willy Desborough have lost their 2 beautiful sons of 25 and 28. There is Shakespearean tragedy in such a double loss as this. They have lost the 2 beings they loved most on Earth. Billy had everything—Courage, brains, good feeling, candour, joy of life. These stupid conscriptionists say you should not take young married men, but idle unmarried ones to fight. I think for the sake of the race these splendid boys should all have children before they are killed.[2]

K. said that we were to blame. The Germans attacked, and we counter-attacked.

K. If you counter-attack, you should do it <u>at once</u>, while your enemy is exhausted. If you can't, then you should wait and reform your plan with deliberation, not wait and then do it impulsively, or you are sure to meet with disaster. A badly thought-out, hesitating counter-attack is always fatal. (I didn't dare ask who was to blame. I told K. H. had thought less well of Joffre in their last meeting.)

[1] Gerald William Grenfell (1890–1915); killed at Hooge, 30 July 1915; his body was never found, and he is memorialized on the Menin Gate. His elder brother Julian had died of his wounds weeks earlier, on 26 May, having also been wounded in the Ypres sector; he is buried in Boulogne eastern cemetery. Margot had once been critical of Billy, writing of 'a delightful and clever boy much spoilt by his worldly upbringing and terrible modern surroundings at Taplow' (diary, 2 Sept. 1912). By Aug. 1915 Kitchener feared a collapse on the Eastern Front, and a French government willing to negotiate a compromise peace: hence his agreement for British participation in operations which might well entail substantial casualties without achieving any success: see Howard, *Continental Commitment*, 56–7.

[2] There was a strong tradition in favour of enlisting unmarried, in preference to married, men. It was not confined to the British Army. It may have been derived partly from dislike of paying separation allowances to wives, and pensions to soldiers' widows. Both of the Grenfell brothers had been unmarried.

K. Did he? Oh! I've always thought him an obstinate little man—not that he is little, he's a huge great creature: not particularly clever, but sound.

M. Is he at all jealous of us?

K. No, I don't think he is: but the French are suspicious and touchy.[1]

M. Which would you rather have under your command, English? French? Or Germans?

K. Oh! English and then Germans. I don't think the French are at all in either German or English class.

Winston, I could see, didn't agree, or at least was much surprised. I can see K. is very disappointed in the French. I'm afraid they are trying allies, and that we shall have great difficulties before we are done with them, but I may be quite wrong. They've fought like tigers individually: it is their generalship that seems a little gappy....

I felt sorry for Winston. He said, with as much bitterness as a man so without bitterness can say, 'I wish I was out of England.'[2] I suggested he should go to the Russian front, but he said he didn't think they would have him. The tragic part about Winston is that I see no place for him <u>anywhere</u>!—the reason being that he draws limelight on to himself in every enterprise. Nothing he can do in silence. He is like people who like arguing, not so much to find the truth as to score....

K. complained to me of the authorities who were arranging the great service in St. Paul's Cathedral for 4th August (anniversary of the declaration of war)—he said the clergy were the most tiresome, unimaginative people in the world, that he had suggested some splendid hymns and all sorts of things, and a <u>very</u> short address etc., to make it a kind of recruiting occasion, but all his ideas had been refused....

---

[1] Joffre's failure to recover the French territory lost to the Germans in 1914 was putting him under pressure. He found the absence of conscription in Britain a handy excuse for disappointments in the field. See Cassar, *Kitchener*, 325 (Chantilly meeting, 29 Mar. 1915).

[2] J. L. Garvin visited Churchill at the offices of the Chancellor of the Duchy of Lancaster that October: 'after the mighty and majestic Admiralty...this sort of small lodging is an incredible come-down, and I realised more than before how Winston feels it. Besides, he has no real executive work to do....' J.L.G. to his son Ged, 25 Oct. 1915: Garvin, *Tomorrow*, 86. Churchill resigned in November and sought active service.

I saw Ll.G. for the first time. Runciman (who settled with help of Ll.G. the painful Welsh colliery strike)[1] and Rufus both told me they thought I should see Ll.G., as he felt deeply aggrieved that I should have thought him capable of intriguing against his Prime Minister. I said it didn't matter a curse what I thought: it was what he had done, and done with singularly little success; so I wrote to him, and asked him to lunch. As I had written before and he had taken no notice, I added to my invitation that I should not discuss the past with him. He arrived and hung on to Puffin's shoulders. He seemed hearty and in good form, but never really looked at me or spoke, except to the company at lunch. I was much amused....

[1] The strike and the efforts of Runciman and Lloyd George to settle it were reported in *The Times* from 16 to 21 July. The settlement was described as 'a personal triumph for the Minister of Munitions' (*Times*, 21 Jul. 1915, 7e).

PART VI

4 AUGUST–
15 NOVEMBER 1915

The anti-conscription activities into which Margot flung herself from mid-August to the end of October 1915 did her husband great harm. As Prime Minister of a Coalition containing all shades of opinion, Asquith's position was a difficult one, and in an important speech in the Commons on 2 November 1915 he attempted to clarify it:

> I have no abstract or a priori objection of any sort or kind to compulsion—in time of war. (Hear, hear.) I have nothing at the back of my mind which would make me go to the stake...in defence of what is called the voluntary principle. I think that in time of war we must get rid of all these predilections, both on the one side and on the other. (Cheers.) It is a pure question of practical expediency—how are we going to bring the war to a successful conclusion?[1]

Conscription would be unworkable, he believed, unless it met with 'with something in the nature of general assent': its introduction 'under existing conditions would forfeit what I regard to be of supreme and capital importance, namely the maintenance of the national unity'. The speech illustrated at once his dexterity and his difficulty: he managed to commit himself to compulsion, as military and political necessity dictated that he must, while upholding the principle of freedom of choice, in deference to the attachment of the majority of Liberals—himself included—to civil liberty. Radicals in the House had cheered at his mention of 'general assent', but The Times was unimpressed by his legerdemain: 'Our own belief is that if Mr Asquith and his colleagues were at any time to tell the country that compulsion was necessary they would find national unity unimpaired.' Nor was that journal approving of his reassurance that he would back conscription 'sooner than not win the war': 'The only comment we have to make is that it is amazing that any British Prime Minister should think it necessary to weigh such alternatives and dissipate any doubts.' Those who bought the Morning Post and the Daily Mail were likely to be less charitable, preferring to believe, not that the anti-conscriptionists deployed some respectable arguments, but that the government was controlled by people who in fact did not want the Allies to win the war. Conscription continued to generate fierce controversy, but in the short term at least Asquith could delay the fateful decision. The introduction of the Derby Scheme in October, which enabled eligible men to 'attest' their willingness to serve, significantly augmented the ranks of the army. Anyone with perception, though, would surely see that losses on the scale of those at Loos, beginning 25 September, would soon negate the Scheme's gains; and, moreover, that if the war were likely to last beyond 1916, as prudence now suggested that it might, the early adoption of a compulsion plan was essential. And towering over any question of

---

[1] For this and other quotations in this paragraph see The Times, 3 Nov. 1915, 12, 14.

political principle was the one that Asquith himself had raised in his speech: 'how are we going to bring the war to a successful conclusion?' To many observers he could no longer provide an adequate answer. The conscription controversy in particular had called for decisive leadership and an open mind. Haldane demonstrated both qualities in the Lords on 8 January 1915.[1] Asquith, though, waited until November to follow his example. By that date Margot had contrived, by her opposition, to make his belated pragmatism sound notably insincere, and his closest advisers were right to think that in 'lobbying people' on this issue she was 'doing no one any good'.

Wednesday 4 August 1915

I Margot Asquith do pledge myself this day not to <u>buy</u> for my own body one single garment till Aug. 4th next year (1916). No clothes: coats, skirts, shirts, underclothes, hats, golfing clothes, shoes, boots, stockings, ribbons, veils or flowers. (I may have to buy 6 pairs of golfing washing gloves, but I will see if I have got any.) <u>Nothing of any kind of fur flowers or clothes</u> will I buy.

Margot Asquith August 4th 1915.[2]

I wrote this in bed at 6 a.m.

It is a year today since Germany forced all of us—Russia, France, Austria[3] and ourselves to draw the sword.... This has been the saddest year in many a man's recollection. Personally my own saddest year was 1913, the year Elizabeth was in Munich and Puffin went to school; the year I was so fearfully ill and weak, and <u>everything</u> seemed to have left me: but outside myself, this has been a Terrible Awefull Year, and

---

[1] See *Parl. Deb.*, Lords, 18.378: 'Therefore compulsory service is not foreign to the Constitution of this country. Given a great national emergency I think it is your duty to resort to it. I can conceive a state of things in which we might resort to it.'

[2] Margot seems not to have recorded whether this pledge was kept; Cynthia Asquith noted in Sept. 1916 that Margot had written to a mutual friend asking her to visit the dressmakers Handley and Jay to adviser her on 'the best crepe-de-chine dress—cut and style': Cynthia thought this 'the most awful letter', not because of the dress, but because it was written on the morning after Margot had news of her stepson Raymond's death: Asquith, C., *Diaries*, 221.

[3] Like many others, Margot could not believe that the politicians in Vienna had been active in pushing those in Berlin into starting the war.

I daresay the next will be as bad in a different way. There will be an awful mess to sweep up in this country after the war (should it end, please God, next year.) Labour difficulties will be the chief ones. People say I'm a radical, but I confess I don't think workmen dislike their employers <u>half</u> as much as employers <u>hate</u> their workmen. I wonder if I'm wrong about this. Strikes in time of War are humiliating, and make me cry.

I have made a few new friends, and lost no old ones.... Etty is...a woman of the world to her finger tips—almost a Court lady—she doesn't know what vagabondage means. She is a very remarkable woman, fundamentally sound and full of the widest sympathies. She has steadied herself for this world—studies and keeps her youth, and covers a great deal of ground. She is modern and full of the Present. She has great and vital effrontery, ambition and method.

She loves books, and has a fine memory and a light humour. Her temperament has no taciturnity or irony: satire is unknown to her. She is fresh as a lark, and almost too agreeable; but with all this accomplishment, she has great powers of loyalty and devotion, and an uncontentious belief in God and Life. She is not puzzled or awe-stricken by the unknown. There are no mists between her and her inner self. Though a trifle vain in a competitive sense, she is not egotistical, and whatever her mood may be, she will make it yours.

I love her dearly: she has been a wonderful friend, even when at times a rival. She is not a country person, and though she can walk for miles with golfers or shooters, she never dreams about in hay or heather without a hat or heels to her shoes. She is a great lady, unshockable except by what is mean or vulgar. She is the best boon companion in the world, as she has no moods....

Till this year, the whole world would have pointed to Etty and Willy Desborough[1] as the most triumphantly happy people. Rich, <u>very strong</u>,

---

[1] William Henry Grenfell (1855–1945), KCVO 1908, cr. 1st Baron Desborough of Taplow 1905; Unionist politician, advocate of bimetallism, and sportsman of great renown; married, 1887, Ethel ('Etty') née Fane (see Biographical Notes).

with 5 splendid children, they never had a shadow of sorrow within the recollection of their friends: now this calamity has fallen like fire from Heaven on them—Julian and Billy <u>both dead</u>—shot—all their glorious possibilities strangled in Death....

Henry, Lucy, Puffin and [I] drove to St. Paul's Cathedral....[1] It was a badly managed service, and a great occasion missed. Our clergy are wonderfully lacking in drama and effectiveness. I wish they would all recruit, and just leave the old ones to train a new lot to read the lessons in proper, manly English voices instead of that 3rd. sex, horrible, indistinct, blurred way of reading which puts people either to sleep, or completely 'away' from what is going on. 'Rock of Ages' is a grand hymn, but it was sung slowly, so that the singers in the Dome were not in time with the choir. It should have been sung loud and straight and not too slow, with a great rush of organ sound to bring all of us in to line. There were long prayers, poor music and a moderate sermon from the Archbishop. I did so long and crave for a short sermon telling us to look up, and not to feel hard and puzzled, or to say things would be the just same in a few years after the war. If it is rather difficult to believe in God, it is <u>more</u> just now to believe in Man....

Friday 6 August 1915—Scotland

10.15 I found Henry and Baker at the Edinburgh Waverley station Hotel. After a night journey from London, and a very fatiguing time, and a bad wasp's sting in his ear, Henry looked wretched—a swollen eye and cheek, and very, very tired, swollen sort of look. His head had been tied up, and he had seen an Edinburgh Dr. on his arrival. I could see his swollen ear and the hot pad made him uncomfortable, but he is a perfect angel and never

---

[1] At noon on 4 Aug. a special commemorative service was held at St Paul's Cathedral to mark the beginning of the second year of war; the King and Queen, and Queen Alexandra, were in attendance, alongside leading public figures: the dominant colour of the assembly was black, interspersed with khaki and the bright blue uniforms worn by the war wounded.

complains or thinks of himself. I wasn't alone with him, so could not ask him if there was any news about Bulgaria, etc:[1] also, it's a bore, a wife who talks of the Balkans before breakfast.

We tucked up all 3 in the open Napier, and motored to Stirling....At 12 the McK[enna] car swung alongside of ours in Stirling. We greeted each other side by side....The Dornie Ferry, and later on Strome Ferry, with neither lunch or tea, proved very exhausting transits. If it had not been for the great up and down stretches of heather and uninhabited scenery through which we motored, I should have felt ill: but if I were dying, this sort of country, in which I was born and bred and lived for 30 years, would put Life into me. I revelled in it. People, politics, platforms, domestic troubles, longings for a home of our own (with Henry, Eliz. and Puffin), impatience at being so easily tired, the sorrow of getting away from youth—all faded; even the war receded from me. I lifted my eyes to the hills and breathed the glory of God. The overmastering horror that the war often inspires me with seemed to go—to evaporate in the mists of the moors, fading between loch and sky....

Sunday 15 August 1915

Henry told me that Bonar Law had talked about himself with the utmost frankness: had told H. how little he enjoyed leading his party, how unambitious he was, and really out of spirits politically, and how he would like much to retire altogether. H. bucked him up and said this was of course unthinkable. He added 'I can't help rather liking B.L., he is _so_ deprecating and diffident, so without temperament. He is rather pathetic.'

I agree. I like B.L., though I really don't quite grasp him, and am never quite sure how straight he is: but I may be wrong—he may be _quite_ straight....

Montagu and Venetia dined with Neil [Primrose]. It was the first time H. and I had seen them since their marriage. This marriage had caused any

---

[1] Bulgaria joined the Central Powers on 6 Sept. 1915; Terraine, _First World War_, 86, 181.

amount of talk, as I think I've said before.[1] The purists would not have minded her being married in a Christian Church: to declare falsely that she was a Christian didn't strike them as being out of the way, but to declare falsely that you are a Jewess shocked Violet, Henry and all her friends profoundly. I think they are made for each other.[2] She is as insensitive as he is sensitive. She has capital health if she doesn't starve herself. They have both great affection and power of devotion, and great intelligence. He has moral courage, she has none. She has physical endurance, he has none.

Montagu told me after dinner he rather hoped H. would come down on the side of Conscription, which need never come into force, as we were recruiting very well: it would be a sop to the agitators, and if the war went on another year we might need it; that Curzon was out for mischief, and the whole gang intended forcing a Gen. Election, and smirching the late Gov, and Henry. I told him I had never discussed Conscription in my life with Henry, but that I was <u>passionately</u> against it, and <u>knew he was</u>.

When we got home, H. showed me an excellent letter from Montagu, putting all the points of the present situation and his (H.'s) personal position (to which H. shows the same inflexible indifference as he did after the coalition was formed) quite admirably. I went to bed unhappy, and I foresee there will be an awful row, and Curzon and Northcliffe will play their tune to very receptive ears. The country is thoroughly unhappy, and we are having a bad time both in the east and west, and the Russian news is alarming.[3] When a nation gets strained, it gets very panicky and

[1] Margot wrote to Violet, 7 June 1915: 'Father is happier over V's marriage tho' not converted—he thinks he w^d mind less were it any-one else but I tell him whoever she married he w^d mind deeply as he has been very much in love—he says if she had only told him he w^d have felt it less.... [Montagu] is <u>wonderful</u> over it all—courageous convinced & <u>very</u> humble. They were both old enough to know their own minds & no one must tease them now. There's a good deal of bosh in the religion campaign au fond, tho' superficially it takes one in....It is Montagu's physique that I c^d <u>never</u> get over not his religion': see Bonham Carter, *Diaries, 1914–45*, 63.

[2] Margot seems not to have realized that any change of religion, when devoid of the slightest sign of conviction, and plainly made for a financial reason, was bound to arouse some disapproval. For her earlier, and far less complimentary, view of Venetia, given in a letter to Edwin, see *Asquith–Stanley*, 13.

[3] Warsaw had fallen, 4 Aug.: Cruttwell, *Great War*, 178–81; see Terraine, *First World War*, 89–90.

deserves a little 'ménagéing'.[1] (H. despises people who get excited: they move me to sympathy, they move him to scorn.) I don't think he would be unsympathetic if it were not that the personal political intrigue against himself and K. makes him rather nuggety and tight-minded.

Tuesday 17 August 1915

I wrote 8 pages to K. and sent my letter very early, before 7 am, to France. I got a wire from Cowans, who is also at the front, to say K. had got my letter that night, which was nice of Cowans. I wish I had kept a copy of my letter, as I never remember what I write clearly. I wrote a very precise letter, explaining the exact situation and what he would find when he came back on 19th Aug. (midnight he arrived).

I said it was purely political: the old gang against the Gov., led by Northcliffe and Curzon. I did not forget K.'s loathing and distrust of Curzon! I told him that he (K.) and H. must work absolutely together. (I think K., H., Crewe, Arthur Balfour, Grey, Runciman, Loulou, McKenna, H. Samuel ought to be able to smash Curzon, FE, Ll.G. and Winston and their small flotilla. I wouldn't mind putting it to the test: if the war wasn't so terrible, I would like a fight, and know who would win.)[2]

K. is so ignorant, he has lived so much abroad, that I had to explain as well as I could what I thought the effect of Conscription would be in this country. I wished I had had one proper talk to H. on the chief arguments before writing; but I put it quite well, and rubbed it well in that only K. and H. can get Conscription in this country, which is true: if it is ever needed, they and they only can get it (I am passionately agin it); that K. must show courage, or there would be an awful split in the cabinet, which some would like, etc. etc.

After sending my letter to K., I wrote to Crewe and McKenna, and sent for Peggy Crewe to see me, and beg her to keep Crewe up to seeing Henry

---

[1] Fr. 'managing'.

[2] Margot could not see that the conscriptionists' strength would grow, not because of their leaders' reputation, but because under war setbacks, a volunteer army was ceasing to look like a war-winning instrument.

about this. Peggy was delightful, and had no idea of what was going on in the inner circle, but was very soon *au fait*. She is an angel. I love her—clever in spite of a certain crudeness, can see very fine shades. She loves Crewe and knows him well. She quite agreed when I said my husband cared more for Crewe's judgement than any one's, but that action was not her man's strong point. He is to my mind strangely devoid of that touch of drama and quickness which in times of great stress are essential in men at the head of things. He is not very strong either vitally, which accounts for this probably.

She promised to back me thoroughly, and see that Crewe saw Grey. I didn't write to the latter: he is so over-laden with responsibility, and so fussy and self-centred since the war. (I don't feel the same necessity to see him, and Pamela[1] is so ridiculously jealous, and minds so passionately him seeing anything of anyone, that all his old women friends have dropt him a little, I think.) I find him useless compared with what he was, though he is, of course, invaluable. I had no idea that in a time of War any beautiful character like Grey's could get so self-enfolded and fidgety!...

Wednesday 18 August 1915

Bonar Law came to see H. this morning. They talked in H.'s room next to the dining-room. I caught a glimpse of his little, insignificant, diffident face and deprecating eyebrows (as he went into the room) from my writing-table. Henry came in and told me what they had been talking about.

H. He began by wanting a Knighthood for Sam Hughes, Canadian Minister of War—a ridiculous man![2]—but at the end of his visit, he lowered his voice and said he didn't suppose that I was in ignorance of what was going on about Conscription, not only among his colleagues but

---

[1] Pamela Tennant (see Biographical Notes), Margot's sister-in-law. Grey's first wife had died in 1906, and in 1922 he married the widowed Pamela, with whom he had long been friendly; her husband, Lord Glenconner, had died in 1920. For Pamela's concern about Grey's well-being see *Asquith–Stanley*, 249, 269, 324.

[2] Sam Hughes (1853–1921), Canadian Minister of Militia and Defence, 1911–16; he was knighted in 1915 despite being thought 'ridiculous' by Asquith.

among mine.[1] He said he wasn't telling any secrets. He himself had never attended any of the deliberations next door (11 Downing St.), but felt it was his duty to tell me he had accepted an invitation to meet the whole lot at dinner on this Friday (20th); that he thought the Conscription agitation was going ahead and must be considered. I smiled and thanked him, and said I had heard about it all, and said goodbye.

Arthur Balfour, Edgar and Crewe lunched.... Arthur was in great form. I can see he really loves the Admiralty. If for this reason only, I should say he will stick to his convictions about Conscription: he can't want to upset the Coalition.

H. told us how wonderfully superior the *Queen Elizabeth* and all oil ships are to the coal lot—50 per cent less labour, and no dirt or smoke.[2] H. 'Jellicoe took me all over the *Queen Elizabeth*, and showed me rather an amusing thing. Just outside the place where coal is generally kept on a battle-ship, I saw a beautiful steel shovel brightly cleaned and shiny nailed up, and written above it by some wag was "Lest we forget"'. A.J.B. said we owed oil and turbines, Fleet concentration, submarines, Dreadnoughts— in fact, all our superiority at sea, to <u>Fisher</u>.

We dined with Cassel that night.[3] Alice Keppel and I played bridge against Winston and McKenna (a funny combination of 2 First Lords who had both been superseded at the Admiralty, and don't like each other <u>at all</u>.) I won £10 from Winston, which I didn't want to do. He is a hopeless player and a gambler, but we only played 1d points....

Edgar, Montagu, Massingham and I at tea on 18th had good talk on Conscription: Massingham said we only saw the forces in its favour, as

---

[1] Margot's phrasing reveals what a disunited body the Coalition was.

[2] See Hough, *War at Sea*, 28: 'There thus came into being the magnificent class of five 15" gunned *Queen Elizabeth* battleships whose service in two wars was pricelessly valuable. And from this time [1912] virtually all new British men-o'-war were fuelled by oil.'

[3] Cassel, Sir Ernest J. (1852–1921), KCMG, 1899, GCB 1909; born in Cologne, moved to Britain, 1869, m. Annette née Maxwell (d. 1881), and became a British subject, 1878; a notable financier and philanthropist, and long-time friend of Edward VII; helped British government during First World War (during which an attempt to cancel his Privy Councillorship, conferred in 1902, was frustrated); of Jewish origin, he became Roman Catholic soon after his wife's death.

they advertised themselves thoroughly. We had no idea what tremendous forces there were in the country against it—that no thinking politician would ever take it up....

Thursday 19 August 1915

Bongie, on announcing Rufus in evening, said to me before Rufus came in 'I'm afraid the Prime Minister is going to be obstinate about Conscription. I'm inclined to think we shall have to come to this.' M. 'Good Heavens, Bongie, are you also wobbly!? Well, I don't know exactly what line H. will take, but I would rather be out of public life altogether if he goes in for Conscription: it would be Insanity.'[1] (The Northcliffe agitation goes on daily in *Times* and *Mail*.)

Friday 20 August 1915

....I went to N. Berwick [by] train from King's Cross. Cowans had just come back from Sir J. French. His first visit to our trenches. He was very interesting over it: told me all our soldiers were Conscriptionists (they would be! I've never known a soldier whose opinion was worth having except Wolseley's).[2]

Mr Runciman got into the train with me, and we talked from 2.30 till 6 without ceasing. I had no idea he was so delightful and so amusing. I've always known he was able, and had a lot of character, but I had an idea he was a trifle touchy and vain. The stupid description of him as 'the alabaster statesman' perhaps put me off, or the height and convictions of his wife, but I found him charming.[3]

[1] There is a marginal note in the diary of July–Nov. 1915 (D. 3213 fo. 157ʳ), at the end of the entry for 19 Aug. 'I was wrong—it had to come.' Margot had come to accept, with time, that her *peacetime* objection to conscription—one widely held among Liberals—was not completely applicable in a long and hard-fought war.

[2] For Field Marshal Sir Garnet Wolseley see above, p. 52 n. 2. Margot's presumption that she could judge better on the conscription issue than the officers and men in the trenches was, and still is, remarkable.

[3] 'The virtuous Runcie ("the alabaster statesman" as someone once called him)'; *Asquith–Stanley*, 409. That 'someone', Margot revealed in her Sept. 1913 diary, was Illingworth, the Chief Whip: 'Like so many little men, [Runciman] is vain and touchy. He is also keener to

He is madly opposed to Conscription, and pointed out all the follies with great clearness and precision. He said we could not afford to take more than 8 hundred thousand men away from imperative war work, even if we could equip them, and we should get them as soon as we could equip them; that there would be a fiendish outcry; that none of the exempt industries—miners, engineers, or railwaymen—would be bought off; that they would stand by their forced fellows and cry out as loud as the rest; that <u>no</u> compulsion for foreign service was feasible; that voluntary heroes and conscript laggers could not [and] would not fight side by side (the latter would have brickbats thrown at them);[1] that the whole problem was far too complicated to be workable, and, most important of all, there would be strikes all over the country. He was pushing on an open door. <u>I agree with every word he said</u>, and am sure Henry does also....

Runciman told me in the cabinet of 17th or 18th George Curzon had perorated a little on Conscription, and some talk had ensued. Some one or other began combating the arguments in favour of Conscription. Ll.G. was restless and not particularly happy. (K. away in France.) Henry spoke very little, but wound up the proceedings by saying 'I have listened to a lot of very unsound talk. I shall have a good deal to say on this subject when we next discuss it.' At this period Ll.G. seems to have said with a shrug 'Oh! then I suppose there is nothing for us to do but to apologize.'—but in the break-up of the cabinet which immediately followed Henry's remark, Runciman said he was not sure how many of them heard Ll.G.

---

keep what he has to say in reserve than to know what you think, so I've really never had any kind of intercourse with him.' Margot may have believed that Mrs Runciman influenced her husband to be a suffragist.

[1] The number of men who could be made available to the army through conscription was hotly disputed, if only because the demands of the new munitions factories were rising all the time. The number of fit young men needed for 'imperative war work' depended on such 'imponderables' as the success of dilution schemes, whereby operations hitherto performed by skilled men could be 'broken down' and performed by half-trained women. In Aug. 1915 the premier told Sylvia Henley that once the needs of war industries, shipping, shipbuilding, and agriculture had been met, 'you may have left for compulsion only a small residuum of the dregs of the nation'. But Runciman should surely have realized that a 'voluntary hero', waiting for relief at the end of a dangerous spell in the trenches, would have been entirely willing to hand over to a 'conscript lagger'.

Runciman said Henry's 2 strong backers outside himself, Grey, Crewe, McKenna and Loulou were of course Arthur Balfour and K: <u>but would they play up</u>?[1] Had Arthur ever played up in a tight place for his friends? He told me he had gone to K. and ragged him about seeing F. E. Smith. He had also dined alone with K., and told him all he could on the subject of Labour and credit, and the English position, etc. etc; and he had ended his talk by pointing out <u>how much</u> K. owed Henry over the Shell Scandal Crusade, and how this intrigue of Curzon's, Ll.G.'s and Winston's was backed by Northcliffe, and his money aimed entirely at getting rid of Henry and K.[2] In fact, Runciman <u>said</u> to K. all that I had written, so I was too glad I had written on my own....

Saturday 21 August 1915   Glenconner, North Berwick

Henry and Baker arrived from London with the Master. The latter and I had a good talk: he is <u>very</u> anxious H. should not allow the Conscription agitation to get out of hand—<u>so am I</u>, of course, but I can see H. is setting himself against doing anything in public. Here he is wrong. Crewe is right: we should not keep an anxious, overstrained country in the dark any longer.

The Master is always amusing, and above all he is in politics what an *homme du monde* would be in a social dilemma. He has a nose like a pointer for spotting where danger lies. We are unluckily without Eric or Hankey, who is in the Dardanelles, and have <u>no</u> one (Montagu also in north of Scotland with Venetia)[3] to tell us the sort of things which I think matter more than Henry thinks. He sees no danger in a Press campaign in which

[1] Runciman's doubts on this were justified. Balfour's argument against conscription concerned the way in which it bore hardest on the working class: Adams and Poirier, *Conscription*, 95–6, 118. For the change in working-class attitudes shown in the Merthyr Tydfil by-election in Nov. 1915 result see *The Times*, 27 Nov. 1915; *Stevenson Diary*, 81–2. Kitchener had undertaken to Joffre, 6 July 1915, without prior consultation, to produce 70 British divisions—a number beyond the capacity of a volunteer army. For the background to Kitchener's statement to the Crewe Committee, 24 Aug. 1915, that a Conscription Act might be needed 'before the end of the year', see Gooch, J., *Plans of War*, ch. 10.

[2] Margot refers to Northcliffe's calls in May 1915 for an acceleration of ammunition making, and presumably also to Kitchener's responsibility in supplying Asquith with misleading information before his disastrous 20 Apr. speech on Tyneside (see above, pp. civ–cv).

[3] The Montagus were on honeymoon at Corrievorrie, near Tomatin, Highland.

up to now rather the <u>rubbish</u> of the Tory party have shone…(Albert Grey, St. John, Esher* [have] all written foolishly to my mind)…, or in letters signed 'Mother of 5 sons' or 'son of a soldier' or 'Lady Huntingdon'.

If Henry thought there was Real political danger to England, like there was when these very same shriekers (except Ll.G. and Winston) tried to sow dissension in the army over the Curragh, he would act with the same Force and Drama that he did then, when he became Minister of War; but he doesn't think there is danger here. I don't agree with him: I think this panic-stricken agitation for Conscription <u>is</u> dangerous. I wonder which of us will be right. The poor Master was rather damped by getting nothing much out of Henry when here.…

Col. Hankey has written letters from the Dardanelles which would be the making of any Historian: he is a remarkable little man of great and perfect character.[1] I love him, and wish he had more to do with the field operations. He would be an ideal staff officer. We thought our generalship bad on our West line—it is worse on our East. Thanks to Stopford, Mahon and another, Hammersley, our Gallipoli surprise landing has been a failure with all its heroism;[2] and following this, de Lisle (of whom I never heard) has had another set-back.[3] When Henry told me that our

[1] Hankey, *Supreme Command*, 378–402.
[2] In an effort to break the deadlock at Gallipoli, after the heroic but costly landings of 25 Apr. 1915, an offensive was mounted in Aug. designed to capture the Sari Bair range, as a preliminary to an advance across the peninsula aimed at the Dardanelles Straits. The main assault of ANZAC forces on the night of 6–7 Aug. stalled in the face of formidable Turkish resistance. The British landings at Suvla Bay, to the north, involved commanders who proved inadequate to the task, and who failed to exploit a clear opportunity to consolidate their position, and advance from it, by securing initially undefended high ground overlooking the bay. Lieutenant-General Sir Frederick William Stopford (1854–1929), KCMG 1900; commander IX Corps at Suvla Bay; the 'most suitable and senior' commander available, he was aged 61, often in ill health, had been living in retirement since 1909. Lieutenant-General Bryan Thomas Mahon (1862–1930), KCVO 1913, commander 10th (Irish) division of new armies, 1914; took a division to Gallipoli, 1915; was relieved of his post at Suvla, but was Commander-in-Chief of the Salonika army, 1915–16, and was Commander-in-Chief in Ireland, 1916–18. Major-General Frederick Hammersley (1858–1924), joined army 1876 and was a veteran of 19th-century campaigns; commanded 11th Division at Suvla Bay; he had suffered a breakdown 'a year or two before' and was removed on 23 Aug. in a state of collapse; see the description of Hankey's visit in Moorehead, *Gallipoli*, 272.
[3] Major-General Sir Beauvoir de Lisle (1864–1955), KCB 1917; served in France and Gallipoli, 1914–19; in June 1915 took command of 29th Division at Gallipoli, which he directed during the failed attempt on Scimitar Hill, 21–3 Aug. 1915, a bitter postscript to the Suvla Bay landings.

great offensive in the Dardanelles had failed (which, <u>had</u> it succeeded, would have seen us in Constantinople in 10 days) tears were in his eyes— he could hardly speak. I myself wish Cavan[1] and Haig could be taken away from the West line and sent to Gallipoli. Hamilton has too many fool generals out there....[2]

The Blazing folly of Northcliffe and Co. are fast killing Conscription: perhaps it is right that H. should have said nothing. It is his way of doing things: he believes in common sense conquering, and fools being given all the rope possible to air their opinions, and knaves left severely alone; but I never feel so sure of this (Of course Ll.G. was a case to leave alone. I dread what his munition outcome will be, and <u>Long</u> for some one to interfere here in case our poor soldiers get murdered for want of artillery.) But I think just now England is going through <u>terrible</u> sorrows and anxieties. Nothing but failures in East and paralysis on West; lines of battle and casualty Lists of a kind that stop my heart beating. I think perhaps Henry might tell the willing public how and where they are best wanted to help.

Saturday 28 August 1915

Charles Lister died of wounds in his pelvis.[3] Charles Lister had genius and a courtesy, sweetness and sense of humour we shall rarely see again. With his death the title of Ribblesdale disappears.

---

[1] Major-General Lord Cavan (1865–1946), s. 1900 as 10th Earl of Cavan, commander, 14th Corps of the BEF, and the Brigade of Guards, subsequently the Guards Division; fought in the battles of Ypres, Loos, and the Somme; CIGS 1922–6.

[2] Margot's view has been generally accepted; but that was not the only cause of the failure: the Dardanelles Commissioners, in Conclusion 5 of their Final Report, 1919, criticized the 'undue delay' which deprived the Suvla landings of the best chance of success. Hamilton's 'appreciation' (asking for 'two fresh divisions'), though forwarded on 17 May 1915, was not considered by the new Coalition cabinet until 7 June. Early in July an attack would have been faced by a numerically inferior enemy: in Aug. 1915 the attackers faced equal numbers: Churchill, *World Crisis*, ii. 452–3; Moorehead, *Gallipoli*, 165.

[3] Charles Alfred Lister (1887–1915), Margot's nephew, the son of Thomas Lister, 4th Baron Ribblesdale, and her sister Charty; since his elder brother's death on active service in the Sudan, in 1904, heir to the Ribblesdale title; a childhood friend of Violet and her brothers, and a Balliol contemporary of Cys Asquith; with the Hood Battalion of the RND, Sept. 1914; severely wounded at Gallipoli, 25 Aug. 1915; died of wounds on a hospital ship off the peninsula, 28 Aug.; Cynthia Asquith was told of the news when she called at Glenconner on 4 Sept. She reported that Margot was looking 'ghastly ill': Asquith, C., *Diaries*, 75.

Sunday 12 September 1915

Henry's birthday....The King sent him a nice telegram, also Queen Alexandra, but the nicest present he got was a wire from his servant George Wicks, who got a commission in the early days of the war and is an officer in [the Middlesex Regiment].[1] I cried when I shook hands with George, and so did Henry. (He had maided me on the *Enchantress* when Violet's maid was ill, and I could hardly move, and was absolutely helpless and more or less alone. George Wicks undid my evening dress at the top, and took care of me, and showed me much quiet sympathy.)...

Beautiful, beloved Alexandra—her telegram brought tears to my eyes and to Henry's: he could hardly read it to me, his voice shook so much. He came in and kissed me in bed, and thanked me for my letter and books. He was sunny and happy, and made everyone feel happy....

At lunch Henry told Frances [Balfour] about the last Zeppelin raid....[2] 'I went with McKenna and Ly Eileen Wellesley,[3] and we went down to Wood St. and saw huge dry goods stores a sheet of flame—quite beautiful; the crowd carefully kept back by City police, and the Fire engines doing wonders. I made the police let us through, and we watched the firemen on terrifically high ladders seemingly run up into the flames. No one luckily in the warehouses. This raid is supposed by gossip to have [destroyed] insured property [by] as much as £3 millions, but I expect this is nonsense. The police took us away from Wood St. and Moorgate St. to St. Bartholomew's' Hospital, where 3 corpses were stretched out, poor innocent old fellows! A huge bomb had fallen 50 yards from the Hospital.' (I could not help wondering what the wobbly world of neutrals would have thought if it had killed all the dying and diseased in the huge Hospital)....

---

[1] George Wicks (1885–1977) had left Asquith's service on 16 Apr. 1915 to join his regiment: *Asquith–Stanley*, 545.

[2] According to a marginal note, this is likely to have been the attack of 8 Sept., during which incendiary and explosive devices were dropped on London and the eastern counties; later reports indicated that 20 were killed, and 86 injured, all but four of them civilians; the dead were 12 men, 2 women, and 6 children.

[3] Lady Eileen Wellesley (1887–1952), daughter of 4th Duke of Wellington; m. 1916 Captain Cuthbert Julian Orde, RFC.

Tuesday 14 September 1915

We went up by night train to London.... I found things here developing rapidly—the Conscription gang making everything very difficult, and most of them behaving abominably. Lloyd George, G. Curzon, F. Guest, Winston, Northcliffe, etc. all doing their d—dest, and making every kind of mischief. George Curzon's part I know little of, except that Bonar Law and K. are down on him.

The Trades Union Congress met at Bristol and passed most moderate but quite unmistakable resolutions against <u>any form of compulsion</u> (I will get the speeches cut out of the Bristol papers, which I took in to get <u>proper</u> reports.)[1] Ll.G. addressed the Congress, and made a very good speech,[2] but alas! as he has allowed Northcliffe and his friends to abuse his Prime Minister every day and night without making any kind of protest, he has made himself loathed by thousands to whom he was a hero before. No man has ever played his cards so badly. 'I know a sweep when I see him!!' John Burns said to me, and all my friends, even dear Bongie who cannot be said to be easily roused to indignation or passion, feel a horror of what Ll.G. has done. The poor Master of Elibank, Ld Murray, still hopes to make things right, but I fear it will be difficult.

The forces are: H., Grey, K., Crewe, Loulou, McKenna, Runciman and Arthur Balfour <u>against</u>, and the rest of the Tory party, plus Winston and

---

[1] *The Times* observed that the Trade Union Congress's resolution on 'National Service ... will be hailed, of course, as an "anti-conscription" vote', adding: 'If the government think compulsion is required, they are ready to listen, but they demand that the need should be fully and openly proved. We do not quarrel with this view. We only point out that the time available grows short': 8 Sept. 1915, 7a.

[2] Lloyd George addressed the Trade Union Congress at Bristol, 9 Sept. 1915, and reminded those gathered of their obligation to the government, and to the nation, to increase the production: 'This is a war of material', he pointed out. His speech, which was fulsomely praised by *The Times*, was 'compounded of stern rebuke, solemn warning, and earnest pleading': 'It put the delegates to shame, for they knew they could not refute the charges it brought. But it also called upon them to repent, and the tumultuous cheers with which they greeted the closing appeal of the speaker was an answer to that call': *The Times*, 10 Sept. 1915, 9f. Four days later Ll.G. released to the press the preface to a collection of his war speeches, *Through Terror to Triumph*, in which he openly identified himself with the conscriptionists: Grigg, *Lloyd George, 1912–1916*, 328–9; for his 9 Sept. speech see 287–93.

Ll.G., <u>for</u> Conscription. (Henry wants to avoid a Gen. Election at all costs.) An abominable debate started Tuesday 14th, ragged and angry.

Wednesday 15 September 1915

Henry, Katharine, Bongie and I motored in Henry's new War Office motor (lent to him, as one of ours is with Violet and the other not quite sound) to the House. A beautiful afternoon. I found Venetia and Pam McKenna in the gallery. H. asked for another vote of credit, and ended up by a magnificent appeal for unity: simple, pathetic and restrained.[1] It made a profound impression on the House. (Northcliffe and Co have started a campaign to stop recruiting in their zeal for compulsion.) Henry spoke with great emotion. I ran across to H. of Lords and heard K. for the first time in the Lords. He is a bad speaker and writer, and can't read his speeches at all well.

I ran in to H.'s room after his speech with Katharine and Pam McK., found him in great form. We told him we were going to the Lords to hear K. H. 'I've heard his speech several times: I may say have cut it down a good deal. It was rather pathetic: when he told me what he was going to say, he said "I thought of rather a good thing in the night. I thought of— <u>what</u> <u>did</u> I think of? I can't remember now what it was." And poor old boy, he never found his good thing. Perhaps you'll notice it. Won't you have tea?'

We got the tea and gulped it down, and flew over to the House of Lords, where we were told we could have places. I sat in Black Rod's pew, and K[atharine] and Venetia below. Ld K., after Henry, was like standing on a stone instead of sitting on a sofa: dry, dull, with no beginning and no end, and not even deploring the abominable agitation. I wonder if K. is afraid of quarrelling with *The Times*....

[1] Asquith spoke in the 'Vote of Credit' debate, 15 Sept. 1915: 'Do not let it be said by our children and our children's children that in the gravest moment in our history our arm was shorn of its strength by any failure on the part either of rulers or ruled to concentrate upon an unexampled task consentient counsels, undivided energy, [and the] unbroken and indomitable will of the British people. (Loud cheers.)' (*The Times*, 16 Sept. 1915, 11a).

Thursday 16 September 1915

Henry came into my room while I was dressing.... Knowing that his great talk to Ll.G., arranged by Eric and the Master, was imminent, I asked him if it had come off.

H. No, only the small one about Munitions (Wed.) before my speech yesterday. I must say he's an unlucky man! always in some little pie. B. Law told me the other day he was a little hurt at not being on some of the Committees (Crewe's, on Munitions).[1] He said he thought as leader of the opposition he ought to be given more to do, etc., and thought he might be deputy leader, perhaps.

M. Who is deputy leader now?

H. Ll.G. was always deputy leader: it was the Chan. of the Exchequer, usually. Ll.G. has kept it. I said I would ask Ll.G., and felt sure he would not object. I got a letter from Walter Long urging me to make Bonar Law deputy leader, so I spoke to Ll.G. who, though rather guarded, said <u>no</u>, he would not mind; a day later I got a letter from Ll.G. saying he had seen B. Law and explained things—that just now, when there was a plentiful crop of rumours, his deposition would water this: so I gave it up....

Saturday 18 September 1915

...*Daily News* Leader, 18 September 1915....[2] I hate newspaper articles, and never think the Press of much importance, but I am no judge of its influence. I never buy patent medicines, but I am no judge of this either. They must be bought by thousands, or it would not pay the owners of patents to spend so much money on advertising them.

---

[1] The omission of Bonar Law from the War Policy Committee was one of the worst of many slights which he suffered at Asquith's hands: for this incident, and Lloyd George's retention of the deputy leadership, see Blake, *Bonar Law*, 262–4.

[2] A. G. Gardiner stressed in an open letter that Lloyd George was incapable of judging the balance of working-class opinion on conscription, as his initiatives against drink and towards industrial conscription had shown.

If this open letter to Ll.G. had come out in another newspaper, it would have made a terrific sensation. Liberal papers don't thrive in London; and the *Daily News* has often been shrieking and exaggerated: I seldom read it. This open letter, I think, put the hands of Death on the Conscription intrigue. I had to tell Henry, as wives who are wise do, that he had scored by his silence and patience, and that his shares were as high as they could be now.[1] I don't however think we are out of the wood. (It will be interesting in the House when Henry makes his announcement on Conscription.)

I am going back to a talk I had with the Master of Elibank (Ld Murray) on 15th, 2 days after I left North Berwick. I heard that he had got Eric Drummond to speak to Ll.G. on his Conscription follies, so I wrote and asked if I might see him. He wrote and said he was laid up, and would I go to him. I went to tea with him....

He worships Henry and is <u>really</u> grateful to him for backing him in his Marconi trouble. He is of all men the most keen to make people get on with each other—a genuine Peacemaker....He talks of McKenna in high praise, and quite genuine, but McK. crosses himself and spits when he talks of the Master. He knows Ll.G. is rotten to the core, and that he has behaved badly to the one man he (the Master) loves, but he still likes Ll.G. very much....He told me it was all important that H. and Ll.G. should have a heart to heart talk....

Ld Murray 'Ll.G. said to me "I'm always being compared to Joe in the papers. There is all the difference in the world between us. Mr G. treated Joe like a dog, he hated and humiliated him. The PM has done <u>everything</u> for me, he has seen me thro awful times like the Marconi: I owe him <u>everything</u>. Why <u>should</u> they, how <u>can</u> they say I intrigue against him?" To this I replied "You must stop Northcliffe. Every day *The Times* abuses your Prime Minister, and you've never made a protest."'

I was very reasonable, listening to this from the Master, and said I was all for them being together again—it was important—but that, in my

[1] Cf. Margot's entry for 21 Aug., above: 'I can see H. is setting himself against doing anything in public. Here he is wrong. Crewe is right: we should not keep an anxious, overstrained country in the dark any longer.'

193

judgement, Ll.G. has lost a <u>great deal</u>. We then talked of my private affairs, in which he took real interest and showed amazing courage and resource.

Monday 20 September 1915

Ll.G., Bongie and H. lunched here, and Ll.G. talked with Henry for an hour afterwards.... Henry told me in the evening that he [Ll.G.] had been at his <u>most</u> emotional—fearfully unhappy, denouncing all the intriguers, protesting his innocence and devotion, etc. etc.

H. I said to him 'Why didn't you come near me? All through Marconi and other difficulties I saw you every day.' I was calm and not much moved by his emotion. He of course said he was too busy, etc. etc: this was, of course, nonsense. When he had his say, I said to him 'There are only 2 men that really count in this crisis: you and me. We can make K. do <u>what we like</u>. We <u>must</u> work together.' He quite sees this, but doesn't like K. and wants to get rid of him. I told him this was madness: the country <u>would not stand it</u>....

M. Your talk was wholly satisfactory then, darling, with the Welshman.

H. Yes, I've got him tight now. He'll do anything I like for the time being....

Tuesday 21 September 1915

I went with H. to hear Budget—a large crowd in front of the H. of Commons, all very excited—masses of pressmen in our street. Brutes, how <u>I loathe them</u>!

I sat next to Venetia and Sylvia Henley. Ll.G. was not there, which gave me rather a ridge[1]—what infinite smallness! He could not face his successor's success. It was a remarkable speech, remarkably well delivered: the House packed, and all looking fit to be hanged, till they saw how little their pockets would suffer.[2] I can easily see, knowing my West End of

[1] i.e. a good feeling.

[2] For the importance of McKenna's budget in the development of Britain's war finance see Strachan, *First World War*, 869–72.

194

London, that McKenna will be what is called a 'general favourite', and highly fashionable. (For some time past Alice Keppel and others through his bridge have taken him up, but now he will cut out Simon in a canter. Nothing is more amusing than social ups and downs!)...

Monday 27 September 1915

We dined with Benckendorffs....I motored back with Grey, who got on to his favourite topic (letting out secrets from here that will help the Germans). He was dry and irritating on it. When I said Good-night to H., and told [him] about this, he said 'I've no patience with Grey about this. He is insane on the subject of spies. In my opinion, a great deal of the concealment and secrecy in this war has been all to the bad.'[1]

Tuesday 28 September 1915

No morning news. Walter Long lunched, and was particularly nice. After we left the dining-room, he told H. that though he was a strong conscriptionist, he would never utter, or allow any one else to utter, unless he (Walter) knew that H. wanted it. Walter is one of the straightest men I know.

We went down to the House. H. made an appeal, in answer to F. Guest's question on Conscription, to the whole house, reminding them that we were in the middle of a serious military crisis, and that to give our allies an impression of disunion just now would be most wrong and unpatriotic. In spite of this dignified and gentle rebuke, [Freddie] Guest spoke (after I had gone) and made his usual Conscription speech. When H. was told in his room by Simon of what was going on, he said 'Clear the House and the front bench, and take no sort of notice of the ass.'[2]

---

[1] Margot invites confusion here between spy mania, which was widespread and mostly unsubstantiated, and withholding information from the public because publication might help the enemy: see *Asquith–Stanley*, 419–20.

[2] Guest claimed the support of 45 Liberal Members, according to Riddell: *War Diary*, 29 Aug. 1915, 120. Margot did not appreciate how mistaken her husband was in treating this influential rebel with disdain.

H. came into my bed-room, as he always does before he dresses, [and] told me he had had an interesting afternoon. H. 'To spike the guns of these silly conscriptionists, I arranged that K. should see the Trade Union Leaders, and tell them what he wanted. After he had had a little talk, he left, and I went in and made them a little speech. I told them that K. and I wanted 30,000 men a week to fight and make shells, and that they must help, and do their <u>utmost</u>. I explained the seriousness of the situation, and made an appeal to them. They cheered me, and one of them—I don't know which—came up and said 'Why don't you come down oftener to us, and speak like that? We'd a deal sooner have you than some who come and talk.' (This was one at Ll.G.!) I saw Henry was happier. He ended by saying '<u>Oh! they're all right!</u>' (Trade Union leaders)....

Wednesday 29 September 1915

We had an interesting dinner party 29th....K. took me in, of course, and Ld Cowdray, the big contractor, sat my other side. The last is a grand fellow—modest, kind, clever and very generous. He has been infinitely kind, and is a remarkable man. K. was in high fettle.

[K.] If we push on, we can get into Brussels, and in any case Lille is certain. No troops in the world ever fought like ours. (His face looked quite soft.) The new army is amazing.[1] I said if the Germans go too far into Russia they are beat, and this is what is happening. They ought to have left Russia, concentrated below Arras and got into Paris.[2]

---

[1] Assuming that Kitchener said this on 29 Sept. it is a remarkable statement. Well as the troops of his new armies had performed in the Battle of Loos, after four days of fighting they were not near Lille, let alone Brussels, and had suffered heavy casualties. Clearly by this date all the doubts about the willingness of London's 'Cockneys', and of other urban Britons, to fight hard in the absence of a strong military tradition had disappeared; for Masterman's doubts before the war about British stamina see Masterman, *Condition of England*, 114–15.

[2] Kitchener's judgement about the German command's strategic error earlier in 1915 was justified. They should have concentrated on the Western Front, instead of achieving easier victories in Russia, where the distances put decisive success out of reach: for K. on this, 24 Nov. 1914, see *Asquith–Stanley*, 319.

M. I doubt if they could break the French lines now. Why, do you suppose, didn't they get into Paris at first?

K. They followed us too quickly. They got too far from their communications and provisions.

M. Do you think this war will go on as long as this day year?

K. Yes, it will go on another year, and the worst fighting of all will be in spring and summer.

M. I bet you are wrong: it will be over in 6 months.

K. I'll bet you £1.

M. That's no good, I want a handsome present.

K. I'll take back if I may, and say the war will last till Aug 1st.

(I felt I ought to have pinned him to his first bet but I said -)

M. <u>Done</u>. I bet the war is over before Aug 1st 1916.

K. Remember, <u>no rotten Peace</u>. We shall go on even if the others stop.

M. Were the Guards much knocked about these 5 days?

K. I've not looked at the casualty lists—I never do.

I turned to Ld Cowdray, who in his quiet way told me just what he thought of Ll.G. Ld Cowdray 'You and your husband know him now. Once you get over the heart-break, <u>nothing</u> can hurt you again. You never return: sentiment is crushed.'...

October 1915

Bulgaria has attacked Servia, and joined the Germans in the war. The Greeks and Roumanians are behaving like curs. We can't move in Dardanelles. Things look bad—very bad....Three cabinet memorandums have been written and circulated to the cabinet—one by K. (<u>quite</u> idiotic! Not having shown it to H. first is so senseless. He is very clumsy and very vain, and is doing his best to sell both anti- and conscriptionists!);[1] one by Ll.G., one by Winston: the last, H. says, one of the most insolent

---

[1] 'Sell', i.e. deceive, cheat.

documents he ever read, and Ll.G.'s that of a maniac! How odd it is that mutual recrimination and violence has set in directly we have failures in the Field. It's only a question of time now—the Government will break. I wonder if Arthur Balfour and Lansdowne and Walter will really be dragged at the heels of 2 such curs as Ll.G. and Winston. They will be <u>mad</u> if they are.

Friday 15 October 1915

I woke up at 5 and wrote to K., Crewe, Ed. Grey and Hankey. I'm never very sure if Grey knows what is going on; he is so self-centred. I can't tell Arthur much. He is rather conventional and inactive, and is angry with me because I wrote and begged him to decorate some of the poor poor devils in Dardanelles (caught as they are, and condemned, in this ill-starred expedition of Winston's). No amateur soldier is decorated in this war, and as most <u>gallant</u> things have been done by them (and more will be expected of them) it is Folly beyond words.

Henry saw all my letters, and entirely agreed with me—thought Admiralty terribly remiss, and the authorities regular old maids! Hankey and Eric Drummond are far our best men outside Henry [and] A. Balfour. Montagu is <u>very</u> clever and <u>devoted</u>, but exaggerated and moody; McKenna loyal, brave and clever, but so <u>terribly</u> over-sharp and suspicious....

The critical cabinet sat till 2. Sir J. Simon lunched. He told me Henry had opened the cabinet by a clear, very firm, admirable, <u>full</u> statement on Conscription. His speech riveted his friends and even his enemies. Crewe then made a dull, halting statement. Ll.G. got very excited and lost both head and temper, not quite but very nearly. He made a mean, caddish, black-mailing speech. <u>He</u> would resign, and go and tell the country the <u>Truth</u>, etc. etc. (This did not worry Henry, but as he said to me afterwards 'We can't have a general election when war is going on, and though I should carry on quite well, it would cause a lot of talk.') I cd. see even the 'correct' Simon was disgusted though he is singularly wooden and cautious....

I thought H. in good form at lunch, though he was very late. Simon said, and I've been told since, that the effect of his statement was tremendous—Lansdowne and Walter really much moved, and B. Law not at all liking it. They are believers in the Conscription Rubbish, and though they dislike Ll.G. and Co., and are fond of Henry, they feel they ought to stick together. I asked about A.J.B....I rather gathered he was all right and would stick to H., but he is not a very robust figure to lean up against!...

Saturday 16 October 1915—The Wharf

Henry came to my bedroom before dinner. He told me Bonar Law had been to see him in the morning to tell him <u>how</u> distressed he was at the situation and how much he disliked the whole thing.

H. I don't think he likes it at all, nor Lansdowne, and to do Curzon justice, I really don't think he does either. I've only got to say 5 words and all would stay except the wild cats Ll.G. [and] Winston.

M. I hope you'll never say them.

H. <u>Not I</u>! I know you can't have Conscription in this country without something very like revolution. I should carry on just the same. Ll.G., Winston and Selborne <u>out</u> would be all to the good, for, nice as Selborne is, he is a donkey, always putting his foot into it: the others are mere wreckers. It's clear to me Ll.G. wants to get out of the whole thing, stump the country to cover his tracks and say how badly this and that has been handled, and press for Conscription. Simon used the right expression: he made a blackmailing speech. I shan't give way <u>one inch</u>!

M. Do you really think they will all go? all tie themselves up to Ll.G. and Winston?

H. They don't want to. Bonar Law came to see me this morning and said 'D'you know, Prime Minister, what impression your speech made on me half way through?' I said 'No'. 'That of a man who wanted to be out of the whole thing—tired, disgusted.'

M. (hastily) A singularly bad shot!

H. I told him that he was wrong: that I intended to stick, and as I say I think we can get on quite well without them.

M. You'll give Bob[1] a seat in the cabinet, and Montagu of course?

H. Certainly, the old lot and Bob: but it's very serious. Edmund Talbot, absolutely loyal, told Gulland he was <u>very</u> sorry about it all.

M. What about K.?

H. Oh, K. has made a real fool of himself—given each lot away in turns to the other; vain and clumsy. The King was very down on him, and told me that K. had confessed to having made a heavy mistake. I said to K. 'You issue a memorandum to the cabinet without showing it to me <u>first</u>, and in less than a week you change your figures. You and I agreed 30,000 men a week was as much as we could equip or spare for soldiers: now you suddenly ask for 35,000—what has changed in the interval? How can I or any one else rely on your word, or on any War Office figures, after this? You promised the Trade Unionists 30,000 was all you needed, and they promised they would get them. How am I to go down to the House and say you've changed your mind?' Naturally the King and I agreed: K. is very trying with his ignorance and inaccuracy.

M. A. Balfour and Masterton think him an awful liar, but I really don't think he is so wicked, as clumsy....

Sunday 17 October 1915—Wharf

...Venetia, Mildred, H. and I went to see Puffin. He was overjoyed, and showed us his little magazine.... Venetia, he and Henry sat on a bench in the playing fields and read it out loud. I watched them rocking with laughter. It was a glorious day.... We all played bridge late Sunday 17th night, and [Henry] talked and laughed, but I thought he looked a little tired. The strain is great, and I never admired Henry more than I ever have these last few days....

[1] (Edgar Algernon) Robert Gascoyne-Cecil (1864–1958), Unionlist Free Trader; joined Asquith's government in May 1915 coalition, entering cabinet as Minister for Blockade Feb. 1916.

Monday 18 October 1915

We all sat down to lunch, and H. came in looking rather tired but not amiss.... (I forgot to say I had been sent for by Stamfordham in the morning to St. James's Palace, and had an excellent talk with him. He opened by saying how <u>devoted</u> to Henry the King was, and how miserable to think that his cabinet might be wrecked by foolish and wild men; and went on by saying Henry had only got to hold up his little finger and tell the country how things were going, and it would stifle <u>all</u> restlessness; that he wasn't prominent enough, and people wanted to hear what <u>He</u> had got to say, and no one else (very much the same as I had written to Henry when he was at Munstead)....[1] When I got to my bedroom Bongie met me 10 to 5 and told me Henry had been 'taken worse' in the middle of the cabinet, and gone to lie down. I felt full of anxiety, and crept into his room. Blinds down, windows shut, and Henry lying in his clothes under those ugly, useless, airless, warmthless things know[n] as cotton counterpanes. 'I found the room like a furnace, and have got a headache.' M. 'Poor darling! I'll see that they always open the cabinet windows.' I kissed him: his head was hot, he was quite silent, and I left him. He slept till 8. E. and I dined in bed, as I could hardly see out of my eyes for throat and nose being so inflamed....

Henry came in after dinner, and walked up and down, looking terribly harassed, I thought. H. 'The King pressed Robertson badly to find out what he thought of Sir J. French, and he ended at last by saying "If you want to know what I think of French, I think he is obstinate, conceited, jealous and stupid"' (this was said on 16th Oc. 1915). I got out of bed and went to his room with him, and kissed him and said good-night 11.30. He didn't go to bed, but was reading as usual. I didn't like the look of his eyes.

At 1 a.m. I was woken by a violent bang of his door, and he came into my bedroom and said 'I feel very ill, and have come to the reluctant conclusion

---

[1] Munstead House, Surrey, a late 19th-century house, remodelled by Lutyens; the home of Sir Herbert and Lady Jekyll (parents of Pamela McKenna).

I must give up.' He spoke very slowly and was quite hoarse. <u>The sky had fallen</u>. I sat bolt upright, and writing now I can hardly believe he is in my garden (Wharf 22nd Oc. 1915),[1] reading the papers, alive and well, though weak. I jumped out of bed, clasped my hands, and prayed for mere physical courage not to break down <u>absolutely</u>. He saw quite well by my attitude what was passing in my mind, and put his hand on my shoulder.

H. I don't propose to take it tragically, but I know I can't go on. I must choose the least of 2 evils. I could perhaps struggle on, but I am on the edge of the precipice.... I see a spectre, and know that greater and permanent evil would come if I don't make up my mind at once... and go right away....[2]

M. (firmly but stunned) Of course, darling, you are <u>worn out</u>. You've been working at high pressure—never 4 days running off since the war began. You've been harried from within, and badgered by outer things, and you are Right. You must knock it <u>all</u> off—think of nothing, read nothing, see <u>no</u> one and not speak a word: just get into bed, and rest your dear head.

He walked up and down for nearly an hour. I watched him and walked with him. He told me it was different to what he had felt last time in the coal strike week (when he had high blood-pressure), and that perhaps in a week he would be right, but that he could not give consecutive thoughts to any thing, or put out his best. His words fell like drops of ice on my heart. He sat down and I sat on his knee. He kissed my hands several times. He told me he had told Violet.

With difficulty I got him to bed, and went to see Violet. I asked her every detail. She was very sweet and tender, and put her arms round me, and we sobbed together. 'He is the linchpin in our lives' she said, upon which all held together or fell. I thought to myself 'You are young, 29[3] and

---

[1] For Margot's sometimes eccentric method of dating her entries see the Editorial Note above.

[2] The ellipses in this paragraph are Margot's.

[3] Violet was in fact 28 (born Apr. 1887).

4 AUGUST–15 NOVEMBER 1915

just going to be married and start real life for the <u>first</u> time. You've seen nothing of Life except glimpses, and the big tragedies in which you have been have not marked you deeply (indeed hardly at all); but for me <u>life must be over</u>, except in such chaperonage or companionship as Elizabeth and Puffin will need. Henry ill—<u>really down</u> and <u>miserable</u>—<u>tired</u>, <u>finished</u>!' Oh! the thought was unbearable.[1]

I told her he could not lie flat, but had asked me to put the other pillow on top of the one he usually slept on, and this had alarmed me. I crept back to his room and found him lying flat, which was a relief. I ran and told her, and Bongy was there, most sweet, wise and sympathetic. I burst into a fury against Ll.G., Winston and Co., who have made things so much more difficult by their intrigues and folly. I could hardly stand for rage, fear and Pity. That such an <u>angel</u> as Henry should be yapped at, criticized, and in any way overwhelmed by such scum! I looked in again at 4 a.m., and found him fast asleep. I had a sleepless night.

Tuesday 19 October 1915

I wrote a lot of early letters to Crewe and Grey. I put the fear of Hell into the latter to shake him out of himself, and said it was touch and go whether H. would ever return to public life again. I telephoned to Buckmaster, and told him to get hold of Simon and make a plan for suspending *The Times* and *Daily Mail*. I said they were all going to kill Henry, and that he could never carry on the war on through another 6 months if things were not <u>radically</u> changed. His voice shook with emotion down the telephone: he begged me to keep my grand courage, and not get ill, and that he would see about it <u>at once</u>.

Dr. Parkinson came in, and assured me Henry could not have had a blood vessel or anything <u>like</u> it burst in his brain, or he could not have walked up and down for so long; and he went in to see him. I waited

---

[1] Margot seems to have assumed in this crisis, as always, that her husband would serve his country best by remaining Prime Minister. A more realistic wife might have surmised that an exhausted premier could give his best service by vacating 10 Downing Street and becoming Lord Chancellor.

breathlessly to hear my fate. When he came out, I saw in a moment that things were not as bad. Bad blood from over-exhaustion, and his secretions not doing proper work, had been feeding his brain poorly; liver out of order, and general fag of brain and body, etc. He must starve and sleep. He slept 36 hours without much break—3 [breaks] for the Dr.—and a little barley water.

At 8 pm o'clock Eliz. and I went into his room to have our big bath, which leads out of his bedroom. We found him reading the Bible.[1] He kissed her and said 'Listen to this, and tell me if it doesn't describe Ll.G.' Elizabeth and I sat silently listening to him reading in what I thought rather a hard voice. I could see how Ll.G. had got on his nerves; how morally stale and unprofitable he felt inwardly towards this man whom he had plucked from the burning. When he had finished reading, I gave him a pencil, and he marked the passage (the Bible belonged to his wife and had 'Helen' written in Henry's handwriting on the first page.)

Wednesday 20 October 1915

Henry slept well. I sent for Carson, who had resigned on our position in the Balkans, and was going to make his statement in the House that afternoon…[2] [He] came, and was charming—very amusing, and full of kindness, even affection, for Henry. I don't think he is a really good politician….

Thursday 21 October 1915

I forgot to say Crewe came to see me while H. was still asleep about 11. The King had asked him to see me to urge the new war committee should be 3 or 5, and I think *au fond* for me to urge the removal of Sir J. French, about

---

[1] During Asquith's illness Margot made notes for him to read afterwards. On the first page Margot wrote: 'After I had told [Rufus] of your illness and of your reading St Peter's betrayal of Christ to me and Elizabeth and saying "Peter was a Celt"….'

[2] *Parl. Deb.*, 74.1812–13. Carson had resigned specifically over Britain's failure to 'save Serbia'. The weakness of his position was his inability to say how the Allies could have gone to Serbia's defence effectively.

whom I fear I have quite lost my confidence. I never liked Crewe better: he is so courteous and understanding, and such a fine friend.

H. and V. motored to Wharf, and I went by train after seeing him in his bedroom, certainly better, lunching alone on [a] little fish while [a] footman packed his bag. Every one was in an anguish while he was ill. Simon lunched, and said it was the best thing that could have happened, as the 3 cabinets have been long and quarrelsome. B. Law told Bongie nothing could be worse than the cabinets without Henry. I felt glad and a little better in my heart that all these men who could not do without him should yet be constantly worrying and threatening him, tiring him out.

We all arrived at Wharf more or less together. H. kissed me, and went to his room. We dined à trois 21st and 22nd at 8, and spent most of our days in bed. As we were alone, I slept in the top room of cottage, not in my Barn bedroom. I felt and indeed was, very ill. I was up all night off and on 18th and 19th, and could not get over the agony of seeing H. ill, and too tired to keep awake....

Wednesday 27 October 1915—The Wharf

H. and Violet went to London. I was in bed with chill, and saw Osler from Oxford.[1] 'You are ill from shock,' he said....

Thursday 28 October 1915

I joined H. and Violet in London, though still very ill. I didn't trust anyone to look after Henry, who was still far from well, and who has got to speak Tuesday 2nd Nov.—his big war Review long-delayed speech. I am sure it will take it out of him. I like to look in and see if his bedroom is too hot or too cold, and make it right; and I love our only little times alone between 11.30 and midnight. I sometimes stay till one, but I don't like making him talk too late, it tires him more than reading....

[1] Sir William Osler (1849–1919), Bt. 1911, Regius Professor of Medicine at Oxford, 1904–19.

Saturday 30 October 1915[1]

> M. The P.M. has let Ll.G. do what he likes too much! But I'll bet he knows his Ll.G. now like you <u>all</u> do and if it's a question of H. or Ll.G. <u>I</u> know and so do you who wins.
>
> R[ufus]. That's quite true but he's a dangerous man going round with his great energy and quality of enthusing men, etc.
>
> M. <u>Let him go round and tell the truth!</u> He is the most discredited man I know, and if you know what all are beginning to know, the <u>chaos</u> of his Munitions, you'll find if H. <u>could</u> get rid of him <u>Everyone</u> would be relieved. I'm as sure as I sit here the best thing that could happen if we are to win this war is to face the danger you fear with courage and get rid of Ll.G. and Winston and muzzle the Northcliffe Press.
>
> R. Ll.G. has got 3 papers, all Liberal: the *Manchester Guardian, British Weekly* (and another I forget).[2]
>
> M. He's not got *D. News* or *D. Chronicle* and the *Manchester Guardian* is hysterical and old-maidish…If H. were to take the country into his confidence by a few big speeches Ll.G. would vanish into Space! Can you deny this? Which is the most powerful man in England? Who would get the biggest audiences?
>
> R. The P.M., but Ll.G. comes next.
>
> M. You overrate this, believe me…Now to go to War Committee,[3] it's <u>impossible</u> to leave McK[enna] out—I feel in my bones this is grossly unjust. McK. is tactless, irritating, common, all you like, but Finance is important though Ll.G. thinks nothing of it.

---

[1] On Saturday, 30 Oct. 1915 Margot travelled to the Wharf with Rufus Isaacs. She wrote an account of her conversation, from which these extracts are taken. It is enclosed in the diary volume in loose sheets, and illustrates the difficulty which this wise friend had in advising Margot.

[2] The third was probably Riddell's *News of the World*.

[3] On 11 Nov., Asquith announced in Parliament the formation of a 'new War Committee of the Cabinet', consisting, in the temporary absence of Kitchener (in the Dardanelles), of himself, Balfour, Llyod George, Bonar Law, and McKenna: see above, p. cxxiv, and *Times*, 12 Nov. 1915, 10a.

R. (keenly) I should think it is!! I told Ll.G. he was a baby not to see it but he says we must sell our last shirt—I say, who is the purchaser? How is money to be paid for the shirt? He laughs at all this and says it's all rot.

M. He doesn't want McK. because he doesn't like him, but would you leave him out?

R. Certainly not—he is very, very able over all this. I assure [you] I talked to Bonar Law and you never heard a man talk such stuff in your life!! He is essential, is McKenna.

M. Well, why not the new War Committee: H., Arthur, Ll.G., and McK. and perhaps Grey—but all this can be settled; McK. must not be left out. I should resign if I were McK.: and he and Ll.G. won't quarrel with H. and Arthur there, and if they do H. will see to it. Rufus, let us be straight. Ll.G. is going to blackmail the P.M. with his 'tell the truth to the country'—this is what you fear.

R. (miserable) I'm sure of it.

M. Is Ll.G. a man of ability? Has he done anything well? Land? Pensions? Finance? Drink?.... Is he a good man? You know he is not. Is he a loyal, grateful, hard-working, courageous Real Friend? (R. shook his head). Well, you can't say 'Yes' to one of my questions. I will put you another—is this the man who with all his fire, energy, insolence, wit, charm and lightning brain is to knock out a man like the Prime Minister and with him the whole old Liberal fighting lot?[1] A man like Henry?—good to the core, Loyal, Patient and by far the ablest, wisest, calmest and cleverest man in England? whose one fault has been over-modesty? Why, what a fault! I know no-one could have minded as much as I that he doesn't come right out and see and speak to sad, over-strained anxious men who are lied to in every paper and kept in the dark

---

[1] This passage encapsulates Margot's inability to see that, while her husband possessed nearly all the qualities needed by a peacetime premier, he lacked the ability, essential in war, to show that he was striving to the utmost to secure the Allies' victory.

by all the great offices—War Off., Admiralty, and Foreign Office. I <u>ache</u> for these poor people, but they would rather be neglected by H. than pawed, patted and roused by Ll.G.! Can you imagine a meaner or more futile indictment than general sweeping criticisms on what is past and over.

R. I agree with all you say and you know who <u>my</u> choice will be and who <u>I</u> shall stick to, but must it come to that?

M. Yes, sooner or later it <u>must</u> and for my part I hope to God it comes <u>Sooner</u>.

This was my talk with Rufus.

<u>Notes for Henry to read.</u>[1] Now, darling, I am not going to bore you but apropos of your speech Tues. (the Ll.G. and K., etc., can wait): If you won't tell the public something quite definite about things on which their minds are not only frightened but sad, your speech, however well expressed, will be a failure. I should be audaciously bold, and say the Dardanelles won't be evacuated, and that we won't let the Servian army be smashed:[2] that in fact that almost <u>Insane</u> speech of Lansdowne's[3] (and, I thought, grossly disloyal) describing the paralysis of England and the Government was <u>not accurate</u>... that we are a nation who may be criticized for being slow, but that we were very tenacious and powerful, and given sufficient provocation, knew how to meet Trouble. Quote the Kaiser's speech

---

[1] These notes, relating to H.H.A.'s important speech in the Commons on 2 Nov., were included by Margot among the loose sheets that she gathered together for Saturday 30 October.

[2] Margot seems never to have recognized how disastrous it would have been had the premier insisted on prolonging these doomed operations. As so often, her wise advice at this juncture about keeping the public informed was apt to be neglected because too much nonsense had been mixed with it.

[3] On 26 Oct. 1915 Lord Cromer had said in the House of Lords that a 'Cabinet of 22' was 'quite incapable of conducting the war properly'; and that the public would prefer 'a small strong executive body chosen from men representing the best talent in the country'. In reply, Lord Lansdowne agreed that 'the efficiency of any body of the kind was apt to vary inversely with its numerical strength'; *The Times*, 27 Oct. 1915, 9. On 2 Nov. 1915 Carson had advocated the kind of arrangement outlined by Cromer: *Parl. Deb.*, 75.533. Margot failed to realize the significance of these calls for a small body, easily summoned, consisting largely of members freed from departmental responsibilities, and equipped with the power of *decision*, even if this applied to no more than a limited area.

in *Westminster [Gazette]* (the men with coolest nerve would be those who would win, or some such saying).

I should also add you intended to make a clear statement every 2 weeks, and announce your War committee. This would revive, re-hearten and Rejoice all hearts. Your silence has been misunderstood by the Court, some of your colleagues, and the Country: but these colleagues <u>like</u> to misunderstand and don't count, and the country, with a little more consideration and sympathy from you, <u>you can get at your feet</u>. Good-night, darling.

Monday 1 November 1915

Henry came to my bedroom 7.40 p.m., and told me he had really had great fun. (His first cabinet since he was ill.) They had all sat down hostile and at 6s and 7s, and got up like lambs! H. 'I found a formula which bridged the Conscription difficulties, and which completely satisfied both lots. At first Curzon groused a little, but Bonar L. and Long sat heavily upon him, so did the others. Ll.G. was charming, and all of them very happy!' (I was told by several members of cabinet that never had anyone handled colleagues of such varying kinds, and with such different views, so well as Henry did at this cabinet. K. seems to have said to my brother Jack Tennant at War Office that he (K.) felt Henry to be the cleverest man in Europe after this cabinet!)

I forgot to say that Sunday night at Wharf, 31st, I ran across and had a long talk to Henry, and I felt rather weepy; he seemed very calm, but rather depressed, I thought. He had had an odious kind of letter from Ll.G. threatening all kinds of things if K. remained in War Council. Henry told me (11.30 p.m.) he had made up his mind K. must go to the East: he wd. make him Commander-in-Chief in the East, which would please him; as it was an undoubtable fact, in spite of K. still being a hero to the public, he was <u>impossible</u> to work with for majority of colleagues. Those who wanted K. to go had no idea of what would be thought in the country, but he (H.) had made up his mind to give K. this very high place, which means nothing much except his opinion, and which will please everyone.[1] 'I rather think Bonar Law will resign tomorrow.' M. 'I must say, you do have a very hard time! I should hate to work with such donkeys!'

H. told B. Law he intended to go to War Office, and send K. to the Dardanelles, etc. B.L. quite approved. H. told him he had told Ll.G., who was quite agreeable. It appears B. Law then said 'I don't want to impute motives, but it is just possible that Ll.G. knows you'll have to bear the odium of K.'s going, which he would prefer to his (Ll.G.) having to bear it.' This H. and I thought characteristic of B. Law's slim side!

Tuesday 2 November 1915

This was the great day.[2] I felt ill from anxiety and the remains of my shock and chill, and woke at 5 am with violent headache.... At 3 Bongie, Violet, Henry and I drove to House: a great crowd in the streets lifting their hats. I had taken the precaution to have a strychnine injection by my Dr., I felt so exhausted and excited. The Speaker's gallery jammed, and the whole House full from top to toe. Great excitement over this speech in Press and public: Northcliffe doing his best to anticipate events, but making out what a lot of 'Truth' H. had to tell about every operation—knowing quite well that his speech could not, in the nature of things, tell the Germans our intentions in Gallipoli or Salonika.

When H. got up I felt physically sick—every female stole a furtive look at me to see how I felt....

A great moment and a great speech. He spoke till 5.30. His voice dropt a little at the end, when he came to the personal part of his speech 'When the war broke out, I was the Head of the Government,' etc. I listened with

---

[1] In fact Kitchener's sojourn in the Mediterranean was only temporary, while he reported on operations there: in his absence Asquith acted as War Secretary: see Maurice Bonham Carter to Violet Asquith, 9 Oct. 1915 (and her reply, 10 Oct.): Bonham Carter, *Diaries, 1914–45*, 82–3.

[2] i.e. the day of Asquith's important speech in the House of Commons on the conduct of the war, which included his statement on conscription; it was one of the longest speeches of his career, and was given after a period of illness, and against the background of Sir Edward Carson's resignation from the government.

strained ears and beating heart. The fine passage on Edith Cavell[1] was lost in the gallery—even Violet heard it wrong: 'What year in our history has done more to justify our faith in the manhood and womanhood of our people? It has brought us, as we cannot at this moment forget, the imperishable story of the last hours of Nurse Cavell, facing a worse ordeal than the battle-field—the moments creeping on slowly and remorselessly, and death already swallowed up in Victory.... Let us endure to the End.'[2] Many who read the speech told me it had brought tears to their eyes. It was received in stunned silence; you could have heard a mosquito, and when he finished there was a roar of applause....

The Conscription part of the speech pleased both lots equally. This was extremely *rusé*, and when I chaffed H. about it he said serenely 'The House never knows when it is being hoodwinked, but I really can't go on having resignations and quarrels.' The speech had a transcendent effect. I had wires from Russia, and heaps of letters of praise. I could only wish it had come 5 weeks sooner, but I daresay I'm wrong, and that it was better to let the grousers get noisier, so as to have a more <u>complete</u> shut-up....[3]

Monday 15 November 1915—Munstead, Godalming

We came here by motor, arriving about 6 Sat 13th; H. wonderfully well. He tells me the mess he has to clear up at WO is awful. K. went away in nick of time.[4] No man was ever so unlike his reputation—muddle-headed,

[1] Edith Cavell (1865–1915), matron of Berkendael medical institute at Brussels, which became a Red Cross hospital in 1914; she helped about 200 allied soldiers to escape from Belgium, 1914–15. She was arrested by the German authorities on 5 Aug. 1915 and placed in solitary confinement: her trial ended on 8 Oct. She was sentenced to death on 11 Oct.; and executed the next day.

[2] This ellipsis is Margot's. See *Parl. Deb.*, 2 Nov. 1915, 75.528–9.

[3] Asquith's speech included, first, a pledge to the married men that they would not be called on to serve until all the bachelors available had been required to do so, even 'in the last resort', by compulsion; secondly, an assurance that if the recently-announced Derby Scheme should fail, with 'men of military age' being found to 'hold back from the service of their country', the voluntary system would have to be supplemented 'by some form of legal obligation'. But the premier dismissed this contingency as one which he did 'not think ever likely to arise': Adams and Poirier, *Conscription*, 129–30.

[4] Kitchener had left for the Dardanelles, via Paris, on the evening of 4 Nov. 1915; he studied operations there 10–16 Nov., and returned to London, via Rome, on 30 Nov.: Cassar, *Kitchener*, 417–29.

secretive, even irresolute, or at any rate saying one thing one day and another the next. The sigh of relief at his departure is <u>universal</u>. Gen. Gough wrote to my Dr. 'Thank God K. is no longer at WO and the PM is, we shall get things done <u>at last</u>.'

What they really want H. to do is, I think, to get rid of Sir John French. I've made up my mind we <u>must</u> do this. Haig may not be a very big man, but Sir John, I regret to say, is a very little one. All the officers have lost confidence in him. <u>This is enough for me</u>....

Winston has finally departed....No one has ever been treated as well as Winston. Time after time all his colleagues have sighed to get rid of him but H. has never budged in his friendship and has shown large hearted loyalty in backing this young man which no Prime Minister has ever extended to anyone in like degree before. (Henry has two colleagues of vision[1]—some would say genius—Vision is a kind of genius). Coupled with this Winston has Industry and affection—one wonders such a fortuitous combination has not put him in direct succession to Henry—but I may be wrong. I see <u>no such future</u> for Winston—I see no political future for him. I would almost say I see death on the battle field. Winston is quite unprincipled—he has no recoil.[2] He has a great hole in his mind and in his character which alas Life, experience [or] whatever you like to call it, does not mend. His mind cannot move quietly from thought to thought: it leaps like a Kangaroo. In consequence his thoughts are astray, he has no mental bump of locality. If your actions are neither guided by morals or mind but simply by temperament, and if added to this you are so self-centred and childishly pleased with shadows as against substance as to give out all the time and never take-in then you can never acquire Judgement. Judgement is character quite as much as Instinct.

I never really loved Winston in old days, Violet did. It didn't bore her, Winston's interest in himself, because it was coupled with interest in her: and no amount of interest in me <u>ever</u> compensates for self-devotion. As

[1] Winston and Lloyd George.
[2] Margot seems to mean that Winston is incapable of responding to comment, so that he never discusses, and adjusts, his views. She lived to see him as Prime Minister, 1940–5.

I got to know him better his childish side has appealed to my maternal instinct and I have found and <u>do</u> find him <u>loveable</u>.[1] He is really a <u>better</u> fellow than Ll.G. but not nearly as clever—I don't mean Able. I think Winston is <u>abler</u> than Ll.G. (who has muddled everything he has ever touched); but Lloyd George is a cleverer, more incalculable and rarer man than Winston. His great speeches are less egotistical. He is <u>infinitely</u> better company. I can exchange ideas with Lloyd George: with Winston you receive or reject his ideas—<u>exchange is impossible</u>. Ll.G. is a far subtler blend of temper, temperament, and intellect.... He is the most mentally and socially resourceful person in the world. Quick, <u>charming</u>, handsome, sympathetic, with vitality that seems to remove mountains, and an odd kind of Faith in an undefined God, he moves rapidly from failure to failure, turning friends into Foes as a man might turn pictures to walls, but never seriously revolting any one.... He has no real Courage, and except a vague preference for the Poor, and the temptation to Help suffering, he has no conviction. All he undertakes drops in chaos and confusion on a floor littered with covered tracks....[2]

Winston made a very clever speech 15th Nov 1915.[3] I listened with pleasure. It was egotistical, as usual, but had to be this, as he was defending himself against all sorts of attacks, and many foolish criticisms which had much better have waited till the end of the war. He opened by praising Carson unnecessarily, I thought, and, while telling the truth about Fisher's folly, he paid the latter a handsome tribute....

[1] For Churchill's views about Asquith at this stage see Soames, *Speaking for Themselves*, 113, 137, 148.

[2] Margot had not asked herself whether anyone except Ll.G. could have raised the money necessary in 1909 for the six Dreadnoughts needed and for the new national pensions over a full year, and, two years later, have secured the passage of contributory National Insurance through both Houses. The Coalition government also depended heavily on his ability to communicate effectively with organized labour, as evidenced by this speech to the TUC at Bristol in Sept.: see *The Times* leader, 'Mr Lloyd George at Bristol', 10 Sept. 1915, 9a; and the news report 'Plain Words to Labour', 9f.

[3] While recognizing that Churchill's speech was an ex parte statement, made in his own defence, *The Times* found much in it to praise: 'Punctuated by cheers from all parts of the House, and accorded an ovation at the close, the speech was an undoubted parliamentary triumph': 16 November 1915, 9a; see *Parl. Deb.*, 75.1499–1521.

PART VII

16 NOVEMBER 1915–
4 MAY 1916

The victory of the pro-conscription candidate, C. B. Stanton, at the Merthyr Tydfil by-election on 25 November 1915 knocked a good deal of nonsense out of the national debate about compulsion. Merthyr was predominantly a mining constituency, and Stanton, 'a miner of miners', stood 'as an independent and patriotic Labour candidate as a protest against the anti-recruiting and pacifist policy of the Independent Labour Party'.[1] Henceforth it would be difficult to argue, as Henderson and Balfour were apt to do, that since military conscription would bear most heavily on society's less affluent ranks it might entail a danger of starting class war. The following month there was another important development in the conscription debate, when Sir William Robertson was appointed to the key post of CIGS. Robertson meant the army's claims for men to take precedence over all others, and his presence added weight to the arguments for conscription, albeit that estimates of the numbers of men likely to be needed, and available to serve, continued to be debated. In the New Year of 1916, however, the pressure finally told, and on 27 January the Military Service Act introduced conscription for single men between the ages of 18 and 41. Very few of those involved expected legislation to be confined for very long to bachelors, but those few included the premier. He was buoyed up by the marvellously successful evacuation of the Dardanelles positions, almost without loss, which had been completed on 9 January 1916, but his problems, external and internal, remained formidable. The furious German attack on Verdun, beginning 21 February, put renewed pressure on the Western Allies, and ensured that Kitchener's new armies would bear the brunt of the great offensive planned for the summer. And by the end of March 1916 Carson was re-emerging as a political force after a period of ill health, taking the chair at the influential Unionist War Committee, a ginger group of MPs who were no more inclined than Robertson and the Army Council to wait any longer for general military conscription. The final phase of that controversy brought Asquith close to resignation, but Margot's diary entry on 10 April revealed something of a lapse into fantasy on his part: her warnings 'that this is the worst crisis in all his political life', though no doubt tiresome, were well justified, but he told Edwin Montagu: 'I think we shall have rather fun with all these silly fellows.' His enjoyment was short-lived: on 27 April he was obliged to introduce a bill for general conscription in the Commons, and Maurice Hankey noted: 'He did not much like the job and was not at his best.'[2] Margot believed that on this issue 'no conjuror could have been cleverer', because her husband had managed to reconcile organized labour to a policy that was objectionable in principle, and likely to bear hardest on working people. There was some truth in her statement; but conjuring was not the only skill needed in a wartime premier.

[1] The Times, 27 Nov. 1915, 8d; 29 Nov., 8b.
[2] Hankey, Supreme Command, 476; Parl. Deb., 81.2611–16.

Tuesday 16 November 1915

Violet and I lunched in Cromwell Road, at Goony Churchill's house, and said good-bye to Winston.[1] He goes to join his regiment tomorrow in France. I felt <u>so</u> sad for Clemmy—poor, lonely, with her husband fallen from his high estate and facing danger. My heart went out to her.... Winston was delightful—gay, talkative and interesting—and Clemmy brave, but no one except Winston contributed anything.

W. You know, Margot, you always said I was in favour of Coalition.
M. I often heard you talk of the advantages of a National Gov., and I passionately minded the idea of it, and no one can say I've not been right! It has been a source of weakness, not strength, as you and Ll.G. said it would be.
W. Oh! but wait. I was all against doing what we did—giving way at a time when we were weak. We should have invited the others in when we are at our strongest as a great favour, etc. etc.

I could not interrupt this flow, but the obvious answer is, if we had been full of strength we should <u>never</u> have asked the second-rate men that we've got from the other side now. Why should we?? <u>We had A. Balfour</u>: what have we gained by having Lansdowne? (charming, courtly, elderly, barren person); Bonar Law? (provincial, ignorant, unreliable); Austen Chamberlain? (sticky and correct); Selborne or Curzon?...

Wednesday 24 November 1915

Gen. Sir Douglas and Ly Haig lunched yesterday. He is handsome and Scotch, and though a very fine soldier a remarkably stupid man to talk to.

---

[1] Lady Gwendeline (Goonie) Churchill née Bertie (1885–1941), m. 1908 Major John Churchill (younger brother of Winston). For Clemmy's pride that Winston was to become 'a soldier, not a politician' see *Churchill Companion*, iii (2) 1375. Churchill served in France from mid-Nov. 1915 to early May 1916, initially with the Grenadier Guards, and, from early Jan. 1916, as commanding officer (Lt. Col.) of the 6th Battalion, the Royal Scots Fusiliers. French had planned a brigade command; but a Parliamentary Question (*Parl. Deb.*, 78.2218) frightened Asquith from pressing this plan on Haig; after much indecision Churchill returned to politics, in May 1916, after his battalion was amalgamated with others because of heavy losses: Soames, *Clementine*, 206.

Sir Douglas Haig	Every soldier felt relieved when they heard K. had gone to the East, Mrs Asquith.
M.	Isn't it strange you should say this: the British public think K. and K. only can win this war!
Sir D.H.	Poor old K.! I know him well. I think we all know him now (silence; a dullish stare from fine grey eyes). I hope K. won't come back anyhow for some time: he hasn't enough decision....I suppose he is a good speaker—in the cabinet, I mean. He can put his case well. (Sir E. Cassel said the same to me when he was, like the others, floundering about to find a reason for K.'s popularity!)
M.	No, he can't speak particularly well.

Henry told me when he announced to the cabinet that K. wd. arrive here on Sat.—this Sat., 27th.—every face fell (He and I winked at each other, and said in the same breath 'Poor Bonar Law, Ll.G. and Co!!') and a sort of hopeless feeling fell over all. He wired K. to go and see King of Italy, but this only gives us a little more breathing space.

Thursday 25 November 1915

Thursday 25th Nov. 1915 a very touching ceremony took place in the Speaker's Library. Through the agency and trouble of Col. Lockwood MP[1] and Mr D. Maclean MP 'over £200 was collected to give the Prime Minister's daughter a wedding present.' I was approached on the subject on the afternoon of 16th, just when I wanted to be with H. and say a proper goodbye (I felt nervous at his crossing the Channel, as a Hospital ship had been blown up by a mine 2 days before, with results too terrible to think or write of!) I said to both Lockwood and [Maclean] that H. would be deeply touched at their kindness.

---

[1] (Amelius Richard) Mark Lockwood (1847–1928), cr. 1st Baron Lambourne 1917; Lt. Col. (retired); Unionist MP 1892–1917.

I was more moved than Violet was on the day of presentation, and felt my voice shake as I thanked them. It was a unique ceremony. I hoped Violet would not have to speak, as I really thought it would agitate her, and make her feel ill. She has been having a <u>highly</u> exhausting time, and will have no real rest (she goes to Esher Sunday, but she can't go to bed ever!) before 30th: but I saw she wanted to speak *au fond*, so I said nothing....

Violet and I motored to the House Thurs. 25th at 4.20. We went to Bongie's room. I went in to see Henry while V. thought of her speech. H. <u>didn't think</u> she would be able to speak. We were fetched by Mr Maclean, and walked to the Speaker's Library (the Speaker [Lowther*] overtook us in the corridor.) The room was densely packed with MPs of every political party, very hot and light. Violet looked extraordinarily pretty—her hair tidy and a charming hat. She wore her red velvet trousseau coat with skunk, and a black jet turban with, I regret to say, the aigrette of old days (I've not bought one for 8 years.)[1] I cd. see Henry was touched.

The Speaker opened by an admirable little speech, both light and earnest; and gave her a large diamond sort of sun wheel (not an ornament I ever care much for, but most beautiful of its kind) and a modern copy of the finest kind of inkbottle with inscription on it (silver gilt official box-inkstand which shuts down.) Then Violet spoke. I could not look at her for nerves and emotion, but I need not have been anxious. Her speech was <u>perfect</u>. Cool as a little cucumber, absolutely without emotion of any kind, she spoke clearly and simply. It was the greatest success possible. Then Henry made a wonderful speech, deeply moved and really grateful. Dear old H. Chaplin thanked the Speaker, and was seconded by Redmond.

When H. came into my room as he always does before dinner he said 'I don't suppose any girl in England could have shown the aplomb Violet did this afternoon! Where my children get their cool heads—(M. 'And hearts')—Yes, where they get them from, God alone knows! for I don't.' (We were much amused when the next day Violet said it was such a bore

---

[1] The 'show and display' at Violet's wedding, on 30 Nov., was criticized on both sides of the Channel; see Asquith, C., *Diaries*, 106; *Stevenson Diary*, 97; and above, p. xcvii–xcviii.

the newspapers saying she had burst into tears at the end of her speech. Poor darling! for once the papers showed more sense of Romance and imagination than Violet.)...

These are terrible [casualty] figures.[1] Will 1916 go on just the same? Shall I hear feet marching from 6 am, tramping, tramping, then see masses of men with little bags in their hands go off from the recruiting tents in the Horse Guards 2 and 2, 2 and 2, preceded by various bands (fifes drums and pipes.). Will I see every morning in the papers 'Killed— Persian Gulf, undated. Killed—Mediterranean. Died of wounds. Died, previously reported missing. Overseas—died, died, missing, etc.' How long, O Lord?

Thursday 9 December 1915

My new Diary opens at a <u>very</u> sad and anxious time.... We dined with Sir Ernest Cassel. I got to bed, after talking to Henry, at 1.30 last night (4½ hours sleep is ridiculous!) In spite of his wonderful courage and fine war temperament, I can see, and indeed I <u>know</u>, Henry is very anxious. He said to me before dinner:

H. I've sent K. and Grey to France. Oddly enough Grey made no demur. His pessimism and nerves are dreadful! <u>I think he is off his head</u>. It's a curious thing, but Grey has developed lately all the defects I thought he could <u>never</u> have! I hardly value his judgement at all now! he is so unstrung and self-enfolded.
M. I suppose the French are impossible—this I've always foreseen.
H. French politics and politicians are rotten to the core! Their expedition to Salonika was purely political: none of our men believed in it (but Carson!).[2] Nothing would have induced me to land such a big force,

---

[1] On 28 Oct. 1915 in a written answer Asquith gave total casualties (killed, wounded, and missing) in all fields of operations as 493,294. Of these 365,046 were 'Western Area' and of these 67,460 or 18.5 per cent were killed; *Parl. Deb.*, 75.367. For the totals by 9 Jan. 1916 see *Parl. Deb.*, 79.1438.

[2] Among the reasons for Sir Edward Carson's resignation from the government, announced 19 Oct. 1915, was his belief that the Salonika campaign should be prosecuted

had it not been for Joffre coming over, and blackmailing us by saying he would have to give up his command and retire if we didn't back the French force;...now that 150,000 Servian soldiers are out of Servia, and the Bulgarians [have] joined the enemy, God knows how many...may attack us any hour! Briand[1] still wants to stick on. The whole cabinet with exception of Bonar Law and Ll.G. looks on this as insanity....[2]

On 5th or 6th Dec 1915 Henry showed me [a] letter...from Sir John French....No one but a very loyal man like my husband could have got rid of Sir John without wounding him to the quick.[3]

When K. went to Gallipoli, Athens, Italy etc., Henry took the War Office. Henry made this great change and many others. In spite of *The Times* and all the croakers (who know nothing, and have never understood that we are fighting this war with allies) my husband is a man of quick decisions—a man absolutely fearless and temperate, who has never made an enemy in his life, and whose brain works with amazing smoothness and rapidity. What I think even more wonderful is his freedom from irritation and moods, and his amazing poise. If he were to die tomorrow, I can't imagine—and no one that I know can tell me—who would take his place. Henry was born for this war, and if I could destroy Robinson, Northcliffe and Co, Kitchener and Ll.G., we should not have a hitch, but win through honourably and nobly.

---

more vigorously, as a demonstration of good faith to the Serbs; Allied forces landed there on 5 Oct. in the hope of making a decisive intervention in the Balkans, but remained largely inactive until the last weeks of the war; the French government and high command backed the campaign as a way of utilizing the controversial General Maurice Sarrail, who was relieved of his command on the Western Front by Joffre.

[1] Aristide Briand (1862–1932), French premier eleven times between 1909 and 1929, notably 1909–11, 1913, 1915–17; from Oct. 1915 he had conducted French foreign affairs.

[2] Asquith was wholly justified in objecting to keeping a British force at Salonika, which the Germans called 'the greatest Allied internment camp'; for the inter-Allied disputes about the base see Cassar, *Kitchener*, 408–11; Cruttwell, *Great War*, 232–5; Moorehead, *Gallipoli*, 322–4.

[3] French had been obliged, by Asquith, to resign his command of the BEF in favour of Sir Douglas Haig.* In this letter, written 4 Dec. 1915, which reached Asquith 6 Dec., French thanked the premier for 'kindness and consideration'. See Holmes, *French*, 312.

Sunday 5 December 1915

Violet & Bongie returned for one night en route to La Mortola Italy.[1] Eliz. Clemmy Goonie & I had gone to St Paul's Cathedral for the communion service—E. & I took the communion—Goonie is a R. Catholic & Clemmy didn't go up. I am so sad for Clemmy. How I should have hated to lose everything as she has done. Position, occupation, money & husband. (Winston is at the front in the Grenadiers now & very likely to be killed. Even if he lives his future will never be a great Political one.) …

Wednesday 15 December 1915

Bonar Law dined with us at home (Aga Khan[2] took me in, and B.L. sat on my other side)—as usual, very deprecating, and head glued on one side, pained puckers in his forehead. He gazed obliquely down at his waistcoat. I praised his excellent speech on plural voting.[3] (I can't imagine anyone thinking it right that faggot votes[4] should still exist: one vote, one value, is the right thing. He offered the stupid Tory party this, but they refused.)

He said Carson, now that he had left the Gov., had a very difficult part to play.

B.L. I don't think he means to be disloyal.

M. (cheerfully) Don't you?

B.L. Carson could at this moment break the Gov. if he chose.

[1] Their honeymoon destination.

[2] The Aga Khan (1877–1957), religious leader; on the outbreak of war he had exercised influence with his Muslim followers in support of the Allied cause.

[3] *Parl. Deb.*, 14 Dec. 1915, 75.1967–73. In his speech Bonar Law had reassured his own party, and given a warning to the Prime Minister's, that he would resign from the government if a Unionist opposition to it emerged, i.e. it failed to command the general confidence of the House. The one-clause bill to abolish plural voting was regarded by Unionists as a partisan measure, and they opposed it accordingly; it had been passed twice by the Commons before the war started and, if passed once more, would become law under the terms of the Parliament Act: see Pugh, *Electoral Reform*, 59–60.

[4] 'Plural voting' referred, not to the creation of a 'faggot' vote, whereby a propertied voter conferred a voting qualification on a dependant, but to the system under which the said voter was himself entitled to cast more than one vote; the Unionist advantage from plural voting was smaller, outside the university seats, than it was then thought to be: see N. Blewett, 'The Franchise of the United Kingdom, 1885–1918', *Past and Present*, 32 (1965), 50.

M. Nonsense! You overrate Carson's powers very much. He is not a statesman at all—[a] crude sentimentalist, so unversed in affairs that he thinks swift decisions are the only merits in conducting war....

B.L. That's true: but in times of war you don't want statesmen so much.[1]

M. I suppose you believe in the journalists' heroes—'dictators' or 'business men'. I was brought up with Glasgow business men, like you, and I can truly say I doubt if any of them would be of much use in tangles like the Balkans, or any other war Problem.[2]

B.L. You are in good company, Mrs Asquith, in despising business men! the majority of the cabinet entirely agree with you.

M. I don't despise business men. We have got several of the best in our cabinet—McKenna, Runciman, Herbert Samuel and others. Don't forget that we have been pretty well let in by 'business men' in this war.

B.L. I could bring you one dozen men now from Glasgow who could run the Gov. better than any of us! and if we were all drowned tomorrow, another lot would take our place, and do just as well.

M. That is one of the business men's illusions. (Rosebery wrote a rotten letter to *The Times* advocating 'more business men', to please Northcliffe, I presume, or from his natural want of insight.) You could never get a better man than McKenna.

B.L. Within his limits (I can see there is no love lost here.) Yes.

M. I don't believe you are a wonderful business man! A Glasgow man I met in the train spoke highly to me of your gift of speaking, and said 'Bonar Law is a very straight man, but we don't consider he is a very good man of business.' (This made him smile.)

---

[1] For Munro-Ferguson's agreement with Bonar (and Rosebery) on this see his letter to Rosebery, 25 Feb. 1916: Rosebery Papers, NLS, 10020 fo. 132.

[2] Bonar saw the premium put by war conditions on rapid decision-making: Margot realized that the most important wartime problems would be extremely complex. Neither seems to have realized the need for a war government which would combine a few planners with a larger body of executives.

B.L. I was a moderately good man of business—perhaps rather more: but my point is that politicians are bound to balance and compromise from the party habit and party standpoint. This is all right in peace, but not good in war times. It's a pity our great war minister should have all the faults of the politicians and none of the directness of the soldier.

Wednesday 29 December 1915

I am writing in bed in 10 Downing St. I felt in my bones yesterday at Easton Grey that Henry was in trouble. I knew when he left me and Puffin (27th, Monday) in bed that early morning that he was worried. I could not stay on in the country.... Walkom (head messenger in 10 Downing St.) told me Henry was alone in cabinet room. I went in and kissed him. He was writing. H. 'Well! this is a surprise: you were to have come Thursday.' M. 'Well! I felt anxious. I knew your colleagues were resigning (which is quite true, but not unexpected). How did the cabinet go off?' H. 'Oh! things are very rocky, very very rocky'.

I saw at a glance that he was busy, and left him, and went into Nash's room and told him to come up and have tea with me. Nash was much distressed. He told me McKenna and Runciman had resigned at 2.15. He thought H. had told me. Montagu came in and joined us, and Nash left me. Montagu told me everything, and stayed an hour. He said he and Rufus had lunched with Henry, and talked over the situation: this being that Runciman, Simon and McK were going, because H., having given a pledge that unmarried men would have to fight first, [and] finding that, in spite of Ld Derby's amazing recruiting success, 250,000 young men had not come forward (how do they know?), is going to bring in a sort of skeleton compulsion, backed by the Labour man in the cabinet (Henderson) and the whole cabinet.

These 3 men—Simon, McK and Runciman—are invaluable to Henry, but not to my mind irreplaceable. Montagu said he was just going to send for Runciman and McKenna after lunch, when they arrived together, and placed their resignations before Henry.[1] (This was 2.30, as I arrived at Badminton Station—at the very time I was <u>sure</u> Henry was in difficulties.) Their reasons for going are, as far as I can gather, constantly changing. They don't want H. to break his pledge to bring unmarried men in first, but they object to the whole thing, because they say we will be taking away too many men, and trying to have too big an army for the nation's needs, etc.

They share Henry's loathing of Conscription, but it is <u>obvious</u> to me that this scheme of Henry's will <u>kill</u> Conscription, and that if he did <u>not</u> bring it in, and we left the shirkers (which are put at 500,000 by some people in the country), real Conscription of a drastic kind would be forced on us: in which case Henry would resign. I know really what is [at] the bottom of all this: it is all inspired by Hate for Ll.G. The latter is a bona fide Conscriptionist. He has also played monkey tricks, and <u>low</u> ones, ever since the coalition; and he is hated and distrusted by all our men for his amazing disloyalty to Henry. It is just a repetition of what has happened before, and will happen again as long as Ll.G. is in the Gov. with Henry.

If K., Ll.G., and Northcliffe, Robinson and Co. (*The Times* newspaper) were to die today, we could win this war with perfect smoothness. These have been our <u>curse</u> from the first. (Winston had no party behind him, and his boyishness aroused a certain sympathy. His resignation hardly made a ripple in our national life: but these resignations will weaken Henry's position very much. They will make ignorant people say H. is a Torified conscriptionist leading a Torified cabinet.) Montagu went on to tell me he had argued for 2 hours with McK., and shown him how fatal it was to desert his chief, his <u>intimate friend</u>, and throw this country into the arms of Germany.

In losing McK. and Runciman and Simon, H. loses his 3 ablest and above all straightest men: Grey is useless (when I say useless, I mean for

---

[1] Neither Walter Runciman nor Reginald McKena infact resigned, but Sir John Simon did: see below, p. 228 n. 1.

the moment), Crewe an angel, but very slow and without initiative of any kind (*au fond* conventional and white-blooded), and Ll.G. is a <u>hound</u>—his 'too late' speech an abomination...for wh. he will never be forgiven.[1] K. was most amusing on this speech.

[K.] I would like to have told Lloyd George to his face that he was a liar.

M. That would have come well from you!

K. (not quite twigging) I told the Prime Minister I should go to the H. of Lords, and say it in a speech: but he said that would be—then he used a very good word. (Thinking hard while munching his mince) <u>What</u> was the word? Gracious! I forget.

M. (suggestingly) Was it 'premature' or 'fatal'?

K. No—much better than that—it was—by Jove! '<u>unedifying</u>'—<u>that's</u> the word.

M. (much relieved at K.'s mental strain being over-past) It was a horrid disloyal speech of Ll.G.'s—an attack upon the Gov. of which he has been a conspicuous member all the time.

K. Ll.G. is a little beast....

Montagu: 'I was rude to McKenna, and argued till I was black, that to throw the PM into the arms of his enemies (Ll.G. and the Tory Party) was a gross breach of loyalty and love, etc. It was all no good, and he went to Munstead after, and only comes back to the Treasury tomorrow morning.'...Montagu went away then, and I wrote a letter to Pamela: I know Pamela's vanity has been a good deal flattered by Henry's letters and his affection for her.

I went downstairs to see how H. was getting on, and sat in Mr Nash's room. At the same time Henry had gone to look for me—to miss a moment of him was dreadful, as I had not had one real word with him

---

[1] In a long-promised Commons statement on the supply of the army, Lloyd George exposed not only the shortcomings of the War Office, but also of workers who failed to back up the men in the trenches, and thus invited the inscription 'Too Late' 'upon the portals of their workshops': *Parl. Deb.*, 87.121, 20 Dec. 1915. *The Times* was eloquent in its praise of Ll.G., and Frances Stevenson, who witnessed the speech, wrote that it had 'created a sensation....The whole House was thrilled at the ending': *The Times*, 21 Dec. 1915, 11b; *Stevenson Diary*, 87.

since I had arrived from E[aston] Grey. He found me talking to Nash, and took me into the cabinet room. He showed me an excellent cutting in *Westminster Gazette....* We roared with laughter at it, and walked up and down arm in arm.

This is intensely characteristic of Henry's sweetness and <u>sense of proportion</u>. There he was! worried to the last degree, having had an endless cabinet in the morning, 2 resignations in afternoon and a third (Sir J. Simon's) pending[1]...a war council at 3 lasting 2 hours, and people ever since. He takes up the *Westminster*, waiting for Simon's arrival, and is quite amused and unrattled. <u>Nothing rattles Henry</u>. Nothing changes the sweetness and perfection of his nature. He never hardens up, or scratches, or even retaliates in an ugly way. God! except Lucy and Viola,[2] I've never seen any man or woman who didn't get home on me,[3] or try to <u>at once</u>, if things went wrong.

What is the bedrock of all this? It is that Henry has <u>no vanity</u> and no <u>self-centredness</u>. <u>He is absolutely detached</u>, patient, full of warmth, and personal interest (children, games, anecdotes, the meaning of words, the history of men and their beginnings, scenery, monuments, heraldry, <u>Everything intellectual</u>, racing—he knows the name and date of every Derby winner, and the breeding—and the Stage, every play, actor and author!)

We read this cutting over each other's shoulders, and he kissed me. I said 'Darling, I've heard <u>all</u> from Montagu and Nash. I am confident you will win through! What an amazing lot you have got to work with!!' H. 'Curious people! Their reason for resigning is so absurd—it is always changing. They don't want me to break my Derby pledge, and don't object to my skeleton scheme. Hate of K. and Ll.G. is, of course, at the bottom of all this. Runciman and McK. hate these men.'...

---

[1] Simon, who had threatened resignation at the outbreak of war, resigned in Jan. 1916 over the introduction of conscription, a decision he later regretted: see above, p. cxxvi.

[2] Viola Parsons (1884–1938), daughter of Sir Herbert Beerbohm and Lady (Maud) Tree, married 1912 Alan Parsons. Attempted opera career without success. A friend of H. H. Asquith over many years, in early days one of the 'little harem' (*Asquith–Stanley*, 1).

[3] Margot means 'make things difficult for me'.

H. and I talked for some time, it was 7.15 pm. I left him as I heard Sir J. Simon was coming....I shut the cabinet door and went into the ante-room: no one there. I looked at the clock and the fire, the half-open door of the little telephone room, the row of pegs round walls where the Ministers hang their coats before going to the cabinet, the photograph of the colonial Premiers at last conference, with H. in the centre of group, the round table on which I often see soldiers' caps—K.'s, Robertson's, Joffre's, etc. etc.—and I wondered when we should leave this house?

If the Gov. is going to break—? Where H., Puff, Eliz. and I would live—Ovington Square[1] on £5000 a year?? Poorer than Violet! and in an uglier house. (Violet has not got £5000 a year—I should say nearly £3000—but she has a small, charming house, 4 servants and 2 selves. I've never had less than 16 servants, sometimes more, and my secretary Miss Way,[2] and will always have masses of people depending on me, and have a bigger course to run, or later on to crawl, than V. will ever have.)...

Whilst I was musing over all this, dear Davies[3] came out, and I told him to watch for Sir John Simon, as I wished to speak to him in corridor before he went into the cabinet room (to see Henry). The front door bell rang at that moment, and I walked down towards Simon. I felt burning in my heart.

M.   Well, Sir John! (Looking intently at his rather smug, good-looking, elderly little face.) Are you a happy man?

Sir J. (with rather a forced smile) None of us can be very happy in times like these.

M.   (bursting out) Sir John! What sort of a man are you? You are going to desert a man to whom you owe your soul—your everything. Where is love, gratitude or patriotism! If you know a better man to get us through this terrible war, forget that I am H.'s wife and tell me who he is. You may be quite sure neither Henry or I would

---

[1] In Kensington between Sloane Street and Brompton Road.
[2] The Asquiths' personal secretary at 10 Downing Street.
[3] David Davies (1889–1964), member of the Downing Street secretariat.

show smallness over a new choice. Who is he? where is he? and if you don't know, then stick to him.

Sir JS   (white and moved) It's not fair of you to say this to me.

M.   (hotly) It may not be fair, but it is true: you owe him everything.

By this time we had got to the red baize door of the cabinet, and he went in. I went in to Nash's room, and told him and Davies while I was still <u>hot</u> with rage, but Davies, who is one of God's own, and who has shown me <u>great</u> sympathy in many miseries, said 'I think you were unfair'.

M.   Da, dear! Simon <u>hasn't</u> got a fine character: he never risks anything.

Da.   Remember he too is giving up a great deal.

M.   You are right. I was horrid to say it, but Simon always comes down on the winning side.

Da.   (getting red and looking sensitive) Of course, Margot, you know him and I don't: but I should say it was hard on him.

M.   <u>You are right</u>. I will tell him I am sorry.

The moment I had said this Simon came into the room, looking for Henry. I jumped up and took him by the arm. I led him out of Nash's room, and, holding him by both arms, told him I was sorry.

Sir JS   You don't know how much I feel all this. Do you think <u>I</u> want to break the Gov., or turn the PM out?

M.   No, but it will amount to this when you 3 resign.

Sir JS   (rather wildly) Do you know what all this has been caused by?— *The Times*, that cursed paper.

M.   You are flattering it!…

Simon wrung my hand and disappeared into the cabinet room, wh. H. had gone into by another door. I went upstairs, and wrote to Runciman. Nash had put himself on to the telephone at my request to find out if R. was in London. I wanted much to see him, and beg him to stay. R. answered himself, and Nash didn't like to say to him 'Come and see <u>Mrs</u> Asquith.' Runciman asked Nash to go and see <u>him</u>. Montagu and I sat in

Henry's big sitting room near the writing table, with one lamp lit and one big picture lighted. I felt anxious and exhausted, and wondered if Sir J. Simon had gone forever (Simon was with H. in cabinet room.) I was much struck with Montagu's cleverness and devotion. He has one principle upon which he goes, in spite of the cleverest and best of reasons for all his actions: 'Stick to the Prime Minister'.

It was past 8 I went into the bathroom thro' Henry's dressing room, and he came into his room at the same moment (We knew each other's ways so intimately that if I had no clock or watch we should meet almost to the moment, in his only spare minutes.) M. 'Well, how did you find Simon?' H. Oh, very much what you would expect. He will go—in fact, he has gone. I think he was a little moved.'

I felt I ought to tell Henry about my interview in the ante-room outside the cabinet room, but I could see he was tired, and he had to dress, and have his bath: it was 8.15. I just said that I knew poor Simon was <u>deeply</u> moved, that I had seen and talked to him. I dined in bed, and finished my letter to Runciman, but I only sent it off next morning at 8 (29th Dec 1915). I wrote this diary, then fell asleep, depressed and tired, but cheered a little *au fond* by Henry's amazing sweetness.

At 12.30 Henry came in from his dinner. He shut my bedroom door with his usual little bang, which I know so well, and walked up and down, quite happy. He had enjoyed wonderful bridge: he and Geoffrey Howard (a very bad player) against Montagu and Ed. Grey. They had 'smashed up' Grey and Montagu—'wonderful hands! very big declarations—5 hearts—only lost one trick—I made 5 diamonds, was doubled and made them!'

I could see he was happy as a boy for the moment, though his face looked tired. I was sorry it was so late, and wished <u>for once</u> he would go to bed, and not read, as he always does every night for 2 hours. I longed to hear more, but said

[M.]   Darling, you should rest your head. You've had a bad day, and will
        have several more: just fly off to your bed.

H. (still walking up and down) Yes, I'll go. To show you what a fellow Grey is: he motored me back here, and on the short way he said 'I must reconsider my position now, unless you put Haldane into one of the vacant cabinet places vacated by Simon, Runciman and McK.' Fancy adding to one's burdens just now! God! I've never seen such selfishness, vanity, egotism and folly as I am surrounded by. Here is Grey—my oldest, most devoted friend, eaten up with vanity: a changed man, hysterical, and I might almost add unfit for his work.

M. It's <u>physical</u>, dearest. Don't fret, he will never go.

H. Who can tell?

He kissed me tenderly, and left me, sleepless and wondering. I slept 4 hours, and then wrote this diary, 5.30 a.m.

Rufus came into the ante-room to my joy, and asked me to speak to him. He looked grave.

Rufus The situation is very grave. I've done my best, and by no means give up. The PM wanted me to go to Munstead and see McKenna last night, but I thought McKenna had better think over it all, and that I was better here. Runciman is breakfasting with Grey this morning.

M. Is he? Well, I hope Grey will use his influence. (I could see in a moment that Rufus either knew or feared the worst about Grey.)

R. We must deal <u>very</u> carefully with Grey. I am very anxious about him: any mishandling now would be fatal.

I had a horrible back thought that Grey had meant what he said to Henry last night. My heart rattled in my boots. Rufus left me, full of sympathy and sweetness. He has a fine nature. I went down to Nash. I love Nash: he has more authority than Bongie, and is not so dilatory. I can get things done in one moment by Nash or Davies, and it's easier in every way for me, as they both love me (so does Bongie, but not in the same way; of course he doesn't think I understand Violet and he is right, I don't).

Raymond (back from France, very well and handsome) Katharine, Buckmaster, Rufus and Montagu lunched. Raymond told us a lot about the trenches and effect on one of the first fire etc. He told it well. I wish he would write just a verbatim account of his experiences in [the] trenches,— like this diary is, an ordinary, indiscreet relation of facts.[1]

I took Nash up to tea with me, and asked him the news. He thought H. had told me that Grey had resigned (just before lunch). I was much shocked at such childish want of patriotism and vision. Poor Mr Nash was sorry he had told me. He is the most discreet man in the world. Mr Nash. 'Let the PM think he has told you himself, Mrs Asquith.'

M. (soothingly) 'My dear friend, do you think H. would mind? Why, it saves poor Henry's time, as he always has told me every trifle and shown me every letter from Kings or colleagues, from the first day he was PM.'[2]

I confess I was done. This was the last straw, Grey going!!! The effect on Germany would be terrible!—worth a new army, and all the food that they were short of, or supposed to be! I really didn't see how Henry could carry on. He wd. have to resign, and what then? a Gen. Election? My blood boiled at Grey's conduct. This splendid Ed. Grey, whom I have really loved, doing this abominable thing....

Nash   I was in the room talking to the PM when Grey's letter arrived.[3] I was really sorry for him. He was distressed beyond words, and said it was a letter you would not treat a dog to! I told him I was

[1] Margot probably did not know that Raymond wrote regularly like that to Katharine (see Jolliffe, *Raymond Asquith*, from 205). For Lady Diana Cooper's reaction when these letters were published see *The Times*, 14 July 1980.

[2] No premier could have told anyone as indiscreet as Margot 'every trifle' *at the time of the event.*

[3] Grey wrote to inform Asquith of his intention to resign (this was not carried through). Asquith was 'stunned and outraged' at the decision, and wrote in reply that Grey's resignation 'on whatever ostensible ground would be interpreted universally as a German triumph': see Cassar, *Asquith, War*, 161. As a wartime Foreign Secretary Grey was ineffectual and 'out of place, though it was still politically expedient that he should remain in office': Keith Robbins, *ODNB*, 'Grey, Edward, Viscount Grey of Fallodon'.

sure, as indeed I am, that it is entirely nerves with Grey. I hope, Mrs Asquith, you won't let the PM be hurt by this, for if he is, it will be very bad. I'm glad to say he was really angry, and wrote Grey a very stiff note. This is a good sign.

M. I love seeing Henry angry much better in a crisis than too calm. This, I'm quite sure, will put the fear of Hell into McK., and will make him think twice before he will resign.

It's a complete smash up & practically gives Germany for the moment the war. We were both horribly distressed & just sipped our tea. Nash was sympathetic to the last degree & could hardly express his sorrow for H. & myself. His onyx eyes & gentle voice pleased me. I felt miles away as if I had heard of someone's death. I had been awake since 5.30 A.M. that morning & was exhausted. Montagu came into the room & told me H. had shown him Grey's letter & that there & then he (Montagu) had sat down & written Grey a snorter asking him if he really intended to delight all our enemies! Was this how he wanted to finish his Foreign Office career—was he sure that the newspapers abusing him (as they always did when things went wrong) over the Balkan situation had not affected him. Had he no loyalty or patriotism. Was he insane? etc. etc. Montagu differed from me—he was convinced it would make McK. & Runciman all the more determined to go—I said I betted it would have the opposite effect[1]—it would steady them & perhaps for a change instead of thinking of themselves & their convictions they would think of the war.

Brother Jack came in to see me before dinner.

Jack 'Well how do things go? K. has just said to me there will be no resignations'. (This showed me how out of things K. always is.)

(H. told me that our new chief of the staff at WO Robertson had not been there a week before he had come into violent collision with K.) H.:

---

[1] Margot was correct: McKenna was then Chancellor, and Runciman President of the Board of Trade, and they opposed conscription on the grounds that by denuding British industry of manpower it would cause economic collapse, and possibly cost Britain the war. They nevertheless remained in the government.

'I can't help smiling when I see all these remarkable men, who think they could do such <u>wonders</u> if they only were given their chance, in any office or situation, and at the very first difficulty all falling foul of each other.' I said I could not help wishing <u>all</u> our critics could have one week of cabinets, war councils, W. Office, Admiralty, Munitions, etc., just to let them have <u>some</u> idea of the difficulties! I remembered what the cabinets were like when Henry was ill—'Chaos', as both Bonar Law and one of the others told me.

Henry showed me Grey's letter.

H. Read this, and tell me what you think of it. In all my career, I never have had such a letter—cold, selfish, stupid!

M. Poor fellow, the sad part of it is that a man who can write and do such hysterical things is quite unfit to remain where he is, and should have proper rest and then come back.

H. Imagine the overwhelming joy of the Germans if Grey left me. The whole of Europe would feel it, in every embassy, friendly and otherwise.

M. <u>You mustn't</u> feel it, darling.

H. Oh! I don't. I know it's purely physical. McKenna was really upset. It may make a great difference to both his attitude and Runciman's. They are a trying lot! I must say....

Thursday 30 December 1915

Henry saw the King,[1] and told him about Grey. H. 'You should have heard the King on Grey!! He was furious, and he ended a delightful talk to me by saying "I'll back you for all I'm worth," and took my hand.'...Henry loves the King. He says he has been admirable throughout the war—unfrightened, sensible, keen to do all he possibly can, and, on the whole, except for his early prejudice against French in favour of K.—a good deal

---

[1] The King assured Asquith that 'he would stand by him and support him, even if all his colleagues were to leave': Nicolson, *George V*, 271.

changed now—very impartial (for a King to be impartial is very rare, as Kings don't hear every side to a question, but only what they are told.)

I dined with Venetia. A sort of clever young modern Tussaud-looking young man called Duff Cooper[1]—hardly a real human being—and I played bridge against Montagu and Masterton Smith. Venetia sat and did needle work. I won £6....

Henry dined with Seymour Fortescue[2] and came back late, 12.30. He and I talked for some little time. He started quite out of the blue when he was praising Seymour by saying, in a sort of sum-up speech 'I consider 3 men have covered themselves with glory this last week in this crisis, particularly Montagu and Rufus.' M. 'The other?' H. 'Little Hankey. Montagu's devotion I shall never forget. Rufus is a perfect angel—loyal, discreet and skilful. Montagu has shown amazing cleverness and courage.'

H. was really moved, and I need hardly say I was enchanted. I above all things love hearing Praise: it revives me like a tonic, specially when it is not only an expression of Love, but coupled with Henry's insight and gratitude. I went and ordered 3 little green cigarette cases, and wrote inside each

'To E Montagu	A real friend
To Rufus	from
To Mr Hankey	Margot Asquith in memory of the last week of 1915'[3]

I wrote to dear Col. Hankey and told him how devoted H. and I were to him....

[1] Alfred Duff Cooper (1890–1954), GCMG, 1948; cr. Viscount Norwich 1952; Foreign Office 1913; Grenadier Guards 1917–18. He married, 1919, Lady Diana Manners.

[2] Sir Seymour Fortescue (1856–1942), KCVO 1910; sergeant at arms of House of Lords, 1910–36.

[3] Margot sent these gifts on 4 Jan. On a later page of the MS Diary, she refers to them again, adding the detail that the inscription was 'printed in a facsimile of my handwriting'—but giving a different version of it ('in memory of the first week of the year 1916'). Hankey wrote in Supreme Command (pub. 1961) that he still had the cigarette case.

H. said to me in my bedroom at midnight, walking up and down: 'This week has been Hellish. I've seen the selfishness and self-centredness of devoted colleagues, and immense stupidity.'...

Tuesday 4 January 1916

I am amused that, now the Viceroyalty of India will be free in March, both Montagu and Jack Islington* are pressing for it personally. People are very wonderful! Vanity governs the world! Montagu is a Jew, which, I am told, makes his appointment impossible. Otherwise he is far the cleverest and most suitable. Islington is not a clever man at all. The poor Aga Khan is in the greatest anguish in case we send 'a Conservative swell—a sort of Lansdowne, charming but quite out of touch with modern India. What a pity Mr Harcourt won't take it.' (H. offered it to Loulou twice, but he doesn't care for grandeur, and loves England.)...

Elizabeth, H. and I went to H. of Commons, and heard H.'s fine dignified speech, and Sir J. Simon's cruel, egotistical oration, which filled my heart with disgust.[1] On Friday 7th Ld Bob Cecil, and G. Curzon, Eric, Kakoo,[2] Granby, Eliz. and I lunched here; and Henry said, when G. Curzon (at lunch) asked what had gone wrong with Simon and talked of his speech—H. 'I felt as if my son had struck me in the face in public.'

It didn't seem bad to listen to though it was far too long & blocks of it so niggly petty & legal to make me laugh. (I could hardly imagine a clever man making such teeny points.) Eliz. sat close to me & Violet next in the Speaker's gallery which was crowded.

After Simon had finished his speech violently opposing the Compulsory Bill I ran down to the secretaries' room. I found Masterton pink &

---

[1] Simon, whose resignation had been formally announced on 4 Jan., followed the Prime Minister in the debate on the Military Service Bill in the Commons the next day (Margot's entry dating is mistaken): Simon spoke at great length, but to little effect, and while he generously acknowledged his personal debt to the Prime Minister, he did not refrain from a forensic examination of the latter's 2 Nov. 1915 speech on conscription, in an attempt to justify his resignation.

[2] Kathleen (Kakoo) Tennant (1894–1989), Margot's niece, was to marry the Marquess of Granby (1886–1940) on 27 Jan. 1916; he succeeded as the 9th Duke of Rutland in 1925.

furious over Simon's speech & our little Davies full of admiration. Violet & Masterton argued together—Masterton 'A vile, low, mean dangerous speech!' Violet 'How can you say such a thing! It was brilliant. I'm sure he feels this deeply & is quite a disinterested person.' Davies backed this opinion—I felt exactly the opposite & said at once it was a cruel speech & might do a lot of harm—on reflection I'm not sure it won't do Simon more harm than Henry but there is no doubt in my mind that Simon is British & amazingly without imagination or knowledge of the world. He had better have stuck to the bar.... Neither Simon, McKenna, or Runciman have sons in the war & their minds are a little stunted by their Departments. That touch of provincialism permanent-officialism will prevent any one leading the Liberal party of this I'm convinced (I wonder if this diary is ever read in years to come whether I shall be right or whether McKenna or Simon will lead our party).[1]

If Henry got ill tomorrow I don't see on whose shoulders his mantle would fall. The one man on whom it might have fallen is finishing himself by his own temper, folly and self-indulgence—Lloyd George. I prophesy that at the end of this war Ll.G. will be a finished man. His last oratorical scream of abusing slackers to please soldiers has put all Labour against him,[2] and I should guess from what I hear that if we could look into his munitions we should find extravagance and chaos on unheard-of scale.

Henry left the front bench and I joined him in his room. The PM's room in [the] House is a very nice one, far the best and quite airy, though no windows appear to be open. Henry and I walked up and down alone together. Henry thought Simon's speech long and wicked....

February 1916

This promises to be the most momentous session of Henry's administration. It opens with everyone in the cabinet at peace. I don't think Ll.G.

[1] Simon became deputy leader after the war, but never leader.
[2] Lloyd George had been much interrupted when speaking in St Andrew's Hall, Glasgow, on Christmas Day, 1915: Grigg, Lloyd George, 1912–1916, 297–300.

or K. will ever be trusted or liked, nor that McKenna will get over his feeling against Ll.G., and a certain longing to have resigned, which may lead him to make trouble again: but his love of his own dislikes has curiously enough reconciled him to Ll.G. for the <u>moment</u>! They have joined forces in their mutual hatred of Kitchener....

Monday 6 March 1916

We dined in Cromwell Road, where Winston, Clemmie and their 3 children[1] share Goonie Churchill's nice house.[2] Winston took Juliet Duff[3] in, and Birrell took me. I sat between Birrell and Winston. Knowing that Winston was going to speak on the Navy estimates the next day, after talking a little about the war and trenches, I said I was sorry he was speaking: at which he said eagerly, without pomposity or touchiness, that it was absolutely necessary; then, in the impressive note I knew so well, with the glare in the eye, 'I have a good deal to say of grave importance about the navy.'[4]

I felt alarmed, and said 'Winston, you made a very fine exit. Even those who dislike you said you did the manly thing—you gave up money and position, and took your place with your fellows, risking your life for your country: don't spoil it all.' I need hardly say he swept this aside, and gave a circular look, to see if he could arrest the attention of some fellow guests—Eddy Marsh, Montagu, young Cripps, Lavery[5]—but no, they were all two-a-twoing.

---

[1] The three Churchill children referred to are Diana (1909–63), Randolph (1911–68) and Sarah (1914–82).

[2] This was 41 Cromwell Road, London.

[3] Lady (Gladys Mary) Juliet Lowther (1881–1965), daughter of 4th Earl of Lonsdale; m. 1903 Sir Charles Michael Duff, 2nd Bt., who was killed in action in 1914.

[4] In a speech in the debate on 'Supply (Navy Estimates)', 7 Mar. 1916, 'Colonel Churchill' voiced his concerns about a lack of driving power in the Admiralty; this resonated with the House, but his accompanying call for the reinstatement as First Sea Lord of Admiral 'Jacky' Fisher caused amazement, given the circumstances surrounding Fisher's abrupt resignation in May of the previous year, and the proposal transformed 'one of the most serious and skilful speeches [Churchill] had ever made into an object of derision' (Gilbert, *Winston S. Churchill*, iii. 722). It also gave Balfour, the implied target of Churchill's criticism, grounds for a scathing reply, which was delivered in the Commons the next day: *Parl. Deb.*, 80.1420–30; 1563–75.

[5] Frederick William Cripps (1873–1959), Kt. 1933; John Lavery (1856–1941), Kt. 1918, portrait painter.

Later. He said would I think a proper opposition a good or bad thing in H. of Commons just now.

M. Oh! I don't think it matters much but I see no elements to make a good opposition—you could get rotters of insignificant judgement—Dalziel…Carson etc. but nothing of any weight.

W. What about Simon—I'm told though his group is small it's quite powerful.

M. You at any rate Winston would never be interested in the Simon group.

W. Oh! I don't know (musingly, as if thinking out loud) Simon might become a very important person.…

M. I doubt it, he isn't an 'Homme du monde'—he's a moderate judge of character dusty & what the French call 'personel' always fatal unless you are a great genius.

Winston who saw himself in the word personel, but still more so in my qualification, was still groping when I said

[M.] Now Winston! Ages ago when I was praising Simon you said he would never really be a political success—you didn't like him.

W. (alertly) By Jove & wasn't I right.

This small bit of conversation convinced me Winston was dreaming of an amazing opposition which he was to lead.

I am glad to say H. spoke to him about his speech for as I came down stairs from winning £2 at bridge…I found H. in his fur coat & top hat talking to Winston in the small boudoir—he had been talking to him for nearly 20 mins. We gave Montagu & Venetia a lift home so H. & I didn't have our accustomed divine talks nevertheless H. when asked by Montagu what Winston was going to say the next day said 'As far as I can see he is going to make a most foolish & pernicious speech—I've done my best—when he told me he proposed to give Fisher a leg-up (this was not H's expression but to this effect) I said he would make himself a laughing stock—the whole world would think it grotesque. I really think he's mad!'

M. I thought Winston nicer & in some ways humbler than he was before he went to war but he is frightfully restless & bored by the trenches.

Venetia I quite agree but I thought he was out of spirits didn't you.

H. No I didn't think so, he was as he always is—excited & self-centred.

Tuesday 7 March 1916

I made Oc go to H. of Commons to hear the great speech the thought of which I confess filled me with alarm. Jenny Churchill (Winston's mother) sat in Violet's old place, & Frances Balfour where Eliz. sometimes sits—next to me. Winston's speaking is always interesting. It is quite different to other peoples'.... Most speakers are guided by something or someone, some motive, some belief—not Winston! He has no creed or convictions & not a first rate comprehension.

People who have not much insight think he has imagination—this is just what he lacks. People who hate him think he is insincere—this is just where they are wrong—he is never a charlatan & <u>never</u> poses. He is a man or rather a boy (never grown up) possessed—possessed by the Evillest of all evil spirits—<u>Self</u>—tempted by his star which he thinks is outside himself & he & other sublime fools think is his Destiny or Career.... He <u>hears</u> what you think but he doesn't heed it. No exchange is possible with egotists except what is merely verbal...no moral truth penetrates because it doesn't appeal—no criticism of an intention changes the resolve because it doesn't apply. You may sometimes think he is standing beside you looking at the same picture—sitting beside you hearing the same music—or mourning beside you seeing the same Dead.

<u>He never is</u>.

But though he idolizes himself he doesn't Love himself particularly. He isn't touchy like the young female egotists I know, or bad-tempered, & he never sulks or gets home on one from pettiness & rancour. This is where he is loveable.

He isn't kind to himself, he is cruel—he doesn't indulge himself, on the contrary—he never spares himself—he doesn't live on his wits like Arthur Balfour does, he is <u>most</u> industrious. He is a gambler who when he has made money does not want to invest it—a burglar who when he has stolen the plate does not want to keep it. He is fond of his friends but gravitates towards a low type of friend. He was always just to his department & in a sense loyal to his subordinates. He is to my mind lacking altogether in intellect & judgement & hazarding a prophecy I should say has no sustained political future but will pop out again [in] the next crisis & make mischief all his Life. Loyalty is a mere inscription like an illuminated manuscript—something to look at admire & try & decipher—nothing more.

The first thing that struck me, listening to [Winston's speech] was its Recklessness: then, its farcical folly! It was also traitorous! To let the Germans think things were seriously wrong with our great navy! was an abominable thing to do. In old days a man would have been shot for less. The speech filled me with indignation, and all my original opinion of Winston—modified by the circumstances of yachting[1] and Henry's affection for him—returned, and now will <u>never</u> change. He is a dangerous maniac, so poor in character and judgement, so insolent and childish, that I hardly even think him a danger. Arthur Balfour was too long but I didn't agree with several…that it was scratching & over done. I think it brilliant—if over-done means length I think it <u>was</u> over-done.

Winston won't mind anything Arthur says & would meet him at dinner with a smile—what he <u>will</u> mind is having made a real Fool of himself.

The inner History of this gigantic error I will now write –

On 2nd March Winston came back on leave from the front. He didn't even know the Navy Estimates were coming on (on 7th March) [until] he dined with his mother that night. She got Garvin (the unbalanced editor

---

[1] That is, enjoying a Mediterranean cruise on the Admiralty yacht *Enchantress* at Churchill's invitation, in 1913, when he was First Lord.

of the Observer) to meet him & Sir Fred Smith[1]—Garvin being well in with the scum of the earth & Ld. Fisher found an easy prey in Winston. They told him he was the one man to save the situation etc. & poor excitable blind boy he rushed into the trap: they wired for Scott of the Manchester Guardian[2]—a Radical of the very greenest. Between Fisher—who is a Press man of the worst type—& the whole lot Winston was easily mobilized. Poor Clemmy realized the folly of it all & behaved very well.

On 7th March the night of Winston's great effort there were 20 or 30 sandwich men walking in couples carrying large printed boards 'We want Jacky back'. This innocent advertisement paid for by Fisher made us all laugh.

After the speech I hurried to Bongie's room. Poor Ed. Marsh—Winston's old secretary—now with us—I found on his way there—I squeezed his hand—he had tears in his eyes. I didn't want to hurt him & thought of Puffin & how he would have spared him—so though my nature & all my critical faculty revolted from the speech I had just heard I refrained from saying much.

E. Marsh Do you think he has done for himself?

  Margot Oh! He is young! If he goes back & fights like a hero it will all be forgotten.

Wednesday 8 March 1916

Henry had a visit from K., who told him that Winston had sent in his resignation—'asked to be relieved of his command in order to grapple with the political situation at home.' This being absolute suicide, H. told K. not

---

[1] i.e. F. E. Smith (see Biographical Notes), who, as Attorney-General in the May 1915 Coalition, had been given the traditional knighthood, 'and became known for the next three years by the unaccustomed title of Sir Frederick Smith' (John Campbell, ODNB, 'Smith, Frederick Edwin').

[2] Charles Prestwich ['C. P.'] Scott (1846–1932), renowned editor of the *Manchester Guardian*, 1872–1929; entered Parliament as a Liberal, 1895; opposed Boer War and also, initially, British intervention in the European war, Aug. 1914; opposed conscription, 1916; favoured a negotiated peace, 1917.

to answer the letter and that he (Henry) would see Winston. After listening to Arthur's castigation of Winston, and the latter's lame retort, I went back to H., who was in the cabinet room, and told him all about it. I passed Winston, walking with head down like a young bull (pale but determined)....

Henry told me he had had a pathetic talk to him. H. 'I said to Winston "I've not sent for you to scold you for your folly; I've sent for you to tell you this. Through one impulsive action, your father committed suicide.[1] I saw this myself. I was fond of him. He lost everything—money, position, power, fame, occupation; and if I can, I am going to save you from doing a precisely similar thing. You will know that nothing but affection prompts me. If I didn't care for you, I could watch with complacency the certainty of your downfall. It is because I care for you that I shall save you." Winston had tears in his eyes'.

Henry was moved when he told me this, and I could not help thinking of the difference between Ld Salisbury and his ruthless joy at having disposed once and forever of his enemy and encumbrance, Randolph, and H.'s desire to save one of the curses, not only of his cabinet, but the country. For Winston to pose as the great critic after his failure in every detail of the Dardanelles (not in its conception, but in its carrying out);[2] to leave the army when every-one is joining it and giving up all they value most in life to serve in it; for him to imagine he will even get a hearing after another speech or two like his one of

[1] Asquith refers to Lord Randolph Churchill's political suicide in Dec. 1886 when, as Chancellor of the Exchequer, he offered his resignation from Lord Salisbury's government in the confident expectation that this would be declined, and his own political influence correspondingly increased. But in thinking that he was the only possible Chancellor Churchill misread the political change that had taken place once the radical leader, Joseph Chamberlain, seceded from the Liberals under Gladstone. Once Chamberlain had become a Liberal Unionist, Lord Salisbury was no longer reliant upon the troublesome Churchill, whose resignation he accepted, appointing the former Liberal George Goschen (1831–1907) in his place. Randolph Churchill's bid for greater power had failed spectacularly: in his own words, he 'forgot Goschen'.

[2] Churchill's greatest failure lay in his 'conception' of the operation as a naval one in which the army would have no more than a subsidiary role. It should have been conceived as a combined operation from the start.

yesterday, shows chronic disability to see things as they are. . . . When Henry told me this, I looked at him with the greatest admiration, and kissed him; but I could not help thinking <u>how</u> amazing it was that he had not given any of his children this <u>wonderful</u> desire to save and protect even their Friend. No one has given more trouble to their PM than Winston and Ll.G., and Henry has <u>saved them both</u> time after time.

We dined with Sir Ernest Cassel that night & H. put Cassel on to talking to Winston. Cassel is very fond of Winston.

<u>Every string was pulled to save Winston.</u>

Just before going to bed Violet came in & said in front of me to her father:

V.   The sad part is when I saw Winston at his mother's house & was persuading him to go back to the front I felt all the time I might be urging him to his death, he might be killed at the front.

H.   Well! It would at any rate be an <u>honourable</u> death—it would be far better he should die like that than live to do what he contemplates.

Henry told me that in talking to Winston it was amazing to find <u>how</u> little he knew of what others thought of him! He told H. he had a great many ardent supporters & admirers who trusted him to which H. answered— 'You have none that count at all'.

M.   If I could have told Winston what Jellicoe said to me the night I sat next to him on the Iron Duke how shocked the poor boy would have been. Jellicoe—who hardly knew me at all—said in answer to my question of how he liked his new chief (A. Balfour) 'I would not have remained one week longer with the last one Mrs Asquith of that I can assure you.'

Henry said to me à propos of Winston's amazing vanity: 'I don't suppose at this moment Winston has a political friend in the world—nor is there a single office in the state that he could be given.

Saturday 11 March 1916

Between Henry, Eddie, Clemmie, Cassel, etc., Winston's resolve was much shaken. I sent for his friend F.E. Smith on Saturday 11th March before going to Walmer. He and I had rather an amusing talk. M. 'It's very good of you to come and see me at such an early hour (15 to 10). I want you to use all your influence, Sir Frederick, not to let Winston do for himself.' FE told me he had done all that was possible, and that H.'s advice had weighed as much as any advice could weigh with a perfectly uninfluenceable man; but that last night, in the Turkish bath (which they seem to have pretty often together!), Winston had told FE <u>definitely</u> that he would return that morning to the front, as his leave was up: but that it would only be for a few days, then he would chuck the army for ever, and resume his Parliamentary duties, etc.

M. Well Sir Frederick which will you back—my husband downstairs who is at this moment seeing Winston for the last time, or Winston?

F.E. Winston—I know him too well. You can't move him once his mind is made up.

M. I totally disagree—he has no mind to make up & I bet you H. wins the day.

F.E. told me that he had lunched with W. Clemmie & Fisher & that Clemmie had said to Fisher:

'Keep your hands off my husband you have all but ruined him once before—leave him alone now.'

F.E. Fisher was toying with a knife at lunch & Mrs Winston looked at him & said 'Yes you would perhaps like to plunge that knife into my heart! Well you may! I don't care but leave my husband alone.'

I like Clemmie for this—it showed great spirit & my heart went out to her when F.E. told me this.

F.E. never looks one in the face: he's not a 'good un', I think. He drinks, which is always ruinous to anyone.

H. told me he had won, and that Winston would stick to his regiment, and return that afternoon. I was delighted, for though I can see this young man will always be a cause of anxiety and worry to H., I would be sorry to see him done....

March 1916

My trial.

I brought an action of Libel against the *Globe* newspaper[1] (a horrible rag) for saying, and printing a series of letters hinting, that I was sending 'Dainties and comestibles' to Donnington Hall, German officer prisoners, etc. etc.—an awful tissue of insolent lies, widely spread and generally believed by the sort of asses that this War has turned up like the sands of the sea! No one shall ever lie about me. I am not at all afraid of anyone or anything—the only fear I have in the world is that I might lose Henry, Elizabeth or Puffin's Love.... All sorts of odious letters, signed and anonymous, came to me, saying I was pro-German and a vile woman, etc., etc. I showed great dash! sent for the public prosecutor, showed him my abominable letters—all saying that my orders to the grocers Fortnum and Mason on a vast scale, to German prisoners in this country, were not denied by Fortnum and Mason's, etc.

The Dss. of Wellington[2] (a vile, vulgar, mischievous woman who, instead of giving up her time to helping the wounded, goes spy-hunting like a truffle dog, to hunt up poor people of German name and hunt down all her political enemies by pretending they are pro-Germans—Terrible Profession!) told everyone in London that both Elizabeth & I harboured German spies in Downing St., etc. etc. E. of course engaged to Tirpitz's

---

[1] *The Globe* was a London newspaper founded in the early 19th century; it came under the effective control of Max Aitken before the outbreak of war in 1914; 'The Libels on Mrs Asquith' and the 'Apology by the *Globe*' were fully reported by *The Times*, 22 Dec. 1915, 5. The long delay before this diary entry was written seems to have resulted from Margot's many preoccupations early in 1916, and to her failure to obtain earlier, or to extract, a newspaper account which she could paste to her page (see d. 3214, fo. 328ᵛ).

[2] Kathleen Emily Bulkeley née Williams (d. 1927); she married, 1872, Arthur Charles Wellesley (1849–1934), from 1900 4th Duke of Wellington.

son, and every sort of rubbish. Darling Elizabeth enjoyed it all, but I confess it made me <u>furious</u>.

Mr Duke, my counsel, and Sir Charles Russell,[1] my solicitor, were angelic. I went to the Law Courts with Elizabeth and Edgar Vincent (Puffin at school, or he would have supported me). Henry had shown the greatest sweetness and encouragement. There was no Defence. I would not take any apology and I got £1,000 damages. I felt nervous when I was called off the bench, where I was sitting next to Edgar and Elizabeth, in the well of the court, under Duke's nose; but I pinched myself very hard, and walked slowly up into the witness-box, and faced both friendly and hostile eyes. I got a little mixed kissing the Bible, and felt a little start at hearing my own voice 'The <u>Truth</u>, the <u>whole</u> Truth, and nothing <u>but</u> the Truth'—an easier oath for me to take on all occasions could not be found....

Directly Elizabeth got over her bronchitis at Walmer Henry was taken ill. Walmer is really unhealthy, because it is not heated, and a fortress on the sea without a heating apparatus can never be healthy. The sea doesn't suit me or Elizabeth, we neither sleep nor eat at Walmer: but the golf and sunshine, sea and place otherwise are all <u>very</u> delicious, and Henry <u>loves</u> it. As he is the <u>most</u> unselfish man in the world, and never asks for <u>anything</u>, and would hardly take a big bath if his family wanted it (which they always do!) I always go to Walmer when he wants me to, and only made one condition: that we should spend the Easter holidays with E. and Puffin at the Wharf (to this he has said <u>Certainly</u>).

He got an awful chill, and though I sent for Dr. Parkinson, he would not see him. He is as unfussy about his health as Cys and Violet are fussy. In consequence, he got really bad, and had to remain in bed 20th to 25th March, being poulticed every hour. I can't <u>bear</u> to see H. ill—it terrifies me, and I miss him every hour: not to be able to pop into his room before he comes up from cabinet room at night, and see that his fire and windows are all right at night; not to sit on his knee in my night-gown and pour myself out to him, or hear him tell me <u>everything</u> in his wonderful

[1] Henry Edward Duke (1855–1939) cr. 1st Baron Merrivale 1925; Q.C. 1899; Unionist MP 1900–06, 1910–18; Chief Secretary for Ireland 1916–18.

way (for I'm ashamed to say how many hours); not to have him come in nightly and chaff Eliz. and me in the bath-room, or ask us all sorts of 'stunners' at lunch, robs life for me of all its detail and pleasure. (I thought when we first married that <u>tiny</u> things would always escape his observation, and undoubtedly none of the Asquiths are acutely observant, or highly sensitive to other people's sensations; but Henry is amazingly observant about some things, and the best judge of character in the world, and far the best company.)

The Northcliffe Press were furious at what they called H.'s 'cold in the head' which, of course, prevented him making his statement on recruiting and Conscription....He no sooner got well than he, Grey, Ll.G., Robertson and K. had to go to Paris for a highly important conference about money and troops, etc., and then on to Rome to put things straight (Allies!!)....

Sunday 26 March 1916—Walmer

Motored to Dover and saw the 'party' and Henry off to Paris. I had bought H. a leather coat, thickly lined, and had a beaver collar put on it. I dreaded his getting straight out of bed to go abroad on a foul day—boisterous wind, and a sea even in Dover Harbour that made my eyes feel pale. Ll.G., Kitchener, Grey and Sir Maurice Hankey (a good haul for German submarines!), and Italian ambassador and his wife—Imperialis[1]—all hanging on to their hats, exchanging chat with an eye on the ship.... [Henry] wired every day. He returned from Rome at 4 am Thursday morning 6th April 1916, Charing Cross station, having had the time of his life—reception the greatest ever given to a British Prime Minister.

Friday 7 April 1916

Henry was quite cured of his bronchitis, and enjoyed himself. During his absence an acute crisis arose. Ll.G. travelled back with Robertson from

[1] Marchese Imperiali (1858–1944), Italian Ambassador in London 1910–20.

Paris, and they shook hands over Conscription. H. is quite open-minded over this d—d stupid unEnglish coercion, but he will take his own time. I venture to prophesy he will do it all as slowly as he can, so as to keep Henderson: if he lost the Labour leader out of his cabinet, he would have to resign....

We kept the 8th anniversary of Henry's Premiership at the Montagus'—E. and I, H., Violet and Bongie all dining at an agreeable dinner. Montagu begged Birrell to speak, but I dissuaded all pressing, as I loathe funny speeches, and no one is really happy enough—except the irresponsible and half-developed—to pull off and enjoy impromptus; luckily Birrell refused....

Monday 10 April 1916

H. answered the German Chancellor's insolent speech at the dinner given to French delegates.[1] In spite of my assuring Henry that this is the worst crisis in all his political life,[2] as B. Law won't have the courage to stay in now that Carson, Northcliffe and Co. are blackmailing him (this means the other Unionists must go), he absolutely disbelieves me, and on 9th (our first Sunday at new Wharf)[3] he said to Montagu 'I think we shall have rather fun with all these silly fellows this week.'

Ll.G. is always to be depended on to make mischief. It is he who first threatens to resign, which puts pressure from within and without on B. Law. They'll either all go, except A. Balfour and Ld R. Cecil, or H. will cajole the lot and keep them: am inclined to think he will succeed in doing this but things look black. (Montagu wired Hankey to return from Paris, and not go on with Henry to Rome. Hankey told me he wished he had

---

[1] On Wednesday, 5 Apr. Bethmann Hollweg, the German Imperial Chancellor, made a long and wide-ranging speech in the Reichstag on the progress of the war, and Germany's plans for post-war Europe: 'It abounds with inconsistencies, pleading in one breath for the right of starved and persecuted Germany to restore to Europe a lasting period of peaceful labour, and revealing in the next her far-flung ambitions: *The Times*, 7 Apr. 1916, 7a, 9a.

[2] Margot refers to the campaign to extend conscription to married men, which resulted in a second Military Service Act, 25 May 1916.

[3] There had been structural alterations to the Wharf, including a new front hall.

come back when he got the wire, as he thought he could have saved things. He sees what we've all watched, the rounding-up of a vicious circle: Ll.G. threatening to resign so as to push Bonar to go also—Northcliffe and Robinson[1] shoving all their papers into the fray—all out to smash the Government.)...

There is an awful bore over here now—Hughes,[2] the Australian PM, who was the Leader of Labour and came from Labour.... Birrell...told me he had said apropos of Hughes to Bonar Law 'Hughes is everything you like: he's a Welshman, a nonconformist, a Labour Leader, a socialist and a Lawyer.' Poor Bonar!—everything he hates most, except music, fine arts, society and scenery, are comprised in this catalogue. He has got a capital sense of humour, and laughed at Birrell.

Saturday 15 April 1916

We went to Wharf—2 Montagus, H. Cust, 2 Benckendorffs, Ilona[3] and Ld Moulton; Montagu and I very unhappy over the Conscription crisis, still going on violently, Henry at his most charming.... Robertson and the Army Council sent their last word, adhering to Conscription, to Henry at the Wharf. I wrote to Lansdowne, Crewe, Loulou, Henderson, Runciman and Walter Long in the train.... I begged them to do their best, as the split of the Gov. would be a tragedy and would lengthen the war. The critical cabinet was to take place at 4.30 in H.'s room in H. of Commons Monday 17th April 1916. We all went to London early....

I forgot to say I had boldly sent for Henderson. Everything depended on this man. Henry had always said if Henderson, a fine fellow and leader of the Labour party, didn't think he (H.) had stuck to his guns over this d—d Conscription, he would resign: he would not stay without Labour.

---

[1] An odd pairing by Margot. Northcliffe held the controlling financial interest in *The Times*, the *Daily Mail*, and other papers. Robinson was the editor of *The Times*. While financially dependent on Northcliffe, and subject to N's instructions, he was, in his ideas, closest to Milner.

[2] William Morris Hughes (1862–1952), then Labour Party leader and premier of Australia; dyspeptic, deaf, and immensely energetic.

[3] Or 'Eilona' (d. 1967), a professional pianist, married to Charles Derenberg.

I didn't suppose I could do much good, but you never can tell. I appealed to Henderson, and asked what PM could carry on a great war with Labour against him? or the soldiers against him? He was extraordinarily nice, rather moved, and said no Minister but Henry commanded the confidence of the working classes in this country.

Monday 17 April 1916

I sat upstairs just above the Cabinet room and prayed things might go right. I felt very anxious. H. came to Eliz. and me in my room at 7.40 and told us he had made a long and moving allocution, pointing out to the whole cabinet the dangers of disruption in the face of Germany at this moment. Ll.G. had come forward with an air of nobility, saying he would have a further talk with Robertson and Co. to beg them to modify their views. K. and Robertson are hopelessly ignorant of what England can afford to put into the field without losing valuable workmen. I wonder if we have not got too big an army....H. told me on going to bed (when I always sit in his room for some time) that, with the exception of Selborne and Curzon, all his Tory colleagues were quite miserable at the idea of having to break with the Gov.

Thursday 18 April 1916

H. was locked up all the morning with Crewe, Robertson, Bonar, Walter, etc....

Donald, editor of *Daily Chronicle*, put himself on to tea. I never know why he comes, he is honest and stupid—perhaps he wants an honour....Donald told me Ll.G. was loathed in the Country; and after we left the House, everyone in the lobby and House was abusing him. The Finance Bill was passed in a buzz of talk. Donald: 'The worst thing Ll.G. has done has been making mischief with France. Repington should never have been allowed to go to the front.' I told Donald nothing. I hate all journalists—it's a vile profession. Nothing is sacred: even corpses are copy. I entirely agree with Donald. I was angry with Robertson for letting

Repington, a hound, (military correspondent of *The Times*) go to the front, and wrote to Stamfordham....

Eric and Bob Cecil think that H. sd. have a special Secretary and member of the cabinet to take down cabinet decisions and see that they are carried out. H. has too much to do; he can't go round like an usher asking colleagues if they have done what is decided upon. Ld Bob offered to be this man, and at first I thought it was a fine idea, but when I found how much dear devoted Montagu felt, I agreed in my mind that it was for Montagu, not for a new man, to take the post. Poor Montagu wrote H. four pages to explain why he could not allow anyone to take the place....

H. and I had a divine dinner alone with Rufus, Buckmaster and Montagu—an excellent talk on most of the great leading men in every country just now being lawyers.

Bonar L. on tapis: H. 'I like him: he has been most straight all the time he has been in my cabinet; Carson <u>most</u> disappointing—ignorant and crabbing: in 6 months he never stopped talking, and never made <u>one</u> suggestion except the silly one on which he resigned—that we should help Servia by bombarding Greece! <u>Every</u> soldier laughed at this!' Montagu told us that Northcliffe's alternative government was Carson, Rosebery, Milner and himself (Northcliffe Air Minister)....

The real excitement was the secret session[1]—the fury of the Northcliffe Press knew no bounds. When, added to this resolve, H. made the King give an order in Council making it penal for any person or newspaper to publish any report describing or referring to the proceedings 'at such session', press passion knew no bounds!!! Here was their man of sloth—their loathed P. Minister—<u>not</u> prompted by <u>them</u> (Northcliffe and Co.) <u>daring</u> to [flout] them all, and act—as he always does—with perfect independence and imperturbability. It amused me very much.

The inequality of the contest between Henry and *The Times* would be pathetic if it were not <u>contemptible</u>. When he is ill he is shamming, when he is Kodaked smiling he is taking things lightly, when he is serious he is

---

[1] The government exposed its recruiting plans to the scrutiny of both Houses in a secret session of Parliament, Tuesday 25 April: see below, p. 255 n. 5.

over-strained, when he is silent he is asleep, when he speaks he is orator-ical—'We do not want oratory, we want deeds.' The perpetual party spite grows daily in volume as they realize that Henry is a somnambulist as far as he himself is concerned....

Monday 24 April 1916

In Easter Sunday's papers we read of the amazing landing of Sir Roger Casement.[1] At lunch on 24th April Henry said to Loulou almost casually:

[H.] It is a curious thing that Spring-Rice[2] should have warned us about this attempt to land guns, and Casement's arrival with the Germans. He was right also about the German Fleet.
Eliz. and Margot (in chorus) What!!!!

  H. (quietly) Yes, it came out and bombarded Lowestoft—raced over and raced back. It opened fire at twelve mile range, killed one child and two old people.

(We heard afterwards that the German guns hit over 100 houses in Lowestoft and only killed these three people!—no doubt God was on our side that day.)[3] I asked why when the Government had been warned by our ambassador in America we had taken no notice to warn Ireland, etc. Henry answered that we were always being warned and scared, and none of these warnings have ever come true. It was a great mistake this time, as

[1] (Sir) Roger Casement (1864–1916), Kt. 1911; born in Dublin; entered British consular service; exposed human rights violations in Africa and South America; joined Irish volunteers, 1913, and during war tried to raise an Irish brigade from prisoners of war in Berlin; captured on the Kerry coast on Good Friday morning, 21 Apr. 1916, after landing from a U-Boat; a shipment of arms that he had helped to secure from Berlin, and which was meant for a rising planned in Dublin, was scuttled; Casement was tried for treason and hanged, 3 Aug. 1916; his diaries, detailing his homosexuality, were covertly used by the state to discredit him.
[2] Cecil Arthur Spring-Rice (1859–1918), KCMG 1906; ambassador to USA, 1913–18.
[3] A German battle cruiser squadron appeared off Lowestoft at 4.30 a.m. on 25 Apr., and engaged in a short fight with the Royal Navy; according to the Admiralty, one man, two women, and one child on shore were killed by the German action: see Hough, *War at Sea*, 198.

it turns out. Our Admiralty knew every movement of the German ship which brought Casement over.

> M. What is Birrell doing?
>
> H. Reading the memoirs of Boufflers in the Athenaeum![1]
>
> M. What has happened to Sir Matthew Nathan?[2]
>
> H. He was taken prisoner in his own house by the Sinn Feinners[3] but has escaped I hear. (Thoughtfully) The Sinn Feins dug a trench opposite the Shelburne Hotel. (We all roared with laughter. None of us had any idea of what had really happened or how serious it was.)[4]
>
> H. 20 Germans and Sir R. Casement our only bag up to now, and as all the wires are cut, we have very little information.
>
> Bongie I wonder if the FO thought of telling the Irish Office of Spring-Rice's wire.

Eliz. and I looked at each other and rocked with laughter. It all seemed like *Alice in Wonderland*. We were in a foolish mood, as Henry was ragging all the time. Everyone is so over-worked in this Hellish war that quite big things look insignificant....

Tuesday 25 April 1916

The secret session.[5] H. made a very long speech, he told me, and dull!— explaining to the House what our resources were, what we are doing for

---

[1] Stanislaus Jean, Chevalier de Boufflers (1783–1815): *The Chevalier de Boufflers: A Romance of the French Revolution* was published in Britain by Nesta Helen Webster in 1916; Birrell shared Asquith's love of literature, and such insouciance was typical of him, but he later resigned (3 May) as Chief Secretary for Ireland over his handling of the Easter Rising.

[2] Lieutenant-Colonel Sir Matthew Nathan (1862–1939), KCMG, 1902; under-secretary to the Lord-Lieutenant of Ireland, 1914–16.

[3] i.e. 'Irish Nationalists' either Irish Volunteers or members of the Irish Citizen Army: Arthur Griffith's Sinn Féin party was not directly involved in the Rising, though it benefited greatly from it.

[4] The week-long rising and its suppression devastated parts of central Dublin, leaving several hundred dead, including civilians, rebels, police, and British troops.

[5] A secret session of Parliament was held on Tuesday, 25 Apr., so that the cabinet, which was widely reported to be in crisis, could lay before both houses the main facts and figures behind its final decision to extend conscription; this information it naturally would not wish to publish, but a factual report of proceedings was released to the press; *Parl. Deb.*, 81.2463–6.

our allies; the men we have got in the field, the men we want, etc., etc.; Blockade, etc. It seems to have been far from exciting.

I was shocked that Birrell only went to Ireland the night of 25th.[1] Poor dear old boy, he never should have been in politics: of this I have been sure for years, much as I love him. He should have gone over the first possible or impossible second. I don't think he will be forgiven this. He knew—so did we all, alas!—how dreadfully tragic and <u>how</u> serious, in spite of failure, this Irish rising is....[2]

Amery, who writes with and without his name for *The Times*, wrote this answer [to a letter from Lord Hugh Cecil].[3] I heard that Amery was in the Intelligence Dep. of the War Office, hence his khaki. I was <u>so</u> shocked that I got at Hankey, and moved Heaven and Earth till he was removed to Servia.[4] (It was his knowledge of Servian that had enabled him to smuggle into WO, where he had a very insignificant post: but a clever man, without the instincts of a gentleman or the feeling or imagination for war, with powers to hate every Liberal and Henry in particular, and always trying to smash the Coalition, is a <u>great</u> danger.)...

Friday 28 April 1916

St. John [Midleton] dined at H.'s invitation. He implored me[5] to send more troops to Ireland, and gave me a terrible account of how he had warned

---

[1] Birrell arrived there on a destroyer at 6 a.m., Thursday, 27 Apr.

[2] Passage probably written on 27 Apr. Margot was right to refer to it *militarily* as a failure, since it had been confined largely to Dublin, and by 27 Apr. was collapsing; but its symbolic value to the Irish Nationalist cause was incalculable.

[3] Leopold Stennett (Leo) Amery (1873–1955), politician, writer, tariff reformer, and imperialist; on *The Times* editorial staff, 1899–1909; Unionist MP for Birmingham South (Sparkbrook) 1911–45; served in intelligence in Flanders and Near East, 1914–16. Hugh Cecil argued that the government was right to keep the Liberals' views in mind when deciding on such issues as conscription. Amery replied that, while the war lasted, all party views were irrelevant.

[4] Amery's War Office post gave him an excessive amount of time to serve the Unionist War Committee, a conscriptionist pressure group hostile to the government, and on 4 May 1916 he attacked the government at a meeting of the committee; his remarkable language skills made him well-equipped for his intelligence work in the Balkans and Salonika: Roskill, *Hankey*, 270; *Riddell War Diary*, 171; Wilson, *Myriad Faces*, 413; *The Times*, 15 May 1916.

[5] See Midleton, *Ireland*, 99–101. Margot had long been friendly with Midleton (St John Brodrick) who spoke for the 'southern' Irish landlords.

everyone of this coming Irish revolt, and how no human being would listen to him. I felt sad, as he is very intelligent and in earnest, and knew the Irish situation; and had he been listened to over here, things might have been different. He told me Birrell and Nathan and all out there except Wimborne thought he (St. John) was over-stating, and quite wrong.

Wednesday 3 May 1916

We went to the House and heard Birrell's resignation speech.[1] It was a little long, but very pathetic, and no doubt Redmond and Carson are closer together. It was a particularly interesting debate....

Thursday 4 May 1916

H. brought in his Compulsion Bill, and Birrell resigned. No conjuror could have been cleverer than Henry has been over Compulsion. *The Times* likes to pretend there never was a crisis, because it failed to break the Gov. Henry's patience and skill in keeping Labour in this amazing change in England have stunned every one. The betting was 100 to 1 against these Islands ever adopting Conscription. I confess I feel anxious about it. The 2nd reading of the Bill had a majority of 292 in the House.[2] (A man called F. S. Oliver wrote a book on the war and has republished it for 1/- —*Ordeal by Battle*. I never read such rot, though quite well written.)[3] ...

---

[1] *Parl. Deb.*, 3 May 1916, 82.31–9; 'For nine years of recurring crisis he has held what is by tradition and bitter experience one of the most difficult of all the administrative posts open to British statesmanship....Mr Birrell at Canossa is a pathetic but not a contemptible figure.' *The Times*, 4 May 1916, 9b.

[2] Hankey noted that the Bachelors' Act had 'produced so few men that trade has not yet suffered. Perhaps after all compulsory service will save the nation'; this was a significant comment from one of the firmest of conscription's opponents; the bill received the Royal Assent on 25 May 1916: Adams and Poirier, *Conscription*, 168–9.

[3] F[rederick]. S[cott]. Oliver (1864–1934), draper and polemicist; made a fortune by transforming Messrs Debenham and Freebody into a leading London drapery business; his biography of *Alexander Hamilton* (1906) established his reputation as a talented historian; *Ordeal by Battle* (1915, republished, abridged, 1916) is not unfairly described by Margot: well written, but marred by the accusation that the Liberals had failed to warn or prepare Britain against German aggression (a point made in Gwynne, *Rasp*, 136). For a clear warning by Grey of the German potential for aggression, and its implications for Britain, see his statement on foreign affairs, 27 Nov. 1911, *Parl. Deb.*, 32.60–5.

PART VIII
5 MAY–29 AUGUST 1916

With the conscription controversy finally settled at the end of May 1916 Margot could have been forgiven for thinking that the political crisis had passed, but during the succeeding months judges as calm and experienced as Bonar Law and Balfour began to take a significantly more critical view of her husband. Where previously they had believed that, with all his faults, Asquith represented the best Prime Minister available, they now contemplated moves directed at replacing him. Both men had been involved in decisions associated with the setbacks of 1916, but both knew that none of those setbacks were in themselves really dangerous. The surrender at Kut on 29 April 1916 had been a humiliation; but it involved relatively small numbers. A tactical victory had eluded Jellicoe in the Battle of Jutland, 31 May–1 June; but it had gradually become clear that he had secured there a strategic success as decisive as Trafalgar. And the British casualties during the first day of the Somme were undeniably appalling; but if the battle were seen as a whole it represented, with the successful defence of Verdun, a severe blow to the German army in the West. Asquith's difficulty lay in the fact that with the war entering its third year there was still no end in sight; and, moreover, the perception was growing that he was incapable of altering this. Lloyd George by contrast was emerging as the man who could win the war. It was he who had reminded the trade unions of their responsibilities to the nation in a tough speech to the TUC in September 1915; and it was he who had delivered home truths to the slackers on the home front with his much discussed 'too late' speech in December. The Times guessed that his admonishments on the latter occasion would be unpalatable in some quarters: 'But they were brave words, and we beg his colleagues to ponder on the fact that he enjoys the confidence of the public more than any of them because he speaks out more than any of them. He is not afraid of the truth or of confessing to mistakes; and his courage inspires confidence.'[1] When Kitchener was drowned early in June, in the sinking of the Hampshire en route to Russia, Bonar Law decided to recommend Lloyd George as his successor as War Secretary. Bonar duly travelled to Sutton Courtenay to press Ll.G.'s claim, but the offhand manner with which he was received by Asquith left a lasting, and strongly negative, impression on him.[2] Margot was mistaken to imagine, as she did, that Ll.G.'s appointment at the War Office would allow him to sideline her husband. That post was no longer the position of power it had once been, nor did Ll.G. enhance his reputation there. But Bonar Law's backing for Ll.G.'s claim was a harbinger of things to come.

---

[1] *The Times*, 21 Dec. 1915, 11b.
[2] For the allegation that Asquith declined to interrupt a hand of bridge when Bonar Law arrived at The Wharf on Whit Monday, *and* its refutation, see Blake, *Bonar Law*, 289–90.

Friday 5 May 1916

Sir Ed. Carson is bidding for Leadership of the strong opposition, and made one of the most disgraceful speeches ever made by an ex-cabinet minister.[1] Lansdowne lunched with us, and told me that Carson and Milner had shocked him very much by their want of Patriotism, and personal vanity. I think Carson, unless he takes this Irish opportunity of settlement, is settled! <u>He</u> will never come again. Henry offered Montagu the Irish Chief Sec.ship—I am much against it: he is far too sensitive, and far too useful to us. He worships H. and me, and is invaluable as a peacemaker, and we love him.

Thursday 11 May 1916

We all went to the House prepared for an awful row from all three sections of the Irish after the terrible executions of the last weeks (not at all too many for what they have done). It was a painful debate but Henry made a very wonderful speech.[2] I went into his room when it was over, and he said 'I averted a row today.'

I wrote to Stamfordham, as I am mad keen for the King to go to Ireland.… Henry told me Wednesday 10th May that he would go to Ireland that night, but he was kept till Thursday by this debate. He and Bongie left Downing St. at 8 that night. I hurried the packing of his clothes. I could not see him off, as we had people dining. Every one enchanted at his

---

[1] By 'the strong opposition' Margot means those Unionists who were not serving in, or did not approve of, the Coalition. Speaking directly after Asquith in the debate on military compulsion, Tuesday, 2 May 1916, Carson had attacked the Prime Minister's overall handling of the conscription issue, and the 'apologetic manner' with which he had outlined the government's legislative response. Asquith had appealed for public confidence in his administration, while acknowledging that people were 'sore and depressed at a deplorable incident, though not one of serious military significance, like the surrender last week of the heroic garrison of Kut'. Carson responded: 'I do not think you can appease their minds and their anxieties by simply perorating and trying by words to mitigate what everybody must know has been a great calamity': *Parl. Deb.*, 81.2611–19.

[2] Asquith spoke in the debate on the continuance of martial law in Ireland, 11 May 1916: *Parl. Deb.*, 82.952–60. In all fifteen of the leaders of the Easter Rising were executed in Dublin 3–12 May 1916.

dramatic turn but *Times* and *M. Post* <u>furious</u>. Robinson wrote that the PM's purely spectacular visit to Ireland would be as futile as his tenure of War Office in Curragh row....

The Times wrote next day of H.'s return 'We hope it is of good omen that the PM, according to information received from our watchdog correspondent (another word for spy), was able to go straight from Cork to a matinée.[1] This looks like a clear-cut policy and a mind at rest. Nevertheless, we should have been glad to see Mr Asquith lose no time in getting together the Irish leaders, etc., etc.',—<u>a sort of reflux of Hate not unlike the German Papers</u>....[2]

Friday 19 May 1916

Henry told me he had seen very sad things, and that the Irish problem was enormously difficult. Chalmers[3] was to take Nathan's place. The Wimbornes had done their very best, and there was nothing against them, but they had to resign and were arriving that night in London.[4] He was impressed by Belfast, and said if he had wished to get up a meeting there among the Ulstermen he would have had the reception of his life. They all wanted a real settlement, and *au fond* don't love us at all!...

I have lost my beloved friend Ann Islington. She has shown the worst form of egotism; accused me of what I <u>never</u> said, just to cover her tracks, and I feel hard about her.... She was furious with Henry for not sending her Jack to India instead of the Chelmsfords,[5] and I've never seen her to

---

[1] Asquith did indeed go to a matinée, to see Viola Tree in *King Lear's Wife* by Gordon Bottomley (1874–1948) (diary, Dec. 1915–July 1916, fo. 418ᵛ).

[2] Margot seems to mean that *The Times'* article reflects the editor's hatred of the premier.

[3] Robert Chalmers (1858–1938), KCB 1908, cr. 1st Baron Chalmers 1919; Governor of Ceylon 1913–16; Joint-Secretary to the Treasury 1916–19, and Under-Secretary for Ireland 1916 (i.e. replacing Lieutenant-Colonel Sir Matthew Nathan).

[4] After the Easter Rising Wimborne resigned, with his chief secretary, Birrell; but whereas the latter's career was over, Wimborne was reinstated as Lord Lieutenant, 9 Aug. 1916, after being exonerated by an official inquiry.

[5] Frederic John Thesiger (1868–1933), s. as 3rd Baron Chelmsford 1905; cr. Viscount 1921; Viceroy of India 1916–21; m. 1894 Frances Charlotte Guest. His appointment, in succession to Lord Hardinge, was announced in *The Times* 15 Jan. 1916 (7b).

speak to except twice since Xmas!!…I had no part in making <u>this</u> Viceroy (<u>I made Hardinge</u>), and I never said one word against Jack, except that you wanted a big and very wise man in India now….[1]

The war has only improved those that have children fighting in it or [who are] nursing in Hospitals. I mean it has done a great deal for men & women who are in <u>real</u> touch with the soldiers. Those who have neither nursed or <u>seen</u> the actual heroes—the maimed, blind, halt, dying & broken men—are just what they were, hard & business-like (on committees) or critical & flimsy—I shudder & I don't want to see half the people I know.

Friday 26 May 1916

H. made his statement on Ireland,[2] and announced that Ll.G. was to do the *pourparlers* (I am sure he could do nothing else) between Redmond and Carson—H. is too busy. The interest of his speech lay in its appeal to the Irish leaders—Carson, Redmond, O'Brien[3]—to refrain from discussion of the rebellion and the present Irish situation. He wrote a private letter appealing to Healy….[4]

There is no folly England has not committed versus Ireland. I have never been a Home Ruler, but I am changed now. I am convinced that if H. had <u>not</u> put the H. Rule Bill on the statute book we should not have had 5000 (or so many Sinn Feiners as there are) but <u>all</u> the Nationalists and Irish in America against us….H. made a coup going over himself at the earliest possible moment, and his shares are very much up. I think his position is very strong just now, in spite of the West End of London….

[1] Only Margot could have thought this an acceptable remark where Lady Islington was concerned, and she may even have said it *to* her.

[2] In fact <u>25</u> (not 26) May 1916: see *Parl. Deb.*, 82.2308–11.

[3] William O'Brien (1852–1928), journalist and Irish Nationalist; long-standing MP, and leader of the non-sectarian and Moderate All-for-Ireland League.

[4] Timothy Michael (Tim) Healy (1855–1931), Irish Nationalist politician, first entered Parliament 1880; land reformer, but later anti-Parnellite; sympathized with Sinn Féin, and was the first governor-general of the Irish Free State; for the letter see Healy, *Letters*, ii. 566.

May 1916

My war work lies chiefly among the blind at St. Dunstan's. Henry is making Mr Arthur Pearson a Bart....[1] He is a fine fellow, with the vitality of my family, and has shown saint-like qualities in helping his fellow blind. Long before the war he was blind. I have taken out in motor a good many of his officers, and would do it oftener, but I am <u>terribly</u> over-worked.

My average day is: I wake 5.30 and doze till 6, then tea. I pull a pile of letters, and all 3 blocks and lists (dinner, lunch, week-ends) near me; and after tea is taken away, put a pile of stylo-pens, envelopes, paper, address-book, red Book Diary, album, gum, towel, scissors, and MS paper on tea bed table; and start off making list for telephone of names to invite for the dinner, lunch or week-ends and filling gaps; writing letters of personal thanks for flowers, fruit, books, 'letters from the front' forwarded by friends as well as written by them (from Egypt, S. Africa, India, France, Flanders, Salonika, etc.), Charity letters, and, what I find <u>most</u> trying, answering letters asking for things—war work which entails my writing to Boards of Trade, Works, Munitions, War Office, Foreign Office and Admiralty. My sec. Miss Way does a heap of things, but it is not the same as if I write myself.

Then I have my Diary (arranging notes, and sorting, sticking, etc.); then my magazine articles (which have all gone to the d---l, as I <u>can't</u> find time to write everything). My housekeeper comes up, and we discuss rooms for week-end or middle-of-week guests in London (<u>always</u> <u>someone</u> sprung on me who wants to stay, or to dine, or lunch, or go to play, or go to public meeting, church or city ceremony). My housekeeper makes a note of the meals and hours and beds and days that are wanted, also all flowers for day by day, and Wharf or Walmer Saturdays to Mondays. After my housekeeper, my cook comes, my nurse who is nursing Lucy, Elizabeth's maid who makes her summer dresses, then my own maid; my

---

[1] Sir Cyril Arthur Pearson (1866–1921), cr. Bt. 1916, newspaper proprietor; having lost his sight in adult life he worked in organizations to help the blind, especially those in the services.

butler outside my door, and at 10 my secretary, Miss Way....Henry comes to my room between seeing people at 10.30 am. We talk over the news and plans, and he tells me if he wants motor to see the King, or who he wants asked to lunch or dinner to save his time....

Friday 2 June 1916

The Naval Battle....[1] The Germans with their usual care of detail & organizing foresight got their news of triumphant victory over the British fleet into America as well as their own country long before we did. We are incorrigible in this way, and will always remain an unpopular nation as we never express ourselves....

Tuesday 6 June 1916: K's death in the North Sea

I told Fitzgerald to tell everyone it was a mine, not a torpedo, that sunk the *Hampshire*, and that if it got out she was torpedoed, and had gone without an escort, the Admiralty windows would be stoned. (I had heard there was no escort of Destroyers.)[2] Arthur's shares were already low. I asked Fitzgerald if he could run to Creedy[3] and stop the word 'torpedo' appearing in the evening papers. We ran down the wide Admiralty passage and found Creedy, who agreed entirely, and ran away, but returned to say the War Council from 10 Downing St. had just sent Jellicoe's telegram as it was, with no comment, to the Press, and it was too late to alter it....

H. said K. had died at the height of his fame, and at the happiest moment of his life. He had said goodbye to him Friday evening (after K. had seen

[1] The Battle of Jutland took place 31 May–1 June 1916. For the release of reports of the battle in Britain see Young, *Balfour*, 363–4; Marder, *Royal Navy*, iii. 190–7. The early German reports did not reveal that one of their battle cruisers and a light cruiser had been sunk after the battle, out of sight of the British. When this came to light German naval reporting was discredited: Cruttwell, *Great War*, 335.

[2] The heading of the 6 June entry is Margot's. She was right, perhaps coincidentally, on what had happened: *HMS Hampshire* had indeed been sunk by a mine, laid by a U-Boat; see Cassar, *Kitchener*, 476–80. The destroyer escort had been withdrawn because of the bad weather and Kitchener had refused Jellicoe's advice to wait until it had cleared.

[3] Herbert James Creedy (1878–1973), Kt. 1919; private secretary to Secretary of State for War, 1913–20.

the King to say goodbye) and he was as pleased as a schoolboy. The experiment, almost inspired, of K. addressing his critics in the H. of Commons in private, though highly dangerous, had gone off magnificently....(I have only seen H. troubled 3 times—1. over the retreat [from Mons] 2. over Hamilton's despatch of Dardanelles fiasco;[1] and now over K.'s death. I hope he won't be bothered over K.'s successor, but I fear it much.)...

Wednesday 7 June 1916

...After dinner the men stopped and talked a long time over K.'s successor. I understand from Montagu that both Bonar and Ll.G. were ruled out....Henry's afternoon was seeing every sort of person about K.'s successor. He told me to my horror at dressing time that he thought *au fond* that Ll.G. had the best claim. Like a perfect fool I was violent, which spoilt all our talk. I said to have a sly, dishonourable, brilliant man in WO, and a Northcliffe, was unthinkable!! The whole army would rebel and WO resign, etc.; that I wd. rather leave Downing St. forever, than see such a hideous blunder. I was sleepless, in spite of our subdued but not dull dinner and mild bridge. I didn't know, for some time after, that H. went against the Ll.G. idea at dinner. H., talking to E. and me when all our guests had gone, just before bed, said that he had the most rapacious colleagues in the world!!

Henry Even Rufus was tactless. I told him not to speak to me about the WO. The poor man's body hasn't yet been found, and they all come boring me over his successor. I call it quite indecent.

    M. I said to Rufus when I said good-night 'Does Ll.G. want WO?' He said 'Yes'. Both Buckmaster and I were shocked, and protested at such a mad and disastrous appointment. Northcliffe and Robinson in the War Office!

---

[1] Probably Hamilton's telegram to Kitchener, 17 Aug. 1915, on the failure of the Suvla Bay landing: Moorehead, *Gallipoli*, 300. It was discussed in the Dardanelles Committee, 19 Aug. Asquith had already received Hankey's report, 14 Aug. (via Vice-Admiral's telegram): Roskill, *Hankey*, 198.

Monday 26 June 1916—The Wharf

26th June in bed at my Wharf. Before I copy out my notes of the last fort-night's events, I must express my <u>intense</u> misery over Ll.G.'s appointment as Sec. of State for War. I look upon this as the greatest political blunder of Henry's lifetime. What I mind terribly is that it is the first <u>acute</u> political difference we have ever had, and now we can't speak hardly on politics. I do just the same things—go to his bedroom before he goes to bed, turn on his lights, see to his windows being open or shut, arrange things and look after him: but I can't really speak on what is going on, as I know in a few days—ten or perhaps more—H. will announce in the House that Ll.G. is to succeed K.

Jack [Tennant] will get into the cabinet, I expect. He deserves it, as he has shown great self-control and goodness and patience throughout all the war, answered thousands of letters with quickness and courtesy. How proud my old father[1] would have been. To have one son a peer would have been a pleasure to him, but Jack in the <u>Cabinet</u>! would indeed have 'done him proud'....[2]

I was so <u>miserable</u> when H. told me he was going to make Ll.G. Secretary for War that I wrote to Lansdowne, and asked him if he thought his son-in-law Victor Devonshire would not make a good successor to K....I also wrote to Gen. Sir William Robertson....He lunched with us after the cabinet (at which Haig was present, discussing our great coming offensive, which is to begin at the end of the month, to relieve the pressure on Verdun which the Germans attack madly day and night).[3] I said to him at lunch 'I don't know what you think, but I think K.'s successor should be a very straight, very hard-working, business-like man, above all <u>not</u> too clever, and a man who despises the Press.' Sir William: 'I <u>quite</u> agree, Mrs

---

[1] Sir Charles Tennant (see Biographical Notes).

[2] H. J. (Jack) Tennant, Margot's younger brother, joined the cabinet as Secretary of State for Scotland. The eldest, Edward, had been cr. Ld. Glenconner, 1911 (see Biographical Notes).

[3] The 'great coming offensive' was the Battle of the Somme, which began on 1 July and continued until 18 November.

Asquith, you are using the very same words as Haig and I used to each other walking down to the cabinet just now.'

All I said in my letter to Robertson was that I hoped, if Henry <u>did</u> speak to him on subject of Ll.G., that he (Robertson) would warn Henry he would not stand a Pressman in the War Office. Robertson had been manoeuvred into dining with Geoff. Robinson, and every effort possible has been made by that gang to collar him. I shall watch with the greatest anxiety every cabinet secret coming out in *The Times* the moment Ll.G.'s appointment is published.

My worry over this appointment, though starting from my own sole responsibility, I soon found was shared by the most important men in the army and the whole of the War Office—one and all begged, prayed Henry to stay on at the War Office. Ld French arrived with a long memorial signed by every big General in England and though official it was private. When Henry told Elizabeth and me this, he had tears in his eyes. The King was in despair when H. told him of his intention. Gen. Cowans said the War Office was in revolt. Ld Charles Montagu told me the City was full of Depression at the very idea of it.

Col. Sir Maurice Hankey refused to believe it and said Rumour was always wrong. Eric Drummond, who was a little uncertain when I first objected to it with Passion, got absolutely of my opinion. The <u>only</u> person who was in favour of it among my near friends was Edwin Montagu! Nothing has ever surprised me more! Montagu has been our <u>wisest</u> counsellor, our <u>truest</u> friend, the <u>most</u> loyal and, in many ways, the cleverest of all H.'s colleagues.... It is the first time I have ever differed from Mr Montagu in politics. I think he thinks Ll.G. would be a terrible danger if he were not given the War Office.[1] I need hardly say the Press made a huge ring, led by Northcliffe, in favour of Ll.G.'s appointment. He was boomed day in, day out, hailed as a Jehovah. The effrontery with which Lloyd G. rigged the Press disgusted me!

---

[1] Montagu thought the War Office *anything but* a comfortable billet for Lloyd George, but this was probably not an argument to be mentioned to the indiscreet Margot.

It is too late now. I played my cards badly with Henry: I said I would rather see him dead before he should make such an appointment; that I would go to Scotland, and cease to take the faintest interest in the cabinet or politics, and was far too vehement and out of proportion. I have cried bitter tears over it, and foresee great trouble. Montagu and all who share his views (I have met none) vastly overrate Ll.G.'s power in the country, they are much too influenced by London opinion. In the country Ll. G. is distrusted universally.

If anything should happen to Henry, I am quite sure as things are now Ll.G. would not lead the Liberal party, and above and beyond all he is not an able man.... He has a beautiful face but it is aged and coarsened; he has a wonderful smile and voice. His genius lies in his sensibility and amazing quickness.... I may be quite wrong but I prophesy that Ll.G.'s appointment to succeed K. at the War Office will turn out to be a great failure![1] If it is a great success, he will take good care to cut Henry out—to pose as the saviour of the soldiers in the greatest war that has ever been, that he has fought for them in the face of sluggishness and 'wait and see' opposition; that thanks to him we had enough guns for our new offensive, and if the latter is successful he, Northcliffe and Robinson will share the victory.

Thursday 15 June 1916—Visit to Rosyth naval dockyard

...There is nothing more pathetic than going over a man of war. The intensity of the men's faces, the happy busy independence, the amazing nippiness, discipline, and aliveness of the whole crew, the prestige and simplicity of the Admirals and swells, the 'common task' and the iron nerve! I remembered what Winston said to me on the Admiralty Yacht *Enchantress* apropos of sea service: 'It is a Priesthood'....

---

[1] Apparently it did not occur to Margot that Montagu's inclination not to oppose Ll.G.'s appointment might be based, partly at least, on the possibility—or, as then appeared, the probability—that Ll.G. would fail as War Secretary. For the latter's doubts about going to the War Office see Grigg, *Lloyd George, 1912–1916*, 356–61; for his failure to visit front-line troops enough as War Secretary see Grigg, *Lloyd George, 1912–1916*, 383–6.

Sunday 18 June 1916

Ld Hugh Cecil spent Sunday 18th June 1916 with us at Wharf. He read the first volume of my political diary....[1] He said it didn't say enough about little things—what people looked like....I quite agree with Ld Hugh Cecil—my diary is dullish, and if he thinks the first volume lacking in colour and too Hansardish, Heaven knows what he will think of the later vols!! But I have no time to write. I am always tired, and if I had not amazing energy I could not get through half or a third of what I do do....

Thursday 20 July 1916

I must finish up this diary[2] and start my new one, which I hope will be more interesting. No intelligent female could have more wonderful opportunities than I have of writing what will be thrilling, one would think, both to one's children and great-grandchildren; but it is possible that they would rather read about the war in proper books, and hear from me of the kind of clothes and manners, foods and amusements of society [rather] than the perpetual political crises....

Thursday 27 July 1916

Arthur Balfour said in the cabinet of 27th July that he despaired of ever making his own colleagues ever understand anything, and there is no doubt, as Henry said, the Tory party just now in England has little or no real brains and a poor education. Eton, that beautiful, divine school, is rotten, full of prejudice, laziness and far too big and fashionable. The new master just appointed, C. Alington,[3] may be better, but I fancy the machinery is too big (like the American Constitution) for the individual.

[1] The volume for 1904–5 was Margot's first 'political' diary, although she had kept a personal diary from the age of 12.
[2] The entry for 20 July 1916 begins a few pages before the end of the diary volume covering Dec. 1915–July 1916.
[3] The Revd Cyril Argentine Alington (1872–1955), Headmaster of Eton College, 1917–33.

The Leader, Bonar Law, is a really great Parliamentary H. of Commons man, but beyond this he is hardly anything (though a <u>very</u> nice fellow) because he is always afraid of Carson and his own side. Curzon is detested, and no doubt he will never get past this. He is not a gentleman, and is not generous or grateful. Arthur Balfour <u>towers</u> above them! Ld Bob Cecil comes next, but no Cecil and no Balfour has a womb....[1]

In this last Home Rule Irish crisis, which alas! has left the cabinet in undiminished numbers, but has shaken Parliament and brought to light an amount of Funk both fatuous and discreditable, Ld Salisbury, Hugh Cecil and the bulk of Unionist party have shown a poverty of mind quite incredible.[2] They see in all rebellion a reason for violent Repression; any idea of removing the causes of revolution is to them a concession to crime. If left entirely to themselves, they would flog criminals who break prison laws; they would make workmen and <u>never</u> employers liable for accidents in workshops; they wd. shoot strikers (in war time, which would be worst of all times); they would retaliate on our German prisoners here; they would do <u>precisely</u> what the Germans do, while condemning the Germans' Barbarity and frightfulness. They would imprison or intern everyone of German name, however many of them had sons fighting in our ranks.

---

[1] Margot uses this odd expression to suggest the absence of deep feeling.

[2] Margot blames the Unionlists for preventing the Government from introducing a bill that would have established a home rule government in Dublin, a measure deemed essential because of the rise in nationalist sentiment and civil unrest in Ireland in the aftermath of the Easter Rising. Unsurprisingly, perhaps, Asquith's administration proved unable to solve during wartime a problem that had proved intractable during peace, and once again Ulster exclusion was the root of the difficulty. But in first seeking a solution, and then finding that this was impossible, his government, according to *The Times*, was 'showing less and less cohesion, grip, and driving power' (1 August 1916, 9a). It has been generally supposed that if Asquith had first established cabinet unity, and then put the issue to Parliament quickly, as a question of confidence, it would have had a reasonable chance of passing, but it is another question entirely whether this would have brought the stable government that was desired. Asquith told Sylvia Henley that John Redmond's Nationalists 'funk Home Rule at present, fearing that they would have to call in English troops to keep their own friends in order': Grigg, *Lloyd George, 1912–1916*, 351–4; Hyde, *Carson*, 402–5; Asquith to Sylvia Henley 24, 25 July 1916, 700, 703; Wheatley, *Nationalism*, 266; Beaverbrook, *Politicians*, 272.

At this point Margot began a new diary, which she introduced with a note written on the inside front cover: 'This Diary was begun July 31st 1916 and ended in August 1917. Its chief interest is the account of our being turned out of Downing St. ...'

Monday 31 July 1916

Starting this new diary in the third year of the war finds Henry's position in the country and in the cabinet stronger than it has ever been. In London itself I don't think it is as strong, because London is made up of the sort of crowd that shouted 'Give us Barabbas! Give us Barabbas!' Both in the East and West Ends of London there is a chronic crowd shouting 'Give us Barabbas!' It would almost seem as if there was a floating substance of evil playing perpetually over crowds ... The Duchess of Wellington (typical of the vulgar in the West-end) continues spreading the same lies about me & mine. I harbour German spies in Downing St., Elizabeth is engaged to the sons of V. Tirpitz and Bethmann Hollweg (German Admiralty & Premiership). I killed Kitchener by betraying his start & ship from these shores by signalling to German ships. I have 'fed all the German prisoners officers etc. with every dainty & comestible' in Donnington Hall (a place whose very whereabouts I don't know!) these lies not only the Dss. of W. spreads but <u>believes</u> & had it not been for my getting £1000 from the Globe for these libels the whole of the Northcliffe Press, Morning Post, Milner, Maxse, Markham group would publish these lies again openly—as it is they mutter incantations—'Give us Barabbas!' & like Pilate 'willing to content the people' the Press releases Barabbas. I am told by J. Morley and other Historians that no greater campaign of calumny was ever conducted against one man than that which has been and is being conducted against Henry by the Low gutter Northcliffe Press by Day and by night.[1] I suppose it is <u>very</u> uncommon for public men to be indifferent to this sort of thing. ...

[1] Britain had not been involved in a great war since widespread literacy had engendered a popular press. *The Times* could hardly be included in 'the low gutter...press', while the *Daily Mail*, in campaigning for a small body to run the war (Thompson, *Northcliffe*, 253), was echoing the views voiced by Carson and Cromer. Northcliffe was not alone in preaching that a Coalition cabinet of 22, meeting without a secretary, could hardly be a war-winning body.

...I <u>know</u> that Henry is as indifferent to the Press as St. Paul's Cathedral is to gnats: this is really what galls their infinite vanity. To be unblackmailable is uncanny to Northcliffe. Henry reads *The Times*, the *Westminster*, and the *Daily News* and *Daily Chronicle* at enormous speed every morning. He misses nothing that is funny, and reads the leading articles last of all. The country Press write very differently of the Government and Henry. If anything happened to Henry—which God forbid—not only I, but every serious person in England, would find it impossible to name his successor....

Friday 4 August 1916

To return to the 4th of Aug. 1916, the anniversary of the War—while E. sat to McEvoy,[1] Puffin was having a music lesson, learning some Schumann with Mme Haas, I went to get some gloves to wear with my grey-silver Russian tea-gown at Henry's big Queen's Hall meeting (to be held that night). After having a wine-coloured tulle toque pinned on, with grapes and a single rose all in purple colouring, I ran in to tell Alice Wimborne that Henry had settled that she and Ivor Wimborne were to go back to the Irish Viceregal lodge. I had worked hard for this, as I thought they were well suited for the horrible place and had been practically promised it by Henry. Bonar Law with his usual funky fussiness at the 12th hour had begged H. to postpone filling the vacant post.[2]

This silly advice, H., out of civility, deferred to, and in consequence the Irish Debate and H.'s announcement was a fiasco.[3] To appoint Mr Duke, a Unionist (excellent man, I should say) and announce this <u>without</u> announcing a Lib. Home Rule Viceroy, made the Irish wild. In any case the Irish were angry with us, as our attempt to conciliate every one, backed by Carson and Redmond, failed completely. <u>Everyone</u> funked!—

---

[1] Ambrose McEvoy (1878–1927), who became fashionable after exhibiting portraits in 1915.
[2] Wimborne was duly reinstated: see above, p. 263 n. 4.
[3] In the debate on 31 July (i.e. *not* 4 August) Asquith declined to nominate a new Lord Lieutenant, but identified Henry Edward Duke as the new Chief Secretary for Ireland.

Lansdowne and Bob Cecil and Walter Long in the cabinet, and Redmond, Devlin[1] and Dillon out of it.

I warn anyone in the future who reads the History of our dealings with Ireland to believe every word I write, as I know every fact. Clumsy as Lansdowne and Co. were, and frightened and suspicious as a small section like Jim Salisbury, Hugh Cecil, Morning Post, etc. were, the H. Rule Bill and Parliament could have been brought into action perfectly with a little more give and take, a little more courage on the part of the Nationalists....

We had our usual strange lunch party...Maud Cunard[2]—rococo, spontaneous, frivolous foreigner of excellent heart and digestion and no occupation, dressed like a girl of 20 in white muslin at night, and decolletée by day; Gen. Sir John Cowans; Mr Gibson,[3] the American who strove to save Nurse Cavell being shot by the Germans, and Bongie....I felt sad at the awful news Tim Eden[4] told me of German brutality, and how many of our poor fellows were going mad daily. Why the Germans, who are very short of food thanks to our Blockade, can be such fools as not to save their reputation and their pockets by sending these wretched non-fighting invalidish English to a neutral country, but prefer keeping them to die or go mad, passes all human imagination....

Cys, Eliz, Puff, Henry, Bongie and I dined early and went to Queen's Hall. Puffin and I were on the platform. E. and an American, Gibson, sat in front row one side of gangway, and Violet, Cys and Da the other. I wore my Russian silver tea-gown and the purple toque with grapes, and looked as well as a face of my kind can look. Ld Derby was in the chair, and read many telegrams from every part of our empire, very

[1] Joseph Devlin (1871–1934), Belfast-born Irish Nationalist politician, and long-standing MP for his home town.

[2] Maud Alice Cunard née Burke (1872–1948), American heiress, renowned London Salonnière, and mother of Nancy (1896–1965).

[3] Hugh Gibson (1883–1954), American diplomat; secretary of the Legation in Brussels, 1914–17. Elizabeth Asquith announced her engagement to him during the political crisis of Dec. 1916; but they never married.

[4] Sir Timothy Calvert Eden (1893–1963), s. as 2nd Bt., 1915; interned in Germany as a civilian, 1914–16; served, European War, 1917–19.

badly—long Botha[1] and Smuts[2] and Canadian messages. I was reminded of 'Reading without tears'![3] He made some curious slips: 'The dastardly—––Government––—no––—Germans', etc.

The hall was well filled, and listened with patience to many long speeches. H. spoke admirably. Bonar Law tried a lighter vein with less success. The best speech after H.'s was a Frenchman from the French Gov....I noticed any vague allusion to retaliating on the Germans was received with great cheers. I thought of Tim Eden, who said it was unthinkable as long as a single English soldier or civilian was in Germany: it would mean their certain Death. It shocked me to think of our people being so inhuman and so Foolish. When the meeting was over, we went to supper with the Montagus....

I got a delightful letter from our boy Raymond dated July 5th 1916 from somewhere near Ypres:[4]

3rd. Gren. Guards.

Dearest Margot, I was delighted to get yr. excellent letter....What you say of the snobbery of soldiers is appallingly true. If you look at any list of honours it's always the same story—the Dukes are proved to be the bravest men of all and after them the Marquesses.... Our men are certainly a very good lot to fight with—mostly miners, farmers, game keepers and policemen—much more comfort at awkward moments than the clerks

---

[1] General Louis Botha (1862–1919), Commander-in-Chief of Boer forces 1900; the first premier of the Union of South Africa, 1910–19.

[2] Jan Christian Smuts (1870–1950), fought against British during the Second South African War (1899–1902); Minister of Defence, Union government, 1910–19; succeeded Botha as Prime Minister, 1919; with Botha conducted successful campaign in South West Africa, 1915; Lt. Gen. in British Army to command imperial forces in East Africa; member of British war cabinet, June 1917–Jan. 1919.

[3] Favell Lee Mortimer's *Reading Without Tears, or, A Pleasant Mode of Learning to Read*, first published in 1861, and doubtless used by Margot and her sisters.

[4] Margot was apt to believe in the 'inhumanity of her step-children' and Raymond wrote to his wife Katharine, 10 July 1916: 'I'm glad that Frances [?Horner] pitched into Margot about the "heartlessness" stunt. As a result I got quite a sensible letter from her (Margot)—the 2nd I have received from Downing Street since the War began. I answered it promptly and at considerable length, but I don't flatter myself that anyone but Margot's maid will read what I wrote': see Jolliffe, *Raymond Asquith*, 274, 286–7.

and counter-jumpers of the new army, and the officers in my company...are a very good lot to live with. Many of them would be pleasant enough in peace time.

We have been having fairly stirring times this last month or so. First of all we were rushed up in motor buses in the middle of our rest-period as an emergency measure to relieve the Canadians after their counter-attack at Hooge.[1] We took over what was in effect a battle-field and a very untidy one at that—mined trenches...craters, bodies and bits of bodies, masses of derelict rifles and equipment, woods turned into a wilderness of short stubby blackened stumps and a stink of death and corruption which was quite supernaturally beastly. You had to pickle your stomach with old brandy to keep it from heaving. As far as abomination and desolation go it was far more impressive than the ruins of Ypres (which are very much like other ruins) or any of the show sights of the war.

The Canadians fought extremely well. They are brave and enterprising but deficient in system and routine. No troops can be first rate unless they are punished for small faults and get their meals with absolute regularity. The Canadians are frequently famished and never rebuked, whereas the Brigade of Guards are gorged and damned the whole time. We stayed among the smells for a week. I had one big bombardment and a gas attack of moderate quality. Then we had a few days rest and were moved to a new part of the line where we are now. It is pretty lively. Something going on all round one most nights.

I had a narrow escape one night. I had taken one man with me to inspect the barbed wire in front of one trench and when we were about 30 or 40 yards out we found ourselves suddenly illuminated by the glare of half a dozen German rockets as so often happens. We bobbed down behind a lump of earth, the next moment a bomb burst a yard away. I was spattered with small fragments but not in the least hurt—the man began rolling about like a porpoise and groaning a good deal. After a minute or two I persuaded him that he wasn't dead and we walked back together

[1] Hooge lies just to the east of Ypres, on the main Ypres–Menin road; Raymond's unit was soon transferred south to reinforce British operations on the Somme.

into the trench where we found some nasty looking holes in his back but no bones or blood-vessels damaged. I suppose he is in England by now and well out of it all.

The next night I hid some bombers in a shell hole 50 yards in front of our parapet and when the Germans came crawling up a ditch our men got in [the] first shot and the enemy made off. We thought we had knocked out one or two more of them and I crawled about with two others for an hour in long wet grass…trying to find them….Now we are back in the second line only about 100 yards from the first, but better dug-outs and less strain. We have ten more days to get through [in] these two lines before we can change our linen or take our boots off. Sixteen days without undressing is excessive in my opinion. But I suppose Philip Sassoon[1] knows best. There is a canal just in front of us which breeds mosquitoes at this season. If the chemists have anything to burn which keeps them down without stinking you might send me some of it.

You'll never get through this letter but I don't write often except to Katharine. One spends as much time as possible asleep when one isn't face to face with the Huns.

Love to all from Raymond…

The clever group of nowadays is very inferior to my clever group called 'Souls'.[2] They are sexless and soulless, and so disloyal that they only hang together by a thread of mutual love of gossip and common capacity to say bright things, read bright and blasphemous novels, modern and very moderate poems (which crop up like weeds every day); and an unimpulsive, uninspired, dry desire to go against authority under the name of anti-cant….

Ll.G. finishes the session to all appearances having regained all his lost ground, but the public knows him, and the Labour party knows him, and I doubt if he will ever be PM, unless put there by a very strong intrigue or

[1] Philip Albert Sassoon (1888–1939), s. as 3rd Bt. 1912; Unionist MP, 1912–39; private secretary to Haig, 1915–19. His influence with the C.-in-C. was resented; and by 1916 nearly all staff officers had become unpopular with those in the trenches. They were suspected of telling the generals nothing except the agreeable news items.

[2] Margot here casts aspersions on the 'coterie', the 'clever group' of the younger generation, of which Raymond was recognized as a leader.

combination of swell, snob and soldier. He and Carson on the other side represent the boomed of the two sides—I might almost add the boomerangs, as it is more than possible Ll.G. will be in the Tory camp, and Carson leading the Irish nation in a Home Rule Dublin Parliament.

The last week of the session was a triumph for the Government. Winston made a ridiculous speech. Carson in Commons and Salisbury in Lords tried hard for a Trench Election.[1] Henry showed amazing patience and skill, stating very moderately the over-whelming objections to this noodle plan, and the opposition collapsed. Only a few wreckers, led by Northcliffe and Milner, want a Gen. Election in the trenches. The reasons against polling booths in Mesopotamia, Egypt, France and Flanders had only got to be stated to make the idea ridiculous. Milner is a stupid man with a good mind—a German....

Tuesday 29 August 1916

Roumania joined the Allies yesterday.[2] I hope and pray it may shorten this Horrible war. Italy declared war on Germany a few days ago, which it had never done before, though it has been fighting Germans and Austrians for a year or more. Quaint people, our allies!! We are eleven to three now....

Poor Winston! His political position is nil—no tenor off the stage was more helpless than he is. He is the most terrible object lesson in the views I hold that to care more for one's self than for any other creature, to believe in oneself more than in any other god, is Death—I would rather be Dead than diseased to such a pitch as this, & in times like these where everyone ceases to have a self at all it has brought a fierce light about his head from which he cannot get away.

He has been writing 4 articles for the Sunday Pictorial £250 each—the same price as I got for my two in Strand & Cornhill—they are very poor stuff. I would be sorry for Winston but he fills me with contempt—I never

---

[1] i.e. an election held while the war was still being fought.
[2] The Germany Army quickly overwhelmed Romania: see Terraine, *First World War*, 119.

made a mistake about this young man's character. Violet & Henry & Venetia always had a soft corner for him & thought him a wonderful talker—he was au fond always a bore & diseased by blighting Egotism.

I was furious with the Admiralty the other day for letting Henry cross over to see Briand at Calais without an escort. After K.'s terrible drowning, you would have thought the Admiralty would have been <u>most</u> careful. The Germans would have had a rich bag if Henry's ship had been torpedoed. There were on board the Prime Minister, Cunliffe, Governor of Bank of England, the Chancellor of Exchequer, Minister of Munitions (Montagu), Ld. Chief Justice (Rufus) and Col. Sir Maurice Hankey. I am glad to say the latter wrote a stiff note to Admiralty.

It was Admiral Bacon[1] at Dover Harbour who behaved like a perfect fool and, most ridiculous of all, kept their ship three-quarters of an hour outside the Harbour at midnight, because it is against Harbour orders to let in any unescorted ship without long and painful delay—this was the *comble*!![2] They all went over to make up the usual financial quarrels between Italy, Russia and France.[3] McKenna, who has been very quarrelsome lately with Rufus and Cunliffe, was heavily spoken to by Henry, and now they are, to quote Henry, like sucking-doves—he did extremely well at the conference....

My house maid Ada (an angel) brought me my tea as usual at 6.30 A.M. & gave me a written telephone message: 'Prime Minister—Lady Diana Manners telephoned at 3 A.M. this morning to say there is a raid on London by 14 Zeppelins & one had been brought down'.

This news caused much excitement when we were all together down stairs. Eliz. & Duff Cooper said 'I <u>must</u> say I've no luck <u>always</u> missing Zeppelins.' Margot (in voice of pride) 'I know! I am just the same! but I saw the only man that was killed that night that Zepp. threw bombs near the Lyceum carried past me in the crowd. I was standing in my evening dress

---

[1] Vice-Admiral Sir Reginald Hugh Bacon (1863–1947), KCB 1916, Commander of the Dover Patrol, 1915–17.

[2] French, meaning, figuratively, 'the height of', 'the last straw'.

[3] For the meeting at Calais, 24 Aug. 1916, see Strachan, *First World War*, 971–2.

after dining at Dudley House all among the broken glass in a big crowd & not a man took his pipe out of his mouth or a woman hurried home'. When the history of the war comes to be written, no one will ever believe how impervious to panic, or even ordinary fear, the British people are. Every child begs its mother to take it out of bed to see the Zepps.

Henry, Bongie and Hankey went to see our army September 5th.[1] They stayed at GHQ with Haig. I wanted H. to go, as he had been pressed by the soldiers, and I like them to see him. No one gets on better or loves soldiers more than Henry. I shall forever thank my stars that he went when he did....He returned about 3 a.m. Saturday 9th morning to London, and went to the Wharf with all of us in the afternoon....

I lose control when I'm ill and tired, and get madly irritable....Irritability, plus a very keen tongue, gets on other peoples nerves, I find, and bores them. I suffer from chronic impatience and irritability, and a sort of dense lack of understanding <u>why</u> people don't and can't make up their minds instantly and <u>do</u> the thing <u>at once</u>. I would not like to be a character part! But there is <u>no</u> doubt! <u>I</u> find it as hard to modify myself as Charty did (Laura was different: she was more *fine mouche*,[2] though quite as impulsive and quick-tempered). I have nothing like Puffin's self-control and gentleness, though he would never agree with this. (I expect Henry has often wondered why, with such a fine natural temper, I am so impressionable and easily upset, and <u>suffer</u> as much as I do. It is really nerves, and a devouring energy: I have several skins too few.)...

[1] Hankey recalled: 'We got out of our cars and hurried to a "dug-out". Just as we arrived a third shell greeted us and landed not fifty yards away....The Prime Minister was as usual quite composed, but I thought his hand was trembling rather, and no wonder': see Hankey, *Supreme Command*, 512–13.
[2] Margot means by this phrase (Larousse: 'personne adroite') to suggest that Laura was more tactful than either herself or Charty, and cleverer, more sensitive to the needs and feelings of others.

PART IX

17 SEPTEMBER–
14 DECEMBER 1916

Throughout Asquith's premiership Margot had avoided certain topics in her diary, and by 1916 the largest of these exclusions concerned the premier's tendency to drink too much, which had for years been notorious enough to give him the nick-name 'Squiff', and to put him into George Robey's repertoire of music hall songs.[1] *When people of the calibre of Balfour, Bonar Law, and Milner looked at their premier in relation to the tasks facing him during the last part of 1916, each was obliged to conclude that, while none looked impossible in themselves, all would demand from Asquith an intensity of effort and innovation which he gave little sign of providing. It would have been something to equip the cabinet with a circulated agenda, a secretary, records, and minutes, so that its members would at least know what the War Committee was doing; but a move towards this in April 1916 had come to nothing, and a last-minute proposal on 1 December for a 'Committee to deal with the purely domestic side of War problems' was condemned as a further generator of delays. Asquith's premiership ultimately foundered on his inability to create what contemporaries recognized as a war-winning governmental machine. Margot believed that if her husband had taken her advice he would never have been ousted by Lloyd George in the palace coup of the first week of December 1916. She was certainly the more aware of the political danger that he faced, but in truth neither understood its full extent or, more importantly, its causes. Asquith's Olympian detachment was a lifelong trait, and he failed to heed Bonar Law's advice not just to be active, but to seem active, during the war. He must, though, have been suffering from the effects of fatigue and stress, a factor that is perhaps not sufficiently emphasized:*[2] *as the war entered its third year he had already been more than eight years in office, and they were among the most demanding of a premier in modern times. It was against this background that he learned of the death of his eldest son, Raymond, on the Somme on 15 September, an event that overshadowed his last weeks in office. Asquith's reserve concealed from all but his closest friends the grinding anxiety that he felt for his three boys at the front; and even those confidantes were given no more than an occasional hint of his forebodings. On 23 April 1915, for example, when he heard of Rupert Brooke's death, he told Venetia: 'It has given me more pain than any loss in the war. . . . In the stress of such an event . . . one gets a dazed, dim, premonitory feeling that the next blow may come even nearer home.'*[3] *Yet in spite of this he was poor at communicating his feelings to his sons. In August 1916, less than a month before he was killed,*

---

[1] Crawford, who joined the cabinet in July 1916 from overseas service, made some journal entries which suggest that Asquith's deterioration from, and dependence on, alcohol had increased during the war: *Crawford Journals*, 356, 358 (12 July, 2 Aug. 1916).

[2] See his letter to Margot, 13 Apr. 1915: 'These last 3 years I have lived under a perpetual strain, the like of which has I suppose been experienced by very few men living or dead': *Asquith–Stanley*, 548. His physical well-being, and air of imperturbability, tend to obscure how stressful his period in office must have been.

[3] *Asquith–Stanley*, 569. Asquith's sons at the front were Raymond, Herbert [Beb], and Arthur [Oc]; Cyril ['Cys'], volunteered for overseas service but was ruled unfit.

Raymond wrote to his wife Katharine: 'If Margot talks any more bosh to you about the inhumanity of her step-children you can stop her mouth by telling her that during my 10 months exile here the P.M. has never written me a line of any description. I don't see why he should. He has plenty of other things to do; and so have I…'[1] Such reticence could too easily be misconstrued as a lack of feeling—an observation as true of Raymond as of his father. When Beb Asquith was on leave in January 1918 his wife Cynthia commented: 'I do think his father is amazing. He is devoted to his sons and it seems so odd that, after Beb has been out for five months—liable to be killed at any moment—he should not address one word of enquiry to him, as to what he has been doing and where he has been.'[2] But Beb understood the depth of emotion that was in play, wryly commenting that his father 'had at times an excessive belief in the powers of the unspoken word'.[3]

Sunday 17 September 1916—The Wharf

Henry went for a long motor drive with Nan—looked well and happy. He was delighted with his visit to the front, and all he saw (our tanks and troops and grand organization). Our offensive was going amazingly well, munitions satisfactory, the French fighting magnificently; the H. of Commons shut, and one of its <u>most</u> mischievous members (Sir Arthur Markham) dead;[4] and the cabinet really stronger and more united than it ever had been. Arnold and Jimmy had played chess. Eliz. had recited Raymond's wonderful poem on girls.[5] Henry had talked a lot about Raymond. He had seen him in France (for the last time) on 6th September

---

[1] RA to KA, 22 Aug. 1916, in Jolliffe, *Raymond Asquith*, 286–7. Raymond disdained conformity to convention, yet died the death (killed in action on the Somme) that seems to epitomize best the sacrifice of his generation; in meeting this end he eschewed opportunities to take a staff position, with the relative security that this implied.

[2] Asquith, C., *Diaries*, 390–1.

[3] Asquith, C., *Diaries*, xviii.

[4] While Margot clearly aimed in this passage at a dramatic contrast, she did not distort the events to any great degree. The offensive of 15 Sept. 1916, though a failure where the Guards Division was involved at Ginchy, proved successful along much of the 15,000-yard front. This, and the sequel, 25 Sept., produced, in Cruttwell's words, 'the most dangerous crisis through which the Germans passed before August 1918' (*Great War*, 273). Sir Arthur Markham (see above, p. 158 n. 4) died of a heart attack on 5 Aug.: 'Never amenable to party discipline, bitterly fearless and honest as the day, [he] came into great prominence last year by his day by day criticism of the Coalition Government': *The Times*, 7 Aug. 1916, 9e.

[5] Arnold Sandwith Ward (1876–1950), son of the novelist Mrs Humphry Ward, and a Balliol contemporary of Raymond Asquith, and a friend of the family; barrister, and Unionist MP, 1910–18; for 'Jimmy' de Rothschild see above, p. 3 n. 2; and for Raymond's light-hearted poem 'In Praise of Young Girls', 'a pastiche of Pope in thirty heroic couplets, contrasting old

1916 at Fricourt[1]—the first village that our offensive took. It was a beautiful happy Sunday.

As Puffin was going to Winchester for 1st time on 20th Sep. Wed. & it was his last Sunday I said he might dine in bed & run over in his pyjamas & play bridge with us before the men came out of dinner. I wore my little grey & silver Ospovat Russian tea-gown wh. Puffin loves. We sat down—Puff & I against Maud Tree & Florry[2] at the bridge table. Eliz & Nan sat talking in the hall. Our hired and clever butler Clouder (of whom Eliz said 'he makes perfect ladies of us all') came in 15 to 10, and asked if I would speak to Davies (our 2nd. secretary) on the telephone. I thought it might be more good war news, but just before lifting the telephone to my ear, I said to myself 'Raymond is killed'.[3] I said down the telephone 'Bad news, I'm afraid, Da—Raymond is dead.'

Da. Terrible, terrible news, Margot—Raymond was shot dead on 15th (Friday). Haig writes—no details—he writes full of sympathy. Where is Katharine? Shall I tell her?

I felt quite physically sick, and said

[M]. Telephone to Frances [Horner] to break it to Katharine: they are at Mells.[4] Let us know all details.
Da. The Guards were in, and Raymond was shot a few moments after going over the parapet leading his men.
M. Oh, Da! <u>poor, poor</u> Katharine!

and new fashions in seduction', see Spender and Asquith, ii. 234–5; Jolliffe, *ODNB*, 'Asquith, Raymond'.

  [1] In his account of the meeting to Katharine, 7 Sept. 1916, Raymond said nothing about what he felt about meeting his father, or indeed any of what passed between them, concentrating instead on the effect of the German artillery barrage, which came uncomfortably close to the PM: Jolliffe, *Raymond Asquith*, 293–4.
  [2] Janet Florence Bridges née Menzies (1867/8–1937), widow of Major W. Marshall, Grenadier Guards, who married, 1907, Lieut.-General Tom Bridges (below).
  [3] Raymond was killed at an early stage of the Guards Division's advance on Lesbœufs, 15 Sept. 1916; see Jolliffe, *Raymond Asquith*, 296.
  [4] A beautiful manor house in Somerset, west of Frome; the Elizabethan original was extensively restored by Sir John and Lady Horner, the parents of Raymond Asquith's wife Katharine.

—and, choked with tears, I put back the receiver and sat down. Elizabeth's delicious laugh & lovely speaking voice chaffing Puffin sounded across the hall thro the open doors—a smell of cigars & the hum of the men talking in the dining room—I wondered how I cd. break in with such Terrible news.——I pulled myself together, got my handkerchief out of my coat pocket in the hall, and went into the sitting room: little Puffin playing bridge in his pyjamas. Maud[1] [Tree] watching on the sofa, and Nan reading in Henry's arm-chair.

M. Terrible news—Raymond is dead: he was shot leading his men on Friday.

Everyone was stunned. Nan burst into tears. Puffin hung his head & came up to me & took my hand. Eliz. bewildered & unbelieving asked a lot of questions; seeing I knew nothing she sat down & sobbed convulsively. I kissed her.... I told the children to leave me, as I would have to tell father. I rang and told Clouder to tell the PM to come out and speak to me. I stood at the end of the dining-room passage—he opened the door, and we stood facing each other. He saw my miserable, thin, wet face, and put his arm round me. M. 'My own darling—Terrible news'—he stopped me. 'I know, I've known it—Raymond has been killed.' I nodded; we walked silently down the little passage into the bridge room. He put his hands over his face for one moment, then asked me in a hoarse voice if I knew how or where. I told him all I knew. We heard Cowans moving his coat in the hall, and went out to say good-bye to him in his great coat. Henry said 'Our boy Raymond was killed on Friday'. Cowans, who has a heart of gold, shook our hands and said he would find out everything, and let us know. He could hardly speak; he went out into the dark, and Henry shut the front door.

---

[1] Maud née Holt (1863–1937), Lady Tree, the actress wife (they married 1882) of the actor and theatre manager Sir Herbert Beerbohm Tree. She owned the Wharf, Sutton Courtenay, which Margot bought from her in 1911 with money given by Pierpont Morgan. She had, as Asquith thought, 'a good, though often disguised, sense of humour'.

We walked back into the bridge room. Henry sat down on the Chinese red arm-chair, put his head on his arms on the table, and sobbed passionately. I flung my arms round him and sat on his knee, silent. H. 'Oh! the awful waste of a man like Raymond!—the best brain of his age in our time, any career he liked lying in front of him. I always felt it would happen—Oc may get off, but not Raymond.' (He had said this to me constantly, over and over again.) He asked me the same questions about what Da had said, what Haig had said, where Katharine was, etc. He was dazed and terribly unhappy. I've never seen any father the least like Henry, and I have known a lot of fathers (Henry is <u>devoted to all his children</u>.) I thought it wiser to send Elizabeth and Puffin to him. I wanted to stop his emotion. E. flung her arms round his neck, and sat on his knees. Puffin brought a chair up close. He was frightened at seeing his father's grief, and rubbed his head against his father's sleeve. I put my arm round him....

Tom (Gen. Bridges)[1] told Elizabeth he wd. show her a card trick & I went into the bridge room to see how Henry looked, and to ask him to go to bed. He was sitting just where he had sat two hours before, his poor face set with tears, but quite simple and natural—a wonderful exhibition of emotion, self-mastery, and unself-consciousness. I was never more struck by the size and depth of his nature, the absence of bitterness and rebuke, the nobility and largeness of his heart and purpose, than I was that night. He saw none of the men, but walked up to his bedroom and talked to me till far into the night, or more accurately morning of 18th....

Wednesday 20 September 1916

Rendall spoke of Raymond....[2] He said he had always deplored Raymond's kind of influence on certain types of young men; that with all his

---

[1] Lieut.-Gen. Sir (George) Tom (Molesworth) Bridges (1871–1939), KCMG, 1919; veteran of Boer War; served in European War, 1914–18, and was (inter alia) commander of the 19th Division. Margot wrote in an unpublished part of her diary for Sept. 1916: 'Tom is a regular Trois Mousquetaire & mercenary—a natural soldier—would fight for any cause against any enemy. 6ft 4—good looking—a strong touch of bounder on the carpet but a hero in the field.'

[2] Montague John Rendall (1862–1950), on staff of Winchester College from 1887; headmaster, 1911–24.

amazing charm, glorious brain, modesty, industry, and great qualities, he lacked a great deal; and he had often felt sad over him. He said of course he didn't mean so much at Winchester, as at Balliol—that there, his influence had been most unfortunate....

I sent a note from Downing St. to Gen. Sir J. Cowans begging for a War Office car as I had bags & papers for Henry—he sent me a fine Rolls Royce open wh. was driven by the devil of a fine driver—except in the King of the Belgians Benz car I've never been so fast in my life. Swinging round a Huge corner we just snapped the cap off our own & the other man's hind wheels—I should have been killed in a twink as we were going 50 miles an our... but we got in to Wharf in dazzling sunshine at 5.30 & I was <u>delighted</u> to be alive & with Henry (who was more dear and selfless, & simple & above all sad[der] than a child. When he talked as he did every day & night to me of Raymond's future I sobbed). He was surrounded by blocks of letters & telegrams—2 good ones from John Buchan & Winston.

I am going to write a character sketch of Raymond as <u>I</u> knew him because I think his death is so fine that both for his own and his father's reputation he will be of interest to another generation. I will do this later on when I have time....

We are heavily over-drawn. It's a real Bore being poor. My father's will gets sillier every day. Eddy and Pamela don't want to entertain except on a very modest scale, and they have no uses to put money to; they don't even <u>like</u> giving (none of the boys of my family <u>like</u> spending or giving: they <u>dislike</u> it, it rankles with them, and shakes their nerve—I <u>love</u> it! it puts me in high spirits and fills me with warmth and courage, even though I know I shall be in debt.) Pamela's screwishness and want of generosity about money has been fatal for Eddy. It is of all defects the most <u>unnatural</u> to me, and yet far the commonest....

Sylvia [Henley] is a great joy to Henry. She is perfectly true and straight, and a fine creature. Eliz. is very fond of her, Violet not—but Violet is not fond of the Sheffield family now, which is a grief to me. Shedding old friends is so tragic, if she only knew it. No new ones make up for this....

I went round to see Katharine for the first time in her own house—I shall never forget her sorrow. Her beauty, and the pain of seeing her will remain with me forever. She was <u>wonderfully</u> generous too, as she knew I had often criticized [Raymond], but she said she knew he had always loved me, and she felt <u>sure</u> of my love for them both. Katharine is a fine creature....

Poor Henry, he never forgets for one moment that Raymond is dead—gone. His courage is touching, and his wonderful simplicity—<u>no</u> self-pity, no pose, no <u>any</u> of the things I have so often seen by which people draw attention to themselves when they are suffering; but he will never get over it.... It is impossible to write of Henry's <u>wonderful</u> sweetness at this time. Every night of his life he cried to me in his bedroom (I always go in and see him, however late he is. We don't sleep together, because I am such a vile sleeper that it would tire him. I am nearly always awake at 5 or 5.30, and I light up at 6 am—this would wake him up; and he never goes to bed before 1, and often at 2 am—this would not suit me.)...

Wednesday 11 October 1916

Henry escaped people and the Cabinet for as long as he could, but Wednesday 11th October he had to face the H. of Commons and make a great speech....[1] This speech...is more characteristic of Henry than almost any utterance he ever made....I had such toothache that I left E. [and] Violet just before the greatest part, and flew to Wimpole St.—just the sort of bad luck I have when I am run down. Everyone told me there was not a dry eye in the House when he said the concluding passages (these were the only two I missed). Everyone saw his emotion and thought of Raymond's death, they admired his self-control and depth of feeling. This it is that removes him from other men....

[1] Asquith spoke in the debate on the Vote of Credit, 11 Oct. 1916, *Parl. Deb.*, 86.95–104. This was his last parliamentary triumph as Prime Minister.

Friday 20 October 1916—The Wharf

Etty Desborough joined me.[1] Her first visit to my home....I never had a more appreciative guest, though Etty is not at <u>all</u> artistic. In fact, if anyone saw Taplow[2] with its flowers in bazaar baskets with large ribbon bows, and stuffed animals holding trays of visiting cards, you would almost think she had <u>no</u> taste. My place bewildered her, but I could see she <u>genuinely</u> admires it. She is fond of colour, and is clever in seeing when things are different to other people's. I was touched by her praise, and amused when she said, departing from her rare and almost overpowering tact, 'My darling, why have I never heard this praised more? Don't people rave about it, Margie? No one has ever told me about its beauty.'

Etty and I have perfectly different techniques in life, but we have a certain resemblance in experience. We have always had men in love with us, and liked the same sort of men, but it so happened I married my superior, and care for things that are not entirely material. I adore people, and parties, and bridge, and week-ends, and clothes: but after that we part a little. I don't care for Wells and Chesterton.[3] I should never have wanted my husband to be a peer, or wanted to be Queen Mary's lady-in-waiting—Royalty stifles me.[4]

Also, in spite of her children adoring her, and the book she has written, and the two glorious boys and their happiness, I would never want boys to be brought up like Billy and Julian were and I think myself they were a little tired of the social deluge in which they were whirled. Water parties, supper parties, the Thames, the visitors' book, the perpetual huge week-end parties (20 and 25, carefully arranged for months beforehand); small children in muslin giving an air of innocence to the two-and-two-ing

---

[1] Ettie was shocked by Margot's 'ebullience after Raymond's death': Davenport-Hines, *Ettie*, 225. Others were equally disapproving: Asquith, C., *Diaries*, 220–1, 223.

[2] Taplow Court, Buckinghamshire, on the Thames near Maidenhead, the home of Lord and Lady Desborough; the original manor house had undergone many alterations, one of them by William Burn, 1855–60.

[3] Herbert George Wells (1866–1946); Gilbert Keith Chesterton (1874–1936), two of the period's best known authors.

[4] From Jan. 1911 Ettie Desborough was extra Lady of the Bedchamber to Queen Mary.

under the trees, older children moving discreetly away, or even helping you to get rid of an awkward third; lawns and lovers, Malmaison and Maidenhead mixed with prize-rings and prize poems—landed Julian in a year of melancholia, and Billy into rather an insolent, wholly beloved, young man struggling with cynicism that sat ill on him.

Etty's book[1] is very interesting and deeply touching, but she seems to me to have eschewed every cloud, and an outsider in the future won't really understand English home life as it is. Raymond's account of the boys is the best thing in the book. I don't deny that they were splendid young men, and that they adored their parents. I only mean they were this in spite, and not because, of the life they led, more or less arranged by their mother.

I asked Etty in the course of our long talks if a certain beautiful young married woman with whom Julian fell in love was his first lapse:[2] she said oh! no, he had his ladies, and, I rather gathered, one settled mistress (melancholy thought for a boy of 21!): but that the lady gave him more bother and sadness by pretending she was going to have a baby by him, when she never was. I surprised Etty by saying it would break my heart if Puffin had a mistress before he married, or before he fell in love. We should never see eye to eye over this either. She would not believe me that none of our boys and no Lyttelton thought this sort of thing a sign of manliness—the best game-players I've ever seen were quite pure about women. Julian told his mother everything: they were very much alike.

We discussed all these things for a long time, also her boys. We cried a great deal, and I found her tremendously brave and simple; also, her religious side has come out. To lose two sons of the most adored and intimate sort in one year makes me shiver. I told her that if Puffin is sent down from Oxford, tragically as I should feel it, I would put it in this diary, and that she should have said this about Billy.[3] It was no real disgrace, and very

[1] *Pages from a Family Journal, 1888–1915* (privately printed, Spottiswoode, Eton, 1916).

[2] For Julian's love for Pamela Lytton, wife of the 3rd Earl of Lytton, see Mosley, *Grenfell*, 175–8.

[3] See Mosley, *Grenfell*, 199–201. Billy Grenfell was a serious student at Oxford but nevertheless took part in rowdyism and was sent down for three terms in 1912. The falsities in their

human; also Billy came out of it finely, as he felt it deeply. Raymond, Norah [Lindsay] and all his friends said he was a grand fellow, and the dons all fools, but Billy didn't agree, and said to me 'I'm glad, Margot, you think I was wrong, and that you've told me so—Mother is always trying to get me out, but father agrees with you. I wish, oh! how I wish, it had been different.' Billy Grenfell was one of the dearest boys that ever lived.

Etty said she had suffered so acutely over it all that she really could not have written of it. Here again we differed, though of course I quite understand: but a diary must be a perfectly true thing, and, if she only knew it, it is just the perpetual Bank Holiday feeling about the Book which spoils it for some of us. She told me that, though she adored Raymond, she thought his influence at Oxford (specially on the younger, imitating generation) unfortunate...

I am going to try and write about Raymond with sincerity and truth and love.[1] I loved him very much & have got several wonderful letters from him. When I first married he was my favourite step-child; he appeared to have the most distinction & to the end was more punctual & less self-indulgent than the rest. He never rang for servants to post his letters at 2 a.m. or to have his pipe or papers brought from 1 room to another by a servant who had to come up 3 storeys high; he didn't break & spoil so many things, & was less clumsy in every way. He had a beautiful face; his mother's eyes & exactly his mother's temperament—otherwise he was singularly unlike her & very different to his father except in his knowledge & sense of literature, style, taste & scholarship.

Raymond Asquith was the kindest man without nature, the cleverest man without ambition, & the most critical without being censorious that I have ever known. Why, with his amazing brains, wit, industry, sense of duty (which was very strong), charm, beauty and health, he did not make the world ring with his success, is an interesting and perplexing problem.

---

elders' attitudes, as exemplified by Ettie, constituted one of the propellants which had driven the younger generation towards the tenets of 'Anti-Cant'.

[1] This passage in the manuscript has obviously been worked over, with underlining in red.

We know why men like A. J. Balfour fail—he is unintelligibly detached and unindustrious: he leaves everything to chance. He does not care much one way or another.[1] <u>Raymond left nothing to chance</u>. We know why Winston fails, why G. Wyndham failed—overblown Egotism, without convictions or common sense, would wreck more powerful brains than either of these.... A man who dies at 37 having swept both Winchester and Oxford of every prize; who took a first in law plus <u>every</u> first, and was a fellow of All Souls; very popular in society, and—above all—<u>adored</u> by officers and men, can never be associated with the word 'failure': but everyone knows that Raymond might have done more with his amazing gifts.[2]

I don't think lack of ambition quite covers the ground, <u>though he was paralysingly deficient in this</u>; or lack of imagination, though he undoubtedly lacked this when compared with his father. No, it was something else. It was a want of nature, 'quickening spirit', <u>passion</u> or <u>compassion</u>. Among the many sorrows of his death to me is the certainty that this would have changed. Henry tells me his hostility to authority had already shown itself before his mother died, and that it had worried her a little. No stepmother can impose authority on her stepchildren without making herself loathed. If she is wise, she trusts that her love, and giving all she has got of protection, pleasure, money and counsel, will give her <u>some</u> influence but Raymond was a very uninfluenceable man: insolently

---

[1] Margot's (and Asquith's) belief about Balfour's indifference on great issues appears constantly in her diary; in her entry of 12 Nov. 1911 she wrote: 'Henry talking to me of Arthur Balfour said: "He is neither a Liberal or a Conservative he is a sceptic".' Margot did not realize, however, the immense importance which Balfour had attached, both before and during the war, to defence issues; for Austen Chamberlain's view see *Down the Years*, 218.

[2] At Winchester Raymond won the Queen's Gold Medal for Latin Essay, the Warden and Fellows' Prizes for Greek Prose and Verse, and the Goddard Scholarship. He gained the top scholarship to Balliol; and at Oxford was awarded 'firsts' in Classical Moderations, 'Greats', and Jurisprudence; he also won the University's Craven, Ireland, Derby, and Eldon Scholarships, and was elected to the presidency of the Union Society, as well as to the fellowship of All Souls which Margot mentions. Being very competitive he was annoyed by his failure to be elected to a Merton College fellowship (where he was runner-up), or to win the Hertford Scholarship, which his brother Cyril won later to fill 'the lacuna in the family annals': Simon, *Retrospect*, 142.

fearless, perfectly sincere, morally, physically and intellectually cool and independent....

No one stood up to Raymond: on the contrary! They retold and retailed the good sayings characteristic of his moral coolness, and intellectual contempt, or veiled Blasphemy, till what was started as an experiment became a habit. It is shy-making to the best of us to have to live up to a reputation of studied brutality and brilliant aloofness when *au fond* you are extremely kind and easily pleased. I saw all this developing in front of me as clear as fish in a bowl.

I don't know who invented the game, but it exactly illustrates what I mean: 'a Raymond', 'a Violet', 'a Margot' were coined perpetually, and became great favourites. They were invented remarks characteristic of all of us. 'A Margot' generally dealt with my social fearlessness or brutality, a sort of Dr. Johnson 'Madam do you wish the child's bladder to burst!!'.[1] 'A Violet' mildly exposed a phase of rather small jealousy or vanity that she was going through at the time. 'A Raymond' was invariably the same kind of thing, sometimes lewd, often blasphemous, always Brilliant.... The 'Margots' were sometimes told before my face—the 'Violets' never: but the 'Raymonds' always; and though he was without any vanity, they made him just a little self-conscious. Cys says it was Raymond's disciples copying him that did harm or that harmed his reputation.

I think Raymond quite unconsciously started a school that hurt a younger lot—Edward Horner, Etty's boys, Patrick and others. 'Anti-cant' these silly young folk called it but this is nonsense...

---

[1] Margot did not like to record, even in the diary, the extent to which the younger generation mocked her. The jokes about her remarks concerned their tactlessness, but also her irrationality and inconsequence: Violet wrote to Venetia Stanley, 2 Feb. 1908, about her stepmother's frequent complaints while on holiday in Switzerland: 'I sympathize & enquire & find that it's invariably a tragedy based on an ointment, woolly, or peppermint issue—& tho' of course I am distressed that M. should be so much upset I can't stretch my imagination sufficiently to take it in quite the right spirit. That is always my difficulty with M.—my pity is arrested by amusement on its way & arrives with half the proper impetus.'

Margot did not claim that her account of the events which marked the ending of her hus-
band's premiership was entirely coherent. At one point in it she wrote: 'I have not time for
anything! I can't write up my notes, so jump about from date to date.' The diary pages about
the crisis days also include two references to a 'separate volume' containing 'the whole corres-
pondence between Ll.G. and Henry and every fact of the crisis'. The thought of this volume
enabled Margot to confine the diary entries about 'those sad days between Sunday Dec. 2nd
[sic] and Monday 11th [to] a few personal happenings'.[1] The 'separate volume' has not sur-
vived among Margot's papers, but its existence would explain the relative brevity of the
account below.

Tuesday 5 December 1916—Friday 15 December 1916

<u>6am Downing Street. My last day there.</u>

I am quite alone in this house. Henry is at Walmer Castle with V. & Bongie.
Elizabeth staying with Alice Wimborne in Dublin. Cys recovering from
flu in Brighton with Beb & Cynthia. Oc with his Naval Hood Battalion in
France (waiting for Death —).

I have gone through deep, <u>deep</u> waters since Saturday, 2nd Dec. 1916.
When a government falls in <u>one week</u>!! or I should say five days, you may
be quite sure its overthrow has been planned long, <u>long</u> before. I have
seen the causes of this <u>staring me in the face for months</u>. Directly Ll.G.
was put in War Office, whatever I may have written in my diary at that
time (which I can't look up now to verify),[2] I can truly say I knew it was
our doom. <u>It has been</u>. It was the <u>first time</u> that Henry gave way to
<u>blackmail</u>.[3]

Henry said to Crewe, Montagu and others the night Kitchener was
drowned, or a few days after, 'I will <u>not</u> put Ll.G. in his place in War Office.'
The very same night Rufus and Montagu and others went to Henry, and

---

[1] Bodleian Library, MSS Eng. d. 3215 fos. 145ʳ, 142ᵛ, 147ʳ.

[2] Margot's fears about Lloyd George's appointment as War Secretary constitute an
important theme in Part VIII; see also Thompson, *Northcliffe*, 258; Gwynne, *Rasp*, 194; above,
5 May–29 August 1916.

[3] Margot was apt to regard any decision made in recognition of political weakness as a
surrender to 'blackmail'. Her husband had never taught her to recognize how often a political
leader had to accept that he lacked the power to act as he would like. Ll.G.'s War Secretaryship
was merely a striking illustration of this.

told him what Ll.G. would do if he <u>didn't</u> get all he wanted. One or 2 others, and Bongie and Violet, <u>all</u> thought it would be an <u>excellent</u> appointment.

I cried and sobbed over it: I could not <u>believe</u> it. All the time of our Rosyth visit (& after) when V., Bongie, Hankey, Montagu H & I were in Scotland seeing the fleet (just after the Jutland battle) & for a long time Henry & I <u>never</u> talked politics, he some times tried when alone with me & of course before the others but I never joined. <u>I was heart broken with the Folly of this appointment</u> & really frightened at the want of wisdom & perception of our immediate surrounders! (Hankey & Eric were the only ones who were very uncomfortable. Everyone Crewe, Nash, Baker, Runciman all told me since that they were sure at the time it spelt our Doom as it has!). H. and I were on bad political terms for three or four weeks. He said, when I asked him why he had given WO to Ll.G., that there was <u>no</u> prominent figure to take K.'s place; and though repeatedly urged by the King and many, many soldiers—a long signed memorial sent him by Ld French and many other requests to take WO himself—<u>Rufus</u>, Bongie and particularly <u>Montagu</u> said that if Ll.G. was denied his way he would stump the country against H., and <u>force a general Election</u>!!!

It was enough to make an angel weep! Ll.G. to stump the country with the backing of the Northcliffe Press against his own PM, who had not only saved him, body and soul, in the Marconi incident with Rufus and Elibank, but who was a thousand times more respected, and loved, and trusted of the people than Ll.G. ever was![1] I shall never be sure in my mind from what reason Rufus was so keen about this appointment. He is a truthful, very honest man, and a wise judge, but he is a <u>coward</u>, and a great friend of Ll.G.'s.

Bongie is a lethargically un-clever man, and [a] <u>very</u> poor judge of men. He is the greatest <u>angel</u> that ever lived, but has no <u>life</u> of any kind in him— no <u>savoir faire</u>; and was no more fit to be first secretary to a man with

[1] Asquith was understandably unwilling to break into Margot's fantasy world over this point. Northcliffe's failure to dislodge Kitchener in May 1915 showed that Northcliffe was ineffective if he attacked a popular leader.

Henry's kind of <u>non-dramatic</u> nature than the dog Tokio.[1] A Prime Minister wants 2 things in a first secretary—a straight, courteous, good man; and a man of <u>rapid action</u> and <u>knowledge of the world</u>. Bongie is born without any sort of <u>indignation</u>, incapable of action of any kind, dilatory, slovenly, <u>very</u> industrious but quite without training of any kind; as second or third quite <u>glorious</u>, but as first secretary to my Henry, <u>Hopeless</u>.

He would have been the best sec. in the world to Ll.G., Carson, Northcliffe, Bottomley or any evil Hasty man & would have got on with them all <u>every-one loves Bongie</u>—one man is the same as another to him except as regards character. He has never seen once in all these years (in spite of my having told him 10,000 times) <u>that Ll.G. would ruin this Gov.</u> He has joined with Montagu, Eric & others in giving H. the most <u>rotten</u> advice—or at any rate approval of all Ll.G.'s schemes but <u>this</u> would not have mattered so much. But what neither Bongie, Gulland (First Whip) nor <u>any</u> of our surrounders saw, was the suicidal Folly of <u>Delay</u>, and neglecting <u>our own army</u>—Liberal MPs, Liberal Press, and Liberals all over England, and <u>our own Press</u>. In a war like this which gets on every one's nerves, and where quarrels of Allies, colleagues, admirals and Generals make things almost <u>Hellishly</u> difficult, delays are unavoidable: but they have been made twice as bad by two <u>avoidable</u> things—the first, by Ll.G. telling Northcliffe <u>every</u> cabinet secret, so that his 52 papers could ramp round and say 'We want this, and <u>intend to get it</u>' (something he knew the cabinet had been settled upon one hour after it had been proposed); and second, that when the thing was fixed, and decisions arrived at, they were never made known or enforced quickly. We had three schoolboys—Bongie, Davies and Ed. Marsh—to push them forward; and a whip, an old Scotch 'budy', running round full of small gossip, without the <u>faintest</u> authority, and <u>unable to stage-manage anything</u>.[2]

---

[1] Margot originally wrote 'stupid' instead of 'un-clever'. Tokio appears with Puffin in a photograph of Aug. 1910. 'Bongie' had been far from inactive during the crisis. See, for instance, his letter to Violet, 22 Nov. 1916, on the need for the premier to arrange a meeting with Lloyd George: Bonham Carter Papers, 258; and, for his earlier efforts in the same direction, Bonham Carter, *Diaries, 1914–45*, 90.

[2] Margot refers to John Gulland (see Biographical Notes).

Henry (full from 10 a.m. to 1 a.m. of work of every kind, and giving an impression of great ease,[1] because he is the quickest man in the world) would no more have suggested that the Press should be dealt with, or taken steps to deal with it, than he would have tried to move the Albert Hall!

The Press either kills you or you kill it, in times of War. Gulland should have got hold of our grand Gardiner[2] (*Daily News*), our idiot Scott (of the *Manchester Guardian*), our weak Donald (of *Daily Chronicle*), etc., etc., and countered the huge, rich, vindictive, personally-loathing-Henry, Northcliffe-Press.[3]

I can't blame Bongie, but he also might have been alive to the dangers of neglecting our own Party and Press. In and out of season I have implored with tears that news should be given to our men. We have kept the Liberal Party starved in the country.[4] Neither H. or I would ever see a Press-man: but it was for H.'s bodyguard to protect him from these kind of small but perpetual crucifixions. Every story told of Ll.G.'s methods caused laughter (V. & Bongie roared with laughter when Ll.G. asked Bongie to be his secretary) that same laughter that rung down the river the night of the pleasure-party steamer when Denis Anson was drowned (the spectators went to bed and the opera while their friend's body was floating and unfound).

[1] Asquith did not give the impression of working from '10 a.m. to 1 a.m.'. Fair-minded observers questioned, not so much his rapidity in dispatching current business, but his readiness to reflect on, and plan for, problems foreseen.

[2] Alfred George Gardiner (1865–1946), Liberal journalist, editor of the Daily News 1902–19; strong supporter of Asquith against Lloyd George in the post-1916 schism.

[3] Gulland and Bonham Carter could have achieved little with the Liberal press at this stage. On 25 Nov. Gardiner's warning in the *Daily News* to those going 'about with lists of new cabinets in their pockets' merely emphasized the seriousness of the crisis. After talks with Lloyd George on 21 and 22 Nov., C. P. Scott concluded (28 Nov.): 'With the present men we shall not win the War.' On 29 Nov. the *Daily Chronicle* defined 'inability to make up its mind' as 'the Ministry's arch-defect': Koss, *Political Press*, ii. 299–300; *Scott, Diaries*, 233. Having quarrelled with Lloyd George over British strategy in Sept.–Oct. 1916, Northcliffe did not have a great part in toppling the government. On 1 Dec. 1916 Frances Stevenson recorded: 'Northcliffe has turned up again, grovelling…if there is anything big happening [he] would hate to be out of the know'; *Stevenson Diary*, 130.

[4] For an instance of Margot's commendable dislike of keeping an 'overstrained country in the dark', and Asquith's inexplicable delay in defining his position on conscription, see the diary entry for 21 Aug. 1915, 186–8 above.

Throughout the whole crisis lasting from Sat Dec 2nd. 1916 till we left Downing St. Friday 15th. Dec. 1916 I can truthfully say I never saw Bongie shocked, distressed, indignant or in the <u>smallest degree surprised</u>. He was kind, busy, sympathetic, understanding & as always—<u>most</u> unselfish in little & big ways but as imperturbable over the whole catastrophe as if it had been of <u>daily occurrence</u>. He saw H. wounded & <u>stabbed to the heart</u>. Me an absolute wreck! <u>morally</u> disgusted & <u>shocked</u>—the Gov. Smashed to atoms in the <u>greatest war</u> & at the most <u>dangerous</u> moment in the life of this country & men put in its place of the lowest possible type (a <u>Press</u> Government—Ll.G., Northcliffe, Rothermere,[1] Aitken[*], Carson, etc.) but <u>not one sign of indignation</u> or any sort did I or any-one else see. The stupidest Tories in London were <u>bewildered</u> & <u>horrified</u> at Ll.G.'s base & long intrigue coming off & expressed themselves freely over it but darling Bongie's temperature was normal!

Thursday 14 December 1916[2]

I walked gingerly into the outer hall, with all the hats on the pegs outside cabinet room....The head messenger always warned me and screened me from meeting any of the cabinet. There he was as usual at foot of stairs to tell me the coast was clear. 'There they all are! any amount of 'em—Ld Milner, Ld Curzon, Ld Derby, Henderson, Jellicoe, Robertson, and there! It makes one's 'eart ache to think of our dear Prime Minister away, and such fellers as Carson and an ignorant little sneak like Ll.G. shoving themselves in his shoes.'...

Henry has had every hour of his time occupied <u>to the full, so much</u> that only a very foolish person would say [that for] any of this breakdown and calamitous smash he himself has been to blame, for not seeing the Press, or speaking in public to his own army enough; <u>not valuing appearances</u> or <u>putting himself forward at all</u>; above all, not informing a <u>very</u> ignorant,

---

[1] Harold Sidney Harmsworth (1868–1940), cr. Baron Rothermere 1919; Viscount 1919; newspaper proprietor and younger brother of Lord Northcliffe.

[2] Part at least of this entry was presumably written late in February 1917. Margot's practice, in evidence here, of treating anyone from her husband's government who agreed to serve under Ll.G. as a 'traitor' or 'deserter' naturally aroused resentment.

very unhappy public, of what has been going on; and not threatening to resign or dismiss a colleague if such and such was not done—no doubt has been his fault: but after all! these are not great faults!

His primary idea has been keeping a united front in the face of Germany, and when History is written, every one will say that no Allies ever kept together so long and with such cohesion in any war as in this; no colleagues in any coalition have ever kept together with so little friction, considering the sort of men it has been composed of (the brains, or rather varying mentality and temperament). Want of stage-management, having to take advice of experts (soldiers and sailors), and the personal as well as National Quarrels have combined to make this Ministry fall (Plus Lloyd George and Northcliffe).

Germany went on her knees and was brought to her knees 12 December 1916 through Henry's guidance and our Blockade [five] days after Lloyd George had kissed hands.[1] (Even Northcliffe can't say it is the new Government that has done this!) It is a curious irony of Fate! that the great 'Warman' who has betrayed and tried to crucify his master under the plausible and perpetually advertised 'Firmer Prosecution of the War'—our Present Prime Minister—should be the man whose first job it is to deal with peace proposals.

In this connection, Jimmy Rothschild said a curious thing to me on Sunday 3rd December 1916 at Walmer: 'It will be easier for Lloyd George than Mr Asquith to deal with peace, as he has never gone so far as the great speech in which Mr A. said we would never sheathe the sword, etc.'[2] I—quite forgetting Lloyd George's vulgar interview given for the sake of America to American Press—said nothing, but pondered in my mind, and came to the conclusion that Lloyd George must have fully discussed this with Neil Primrose (whom Jimmy Rothschild believes will be the

---

[1] On 12 Dec. 1916 Germany for the first time made direct peace overtures to the Allies, by means of a note sent through neutral powers. The economic conditions obtaining in Germany, and in particular shortages of basic food supplies, arising from the British blockade of her ports, was widely seen as creating the conditions for this peace initiative.

[2] 'We should not sheath the sword…until the Military domination of Russia was fully and finally destroyed': H.H.A., Guildhall speech, Monday 9 Nov. 1914 (*Times*, 10 Nov. 1914, 9e).

future PM of this country!!) and Mr. Beck[1] (two of our deserters). It will be curious to see if I am right—I have <u>nothing</u> to go upon....

<u>I was on telephone at Walmer Castle 6.30 on night of Dec. 12th</u> Tuesday 1916 when Evelyn Fitzgerald at War Office read out loud to me these words 'Germany together with her allies, conscious of her responsibility before God, their own nation and humanity, have proposed this morning to the Hostile powers peace negotiations.'

I said them out loud for V. to write down and ran to Henry who... was in bed from pure exhaustion and liver poisoning but which <u>we</u> (Dr. Parkinson and I) called 'influenza', on purpose to prevent the Northcliffe Press plus Ll.G. saying he was a broken finished man (and Robinson and D. Mail printing veiled suggestions that he had cancer—the wish being father to the thought). I opened the door of H.'s bedroom at Walmer Tuesday 12th Dec 1916 read out loud what Evelyn Fitzgerald had told me—6 p.m. Henry sat up in bed, very excited (being very unexcitable though always enormously interested in everything).

[H.]   This transforms everything! Germany does these things well. The moment is well chosen—Christmas, and every nation dog-tired of the war. Everything depends on the terms, <u>what</u> they are.

M.   They'll clear completely out of the West, I suppose, and retain the whole East! but can Russia have Constantinople?

H.   One can't tell, but I should not be surprised if later on, when the Germans are <u>really</u> on their last legs, which they <u>aren't now</u>,—if Germany, with <u>every</u> right of way and safeguard, bribed Russia with Constantinople. (He was much excited, and it rejoiced my heart to see him. He looked terribly ill nevertheless—tired and flattened out.)

M.   Thank God it was under <u>your</u> leadership that Germany has been brought to her knees—no one can say Ll.G. brought this about.

H.   (sweetly) No, they can't say that.

---

[1] Arthur Cecil Beck (1878–1932), Kt 1920; Liberal MP 1906–Jan. 1910, Dec. 1910–22.

M. (very sadly putting face down to his) Oh! if it had only come in your
     time! But now they must consult you. I thank God you never fell
     into the trap of the 'noble role' urged on you by the King, Bonar,
     Ll.G., etc.[1]

(H.'s second remark after hearing of Germany Peace soundings: 'It's our
navy that has done this. We have throttled them slowly but surely by our
Blockade.[2] No one can say they have been beaten on land: except for the
Somme offensive they have had no failures.[3] Haig's success on the Somme
had 3 great values. It relieved Russia in East; France at Verdun; and our
Gen. Staff think the French and ourselves have killed more Germans than
we have had killed.')[4] ... I kept my face next to him in silence till I thought
my tears would upset him. The news had excited him; but his first words
to me, when he spoke of what had happened, haunted me—'I feel as if I
had been stabbed.' He kissed me, and I felt his tears.

   (If Bongie had only kept me au fait, like Nash did in the Conscription
crisis, I would have done much. I would have seen Crewe, Runciman,
McK. and Grey, who would all have resigned than let H. fall in with the
idiotic Ll.G.'s 'in and out' clause, apropos of the war committee.[5]

   Man after man on our side tumbled on top of each other into Ll.G.'s
simple trap of getting rid of Henry. Bongie should have sent for Crewe

---

[1] i.e. H.H.A.'s acceptance of a subordinate office in a government led by Ll.G.
[2] Bethmann Hollweg's peace initiative was stillborn, because Hindenburg (Chief of Staff
since 28 Aug. 1916) and Ludendorff were already sapping his authority. He could not offer to
withdraw completely from Belgium: Craig, Germany, 376–7. Asquith and Lloyd George both
dismissed the initiative when speaking in the Commons, 19 Dec.; Asquith was right to stress
the effect of the blockade: see Offer, Agrarian Interpretation, 28–31, 61–3.
[3] This seems like one of Margot's exaggerations. Asquith would surely have allowed that
the Battle of the Marne, 'First Ypres', and Verdun had been German failures.
[4] The Somme casualties remain controversial because of German concealment and loss
of records. See also Asquith in the Commons, 19 Nov. 1917: Spender and Asquith, ii. 292–3.
[5] Margot refers to the 25 Nov. proposals put forward by Bonar Law, Ll.G., and Carson (her
'little gang of brigands') as the basis of a rearrangement of the government, devolving greater
power on a smaller war committee of four; in theory the premier would preside over this, but
since it would sit in continuous session, and the premier's other responsibilities would pre-
clude his regular attendance, Lloyd George would effectively take the chair; it represented a
reduction in the role and authority of the Prime Minister, which Asquith strongly resented.

and the others. The colleagues felt this, and said so to me, not with any bitterness, as they are all fond of Bongie, but they blamed him very much. Nash took Bongie's place at the time of Bongie's honeymoon [and] managed the conscription crisis with Montagu's help and mine (in a small way) <u>wonderfully</u>.

The Political Crisis began by Ll.G. putting forward certain proposals to Henry Friday night Dec. 1st 1916. <u>I had never heard of these proposals</u> which had been for some time on the *tapis*. Having formed a low opinion of Ll.G. as a loyal colleague, or even as a man of intellect, education, or capacity, I had, alas! lost touch with Henry and several others (Montagu, Bongie, Violet, Eric, etc., all <u>tremendously attracted</u>, and partly taken in, and half afraid of him);[1] so that I was not in the confidence of any <u>new</u> giving-way to Ll.G. I may be vain, but I shall <u>always</u> regret this. I am well backed up in this view by Crewe, who told Peggy that I had been wonderfully right all through the war in my <u>political advice</u>; and that if Henry had taken it latterly (of course he didn't mean about big things of the war! but merely the political government situations) Ll.G. would <u>never</u> have ousted him (Henry).[2]

In consequence of this, it came like a bomb to me on Saturday morning 2nd Dec 1916 that the Government was tottering, and on the eve of collapse. I begged H. (and even Bongie was against our going to Walmer Castle, an arctic place where I and Eliz always feel ill) not to go to Walmer:

---

[1] Bringing Margot into the picture would have been far riskier for Bongie in Dec. 1916 than it had been for Nash during the last days of 1915. The later crisis, unlike the earlier, involved members of both parties, and Bongie had found in Aug. 1915 how indiscreet and maladroit Margot's interventions could be: 'Tomorrow of course we have a meeting of the Dardanelles Committee & I suppose that I must be ready to face Margot. I think that I shall ask her to stop lobbying people about the conscription question. She is doing no one any good. I wish she were not coming down': MBC to VA, 30 Aug. 1915, Bonham Carter, *Diaries, 1914–45*, 74. Bongie made efforts to promote more frequent meetings between the premier and Ll.G.: and, as Margot records, it took Bongie's arrival by car at Walmer, a.m. 3 Dec., to persuade Asquith to return to London that afternoon and see Bonar Law.

[2] Crewe may well have told his wife that Margot was less complacent than the premier about the precariousness of the latter's position. Unfortunately, Margot, though alert to political danger, could be quite unrealistic on the way to react to it.

but the idea that sea air and rest from the awful strain of colleagues, etc, must on <u>no</u> account be sacrificed prevailed, and we went down as usual....

I was so exhausted & anxious & <u>miserable</u> that I pretended I wanted to sleep & got into my own reserved carriage & let B. Cowans and Beatrice[1] get into the next carriage. I was alone & very sleepless. I felt all through my bones that it was <u>all up</u>—a horrible sensation (that I have had <u>all my life</u>, and by which I suffer double pain) <u>that I was living among the blind</u>, that Henry was going to be betrayed. I remember the same kind of stomach-less, stabbing feeling, when I heard that Carson and Ll.G. had dined <u>together</u> the night Carson attacked the Government, and particularly Bonar Law, Carson's old friend, in the Nigerian Debate. That night Ll.G. gave Bonar away: he didn't vote for him, or go near the House. From <u>that night it was quite clear that</u> Northcliffe, Rothermere, Bonar, Carson, Ll.G. (and, I've been told since, a man called Max Aitken, lately elevated by Ll.G. to the peerage) were going to run the Government. I felt it <u>less</u> strongly over Carson and Ll.G.'s sudden friendship, but going to Walmer that afternoon <u>I knew it was the end.</u>

Henry was in fair form. B. Pembroke[2] looked handsome. She is a regular Paget & just a little tired of the stupid Tory Party. She has a touch of social & intellectual snobbishness. Haughty over Home Rule—humble when we were in Downing St. & now we are out—<u>kind</u>—but I shall not expect her to run after us as quickly as she did.

Sunday morning 3 December Bongie came down in a WO car to fetch H. to London. I made up my mind to go, though I had <u>no</u> illusions as to how much good I could do!...H. was quite surprised at the very idea of my going to London—I could see he shared none of my fears....We arrived late—2.30 in Downing St....I never went out all the afternoon, but saw several people and wrote a lot of letters....I felt ill with suppressed excitement and misery, and found myself looking at Disraeli's hideous chairs in

[1] (Jane) Beatrice née Mills (1883–1972), American–born heiress; she had married the 8th Earl Granard in 1909; Forbes House was in Halkin Street, Westminster.
[2] Lady Beatrice née Paget, who married, 1904, Reginald Herbert, 15th Earl of Pembroke.

H.'s room, and out of the windows on to the tops of the recruiting sheds in the Horse Guards parade, and wondered if I would look out of the windows or observe the ugly furniture for many more days in 10 Downing St.

H. came to my bedroom 15 to 8 p.m., and told me he thought the crisis looked like being over, though he was not very confident.

[H.]   When Ll.G. came into the room, he almost put his arm round my neck, and begged me not to believe all the stories that McKenna was spreading about—that he (Ll.G.) wanted to take my place, and was disloyal, etc., etc. I told him to sit down, that I never heard any of the stories he referred to, and cared little for gossip. He almost had tears in his eyes.

We went through his proposals. I told him I would not include Carson, as both he and I knew how useless, ignorant, sentimental and talkative he had been before he resigned. I would not oust A. Balfour, though later on in my reconstruction I might put him in FO. Arthur gets on curiously well with the three men who fight like the soldiers, quite as bad—Madden,[1] Beatty[2] and Jellicoe (H. blamed Jellicoe the most he said to me another day.)[3] Apropos of my not attending every War Council, we might come to some arrangement. I said I need not attend every time, but that I would let him know it all in writing.

M.   You will never never let Ll.G. oust you from the War Council!—this is quite obviously his design: and to keep you in so as to give weight, Honour and Respectability to his lot. But no human being outside will ever ever forgive you or him, or believe in you again, if you sit in the next room while the war is conducted without you. They are all mad to have advised this—Montagu, Hankey, Eric. To do Rufus

---

[1] Rear-Admiral Charles Edward Madden (1862–1935), KCB 1916, cr. Bt. 1919; Chief of Staff to Jellicoe, 1914–16; second in command to Beatty, 1916–19.

[2] Vice-Admiral David Beatty (1871–1936), KCB 1914, 1st Earl 1919, OM 1919; commanded 1st Battle Cruiser Squadron 1912–16; Grand Fleet 1916–19; Admiral of the Fleet 1919; First Sea Lord 1919–27.

[3] Margot means that these three great sailors quarrelled between themselves as much as the generals were prone to do.

justice, he told me he was <u>always</u> against your giving up chairman-ship of War Council.

(Rufus was a very unhappy man all these days. He served both Henry and Ll.G. No one can serve two masters. 'He that is not for me is against me.'[1] I told Rufus in a <u>letter</u> just what I thought. I've been more than straight with the enemy, also with Montagu, Derby and all of them. It is easier to be straight to enemies than friends. Rufus brought this letter of mine back to me, and burnt it in my drawing-room fire in 10 Downing St. I never turned a hair <u>or took back a word of my letter</u>. I only said and <u>felt</u> sorry that I had hurt him.)

But, though they varied in their method, most of the cabinet seemed to think H.'s decisions were not registered with violence, and that he did not stop the quarrels (How any human being can stop quarrels!!) between Ll.G. and McKenna, A. J. Balfour and Curzon. H. told me Arthur was much the worst, that he kept <u>everything</u> hanging up—Hankey also said the same; and though they <u>all</u> (except Ll.G.) wanted H. to be <u>complete</u> boss of War Council, they seemed to think some of the talk on civil de-tails waste of time for a man as busy as he was....

I <u>persisted</u> in this short talk at dressing-time (Sunday 3d December 1916) that Ll.G. wanted to oust Henry in his own fascinating way, or rather <u>not oust</u> him, but put him in the <u>back garden</u>; and then run [in] his big Press—'Nothing done today, as the PM presided', 'Great Progress done in Downing St., Mr Ll.G. presided' etc, etc. Henry practically agreed with me, and said he had not the '<u>faintest</u> intention of giving up the direction of the war to Ll.G. or any-one else!!'

I felt sure that Henry had not made it <u>clear</u> to Ll.G. that as President of War Council he—H.—<u>was</u> controlling the war & that <u>nothing</u> would in-duce him to abandon this position though he was quite willing if the Council had merely to register decisions of transport & unimportant things to let Ll.G. take the chair in his absence. Henry swore to me he had made it clear enough & that I was quite wrong Ll.G. did <u>not</u> want to oust

---

[1] 'He that is not *with* me...': Matthew 12: 30; Luke 11: 23.

him (once someone sets themselves to think <u>all</u> you say is prejudice! and all they think is correct! you are helpless).

We dined with Montagus....I was paralysed by misery, and could not look at H. for fear of tears. Hugh Godley[1] was there—Montagu in quite fair spirits—also Henry.

When we got home, H. and I talked till far into the morning. I sat on his knees. I asked him if he had made it <u>quite</u> clear to Ll.G. about his (Henry's) never giving up the direction of the war. He was quite surprised and almost irritable. He asked me if I took him for a fool. I said 'No,' but I took Ll.G. for a knave.

He went into greater detail over his afternoon's talk with Ll.G. He told me that Ll.G., after putting his arms round H.'s neck and protesting his perpetual <u>devotion</u> and <u>loyalty</u> (was ass enough to do it twice!), walked up and down the cabinet room, in spite of H. saying he had not motored up from Walmer to listen to gossip.

When he did sit down, Henry went through the proposals with Ll.G. He said he would <u>not</u> give way to a Press campaign over A. Balfour. He (H.) had got rid of Jackson,[2] and brought Jellicoe up to Admiralty, and that Arthur had the confidence of the two quarrelsome heads (Beatty and Jellicoe) which was useful, as they did not want the Fisher–Beresford[3] rows over again: <u>so Arthur was to stay</u>. Ll.G. abused Arthur, said he was gaga, useless, etc., and would have to go; but as H. didn't <u>budge</u>, they rapidly turned to Carson, over which (as the whole correspondence shows) H. was <u>quite</u> clear. <u>He wd. not include him</u>. Carson's friendship with Ll.G. had dated back some time. He was the instrument with which Ll.G. knew he cd. break the cabinet.

---

[1] Hugh John Godley (1877–1950), eldest son of 1st Baron Kilbracken (s. 1932); a Balliol friend and contemporary of Raymond Asquith, and of Bongie; called to the Bar, 1902; Assistant Parliamentary Counsel to the Treasury.

[2] Admiral Sir Henry Bradwardine Jackson (1855–1929), KCVO 1906; First Sea Lord, 1915–16; succeeded by Jellicoe; Admiral of the Fleet, 1919. Balfour had wished to bring Jellicoe to the Admiralty, but also to retain Jackson: see Young, *Balfour*, 364; Marder, *Royal Navy*, iii. 283–4.

[3] Admiral Lord Charles Beresford (1846–1919), cr. Baron 1916. Had a naval career of great distinction, but as second in command to Fisher 1900–2 fell out with him and opposed his reforms. This gave rise to a long series of public quarrels.

Bonar Law, being a <u>poor</u>, weak, ambitious creature, has always been terrified, as a bird with a snake, of Carson.[1] On the night of the Nigerian debate, Bonar was subjugated, the thing was over! Carson and Ll.G. made up their minds to get Bonar out of the cabinet. They dined together *à deux*. Ll.G., instead of supporting B. Law (like the Prime Minister and <u>all</u> the others did) <u>the leader of the opposition</u>, saw his opportunity of getting rid of him, breaking the Gov., and either making <u>himself</u> P.M. (<u>which I don't think was at all his original intention</u>); or of gradually shoving Henry into the background, discrediting him in a more violent Press intrigue than ever before ('New submarine menace!') and making himself Inevitable and adored, plus collaring the <u>Party machine</u> and <u>party funds</u>. The little gang of brigands—Northcliffe, Rothermere, Aitken, (a vulgar Canadian of lowest reputation and charming wit, I am told, whom I have never seen) Carson, Bonar, Ll.G., plus *officiers de liaison* like Rufus, and, in an innocent way, several others, have achieved a good deal, but not <u>all</u> <u>they wanted</u>!...

Tues 5th December 1916 Henry said at lunch to Eric, Hankey, Masterton Smith, Eliz., Oc and Bongie 'Grey and I are symbols: we represent what is to the foreigner strength and unity. A break in this Government will plunge every embassy in despair, and peace meetings, or anyway peace talk, will start off at a great pace. Everyone is war-weary.' Eric said no one in London had any idea how much Grey was loved by all the foreign ambassadors. Hankey and Masterton more than agreed with H. They were both in the lowest of spirits....[2]

---

[1] To interpret Bonar's conduct in the Nigerian debate, 8 Nov. 1916, as exemplifying 'terror' was one of Margot's more notable extravagances. If Bonar had been 'terrified' of Carson, he would not have treated the amendment to the Coalition's proposal on the captured Nigerian properties as a confidence question. He treated it like that because he could not allow half of the Unionist MPs to defy the Coalition government with impunity.

[2] Asquith seems to have overrated Grey's indispensability almost as much as his own; but the importance of Balfour's acceptance of the Foreign Office under Ll.G. can hardly be exaggerated. Balfour was the only 'alternative Foreign Secretary' whose international prestige matched Grey's. Robert Donald, editor of the *Daily Chronicle*, recorded that on 6 Dec. 1916 Asquith foresaw little stability in a Lloyd George government. He expected, according to this account, to be recalled. Then, he said, 'Mr Lloyd George will have to come in on <u>my</u> terms': Wilson, *Downfall*, 102–3.

(I shall be curious to see if the new 'Business Government' will command real confidence in this country for any length of time.) Ll.G. is Prime Minister. Bonar Law leads the House as Chancellor of Exchequer.[1] Aitken is a peer;[2] Carson, Admiralty. The gaga-gone old man Balfour is at Foreign Office. Labour has lots of seats, in a cabinet which is to be broken.[3] Pledges to induce Labour to take those seats have been given of an American exaggeration, which are bound to be broken: if they are kept, England won't be a white man's country!—if broken, there will be Hell to pay with Labour, I've got the greatest contempt for 'business men' outside their sphere: when anyone says to me 'from a business point of view I can tell you', etc., I know he is going to utter a platitude or fallacy.

I have no time for anything! I can't write up my notes so jump about from date to date.

10th Dec. 1916 I wrote to the King: 'Mrs Asquith presents her humble devotion to your Majesty. She cannot resist writing to say how deeply moved she and her husband have been by the fine backing and wonderful, gracious affection you have shown to him. There is only one thing to hope for now, which all true Englishmen and subjects of your Majesty must feel. It is that the changes of the Prime Minister, Sir Edward Carson, Ld Milner, Mr Bonar Law, Mr Henderson (Labour) from Mr Asquith, Ld Grey, (Edward, now Viscount Grey of Fallodon) Mr McKenna, Mr Runciman and Lord Crewe will fill the enemy with terror, the army and navy with enthusiasm, the allies with Confidence, and the cabinet with concord. Then, and then only, will we beat the most unscrupulous enemy

[1] Bonar Law was the only one of the five original War Cabinet members who would have substantial responsibilities outside that body (as Leader of the Commons and Chancellor of the Exchequer).

[2] Aitken apparently expected the post of President of the Board of Trade in the new administration; no job emerged, but he was given a peerage, 'despite the king's objections' (D. George Boyce, *ODNB*, 'Aitken, William Maxwell').

[3] Margot seems to mean that the Labour Party's ministers in the new Departments of Labour and Pensions, although of 'cabinet rank', would not be cabinet ministers in the accepted sense; i.e. they would not be serving on this new 'small body' which was to control everything.

that ever waged war. Your Dear Majesty will forgive this letter of gratitude and everlasting devotion.'[1]

7th Dec. 1916 Henry said to me at night 'A man who has no capacity for concord, a man who lives in low society, works every Pressman and blackguard to his advantage, and who is not trusted by anyone who has ever served in his office, or in a cabinet with him, can never be Prime Minister of this country for long.'...

The crisis came. We were turned out of Downing St. Saturday 16th Dec. 1916,[2] and all went to Walmer, where Henry had been ill all the week—that agonizing illness which I shall never forget.... Monday 18th Henry and I went to Forbes House, Lady Granard's, where I remained till Jan 13th. 1917, when I went to live with Alice Keppel[3] till February 26th 1917.

We had nowhere to live, as my own house 20 Cavendish Square was still let to Maud Cunard. Violet and Bongie went to live in his mother's house, as she let 1 Dorset St. Elizabeth went to Mrs Cavendish Bentinck's, Richmond Terrace, and Cys to the Crewes. Maud Cunard behaved splendidly—scrambled out of 20 Cav. Sq, and Puffin and I went there alone to get the house ready till he went back to Winchester. (Poor 20 Cav. Sq., I cried daily over its ugliness and filthy condition!!!)

We all went to Easton Grey Fri. 22nd Dec. 1916 for Christmas till Wed 27th. Sat. 30th we went to the Wharf all together till Tues. 9th Jan. 1917. Christmas with Cys, Puffin, Elizabeth, V., and Bongie was sad but delightful. Henry looked ill, and I was broken down, and remained in bed most of the time.[4] Lucy was an angel. There was snow, so Puff, Cys and Bongie had fun tobogganing and snow-balling. Puff came back for Xmas

---

[1] Rumour suggested that, during these days, Margot's letters to the palace were not treated as worthy of much attention: *Belloc Lowndes Diaries*, 78.

[2] 'Dame Margaret [Lloyd George] wrote...to Mrs A. to tell her to take her time'; but, according to Frances Stevenson, Margot said that they would soon be moving in again in any case: Stevenson, *Years Past*, 99.

[3] At 16 Grosvenor Street, Mayfair. For these moves see *Autobiography*, i. 106–7.

[4] Violet describes Margot at Christmas as 'worn and feverish and her nerves sticking out of their sheathes and indeed out of her body altogether': Bonham Carter, *Diaries, 1914–45*, 97.

Holidays on Wed. 20th. (9.42 Paddington) I went to meet him, and con-soled him, and explained as well as I could the crisis and all that had hap-pened. He understood *à demi*,[1] but he is so sensitive and quick and could only ask how father was.

[1] Fr. 'in part'.

EPILOGUE

1. Lloyd George's War Cabinet

When Asquith met the other Liberal ex-ministers late in the afternoon of 6 December 1916, and they decided not to serve under Lloyd George, they were influenced by three beliefs.[1] These were, first, that, although Ll.G. might well succeed in forming a government, it would be short-lived; secondly, that Asquith's influence was still, in Crewe's phrase, 'powerful and pervading';[2] and thirdly, that the Liberals in the constituencies would not want Lloyd George to take over their party's organization.[3] All three of these convictions were held by both Asquith and Margot. The basis for the first was undermined within twenty-four hours. By the evening of 7 December Lloyd George held Balfour's acceptance of the Foreign Secretaryship and the degree of Labour support which he needed; and a rise in sterling, with a fall in the German mark, showed that he had the confidence of the financial markets.[4] On 10 December Northcliffe predicted to a worldwide readership that the new premier would be victorious in the war.[5]

The second and third convictions were half-truths at best. Although Asquith was better liked by Liberals than by the population as a whole, his backing even in his own party had become reluctant. Some Liberals thought Asquith almost as blameworthy for conceding conscription as Lloyd George had been for joining the Unionists in pressing for it. The situation was made impossibly difficult by the failure of both Asquith

[1] In the formal sense the question was whether to take office under Bonar Law; but it was known that Bonar, unlike Lloyd George, would not try to form a government if Asquith declined to serve as one of his subordinates.

[2] For this view see 6 Dec. 1916 Cowans, 7 Dec. Leith-Ross, both to Margot: Margot Asquith Papers, c. 6674 fo. 62; c. 6678 fo. 91.

[3] Asquith, C., *Diaries*, 242; Wilson, *Downfall*, 102–3; Asquith, *Memories*, ii. 136. The party's leader appointed the Chief Whip in the Commons and controlled the party funds. As Crawford noted, with a hint of surprise, Asquith made clear in his Reform Club speech that he was retaining the leadership with the functions attached to it: *Crawford Journals*, 376.

[4] Koss, *Asquith*, 225.

[5] *Weekly Dispatch*, 10 Dec. 1916, distributed through Northcliffe's United Press. Northcliffe had played no great part in the events of the preceding fortnight: Beaverbrook, *Politicians*, 402–3.

and Margot to face it with realism: neither had much idea of how unpopular they had become.[1] Asquith's carapace of political complacency during 1916 has already been mentioned; and despite an acute awareness of danger Margot had been largely mistaken about its sources and nature. Until September 1918 she encouraged and applauded all his refusals of subordinate office.[2] The result was the failure of the ex-ministers to envisage the likely results of the policy which they favoured. On Crewe's definition they were to give the new government steady support while 'criticizing when necessary, and in the last resort offering an alternative administration'. It was not hard to discern that, while they would look ineffective as long as they supported Lloyd George's government, they would be seen as a dangerous challenge whenever they criticized it.[3]

At the Liberals' meeting on 6 December it was agreed that for Asquith to serve under Bonar Law or Lloyd George would 'be an unworkable arrangement'. This was a blinkered view. Asquith's acceptance of an office directly concerned with war policy would certainly have proved unworkable:[4] but the office most often suggested for him, the Lord Chancellorship, was not of that kind. There had been a rumour in August 1916 that financial troubles might induce him to move to this office; and doing so had been mentioned during Bonar Law's conversation with him on 3 December.[5] While that had been common talk among Unionists, the Liberal leaders do not seem to have referred to the possibility. This can hardly have been a coincidence. Most of the Liberals present on 6 December abhorred the prospect of Lloyd George

[1] *Crawford Journals*, 371, 376.

[2] Wilson, *Downfall*, 122. Margot, though conceding that to work for the downfall of a respectable government would have been unpatriotic in wartime, maintained that this did not apply when a 'little gang of brigands' (Diary, 14 Dec. 1916, p. 310 above) had seized power. She did not allow George V's wishes, or those of men with a reputation for probity, such as Balfour, Austen Chamberlain, Long, and Milner, to affect this view.

[3] See, for example, Gwynne's explanation of Ll.G.'s appointment of Churchill to office, 'to deprive the Asquithian lot of a man of energy and authority': Gwynne, *Rasp*, 225.

[4] Asquith to Bonar Law, 6 Dec. 1916: Blake, *Bonar Law*, 338; Crewe memo.: Asquith, *Memories*, ii. 136.

[5] Addison, *Years*, i. 237; *Crawford Journals*, 371; Spender and Asquith, ii. 287.

succeeding to the Liberal leadership in the Commons and to the control of the party's funds.

It was soon clear that Lloyd George was as prone to misjudgement as his predecessor. His strong support in January 1917 for Nivelle's proposed offensive on the Western Front was injudicious, and a few of his ministerial appointments proved unfortunate; the combination of Carson and Jellicoe at the Admiralty, for example, turned out badly. Both were ultra-cautious administrators, and this was not the best stance for defeating the U-Boats.[1] Among the 'new style' appointments, made from outside the ranks of leading parliamentarians, Devonport and Neville Chamberlain were failures, though whether Chamberlain was to blame for not devising his own instructions in a task as tricky as manpower allocation must be questioned;[2] but the successes soon outnumbered the failures by a large margin. Sir Joseph Maclay, for instance, produced a remarkable improvement in the use of British shipping while declining membership of either the House of Lords or the Commons.[3]

For some weeks the War Cabinet functioned poorly. Lloyd George had a proper system in place for wartime government; but, unlike Asquith, he was not personally systematic. He would neither stick to the agenda nor initial, and so authorize, the minutes. On 18 March 1917 Hankey noted: 'The War Cabinet... is not working satisfactorily.... The work is dreadfully congested—far worse than it ever was under the so-called "Wait and See" Government';[4] but after four or five months the improvements brought by the new regime were hardly deniable. Charteris, Haig's Chief Intelligence Officer, wrote in his diary (Sept. 1917):

---

[1] See Hough, *War at Sea*, 307–10. Asquith and Balfour had made Jellicoe First Sea Lord, Nov. 1916. For Carson's appointment as First Lord see Grigg, *Lloyd George, 1912–1916*, 483–6. The convoy system, which Jellicoe was slow to adopt, had been expounded, as a defence against surface attacks, to the cabinet by Churchill, 5 Aug. 1914: Pease, Gainford Papers 35/2 (5 Aug. 1914).

[2] Grigg, *Lloyd George, 1916–1918*, 212. (Arthur) Neville Chamberlain (1869–1940); Hudson Ewbanke Kearley, Visc. Devonport (1856–1934).

[3] Joseph Paton Maclay (1857–1951), Bt. 1914, cr. Lord Maclay 1922 (in Resignation Honours List, i.e. after leaving office); Minister of Shipping, Dec. 1916–Oct. 1922.

[4] For the origin of 'wait and see', 3 mar. 1910, see Spender and Asquith, i. 275.

[Asquith] is, to my mind, the greatest of all the politicians and perfectly straight. If he were P.M. now, with the same powers and the same organization that L.G. has devised to make the P.M. virtual dictator, the outlook would be far more cheerful.[1]

At last Britain's war effort was directed by a body which was easily assembled, small enough to take decisions with the rapidity often required in war, largely free from departmental responsibilities, and equipped with a secretariat able to communicate them accurately, and at once, to the executive agencies concerned. At least one of the changes introduced was needed in both war and peace. Since December 1916 no British cabinet has reverted to holding all of its meetings in the absence of a secretary to take the minutes.[2]

By May 1917 it was evident that Lloyd George had survived his government's early difficulties, and that month Lord Reading arrived at the Wharf with an offer of the Lord Chancellorship for Asquith. Like all of the later offers it was refused. Asquith told Lady Scott that he would not serve under a premier whom he thought 'unsuited' to running the government.[3] He maintained this stance throughout the various vicissitudes in Lloyd George's wartime fortunes. It outlasted his own urge to return to 10 Downing Street.[4] On 26 September 1918 he refused to consider a proposition brought by Elibank that he and his Liberal followers should accept the Lord Chancellorship, two Secretaryships of State, and six under-secretaryships in Ll.G.'s Coalition. An immediate general election was part of the arrangement proposed. Elibank suggested that the premier, who was in a position to 'sweep the country' at the polls, wanted to strengthen his personal position vis-à-vis the Unionists who dominated the Coalition.

---

[1] Roskill, *Hankey*, 370–1. See also Roskill, *Hankey*, 353, and *Tom Jones Diary, 1916–1925*, 15–16; Charteris, *At GHQ*, 252.

[2] During the Second War Churchill held some War Cabinet meetings in the absence of any secretary. At those no decisions were taken. They were convened so that difficult issues could be given some preliminary discussion.

[3] Kennet, *Self-Portrait*, 155–6.

[4] Asquith's strategy over the 'Maurice Debate', May 1918, suggests that his objective by then was to discredit Lloyd George rather than to regain power. Ch. 27 of Grigg, *Lloyd George, 1916–1918* is devoted to this episode.

Asquith thought an immediate election the policy of 'a reckless gambler'. He doubted whether the proposals would be accepted by the Liberal Party. He said that his information 'by no means tallied' with the prediction about Lloyd George sweeping the country.[1]

2. The War Service Medals

Meanwhile Margot's attitude to overtures from the government seems to have been changing. On 30 July 1918 she had noted that there was talk of a general election before the end of the year. In her 'heart of hearts', she added, she was afraid that Lloyd George would win it.[2] Three weeks later she wrote: 'Our political life is behind us, I am pretty sure.... I don't think Henry is even very keen now.... Politics seem to bore him.' He was not, in her view, one of the 'natural fighters. I am but the Asquiths have not one drop of wild blood in their veins.'[3] Riddell was told that the offer brought by Elibank on 26 September had the approval of 'Mrs A'.[4]

This final wartime decision by Asquith that he and his group should remain independent was even more dangerous than Margot can have thought. Three days after the conversation of 26 September 1918 the Allies secured an unexpected triumph: the southern part of the Hindenburg Line fell to Britain's Fourth Army: and on 3 October Prince Max of Baden, the newly installed German Chancellor, asked the President of the United States 'to arrange the immediate conclusion of an armistice'.[5] This was achieved on 11 November; and Lloyd George was presented with the prospect, not of a war election, but of one celebrating victory. The urgent need for a well-supported British delegation at the peace conference had made the case for replacing the 1910 House of Commons

[1] Murray, *Master*, 172–8. The 'immediate election' was neither new nor surprising as a condition of joining. It had been virtually announced by Ll.G. in his speech, 12 Sept. 1918.

[2] Margot Diary, d. 3216, fo. 185ᵛ. The registration arrangements under the Representation of the People Act, Feb. 1918, would be ready in October. Manhood suffrage, and the enfranchisement of some six million women, had increased the electorate from 8 million to some 20 million voters.

[3] Margot Diary, d. 3216, fo. 188ʳ.

[4] *Riddell War Diary*, 358.

[5] Cruttwell, *Great War*, 575.

overwhelming.[1] By 4 November 1918 Margot's fears for her husband had become acute. She wrote: 'I feel in spite of the grand speeches and great character he will be beaten in [the] Gen. Election.'[2] She was now facing, not only the loss of political influence, but the comparative penury from which her Henry's acceptance of office would have saved her. In future she would have to put her thoughts, not into a private diary, but into publications which seemed likely to sell well.[3] She is unlikely to have realized that her talents as a diarist exceeded those which she could command as an author, or what resentments she would arouse in society when her indiscretions, long known among the elite, were revealed to the world.[4]

In the December election Lloyd George, helped by a discreditable campaign, secured an overwhelming victory. The 'unfettered' Liberals were reduced to a mere 28 MPs, Runciman, McKenna, and Samuel being left at the foot of the poll. Asquith's opponent in East Fife secured a majority of 2,000, although he was standing against the wishes of the Unionists' HQ and had been refused the 'coupon'. Lloyd George was alarmed by the scale of his success, and 'genuinely upset', in Frances Stevenson's words, by Asquith's defeat.[5] He had needed a substantial majority for the peace conference, not a crushing one. He realized that the chances of Liberal reunion had been badly damaged, and later episodes such as the conduct of the irregular forces, the Black and Tans, during the Irish War of Independence,

[1] Nicolson, *Peacemaking*, 14. Balfour called the election of Dec. 1918 'a very inconvenient necessity': Dugdale, *Balfour*, ii. 263. Lloyd George obtained the King's reluctant leave for an immediate dissolution, 5 Nov. 1918: Nicolson, *George V*, 328–30. By then the King's arguments against an early election had come up against the need for the British delegation to be armed at the peace conference with a convincing popular mandate. Without that they would not (as was feared) be able to cope with President Wilson and Clemenceau.

[2] D. 3216, fo. 237^r.

[3] For information about Margot's earnings from authorship see Bennett, *Margot*, chs. 31, 32, 34, 37. For her statement about this to Donald Maclean see Koss, *Asquith*, 282–3.

[4] For the King's anger when the first volume of Margot's *Autobiography* was announced see Nicolson, *George V*, 342. Curzon, who much resented the passages about himself, listened to a royal diatribe about Margot's 'scandalous chatter' being published: Rose, *George V*, 314. Margot was invited to dinner by Curzon in 1925; but he died on the day of this intended reconciliation: Rose, *Curzon*, 376.

[5] *British Political Facts*, 206. Wilson, *Downfall*, 175; Roskill, *Hankey*, ii. 39–40; *Stevenson Diary*, 319–20 (17 Nov. 1935). Deposits had been instituted in the 1918 Electoral Reform Act to discourage 'freak' candidates. The certificate held by candidates certified as being Coalition supporters was nicknamed the 'coupon'—a term made familiar by wartime rationing.

and the sale of honours scandal, increased this damage to his reputation and prospects. The electorate's impression that Ll.G.'s splendid Coalition had succeeded an administration which had been unequal to the demands of war was justified chiefly in relation to the last months of Asquith's premiership.[1] While Lloyd George's team exerted—and, above all, displayed—more grip on events than Asquith's, both administrations made serious mistakes;[2] but Lloyd George, while personally less businesslike than his predecessor, was nimble and imaginative enough to see that the war demanded a drastic adaptation of Britain's governmental structure and methods. By 1918 Ll.G. had been widely criticized; but none of the critics were prepared to see his small War Cabinet replaced by an Asquithian cabinet containing some twenty-two members,[3] and lacking any systematic record of its doings, as the only body entitled to take decisions.

Asquith's actions after he had lost office cannot detract from his remarkable achievements while holding it. That he was, by December 1916, a less effective wartime premier than his successor can hardly be disputed, although the discrepancy between the problems of 1914 to 1916 and those of 1917 and 1918 makes the comparison more difficult than is sometimes supposed. George V was generous and just when he ordered that the two wartime Prime Ministers, unlike any other civilians, should each receive the three war service medals.[4] Asquith was not powerful

[1] Observers of good judgement such as Hankey and Crawford give a strong impression that by Oct. 1916 the combined effect of a long spell in high office, an unsuitable lifestyle, and Raymond's death had reduced Asquith's ability to cope with accumulating war problems. For the 1922 honours scandal see Searle, Corruption, ch. 15.

[2] For instance Asquith's Tyneside speech. Lloyd George's reliance on Nivelle was mentioned earlier: Cruttwell, Great War, 398.

[3] On Ll.G.'s slipshod habits see Roskill, Hankey, i. 371. Northcliffe, replied, 10 Apr. 1918 to Maxse's criticisms of Ll.G.'s performance, that, while he had heard many such strictures, 'I never hear the names of any persons with whom to replace the present government': Thompson, Northcliffe, 301. See also Gwynne, Rasp, 243–50, 272–3.

[4] Grigg, Lloyd George, 1912–1916, 474. George V's treatment of Asquith was marked throughout by considerate kindness. An offer of the Garter in Dec. 1916 was declined, perhaps because Asquith was reluctant to accept any honour which might have suggested his impending retirement from the leadership of the Liberal Party: Nicolson, George V, 292–3. Early in 1925 offers of an earldom, and, shortly afterwards, of the Garter, were accepted: Spender and Asquith, ii. 355–6.

enough during 1917 and 1918 to impair national unity by refusing office. By declining the Lord Chancellorship, however, he initiated the Liberal split which was to hasten the party's decline between the wars.

Asquith's premiership has been subjected for many years to what Churchill called 'the grievous inquest of history'; he has been charged, as the Prime Minister, with subjecting his country to an eventual 'victory worse than a defeat'.[1] Even if that description of the event is accepted, was Britain's decision to intervene in the war on land and sea Asquith's responsibility in more than a formal sense? By 30 July 1914 he could not have agreed to British neutrality while Germany attacked France through Belgium without being repudiated by many of his followers. If he had tried on 4 August, and the two days after that, to limit British intervention to the sea, he would have been swept from power at once.[2] His part in causing the agonies and losses which followed should therefore be classed as an appalling misfortune, not as a mistake. In 1917 he could have said with Abraham Lincoln: 'I claim not to have controlled events, but confess plainly that events have controlled me.'[3]

In 1914 the British were plunged into a world utterly unlike anything which they had known or even envisaged. The Prime Minister, who bore the brunt of this, and his wife, deserve sympathetic treatment. In 1964 Violet Bonham Carter wrote of the 'exasperation' which Margot had often caused her father. Anyone reading this book will recognize the force of that; but, considering the harsh realities of political life at the top, exacerbated by war's horrors, which are revealed in Margot's account, it is possible to admire what Violet acknowledged to have been 'her <u>unwavering</u>, though blind, devotion' to him.[4]

---

[1] Churchill, *Great Contemporaries*, 342 (ch. on Fisher); Professor Brian Bond, Annual Lecture, Liddell Hart Centre for Military Archives, King's College, London, 20 Nov. 1997.

[2] For Professor Niall Ferguson's contention in *The Pity of War* (1998) see especially chs. 6 and 7, and pp. 433–62. In Prof. Ferguson's view, for Britain, standing aside would have been preferable to an intervention which could not have been conclusive in the absence of a much bigger British army, since German objectives, had Britain remained out, 'would not...have posed a direct threat to the [British] Empire'.

[3] Open Letter to Albert G. Hodges, 4 Apr. 1864, Lincoln, *Collected Works*, ed. R. P. Basler (9 vols, 1953–5), vii. 282. Quoted in Morley, *Gladstone*, i. 871.

[4] *Bonham Carter Diaries, 1946–1969*, 286.

APPENDICES

ASQUITH AND TENNANT FAMILY TREES

Note: these Family Trees are intended, first, to identify members of the Asquith and Tennant families *mentioned* in this edition; and, secondly, to give a view of the two families as they were in 1916, when the Asquiths left Downing Street. For reasons of space, some omissions have been necessary.

The Asquiths

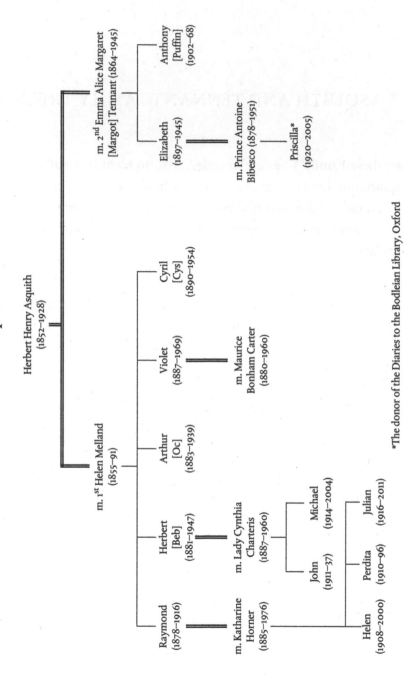

Herbert Henry Asquith
(1852–1928)

m. 1st Helen Melland
(1855–91)

m. 2nd Emma Alice Margaret
[Margot] Tennant (1864–1945)

Raymond
(1878–1916)

m. Katharine Horner
(1885–1976)

Herbert
[Beb]
(1881–1947)

m. Lady Cynthia Charteris
(1887–1960)

Arthur
[Oc]
(1883–1939)

Violet
(1887–1969)

m. Maurice Bonham Carter
(1880–1960)

Cyril
[Cys]
(1890–1954)

Elizabeth
(1897–1945)

m. Prince Antoine Bibesco (1878–1951)

Anthony
[Puffin]
(1902–68)

John
(1911–37)

Michael
(1914–2004)

Helen
(1908–2000)

Perdita
(1910–96)

Julian
(1916–2011)

Priscilla*
(1920–2005)

*The donor of the Diaries to the Bodleian Library, Oxford

The Tennants

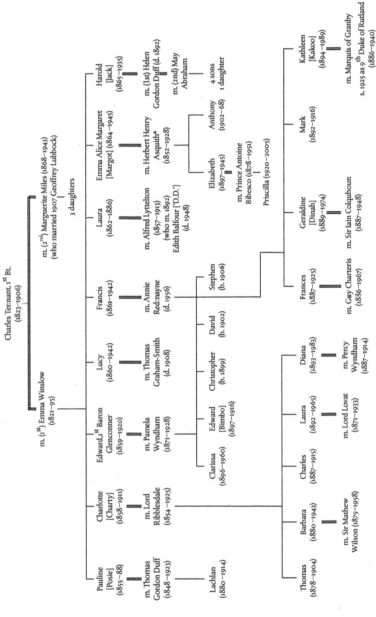

Charles Tennant, 1st Bt. (1823–1906)

m. (1st) Emma Winslow (1821–95)

m. (2nd) Marguerite Miles (1868–1943) (who married 1907 Geoffrey Lubbock)

3 daughters

Pauline [Posie] (1855–88)
m. Thomas Gordon Duff (1848–1923)

Charlotte [Charty] (1858–1911)
m. Lord Ribblesdale (1854–1925)

Edward, 1st Baron Glenconner (1859–1920)
m. Pamela Wyndham (1871–1928)

Lucy (1860–1942)
m. Thomas Graham-Smith (d. 1908)

Francis (1861–1942)
m. Annie Redmayne (d. 1956)

Laura (1862–1886)
m. Alfred Lyttelton (1857–1913) (who m. 1892 Edith Balfour ['D.D.'] (d. 1948)

Emma Alice Margaret [Margot] (1864–1945)
m. Herbert Henry Asquith* (1852–1928)

Harold [Jack] (1865–1935)
m. (1st) Helen Gordon Duff (d. 1892)
m. (2nd) May Abraham

Lachlan (1880–1914)

Clarissa (1896–1960)

Edward [Bimbo] (1897–1916)

Christopher (b. 1899)

David (b. 1902)

Stephen (b. 1906)

Elizabeth (1897–1945)
m. Prince Antoine Bibesco (1878–1951)

Anthony (1902–68)

Priscilla (1920–2005)

4 sons
1 daughter

Thomas (1878–1904)

Barbara (1880–1943)
m. Sir Mathew Wilson (1875–1958)

Charles (1887–1915)

Laura (1892–1965)
m. Lord Lovat (1871–1933)

Diana (1893–1983)
m. Percy Wyndham (1887–1914)

Frances (1887–1925)
m. Guy Charteris (1886–1967)

Geraldine [Dinah] (1889–1974)
m. Sir Iain Colquhoun (1887–1948)

Mark (1892–1916)

Kathleen [Kakoo] (1894–1989)
m. Marquis of Granby s. 1925 as 9th Duke of Rutland (1886–1940)

*For H.H. Asquith's first wife, Helen (d. 1891), and their family, see Asquith tree

North Sea

THE NETHERLANDS

Zeebrugge
Blankenberghe
Ostend
Nieuport
Dunkirk
Calais
R. Yser
Boulogne
St Omer
Ypres
Neuve Chapelle
Lille
Abbeville
Arras
Douai
Cambrai
Valenciennes
Le Cateau
Péronne
Amiens
St Quentin
Noyon
La Fère
Compiègne
Soissons
R. Oise
R. Ourcq
Rheims
R. Marne
PARIS
FRANCE
R. Seine
Bruges
Ghent
R. Schelde
Termonde
Courtrai
BRUSSELS
BELGIUM
Tournai
Mons
Longueville
Landrecies
Rocroi
Zelzate
Antwerp
Louvain
Liège
GERMANY
R. Sambre
Namur
R. Meuse
Maubeuge
A R D E N N E S
LUXEMBOURG
R. Aisne
R. Meuse
Verdun
Vitry
Nancy

0   10   20   30 miles
0   10   20   30   40   50 km

Location of Western Front 15th December 1914

Map of the Western Front

CHRONOLOGY

Events relating to the personal and family life of Margot and Henry Asquith are given in italics. For reasons of concision, political events are mostly confined to the period of Asquith's premiership, 1908 to 1916.

1852	12 Sept.	*Asquith born, at Morley in Yorkshire*
1864	2 Feb.	*Margot born at The Glen, Innerleithen*
1869	Nov.	*Asquith wins a classical scholarship to Balliol, going up in 1870*
1874		*Asquith president of the Union at Oxford, and gains first in literae humaniores.*
1877	7 Apr.	*Charlotte ('Charty') Tennant marries Lord Ribblesdale*
1877	23 Aug.	*Asquith marries Helen Melland*
1879		*Charles Tennant (Margot's father) elected MP*
1880		*Margot's first hunting season; Charles Tennant buys London house*
1881–2		*Margot at Dresden; her 'coming out'*
1885	May	*Wedding of Laura Tennant to Alfred Lyttelton*
1885	July	*Charles Tennant created baronet*
1886	24 Apr.	*Death of Laura Lyttelton*
1886		*Asquith first elected to Parliament for East Fife (represents the constituency until 1918)*
1886	June	Defeat of Gladstone's 1st Home Rule Bill
1890		*Margot meets H. H. Asquith, who becomes QC in Feb.*
1891	July	*Asquith writes to Margot in terms of intimate friendship*
1891	11 Sept.	*Death of Asquith's first wife, Helen Melland*

1892	18 Aug.	Asquith appointed Home Secretary in Gladstone's last government
1893		Publication of *Dodo* (by E. F. Benson)
1893	Sept.	Crushing defeat of Gladstone's 2nd Home Rule Bill in the Lords
1894	Mar.	Gladstone resigns; succeeded as Prime Minister by Rosebery
1894	10 May	*Margot's marriage to H. H. Asquith*
1895		*Birth and death of a daughter; death of Margot's mother*
1895		Formation of the Salisbury government
1895	June	*Asquith returns to the Bar after the fall of the Rosebery government*
1897		*Birth of Elizabeth Asquith*
1898		*Sir Charles Tennant marries Marguerite Miles*
1900		*Birth and death of a daughter*
1902	9 Nov.	*Birth of Anthony Asquith*
1903	May	Chamberlain declares for Tariff Reform and resigns from cabinet (Sept.)
1904		*Entente Cordiale* between Britain and France
1905	Dec.	Balfour resigns; formation of Liberal Government under Campbell-Bannerman; Asquith becomes Chancellor of the Exchequer
1906	Jan.	Landslide General Election victory for Campbell-Bannerman's Liberals
1906	4 June	*Death of Sir Charles Tennant*
1906	Dec.	*For the third and final time, Margot loses her child, a boy, soon after birth*
1907	18 Apr.	Asquith's budget makes provision for Old Age Pensions the next year
1908	8 Apr.	Asquith becomes Prime Minister, 'kissing hands' in a hotel room at Biarritz, where Edward VII was staying

1909		Lloyd George introduces his 'People's Budget'
1910	Jan.	General election returns Liberal government dependent on Irish Nationalists
1910	14 Apr.	Asquith introduces Parliament Bill
1910	6 May	Death of Edward VII; succeeded by George V
1910	17 June (to 10 Nov.)	Conference convened to try to resolve the crisis over House of Lords' reform
1910	Dec.	General election results in little change between the parties
1911	July	German gunboat *Panther* arrives at Agadir
1911	10 Aug.	Parliament Bill passed in House of Lords
	23 Aug.	War Office and Admiralty present their war plans to CID
1911		*Death of Lady Ribblesdale (Charlotte Tennant)*
1912	Jan.	*Asquith forms a romantic attachment to Venetia Stanley*
1912	11 Apr.	Asquith introduces the 3rd Home Rule Bill
1912	July	*Asquiths move into The Wharf, Sutton Courtenay, on the Thames near Oxford*
1914	Mar.	'Curragh mutiny' of army officers in Ireland
1914	12 May	Home Rule Bill passes its third reading in the Commons; focus shifts to the content of an Amending Bill detailing the provisions for Ulster Protestants
1914	28 June	Assassination of the Archduke Franz Ferdinand, heir apparent to the Austro-Hungarian throne, and his wife in Sarajevo; Austria-Hungary holds Serbia responsible
1914	6 July	Germany communicates support for Austria-Hungary
1914	24 July	Cabinet discusses Home Rule amendment, when Sir Edward Grey announces Austria-Hungary's ultimatum to Serbia

1914	25 July	Austrian ultimatum due to expire 6 p.m.; Serbian reply delivered in Austrian Legation in Belgrade a few minutes before
1914	28 July (Tuesday)	Austria-Hungary declares war on Serbia and bombs Belgrade; the Tsar orders partial Russian mobilization
1914	29 July (Wednesday)	Midday—cabinet agrees to declaration of 'Precautionary Period' in case of war
1914	30 July (Thursday)	6.00 p.m.—Russian government orders general mobilization
1914	31 July (Friday)	Austria decrees full mobilization; German ultimatum to Russia to stop mobilization; Britain seeks assurances from Germany and France regarding Belgian neutrality: France gives reassurance, Germany does not
1914	1 Aug. (Saturday)	France and Germany begin general mobilization; Belgian government orders mobilization in defence of its neutrality; 7.00 p.m.—Germany declares war on Russia
1914	2 Aug. (Sunday)	Britain assures France its Fleet will 'give all protection in its power' to prevent German hostilities towards French coast or French shipping: cabinet will not go further without first consulting Parliament; Asquith approves Churchill's mobilization of the Fleet.
		Evening: German ultimatum delivered in Brussels 'requesting' free passage for its troops through Belgium: Belgian government replies that it will resist encroachment from any quarter

1914	3 Aug. (Bank Holiday Monday)	Morning: Asquith learns of German ultimatum, through news agency message. Afternoon: Grey makes the case for intervention on the side of France. 6.45 p.m. Germany declares war on France, falsely alleging a violation of her frontier by French patrols. Night (3/4 Aug.)—becomes clear that Germany intends to advance in force through Belgium.
1914	4 Aug. (Tuesday)	Morning—German cavalry cross Belgian frontier. Britain issues ultimatum to Germany to observe Belgian neutrality. 4.00 p.m.—War Office sends by telegraph, *en clair*, message 'MOBILIZE' 11.00 p.m.—Britain at war with Germany (midnight, central European time) after ultimatum expires.
1914	5 Aug.	Officially 'the first day of mobilization'
1914	6 Aug.	Kitchener becomes Secretary of State for War; cabinet sanctions the dispatch to France of BEF
1914	7 Aug.	Kitchener appeals for 'the first 100,000' volunteers for the new armies
1914	9 Aug.	Embarkation of BEF begins (completed by 17th)
1914	22 Aug.	Dawn—C Squadron, 4th Dragoon Guards, fires on German piquet while pushing north from Obourg towards Soignies—the first shots fired by British in the war
1914	23 Aug.	Morning: von Kluck's First Army engages BEF at Mons

1914	24 Aug. (to 4 Sept.)	BEF's retreat from Mons
1914	26 Aug.	Smith-Dorrien's 'stopping blow' halts von Kluck's First Army at Le Cateau; German victory over Russians at Tannenberg (to 30 Aug.)
1914	29 Aug.	Kitchener's First New Army ('K1') created from first six volunteer divisions
1914	6–12 Sept.	Battle of the Marne
1914	10 Oct.	Fall of Antwerp
1914	19 Oct. (to 22 Nov.)	1st Battle of Ypres
1914	29 Oct.	Turkey attacks Russia; on 5 Nov. Britain declares war on Turkey
1914	16 Dec.	German navy bombards Scarborough and other east coast towns
1915	8 Jan.	Haldane accepts principle of conscription in speech in Lords
1915	19–20 Jan.	First Zeppelin raid on Britain, over East Anglia: four killed and sixteen injured
1915	28 Jan.	War Council approves plan for a naval attack on Dardanelles
1915	4 Feb.	Germany announces unrestricted submarine warfare in British waters (begins 18 Feb.)
1915	10 Mar.	Battle of Neuve Chapelle begins
1915	11 Mar.	Britain bans all 'neutral' parties from trade with Germany
1915	18 Mar.	Naval bombardment of Turkish forts on Dardanelles Straits begun, and suspended
1915	20 Apr.	Asquith's Tyneside speech to munitions workers and employers
1915	22 Apr. (to 25 May)	2nd Battle of Ypres; first use of gas, by Germans at Langemarck in Ypres salient

1915	25 Apr.	Gallipoli landings
1915	7 May	Sinking of the *Lusitania* off Ireland, with the loss of 1,198 lives
1915	9 May	Aubers Ridge offensive: British attack impeded by shortage of shells
1915	11 *May*	*Venetia Stanley writes to Asquith of her engagement to Edwin Montagu*
1915	14 May	*The Times*' military correspondent alleges shortage of shells on Western Front
1915	15 May	Fisher resigns as First Sea Lord
1915	17 May	Asquith visited by Bonar Law: agrees to a coalition
1915	23 May	Italy declares war on Austria-Hungary
1915	30 May	Asquith's first visit to the Western Front
1915	31 May	First Zeppelin raid on London
1915	4 June	Allies attack on all fronts in Gallipoli
1915	6 Aug. (to 10 Aug.)	Landings at Suvla Bay in Gallipoli
1915	11 Aug.	Crewe Committee on enlistment figures convenes
1915	25 Sept. (to 14 Oct.)	Battle of Loos
1915	12 Oct.	Execution of nurse Edith Cavell by the Germans
1915	19 Oct.	Asquith's health breaks down; recovers after a couple of weeks; Derby Scheme to encourage voluntary enlistment announced
1915	2 Nov.	Asquith's key statement in Commons on conscription
1915	25 Nov.	Victory of conscriptionist Labour candidate at Merthyr Tydfil by-election
1915	*30 Nov.*	*Violet Asquith marries (Sir) Maurice Bonham Carter*

1915	7 Dec.	Anglo-Indian forces besieged in Kut, Mesopotamia
1915	18–19 Dec.	Evacuation of Suvla Bay and Anzac Cove, Gallipoli
1915	19 Dec.	Haig officially appointed C.-in-C. on Western Front, replacing French
1915	31 Dec.	Cabinet approves the Military Service Bill; Sir John Simon later resigns
1916	4 Jan.	Asquith introduces the first Military Service Bill in Commons
1916	8–9 Jan.	Evacuation of Cape Helles, Gallipoli
1916	27 Jan.	First Military Service Act—conscription of single men aged 18–41
1916	21 Feb.	Battle for Verdun begins (to Dec.)
1916	26 Mar. (to 6 Apr.)	Asquith visits France and Italy to discuss progress of the war
1916	24 Apr. (to 1 May)	Easter Rising in Dublin
1916	29 Apr.	Fall of Kut
1916	2 May	Asquith introduces the second Military Service Bill in Commons
1916	3–12 May	Execution of the leaders of the Easter Rising in Dublin
1916	25 May	Second Military Service Act—extends conscription to married men
1916	31 May–1 June	Battle of Jutland
1916	5 June	Kitchener drowns in sinking of HMS *Hampshire*
1916	24 June	Beginning of bombardment of German positions on the Somme
1916	1 July (to 18 Nov.)	Battle of the Somme; 19,026 British dead on the first day of fighting

1916	4 July	Lloyd George becomes Secretary of State for War
1916	6 Sept.	*Asquith visits the front; sees his son Raymond at Fricourt*
1916	15 Sept.	*Raymond Asquith killed leading his men as the Guards' Division advanced from Ginchy on Lesboeufs;* tanks used for first time, at Flers-Courcelette, on Somme
1916	17 Sept.	*News of Raymond's death reaches the Wharf*
1916	23 Sept.	Germans begin construction of the Hindenburg Line
1916	8 Nov.	Vote in the 'Nigerian debate' in Commons shows Unionist dissatisfaction with Coalition government
1916	18 Nov.	Somme offensive ends: casualties in region of 419,000 British and 204,000 French, while estimates of German losses vary greatly
1916	25 Nov.	Bonar Law, Lloyd George, and Carson put to Asquith their proposals for a rearrangement of the government
1916	26 Nov.	Asquith rejects their proposals
1916	2 Dec.	News of the Bonar, Ll.G., Carson initiative reported in the press
1916	4 Dec.	*The Times* publishes details of the trio's plan, including a strong attack on Asquith
1916	5 Dec.	Asquith submits his resignation to the King, 7 p.m.
1916	7 Dec.	7.30 p.m. Lloyd George informs the King that he can form a government, and becomes Prime Minister
1918	9 Nov.	Kaiser flees to Holland, and abdicates; republic proclaimed in Berlin

1918	11 Nov.	German delegation signs armistice of surrender; armistice on all fronts
1918	14 Dec.	Asquith defeated at East Fife in the 'khaki' general election
1919		*Elizabeth Asquith's wedding; Asquiths sell their Cavendish Square house and move to 44 Bedford Square*
1920		*Volume One of Margot's Autobiography published*
1920	25 Feb.	Asquith elected for Paisley (re-elected 1922, 1923)
1922		*Volume Two of Margot's Autobiography published*
1924	30 Oct.	Asquith defeated at Paisley
1925		*Places and Persons*
1925	9 Feb.	*Asquith created Earl of Oxford and Asquith (gazetted)*
1927		*Lay Sermons published*
1928		*Octavia published*
1928	15 Feb.	*Death of H. H. Asquith, at the Wharf*
1932		*The Wharf sold*
1933		*More Memories published*
1938		*Myself when Young published*
1943		*Off the Record published*
1945	7 Apr.	*Death of Elizabeth Asquith*
	28 July	*Death of Margot Asquith, at 14 Kensington Square, London*
1968	21 Feb.	*Death of Anthony Asquith*

BIOGRAPHICAL NOTES

The following Biographical Notes refer to Asquith and Tennant family members and prominent historical figures mentioned in the diary. The notes are concise and mostly restricted to the period in view. Names in square brackets are nicknames, or abbreviations commonly used by Margot; those in rounded brackets are unused given names. A hereditary peer is identified by his family name, and his peerage is cross-referenced (i.e. Esher, Lord *see* Brett, Reginald Baliol).

Aitken, William Maxwell [Max] (1879–1964), like Bonar Law a son of a New Brunswick manse. Acquired a substantial fortune chiefly from his skill in forming combines, culminating in creation of the Canada Cement Company, 1909. Settled in England, and became an MP, 1910: knighted, 1911, Bt. 1916. Played major part, Nov.–Dec. 1916, in bringing Bonar Law and Lloyd George together and ousting Asquith from the premiership, his *Politicians and the War* (2 vols, 1928, 1932) being largely an account of this episode. Cr. Lord Beaverbrook 1917.

Alexandra, Queen (1844–1925), Princess Alexandra of Denmark; she married, 1863, Albert Edward, Prince of Wales (Edward VII), who died 1910; thereafter she struggled to adjust to the role of dowager, her special status signified by the title Queen Mother; although she had family on both sides of the conflict during the Great War, the fighting brought out her 'fervent anti-German feeling', and she demanded that the Garter banners of enemy sovereigns be removed from St George's Chapel at Windsor; her war work was spent mostly visiting hospitals; she was the aunt of

Tsar Nicholas II of Russia (A. W. Purdue, *ODNB*, 'Alexandra, [Princess Alexandra of Denmark]').

Asquith, Anthony [Puffin/Puff] (1902–68), only son and second (surviving) child of H. H. Asquith and Margot. His childhood was lovingly documented by Margot in the 'Family' Diaries which she composed in parallel to her 'Political' narratives. Margot lost three children who died at, or soon after, birth; this experience probably contributed to making her an over-protective mother, who attempted, in Puffin's case, to prolong his childhood. (One of her stepsons wrote to ask her to stop dressing Puffin in white suits.) Puffin was however allowed to go to Summer Fields Preparatory School in Oxford, even if Margot bought the Wharf, Sutton Courtenay, in order to be near him. He went on to Winchester College and Balliol College, Oxford. He had inherited the artistic eye that had enabled his grandfather, Sir Charles Tennant, to assemble a remarkable collection of paintings. He developed an interest in the cinema, and became a distinguished film director, his principal successes being *The Winslow Boy* (1948), *The Browning Version* (1950), and *The Importance of Being Earnest* (1951).

Asquith, Arthur [Oc] (1883–1939), 3rd son of H. H. Asquith and his first wife Helen; educated at Winchester College and New College, Oxford; Sudan Civil Service 1906–11. Joined Royal Naval Division 1914, served in Gallipoli and France, severely wounded 1917; DSO and two bars; retired, honorary brigadier-general, 1918. Married 1918 Betty Constance Manners, daughter of Margot's old friends 'Hoppy ' and 'Con' Manners. Margot thought Oc 'so much the best regulated of Henry's children and with far the finest character—the only one like Henry in being <u>absolutely</u> without any self'. He was also his father's favourite. When awarded the second bar to his DSO he had been recommended by his own battalion for a VC.

Asquith, Lady Cynthia née Charteris (1887–1960), eldest daughter of Lord Elcho (succ. as 9th Earl of Wemyss 1914) and his wife Mary, both old friends of Margot and members of 'the Souls'. Married 1910 Herbert [Beb]

Asquith. Margot found her daughters-in-law, by comparison with the Tennant family, lacking in 'Life'; Cynthia in her turn was severely critical of Margot in her diary (pub. 1968), giving many instances of Margot's tactlessness. Cynthia was private secretary to J. M. Barrie 1918–37, and inherited a considerable sum of money on his death.

Asquith, Cyril [Cys] (1890–1954), cr. life peer 1951. 4th son of H. H. Asquith and his first wife Helen; educated at Winchester College and Balliol College, Oxford (Hertford, Ireland, Craven and Eldon Scholar). Unfit for overseas service, served in Britain, 1914–18; married 1918 Anne Pollock. KC 1936; judge of high court of justice, King's Bench, 1938–46; lord of appeal in ordinary 1945. Cys was sympathetic to Margot's problems as a stepmother: 'I've always noticed that you and Lucy are moved to tears at the kind of thing that moves all of us to laughter.'

Asquith, Elizabeth Charlotte Lucy [Eliz.] (1897–1945), only daughter and first (surviving) child of H. H. Asquith and Margot. Margot's 'Family' Diaries contain a photographic record of her childhood. She was a clever and precocious girl, with some talent for writing. In 1916 Margot intervened to prevent her from marrying a young American to whom she had engaged herself. In 1919 Elizabeth married the Romanian Prince Antoine Bibesco, and their daughter Priscilla, Margot's only grandchild, was born in 1920. (Margot dedicated *More Memories* to 'One of the loves of my life, Priscilla Bibesco'). After her marriage Elizabeth lived mostly abroad, and was caught by the outbreak of war in 1939 in Romania: no communication with her mother was possible throughout the war. In Mar. 1945 a Red Cross letter brought news that she was about to return to England; but this was followed by the report that she had died on 7 Apr. Margot never recovered fully from the distress that this caused her.

Asquith, Helen Kelsall née Melland (1854–91), daughter of a Manchester doctor; first wife of H. H. Asquith, married 1877. Helen preferred a quiet domestic life with her family to going into 'society'. Died suddenly of typhoid fever in 1891 while on holiday on the island of Arran, leaving five children, ranging in age from 12 years to eighteen months. Margot's early impression, later revised, had been: 'No wife for him. She lives in Hampstead, and has no clothes.'

Asquith, (Helen) Violet (1887–1969), the fourth child, and only daughter, of H. H. Asquith and his first wife, Helen. Violet was only 4 when her mother died, and this loss intensified her attachment to her father, whom she idolized. She wrote to him on the day after her wedding (to Maurice Bonham Carter, in Nov. 1915) that their relationship had been 'the *romance* of my life.... There has never been such a Father—there has never been such a friend.' Violet inevitably saw Margot as a competitor, and in 1909 Asquith lamented that the pair were 'on terms of chronic misunderstanding'. For her part, Margot later wrote: 'I always tell everyone of temperament *never* to be a stepmother.' She was nevertheless an important influence on her stepdaughter, helping to cultivate the taste, sophistication, and above all social confidence that carried Violet successfully through life. Violet possessed, in her father's opinion, 'a first-rate masculine mind of the same order as Raymond's', but this intellectual approach made the irrationality of Margot exasperating to her. They viewed one another with incomprehension, though not without sympathy, and Margot wrote to Oc, 19 May 1915: 'I love Violet though I know I don't understand her and I would, as she knows, do anything for her.' Bonham Carter MS, 154).

Asquith, Herbert [Beb] (1881–1947), 2nd son of H. H. Asquith and his first wife Helen; educated at Winchester College and Balliol College, Oxford. Called to the Bar 1907; war service 1914–18; poet, author, and publisher. Married 1910 Lady Cynthia Charteris.

Asquith, Herbert Henry [H.H.A.] (1852–1928), cr. Earl of Oxford and Asquith 1925. Born Morley, Yorkshire; lost his father, a small employer, at age of 8. Relatives paid (partly on a loan basis) for his education at City of London School. As a scholar of Balliol College, Oxford, 1870–4, he had a successful undergraduate career; called to the Bar 1876; QC 1890. In 1877 he married Helen Melland; they had four sons and one daughter. Asquith had first met Margot in 1890, and after Helen's sudden death from typhoid in 1891, he and Margot were married in 1894; of their five children, only two survived. Asquith, who had entered Parliament in 1886 and had risen rapidly to prominence in the Liberal Party, was Home Secretary, 1892–5, and a leader of the Liberal Imperialist group during the party's Boer War troubles; Chancellor of the Exchequer, Dec. 1905–Apr. 1908; succeeded Campbell-Bannerman as Prime Minister in 1908; he took on the job of Secretary of State for War following 'Jack' Seely's resignation over the Curragh 'mutiny' in Mar. 1914, but relinquished this role on the outbreak of war in Aug. 1914, when he was succeeded by Kitchener. Margot's Diaries provide the background to the successive political crises of Asquith's premiership, ending with his fall from power in Dec. 1916. Asquith was MP for East Fife 1886–1918, and for Paisley 1920–4. KG, 1925. Resigned the leadership of the Liberal Party in 1926. He died in Feb. 1928.

Asquith, Katharine née Horner (1885–1976), daughter of Sir John and Lady (Frances) Horner, old friends of the Asquiths, and members of 'the Souls'. Married 1907 Raymond Asquith. Their son Julian succeeded to the earldom on the death of H. H. Asquith.

Asquith, Margaret Emma Alice [Margot] née Tennant (1864–1945), Countess of Oxford and Asquith from 1925. Political hostess and diarist. Born on 2 Feb. 1864, the sixth (surviving) daughter of Sir Charles Tennant and his first wife Emma. Passed a happy childhood at Glen, Peeblesshire, and from the age of 16 was a fearless rider to hounds. With her sister Laura she had a resounding success on entering society. Laura (Mrs Alfred Lyttelton) died after the birth of her child in 1886. Margot became a prominent member of the group of friends, originally united in mourning Laura, known as 'the Souls'. She was lively and self-assured, and is nowadays thought of as having been a 'wit': but according to the late Lord David Cecil, who had known her, it was rather that she resembled a precocious child, who makes a clever remark and is surprised when people laugh. She first met H. H. Asquith in 1890; the following year his wife

Helen died suddenly from typhoid fever, leaving four sons and a daughter. After a long courtship Asquith proposed to Margot, who hesitated for some months before accepting him: the wedding took place in 1894. She gave birth to five children, but only two, Elizabeth and Anthony, survived. Relations with her stepchildren, especially Raymond and Violet, were never easy. Asquith succeeded Campbell-Bannerman as Prime Minister in 1908. Margot was wholly committed to keeping the Liberal Party in power, with her husband as premier. Her diaries reveal the remarkable degree to which she interfered to this end in political matters; it is difficult, however, to judge how much real influence she had on the course of events. She did not modify her habitual outspokenness, and her arrogance and extravagance as the Prime Minister's wife were much resented and criticized. After Asquith ceased to be Prime Minister, Margot, partly impelled by shortage of money, wrote her *Autobiography* (2 vols, 1920, 1922). Her excessively candid remarks about her friends and others gave great offence, but the book sold well. After her husband's death she occupied herself with writing. Her daughter had passed the Second World War in Romania, and Margot looked forward to being reunited with her in 1945: the news that Elizabeth had died, 7 Apr. 1945, was a tragic blow from which Margot never fully recovered. She died on 28 July 1945.

Asquith, Raymond (1878–1916), eldest child of H. H. Asquith and his first wife Helen; educated at Winchester College and Balliol College, Oxford, where after obtaining first class honours in both Greats and Jurisprudence, he won the Ireland, Craven, and Eldon scholarships, and a fellowship of All Souls College, Oxford; called to the Bar 1907. 'To him', Churchill wrote, 'the [Asquith] inheritance passed in extraordinary perfection.' Adopted Liberal candidate for Derby 1913. Joined Queen's Westminster Rifles, transferred to 3rd Battn Grenadier Guards, 1915. Died of wounds during Somme Battle, 15 Sept. 1916. What Margot wrote in her diary after Raymond's death revealed why she so despised the 'Corrupt Coterie' of which he had been a leader, and how deeply she was hurt by the mockery of her stepchildren.

Balfour, Arthur James [A.J.B.] (1848–1930), cr. Earl 1922. Entered Parliament 1874; made his name as Chief Secretary for Ireland 1887–91. Prime Minister 1902–5, succeeding his uncle, Lord Salisbury. Led the Conservatives in the Commons 1891–1911; then was forced to resign, replaced by the more obviously combative Bonar Law. First Lord of the Admiralty in Coalition government 1915; Foreign Secretary 1916–19 (Balfour Declaration in favour of Jewish national home in Palestine, 1917); at Peace Conference, 1919; President of British Association 1924; of British Academy 1921–30. Published several works of philosophy. As a member of 'the Souls', Balfour was an old, but not a completely trusted, friend of Margot. Against a paragraph praising him in her Diary of 1904–6, which ends 'Arthur has neither self-consciousness or obstinacy', she wrote in 1921: 'I think I am wrong here, he is an obstinate man and a bitter jealous and even unfair enemy.'

Beaverbrook, Lord *see* Aitken, William Maxwell.

Bethmann Hollweg, Theobald von (1856–1921), Imperial Chancellor of Germany, 1909. In the final dispatch by the British Ambassador to Berlin (28 Aug. 1914), Bethmann-Hollweg is quoted as referring to the 1839 treaty on Belgium as 'a scrap of paper', although it is not clear whether these were his exact words. He was dismissed in 1917. He stated in his memoirs that no meeting had ever been held during his pre-war chancellorship at which the politicians could participate in Germany's military planning (Craig, *Germany*, 317). Once compared ineptly by Asquith with Abraham Lincoln.

Bigge, Sir Arthur John (1849–1931), KCB 1895, cr. Baron Stamfordham 1911. Military career 1869–79. PS to Queen Victoria 1895–1901, PS to George V as Prince of Wales and later as King 1901–31 (jointly with Knollys, 1910–13). In 1910 Margot quoted Lord Esher as saying that Bigge 'was clever but had no kind of judgement'; she added 'I told him I had never met a soldier that had.' In Sept. 1913 she recorded: 'That ass, Stamfordham…knows nothing of constitutional history.' She found the more Liberal Lord Knollys more congenial.

Birrell, Augustine (1850–1933), barrister and author (*Obiter Dicta*, 1884, 1887, 1924). Entered Parliament, 1889; Chief Secretary for Ireland, 1907–16; resigned after the Easter Rising, 1916, which tarnished what may be considered, at least until 1912, a fine record of administrative achievement in Ireland. One of Asquith's oldest friends. Hobhouse, a cabinet colleague, thought him (Aug. 1912) 'cynical, amusing, a bad administrator, but high principled and with plenty of courage'.

Bonham Carter, Maurice [Bongie/Bongy] (1880–1960), Kt. 1916; close friend of Asquith's sons, educated at Winchester College and Balliol College, Oxford. Private Secretary to Asquith, 1908–16; Principal PS, 1912–16. Married Violet Asquith, 1915. Margot was fond of Bongie, whom she preferred to 'all Violet's [other] admirers'. She considered him, however, inadequate as 'first secretary' to Asquith in the critical days of late 1916, and wrote severely then about his supposed shortcomings.

Bonham Carter, (Helen) Violet *see* **Asquith, (Helen) Violet. From Dec. 1964 Baroness Asquith of Yarnbury.**

Brett, Reginald Baliol (1852–1930), succeeded as 2nd Viscount Esher 1899. Liberal MP 1880–5. Superintended Diamond Jubilee, 1897, and coronation of Edward VII, 1902. Member of Royal Commission on South African War; War Office Reconstruction Committee, 1903; Committee of Imperial Defence, 1905. Advocate of army reform, and supporter of the Territorial Army. Preferred influencing events at the centre to accepting the 'parochial' appointment of Indian Viceroy. According to Margot (1912): 'Likes to know everything, and knows much more than he ought'.

Brodrick, (William) St John (1856–1942), succeeded as 9th Viscount Midleton 1907, cr. Earl 1920. Unionist MP 1880–1906; Secretary of State for War 1900–3; for India 1903–5. His tenure at the India Office was marred by serious disputes with Curzon, then Viceroy, over Younghusband's treaty with Tibet, and the control of the Indian Army. One of Margot's oldest friends and a member of the Souls, he is warmly praised in the *Autobiography*.

Burns, John Elliott (1858–1943), Labour MP for Battersea, 1892–1918; President of Local Govt. Board, 1905–14; President Board of Trade, 1914. For his resignation on outbreak of war see *Asquith–Stanley*, 146–7.

Campbell-Bannerman, Sir Henry [C.B.] (1836–1908), GCB 1895. Born Glasgow, son of wholesale draper, partner in family business till 1868. Liberal MP for the Stirling Burghs, 1868–1908. Entered cabinet in Gladstone's 3rd administration, Feb.–June 1886. Secretary of State for War in Gladstone and Rosebery administrations, 1892–5. Leader of Liberal Party in opposition, Jan. 1899–1905. Prime Minister, 1905–8.

Carson, Sir Edward (1854–1935), cr. Baron 1921. Barrister. Born in Dublin. Unionist MP for Dublin University, 1892–1918; for Belfast (Duncairn) 1918–21. QC, 1894 (Oscar Wilde trial, 1895); Solicitor-General, 1900–5. Leader of Ulster Unionist MPs 1910. Ulster Volunteers and Covenant, 1912. Attorney-General, May 1915–16; First Lord of the Admiralty, Dec. 1916; War Cabinet, July 1917–Jan. 1918. The 'uncrowned king of Ulster'. 'By temperament opposed to every government' (Beaverbrook).

Chamberlain, Joseph [Joe] (1836–1914), moved in 1854 from London to Birmingham to join a firm of screw manufacturers. Mayor of Birmingham, 1873–5. Entered Parliament as Radical reformer. Liberal MP 1876–86, Liberal Unionist 1886–1914. President of Board of Trade 1880–85; President of Local Government Board Feb.–Mar. 1886 when he resigned over Home Rule Bill. Secretary of State for Colonies 1895–1903; accused of complicity in Jameson Raid. Resigned 1903, to further his campaign for tariff reform. The stroke which he suffered in July 1906 ended his political career, although he continued to advise the Unionists for some years.

Chamberlain, Sir (Joseph) Austen (1863–1937), KG 1925; son of Joseph Chamberlain. Liberal Unionist MP 1892–1914, Conservative MP 1914–37. Chancellor of the Exchequer 1903–5. On resignation of Balfour, 1911, he and Walter Long, as rivals for the leadership of the Unionist Party, stood down in favour of Bonar Law. Secretary of State for India 1915–17; War Cabinet, 1918; Chancellor of the Exchequer 1919–21; Leader of Conservatives,

House of Commons, 1921–2; Foreign Secretary, 1924–9. 'Straight as a die' (Selborne). Margot thought him, Mar. 1911, 'a thoroughly second-rate politician'.

Churchill, Clementine Ogilvy Spencer-, née Hozier [Clemmie/ Clemmy] (1885–1977), second of four children of Sir Henry and Lady Blanche Hozier. Married 1908 Winston Churchill; they had four girls and one boy; Margot's relations with 'Clemmie' were never warm, and after Winston's demotion in 1915 they deteriorated considerably.

Churchill, Winston Leonard Spencer (1874–1965), KG 1953. Elder son of Lord Randolph Churchill and of Jennie, daughter of Leonard Jerome of New York. Married 1908 Clementine, daughter of Sir Henry and Lady Blanche Hozier. Conservative MP 1900. Opposed tariff reform, and joined Liberals May 1904. Colonial Under-Secretary 1905–8. President of Board of Trade 1908–10. Defeated NW Manchester, elected Dundee (May 1908). Home Secretary 1910. First Lord of Admiralty 1911–15. Instituted Admiralty War Staff, Jan. 1912; demoted on formation of coalition government, May 1915 and resigned later that year. War service in France. Minister of Munitions 1917–19; Secretary for War and Air 1919–21; Colonial Secretary 1921–2. Rejoined Conservative Party after short period as a 'Constitutionalist': MP for Epping, and later Woodford 1924–45; Chancellor of Exchequer 1924–9; Conservative Prime Minister 1940–5, 1951–5. Although Margot found Winston frequently exasperating ('a child who will never grow up', 1912) she admired his 'courage and colour, his amazing mixture of industry and enterprise' (1914); but in Nov. 1915 she could 'see no political future for him'.

Crewe, Lord *see* **Crewe-Milnes, Robert Offley.**

Crewe-Milnes, Robert Offley (1858–1945), cr. Earl of Crewe 1895; Marquess 1911. Never an MP. Succeeded to his father's barony, 1885. Married as his 2nd wife, 1889, Lady Margaret Primrose [Peggy], daughter of 5th Earl of Rosebery. Lord Lieutenant of Ireland, 1892. Lord President of Council, 1905–8, 1915–16; Secretary of State for Colonies, 1908–10; Lord Privy Seal,

1908–11 and 1912–15; Secretary of State for India 1910–15. When in Feb. 1915 Asquith sent Venetia Stanley a 'class list' (i.e. arranged in order of merit) of his cabinet colleagues, he placed Crewe first. Jenkins comments in *Asquith*, 341, that Crewe could never have run a government—'but partly perhaps for this reason, he was an almost ideal colleague to a Prime Minister'.

Curzon, George Nathaniel (1859–1925), Baron Curzon of Kedleston (Irish peerage) 1898, Irish representative peer 1908; cr. Earl 1911; Marquis, 1921. President of Oxford Union, prize-winner and fellow of All Souls College, Oxford. An old friend of Margot and a member of the Souls. Unionist MP 1886–98. Travelled widely and became a leading authority on Asiatic affairs. Under-Secretary for India 1891–2. 1895 married Mary Leiter (who died 1906). Under-Secretary for Foreign Affairs 1895–8. He became Viceroy of India in 1898, but was involved in serious disputes with St John Brodrick, Secretary of State for India, and Lord Kitchener, Commander-in-Chief India; he resigned in 1905. Lord Privy Seal in coalition cabinet 1915–16; War Cabinet, 1916–19; Foreign Secretary 1919–24, Lord President of the Council, 1916–19 and 1924–5. Margot, who looked upon Curzon as 'almost like … one of the family' was angry when in May 1914 he gave a ball to which he did not invite her, Violet, or Elizabeth. He, in turn, was offended, when Margot's *Autobiography* appeared, at being said to have 'a childish love of fine people'. He died before a planned reconciliation could take place.

Davidson, Randall Thomas (1848–1930), cr. Baron 1928. Dean of Windsor, 1883; Bishop of Rochester 1891–5; of Winchester 1895–1903; Archbishop of Canterbury 1903–28.

Desborough, Lady [Ettie] *see* **Grenfell, Ethel.**

Dickson-Poynder, Ann Beauclerk, née Dundas (1869–1958), married 1896 Sir John Dickson-Poynder (see below). She and Margot were good friends for many years, until a quarrel took place in 1916 over the viceroyalty of India, apparently as a result of Margot's tactlessness.

Dickson-Poynder, Sir John Poynder [Jack] (1866–1936), succeeded as 6th Bt. 1884, cr. Baron Islington 1910. Married 1896 Ann Beauclerk (d. 1958), third daughter of Robert Dundas. MP (Unionist) 1892–1905, (Liberal) 1906–10. Governor of New Zealand 1910–12; Under-Secretary for Colonies 1914–15; for India 1915–18.

Drummond, Sir (James) Eric (1876–1951), KCMG 1916, succ. as 7th Earl of Perth, 1937. Private Secretary to Asquith 1912–15, and to Foreign Secretaries Grey and Balfour 1915–18. First Secretary-General of the League of Nations 1919–33. Asquith told Venetia on 22 Feb. 1915 that he was having to let Drummond go back to Grey: 'It will be a terrible mutilation of my staff. He is in some ways the best PS I have ever had: careful, capable, admirable in dealing with bores…'

Edward VII, King (1841–1910), eldest son of Queen Victoria and Prince Albert. Married 1863 Princess Alexandra, daughter of King Christian IX of Denmark, succeeded to throne 1901. Unlike his mother favourable to the Liberals (though hardly to Margot), but in first 1910 election obstructed lessening of Lords' powers. Suffered severe bronchial trouble in spring of 1910, and died at Buckingham Palace on 6 May.

Elibank, The Master of *see* **Murray, Alexander.**

Enver Pasha (1881–1922), leader of Young Turks in revolution of 1908. Turkish Minister of War 1914; formed a secret alliance with Germany. In 1918 fled to Russia, and was killed in an uprising in Turkestan.

Esher, Lord *see* **Brett, Reginald Baliol.**

Fisher, (Admiral of the Fleet) John Arbuthnot [Jacky] (1841–1920), KCB 1894, OM 1904, GCVO 1908, cr. Baron 1909. Served in Baltic Fleet during Crimean War. 3rd Sea Lord and Controller of Navy, 1892–7: devised programme of shipbuilding following Naval Defence Act, 1889. 2nd Sea Lord, 1902; First Sea Lord, 1904–10 and Oct. 1914–May 1915. Responsible for Britain's lead in 'all-big-gun' battleships and battle cruisers (Dreadnought launched Jan. 1906). Flamboyant, creator of greatly needed changes and of much discord. The scene in May 1915 when Margot and Fisher discuss the dangerous situation in the Dardanelles, and end up waltzing round the room, is one of the most bizarre in the diary. In Aug. 1915 Balfour told Margot that 'we owed all our superiority at sea to Fisher'.

Foch, (General) Ferdinand (1851–1929), the great star of the École de Guerre. Aged 62 at the outbreak of war. Apostle of the offensive, but learned much about defensive warfare round Nancy in Aug. 1914, and south of the Marne when the German advance was at its limit. Sent Oct. 1914 to northern part of Front as 'deputy' to Joffre, to coordinate French, British, and Belgian forces there. Commanded Allied armies, 1918.

French, (Field Marshal) Sir John Denton (1852–1925), cr. Viscount 1916; Earl of Ypres 1922. Entered navy at 14, but left to join army, 1870. After success in Boer War, Lt.-Gen. and KCMG, 1902. Inspector-General of Forces 1907; CIGS 1912; Field Marshal 1913. Resigned after Curragh 'mutiny' 1914. Commander in Chief BEF from 1914 till superseded Dec. 1915. In May 1915 Kitchener told Margot (who had been inclined at first to hero-worship French) that the Commander in Chief was 'the greatest soldier living in the field', but also 'the worst organizer, and a stupid man'.

George V, King (1865–1936), 2nd son of Edward VII. Cr. Duke of York on elder brother's death, 1892. Married Princess Victoria Mary of Teck, 1893. Prince of Wales, 1901. Succeeded to throne, May 1910. Unabashed Unionist in sentiment until succeeding to the throne, but thereafter took an impartial line, at first in very difficult circumstances.

Glenconner, Lady *see* **Tennant, Pamela.**

Glenconner, Lord *see* **Tennant, Edward.**

Graham-Smith, Lucy Katharine née Tennant (1860–1942), third (surviving) daughter of Sir Charles Tennant; married 1879 Thomas Graham-Smith, who died 1908. Lucy was a member of the Souls, and a talented artist. She owned the Manor House in Easton Grey, Wiltshire, where she frequently provided hospitality for Margot and her family.

Grenfell, Ethel Anne Priscilla [Ettie/Etty] née Fane (1867–1952), married 1887 William Grenfell, cr. Baron Desborough 1905. Having inherited considerable wealth, she became a famous hostess at their house, Taplow Court, near Maidenhead, and was a prominent member of the Souls. Extra Lady of the Bedchamber to Queen Mary from Jan. 1911. Two of her sons, Julian and Billy Grenfell, were killed in 1915. Margot includes character sketches of her in the diary, Aug. 1915 and Oct. 1916. Fully described in biography by R. Davenport-Hines. This may be supplemented from N. Mosley, *Julian Grenfell* and from the *Balfour-Elcho Letters*.

Grenfell, Julian (1888–1915), eldest son of Lord and Lady Desborough. Educated at Summer Fields and Eton, and at Balliol College, Oxford, where he was renowned for athletic and sporting prowess but took a pass degree. Army service in India and S. Africa. Western Front 1914; died 26 May 1915 of wounds received at Ypres. His brother Billy (1890–1915) was killed, also at Ypres, on 30 July 1915.

Grey, Sir Edward (1862–1933), succ. as 3rd Bt. 1882, KG 1912, cr. Viscount 1916. Sent down from Balliol College, Oxford, for idleness, 1884, but later took degree. Liberal MP 1885–1916. A mainstay, with Asquith and Haldane, of the Liberal Imperialist group during party splits occasioned by Boer War. Foreign Secretary from 1905 until Asquith's fall. Married (1) 1885 Dorothy Widdrington, who d. 1906; (2) 1922 Pamela, widow of Baron Glenconner. Margot and her husband admired him greatly in pre-war days. Henry had told her (28 Feb. 1909): 'Grey and Crewe are worth all the others [in the cabinet] put together.' Both admirers became disillusioned when, his eyesight failing, Grey seemed less successful and cooperative in wartime; but his tact with the United States over the blockade of Germany proved valuable.

Guest, Ivor Churchill (1873–1939), s. as 2nd Baron Wimborne 1914, cr. Viscount 1918. Unionist MP 1900, Liberal MP 1906. Paymaster-General 1910–12; Irish Viceroy 1915–18. Cynthia Asquith's *Diaries* contains an unflattering portrait of him. Married 1902 Alice Katherine Sibell Grosvenor, daughter of 2nd Baron Ebury.

Gulland, John (1864–1920), Scottish Whip under Illingworth; appointed Chief Whip after Illingworth's sudden death on 3 Jan. 1915. Asquith was not enthusiastic about this promotion ('…It will be the line of least resistance'). Gulland was not a success in the post, but he inherited an inadequate Whips' Office, and received little help from the premier.

Haig, (General) Sir Douglas (1861–1928), KCVO 1909, cr. Earl 1919. Married 1905 Dorothy Maud Vivian. Staff Officer to Sir John French, Boer War, both being cavalrymen. Summoned by Haldane to work on military organization, 1906. Commanded 1st Corps BEF Aug. 1914; came into national prominence after 1st Battle of Ypres (Oct.–Nov. 1914). Commanded 1st Army Jan. 1915. Succeeded French as Commander-in-Chief, Dec. 1915. C. R. M. F. Cruttwell described him as 'reserved and almost grotesquely inarticulate', but greatly admired his 'profound calm of spirit maintained during the worst days of Mar. 1918'.

Haldane, Richard Burdon (1856–1928), cr. Viscount 1911. Barrister. Liberal MP 1885–1911. Secretary of State for War 1905–12; Lord Chancellor 1912–15, (in Labour government) 1924. FRS 1906; FBA 1914. One of Asquith's closest friends in the 1880s, but later told his mother (Feb. 1920) that Margot had 'done much to make it difficult in the years gone by for Asquith to rise to the occasion'.

Hamilton, (General) Sir Ian Standish (1853–1947), KCB 1900. Notable service in Boer War (chief of staff to Kitchener); QMG 1903–4; headed military mission to Japanese in Russo-Japan War 1904–5; commanded anti-invasion forces 1914–15. Dardanelles army Mar.–Oct. 1915. Distinguished and intelligent, he lacked the tough, ruthless realism of the great commander.

Hankey, Sir Maurice Pascal (1877–1963), KCB 1916; cr. Baron 1939. Commissioned Royal Marine Artillery: transferred 1902 to Naval Intelligence. Committee of Imperial Defence, Assistant Secretary 1908, Secretary 1912. Acted as Secretary to War Council from its formation Nov. 1914. Creator of the cabinet secretariat. 'Without Hankey we should not have won the war' (Balfour).

Harcourt, Lewis [Loulou] (1863–1922), cr. Viscount 1917. Liberal MP 1904–16. First Commissioner of Works 1905–10 and 1915–16; Secretary of State for Colonies 1910–15. Married 1899 Mary Ethel, daughter of Walter H. Burns of New York.

Harmsworth, Arthur Charles (1865–1922), cr. Baron Northcliffe 1905, Viscount 1917. Father of modern popular journalism. Proprietor of *Daily Mail* 1896, *The Times* 1908, and other papers. Gave warnings of Germany's warlike intentions and campaigned before and after the outbreak of war for compulsory military service, but had little notion of how Britain could work effectively with her Entente partners. Greatly distrusted by Asquith, by almost all other Liberals, and by a number of Unionists. Close to insanity when he died.

Henley, Sylvia née Stanley (1882–1980): 2nd daughter of 4th Baron Sheffield and sister of Venetia Stanley; married 1906 Anthony Henley (1873–1925). When Asquith's correspondence with Venetia Stanley was suddenly broken off in May 1915, he was in desperate need of a confidante, and by the end of May her sister Sylvia had become his 'sheet-anchor'. Sylvia, a married woman with small children, was sometimes disconcerted by Asquith's dependence on her: her recurrent discomfort is expressed in her letters to her husband (see extracts, May and June 1915, paperback edition of *Asquith–Stanley*, 610–13). At no point was this friendship as intense as the one with Venetia. The correspondence, which was given to the Bodleian Library in 1982 by Sylvia's daughter, the late Mrs Juliet Daniels, consists of 339 letters written by Asquith (with a few enclosures). The quota of comment on politics and world events increased from about Mar. 1916, and as affairs became more critical and tragic the letters naturally reflected this.

Herbert, Auberon Thomas [Bron] (1876–1916), 8th Baron Lucas, 1905. Wounded and lost foot, South African War. Private Secretary to Haldane when Secretary of State for War 1905–6; President of Board of Agriculture and Fisheries 1914–15. Joined Royal Flying Corps and became a pilot although one-footed and above the standard age. Was reported missing Nov. 1916.

Hobhouse, Sir Charles Edward (1862–1941), succ. as 4th Bt., 1916. Liberal MP 1892–5, 1900–18. Under Secretary for India 1907–8, Financial Secretary to Treasury 1908–11, Chancellor of Duchy of Lancaster 1911–14, Postmaster General 1914–15. Hobhouse kept diaries 1893–8, and 1904–15: selections from the latter, edited by Edward David, were published in 1977 under the title *Inside Asquith's Cabinet.*

Illingworth, Percy (1869–1915), chairman, Yorkshire Liberal Federation. Liberal MP 1906, Chief Whip from 1912. Nonconformist; sportsman; formerly Capt. in Imperial Yeomanry. His death in Jan. 1915 was a serious blow to Asquith.

Isaacs, Sir Rufus Daniel (1860–1935), Kt. 1910, cr. Baron Reading 1914, Viscount 1916, Marquess 1926. KC 1898. Liberal MP 1904–13; Solicitor-General 1910; Attorney-General 1910. Implicated in Marconi controversy 1912–13. Lord Chief Justice 1913–21. Viceroy of India 1921–6. A most talented negotiator.

Islington, Ann *see* **Dickson-Poynder, Ann.**

Islington, Lord [Jack] *see* **Dickson-Poynder, Sir John Poynder.**

Jellicoe, John Rushworth (1859–1935), OM 1916, cr. Visc. 1918, Earl 1925, Admiral of the Fleet 1919. Commander-in-Chief, Grand Fleet, by Fisher's design, 4 Aug. 1914. Secured at Battle of Jutland, 31 May–1 June 1916, strategic, though not tactical, victory as sweeping as Trafalgar. British ship losses exceeded German; but many more German ships were damaged; and the British Grand Fleet was ready to put to sea three days after the battle. British naval supremacy was shown to have been at risk from mines or torpedo attacks by surface ships or submarines, rather than by fire from German Dreadnoughts. First Sea Lord, Dec. 1916. Implemented convoy system when USA joined Allies, but dismissed Dec. 1917. Governor-General of New Zealand, 1920–4.

Joffre, Joseph Jacques Césaire (1852–1931), took part in defence of Paris, 1870. Vice-President of Supreme War Council, and thus C. in C. in case of war, 1911 (third choice for the post). C. in C. French armies, Western Front, Aug. 1914–Dec. 1916. President of Allied War Council, 1917.

Jowett, Benjamin (1817–93), ordained 1845; tutor at Balliol College, Oxford 1842–70, and Master 1870–93; aroused controversy with his contribution to the liberal *Essays and Reviews*, 1860; advocate of university reform and university extension. A mentor of the young Margot and a profound influence on the young Asquith.

Kaiser, The *see* **Wilhelm II.**

Keppel, Alice Frederica née Edmonstone (1868–1947), married 1891 George Keppel, brother of 8th Earl of Albemarle. After meeting King Edward VII in 1898 she quickly became his 'favourite', exercising a good influence and being trusted for her discretion. When war broke out in 1914, Margot's 17–year-old daughter Elizabeth was staying with Mrs Keppel in Holland. Margot described her (diary, 19 Aug. 1914, p. 22 above) as 'a "typical *femme maitresse*"…coarse, kind, truthful and gay…clever, and essentially kind and good-hearted'.

King, the *see* **George V, King.**

Kitchener of Khartoum, (Field Marshal) Earl, Horatio Herbert [K. of K.] (1850–1916), KCMG 1894, cr. Baron 1898, Viscount 1902, Earl 1914, KG 1915. Served briefly in French Army in latter part of Franco-Prussian War, 1871, after qualifying for a commission in Royal Engineers. Successful campaigns in Egypt and Sudan (Battle of Omdurman 1898). Roberts's Chief of Staff, then C.-in-C., in Boer War. C.-in-C. India 1902–9, where he worsted the Viceroy (Curzon). Esher discerned signs of 'demoralization' in him, June 1911. British Agent and Consul-General, Egypt 1911–14. Secretary of State for War, Aug. 1914 to 1916. Drowned on HMS *Hampshire*, en route to Russia, June 1916. His creation of the New Armies during the war ranks, in Churchill's phrase, 'among the wonders of the time'.

Kühlmann, Richard von (1873–1948), staff of German Embassy, London, 1908–14. German Secretary of State for Foreign Affairs 6 Aug. 1917–June 1918, when Supreme Army Command forced his dismissal for telling Reichstag that war could not be won by military means alone. In 1914 Margot thought him 'after Cambon...the cleverest of our foreigners'. Others were more resistant to his flatteries.

Lansdowne, Lord *see* **Petty-Fitzmaurice, Henry Charles.**

Law, Andrew Bonar [B.L.] (1858–1923), born in Canada, brought up from the age of 12 in Glasgow. Joined his mother's family firm, and later William Jacks and Co., iron merchants. Entered Parliament, 1900. Profiting from the split between Austen Chamberlain's supporters and Long's, became Unionist leader in the Commons, 1911. Much underrated by Asquith (and Margot). Colonial Secretary May 1915. Member of War Cabinet Dec. 1916–Oct. 1919. Chancellor of the Exchequer Dec. 1916–Jan. 1919. Leader of the Commons, Dec. 1916–Mar. 1921. Prime Minister, 23 Oct. 1922–20 May 1923. A sad figure after his wife's death, 1909. In politics a bleak realist. After attending his funeral in Westminster Abbey Asquith is said to have commented that it was fitting to 'have buried the Unknown Prime Minister by the side of the Unknown Soldier' (Blake, *Bonar Law*, 13).

Lichnowsky, Prince Carl Max (1860–1928). German diplomat, served in various legations, 1884–9; recalled to Foreign Office by von Bülow. German Ambassador in London, 1912. Worked hard for pacific relations between England and Germany, but had warned the Kaiser about the danger of antagonizing Britain soon after arrival, and thereafter carried no weight in Berlin.

Lichnowsky, Princess Mechtilde (1879–1958) was described by Margot in the *Autobiography* as 'a handsome woman of talents and character' who 'detested the influence of the Prussian Court' (see also *Asquith–Stanley*, 86, 87, and 157).

Lister, Charlotte Monkton[Charty], Lady Ribblesdale née Tennant (1858–1911), elder sister of Margot. Married 1877 Thomas Lister, 4th Baron

Ribblesdale. They had five children: their elder son, Thomas, was killed on active service in Somaliland in 1904, and their younger son, Charles, a close friend of the younger Asquith children, died at Gallipoli in Aug. 1915, when the peerage became extinct. Charlotte was described by Margot as 'the only beauty of our family'; she was a member of the Souls. She died in 1911 after a three-year fight against tuberculosis.

Lloyd George, David [Ll.G.] (1863–1945), cr. Earl 1945. Schoolmaster's son, orphaned in infancy, brought up by uncle, a shoemaker and Baptist preacher in the radical Welsh tradition. Solicitor, 1884. MP, Carnarvon Boroughs, 1890 (to 1945). Became a national figure, and the radicals' standard-bearer, by championing the Boers against Joe Chamberlain's imperialism, and the Nonconformists against Balfour's Education Bill. President Board of Trade 1905; Chancellor of Exchequer 1908. Introduced People's Budget 1909; National Insurance 1911. Under slight cloud from the end of 1912 to the outbreak of war from Marconi scandal and fiasco of 1914 Budget. Minister of Munitions May 1915; Secretary of State for War July 1916; resigned 5 Dec. 1916. Prime Minister 7 Dec. 1916–Oct. 1922. Introduced energetic new measures for prosecution of the war, and negotiated peace treaty, 1919. Headed National Liberal Party in 1922 election. Dispute with Asquith over General Strike led to Asquith's resignation from party leadership, 1926. Margot was at first disposed to be friendly with Lloyd George, and some of her best 'character sketches' are those describing him; but her growing, and eventually obsessional, distrust is evident in the diary, and she was appalled by his appointment as Secretary for War in 1916. Diary entries after Dec. 1916 have an almost frantic tone: her opposition to Lloyd George and to all who agreed to serve under him is very bitterly expressed.

Long, Walter Hume (1854–1924), cr. Viscount 1921. Unionist MP (7 constituencies) 1880–1921; as parliamentary Secretary to Local Government Board was largely responsible for Local Government Act 1888; President Local Government Board 1900–5; Chief Secretary for Ireland 1905; Sec of

State for Colonies 1916–18; First Lord of Admiralty 1918–21. Margot thought him (1911) as 'a fine old fighting sort with a clear crude "up-and-at-'em" kind of mind'.

Lowther, James William (1855–1949), cr. Viscount Ullswater 1921. Unionist MP for Rutland 1883; for Cumberland (Penrith) 1886–1921. Speaker of the House of Commons 1905–21.

Lyttelton, Alfred (1857–1913), athlete, sportsman, and successful lawyer. Margot and her sister Laura vied for his affections, and he married Laura in 1885. She died the following year. In 1892 he married as his second wife Edith (D. D.) Balfour. Liberal Unionist MP for Leamington 1895–1905; Colonial Secretary 1903–5; MP for St George's Hanover Square 1906. In an obituary speech on Lyttelton in the House of Commons, Asquith said that 'wherever he moved, he seemed to radiate vitality and charm.... He has left behind him no resentments and no enmities, nothing but a gracious memory of a manly and winning personality.' For text see Asquith, *Addresses*, 187–8.

Lyttelton, (Octavia) Laura née Tennant (1862–86), the elder sister nearest in age to Margot. Although very different in character—Laura was quieter, more devout, and more concerned about moral problems than her impetuous sister—the two girls were devoted to each other, and together they enjoyed a great success in society. Lord Bonham Carter wrote (Introduction to *Autobiography*, abridged edition, xxi–xxii) that Margot's feeling for Laura 'was probably the deepest, the most unselfish and the most important in her life'. Laura married Alfred Lyttelton in 1885, but died a few days after their son was born in 1886. This loss had a profound effect on Margot, who referred frequently to Laura in her diaries thereafter, always underlining her name. More immediately, Margot was one of the circle of friends, soon to be known as 'the Souls', who were drawn together in mourning for Laura. On 19 May 1915 Margot listed in her Diary the 'Fateful Days' of her life: these include Laura's engagement and her death.

McKenna, Reginald [McK.] (1863–1943), barrister. Entered Parliament 1895. President, Board of Education 1907; First Lord of Admiralty 1908. Married 1908 Pamela Jekyll (1889–1943), younger daughter of Sir Herbert Jekyll and his wife Dame Agnes née Graham. Home Secretary 1911–15; Chancellor of Exchequer 1915–16. Asquith admired his courage, but thought him 'singularly rasping and unpersuasive in argument'. His appearance seemed to Margot 'ugly in a pathetic and insignificant way'.

Mary, Queen (1867–1953), born Princess Mary of Teck in Kensington Palace, in the room in which Queen Victoria was born; she married, 1893, Prince George Frederick Ernest Albert, Duke of York (George V); during the war her natural sense of duty, and of social responsibility, came to the fore, and she was noted for her philanthropic initiatives, 'a charitable bulldozer, clearing a path for hundreds of thousands of volunteers': 'At the palace, meanwhile, she and the king imposed a regime of legendary frugality, in keeping with the national sense of crisis' (Frank Prochaska, *ODNB*, 'Mary, [Princess of Teck]').

Masterman, Charles Frederick (1874–1927), Liberal MP 1906–14, 1923–4. Married 1908 Lucy Blanche Lyttelton (1884–1977). As Under Secretary of the Local Government Board, assisted John Burns in carrying through the Housing and Town Planning Act 1909; Under Secretary, Home Office 1909, and Financial Secretary to Treasury 1912. First Chairman of National Insurance Commission. On becoming Chancellor of the Duchy of Lancaster, 1914, he stood for re-election at Bethnal Green, but was defeated, and, lacking a parliamentary seat, resigned from cabinet 1915; see *Asquith-Stanley*, 74–5.

Midleton, Lord *see* **Brodrick, (William) St John.**

Milner, Alfred (1854–1925) KCB 1895, cr. Viscount 1902. After early education in Germany, gained many distinctions at Oxford. High Commissioner for South Africa 1897–1905; signed, with Lord Kitchener, Treaty of Vereeniging 1902. Opposed the Parliament Bill and Home Rule; supported wartime conscription. Member of Lloyd George's small War

Cabinet 1916. An old friend and admirer of Margot, he had once proposed marriage to her. Had been enabled to opt for British nationality under a statute of 1773, repealed 1914, on ground that a grandfather had originally been British.

Montagu, Edwin Samuel (1879–1924). 2nd son of a wealthy merchant banker who was cr. Lord Swaythling 1907. Married 26 July 1915 Venetia Stanley. Liberal MP 1906–22. Parliamentary Private Secretary to Asquith when H.H.A. was Chancellor of Exchequer and Prime Minister. Under-Secretary for India 1910–14 (toured India 1912–13). Financial Secretary to Treasury 1914–15; Chancellor of Duchy of Lancaster 1915; Minister of Munitions 1916; Secretary of State for India 1917 till resignation, Mar. 1922. In 1912 Margot judged him to be 'emotionally affectionate, wonderfully clever and inordinately ambitious'.

Montagu, (Beatrice) Venetia née Stanley (1887–1948). Youngest daughter of Lyulph Stanley, who succeeded as Lord Stanley of Alderley, 1903, and as Lord Sheffield, 1909. A member of a prominent Liberal family, and a contemporary and friend of Violet Asquith, she became the confidante of H. H. Asquith, who wrote to her in 1914 and 1915 a remarkable series of personal letters, describing the political events of these years (see *Bibliography*). The correspondence ceased when in 1915 Venetia became engaged to Edwin Montagu. By the terms of his father's will, Montagu would forfeit his inheritance if he did not marry a Jewess: Venetia converted to Judaism, and they were married in July 1915.

Morley, John (1838–1923), cr. Viscount 1908. Editor of *Fortnightly Review* 1867–82, and of *Pall Mall Gazette* 1880–3. Author of *Life of Gladstone* 1903, and other biographies. Liberal MP 1883–1908. Chief Secretary for Ireland 1886, 1892–5; Secretary of State for India 1905–10; Lord President of the Council 1910–14. Resigned from cabinet on government's decision to enter war, 1914. Handing this resignation letter to Margot, Asquith remarked, 'I shall miss him very much; he is one of the most distinguished men living': *Autobiography*, ii. 195.

Murray, Alexander (1870–1920), entitled The Master of Elibank as the eldest son of a pre-Union Scottish Baron (the 10th Lord Elibank), cr. Lord Murray of Elibank 1912. Liberal Chief Whip Feb. 1910–Aug. 1912. Predeceased his father, who had been cr. Viscount Elibank 1911. When he became Chief Whip Margot welcomed the news as 'the best of all Henry's appointments', adding: 'He is a very clever fellow, full of energy and shrewdness—a regular Scot, as Henry would say' (diary, 17 Feb. 1910). He was also an expert flatterer, and, as such, fairly sure of Margot's vote. Jack Pease, though recognizing the Master's qualities, thought him 'a bit too scheming', and in need of 'a steady hand over him'. Seely had been Pease's choice for the post: Hazlehurst and Woodland, *Gainford Diary*, 156.

Northcliffe, Viscount *see* **Harmsworth, Arthur Charles.**

Oxford and Asquith, Earl and Countess of *see* **Asquith, Herbert Henry, and Asquith, Margot.**

Pease, Joseph Albert [Jack] (1860–1943), cr. Baron Gainford 1917. Quaker. Liberal MP 1892–1900, 1901–16. Chief Whip 1908; Chancellor of Duchy of Lancaster 1910–11; President Board of Education 1911–15; Postmaster General 1916.

Petty-Fitzmaurice, Henry Charles Keith (1845–1927), succ. as 5th Marquess of Lansdowne 1866. Married 1869 Lady Maud Evelyn Hamilton, daughter of 1st Duke of Abercorn. Foreign Secretary Nov. 1900–Dec. 1905. In House of Lords, Leader of Unionists, 1903–5; (opposition) leader, 1906–May 1915; joint Leader (with Crewe) May 1915–Dec. 1916.

Primrose, Archibald Philip (1847–1929), succ. as 5th Earl of Rosebery 1868. Married 1878 Hannah, eldest daughter and heiress of Baron Meyer de Rothschild. Foreign Secretary 1886, 1892; Prime Minister 1894: his government collapsed, June 1895; resigned Liberal leadership, Oct. 1896. Formed Liberal League 1902, and detached himself from Liberal Party 1905. Resigned presidency of Liberal League, Sept. 1909. Margot wrote of him in 1904: 'In my young days I was vastly impressed by him and even rather in love.' Asquith wrote, 1920: 'The most tragic example in our time of a wasted and ineffectual life'.

Queen, the *see* **Mary, Queen.**

Reading, Marquess of *see* **Isaacs, Sir Rufus Daniel.**

Redmond, John (1856–1918), barrister; from a family of Catholic gentry in Wexford. Entered Parliament, 1881. Leader of the Parnellite group after the Irish party split, 1891. Chairman of the reunited Irish MPs 1900. Able and patient parliamentarian, but knew little of Ulster, and not much of extremist movements, such as Sinn Fein, in the rest of Ireland. His speeches bored Margot.

Ribblesdale, Lady *see* **Lister, Charlotte.**

Roberts of Kandahar (Field Marshal) Earl, Frederick Sleigh (1832–1914), VC 1858, KCB 1878, Baron 1892, cr. Earl 1900. Service in India, supreme command in S. Africa, 1899. In retirement campaigned for conscription, Chairman of National Service League 1905. Colonel-in-Chief of Indian Expeditionary Force, 1914; died at St Omer, 14 Nov. 1914, while en route to inspect troops at the Front (aged 82). Margot thought him 'a cheerful, charming little man of sweet temper, good manners, and no mind of any kind'.

Robinson, Geoffrey (1874–1944), assumed surname of **Dawson** by royal licence, 1917; fellow of All Souls College, Oxford, 1898–1944; member of Milner's staff in S. Africa 1901–5; editor of *The Times* 1912–19, 1923–41. Margot called him, Apr. 1915, 'a real blackguard of the lowest kind, [who] has openly boasted he will do for Henry'. In Mar. 1914 she had thought him 'a charming fellow'. A 'Milnerite'.

Rosebery, Earl of *see* **Primrose, Archibald Philip.**

Runciman, Walter (1870–1949), cr. Viscount 1933. Entered Parliament 1899. President of Board of Education 1908; Board of Agriculture and Fisheries 1911; Board of Trade 1914–16 and 1931–7. With McKenna, core of opposition to conscription, 1915–16.

St John Midleton/Brodrick *see* **Brodrick, (William).**

Samuel, Herbert Louis (1870–1963) cr. Viscount 1937. A first cousin of Edwin Montagu. Liberal MP 1902–18; Chancellor of Duchy of Lancaster 1909; Postmaster General 1910–14, 1915–16; President of Local Government Board 1914–May 1915; Home Secretary 1916. Declined invitation to serve under Lloyd George, Dec. 1916. First High Commissioner, Palestine, 1920–5. Hobhouse thought him (Mar. 1915): 'Very able, not liked or trusted by anyone, but much used, and his wits often drawn on.'

Simon, Sir John Allsebrook (1873–1954), Kt. 1910, cr. Viscount 1940. Fellow of All Souls College, Oxford, 1897. Called to Bar, 1899; a brilliant advocate, he took silk only nine years later. Entered Parliament 1906. Solicitor-General, 1910; Attorney-General, and in cabinet 1913; Home Secretary 1915, resigned on conscription issue Jan. 1916. Foreign Secretary 1931–5; Home Secretary 1935–7; Chancellor of the Exchequer 1937–40; Lord Chancellor 1940–5.

Smith, Frederick Edwin [F. E.] (1872–1930), cr. Bt. 1918; cr. Lord Birkenhead 1919; Visc. 1921; Earl 1922. Unionist MP 1906–18, established reputation with a brilliant maiden speech. KC 1908, with a large and lucrative legal practice. Deeply involved in resistance to Parliament Bill and to Home Rule. Drank heavily. Head of Press Bureau 1914. Solicitor-General in first Coalition government 1915; Attorney-General 1915; Lord Chancellor 1919: Margot called this last 'a very cynical and <u>disgraceful</u> appointment'.

Spender, John Alfred (1862–1942), journalist and author; editor of the influential *Westminster Gazette* 1896–1922; in collaboration with Cyril Asquith wrote life (2 vols, 1932) of H. H. Asquith, many of whose views he had shared.

Stamfordham, Lord *see* **Bigge, Sir Arthur John.**

Stanley, (Beatrice) Venetia *see* **Montagu, (Beatrice) Venetia.**

Tennant, Sir Charles (1823–1906), cr. Bt. 1885. Father of Margot and eleven other children by his first wife Emma, and of three daughters by his second wife, Marguerite. Scottish industrialist. Liberal MP 1879–86. His house, The Glen, Innerleithen, in which Margot spent much of her childhood, was built in 1854–8. At the time of his death, Margot wrote in the diary of his impulsiveness and tactlessness: it is clear that she inherited his temperament in large part. For the financial help he gave to Asquith and Margot, see Introduction, Part 2, 'Margot and Henry'.

Tennant, Edward Priaulx (1859–1920), cr. Baron Glenconner 1911. Eldest brother of Margot. Married 1895 Pamela Wyndham. Their eldest son, Edward, was killed in the Battle of the Somme, 1916, one week after Raymond Asquith.

Tennant, (Harold) John [Jack] (1865–1935), 3rd son of Sir Charles Tennant, and brother of Margot. Liberal MP 1894–1918. Assistant Private Secretary to Asquith when Home Secretary, 1892–5. Parliamentary Secretary to Board of Trade 1909; Financial Secretary to War Department 1911–12; Under-Secretary of State for War 1912–16; Secretary of State for Scotland July–Dec. 1916.

Tennant, Pamela née Wyndham (1871–1928), Lady Glenconner, Margot's sister-in-law. She and her husband built Wilsford Manor, near Salisbury. After Lord Glenconner's death Pamela married, 1922, Viscount Grey of Fallodon. Margot's diary records frequent disagreements between the sisters-in-law.

Wilhelm II, German Emperor and King of Prussia (1859–1941), The Kaiser. A grandson of Queen Victoria, and thus related to both the British and Russian royal families, he succeeded his father as Emperor in 1888. After Germany's defeat in 1918 he abdicated and retired to the Netherlands. Gifted, but superficial: there were recurrent doubts about his mental stability.

Wimborne, 2nd Baron *see* **Guest, Ivor Churchill.**

BIBLIOGRAPHY AND LIST OF SHORT TITLES OF THE SOURCES CITED IN THE TEXT

Below is an alphabetical list of the short titles used to identify the manuscripts and printed works that are cited in footnotes. Also included are the full titles of many (though not all) of the works that were found to be especially useful in the preparation of the edition, but which might not be cited in footnotes. Unpublished items are underlined. The first items are those referring to (i) Margot Asquith, from 1925 entitled 'the Countess of Oxford and Asquith' or 'Margot Oxford'; and (ii) H. H. Asquith, from 1925 entitled 'the Earl of Oxford and Asquith'.

MGB, EHB

1. Margot Asquith

(i) Autobiography
Margot Asquith, *Autobiography* (2 vols, 1920, 1922; serialized in the press before publication in these 2 vols; paperback published later). Abridged single volume edition, with introduction by Mark Bonham Carter, 1962; paperback, 1985. (Both of these editions have been reissued.)

(ii) Margot Asquith Papers
The papers of Emma Alice Margaret (Margot) Asquith, *which include her diaries,* are to be found in the Bodleian Library, Oxford, reference: MSS Eng. c. 6665–6720, c. 6729, c. 7098; d. 3198–3218, Diaries; d. 3262–319; e. 3256–7, e. 3280–92; Photogr. c. 120–1, e. 11. The diary volumes presented here are d. 3210 to d. 3215. When unpublished passages are cited from these volumes they are preceded by the word 'diary'. For convenience

'MSS Eng.' is often omitted from references in this volume. References to Margot are also to be found in: Asquith Papers, Asquith–Henley Letters, Asquith–Stanley Letters, Bonham Carter Papers. H. H. Asquith's letters to Margot for the years of his premiership are contained in c. 6690 for 1908–11, and in c. 6691 for 1912–16. Asquith dated his letters carefully and folio references are not given for some of these letters.

(iii) Published works

Lay Sermons	Margot Oxford, *Lay Sermons* (1927)
Little Journey	Margot Tennant, *A Little Journey, 1891* and *A Week in Glasgow, 1892* (privately printed, 1892)
More Memories	Margot Oxford, *More Memories* (1933)
Myself When Young	Margot Asquith (ed.), *Myself When Young* (1938)
Octavia	Margot Asquith, *Octavia* (1928)
Off the Record	Countess of Oxford and Asquith, *Off the Record* (1943)
Places and Persons	Margot Asquith, *Places and Persons* (1925)

2. H. H. Asquith

(i) H. H. Asquith Papers

The papers of Herbert Henry ('H. H.') Asquith are to be found in the Bodleian Library, Oxford, reference: MSS Asquith 1–152. The Library also holds: (i) the Asquith–Henley MSS Letters, H. H. Asquith's letters to Sylvia Henley, Bodleian Library Oxford (MSS Eng. LETT., c. 542/1–5, each letter being numbered). (ii) H. H. Asquith's letters to Venetia Stanley, Bodleian Library, Oxford (MS Eng. 7098). (See also Margot Asquith Papers, Bonham Carter Papers, Venetia Stanley Correspondence.)

(ii) Published works

Asquith, *Addresses*	H. H. Asquith, *Occasional Addresses* (1918)
Asquith, *Fifty Years*	H. H. Asquith, *Fifty Years of Parliament* (2 vols, 1926)
Asquith, *Genesis*	H. H. Asquith, *The Genesis of the War* (1923)

Asquith, *Memories*   H. H. Asquith, *Memories and Reflections* (2 vols, 1928)

Asquith, *Studies*   H. H. Asquith, *Studies and Sketches* (1924)

Asquith, *War*   H. H. Asquith, *The War: Its Causes and its Message: Speeches Delivered by the Prime Minister, August–October 1914* (1914)

Asquith–Harrisson   H. H. A.; *Letters from Lord Oxford to a Friend* (2 vols, 1933, 1934, 1st series, 1915–22, 2nd series, 1922–1927). This friend was Mrs Hilda Harrisson.

Asquith–Stanley   M. G. and E. Brock (eds), *H. H. Asquith, Letters to Venetia Stanley* (1982, 1985). Pagination is the same in hard cover and paperback editions. Venetia's replies do not seem to have survived. For the extent to which Asquith's letters in the Bodleian (MS Eng. 7098 above) were published (in whole or part) in *Asquith–Stanley* see pp. 618–20 of that work.

3. Other Works and Collections Cited and Used (unpublished items are underlined)

Adams, R. J. Q., *Arms and the Wizard: Lloyd George and the Ministry of Munitions, 1915–1916* (1978)

Adams and Poirier, *Conscription*: R. J. Q. Adams and Philip Poirier, *The Conscription Controversy in Great Britain, 1900–1918* (1987)

Addison, *Politics*: Christopher Addison, *Politics from Within, 1911–1918* (2 vols, 1924)

Addison, *Years*: Christopher Addison, *Four and a Half Years* (2 vols, 1934)

Albertini, Luigi, *The Origins of the War of 1914* (trans. and ed. J. M. Massey, 3 vols, 1952–7)

Amery, Julian, *Chamberlain*: Julian Amery, *Joseph Chamberlain, 1901–1914*, vols iv–vi (1951–69). For vols i–iii see Garvin.

Amery, *Diaries*: John Barnes and David Nicholson (eds), *Leo Amery Diaries, 1896–1929* (1980)

Amery, Leo, *My Political Life* (3 vols, 1953–5)

Arthur, *Kitchener*: Sir George Arthur, *Earl Kitchener* (3 vols, 1920)

Arthur Asquith Papers: Private collection, Clovelly Court, Devon

Asquith, C., *Diaries*: Cynthia Asquith, *Diaries, 1915–1918* (1968)

Asquith, C. *Remember (ii)*: Cynthia Asquith, *Remember and Be Glad* (1952)

Asquith, Cynthia, *Haply I May Remember* (1950)

Asquith–Henley: see under '2. H. H. Asquith … (i) Papers'

Asquith–Stanley: see under '2. H. H. Asquith … (ii) Published Works'

Attenborough, *Living Memory*: John Attenborough, *A Living Memory* (1975)

Ayherst, David, *Garvin of the Observer* (1985)

Bacon, R. H., *Fisher* (2 vols, 1929)

Bacon, R. H., *Jellicoe* (1936)

Bagehot, Walter, *Collected Works of Walter Bagehot* (15 vols, 1965–86)

Baker, R. S., *Woodrow Wilson* (8 vols, 1927–39)

Balfour, *Autobiography*: Arthur James Balfour, *Chapters of Autobiography*, ed. B. E. Dugdale (1930)

Balfour–Elcho Letters: Jane Ridley and Clayre Percy (eds), *The Letters of Arthur Balfour and Lady Elcho* (1992)

Balfour, Lady Frances, *Ne Obliviscaris* (2 vols, 1930)

Balfour Papers, BL: Papers of A. J. Balfour: British Library, Additional MSS

Balfour Papers, Whitt.: The A. J. Balfour MSS from Whittingehame, now in the National Archives of Scotland

Barraclough, Geoffrey, *From Agadir to Armageddon* (1982)

Battersea, Constance, Lady Battersea, *Reminiscences* (1922)

BDW: G. P. Gooch and H. Temperley (eds), *British Documents on the Origins of the War, 1898–1914* (vols i–xi in 13 bound vols, 1926–38)

Beaverbrook, *Politicians*: Lord Beaverbrook, *Politicians and the War* (1960, originally in 2 vols, 1928, 1932)

[Begbie], *Mirrors*: [Harold Begbie], *The Mirrors of Downing Street* (1922 edn; first pub. 1920)

Bell, G. K. A., *Randall Davidson*, 2 vols (1935)

Belloc Lowndes Diaries: Susan Lowndes (ed.), *Diaries and Letters of Marie Belloc Lowndes, 1911–1947* (1971)

Benckendorff, Constantine, *Half a Life* (1954)

Bennett Letters: Letters of Sir John French to Winifred Bennett: Imperial War Museum

Bennett, *Margot*: Daphne Bennett, *Margot* (1984)

Bentley, *Those Days*: E. C. Bentley, *Those Days* (1940)

Bickersteth, John (ed.), *The Bickersteth Diaries, 1914–1918* (1995, paperback 1996)

Bidwell, Shelford, and Graham, Dominick, *Fire-power: British Army Weapons and Theories of War, 1904–1945* (1982)

Birkenhead, *Churchill*: The (2nd) Earl of Birkenhead, *Churchill, 1876–1922*, ed. Sir John Colville (1989)

Birkenhead, (2nd) Earl of Birkenhead, *Frederick Edwin, Earl of Birkenhead*, 2 vols (1933, 1936)

Birrell, Augustine, *Things Past Redress* (1937)

Blake, *Bonar Law*: Robert Blake, *The Unknown Prime Minister: Life and Times of Andrew Bonar Law* (1955)

Blewett, Neal, *The Peers, the Parties, and the People: The General Elections of 1910* (1972)

Blunt, Wilfrid, *My Diaries [part 2], 1888–1914* (single volume edn, 1932)

Bogdanor, Vernon, *The British Constitution in the Twentieth Century* (2003)

Bogdanor, Vernon, *The Monarchy and the Constitution* (1995)

Bond, Brian, and Cave, Nigel (eds), *Haig: A Reappraisal 70 Years On* (1999)

Bonham Carter, *Churchill*: Violet Bonham Carter, *Winston Churchill as I Knew Him* (1965)

Bonham Carter, *Diaries, 1904–14*: Mark Bonham Carter and Mark Pottle (eds), *Lantern Slides: The Diaries and Letters of Violet Bonham Carter, 1904–1914* (1996, paperback 1997)

Bonham Carter, *Diaries, 1914–45*: Mark Pottle (ed.), *Champion Redoubtable: The Diaries and Letters of Violet Bonham Carter, 1914–1945* (1998, paperback 1999)

Bonham Carter, *Diaries, 1946–69*: Mark Pottle (ed.), *Daring to Hope: The Diaries and Letters of Violet Bonham Carter, 1946–1969* (2000)

Bonham Carter Papers: Bonham Carter MSS, 1–803, Bodleian Library, Oxford. For Maurice Bonham Carter's correspondence, 1908–16, see items 248–58. See also Asquith Papers, Margot Asquith Papers, Asquith–Henley Letters

Boyce, George (ed.), *The Crisis of British Unionism: Lord Selborne's Domestic Political Papers, 1885–1922* (1987)

Bradley, *Lady Curzon*: John Bradley (ed.), *Lady Curzon's India* (1985)

Bright's Speeches: J. E. T. Rogers (ed.), *Speeches of John Bright* (2nd edn 1869)

British Political Facts: David Butler and Gareth Butler (eds), *Twentieth-Century British Political Facts, 1900–2000* (8th edn, 2000)

Brittain, Vera, *War Diary, 1913–1917*, ed. A. Bishop and T. Smart (1981)

Brock, *Britain Enters*: Michael Brock, 'Britain Enters the War', ch. 7 (pp. 145–78) in Evans and Pogge von Strandmann, q.v.

Brock, Michael, *The Great Reform Act* (1973, 1993)

Brock, M. G. and E. H. (eds) see *Asquith–Stanley*

Brock, *Raymond Asquith*: Michael Brock, '"The Eternal Lack of Motive": Raymond Asquith's Buried Talents', ch. 14 in *Winchester College: Sixth Centenary Essays*, ed. Roger Custance (1982)

Buchan, *Grenfells*: John Buchan, *Francis and Riversdale Grenfell: A Memoir* (1920)

Buchan, *Memory*: John Buchan, *Memory Hold-the-Door* (1940)

Buckmaster, Owen Stanley, 2nd Visc. Buckmaster, *Roundabout* (1969)

Bülow, Prince Bernhard von, *Imperial Germany* (1914)

Callwell, C. E., *Field-Marshal Sir Henry Wilson: His Life and Diaries* (2 vols, 1927)

Cammaerts, Emile, *Albert of Belgium* (1935, translated)

Campbell, *Frances*: Campbell, John, *If Love Were All…: The Story of Frances Stevenson and David Lloyd George* (2006)

Campbell, John, *Birkenhead* (1983)

Cannadine, David, *Aspects of Aristocracy: Grandeur and Decline in Modern Britain* (1994)

Carlyon, L. A., *Gallipoli* (2002)

Carrington, Charles, *Rudyard Kipling* (1955)

Cassar, *Asquith, War*: George H. Cassar, *Asquith as War Leader* (1994)

Cassar, *Kitchener*: George H. Cassar, *Kitchener: Architect of Victory* (1977)

Cecil, Lamar, *Wilhelm II*, ii: *1900–1941* (1996)

Cecil, Visc., Cecil of Chelwood (Robert Cecil), *All the Way* (1949)

Chamberlain, *Down the Years*: Austen Chamberlain, *Down the Years* (1935)

Chamberlain, *Politics*: Austen Chamberlain, *Politics from Inside: An Epistolary Chronicle, 1906–1914* (1936)

Chamberlain, Joseph see Amery, Julian, and Garvin

Chamberlain Papers: Austen Chamberlain MSS, University of Birmingham

Charteris, *At GHQ*: John Charteris, *At GHQ* (1931)

Chesterton, G. K., *Autobiography* (1937)

Childers, Erskine, *The Riddle of the Sands: A Record of Secret Service* (1998 edn ed. David Trotter; originally published 1903)

Churchill: Randolph S. Churchill (vols i–ii) and Martin Gilbert (vols iii–viii), *Winston S. Churchill*, 8 vols (1966–88)

Churchill Companion: Winston S. Churchill: Companion Volumes (documents) 16 vols, covering vols i–vi of the biography, 1874–1941 (1967–2000)

Churchill, *Great Contemporaries*: Winston S. Churchill, *Great Contemporaries* (1939; first published with fewer articles, 1937)

Churchill, Winston S., *Lord Randolph Churchill*, 2 vols (1906)

Churchill, *World Crisis*: Winston S. Churchill, *The World Crisis*, 6 vols (1923–31)

Churchill, Randolph S., *Lord Derby* (1959)

Clark, Christopher M., *The Sleepwalkers: How Europe Went to War in 1914* (2013)

Clark, *Echoes*: James Munson (ed.), *Echoes of the Great War: The Diary of the Reverend Andrew Clark, 1914–1919* (1985)

Clarke, P. F., *Lancashire and the New Liberalism* (1971)

Clarke, Tom, *My Northcliffe Diary* (1931)

Clifford, *Asquiths*: Colin Clifford, *The Asquiths* (2002)

Colvin, Ian, *Life of Lord Carson*, 3 vols (1932–6)

Cooper, Artemis (ed.), *A Durable Fire: Letters of Duff and Diana Cooper, 1913–1950* (1983)

Cooper, Duff, *Old Men Forget* (1953)

Cooper, *Rainbow*: Diana Cooper, *The Rainbow Comes and Goes* (1958)

Craig, *Germany*: G. A. Craig, *Germany, 1866–1945* (corrected edn, paperback 1981)

Crathorne, Nancy, *Tennant's Stalk* (1973)

Crawford Journals: John Vincent (ed.), *The Journals of David Lindsay, 27th Earl of Crawford and 10th Earl of Balcarres, 1871–1940* (1984)

Crewe Papers: Correspondence and papers of the 1st Marquess of Crewe: Cambridge University Library

Cruttwell, *Great War*: C. R. M. F. Cruttwell, *History of the Great War, 1914–1918* (1934)

D'Abernon, Visc. (Edgar Vincent), *Portraits and Appreciations* (1931)

Dalton War Diaries: Ben Pimlott (ed.), *The Second World War Diaries of Hugh Dalton, 1940–1945* (1986)

Dangerfield, George, *The Strange Death of Liberal England* (1935 New York, 1936 London, etc.)

Darroch, *Ottoline*: Sandra Jobson Darroch, *Ottoline: The Life of Lady Ottoline Morrell* (1976)

Davenport-Hines, *Ettie*: Richard Davenport-Hines, *Ettie: The Intimate Life and Dauntless Spirit of Lady Desborough* (2008)

Desborough, *Family Journal*: Lady Desborough (Ethel Priscilla), *Pages from a Family Journal, 1888–1915* (privately printed, Spottiswoode, Eton, 1916)

Desborough Papers: Correspondence and papers of Lady Desborough, Ethel Priscilla Grenfell (née Fane): Hertfordshire Record Office

Drew, *Acton*: Mary Drew, *Acton, Gladstone, and Others* (1924)

Dugdale, *Balfour*: B. E. C. Dugdale, *Arthur James Balfour* (2 vols, 1936)

Dutton, David, *Simon* (1992)

Edmonds, J. E., *Military Operations, France and Belgium, 1915*: vol. i, with G. C. Wynne (1927); vol. ii, with C. Becke (1928): in *History of the Great War*, for which also see C. E. Fayle, *Seaborne Trade*; Edmonds wrote nine other vols in the *Official History*, which was published between 1922 and 1947.

Edward VIII, *King's Story*: Edward, Duke of Windsor, *A King's Story: the Memoirs of H.R.H. the Duke of Windsor, K.G.* (1951)

Egremont, Max, *Balfour* (1980)

Ellenberger, thesis: Nancy W. Ellenberger, 'The Souls: High Society and Politics in Late Victorian Britain': typescript, Ph.D. thesis, University of Oregon, 1982

Ellenberger, Nancy W., 'The Souls and London "Society" at the End of the Nineteenth Century', *Victorian Studies*, 25 (1982), 133–60

Ensor, *1870–1914*: R. C. K. Ensor, *England, 1870–1914* (1936)

Esher Journals: 3rd Visc. Esher (ed.), *Journals and Letters of Reginald, Visc. Esher, 1870–1930* (4 vols, 1934–8)

Evans and von Strandmann, *First World War*: R. J. W. Evans and H. Pogge von Strandmann (eds), *The Coming of the First World War* (1988). For ch. 7 see under Brock, *Britain Enters.*

Eyck, *Gooch*: F. Eyck, *G. P. Gooch* (1982)

Farrar-Hockley, Anthony, *Death of an Army* (1967)

Fay, *World War*: S. B. Fay, *The Origins of the World War* (revised edn, 1930, two vols in one cover)

Fayle, C. Ernest, *Seaborne Trade* (3 vols, 1920–4), in *History of the Great War* (for which see also J. E. Edmonds)

Ferguson, Niall, *The Pity of War* (1998)

Fergusson, Sir James, *The Curragh Incident* (1964)

Fischer, Fritz, *War of Illusions: German Policies from 1911 to 1914* (1975)

Fisher Correspondence: A. J. Marder (ed.), *Fear God and Dread Nought: Correspondence of Admiral of the Fleet Lord Fisher of Kilverstone* (3 vols, 1952–9)

Fisher, Lord, *Memories* (1919)

Fitzherbert, Margaret, *The Man Who Was Greenmantle* (1983)

Fortnightly Review (old style volume numbers are cited)

French, *1914*: Visc. French (later Earl of Ypres), *1914* (2nd edn, 1919)

French, *Despatches*: Visc. French (later Earl of Ypres), *The Despatches of Lord French* (1917)

French, David, *British Economic and Strategic Planning, 1905–15* (1982)

French Papers: Papers of the 1st Earl of Ypres, Imperial War Museum, London

Gainford Papers: The Papers of J. A. Pease (cr. Lord Gainford 1917); Nuffield College. See also Pease, *Journals*, 1908–10 and July–August 1914.

Gardiner, *People*: A. G. Gardiner, *Certain People of Importance* (1926). Most of the portraits in this book, and all of those in the two which follow, appeared first in the *Daily News*.

Gardiner, A. G., *Pillars of Society* (1913)

Gardiner, *Prophets*: A. G. Gardiner, *Prophets, Priests, and Kings* (1914; first pub. 1908)

Garvin, *Chamberlain*: J. L. Garvin, *Joseph Chamberlain, 1836–1900*, vols i–iii (1932–4). For vols iv–vi see Amery.

Garvin, *Tomorrow*: M. Pottle and J. G. G. Ledingham (eds), *We Hope to Get Word Tomorrow: The Garvin Family War Letters, 1914–1916* (2009)

Gerard, James W., *My Four Years in Germany* (1917)

Gilbert, B. B., *David Lloyd George, 1863–1912* (1987)

Gilbert, B. B., *David Lloyd George, 1912–1916* (1987)

Gilmour, David, *Curzon* (1994)

Glenconner Papers: Glenconner Papers, Glen, Scottish Borders: National Register of Archives for Scotland, NRAS 1369

Gollin, *Garvin*: A. M. Gollin, *The Observer and J. L. Garvin, 1908–14: A Study in a Great Editorship* (1960)

Gollin, A. M., *Proconsul in Politics* (1964)

Gooch, G. P., *Recent Revelations in European Diplomacy* (1923)

Gooch, G. P., *Under Six Reigns* (1958)

Gooch, J., *Plans of War*: John Gooch, *The Plans of War* (1974)

Goschen Diary: C. H. D. Howard (ed.), *The Diary of Edward Goschen, 1900–1914* (1980)

Grenfell, *Memoirs*: Lord Grenfell, *Memoirs* (1925)

Grey, *Twenty-Five Years*: Visc. Grey, *Twenty-Five Years* (2 vols, 1925, and other edns)

Grieves, Keith, *The Politics of Manpower, 1914–1918* (1988)

Grigg, *Lloyd George, 1902–1911*: John Grigg, *Lloyd George: The People's Champion, 1902–1911* (1978)

Grigg, *Lloyd George, 1912–1916*: John Grigg, *Lloyd George: From Peace to War, 1912–1916* (1985)

Grigg, *Lloyd George, 1916–1918*: John Grigg, *Lloyd George: War Leader, 1916–1918* (2002)

Guinn, Paul, *British Strategy and Politics, 1914 to 1918* (1965)

Gwynn, *Redmond*: Denis Rolleston Gwynn, *John Redmond* (1932)

Gwynne Papers: Gwynne Papers, Bodleian Library, MSS Gwynne dep.

Gwynne, *Rasp*: K. Wilson (ed.), *The Rasp of War: Letters of H. A. Gwynne to the Countess Bathurst, 1914–1918* (1988)

Haldane, *Autobiography*: Richard Burdon, Visc. Haldane, *An Autobiography* (1929)

Haldane, *Before the War* (1920): Visc. Haldane, *Before the War* (1920)

Haldane Papers: Papers of Visc. Haldane, National Library of Scotland

Hale, O. J., *Great Illusion, 1900–1914* (1971)

Hamilton Diary: Dudley W. R. Bahlman (ed.), *Diary of Sir Edward Walter Hamilton, 1885–1906*, (1993)

Hamilton, General Sir Ian, *Gallipoli Diary* (1920)

Hankey, Diary: Hankey diary, in Hankey Papers, Churchill College, Cambridge (HNKY 1)

Hankey, *Student in Arms*: Donald Hankey, *A Student in Arms* (1st Series, Apr. 1916, 2nd Series, Apr. 1917, both often reissued)

Hankey, *Supreme Command*: Lord Hankey, *The Supreme Command, 1914–1918* (2 vols, 1961: continuous pagination, pp. 1–435, vol. i; pp. 436–906, vol. ii)

Hart-Davis, Duff (ed.), *Diary of A. F. Lascelles, 1887–1920: The End of an Era* (1986)

Hawarden Letters: L. March Phillips and B. Christian (eds), *Some Hawarden Letters, 1878–1913* (1917)

Hazlehurst, Cameron, 'Asquith as Prime Minister', *EHR* 85 (July 1970), 502–31.

Hazlehurst, *Politicians at War*: Cameron Hazlehurst, *Politicians at War, July 1914 to May 1915* (1971)

Healy, *Letters*: T. M. Healy, *Letters and Leaders of my Day* (2 vols, 1928: continuous pagination)

Henley Letters: Letters of Anthony and Sylvia Henley; Bodleian Library MSS Eng. Lett. c. 641–9.

Herbert Samuel Papers: Papers of Herbert (1st Visc.) Samuel, House of Lords Record Office (Historical Collection 128)

Hewins, W. A. S., *The Apologia of an Imperialist*, 2 vols (1929)

History of the Great War: Brigadier-General Sir James E. Edmonds, *History of the Great War: Military Operations, France and Belgium, 1914* (3rd edn, 2 vols, 1933)

Hobhouse Diaries: E. David (ed.), *Inside Asquith's Cabinet: From the Diaries of Charles Hobhouse* (1977)

Holmes, *French*: Richard Holmes, *The Little Field-Marshal: Sir John French* (1981)

Holroyd, *Strachey*: Michael Holroyd, *Lytton Strachey: A Biography* (1971)

Holt Diary: Odyssey of an Edwardian Liberal: The Political Diary of Richard Durning Holt, ed. D. Dutton (Gloucester, for Record Soc. of Lancs. and Cheshire, 1989)

Horner, *Time Remembered*: Frances Horner, *Time Remembered* (1933)

Hough, *War at Sea*: Richard Hough, *The Great War at Sea, 1914–1918* (1983)

House, *Intimate Papers*: C. Seymour (ed.), *The Intimate Papers of Colonel House* (4 vols, 1926–8)

Howard, Christopher, *Splendid Isolation* (1967)

Howard, Michael, *The Continental Commitment* (1972; paperback 1974)

Howard, Michael, *The First World War* (2002)

Howard, Michael, *War and the Liberal Conscience* (1981 paperback; first pub. 1978)

Huguet, A., *Britain and the War* (1928)

Hurwitz, *Intervention*: Samuel J. Hurwitz, *State Intervention in Great Britain: A study in economic control and social response, 1914–1919* (1949)

Hyde, *Carson*: H. Montgomery Hyde, *Carson* (1953)

Hyde, *Other Love*: H. Montgomery Hyde, *The Other Love: An Historical and Contemporary Survey of Homosexuality in Britain* (1970)

Jalland, Patricia, *The Liberals and Ireland* (1980)

Jeffery, Keith, *Sir Henry Wilson, a Political Soldier* (2006)

Jenkins, *Asquith*: Roy Jenkins, *Asquith* (3rd edn, revised, 1986)

J. Mod. H.: *Journal of Modern History*

Joll, James, *The Origins of the First World War* (1984)

Jolliffe, *Raymond Asquith*: John Jolliffe, *Raymond Asquith: Life and Letters* (1980)

Kellett, Richard, *The King's Shilling: The Life and Times of Lord Kitchener* (1984)

Kennedy, *War Plans*: P. Kennedy (ed.), *War Plans of the Great Powers* (1979)

Kennet Diaries: Diaries of Lady Scott, later Lady Kennet (Cambridge University Library). References from copies in Bodleian Library, Oxford, Asquith Papers 152. Much of this material appears in the next item, *Self-Portrait*.

Kennet, *Self-Portrait*: Kathleen Kennet (previously Scott), *Self-Portrait of an Artist* (published posthumously, 1949)

Kipling, *Letters*: Thomas Pinney (ed.), *The Letters of Rudyard Kipling*, iv: 1911–1919 (1999)

Koss, *Asquith*: Stephen Koss, *Asquith* (1976)

Koss, *Haldane*: Stephen Koss, *Lord Haldane: Scapegoat for Liberalism* (1969)

Koss, *Nonconformity*: Stephen Koss, *Nonconformity in Modern British Politics* (1975)

Koss, *Political Press*: Stephen Koss, *The Rise and Fall of the Political Press in Britain*, vol. ii (1984)

Lee Diaries: Alan Clark (ed.), *A Good Innings: Private Diaries of Visc. Lee* (*c*.1974)

Lees-Milne, James, *The Enigmatic Edwardian* (1986)

Lees-Milne, *Nicolson*: James Lees-Milne, *Harold Nicolson* (2 vols, 1980, 1981)

Leveson Gower, George, *Endeavour, 1886–1907* (1942)

Lichnowsky, Prince Karl Max von, *Heading for the Abyss* (1928)

Liddell, *Notes*: A. G. C. Liddell, *Notes from the Life of an Ordinary Mortal* (1911)

Lister, Charles, *Letters and Recollections*, ed. Lord Ribblesdale (1917)

Lloyd George, *War Memoirs*: David Lloyd George, *War Memoirs* (2 vol. edn., with additional material, continuous pagination, 1938; originally 6 vols, 1933–6)

McCallum, *Asquith*: R. B. McCallum, *Asquith* (1936)

MacCarthy, Desmond (ed.), *H.H.A. Letters to a Friend*, 1915–27 (2 vols, 1933, 1934)

MacCarthy, Desmond, *Portraits* (1931)

McEwen, *Riddell Diaries*: J. M. McEwen (ed.), *The Riddell Diaries, 1908–1923* (1986) (i.e. important for passages not published in entirety by Riddell in the original)

McKibbin, Ross, *The Evolution of the Labour Party, 1910–1924* (1991 impression)

Magnus, P., *King Edward VII* (1964)

Magnus, *Kitchener*: P. Magnus, *Kitchener* (1958)

Marder, *Royal Navy*: A. J. Marder, *From the Dreadnought to Scapa Flow: The Royal Navy in the Fisher Era, 1914–1919* (5 vols, 1961–70)

Marwick, Arthur, *Deluge: British Society and the First World War* (1915)

Massie, *Dreadnought*: R. K. Massie, *Dreadnought* (1993)

Masterman: L. Masterman, *C. F. G. Masterman* (1939)

Masterman, *Condition of England*: C. F. G. Masterman, *The Condition of England* (cheap edn 1911; first pub. 1909; reissued 1960)

Masterman Papers: C. F. G. Masterman MSS, University of Birmingham: including Mrs (Lucy) Masterman's Diary

Matthew, H. C. G., *The Liberal Imperialists* (1973)

Maurice, *Haldane*: Sir F. Maurice, *Visc. Haldane* (2 vols, 1937, 1939)

Maurice, *Rawlinson*: Sir Frederick Maurice, *The Life of General Lord Rawlinson of Trent...from his Journals and Letters* (1928)

Maxse Papers: Papers of Leo Maxse, West Sussex Record Office

Midleton, *Ireland*: William St. John Fremantle Brodrick, Earl of Midleton, *Ireland: Dupe or Heroine* (1932)

Millar, S. E., Lynn-Jones, S. M., and Van Evera, S., *Military Strategy and the Origins of the First World War* (revised edn, 1991)

Miller, J. D. B., *Norman Angell and the Futility of War* (1986)

Milner Papers: Papers of Visc. Milner, Bodleian Library, Oxford

Minney, R. J., *'Puffin' Asquith* (1973)

Monger, G. W., *The End of Isolation: British Foreign Policy, 1900–1907* (1963)

Montagu Papers: Papers of Edwin Samuel Montagu, Trinity College, Cambridge

Montague, *Disenchantment*: C. E. Montague, *Disenchantment* (1922)

Moorehead, *Gallipoli*: Alan Moorehead, *Gallipoli* (1956)

Morgan, Kenneth and Jane, *Portrait of a Progressive; The Political Career of Christopher, Visc. Addison* (1980)

Morley, Visc., *Recollections* (2 vols, 1917)

Morley, *Memo.*: John, Viscount Morley, *Memorandum on resignation, August 1914* (1928)

Morrell, R. Gathorne Hardy (ed.), *Ottoline: Early Memoirs of Ottoline Morrell* (1963)

Morris, *Scaremongers*: A. J. A. Morris, *The Scaremongers: The Advocacy of War and Rearmament, 1896–1914* (1984)

Mosley, *Grenfell*: Nicholas Mosley, *Julian Grenfell* (1976)

The Nation: The Nation (28 vols., London, 1907–21)

National Review, monthly issues from 1883

Newton, Lord, *Lord Lansdowne* (1929)

Nicolson, *Carnock*: Harold Nicolson, *Sir Arthur Nicolson, Bart: 1st Lord Carnock* (1930)

Nicolson, *George V*: Harold Nicolson, *King George V* (1952)

Nicolson, *Peacemaking*: Harold Nicolson, *Peacemaking* (with new introduction, 1945; first pub. 1933)

Nineteenth-Century Oxford (i)/(ii): M. G. Brock and M. C. Curthoys (eds) in *The History of the University of Oxford* (8 vols, 1984–2000); volume vi: *Nineteenth-Century Oxford (part 1)* (1997); volume vii: *Nineteenth-Century Oxford (part 2)* (2000)

NLS: National Library of Scotland

O'Day, Alan (ed.), *The Edwardian Age: Conflict and Stability, 1900–1914* (1979)

ODNB: *Oxford Dictionary of National Biography* (2004: online edition under continuous revision)

Offer, *Agrarian Interpretation*: Avner Offer, *First World War: An Agrarian Interpretation* (1987)

Offer, Avner, 'Going to War in 1914: A Matter of Honour?', *Politics and Society*, Canberra, 23 (1995)

Oliver, *Anvil*: F. S. Oliver, *The Anvil of War* (1936)

Oliver, F. S., *Ordeal by Battle* (abridged edn, 1916; first pub. 1915)

OWH: *Official War History*. See also Edmonds, J. E.

Packer, Ian, *Liberal Government and Politics, 1905–1915* (2006)

Page Letters: Burton J. Hendrick, *Life and Letters of Walter H. Page* (2 vols, New York, 1923)

Parl. Deb.: Parliamentary Debates. In the absence of an indication the reference is to the Commons series.

Parl. Pp.: *Parliamentary* Papers, with annual vol. nos.

Pease, J. A. see Gainford Papers

Pease, *Journals, 1908–1910*: Cameron Hazlehurst and Christine Woodland (eds), *A Liberal Chronicle: The Political Journals and Papers of J. A. Pease, 1st Baron Gainford*, i: 1908–1910 (1994)

Pease, *Journals, July–August 1914*: K. M. Wilson (ed.), 'The Cabinet Diary of J. A. Pease, 24 July–5 Aug. 1914', *Proc., the Leeds Philosophical and Literary Society*, 19. pt iii (1983), 41–51

Peel, *How We Lived*: C. S. Peel, *How We Lived Then, 1914–1918* (1929)

Petrie, Charles, *Austen Chamberlain* (2 vols, 1939, 1940)

Ponsonby, Frederick, *Recollections of Three Reigns* (1951)

Pope-Hennessy, James, *Lord Crewe* (1955)

Pound, R., and Harmsworth, G., *Northcliffe* (1959)

Pugh, *Electoral Reform*: Martin Pugh, *Electoral Reform in War and Peace, 1906–1918* (1978)

Punch: Punch, or the London Charivari

Reading Papers: Papers of the 1st Marquess of Reading (1860–1935), India Office Records, British Library

Rhodes James, *Churchill*: R. Rhodes James, *Churchill: A Study in Failure, 1900–1939* (1970)

Rhodes James, *Rosebery*: R. Rhodes James, *Rosebery: A Biography of Archibald Philip, Fifth Earl of Rosebery* (1963)

Riddell, Lord, *More Pages from my Diary, 1908–1914* (1934)

Riddell, Lord see also McEwen

Riddell War Diary: Lord Riddell, *War Diary, 1914–1918* (1933)

Ritter, *Schlieffen Plan*: G. Ritter, *The Schlieffen Plan: Critique of a Myth* (trans. A. and E. Wilson, 1958)

Ritter, *Sword and Sceptre*: G. Ritter, *The Sword and the Sceptre*, trans. H. Nordan (4 vols, 1972–3)

Robbins, Keith, *Sir Edward Grey* (1971)

Robertson, Sir William, *Soldiers and Statesmen*, 2 vols (1926)

Robertson, Sir William, *From Private to Field-Marshal* (1921)

Ronaldshay, Earl of, *Curzon* (3 vols, 1928)

Rose, *George V*: K. Rose, *George V* (1983)

Rose, K., *Curzon* (1969)

Rosebery, Earl of, *Miscellanies, Literary and Historical* (2 vols, 1921)

Rosebery Papers: Papers of the 5th Earl of Rosebery, National Library of Scotland (NLS)

Roskill, *Hankey*: S. Roskill, *Hankey, Man of Secrets* (3 vols, 1970–2: vol. i for 1877 to 1918)

Rowland, Peter, *The Last Liberal Governments: The Promised Land, 1905–1910* (1968)

Rowland, Peter, *The Last Liberal Governments: Unfinished Business, 1911–1914* (1971)

Samuel, *Memoirs*: Visc. Samuel, *Memoirs* (1945)

Schmitt, B. E., *The Coming of the War* (2 vols, 1930, reissued 1966)

Scott, Diaries: Trevor Wilson (ed.), *The Political Diaries of C. P. Scott, 1911–1928* (1970)

Scott Papers: C. P. Scott MSS, British Library, Add. MSS 50901–09

Searle, *Corruption*: G. R. Searle, *Corruption in British Politics, 1895–1930* (1987)

Searle, *1886–1918*: G. R. Searle, *A New England? Peace and War, 1886–1918* (New Oxford History of England, 2004)

Selborne Papers: Papers of 2nd Earl of Selborne (1859–1942), Bodleian Library, Oxford

Silkin, *Out of Battle*: Jon Silkin, *Out of Battle: The Poetry of the Great War* (1972)

Simkins, Peter, *Kitchener's Army: The Raising of the New Armies, 1914–1916* (1988)

Simon Papers: Papers of Visc. Simon, Bodleian Library, Oxford (MSS Simon 1–284, Adds 1–5)

Simon, *Retrospect*: Visc. Simon, *Retrospect* (1952)

Soames, *Clementine*: Mary Soames, *Clementine Churchill* (2002, first pub. 1979)

Soames, *Speaking for Themselves*: Mary Soames (ed.), *Speaking for Themselves: The Personal Letters of Winston and Clementine Churchill* (1998)

Sommer, Dudley, *Haldane of Cloan: His Life and Times* (1960)

Spender, *Fifty Years*: J. A. Spender, *Fifty Years of Europe* (revised edn, 1936)

Spender and Asquith: J. A. Spender and Cyril Asquith, *H. H. Asquith, Lord Oxford and Asquith* (2 vols, 1932)

Spender Papers: John Alfred Spender MSS, British Library, chiefly in Add. MSS 64386–94

Stanley see *Asquith–Stanley*, Venetia Stanley Correspondence

Steed, H. Wickham, *Through Thirty Years, 1892–1922* (2 vols, 1924)

Steiner, *First World War*: Zara S. Steiner, *Britain and the Origins of the First World War* (1977)

Steiner, *Foreign Policy*: Zara S. Steiner, *The Foreign Office and Foreign Policy, 1898–1914* (1969)

Stevenson Diary: A. J. P. Taylor (ed.), *Lloyd George: A Diary by Frances Stevenson* (1971)

Stevenson, *Years Past*: Frances Stevenson, *The Years that are Past* (1967)

Stewart, A. T. Q., *The Ulster Crisis* (1967)

Strachan, *First World War*: H. Strachan, *The First World War*, i: *To Arms* (2001)

Sutherland, *Ward* : John Sutherland, *Mrs Humphry Ward* (1990)

Sylvester, A. J., *The Real Lloyd George* (1947)

Symonds, Letters: *The Letters of John Addington Symonds*, ed. H. M. Schueller and R. L. Peters, 3 vols (1967–9)

Taylor, *1914–1945*: A. J. P. Taylor, *English History, 1914–1945* (1965)

Taylor, *Beaverbrook*: A. J. P. Taylor, *Beaverbrook* (paperback 1974, first pub. 1972)

Taylor, *Struggle*: A. J. P. Taylor, *The Struggle for Mastery in Europe, 1848–1918* (1954)

Taylor, *Trouble Makers*: A. J. P. Taylor, *The Trouble Makers: Dissent over Foreign Policy, 1792–1939* (1957)

Taylor, *War Politics*: A. J. P. Taylor, *Politics in Wartime* (1964)

Terraine, *First War*: John Terraine, *The First World War, 1914–1918* (paperback with new introduction, 1984)

Terraine, *Mons*: John Terraine, *Mons, the Retreat to Victory* (1972; 1st edn, 1960)

Terraine, *Smoke*: John Terraine, *The Smoke and the Fire* (1980)

Theodore Roosevelt Letters: E. E. Morison (ed.), *The Letters of Theodore Roosevelt*, 8 vols (1951–4)

Thompson, *Northcliffe*: J. Lee Thompson, *Northcliffe* (2000)

The Times, accessed online through the Times Digital Archive 1785–2007

Tom Jones Diary, 1916–1925: K. Middlemass (ed.), *Whitehall Diary, 1916–1925* (1969)

Tom Jones Diary, 1926–1930: K. Middlemass (ed.), *Whitehall Diary, 1926–1930* (1969)

Tom Jones Diary, 1931–1950: K. Middlemass (ed.), *A Diary with Letters, 1931–1950* (1954)

Trevelyan, *Grey*: G. M. Trevelyan, *Grey of Fallodon* (1937)

Tuchman, *Guns*: Barbara W. Tuchman, *The Guns of August* (paperback edn. 1964, 1st pub. 1962)

Venetia Stanley Correspondence: Correspondence of Venetia Stanley (from 1915 Mrs E. S. Montagu), Bonham Carter Papers, Bodleian Library, MS Bonham Carter B. 150–5 (See also Asquith–Stanley Letters; *Asquith–Stanley*)

Waley, S. D., *Edwin Montagu* (1964)

Ward Letters: Letters of Arnold Sandwith Ward, University College, London

Wasserstein, *Samuel*: Bernard Wasserstein, *Herbert Samuel* (1992)

Webb Diary (ii): N. and J. MacKenzie (eds), *The Diary of Beatrice Webb*, ii: *1892–1905* (1983)

Webb Diary (iii): N. and J. MacKenzie (eds), *The Diary of Beatrice Webb*, iii: *1905–1924* (1984)

Wemyss, Countess of, *A Family Record* (privately printed, 1932)

Wemyss, *Wester Wemyss*: Lady Wester Wemyss, *Life and Letters of Lord Wester Wemyss* (1935)

Wheatley, *Nationalism*: Michael Wheatley, *Nationalism and the Irish Party: Provincial Ireland 1910–1916* (2005)

(Wilfred) Owen, *Poems*: Jon Stallworthy (ed.), *The Complete Poems and Fragments*, 2 vols (1983)

Williamson, S. R., *The Politics of Grand Strategy: Britain and France Prepare for War, 1904–1914* (1969)

Wilson, Diary: Henry Wilson, Diary: Imperial War Museum Papers

Wilson, John, *CB: A Life of Sir Henry Campbell-Bannerman* (1973)

Wilson, *Decisions*: Keith Wilson (ed.), *Decisions for War* (1995, paperback 1996)

Wilson, *Empire and Continent*: Keith Wilson, *Empire and Continent: Studies in British Foreign Policy* (1987)

Wilson, Keith, *The Policy of the Entente* (1985)

Wilson, *Downfall*: Trevor Wilson, *The Downfall of the Liberal Party, 1914–1935* (1966)

Wilson, Trevor, *The Myriad Faces of War* (1986)

Winter, Denis, *Death's Men: Soldiers of the Great War* (1978)

Winter, J. M., *The Great War and the British People* (1985)

Wolfe, *Labour Supply*: Humbert Wolfe, *Labour Supply and Regulation* (1923)

Woodward, D. R., *Field Marshal William Robertson, CIGS in the Great War* (1998)

Woodward, E. L., *Great Britain and the German Navy* (1935, 1964)

Woodward, E. L., *Great Britain and the War of 1914–1918* (1967)

Wrench, Evelyn, *Milner* (1958)

Young, *Balfour*: K. Young, *Arthur James Balfour* (1963)

Ziegler, *Diana Cooper*: Philip Ziegler, *Diana Cooper* (1981)

Ziegler, Philip, *Edward VIII* (1990)

Zuber, Terence, *Inventing the Schlieffen Plan: German War Planning, 1871–1914* (2002)

INDEX

Bold page numbers refer to illustrations, while *italicized* page numbers indicate where basic biographical information (i.e. for the individual in question) is provided in a footnote. Margot Asquith is referred to throughout as simply Margot and Herbert Henry Asquith is referred to as HHA.